ANCIENT GREECE

ANCIENT GREECE
A Political, Social, and Cultural History

Sarah B. Pomeroy
*Hunter College and
the City University of New York
Graduate Center*

Stanley M. Burstein
*California State University,
Los Angeles*

Walter Donlan
*University of
California, Irvine*

Jennifer Tolbert Roberts
*City College and
the City University of New York
Graduate Center*

New York • Oxford
OXFORD UNIVERSITY PRESS
1999

Oxford University Press

Oxford New York
Athens Auckland Bangkok Bogotá Buenos Aires Calcutta
Cape Town Chennai Dar es Salaam Delhi Florence Hong Kong Istanbul
Karachi Kuala Lumpur Madrid Melbourne Mexico City Mumbai
Nairobi Paris São Paulo Singapore Taipei Tokyo Toronto Warsaw

and associated companies in
Berlin Ibadan

Published by Oxford University Press, Inc.
198 Madison Avenue, New York, New York 10016

Library of Congress Cataloging-in-Publication Data

Ancient Greece : a political, social, and cultural history / by Sarah
   B. Pomeroy, Stanley M. Burstein, Walter Donlan, Jennifer Tolbert
   Roberts.
      p. cm.
   Includes index.
   ISBN-13 978-0-19-509743-6
   ISBN 0-19-509742-4 (cloth). — ISBN 0-19-509743-2 (pbk.)
   1. Greece—Civilization—To 146 B.C. 2. Hellenism. I. Pomeroy,
Sarah B.
DF77.A595 1998   98-14544
938—dc21   CIP

19 18 17 16 15

Printed in the United States of America
on acid-free paper

For
Bob, Dorothy, Gail, and Jordana

CONTENTS

LIST OF MAPS AND BATTLE PLANS

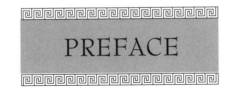

PREFACE

This book is designed to share with readers a rich and complex vision of ancient Greece that has been forged by the collaboration of four scholars with different backgrounds and varying interests. We undertook it because of our frustration in the search for a single volume that provided readers with a comprehensive history of Greek civilization from its first beginnings in the second millennium BC through the Hellenistic era. It has been more than a quarter of a century since the last attempt to tell this story in depth; all recent textbooks have either focused on political and military developments or omitted the Hellenistic era. We hope that what we have written will be useful and will give pleasure both to the general reader and to the student who is asked to read it in college. We have strived for a pace and a length that are suitable for a course lasting for a semester or a quarter devoted to the history and civilization of Greece—long enough to provide depth and detail, and short enough to enable the instructor to assign primary sources that will expand the student's understanding of a world that is both familiar and alien. Incorporating the fruits of the most recent scholarship, we have aimed for a balance between political, military, social, cultural, and economic history. The Athenian lawgiver Solon, who sought to reconcile the feuding political parties of his day, lamented that in trying to please everybody he seemed to have pleased nobody. We are optimistic that we will not be driven to such lamentations by the challenges we faced in our quest to integrate the various aspects of Greek civilization.

Greek culture was forged in the crucible of the Bronze Age civilizations that cropped up in worlds as diverse as unified Egypt and fragmented Mesopotamia. Absorbing key skills from these highly developed neighbors—metallurgy, for example, and writing—the Greeks built a distinctive culture marked by astonishing creativity, versatility, and resilience. In the end this world dissolved as Greek civilization, having reached from France and Italy in the west to Pakistan in the east, merged with a variety of other cultures—Macedonian, for example, Syrian, Iranian, Egyptian, Roman, and finally Byzantine. Greek became the common language throughout the Near East and was the language in which the texts collected in what we call the New Testament were written. Through its incorporation into the Roman empire and the fusion of Greek and Italian elements in mythology and architecture, a hybrid culture known as "Classical" came to hold an important place in the traditions of Europe and the Americas.

Between the decline of the Bronze Age and the diffusion of Greek culture throughout the Mediterranean world, Greek civilization attained an extraordinary richness marked by diversity within unity. The world of the Homeric epics the *Iliad* and the *Odyssey* was radically different from that of the fifth and fourth centuries, yet the epics remained the texts most commonly taught in schools, and Alexander was rumored to have carried a copy of Homer's work as he traveled, and lamented that he had no great poet to immortalize him as Homer had immortalized Achilles. Though religion inspired much of architecture, literature, and even athletic competitions, which were held to honor the gods, Greek government and society often seemed to function in an entirely secular manner. Marriage, for example, was a purely secular affair, and divorce was not believed to distress the gods at all. The gods were nowhere and everywhere. Ideals of equality were preached by men who usually owned slaves and believed in the inferiority of women. Stolid, warlike Sparta and cultivated, intellectual Athens considered themselves polar opposites; Thucydides encapsulated many of the differences seen from the Athenian point of view in the funeral oration for the war dead he put in the mouth of the Athenian statesman Pericles. Yet people in both cities lived by agriculture, worshipped Zeus and the other Olympian gods, subjected women to men, believed firmly in slavery (provided they were not slaves themselves!), sacrificed animals, considered war a constant in human life, preached an ethic of equity among male citizens, cherished athletics and delighted in the Olympics and other competitions, enjoyed praising the rule of law, considered Greeks superior to non-Greeks, and accepted as axiomatic the primacy of the state over the individual.

The history of the ancient Greeks is one of the most improbable success stories in all of world history. A small people inhabiting a poor country on the periphery of the civilizations of Egypt and the Near East, the Greeks created one of the world's most remarkable cultures. In almost every area of the arts and sciences they made fundamental contributions, and their legacy is still alive in western and Islamic civilizations. Throughout the Renaissance and the eighteenth century, Sparta was cherished as the model of a mixed and therefore stable constitution. In the nineteenth and twentieth centuries, more attention has focused on Athens, where it is possible to witness the gradual erosion of privilege based on wealth and lineage and the growth of democratic machinery—law codes and courts, procedures for selecting officials and holding them accountable, and public debates and votes on matters of domestic and foreign policy. Athens and Sparta fought ruinous wars with one another, and the propensity of the Greek states for fighting one another shaped much of their history. The devastating Greek world war of 431–404 known as the Peloponnesian War (because of Sparta's location on the peninsula of the Peloponnesus) placed a damper on the extraordinary burst of creativity that had marked the fifth century—the tragedies of Aeschylus, Sophocles, and Euripides; the comedies of Aristophanes; the building of the Parthenon at Athens and the temple of Zeus at Olympia. Throughout this painful era and the decades that followed, thinkers continued to explore the questions that had intrigued Greek intellectuals at least as far back as the sixth century—the origins of the universe and the mechanisms by which it functioned; the relation between *physis*, "nature," and *nomos*, "custom" or "law"; how and what mortals can know about the gods; what these gods might want from people; whether indeed true knowledge was possible for humans; what the best rules might be by which people could live together in society; what the best form of education was—who was most qualified to direct it, and how many could profit from it; under what circumstances the rule of a single wise man might after all be best. New questions were also posed—whether involvement in politics ought really to be the focus of a man's life; whether the individual might find identity separate from the state; whether war was worth the sacrifices it entailed; and even whether slavery and the disfranchisement of women were necessary (though those radical speculations did not result in social change). Inevitably, the conquests of Alexander, the mass marriages he celebrated between Macedonian soldiers and women from Persia and Media in 324 BC, and the hybrid culture that was forged throughout western Asia and Europe challenged conventional Greek assumptions about the clear line that divided Greeks from the non-Greek peoples they called "barbarians"—people whose language sounded like "bar, bar, bar." In some of the lands incorporated into the new Macedonian empires, women enjoyed higher status than in most of the Greek world, and this sometimes rubbed off on the colonial Macedonian aristocracy, changing long-entrenched mores.

The country that the poet Byron labeled the "land of lost gods" continues to live on in the modern imagination. It is our hope that this book will flesh out these romantic images with historical realities. During the past decades our understanding of ancient Greece has vastly expanded. Thanks to the work of a generation of talented scholars, our knowledge of numerous aspects of Greek history and life has been transformed and is still being transformed today. Archaeology has revealed the critical importance of the Dark Ages, while comparative anthropology has illuminated the nature of Archaic society and made clear the oral character of early Greek culture. At the same time, social historians have veered away from the traditional preoccupation with the elite, who left written records of their doings, and have been tireless in ferreting out evidence that throws light on the lives of those who do not generally speak for themselves—women, for example, and slaves.

Synthesizing the results of this scholarship has been an exciting and challenging task made possible only by the help of many people. We have, of course, profited enormously from the work of innumerable scholars whose names never appear in our volume; that is the nature of historical writing. We are also greatly indebted to Robert Miller of the Oxford University Press and his energetic staff who dragged us through a series of seemingly impossible deadlines, and to the readers who took time out from busy schedules to examine our work and make numerous useful criticisms and suggestions. Beth Cohen and H. Alan Shapiro gave careful scrutiny to the visual images presented here but are in no way responsible for any errors of judgment the authors may have exercised. We are grateful also to Jørgen Mejer for his advice on the Presocratics and to Margaret Miles for bringing up to date the plan of the Archaic agora of Athens.

Finally, we must thank Gail Davis, whose editorial sagacity has smoothed the rough edges from several of these chapters; Robert Lejeune, who offered computer assistance when it was most needed and endured our assorted technoflubs with remarkable patience; and Miriam Burstein, who not only undertook to obtain the necessary permissions from various publishers but also handled with grace and firmness the challenging task of reminding us that we were writing for ordinary mortals, not omniscient deities.

We acknowledge with thanks the publishers who have granted permission to quote translations. Unattributed translations in the text are by the authors.

The authors would also like to call the reader's attention to the extensive glossary at the end, which provides capsule descriptions of many of the terms that occur in the book.

Jennifer Roberts, New York City
Stanley Burstein, Los Alamitos, California

Walter Donlan, Irvine, California
Sarah Pomeroy, New York City

ACKNOWLEDGMENTS

The authors wish to acknowledge the following publishers for their kind permission to reprint material from their publications.

American Historical Association: From *The Hellenistic Period in World History*, by Stanley M. Burstein. Copyright © 1996.

Aris & Phillips, Ltd.: From *Plato: Phaedrus*, edited and translated by C. J. Rowe. Copyright © 1988.

Cambridge University Press: From *The Hellenistic Age from the battle of Ipsos to the death of Kleopatra VII*, edited and translated by Stanley M. Burstein. Copyright © 1985.

Columbia University Press: From *Zenon Papyri. Business Papers of the Third Century B.C. Dealing with Palestine and Egypt*, vol. 2, edited by W. L. Westermann, C. W. Keyes, and H. Liebesny. Copyright © 1940.

Harvard University Press and the Loeb Classical Library: From *Isocrates*, vol. 1, translated by George Norlin. Copyright © 1928.

Johns Hopkins University Press: From *Hesiod: Works and Days*, translated by Apostolos N. Athanassakis. Copyright © 1983. From *Pindar's Victory Songs*, translated by Frank Nisetich. Copyright © 1980.

Oxford University Press: From *The Republic of Plato*, translated by Francis MacDonald Cornford. Copyright © 1945. From *The Politics of Aristotle*, translated by Ernest Barker. Copyright © 1946. From *Xenophon: Oeconomicus: A social and historical commentary*, edited and translated by Sarah B. Pomeroy. Copyright © 1994.

Penguin Books: From *Plutarch: The Age of Alexander*, translated by Ian Scott Kilvert. Copyright © 1973. From: *Plutarch on Sparta*, translated by Richard Talbert. Copyright © 1988.

Schocken Books: From *Greek Lyric Poetry*, translated by Willis Barnstone. Copyright © 1972.

University of California Press: From *Sappho's Lyre*, translated by Diane J. Rayor. Copyright © 1991.

University of Chicago Press: From *Aeschylus: The Persians*, translated by S. Bernardete and *Aeschylus: The Oresteia*, translated by R. Lattimore in *The Complete Greek Tragedies*, vol. 1, edited by D. Grene and R. Lattimore. Copyright © 1959. From *Antigone,* translated by Elizabeth Wyckoff in *Greek Tragedies, Vol. 1,* edited by David Grene and Richmond Lattimore. From *The History of Herodotus,* translated by David Grene. Copyright © 1987. From *The Iliad of Homer,* translated by R. Lattimore. Copyright © 1951.

University of Oklahoma Press: From *Alexander the Great and the Greeks* by A. J. Heisserer. Copyright © 1980.

W. W. Norton and Company, Inc.: From *Herodotus: The Histories,* edited by Walter Blanco and Jennifer Tolbert Roberts, translated by Walter Blanco. Copyright © 1992. From *Thucydides: The Peloponnesian War,* edited by Walter Blanco and Jennifer Tolbert Roberts, translated by Walter Blanco. Copyright © 1998.

Yale University Press: From *Royal Correspondence in the Hellenistic Period: A Study in Greek Epigraphy,* edited and translated by C. B. Welles. Copyright © 1934.

TIME LINE

Period	Military Events	Political/ Social Events	Cultural Development
6500–3000 **Neolithic**		Permanent farming villages	Domestication of plants and animals; pottery
3000–2100 Early **Bronze Age** (Early Helladic 2800–1900)		Social ranking emerges; villages and districts ruled by hereditary chiefs	
			2500 Widespread use of bronze and other metals in Aegean
2100–1600 **Middle Bronze Age** (Middle Helladic 1900-1580)	2100–1900 Lerna and other sites destroyed	2100–1900 Incursions of Indo-European-speakers into Greece	2100–1900 Indo-European gods introduced into Greece
			2000 First palaces in Crete
			1900 Mainland contacts with Crete and the Near East
			1800 Cretans develop Linear A writing
1600–1150 Late Bronze **Age** (Late Helladic 1580–1150)		1600 Mycenae and other sites become power centers; small kingdoms emerge	1600 Shaft graves

continued

Period	Military Events	Political/ Social Events	Cultural Development
	1500–1450 Mycenaeans take over Crete		1500 Tholos tombs
			1450 Linear B writing
	1375 Knossos destroyed	1400–1200 Height of Mycenaean power and prosperity	1400 New palaces in Greece
	1250–1225 "The Trojan War"		
	1200 Invaders loot and burn the palace centers	1200–1100 Palace-system collapses	1200 Cultural decline
1150–900 Early Dark Age (Submycenaean 1125–1050) (Protogeometric 1050–900)		1050 Small chiefdoms established; migrations of mainland Greeks to Ionia	1050 Iron technology
		1000 Dorian Greeks settled in the mainland and the islands	1000 Monumental build-ing at Lefkandi
900–750 Late Dark Age (Early Geometric 900–850) (Middle Geometric 850–750)		900 Population increases; new settle-ments established; trade and manufacture expand	
		800 Rapid population growth	800 Greeks develop an alphabet; earliest temples built
			776 Traditional date of first Olympian games
750–490 Archaic Period (Late Geometric 750–700)	730–700 First Messenian War; Lelantine War	750-700 City-states emerge	750–720 *Iliad* and *Odyssey* composed
		750 Overseas coloniza-tion to the West begins	720 "Orientalizing pe-riod" in art begins

continued

Period	Military Events	Political/ Social Events	Cultural Development
	700–650 Evolution of hoplite armor and tactics		700 Hesiod; period of lyric poetry begins
	669 Battle of Hysiae	670–500 Tyrants rule in many city-states	
	650 Second Messenian War	650 Colonization of Black Sea area begins; earliest known stone inscription of a law; "Lycurgan Reforms" at Sparta; the "Great Rhetra" (?)	650 Temples built of stone and marble; Corinthian black-figure technique
		632 Cylon fails in attempt at tyranny in Athens	
		620 Law code of Draco in Athens	
		600 Lydians begin to mint coins	600 Beginnings of science and philosophy (the "Presocratics")
			582–573 Pythian, Isthmian, Nemean games inaugurated
		560–514 Peisistratus and his sons tyrants of Athens	Peisistratus expands religious festivals at Athens
		550 Sparta dominant in the Peloponnesus	
			530 Athenian red-figure technique
		507 Cleisthenes institutes political reforms in Athens	
	499 Ionian Greeks rebel from Persian Empire		

continued

Period	Military Events	Political/ Social Events	Cultural Development
	494 Defeat of Argos by Peloponnesian League in Battle of Sepea		5th century rationalists and scientists; Hippocrates; advances in medicine; increase in literacy
490–323 Classical Period	490 Battle of Marathon	489 Trial of Miltiades	Classical style in sculpture
		486 Decision to choose Athenian archons by lot	
		483 Ostracism of Aristides	
	480–479 Battles of Thermopylae, Artemisium, Salamis, Plataea, Mycale; Xerxes driven from Greece		
		477 Foundation of Delian League	
			470–456 Construction of temple of Zeus at Olympia
		Growth of democracy in Athens; Themistocles driven out of Athens, flees to Persia	
	463 Helot rebellion in Sparta	460s Prominence of Cimon	
		461 Reforms of Ephialtes at Athens; Pericles rises to prominence	
	460–445 "First" Peloponnesian War		
			458 Aeschylus' *Oresteia*
		454 Athenians move treasury from Delos to Athens	

continued

Period	Military Events	Political/ Social Events	Cultural Development
		Flourishing of Greek trade and manufacture	451 Pericles carries law limiting citizenship at Athens
			Herodotus at work on his *Histories*
			447–432 Construction of Parthenon at Athens
			Sophists active in Athens
	431–404 Peloponnesian War		Thucydides begins his *History*
		429 Death of Pericles	428 Sophocles' *Oedipus Tyrannus*
			425 Aristophanes' *Acharnians*
		423 Thucydides exiled from Athens	
		422 Deaths of Brasidas, Cleon	
		421 Peace of Nicias	
	415–413 Sicilian campaign		415 Euripides' *Trojan Women*
		411–410 Oligarchic coup in Athens; establishment of Council of 400; regime of the 5000	411 Aristophanes' *Lysistrata*
		407 Ascendance of Dionysus I at Syracuse	
	403–377 Sparta the most powerful state in Greece	404–403 Regime of the Thirty Tyrants in Athens	
		399 Trial and execution of Socrates	399–347 Dialogues of Plato; foundation of the Academy

continued

Period	Military Events	Political/ Social Events	Cultural Development
	395–387 Corinthian War	Fourth century: Rise of class of *rhetores* at Athens; economic inequalities and social *stasis* throughout Greece	
	377 Establishment of Second Athenian Naval Confederacy		
	377–371 Athens the most powerful state in Greece		
	371 Theban victory over Spartans at Leuctra		
	371–362 Thebes the most powerful state in Greece		
		Serious population decline in Sparta; impoverished class of "Inferiors" at Sparta; increasing amount of property in hands of Spartan women	
	359 Defeat of Perdiccas III	359 Accession of Philip II	
	357 Siege of Amphipolis	357 Marriage of Philip II to Olympias	
		357–355 Social War	
		356 Birth of Alexander the Great; outbreak of Third Sacred War	356 Philip II's Olympic victory
			355 Demosthenes' first speech
	352 Battle of Crocus Field		
	348 Capture of Olynthus		
			347 Death of Plato
		346 End of Third Sacred War; Peace of Philocrates	346 Isocrates' *Philippus*

continued

Period	Military Events	Political/Social Events	Cultural Development
	340 Athens and Macedon at war		
	338 Battle of Chaeronea	338 Assassination of Artaxerxes III; foundation of Corinthian League; marriage of Philip II and Cleopatra	338 Death of Isocrates
		338–325 Administration of Lycurgus at Athens	
	336 Invasion of Asia by Philip II	336 Accession of Darius III; assassination of Philip II; accession of Alexander III	
	335 Revolt of Thebes	335 Destruction of Thebes	335 Aristotle returns to Athens; founding of Lyceum
	334 Battle of Granicus		
	333 Battle of Issus	333 Alexander at Gordium	
	331 Battle of Gaugamela	331 Foundation of Alexandria	331 Visit to Siwah by Alexander
	330–327 War in Bactria and Sogdiana	330 Destruction of Persepolis; death of Philotas	
		329 Assassination of Darius III	
		328 Murder of Clitus	
	327–325 Alexander's invasion of India	327 Marriage of Alexander and Roxane	
	326 Battle of the Hydaspes		
		324 Exiles Decress	
323–30 Hellenistic Period		323 Death of Alexander III; accession of Philip III and Alexander IV	

continued

Time Line

Period	Military Events	Political/ Social Events	Cultural Development
	323–322 Lamian War	322 Dissolution of the Corinthian League	322 Deaths of Aristotle and Demosthenes
	321 Invasion of Egypt	321 Death of Perdiccas; Antipater becomes regent	321–292 Career of Menander
	318–316 Revolt against Polyperchon		
		317 Demetrius of Phaleron becomes tyrant of Athens	
	315–311 Four-year war against Antigonus	315 Freedom of Greeks proclaimed by Antigonus the One-Eyed	
		311 Peace between Antigonus and his rivals	
	307 Demetrius invades Greece	307 End of tyranny of Demetrius of Phalerum at Athens	307–283 Foundation of the Museum
	306 Battle of Salamis	306 Antigonus and Demetrius acclaimed kings	306 Epicurus founds Garden
	305–304 Siege of Rhodes	305 Ptolemy, Seleucus, Lysimachus, and Cassander declare themselves kings	
	301 Battle of Ipsus	301 Death of Antigonus; division of his empire	301 Zeno founds Stoa
			300–246 Construction of the Pharos
		283 Death of Ptolemy I; accession of Ptolemy II	
	281 Battle of Corupedium	281 Deaths of Lysimachus and Seleucus	
	279 Invasion of Gauls		
		237–222 Reign of Cleomenes III at Sparta	

continued

Period	Military Events	Political/ Social Events	Cultural Development
	222 Battle of Sellasia	222 Exile of Cleomenes III; end of his reforms at Sparta	
	200–197 Second Macedonian War		
		196 Flamininus proclaims freedom of the Greeks at Isthmian games	
	171–168 Third Macedonian War		
		167 End of the Macedonian monarchy	167 Polybius comes to Rome
	146 Sack of Corinth	146 Rome annexes Macedon and Greece	
	31 Battle of Actium		
		30 Suicide of Cleopatra VII; Rome annexes Egypt	

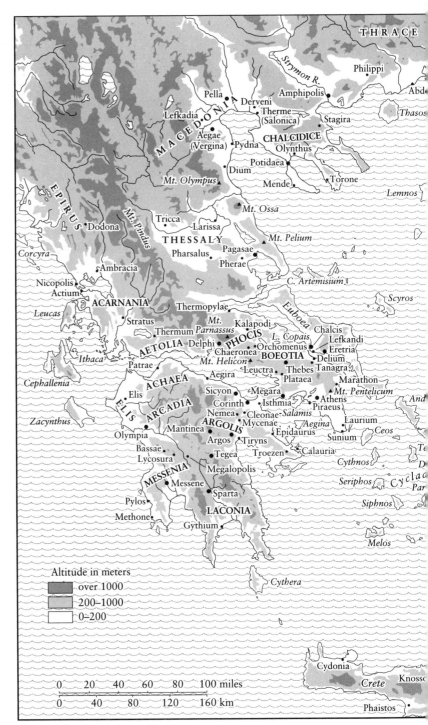

Greece and The Aegean World

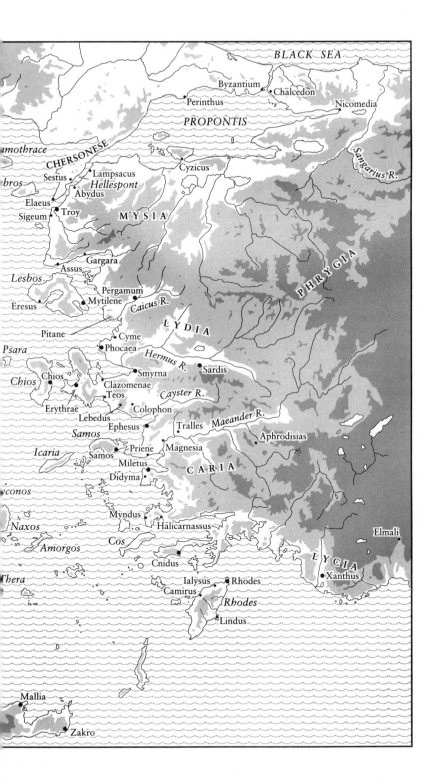

EARLY GREECE AND
THE BRONZE AGE

One of the greatest of the Greek cultural heroes was Odysseus, a man who "saw the towns of many men and learned their minds, and suffered in his heart many griefs upon the sea . . ." (*Odyssey* 1.3–4). Like their legendary hero, the Greeks were irresistibly drawn to distant shores. From early in their history and continually throughout antiquity they ventured over the seas to foreign lands seeking their fortunes as traders, colonizers, and mercenary soldiers. Their limited natural resources forced the Greeks to look outward, and they were fortunate in being within easy reach of the Mediterranean shores of Asia, Africa, and Europe. By the fifth century BC, they had planted colonies from Spain to the west coast of Asia and from north Africa to the Black Sea. The philosopher Plato (c. 429–347 BC) likened the hundreds of Greek cities and towns that ringed the coasts of the Mediterranean and Black seas to "frogs around a pond" (*Phaedo* 109b). Those far-flung Greeks left a priceless legacy of achievements in art, literature, politics, philosophy, mathematics, science, and war. Their story is a long and fascinating one.

THE LAND OF GREECE

A history of the Greeks (*Hellēnes*) must begin with the land, for the natural environment of a people—the landscape, the climate, and the natural resources—is a major factor in determining the way they live and how they develop socially. Greece (*Hellas*) occupies the southern portion of the Balkan peninsula, which juts far into the eastern Mediterranean Sea. Its reach was further extended by the Greek islands to the west and east of the mainland, embracing the large islands of Crete and Rhodes to the south.

Greece is about the size of England in Great Britain or the state of Alabama in the United States. The landscape is very rugged, with mountains covering almost 75 percent of the land. Only about 30 percent of the land can be cultivated at all, and only about 20 percent is classified as good agricultural land. Except in the northern mainland, where there are extensive plainlands, the mountains and lower hills cut the land into many narrow coastal plains, and upland plains and valleys. The mountain ranges, which are not terribly high (3000–8000 feet) but quite steep and craggy, made overland travel very difficult in antiquity, and somewhat isolated the small valleys and their people from one another.

By far the easiest way to travel was by sea, especially in the islands and the southern mainland, where the coast is never more than 40 miles away. The chains of islands in the Aegean Sea facilitated sea voyages. It is true that the rugged coastlines offer relatively few good harbors, and those choice locations were continuously occupied from earliest times. Yet sailors were seldom far from safe landfalls, where they could beach their boats for the night or find haven from a threatening storm. Throughout antiquity, the narrow Aegean tied the Greeks to the Near East and Egypt, commercially, culturally, politically, and militarily. The commercial contacts were vital, for, with the exception of building-stone and clay, Greece is not well endowed with raw materials. The necessity to trade overseas for raw materials, especially for bronze, destined the Greeks very early in their history to take to the sea and mingle with people from the other, older civilizations to the east and south.

The Mediterranean climate is semiarid, with long, hot, dry summers and short, cool, moist winters, when most of the rain falls. This general pattern varies from region to region in Greece. Northern Greece has a more continental climate, with much colder and wetter winters than the south. More rain falls on the western side of the Greek mainland than on the eastern side, while the Aegean islands receive even less. The generally mild weather permitted outdoor activity for most of the year. The soil in Greece though rocky is fairly rich, the most fertile plowland being in the small plains where, over the ages, earth washed down from the hills has formed deep deposits. The lower hillsides, which are rockier, can be cultivated through terracing, which prevents the soil from washing further down the slope and captures soil from above. The mountains, with their jagged limestone peaks and steep cliffs, support only wild vegetation, but some enclose mountain valleys suitable for farming and for grazing animals. Wood, essential for fuel and construction, especially shipbuilding, was originally abundant in the highland areas. As time went on, however, forests became depleted and by the fifth century BC the more populous regions were forced to import timber. Water, the most precious natural resource, is scarce in Greece, because there are very few rivers that flow year round and few lakes, ponds, and springs. Unlike in the huge river valleys of Egypt and Mesopotamia, irrigation on a large scale was not possible; farming depended on the limited annual rainfall.

It should be emphasized that this description of the land and resources of Greece is a generalized one. Though small in area, Greece has a variety of local landscapes and micro climates in which the rainfall, the quantity and quality of farmland, the pasture land, and raw materials are decidedly different. On the whole, however, the land, which the Greeks called Gaia ("Mother Earth"), allowed the majority of the farmers a decent though modest living. But she offered no guarantees. Drought, especially in the more arid regions, was a constant and dreaded threat. A dry winter meant a lean year, and a prolonged drought meant hunger and poverty for entire villages and districts. Torrential rainstorms, on the other hand, could send water rushing down the hillsides and through the dry gullies, suddenly wiping out the terraces, flooding the fields, and destroying the crops. Life on the sea was equally unpredictable. The Aegean, though often calm with favoring winds, could just as suddenly boil up into ferocious storms sending ships, cargo, and sailors to the bottom. (Drowning at sea, unburied, was a hateful death for the Greeks.) It is no wonder, considering the extent to which the Greeks were at the mercy of the land, sky, and sea, that the gods they worshipped were personifications of the elements and forces of nature.

Food and Livestock

In general, the soil and climate amply supported the "Mediterranean triad" of grain, grapes, and olives. Bread, wine, and olive oil were the staples of the Greek diet throughout antiquity and for long afterward. Grains—wheat, barley, and oats—grow well in Greek soil, having been cultivated from native wild grasses. Olive trees and grapevines, also indigenous to Greece, flourished in their cultivated state. Legumes (peas and beans) and several kinds of vegetables, fruits (especially figs), and nuts, rounded out and varied the basic components of bread, porridges, and olive oil. Cheese, meat, and fish, which are rich in proteins and fat, supplemented the diet; however, meat provided a very small part of the average family's daily food intake, and because fish are not abundant in the Mediterranean, they were usually eaten as a small "relish" with the meal. The Greeks did not like butter and drank little milk. Their beverages were water or wine (usually diluted with water). Honey was used for sweetening, and various spices enhanced the flavor of food. Though it might appear monotonous to modern tastes, the Greek diet was healthful and nourishing.

The pasturing of small animals did not interfere with agriculture. Flocks of sheep and goats grazed on hilly land that could not be farmed and on the fallow fields, providing manure in return. As suppliers of wool, cheese, meat, and skins, they had great economic importance. The Greeks also kept pigs, relished for their meat, and fowl. The two largest domesticated animals, horses and cattle, occupied a special niche in the economy and the society. Oxen (castrated bulls) or mules (hybrids of the horse and donkey) were necessary for plowing and for drawing heavy loads. A farmer without ready access to a yoke of oxen or a pair of mules would be classified as poor. Herds of cattle and horses did compete with agriculture, since the stretches of good grazing land they required were also prime farmland. Practically speaking, there could be large-scale ranching of cattle and horses (except in the northern plains) only in times of low population density. Because they were such costly luxuries, cattle and horses were a status symbol for the rich. Cattle were raised mainly for their meat and hides. Horses were the primary markers of high social status: beautiful creatures, very expensive to maintain, and useful only for riding and for pulling light chariots.

This agricultural and pastoral way of life remained essentially unchanged throughout Greek history. The fundamental economic fact that ancient Greece was essentially a land of small-scale farmers (most of whom lived in farming villages and small towns) governed every aspect of Greek society, from politics to war to religion. It has been estimated that even in the fifth to third centuries BC, the peak population period, up to 90 percent of the citizens of a city-state were engaged in agriculture. One of the major unifying forces within the Greek city-states was the citizen-farmers' devotion to their small agricultural plain and its surrounding hillsides, and their willingness to die defending their "ancestral earth," as the poet Homer called it. And the primary disunifying force throughout Greek history was the perpetual tension between those citizens who had much land and those who had little or none.

SOURCES FOR EARLY GREEK HISTORY

True history in the sense of specific events involving specific persons would not begin until the seventh century BC, when writing made it possible to record what was happening in the Greek world. Knowledge of what had happened earlier came in the form of ancient *mythoi* ("stories"), which were transmitted orally from generation to generation for hundreds of years. The ancient Greek historians accepted these myths, many of which had been committed to writing, as historical fact and used them to reconstruct the early history of the Greeks. Modern historians, however, realizing how much old stories can change in their countless retellings, are generally skeptical of their historical value, although it is possible that some of them contain elements of truth.

The primary legend of the Greek past was the story of the Trojan War, a ten-year assault against the large fortified city of Troy in northwest Anatolia (modern Turkey) by a huge armada of Greeks led by Agamemnon, king of Mycenae, a large city in the Peloponnesus. If such a war had actually occurred (modern historians are divided on the question), it would have taken place during the thirteenth century BC, at the height of Bronze Age prosperity and military might. For later Greeks, the chief repositories of knowledge concerning the world of the Trojan War were the *Iliad* and the *Odyssey*, two long narrative poems attributed to Homer, the poet whom they regarded as the greatest of all. The poems, however, were composed five centuries after the time of the Trojan War, around 750 to 700 BC. They correctly portrayed the era of the Trojan War as one of great wealth and architectural splendor, but in the long process of oral transmission the actual society of the Late Bronze Age was completely forgotten. The type of society reflected in the poems is in fact much closer in time to that of the poet.

The discrepancy between the way the eighth-century Greeks imagined the world of the Bronze Age and what that world was really like has been revealed by archaeological discoveries. Almost everything we know of early Greece has come from the study of the excavated remains. Scientific or systematic archaeology (the study of *archaia*, "ancient things") goes back a little more than a century.

Before the late nineteenth century antiquarians had tunneled and dug in ancient graves and settlements, but they were primarily interested in uncovering precious art objects, not in using the artifacts and other finds to reconstruct the nature and history of the excavated site. Today, archaeology is a science, which employs highly sophisticated methods and equipment to wring every bit of information from the material remains. It has come a long way from the early organized expeditions, whose techniques appear crude by today's standards. Yet, we must admire the achievements of those pioneer archaeologists who, inventing the discipline as they went along, were the first to uncover and describe the ancient civilizations of the Near East, Egypt, and Greece.

Thanks to the science of archaeology, scholars today know infinitely more about the society and culture of early Greece than did the ancient Greeks themselves, who knew it only through the myths and legends. Even so, many questions remain unanswered or only partially answered. Prehistoric archaeology has only the silent fragments of ancient civilizations. The sites are buried deep under the surface, each level of habitation crushed under the enormous pressure of the succeeding layers and eroded by time and the forces of nature. By piecing together the evidence (in many cases literally), archaeologists can reconstruct with fair accuracy the material aspects of life and society. It is much more difficult, however, to make inferences about social behavior and beliefs from the archaeological remains. In this respect, Aegean archaeologists are fortunate, for they have not only a large amount but also a wide variety of material from which to reconstruct the society, including painted pottery, murals, engravings, sculptures, and, most important, written records, preserved on clay tablets. Those kinds of evidence have added immeasurably to our understanding of the early Greek culture.

GREECE IN THE STONE AGES

The archaeology of primitive Greece has made great strides in this century; nevertheless, the sparsely populated Stone Ages remain very obscure. Humans have lived in Greece since at least the Middle Paleolithic (Old Stone) Age (c. 55,000–30,000 BC). These earliest inhabitants lived mainly by hunting and some gathering of wild plants, using finely crafted tools and weapons of stone, wood, and bone. At the end of the Ice Age, when the glaciers that had covered much of Europe were receding (c.12,000 BC), the climate of Greece warmed considerably; in the process the landscape and its plants and animals were altered into their present forms. Evidence from a cave in southern Greece, at a place called Franchthi, shows that the inhabitants at the end of the Ice Age hunted deer and smaller game, caught fish in the coastal waters, and gathered wild cereals, wild peas and beans, and nuts. They probably also had some experience with going to sea in small boats made of reeds and skins.

Early in the Neolithic (New Stone) Age (c. 6500–3000 BC) the people learned to cultivate the wild cereals and other plants and to domesticate animals, beginning the farming and herding economy that was to be the mainstay of Greek life until the modern era. This new way of life, which repeated a process that had begun in the Near East nearly two thousand years earlier, may have been introduced by newcomers from western Anatolia. The cultivation of plants is a watershed event in the lives of a people. It allows population to increase and forces them to settle down permanently. The Neolithic Age saw the first appearance of small, permanent farming villages, made up of one-room houses similar in construction to those of the Near East. Houses were built of sun-dried mud bricks laid over low stone foundations, with floors of stamped earth and flat or pitched roofs made of thatch or brush. The Neolithic house style and the custom of clustering houses together in small communities would persist with little change for millennia in Greece and the Near East. In the favorable conditions of the warm New Stone Age, villages grew larger and new village communities were formed.

The social organization of the small Stone Age villages was probably very simple. Families cooperated and shared with their neighbors, most of whom were also their kinfolk. We may assume that by this time division of labor by gender and age and the dominance of males over females had become established, and although no one individual or family held a dominant position, temporary leadership was probably assumed now by this man, now by another, as the need arose. At a certain point in the growth of population, however, leadership roles emerged that were more formal and more lasting. This semipermanent position of leadership was held by a type of person anthropologists call the "big man" or the "head man," one who is better at "getting things done." His force of character, sense of responsibility, wisdom in solving disputes, courage in the face of danger, and like qualities propel him to the front and keep him there. In time this position becomes a sort of "office," into which a new man, having demonstrated that he is better suited than the other would-be leaders, steps when the old head man retires or dies (or is pushed out). That this kind of political and social "ranking" occurred in the Neolithic period is almost certain. Thereafter, the division into two groups, the very small group of those who led and the large group of those who were led, would be a permanent feature of Greek political life.

THE ANCIENT CIVILIZATIONS OF THE NEAR EAST

While rank societies were evolving in Greece and elsewhere on the European continent, a new kind of society was forming in western Asia and northern Africa: the "state" and "civilization." When the Greeks attained a high civilization (around 1600 BC), the civilized cultures of the Near East and Egypt were already 1500 years old. The direct teachers of the Greeks would be the Cretans, who had attained this level by about 2000 BC, but the growth of civilization on Crete was itself a product of contact with the older civilizations. The history of ancient Greek civilization is entwined with the civilizations of the East.

The region where the earliest civilization emerged was called by later Greeks Mesopotamia, "the land between the rivers" Tigris and Euphrates. In that wide, fertile river plain the ability to organize and control the natural and social environments was advancing to a higher level around 3500 BC. There appeared, for the first time in the history of the world, large-scale irrigation, metal technology, large cities, bureaucratic administration, complex trade networks, and writing.

Most of these new features had their roots in earlier Mesopotamian culture. The progression to civilization was the result of the concurrent advancement and interaction of certain features, which created a spiraling effect. Advancements in the technology of irrigation increased food production, which enabled population to increase further. The responsibility of the leaders to mobilize labor and resources for increasingly ambitious irrigation projects gave them more power and turned them into a privileged ruling class, sharply differentiated from the mass of the people. The growing appetite of the governing elites for luxury goods befitting their high status increased the quantity and quality of manufacture at home and led to the rapid expansion of long-distance trade for raw materials and exotic items. These goods were paid for with ever-increasing surpluses from the land, more and more of which came under the control of the rulers.

The Egyptian civilization, which emerged around 3200 BC along the long, narrow valley of the Nile, followed the same trajectory as civilizations of the Near East, except that very early on Egypt became a united kingdom under a single pharaoh (king). The Aegean civilizations of Crete and Greece would pattern themselves on the Near Eastern model of separate city-states and kingdoms.

City-States and Kingdoms

In Mesopotamia, as advances were made in agricultural production, towns with hundreds of people grew into cities with thousands, and even tens of thousands, of inhabitants. In the fertile irrigated areas, the largest and most powerful city dominated the towns and villages and drew them into a single political unit, administered from the capital. The territories of those earliest city-states, as they are called, were fairly small, usually no more than a few hundred square miles; yet the step from a loose community of towns and villages into a centralized state changed the course of human history.

With civilization, society became highly stratified. The leader and his immediate subordinates made all the decisions, which were carried out by lower-status officials and their assistants. The wide base of the social pyramid was made up of the primary producers, free farmers and herdsmen, who were required to give to the state (i.e., the palace) a portion of their annual production, contribute their labor to irrigation and construction projects, and serve in the army. Many of them were dependents of the ruling class, working as tenants on land that belonged to the palace and to the temples of the gods. Some craftsmen also worked directly for the state. At the very bottom, below the free but dependent population, were slaves. Although slavery predated the advent of civilization, it was only after the formation of the state that it became economically important and practiced on a large scale.

The formation of states transformed Mesopotamian society in all sorts of ways. Artistry and craftsmanship made gigantic strides, writing was invented, architecture took on a monumental character. All of these cultural refinements served the elites as tools of social control. The kings and the high nobles, using a huge portion of the surplus wealth from agriculture, manufacture, and trade, as well as millions of hours of human labor, built massive defensive walls and temples, and luxurious palaces and elaborate tombs for themselves and their families. Architecture especially served religion, which became the most important means of control, for it identified the will of the ruler with the will of the gods. Vast wealth and increased population allowed battles to be fought on a large scale by well-organized armies; and war progressed from spontaneous actions inspired by revenge or greed for booty into deliberate campaigns of punishment or conquest by one ruler against another.

The natural reflex of states that border on one another is to try to gain dominion. In early Mesopotamia, a powerful city-state would intimidate and conquer its weaker neighbors, becoming the capital city. Its ruler would then become the great king over a number of vassal states. These kingdoms were inherently unstable, both because the core city-state itself was continually beset by internal struggles for power, and because the subject cities were constantly asserting their independence. Moreover, there was an ongoing threat of raids from people on the fringes of civilization. Large groups of warriors would sometimes move en masse out of the mountains or deserts to take over cities and kingdoms. Such was the geopolitical world in which the civilizations of Crete and then of Greece emerged in the second millennium BC.

GREECE IN THE EARLY BRONZE AGE (c. 3000–2100 BC)

The technology of smelting and casting copper appears to have originated independently in both western Asia and southeastern Europe before 6000 BC. The crucial next step, of adding 10 percent of tin to the copper to produce bronze, a much harder metal, was taken in the Near East during the fourth millennium. The technique came to Greece around 3000 BC; by about 2500, the use of bronze as well as other metals such as lead, silver, and gold became widespread throughout Greece and the Aegean.

The introduction of metallurgy was a major technological advance, for tools and weapons of bronze were considerably more efficient than those made of stone, bone, or copper. The impact was not just utilitarian, however; the movement into the Bronze Age marked a turning point in Greek social and economic relations, just as it had in the East. It was the high-ranked individuals and families, those with greater surpluses of wealth, who had the most access to bronze and scarce metal products. Possession of these and other prestige items set them further apart from the mass of the population. Their increasing demand for metal goods gave rise to local specialists and workshops and accelerated trade for copper and tin and other metals, not only with the East, but also with the peoples of central and western Europe. Early Bronze Age Greece was edging its way into the wider economy and culture of the Mediterranean world. And as the economy expanded and the settlements grew larger, so did the wealth, power, and authority of their leaders, now established as hereditary chiefs who ruled for life and were accorded exceptional honors and privileges.

A major Early Bronze Age settlement was the town of Lerna in Argolis, where the remains of strong stone fortifications and some monumental buildings have been found, the largest of which may have been the house of the ruling chief. The sophistication of the architecture and the quality of the artifacts betoken a fairly complex political and economic system, though far less advanced than those of the Near East and Egypt. Lerna flourished from about 3000 to about 2100, when it was destroyed along with a number of other towns and villages in Argolis, Attica, and Laconia. Similar devastation of settlements occurred throughout much of Europe at this time.

GREECE IN THE MIDDLE BRONZE AGE
(c. 2100–1600 BC)

After the destructions, Greece entered what appears to have been a period of cultural stagnation. During the next five hundred years the archaeological record is both sparse and generally unimpressive. Most historians connect both the destructions of the sites and the ensuing cultural lag to the incursion of a new people into the central and southern mainland of Greece. The arrival of these newcomers, who spoke a very early form of Greek, marked a decisive turning point in the history and culture of Greece and the Aegean.

As is usual with events that occurred so early in prehistory, there is uncertainty about when the speakers of proto-Greek entered Greece. It may have been as early as 2100 BC, or two centuries later, when there is evidence of a new type of pottery and other possibly new cultural features. On the basis of such material, archaeologists have labeled this intermediate cultural stage the "Middle Helladic" period (c. 1900–1580). The picture is confused by a third theory, which places the arrival of the Greek-speakers at the end of the Middle Helladic period, around 1600 BC. Despite the ongoing controversy about when they entered, however, it is unanimously agreed that the newcomers were part of a huge wave of migrating groups from the north and east known collectively as the Indo-Europeans. This knowledge was the result of modern linguistic discoveries.

The Indo-Europeans

In the eighteenth century AD, scholars began to recognize that ancient Greek bore many similarities to other dead languages, such as Latin, Old Persian, and Sanskrit (the language of ancient India), as well as to entire families of spoken languages, such as the Germanic and Slavic. They observed, for example, a striking similarity in words such as "mother": Sanskrit *mātar*, Greek *mētēr*, Latin *mater*, Anglo-Saxon *mōdor*, Old Irish *mathir*, Lithuanian *mote*, Russian *mat'*. The close likenesses in vocabulary and grammatical structure among ancient languages and their descendants soon led to the insight that they had all sprung from a common linguistic ancestor, which was termed "Proto-Indo-European." It was reasoned that there had once been a single Indo-European homeland, located perhaps in the vast steppes north of the Black and Caspian seas (one of several suggested homelands), and that the separate languages developed in the course of emigrations from the homeland into distant places. The speakers of proto-Greek were thus a part of a great and lengthy ancient exodus of peoples, which gradually over the centuries spread the Indo-European languages across Europe and Asia, from Ireland to Chinese Turkestan.

The First Greek-Speakers

Eventually, the language of the Greek-speaking newcomers replaced the non-Indo-European "Aegean" languages, which survived in Greek primarily in place names (e.g., *Korinthos*) and in names for indigenous animals and plants, such as *hyakinthos*, ("hyacinth"). This would seem to indicate that the Greek-speakers were the dominant group within the society, but one language may displace another for reasons other than conquest and dominance. At any rate, the process of displacement was probably a long one, with both Greek and indigenous languages existing side by side for centuries.

During the nineteenth and early twentieth centuries, there was considerable conjecture about the nature of the social organization and culture of these earliest Greek-speakers. It was assumed that the Indo-Europeans were a superior race of northern horse-riding "Aryan" warriors, who swept down into southern Europe and violently imposed their languages and customs on the weaker, unwarlike, agrarian natives. Such suppositions were the products of a racially biased Eurocentrism. No scholar today accepts any part of this "Aryan myth," which was the pretext for so many crimes against humanity in the nineteenth and twentieth centuries, culminating in the horrors perpetrated by the Nazis and Fascists in the 1930s and '40s.

The most we can safely say about these incoming Indo-European Greek-speakers is that for subsistence they practiced herding and agriculture, and they knew metallurgy and other crafts, such as pottery and cloth-making. Of their society, we can surmise only that they were organized in families and larger groups (clans and tribes) that were patriarchal (the father was the supreme authority figure) and patrilineal (descent was reckoned in the male line). Their primary divinity was Zeus, a powerful male god; and they were a warlike people with a hierarchical leadership system. The once common notion that the pre-Indo-European societies of Greece around 2000 BC were polar opposites—peaceful, nonhierarchical, and matriarchal (where descent, inheritance, and authority came down through the mother)—is now discredited. In most respects, except for language, religion, and some relatively minor features (such as architecture and pottery), the two peoples were probably very similar.

The drop in the cultural level during the archaeological Middle Helladic period (c. 1900–1580 BC) is best explained as a long stage of adjustment, during which the native people and the newcomers gradually merged into a single people through generations of intermarriage, and their two cultures fused into a single Greek-speaking culture that contained elements of both. Nor in fact was the Middle Bronze (Middle Helladic) period totally static. Population increased, new settlements grew up, there were advances in metallurgy, and contacts with the civilizations of Crete and the Near East began. These would lead, toward the end of the period, to a sudden cultural quickening that ushered in the high civilization of the Late Bronze (Late Helladic) period.

THE DISCOVERY OF AEGEAN CIVILIZATION: TROY, MYCENAE, KNOSSOS

That advanced civilizations had existed in the Aegean during the Bronze Age was not known until the unearthing in the late nineteenth century of three famous cities from the mythical Age of Heroes. First, in 1870, Heinrich Schliemann, a wealthy German businessman turned archaeologist, discovered the city of Troy. In Schliemann's day, most historians dismissed the Mycenaeans' war against Troy (the central event of the Greeks' ancient past) as just another mythical tale. Schliemann, however, was convinced that the Trojan War had happened exactly as it was told in the early epic poems, the *Iliad* and the *Odyssey*. Using his beloved Homer as a guide, he dug at a place called Hissarlik on the northeast coast of Anatolia and revealed the massive ruins of a Bronze Age city, which he identified as the fabled Troy. The news electrified the scholarly world and captured the public's imagination. There really had been a Troy, found where Homer said it was located!

Four years later, Schliemann began his excavations of Bronze Age Mycenae itself. Though a small, rather insignificant town throughout recorded Greek history, prehistoric Mycenae turned out to be more than worthy of the legendary hero Agamemnon, its king and the leader of the Greek invasion of Troy. Although Schliemann's discoveries are not conclusive evidence of a large-scale war between Troy and Mycenae, the impressive ruins unearthed at both sites, with their immense wealth in gold and other costly things, do prove correct the Greeks' remembrance of their Heroic Age (i.e., the Late Bronze Age) as a time of fabulous wealth and splendor. Because Mycenae was the richest (as well as the first) site explored in mainland Greece, archaeologists refer to the entire culture of Greece in the Late Bronze (Late Helladic) period (c. 1580–1150 BC) as the Mycenaean Age.

MINOAN SOCIETY AND CULTURE (c. 1700–1500 BC)

No less spectacular was the discovery in 1899 of the third fabled site, the "palace" complex of Knossos on Crete, by the English archaeologist Arthur Evans. Evans called the civilization on Crete "Minoan," after the mythical king Minos of Knossos, who lived, according to Homer, three generations before the Trojan War. In the *Iliad* and the *Odyssey* Knossos is the dominant city of a rich and populous land. Odysseus, the hero of the *Odyssey*, describes it as follows:

> There is a land called Crete, in the middle of the wine-dark sea,
> beautiful and fertile, surrounded by water; and in it
> there are many people, countless, and ninety cities. . . .
> and among them is Knossos, the great city, where Minos
> was king . . . and conversed with great Zeus.
>
> (Odyssey *19.172–179*)

Very little is known about the early history of this large, mountainous island (3400 square miles). Around 7000 BC, the earliest inhabitants, people of unknown language and origin, settled in the central and eastern parts, where there were fairly large fertile plains, and practiced farming and stock raising. During the fourth millennium, new settlements sprang up and some of the small farming villages grew into substantial towns. With population growth and increasing production, the chiefs gained considerably greater powers in their towns and villages. And just as in the Near East, the chiefs of the major settlements emerged as the single rulers over the other chiefs and people in the various districts. Thus Crete became a land of small city-kingdoms.

The first royal palace in Crete was built about 2000 BC at Knossos, which by then was a large town with several thousand inhabitants. Other major palaces, though not as big or as magnificent as Knossos, followed at Phaistos, Mallia, Zakro, and elsewhere, each center controlling an area of a few hundred square miles. The political and cultural flowering in Crete (and on other Aegean islands as well) probably can be attributed to their inclusion in the international trade, which was a major component of the state economies of the East. Cretan contact with Egypt and western Asia was both heavy and direct, because the island's location and natural harbors made it an important crossroad in the trade routes across the Mediterranean Sea. The palace-centered economies that emerged in Crete, accordingly, were replicas, on a much smaller scale, of the state economies of the Near East.

Whether the small Minoan kingdoms were consolidated into larger political units, as happened in the Near East, remains an open question. One opinion is that by the sixteenth century BC the island, or most of it, was a unified kingdom, ruled by the king of Knossos. Others suggest that Knossos was the dominant center of a looser federation of self-ruling states, which seems more likely.

The Minoan Palace Economy

The palace-complex that we see today at Knossos was begun around 1700 BC, after the first palace was destroyed by an earthquake. During its existence it underwent numerous restorations and additions until its final destruction around 1375. Knossos and the other smaller Cretan palaces consisted of a maze of rooms—residential quarters, workshops, and storerooms—clustered around a large central courtyard. As in the East, the palace was the central place of the entire society. The impressive residence of the ruler and his high-ranking subordinates appears to have been the political and administrative center and the focal point of economic activity, state ceremony, and religious ritual for the entire kingdom.

The type of economy that developed around Knossos and the other Cretan centers is called a redistributive economy. The center—the king and the palace—probably had considerable control over the allocation and use of the surrounding land, much of which belonged directly to the palace. Produce from the palace's lands along with produce from private farms and herds, paid as taxes, was funneled into the palace, where it was stored. The king could distribute these as he willed. The influx of food and raw materials provided his family and his entourage with a luxurious lifestyle and also supplied the needs of the low-status workers in the palace complex. In addition, the great quantities of grain and olive oil stored in the palace formed a reserve for distribution to the populace in times of famine or other calamity.

The king's main use of his surplus, however, was for trade. The large areas of the palace devoted to storage and workshops indicate that a significant portion of what was produced was meant to be sent out in exchange for other things. The palace's workshops were kept busy turning raw materials from the countryside, such as wool, flax, and hides, as well as bronze, gold, ivory, and amber from abroad, into material goods. No doubt some of these were traded internally, among the city-kingdoms. Throughout the island, traces have been found of networks of good roads, along which food, animals, and goods would have passed between the centers and into the smaller towns and villages. It was the exchange of materials and goods on the Mediterranean-wide market, however, that made Knossos and the other Cretan centers so rich.

The increasing diversity and complexity of the Cretan palace economies is shown by their adoption of writing for the purpose of management. About 1900 BC the Cretans developed pictographic writing, perhaps inspired by Egyptian hieroglyphics, in which a picture symbolizes an object or idea (as in "I [heart symbol] New York"). This evolved around 1800 BC into a more stylized linear script made up of specific signs that stood for syllables and were joined together to form the sound of the words themselves. Although this script (called "Linear A" by archaeologists), preserved on small clay tablets, remains largely undeciphered, it is clear that it was used for keeping the economic records in the palaces.

The Social Classes of Crete

Evidence of a class society shows up archaeologically as a huge difference in the living standards, lifestyles, and social status of the privileged few and the rest of the people. The architecture and the finds at Knossos and other centers give us a good idea of the enormous luxury enjoyed by the royal family and the nobility. Archaeologists have also found in towns outside the palaces comfortable two- and three-story houses, which indicate the existence of a lower tier of elite families. This group of well-off townspeople probably formed a very small segment of the free population, and was possibly part of the administrative and commercial sectors. On the other hand, the thousands of ordinary farmers and crafts workers have left almost no trace in the archaeological record. What little evidence there is indicates that they lived in small, sparsely furnished houses in small villages and were buried with meager funerary gifts in simple graves. In other words, they lived much as their ancestors had. It was only the high-ranked families that enjoyed vastly increased wealth and more luxurious lifestyles, benefits derived from the taxes and labor extracted from the people.

In all probability, ordinary Cretan people, like the common people in Egypt and in the Near East, accepted their roles as exploited subjects willingly, in the belief that the rigidly hierarchical arrangement was quite proper. It is true that people received benefit in the form of protection from famine and from outside aggressors. Still, their willing acceptance of the heavy interference in their lives by the center indicates something more—their positive identification with the center, that is, the king. In Crete, as in all ancient kingdoms, the king was a symbol as well as the actual ruler. He was the embodiment of the state: supreme war leader, lawgiver and judge, and, most important, the representative of the land and people to the gods.

This enlargement of the ruler's priestly function, cultural historians believe, was one of the key factors in the rise of monarchical power. Certainly the kings of ancient Egypt and the Near East derived much of their legitimacy from the official equation of royal power with the will of the gods. The Egyptians expanded this principle by identifying each new pharaoh as the human incarnation of the god Horus. Some Mediterranean scholars believe that the Minoan kings ruled as priest-kings like the Mesopotamian kings. A major difference, though, is that Bronze Age Crete lacked the huge temple complexes of the Near East; rather the palaces themselves appear to have been the religious centers of the society.

Slavery

Occupying an economic and social level below the free farmers and palace dependents were the slaves. What differentiates true slaves from others who work by compulsion is not so much how they are treated as the fact that they are possessions, not persons. Though they live in a community, they are not members of it and thus lack even the most rudimentary protections against arbitrary use of their bodies. Because most slaves in the ancient world were war captives, that is, outsiders, it was easy to set them apart as non persons. Although the practice of capturing people and making them slaves undoubtedly went back to the Stone Ages, it was only with the emergence of civilization and the state in the fourth millennium that enslavement occurred on a large scale as a matter of policy and economic necessity. We have no way of estimating the proportion of slaves to the rest of the population in the Aegean societies. It is probable, however, that the majority of them belonged to the palaces.

Minoan Culture

Minoan art and architecture owed a large debt to the civilizations of the Near East, and especially Egypt. The Cretans developed extensive commercial and diplomatic relations with Egypt and the states along the Syrian and Phoenician coasts, and they adopted both the techniques and styles of the older civilizations. The spirit of Minoan art and architecture, however, was very different. The predominant function of palace art in the East was to glorify the royal household. The kings were depicted as mighty conquerors and powerful rulers. In Minoan art, on the other hand, there are no scenes that show the king as a conquering warrior and indeed very few, if any, images of royal pomp. The subjects and motifs of the wall paintings are much the same as those in the "middle class" villas. Nature motifs are everywhere. The spirit of Minoan palace art is serene and happy, even playful at times. It was meant to make the palace a place of beauty and charm.

Visitors to the ruins of Knossos, which was greatly restored by Arthur Evans in the early twentieth century, are dazzled by its size and complexity (it covered 3.2 acres with perhaps three hundred rooms) and the elegance of its architecture. The palace was well constructed of stone and mud brick, reinforced with timbers (to help withstand earthquakes); it stood two and three stories high with basements beneath. Porticoes (with columns that seem upside down to us) and numerous balconies and loggias, all brightly painted, gave the exterior a theatrical look. Light wells brought daylight and fresh air into the interior of the palace. A system of conduits and drains provided many of the rooms with running water and waste disposal. Walls and passageways were adorned with brilliantly colored paintings of plant and animal life and with scenes of human activity, often religious processions or rituals.

Minoan paintings are much admired today for their sophistication, vitality, and exuberance and stand comparison with the best of contemporary ancient art. Although Egyptian scene paintings were more accurate in detail, Cretan painters were more skillful at conveying a sense of movement and life. Minoan pottery, jewelry, and metal and ivory work display equal technical and artistic skill. Minoan frescoes and small sculptures have preserved a visual image of what the people looked like, that is to say the rich and powerful inhabitants of the palaces and "villas." Men and women both are depicted as young, slender, and graceful. The men are smooth shaven and wear only a short kilt, similar to the Egyptian male dress. The women wear elaborate flounced skirts and a tight, sleeved bodice

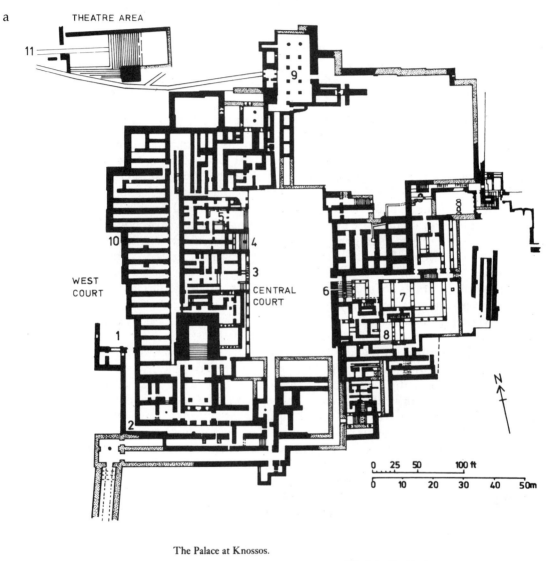

a

THEATRE AREA

11

9

10

WEST
COURT

4

3

CENTRAL
COURT

6

7

1

8

2

N

```
0    25   50        100 ft
├────┼────┼──────────┤
0   10   20   30   40   50m
```

The Palace at Knossos.

1 West Porch
2 Corridor of the Procession
3 Palace Shrine
4 Stepped porch
5 Throne Room
6 Grand Staircase

7 Hall of the Double Axes
8 'Queen's Megaron'
9 Pillar Hall
10 Store-rooms
11 Royal Road, to Little Palace

Figure 1.1a. Ground plan of the Minoan palace at Knossos, Crete. **Figure 1.1b.** View of the ruins of the Minoan palace at Phaistos, Crete.

b

that exposes their breasts. Both men and women have long hair, stylishly curled, and wear gold bracelets and necklaces.

The placid and carefree outlook of Minoan art, the fact that none of the Cretan palace-complexes was walled, and the later Greek tradition that Knossos under king Minos had been a mighty sea power, led earlier generations of scholars to picture Crete as a peaceful, secure island, untouched by internal and external conflict. However, more recent discoveries of depictions of land and naval battles and some remains of fortification walls have largely dispelled that romantic view.

Minoan Influence in the Aegean: Thera

That the Cretans exercised actual political control outside of Crete is doubtful. They did, however, exert considerable economic and cultural influence in the Cycladic islands. A remarkable example of Minoan cultural hegemony was discovered on the island of Thera (modern Santorini), 80 miles north of Crete. In 1967, the Greek archaeologist Spyridon Marinatos began excavation of a thriving city of several thousand inhabitants, which lay buried under 50 yards of volcanic ash. The explosion that tore apart the tiny island—considered the most powerful volcanic eruption in all of history—occurred, according to the latest scientific dating, around 1630 BC. As in Pompeii (the Roman provincial city buried by an eruption of Mount Vesuvius in 79 AD), the hardened ash formed a protective envelope, allowing us today a detailed picture of town life at the height of the Minoan civilization. The frescoes that adorn the walls of a number of houses are very similar in style and also equal in imagination and execution to the finest paintings from Crete. Less spectacular finds from other Cycladic islands show a similar "Minoanization" in such things as art, religion, dress, and lifestyles. Nevertheless, several distinctly "local" features among the island cultures indicate that those prosperous islands were independent societies, trading partners, not colonial outposts of a Cretan empire.

THE MYCENAEANS

About the time Thera was destroyed, the Greeks were just emerging into their civilizational stage. They too were heavily influenced by the Cretans and even adopted the model of the Minoan state. A century or so later Minoanized Greeks from the mainland, the Mycenaeans, ungratefully repaid their teachers by invading Crete and taking over their power centers.

As was noted earlier, "Mycenaean" refers to the entire civilization of Greece during the Late Bronze (Late Helladic) period (c. 1580–1150 BC). The emergence in mainland Greece of a hierarchical political and social system, based on centralized control of the economy, recapitulated the process of state formation in the Near East and Crete. Before 1600 Greece had gone through the preparatory steps: rise in population, increased productivity, expansion of trade with the out-

Figure 1.2. Fresco of a fisherman from Thera.

side, and the strengthening of the economic and political power of the leaders. As the southern mainland Greek states became full participants in the Mediterranean trading economy, they put on the ready-made cloak of Minoan administration.

Contacts between mainland Greece and Crete had begun as early as 2000 BC and increased steadily thereafter. The evidence of Minoan influence over Greece was so overwhelming that Arthur Evans, the excavator of Knossos, was convinced that the mainland Greek palaces of the fourteenth and thirteenth century had been occupied by Cretan kings, loyal subjects of the king of Knossos, whose mighty "sea power" had conquered Greece. Evans' reasonable conclusion turned out to be just the opposite of what happened: it was the Mycenaeans who did the conquering. Wealthy Crete must have seemed a juicy prize to the warlike Mycenaeans, who had intimate knowledge of the island and its defenses. Yet, the Mycenaeans were certainly not out to destroy Crete. Once they had beaten the

Cretan forces, sacked some palaces and towns, and killed the leaders, the main-landers took over Knossos and other centers and ruled in place of the old rulers.

The Mycenaean takeover is dated to around 1500 to 1450. About that time, a number of important Cretan sites were badly damaged, though Knossos itself suf-fered little harm. There are also signs that about 1500 BC Minoan exports to places around the Aegean declined, while Mycenaean exports rose; and on several Cy-cladic islands Mycenaean cultural influences appear more prominently. Cretan so-ciety and culture under the rule of the already Minoanized Mycenaean invaders did not change much, however. For the mass of the people life went on as before, al-though they now paid their taxes to kings who spoke Greek. And the new kings ruled and lived in the manner of Cretan kings, although they did keep to certain mainland ways (in burial rites, for example). From the fifteenth century onward we can speak of a Minoan-Mycenaean culture, a dynamic fusion of the two cultures, which was further enriched by continuing influences from the Near East and Egypt.

There is some reason to believe that under Mycenaean rule Knossos controlled much of central and western Crete (an area of perhaps 1500 square miles), hav-ing incorporated the territories of the formerly independent or semi-independent palace centers. But their success was relatively short-lived. Around 1375, Knos-sos was burned and looted, and although the ruined palace continued to be oc-cupied, Mycenaean Crete sank in importance while Mycenae and the other main-land centers reached the zenith of their prosperity and influence in the Aegean. It is not known who destroyed Knossos and set off the irreversible decline of the entire Cretan economy and culture. The most likely suspects are mainland Myce-naeans tempted by the riches of the Cretan palaces and perhaps eager to get rid of their biggest rival in the Mediterranean trade.

The Famous Clay Tablets

As we saw earlier, the Minoans had developed a pictographic writing system to keep records of their palace economies, which was in use from about 1900 BC. The pictographs were mostly incised on small stones used as seals (when pressed on wax or clay they leave an impression of the symbols) and were probably used as labels and marks of ownership. This picture writing, which could convey only minimal information, was replaced by a syllabic writing system incised on small clay tablets, used from about 1800. Arthur Evans found a few tablets with this writing in Knossos; small quantities were later discovered at Phaistos, Mallia, and other sites in Crete and the Cycladic islands, showing that it was widely used in the area during the eighteenth to fifteenth centuries BC.

In the destruction level at Knossos, Evans found a huge number (around three thousand) of clay tablets inscribed with a more elaborate version of the linear script. Evans named the earlier script "Linear A" and this later one "Linear B." He assumed without question that the language of both was Cretan. The discov-ery in 1939 of many hundreds of the Linear B tablets at the palace complex of Py-los on the southwestern Greek mainland seemed to strengthen his theory that mainland Greece was controlled by the Minoans.

There was now a sufficient amount of material to allow serious attempts at deciderment of the Linear B tablets. Even so, the tablets presented an enormous challenge, because the script was totally unlike any of the other writing systems in use among the Late Bronze Age civilizations, and no one knew what the underlying language was. Relatively little progress was made until the early fifties, when a young British amateur, Michael Ventris, broke the code. Working from the hypothesis that the signs stood for whole syllables rather than single letters and that the language might possibly be Greek (and not Minoan, after all), Ventris was gradually able to obtain the phonetic values of some of the signs. For example, a combination of three signs—*ti-ri-po*—yields the syllabic equivalent of the Greek word *tripous* ("tripod").

In 1953, Ventris and a collaborator, John Chadwick of Cambridge University, jointly published their findings in a famous article that has completely changed our picture of the Bronze Age Aegean. It is now certain beyond any doubt that (1) Greek was the language of the Mycenaean culture, (2) the Mycenaeans had adapted the Cretan Linear A script to their own Greek language and used it for the same purpose as Linear A, to keep palace records, and (3) Mycenaeans were ruling in Crete by at least the fifteenth century BC.

More recent finds of Linear B tablets at Pylos (in 1952) and at Mycenae, Tiryns, and Thebes on the mainland, as well as at Chania on Crete have increased the fund of texts. Today, most of the more than five thousand Linear B inscriptions have yielded up most of their secrets. Despite some successes, however, Linear A, the script of the unknown Cretan language, has not yet been deciphered.

THE EARLY MYCENAEANS (c. 1600–1400 BC)

Hundreds of Bronze Age habitation sites have been found in mainland and island Greece, many of which can be identified by name from the ancient legends. Archaeology has confirmed that the famous mainland cities of epic poetry, such as Mycenae, Tiryns, Pylos, Thebes, and Athens, were in fact the major Bronze Age centers. Their grand palaces, however, were built in the fourteenth and thirteenth centuries, over the remains of the older, less imposing structures of the early Mycenaeans. Accordingly, what we know of the early stage of the Mycenaean civilization, roughly 1600 to 1400, is revealed chiefly through graves and the offerings interred with the bodies of the deceased men, women, and children.

The Rise of Mycenaean Power: The Shaft Graves and Tombs

The contents of two circular burial grounds, reserved for the elite families, have shed much light on Mycenae's early development. The older of the two grave circles, which was discovered outside the citadel in 1952, was used from the late seventeenth century (Middle Helladic) to about 1500. It overlaps in time with the later grave circle located at the edge of the citadel, discovered by Schliemann.

This later, richer group was in use from the early sixteenth century until after 1500.

The graves in the two circular burial grounds are called "shaft graves," because the bodies were lowered into deep rectangular pits cut into the soft bedrock. The earlier circle contained many bronze weapons (swords, daggers, spearheads, and knives) and quantities of local pottery, but little gold or jewelry. By comparison, a single one of the graves from the later cemetery, containing the bodies of three men and two women, held not only an arsenal of weapons (43 swords, for example), but also hundreds of other expensive objects, including exquisite gold jewelry adorning the bodies of the women. These burial gifts exhibit superb workmanship and are made of precious materials, such as gold, silver, bronze, ivory, alabaster, faïence, and amber, imported from Crete, Cyprus, Egypt, Mesopotamia, Syria, Anatolia, and western Europe. The styles and techniques are an eclectic mix of traditional Helladic and foreign elements.

The increasing wealth of the shaft graves reveals the evolving power of the ruling class in Mycenae over roughly 150 years. Burial goods show that during the Middle Helladic period warrior-chiefs and their close supporters were already in control of the local economy and were in contact with the established civilizations. Their grandsons and great-grandsons became powerful warlords who, with the help of their close subordinates, tightly organized and expanded their local economies, becoming significant players in the pan-Mediterranean economy.

Shortly before 1500, the Mycenaean elites adopted a different type of tomb, called a *tholos*, which provides further evidence of their growing power and resources. The *tholoi* (plural), which have been found throughout Greece, were the highest achievement of Mycenaean engineering. They were very large stone chambers, shaped like beehives, cut horizontally into a hillside. The high vaulted burial and ceremonial chamber was approached through a long stone-lined passageway and huge bronze doors and was covered over by an earthen mound. The tholos, represents the height of Mycenaean upper-class ostentation. We may see it as a conspicuous statement of their "arrival" on the wider Mediterranean scene. Unfortunately, most of the tholoi were robbed centuries ago, but the few that remained unplundered have yielded burial gifts even more numerous and beautiful than those of the shaft graves. The royal and noble families that owned those tombs appear just as warlike as their forebears, but far richer and more thoroughly Minoanized. Many of the later burials in the tholoi overlap in time with the construction of the great palaces in the fourteenth and thirteenth centuries, whose ruins we see today.

THE LATER MYCENAEANS (c. 1400–1200 BC)

With the new palaces the Mycenaeans entered the final phase of their wealth and power. The architecture and decoration of the Mycenaean palaces closely followed the Minoan style, though with some notable differences. For one, the Mycenaean centers were much smaller and were usually located on a commanding hill and

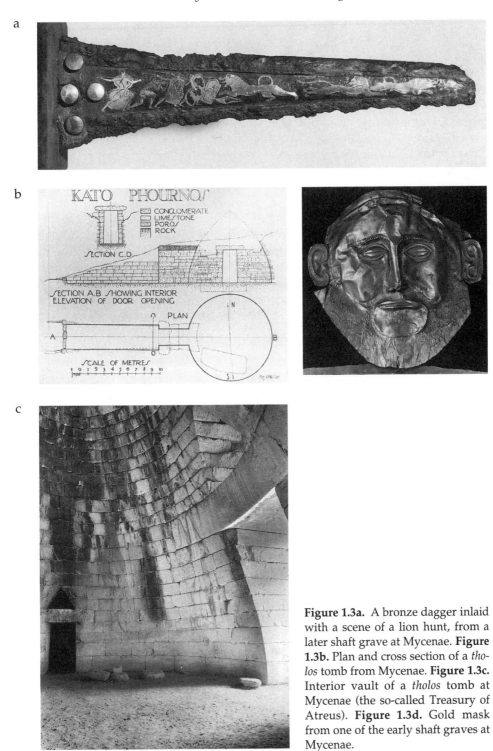

Figure 1.3a. A bronze dagger inlaid with a scene of a lion hunt, from a later shaft grave at Mycenae. **Figure 1.3b.** Plan and cross section of a *tholos* tomb from Mycenae. **Figure 1.3c.** Interior vault of a *tholos* tomb at Mycenae (the so-called Treasury of Atreus). **Figure 1.3d.** Gold mask from one of the early shaft graves at Mycenae.

fortified by high, thick walls. Whereas the Minoan palaces had had little defensive function, defense seems to have been the paramount consideration in the Greek palaces. The immensely strong fortification walls of Mycenae and Tiryns, built of enormous stone blocks, are an impressive sight even in their ruined state. The later Greeks referred to them as Cyclopean walls, so massive that they could only have been built by the mythical race of giant Cyclopes. The fortifications were well engineered, taking full advantage of the natural slopes, with refinements that allowed defenders to fire down on two sides at attackers storming the gates.

To construct, maintain, and repair the defenses called for huge expenditures of material resources and the mobilized labor of many hundreds of people. The walled citadel provided not only protection for the palace, but also a place of refuge for the inhabitants of the unfortified town below. But these Mycenaean fortifications were as much a boast by the king of his wealth and military might as they were a defense for his palace and people. Such huge walls, 20 feet thick in many places, were much more than was necessary to stave off an enemy assault. The city walls that were built in the later periods were far less immense, yet remained impregnable until the advent of workable siege machinery in the fourth century BC.

The Mycenaeans also utilized space within the palaces in one notably different way from the Minoans. In place of the open paved courtyard of the Cretan complexes, they made the focus of their palaces the *megaron*, a large rectangular hall, with a smaller anteroom, and a portico in the front, opening onto a courtyard. In the middle of the great hall stood a large, raised circular hearth, flanked by four columns that supported a balcony; a kind of chimney was built into the roof above the hearth to draw off the smoke. For the Mycenaeans the megaron was clearly the ceremonial center of the palace; they used it for feasts, councils, and receptions of visitors. The megaron room would survive in the form of a chieftain's house during the long Dark Age that followed, and as the essential plan of the Greek temple, the god's house, from the eighth century onward.

The final Mycenaean palaces provided their inhabitants a standard of luxury, refinement, and beauty almost as high as that of the Minoans. Although they had fewer rooms and lacked some of the architectural embellishments of their Cretan models, the Mycenaean palaces boasted such Minoan refinements as indoor plumbing and beautiful wall paintings. The frescoes are completely Minoan in style, though reproduced in a more formalized manner, and show a preference for martial themes, such as personal combats, sieges, and hunting scenes. In the wall paintings, women and men are usually shown wearing the traditional Minoan costume, but other depictions, as on painted vases, reveal that mainland men normally wore a loose woolen or linen tunic, cinched by a belt, and women wore a longer version of the same tunic.

Relations Among the Palace-Centers

Scholars no longer believe in a united "Kingdom of Greece," ruled by the king of Mycenae. The extent of political or military expansion in Greece was the formation of small regional kingdoms under a single center; the kingdom of Pylos in

Messenia presents a clear example. The picture is less certain in those regions where major centers were close together, as in Argolis, which held ten important towns, including the impregnable fortresses of Mycenae and Tiryns, only a few miles apart. It is possible that the king of Mycenae was the sole and absolute ruler of the region, just as the king of Pylos was of Messenia. In that case, we should see the palace at Tiryns as an outpost of the palace at Mycenae. We must not assume, however, that all Mycenaean kingdoms were structured alike. It is equally possible that Tiryns and the other strongholds were semi-independent settlements, whose leaders acknowledged the ruler of Mycenae as their superior and pledged their loyalty to him. The palace-towns of Athens and Thebes may have had similar dominant positions in the regions of Attica and Boeotia.

It appears, at any rate, that from 1600 until 1200, relations both within and between regions were generally stable. Undoubtedly there were battles between rival palace-towns as they feuded and fought for hegemony in their region, but archaeology reveals very few examples of all-out warfare. The burning of Thebes early in the thirteenth century may have been the work of a neighboring center, possibly Orchomenus, which was a rich and populous site and would later be Thebes' perennial rival during the Classical period.

Mycenaean Influence in the Mediterranean

In their heyday, around 1300, Mycenaean kingdoms were actively trading all across the Mediterranean, from Sardinia, southern Italy, and Sicily in the west to Troy down to Egypt in the east, as well as to Macedonia in the north. Mycenaean settlements and trading posts were strung along the Asian coastline and throughout the islands, including Rhodes and Cyprus. Across this wide expanse the Mycenaean culture exhibits a remarkable uniformity; even the experts find it difficult to determine whether a vase or a dagger found, say, in Miletus in Anatolia was made locally or came from a palace workshop in Greece or Crete.

The immense wealth of the Mycenaean kings and nobles came not only from peaceful trade but also from international piracy. The generations of warriors buried in the weapon-laden graves and tombs of the Late Helladic period were wealthy marauders who could easily afford to mount large seaborne expeditions for booty. Though they were few in numbers compared with the vast populations of the East, and were divided into small states, the Mycenaean Greeks were the third power in the Mediterranean, after the huge Hittite empire, which covered Anatolia and Syria, and the brilliant and aggressive New Kingdom of Egypt. Hittite archives of the fourteenth and thirteenth centuries mention a people they called Ahhiyawan, which many believe is the cuneiform version of Mycenaean Akhaiwoi, that is, "Achaeans," an inclusive term for "Greeks" in the eighth-century-BC epic poems. In a letter, the king of the Hittites addresses his "brother, the king of Ahhiyawa (Achaea)." Other records speak of an exchange of gifts between the king of Hatti and the king of Ahhiyawa; Ahhiyawans are sent to Hatti to learn chariot warfare; a god of the Ahhiyawans is summoned to cure a Hittite king. Relations were not always peaceful; in the thirteenth century "a man from

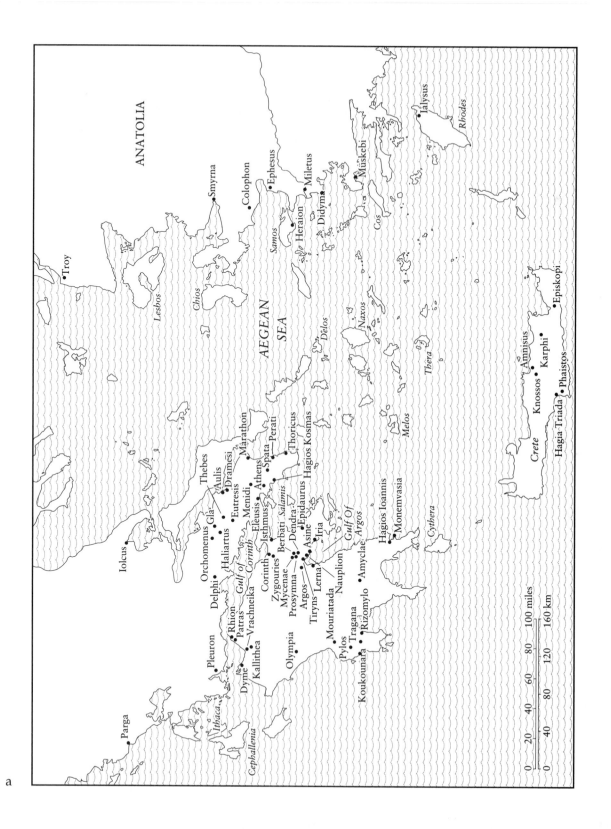

ANATOLIA

Troy

Lesbos

Chios

Smyrna

Colophon

Ephesus

Samos · Heraion

Miletus

Didyma

Müskebi

Cos

AEGEAN

SEA

Delos

Naxos

Thera

Melos

Ialysus

Rhodes

Episkopi

Amnisus

Karphi

Knossos

Hagia Triada · Phaistos

Crete

Cythera

Monemvasia

Hagios Ioannis

Thebes

Aulis

Dramesi

Eutresis

Menidi

Marathon

Spata · Perati

Thoricus

Athens

Hagios Kosmas

Eleusis

Isthmus

Salamis

Epidaurus

Iria

Orchomenus Gla

Haliartus

Delphi

Gulf of Corinth

Berbati

Dendra

Asine

Gulf Of Argos

Iolcus

Corinth

Zygouries

Mycenae

Prosymna

Argos

Tiryns Lerna

Nauplion

Amyclae

Rhion

Patras

Vrachneika

Kallithea

Pleuron

Dyme

Olympia

Mouriatada

Pylos

Tragana

Rizomylo

Koukounara

Parga

Ithaca

Cephallenia

0   20   40   60   80   100 miles

0 40 80 120 160 km

a

b

c

Figure 1.4a. (facing page) Mycenaean sites in the thirteenth century BC. **Figure 1.4b.** View of the ruins of the *megaron* hall of the Mycenaean palace at Pylos. **Figure 1.4c.** The "Lion Gate" entrance to the citadel of Mycenae.

Ahhiyawa" was invading Hittite territory in western Anatolia. These references were probably not to mainland Greeks but to one or more of the nearer Mycenaean kingdoms, located in the islands or on the Asian coast. Nevertheless, the mentions of Greeks in the Hittite records (and possibly also in Egyptian records) supplement the archaeological evidence that Mycenaeans were a significant presence in the world of the fourteenth and thirteenth century.

The Administration of a Mycenaean Kingdom

One of the important leaders in the Trojan War, as told in the *Iliad* and *Odyssey*, was Nestor, who, Homer tells us, lived in a magnificent many-roomed house in a town called Pylos, from which he ruled over a large kingdom in Messenia. The discovery of the "palace of Nestor" by the American archaeologist Carl Blegen in 1939 was as momentous as the earlier discoveries of Troy, Mycenae, and Knossos. It not only confirmed that a Bronze Age center known only in legend had actually existed, but it also revealed that a center far away from the great palaces of eastern and central Greece could be just as rich and important.

The fertile and well-watered region of Messenia in the southwest corner of the Peloponnesus was one of the most heavily populated parts of Mycenaean Greece. According to a recent survey, population there rose from about 4000 in Early Helladic to 10,000 in Middle Helladic and surged to well over 50,000 in Late Helladic. Some estimates put the figure as high as 100,000. Pylos (written Pu-ro in the Linear B script) became a regional center of power around the time Mycenae and the other centers did, reaching its height during the Late Helladic IIIA and IIIB periods (roughly 1400–1200 BC). The palace, located on a hill 5 miles from the sea, was built around 1300 BC on the ruins of an earlier, smaller complex of buildings.

Blegen's meticulous excavation of the site, which had lain undisturbed since its destruction around 1200 BC, and the huge numbers of Linear B tablets found in the archive rooms, provide our clearest picture of the organization and workings of a Mycenaean kingdom. The Pylos tablets, together with those from Mycenaean Knossos, reveal much of the day-to-day administrative details of the highly regimented production and distribution system of Mycenaean palaces.

The sun-dried tablets from Pylos and Knossos were temporary records, meant to last only until the information on them was transferred onto larger, permanent records. They were preserved only because they were baked hard in the fires that destroyed the palaces. What we have, in other words, are palace scribes' notes on personnel and production which pertain to only a small part of the last year of the palaces where they were found. Nevertheless, they are representative of palace administration throughout the time span of the later palace period.

The tablets give us some idea of the Mycenaean ruling hierarchy. At the top was the *wanax*, which perhaps meant "lord" or "master." Next in rank, apparently, was a man called *lawagetas*, which seems to be a combination of the words for "people" and "leader," and is commonly believed to have designated the commander of the army. There was also a high-ranking group called *telestai*, who received the same allotment of land as the lawagetas. Their function is unknown;

a

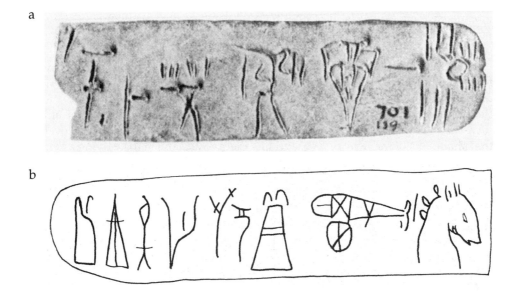

b

Figure 1.5a. A Linear B tablet from Mycenaean Knossos. **Figure 1.5b.** Drawing of a chariot tablet from Knossos.

some believe they were priests. Other individuals, with the title *hequetas* (possibly meaning "follower"), may have been high-ranking military officers.

Below this top echelon were lesser officials, who appear to have been in charge of the outlying areas. The kingdom of Pylos was about 1400 square miles in extent and contained over two hundred villages and towns. It was divided administratively into two "provinces," each subdivided into several "districts," named after the principal town in the district. The titles *korete* and *prokorete* found on the tablets may have belonged to the governor of a district and his deputy. Finally, there was an apparently large group of officials with the title *pasireu*, who seem to have been in charge of affairs at the town and village level. The officials and military officers named in the tablets represent only the tip of a large bureaucracy. Subordinate to them were numerous low-level functionaries, who were just as dependent on them as they themselves were dependent on the wanax. The tablets reveal that the higher officials received land from the wanax in return for their service to the palace and a share of their crops; a similar relationship undoubtedly existed between such officials and their subordinates.

The highest officials, and perhaps some portion of the lower ranking ones, occupied substantial private houses, some quite large, found on the citadels, in the lower towns, and also out in small country towns. Only the highest ranking families could afford (or, perhaps, were permitted) to be buried in the ostentatious tholoi. The families of the lesser elite were laid to rest in smaller, simpler tombs, rectangular crypts cut into the soft rock. Like the tholoi, some of these "chamber tombs" were grander than others and they contained greater or lesser amounts of expensive grave goods. It is possible that some of the inhabitants of the rich houses and chamber tombs were private merchants and traders, acting as agents of the palace.

However, the great majority of the people, as usual, lived in small, modestly furnished houses with few amenities, and they were buried in simple graves with only a couple of vases or other small items. Their standard of living was much the same as their ancestors', no better or worse. In fact, throughout later antiquity, the majority of Greeks would live at essentially the same material level as the inhabitants of the Bronze Age, and like them would make their living as farmers, herders, and artisans. In the Mycenaean Age, as later, most of the farmers and herders lived in rural villages, while most of the crafts specialists were concentrated in the regional centers and the larger settlements. It appears from the tablets that many families farmed as tenants on land belonging to the nobles, some of whose holdings were very large. Other nonelite families held plots of land in their own names; craftsmen and herders are listed as "owners" of private land. It appears that the fifty to seventy-five families that made up a typical Mycenaean village either had shares in the village's land or else rented land that was allocated to high officials.

The palace's supervision over the people was very thorough. Officials were sent out into the countryside on regular inspections, and the taxes in produce and animals levied on individuals and villages were meticulously recorded, including deficiencies in the assessments. One tablet from Knossos reports: "Men of Lyktos 246.7 units of wheat; men of Tylisos 261 units of wheat; men of Lato 30.5 units of wheat." Although estimations of what constituted a "unit," are uncertain, it does appear that the farmers from those villages were not too heavily taxed. All in all, the evidence of the tablets does not support the once common view that the mass of the population were oppressed peasants, toiling in misery on the estates of their noble masters. The men of the village farmed their plots and tended to their trees, vines, and livestock; they paid their taxes, contributed some labor to the palace, and served in the army. The women probably helped with the farm chores and performed the domestic tasks of spinning and weaving, food preparation, and child care. A number of the village women were also engaged as textile workers for the palace, for which they received rations of wool and flax.

As in Minoan society, slaves were at the bottom. References to "captives" and "bought" show that the Mycenaean warrior-aristocrats were active in the slavery business. The numbers of slaves were high, very many of whom were female. Tablets from Pylos, for example, record over six hundred slave women, and about the same number of children. The women named on the tablets worked as grinders of grain, bath attendants, flax workers, weavers, and so on. Most of the women listed were attached to the palace; some lived in other towns in the kingdom and received rations of food from the palace. High-ranking individuals also owned slaves, though in far fewer numbers than the wanax. Slaves were valuable possessions, both as producers and as commodities to sell for profit. Some also served as domestic slaves, freeing their owners from every sort of menial labor. Throughout antiquity Greeks would find this combination of benefits irresistible. Indeed, it is commonly said that Greek civilization was "based on slavery." While this is an oversimplification, it is true nonetheless that slavery was a central institution, and with few exceptions its morality remained unquestioned. It was practiced everywhere in the Greek world and at all periods. The practice of slavery on a really massive scale, however, would not come until about the sixth century BC.

It is also possible that some of the lowest-status workers listed on the tablet were not true slaves, that is, foreigners captured or bought, but were native individuals and families who were reduced to a state of permanent dependence on the palace. If so, they would be recognized as persons, not chattels, yet their condition would be hardly different from that of slaves. In later Greek history such "semislaves" were not uncommon, the most famous being the "helots" of Laconia and Messenia owned by the state of Sparta.

Manufacturing and Commerce

The Linear B tablets also demonstrate the size and complexity of the manufacturing operations of Mycenaean kingdoms. A wide array of specialists is listed for the palaces and other locations. Men were engaged as carpenters, masons, bronze smiths, goldsmiths, bow-makers, armorers, leather workers, perfume-makers, and more. On one tablet a physician is mentioned. Women worked mostly in the textile sector, as carders, spinners, weavers, and embroiderers. The workshop areas of the palace must have been noisy, bustling places with interesting smells. The wanax kept a close eye on the workshops, and his scribes scrupulously wrote down how much raw material was provided to the crafts specialists, the objects they produced, and the rations of food they received in return. The tablets attest both to the skills of the specialists and the careful accounting by the scribes. Dozens of entries go like this: "one ebony footstool inlaid with figures of men and lion in ivory." Most kinds of labor-intensive objects, such as this one, made of expensive imported material, are known only from their descriptions in the tablets; the objects themselves long ago crumbled into dust. The inventories are exhaustive. For example, individual chariot wheels are listed, and their condition ("serviceable," "unfit for use") is noted. Even damaged bronze cauldrons were inventoried.

Several industries were on a large scale. About a third of the Knossos tablets are concerned with sheep and wool. The quantities of sheep are impressive; 19,000 are recorded from one district alone. And large numbers of women were employed at Knossos and the surrounding towns in spinning yarn and weaving and decorating the woolen cloth. The wanax of Pylos also controlled a large textile industry, both in wool and in linen. Metalworking was another important industry at Pylos, where the large number of bronze smiths (estimated at 400) receiving rations of bronze indicates that the production of bronze manufactures, including weapons, far exceeded local consumption needs.

The size of these manufacturing operations reveals that textiles and metalwork were the two leading exports of the palace economy. To these we may add olive oil (both plain and perfumed), wine, hides, leather, and leather products. High-quality manufactures, such as painted ceramics, jewelry, and other costly items (like the decorated footstool mentioned above), competed well in the international luxury trade. It is mainly ceramics (which are virtually indestructible), that have been found in distant locales. But the presence of those items means that other, more perishable goods also reached the trading centers around the Mediterranean. In return, the palaces imported things lacking in Greece, such as copper, tin, gold, ivory, amber, dyes, and spices, as well as foreign varieties of things that they did have, such as wine, textiles, ceramics, jewelry, and other exotic luxury items. Needless to say, very few luxury goods made their way into the houses and graves of the common people.

Religion

The belief in supernatural forces and beings that control the natural world is probably as old as humankind. Nearly as old as the belief in gods are the practices of religion: cult and ritual, which are the worship and acts of devotion performed by the worshippers, and religious myths, the suppositions about the gods told in story form as part of ritual activity. The specific content of cult and ritual develops and changes through the ages, but the essence and purpose remain the same: to maintain harmonious relations between human society and the gods.

Among agricultural people, the relationship of mortals to immortals revolves around the continuation of the fertility of the land and animals. To appease the gods, who can bestow or take away the blessings of nature at will, the people make communal displays of respect, including sacrifices of food and animals and, in some cultures, even humans. The larger and more complex the society becomes, the more elaborate the displays. Archaeology reveals that the Bronze Age peoples of Crete, the other islands, and the Greek mainland were no different from other agrarian cultures. They honored their gods with processions, music, and dance, and propitiated them with gifts and sacrifices. The slaughter and butchering of animals on outdoor altars was the most solemn ritual. There may possibly have been human sacrifice among the early Minoans.

The principal recipient of worship depicted in Minoan art is a goddess, pictured as a woman dressed in the Minoan style and placed in outdoor settings that feature trees and other vegetation, and animals. The same kinds of scenes of worship were reproduced in Mycenaean frescoes and on gold and silver rings. Minoan religious symbols (whose meaning is not well understood) also recur in mainland and island art: snakes, birds, bulls, stylized bullhorns, and axes with double heads. However much these similarities show Minoan influence on Mycenaean religion, there were significant differences in rituals and practices. For example, much of the Minoan worship of gods took place in caves and in sanctuaries built on mountain peaks, while the mainland Mycenaeans did not construct shrines outside of the centers. Moreover, Cretan palaces contained more shrines, and more elaborate ones, than the Mycenaean palaces, where the megaron complex appears to have been the main place for religious ceremony.

a

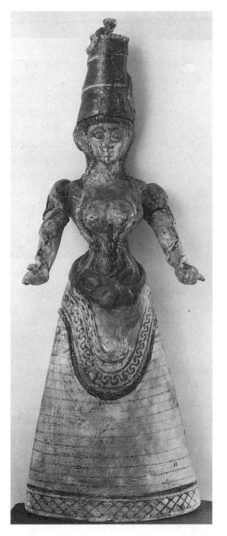

Figure 1.6a. Statuette of a goddess figure from Knossos, Crete. **Figure 1.6b.** Gold ring from Knossos showing women worshiping a goddess.

b

The ubiquitous goddess figures depicted in Minoan-Mycenaean art were originally identified as representations of a single, pan-Aegean mother goddess, who ruled over all of nature. It now appears more likely that they were representations of different goddesses, some of whom were local deities. They may have exercised specialized fertility functions within the community of worshippers, or presided over other aspects of life besides fertility. The tablets assign the title *potnia* ("lady" or "mistress") to the female deities. They also reveal that male gods were almost as numerous and equally important as the female gods, although they were very rarely depicted in art. There is no explanation for this curious fact.

Names of around thirty gods and goddesses have been firmly or tentatively recognized on the tablets from Mycenaean Knossos and Pylos. Many of these were unknown in later times, but quite a few are the names of the major gods of later Greek religion: Zeus, Hera, Poseidon, Hermes, Athena, Artemis, and possibly Apollo, Ares, and Dionysus, as well as some minor divinities. Zeus, the supreme god of the later Greek religion, is plainly the Indo-European "sky-father," and was brought in by the earliest Greek-speakers. *Zeus patēr* ("Zeus the father") is the same deity as the Indic *Dyaus pitar*, Roman *Iuppiter*, and Germanic *Tiew* (who gives us Tues-day). The names of Hera, Poseidon, and Ares are also formed from Indo-European roots.

It is generally believed that some of the gods the Mycenaeans worshipped, in particular the "lady" goddesses, were pre-Greek (i.e., not Indo-European) in origin, and that the deities, rituals, and beliefs of the Mycenaeans were the result of a fusion of the Aegean fertility-and-mother religions and the Indo-European worship of sky-and-weather gods. Of course, the Mycenaean religious tradition that we now observe had evolved over a span of seven centuries, much too long for us to say for certain what elements in the thirteenth-century Mycenaean religion were originally Indo-European, or Aegean, or Cretan, or, for that matter, Near Eastern.

It is certain, however, that the palace controlled the religious organization of the kingdom. The tablets list the gifts of land, animals, precious objects, and human labor from the palace to the gods to be used for the maintenance of their sanctuaries and of the priests and priestesses. The tight economic and political control exercised by the king over the sanctuaries and the priesthoods is an indication that he was able to claim divine sanction to rule as the undisputed sovereign. When the king officiated at religious ceremonies and sacrifices, he did so as the special representative of the community to the gods. There is nothing in the written or material evidence, however, to suggest that the wanax was considered divine himself either in his lifetime or after death, or that he functioned as a priest-king over a theocratic state.

Warfare

That the Mycenaean kings were the commanders-in-chief of their military forces is beyond doubt. By analogy with other small warrior-states, the wanax and his military commander (lawagetas) would have been present on the field in major battles, and would probably have taken part in the fighting along with his sub-ordinate commanders. The military was socially stratified; the officers came from the nobility while the ranks were levied from among the farmers and craftsmen. The palace directed all military operations. Troop movements of "rowers" and "[coastal] watchers," and the disbursements of weapons and rations for the sol-diers are recorded on the tablets. The actual organization of the military is be-yond our knowledge, though it appears that it was made up of units from all over the kingdom.

Weapons and armor are fairly well known from the material evidence, depic-tions, and the Linear B tablets. A fully equipped soldier was protected by a leather helmet with bronze strips sewed on, body armor of leather or padded linen, and a large shield made of ox hide stretched over a wooden frame. Offi-cers wore more elaborate body armor: helmets made of bronze or of boars' tusks,

Figure 1.7. Bronze plate armor and boar's tusk helmet from Dendra in Argolis, c. 1400 BC.

corselets of bronze plates, and bronze greaves (knee and shin protectors). The weaponry consisted of bronze swords and daggers; heavy, bronze-tipped thrusting spears and shorter, lighter throwing spears; and bows and arrows. How these weapons were combined in battle, and the tactics employed by the commanders, are poorly understood. The greatest puzzle, however, is the military use of the chariot by the Mycenaeans.

The Chariot

The chariot was invented early in the second millennium (just where is uncertain), and, because of its speed, it soon became very popular in the civilizations of Mesopotamia, Anatolia, Syria, and Egypt. A small platform set atop two high, spoked wheels, and pulled by two horses, the chariot was a magnificent innovation in wheeled transport. Horses could not pull the heavy four-wheeled carts that had been in use for centuries, because the harnesses constricted their necks and chests (a problem not solved until the invention of the horse collar in the Middle Ages). Because the chariot was extremely light (one man could easily lift it), a pair of horses could draw it and two passengers for many miles at a pace previously unknown on land. A horse and rider could go faster, but only for a short distance. Used at first by the nobility only for fast communication, hunting, ceremony, and racing, the chariot acquired a military function in the seventeenth century BC, and eventually the chariot corps became the primary military arm throughout the Near East. The essential maneuver was the massed chariot charge against an enemy's chariots, one man driving and the other shooting arrows. Cavalry, mounted warriors fighting in formation, was not known in the Bronze Age.

Chariots appeared in Greece around 1600 BC, after the difficult art of chariotry had already been perfected among the Hittites and other major states. From the very first, the Mycenaeans used it in battle as well as for the whole range of peaceful purposes. It is generally believed, however, that its military use was restricted to conveying heavily armored elite warriors to and from the fighting. That is the sole function ascribed to the war chariot in the eighth-century Homeric epics. Indeed, it is hard to imagine mass formations of chariots charging across the broken terrain of Greece. Yet, while it is true that Greece was not like the vast plains countries of the East, it is conceivable that mini-versions of eastern chariot warfare took place on the plains that lay below the Mycenaean fortresses. The wanax of Knossos had a chariot corps with perhaps 200 chariots, and Pylos may have had nearly as many. These numbers are small compared with the 3500 Hittite chariots that the pharaoh Rameses II (1298–1232 BC) claimed to have defeated in a single battle, but they fit the scale of the small Mycenaean kingdoms.

In any case, the significance of the chariot was not its use in battle, but rather its high prestige value. Like the grand palaces and the tholos tombs with their rich burial offerings, the adoption of chariotry proclaimed that the semibarbarous warrior-chiefs of Late Bronze Age Greece were the cultural equals of the great kings of Asia and Egypt. The chariot, the most intricate and costly item of manufacture known to the Greeks, would retain its importance as a prestige symbol for many centuries after it ceased to have any military function.

THE END OF THE MYCENAEAN CIVILIZATION

At the height of its prosperity, the Mycenaean civilization suffered a fatal blow. Over the course of a few decades around 1200 BC, almost every center, major and minor, from Iolcus in Thessaly to the southern Peloponnesus, was attacked, plundered, and burned by invaders. This devastation began a rapid downward spiral so severe that by the end of the twelfth century there is scarcely a trace in the archaeological record of the great Mycenaean civilization and culture.

Some of the centers, Pylos among them, were never reinhabited after the initial onslaught. Others, such as Mycenae and Tiryns, were quickly reoccupied and even enjoyed a brief resurgence, but the revivals were short-lived. Mycenae succumbed to new attacks around 1150, from which it did not recover. Tiryns actually grew considerably in size and population in the twelfth century (probably by an influx of refugees), but by 1100 it too had declined into a group of small villages surrounding the acropolis. The places that were not destroyed were either abandoned completely or shrank drastically in size. A notable example is the major Bronze Age center of Athens in Attica, which lapsed into a collection of small villages within sight of the acropolis, even though its palace and town had escaped destruction. The destructions also caused large movements of people to other, presumably safer, areas, such as eastern Attica, southern Argolis, Achaea (which preserved the Mycenaean name of Achaeans), the western island of Cephallenia, and far-off Cyprus.

The collapse of Late Bronze Age Greek civilization was actually part of a wider catastrophe that overwhelmed the entire eastern Mediterranean region and was felt even in the west, in Italy, Sicily, and the adjacent islands. Around 1200 the mighty Hittite empire fell apart; its capital Hattusas and many of the cities and towns in Anatolia and Syria were crushed. The invaders were apparently barbarian tribes from north and east of Anatolia and another group of marauders whom Egyptian inscriptions refer to as "the land and sea peoples," and "northerners from all lands."

This latter group, commonly referred to today as the Sea Peoples, attacked Egypt in 1232 and again early in the twelfth century, both times repelled at great cost. The Kingdom of Egypt survived but never fully recovered its former power. In Anatolia civilization languished for almost four centuries. Among the casualties was Troy, which was besieged and burned between about 1250 and 1200. There is no way of knowing whether the destroyers were really the Mycenaean Greeks, as the legend of the Trojan War said, though there is some evidence that Mycenaeans did take part in the general havoc that engulfed the Mediterranean in the late thirteenth and early twelfth centuries.

Egyptian inscriptions recorded the names of the raiding and migrating warrior-bands from around the Mediterranean who made up the attacking Sea

Peoples. Among the peoples that have been tentatively identified were Libyans from North Africa; Philistines, who gave their name to Palestine; and groups from Anatolia, Sicily, and Sardinia. Also listed were a people called Ekwesh, who were possibly the Achaioi (the name by which the Mycenaeans were known). Thus, although the picture is hopelessly confused, the destructions in the Mediterranean may have been linked to migrations of northern populations who displaced populations further to the south, setting off convulsive raids among the latter and sparking migrations that ended centuries of relative stability in the region.

The "Dorian Invasion" and Other Guesses

Starting in the mid-thirteenth century, the Mycenaean kingdoms show apparent signs of anxiety concerning the threat of attack. There is a great increase in fortification building in Greece, with previously unwalled centers constructing defenses. Mycenae, Tiryns, and Athens considerably strengthened their circuit walls, and also took elaborate measures to ensure a water supply within the citadels by sinking new wells. A fortification wall was even constructed across the narrow Isthmus of Corinth, presumably to defend the Peloponnesus from invasion from the north. Centers throughout Greece were taking precautions, which would prove to be of no avail.

The identity of the attackers of 1200 BC remains one of the great unsolved mysteries of Greek history. Until fairly recently there was unanimous agreement: they were "Dorians," tribes of Greek-speakers who lived in northern Greece in the area of the Pindus Mountains in Epirus and Thessaly. Situated on the fringes of the Mycenaean world, but not really part of it, the warlike Dorians, according to the theory, came south in a series of migrations, first plundering the palaces and then settling down in rich plains of the Peloponnesus.

The modern "Dorian invasion" theory is largely based on the claims of later Dorians in antiquity. Doric was one of the three main dialects of Greek, spoken in the Peloponnesus, from where it had spread to Crete, Rhodes, and other Aegean islands and to the southwestern coast of Anatolia. These Dorian-speakers claimed that their ancestors were the Heraclids, "descendants of Heracles," son of Zeus and a mortal, Alcmene, and the greatest of the mythical Greek heroes. After Heracles' death, so the story went, his sons were expelled from the Peloponnesus and went north. Then, several generations after the Trojan War, his descendants returned south to reclaim by force their rightful ownership of the Peloponnesus, asserting that they were the true "Achaeans." The legends of later Greeks from Ionia and Attica lend additional credence to the Dorian invasion theory. They told that the desire to escape the "Returns of the Heraclids" had caused some of their ancestors to relocate into remoter parts of the mainland (for example into Achaea, which preserved their name), while other groups—for example, fugitives from the kingdom of Pylos—fled to Athens, which was spared destruction, and from there migrated across the Aegean to settle the central coast of Anatolia, which they called Ionia. These migrations correspond to the dialect map, which situates speakers of the Ionian dialect in Attica, the Aegean islands, and on the Anatolian coast, in a north-south band from Smyrna down to Miletus. Archaeology confirms that migrations to Ionia occurred around 1050 BC.

Archaeologists have found, however, that the features that were once thought to have been brought in by the invading Dorians (such as iron, cremation, and new types of weapons) were in fact not introduced by new people during a single circumscribed period; and the only material signs of Dorians are now dated much later than the destruction period, to around 1000 BC or later. Other theories have been brought forth to account for the destructions of the Mycenaean centers: devastating earthquakes, marauding bands of the sort that made up the Sea Peoples, fierce wars among the kingdoms that resulted in mutual destruction, or revolts of the Mycenaean peasants and slaves who rose up against their oppressive masters.

A more likely explanation is that the Mycenaeans, and other Mediterranean civilizations as well, experienced "system collapse," a breakdown of their economic and social systems. These, it is suggested, were triggered by problems such as prolonged drought, overpopulation, soil exhaustion, reliance on too few crops, and similar internal difficulties, which the ponderous bureaucracies were unable to correct. As one area of the governmental system faltered, other areas were affected, until the entire ruling structure broke down and the strongholds became easy prey for various invaders. Compounding internal problems was the almost total interruption of Mediterranean commerce during and after the general upset of the late thirteenth century. The cessation of foreign trade—and the lucrative opportunities for booty it offered—might alone account for the inability of the Mycenaean economy to recover and also may explain why the centers and sub-centers that did not suffer physical damage declined and stagnated just the same as those that had been burned to the ground.

The coming of the Dorians, then, was perhaps not really an invasion but an intrusion into a political vacuum created by the obliteration of the Mycenaean kingdoms. Groups of Doric-speakers from the north may have filtered in over a long period and taken over the Peloponnesus and some of the islands, including Crete, using force to subjugate the remnants of the Mycenaean populations.

*   *   *

From the New Stone Age until the Late Bronze Age, Greece was a stateless society of farmers and shepherds led by local chieftains, while the civilizations of the East emerged and became mighty. Propelled by contact with Crete, Greece made a sudden leap into civilization and statehood around 1600 BC. The Mycenaean states reached their height of power and sophistication around 1300. For a brief period they were an important presence in the eastern Mediterranean and attained a level of cultural refinement approaching that of the older civilizations. Then around 1200 the Mycenaean civilization disintegrated completely.

With the destruction of the palaces, the Near Eastern type of social and economic organization would disappear forever from Greece. Yet, in Egypt and the Near East, which also suffered severe shocks in the late thirteenth century, the ancient pattern of highly centralized, rigidly hierarchical, monarchical states continued. This is a good indication that underneath the veneer of great wealth and stability the Mycenaean economy and government were shallowly rooted, essentially fragile systems.

We will probably never know for certain why the Mycenaean civilization ended so abruptly and with such finality. This we do know: with the end of the first stage of Greek civilization came the beginning of a new era, so different that when the Greeks looked back upon their Late Bronze Age past they could only imagine it as a kind of mythical dream world, a time when gods and humans mingled together.

SUGGESTED READINGS

Barber, Elizabeth Wayland. 1994. *Women's Work: The First 20,000 Years. Women, Cloth, and Society in Early Times*. New York and London: Norton. The history of textile manufacture as women's work and art from the Paleolithic through the Iron Age, including weaving techniques and myths about weaving. A major study of women's principal contribution to the ancient economy.

Chadwick, John. 1967. *The Decipherment of Linear B*. 2nd ed. Cambridge, Eng.: Cambridge University Press. The story of how the Linear B tablets were deciphered told by one of the principal investigators.

Chadwick, John. *The Mycenaean World*. 1976. Cambridge, Eng.: Cambridge University Press. A lavishly illustrated description of the workings of the palace societies of Mycenaean Greece, with emphasis on the kingdom of Pylos.

Dickinson, Oliver. 1994. *The Aegean Bronze Age*. Cambridge, Eng.: Cambridge University Press. A scholarly, but accessible, survey of all aspects of the prehistoric Aegean cultures from the Early Bronze Age to the collapse of Mycenaean civilization.

Drews, Robert. 1993. *The End of the Bronze Age: Changes in Warfare and the Catastrophe ca. 1200 B.C.* Princeton, N.J.: Princeton University Press. An overview and detailed analysis of the latest theories of the fall of the great civilizations of the Late Bronze Age.

Hooker, J.T. *Mycenaean Greece*. 1976. London: Routledge. A good general introduction to the ancient Aegean societies.

McDonald, William A. and Carol G. Thomas. 1990. *Progress into the Past. The Rediscovery of Mycenaean Civilization*. Bloomington: Indiana University Press. An account of the major and minor discoveries of the Minoan and Mycenaean civilizations written from the point of view of the archaeologists themselves, from Evans and Schliemann to the present.

van Andel, Tjerd and Curtis Runnels. 1987. *Beyond the Acropolis: A Rural Greek Past*. Stanford, Calif.: Stanford University Press. A description of the topography, flora and fauna, and subsistence strategies of ancient Greek farming life.

Vermeule, Emily. 1972. *Greece in the Bronze Age*. Chicago: University of Chicago Press. One of the foremost experts of early Greek culture describes the land, art, culture, and life of prehistoric Greece from the Stone Age to the end of the Bronze Age.

THE "DARK AGE" OF GREECE AND THE EIGHTH-CENTURY "RENAISSANCE" (c. 1150–700 BC)

The archaeological remains from the late twelfth century give the impression that a giant hand had suddenly swept away the splendid Mycenaean civilization, leaving in its wake only isolation and poverty. By 1100 BC the palace-centers were in ruins or uninhabited; so were the scores of once bustling towns and villages across the entire Greek world. The cultural losses were catastrophic and long lasting. For the next 450 years no monumental stone structures would be built in Greece. The art of writing was forgotten, and would not return until the eighth century. Supplies of bronze and other metals dwindled to a trickle, as vital trade links were broken. It would be two hundred years before Greek craftsmen again turned out objects and jewelry of gold, silver, and ivory. And the kinds of luxury goods and weapons that the Mycenaean elite had taken with them into the earth are not found in the graves of the postdestruction period. By contrast to the brilliant age that had gone before, Greece had truly descended into a dark age. Yet during those obscure centuries, a new Greece was rising, radically different from both the old Greece and the other societies of the ancient Mediterranean. The patterns of social and political integration that emerged from the shattered palace-states would set the path to a new kind of state government in Greece, the city-state (*polis*), which arose in the eighth century BC. The roots of the Greek city-state, considered by many to have been the cradle of western democracy and legal equality, were firmly planted in the Dark Age.

It took many years for Greece to recuperate fully from the shocks of the destructions and their aftermath. In the early part of the Dark Age, from about 1150 to about 900 BC, Greece was disturbed by sporadic incursions and movements of people. Yet it is during this period of dislocation and turbulence that evidence of

41

recovery and material progress appears. The later part of the Dark Age, from about 900 to about 750 BC, saw a slowly accelerating revival, culminating in the remarkable cultural leap of the "eighth-century renaissance" (c. 750–700).

SOURCES FOR THE DARK AGE

The principal reason for calling this a "dark" age is not so much for cultural decline as for archaeological obscurity. The rich material record of the Late Bronze Age turns nearly blank in the eleventh and tenth centuries. And though the material finds increase after 900 BC, they are still relatively meager until about 700. Even so, the archaeology of the Dark Age has made significant progress since the 1960s. A number of new Dark Age settlements have been discovered. A technique called survey archaeology, in which a team of investigators systematically walks large areas of the terrain, is providing a picture of the sparsely populated Dark Age countryside. Moreover, the increasing use of the comparative methods of anthropology and sociology to analyze the material evidence has furthered our knowledge of how these societies functioned.

A very rich source of information about the later part of the Dark Age are the Homeric poems, the *Iliad* and the *Odyssey* (c. 750–720 BC). As we saw in Chapter 1, although they take place in the glory days of the Mycenaean period, the poems do not describe the society revealed by the material remains and the Linear B tablets. The social background of the Homeric narratives fits instead the archaeological picture of the late Dark Age. The question of where in the period from 1100 to 700 BC to place "Homeric" society is far from settled, but there is a growing belief that it largely reflects the actual society of the late ninth and early eighth century BC.

The two poems of Hesiod offer a wealth of information about Greek life and thought around 700 BC, the time of their composition. The *Theogony*, in conjunction with the Homeric epics, provides a comprehensive picture of early Greek religious beliefs. Hesiod's other poem, *Works and Days*, which reflects the social and economic relations of his own day, will be an important source for the next chapter.

DECLINE AND RECOVERY (c. 1150–900 BC)

The near total absence of finely made and expensive artifacts is the strongest evidence for the decline of Greek civilization after 1200. Through painted pottery, however, which is relatively abundant, we can chart the general course of decline and recovery. The periods of the Dark Age in fact are named after the stages of pottery shapes and ornamentation. Luckily for historians, the Greeks continued to take the art of making and painting vases very seriously, and so their clay containers furnish a reliable index to the general state of culture.

The pottery dating from about 1125 to about 1050, the low point in the aftermath of the destructions, is called Submycenaean, since it is still recognizably Mycenaean yet is much inferior in quality. It has been aptly called a "style of exhaustion." Potters were content to replicate a mere handful of the large repertoire of shapes and decorative elements that had been available to their grandparents. The clay is often poorly prepared. The vessels are smaller, less well formed, and poorly fired. The execution of the traditional motifs and decorations is clumsy and irregular. Yet these vases, wretched by comparison with those of the thirteenth century and feeble even by the lowered standards of the destruction period, are the main wealth of the Submycenaean graves in which they were found. Nothing else of value was buried except for an occasional gold ring or bronze dress pin, and even the pottery was not abundant. (For example, only 160 vases were found in 220 graves in Athens and Salamis, places that were not destroyed or abandoned.) The evidence both from the graves and from above ground reveals a society in a deep depression, both economic and cultural.

Across the Greek world, population levels had dropped precipitously. Estimates of the decrease vary, according to region, from 60 to 90 percent, a picture of almost inconceivable depopulation. The Aegean island of Melos, for example, heavily populated in the Late Bronze Age, appears to have been virtually empty for the next two hundred years. Even in Attica, which was not invaded successfully, the number of settlements dropped by 50 percent. The population of Greece at the end of the eleventh century was probably the lowest it had been in a thousand years.

The cause of the dramatic drop in population is not fully understood, but it seems to have been connected to the collapse of the redistributive system and the general economic lethargy that gripped Greece at the beginning of the Dark Age. The insecure conditions caused by large movements of peoples, often accompanied by violence, may also have been a factor. At the same time, however, movements and relocations of people can give an exaggerated impression of overall depopulation. The desertions of some of the smaller Bronze Age settlements were the result of their inhabitants moving to another, more secure, village. Recent excavations at Tiryns, for example, have revealed that its population actually increased after 1200. In addition, substantial numbers fled to Achaea and Arcadia and other regions not heavily populated earlier, while others relocated overseas.

What survived from the world of the thirteenth century into the world of the eleventh, and what was lost? Plainly, the centralized economic and political organization had disappeared along with the palaces. The powerful *wanax* ("king") and his small armies of officials, scribes, and workers that had supported the elaborate redistributive system were gone forever. Within a few generations all knowledge of those things disappeared, leaving only the memory of legendary warrior-chiefs, powerful rulers of once large and prosperous kingdoms, imagined as better men in every way than their puny descendants.

The disappearance of the political and economic systems and the high culture that accompanied it does not mean, however, that Greece had lapsed into a primitive state. Despite the collapse of the palace organization, everything that mattered in daily life at the level of the household and the village continued without interruption. As they had in the Mycenaean Age, the Dark Age Greeks grew wheat and barley, olives, figs, and grapes; they made wine and cheese, tanned hides, sheared their sheep, spun and wove their wool and flax, using the same methods and equipment as before. So too, the basic technical crafts of the potter, weaver, metalworker, and carpenter-builder survived, though at a lower level of skill and refinement. To be sure, there was no longer any demand for metal inlay or blue glass paste or fresco paintings, which, like the art of writing, had disappeared with the palaces. For central manufacturing, storage, and distribution had been eliminated, along with luxury goods, trade, and the tax collector. Yet the timeless rhythm and activities of the agricultural year and the farming village went on unchanged and would remain constant over the following centuries.

Similarly, in the realm of religion, the Dark Age was a period of both continuity and discontinuity. The names of six or seven of the later twelve "Olympian" gods are found in the Linear B tablets. On the other hand, many of those named in the tablets did not survive, such as "Drimios, son of Zeus," and "Dia," a feminine form of Zeus, presumably his consort. The general manner of worshipping and placating the gods through prayer and sacrifice and gifts remained much the same. In the Dark Age, however, religious worship was no longer centered in the palaces but was diffused among the villages, and many of the cults and festivals for specific deities were founded then. Ideas about the nature and personalities of the gods probably also changed. Though many of the stories (*mythoi*) about gods and heroes that formed the core of later literature and art originated in the fourteenth and thirteenth centuries BC and did survive more or less intact through the destruction period, others were probably made up or borrowed from the East during the Dark Age.

Paradoxically, signs of recovery appear at a time when the material culture was at its lowest ebb. Beginning around 1050, different dialect groups from the mainland began migrating to the Aegean islands and to the coast of Asia Minor, settling in a north-south band from the Hellespont to Rhodes. As we saw in Chapter 1, according to the legends the settlers of the central portion, the Ionians, were Achaean refugees from the Peloponnesus who, to escape the Dorians, fled first to Attica and later set out across the Aegean. Dorians also participated in the movements, taking over the southern Aegean islands and the southwest coast of Asia Minor. The numerous coastal and island towns created, for the first time in history, a large permanent Greek presence in Asia Minor and ensured that the Aegean Sea would one day be known as the "Greek Sea."

Another indication of recovery was the mastery of the difficult process of smelting and working iron, which produced weapons and tools that were harder than those made of bronze and kept their edge better. Although Greece is fairly rich in iron ore, and the technology for exploiting it was long known in the East, the Mycenaean Greeks had preferred to import from abroad copper and tin (resources largely lacking in Greece) to make bronze. But when the collapse of trade cut off the supply of bronze, necessity proved the mother of invention. From 1050 on, small local iron industries sprang up all across the mainland and the islands. Archaeology shows that by 950 most of the weapons and tools were made of iron, not bronze. The Iron Age had dawned in Greece.

Renewed energy is revealed in a new style of pottery called Protogeometric (1050–900), which seems to have originated in Attica and very quickly spread into other regions. Although Protogeometric bears clear affinities to the decadent Submycenaean style from which it evolved, there are remarkable differences. The

a

b

Figure 2.1a. A Submycenaean vase from the Kerameikus cemetery in Athens. Note the barely recognizable octopus, which had been a standard motif on Minoan-Mycenaean vases. **Figure 2.1b.** A Late Protogeometric vase from the same cemetery, foreshadowing the Geometric style.

vases become better proportioned, slimmer and less squat. New varieties of shapes appear. The abstract decorative designs inherited from Submycenaean— horizontal lines and bands, arcs, half-circles, and concentric circles—are now crisply drawn and fit the shapes of the vases more pleasingly. The overall effect is one of balance, order, and symmetry.

The aesthetic refinement was partly a result of advances in technique. Potters had developed a faster wheel, which allowed them to improve the shapes of the vases. And they no longer drew their lines and circles freehand. For lines and bands they used a ruler; for circles they invented a multiple brush and compass (several brushes on a single arm affixed to a pair of dividers). Moreover they prepared the clay better and achieved a finer, more lustrous glaze by firing at a higher temperature.

Beginning around 1000 BC, population slowly began to inch upward, although even at the end of the Protogeometric period (c. 900 BC) population levels were still quite low and the number of settlements had increased only slightly. Archaeologists label as "prominent" any tenth- or ninth-century site that held more than two hundred people; the smaller sites were mere hamlets containing a handful of families, a total of twenty to forty people. Many of these sites had been flourishing towns and villages in the Late Bronze Age. They were destroyed or abandoned in the twelfth century and left totally or nearly uninhabited for several generations, and then were reinhabited (though not always on the exact site) on a much smaller scale in the Protogeometric period. A few major settlements like Athens or Corinth may have had populations of a thousand or even substantially more at this time. However, because such places have been continuously inhabited and built over, there is no way to judge their size or growth in the Dark Age without stripping away the modern buildings or demolishing the excavated Classical structures.

Although recovery was slow and its pace varied from region to region, progress was steady. Abandoned Mycenaean villages came back to life, and, though few and small, new settlements appeared. Communication improved as well, both between the various regions of Greece and between the Greeks and the East. Foreign trade, which had virtually ceased by the end of the twelfth century, resumed, though at much reduced levels. By the end of the tenth century, the major movements of people into and within Greece had slackened. Greece had achieved a stability it had not known since the destruction phase. In 900 Greek civilization stood at the threshold of a new era.

SOCIETY IN THE EARLY DARK AGE

Material and social conditions in the early Dark Age were vastly different from what they had been in the highly populated and highly regulated regimes of the Mycenaean Age. With the dissolution of the intricate ties that had bound the outlying settlements to the palace-complexes and to one another, the former centers and peripheral villages found themselves largely on their own politically and economically. With the decline of population, land was plentiful. The fertile plains were more than sufficient for the inhabitants of the small farming communities. The less fertile farmland provided a reserve. Distant upland plains and mountain valleys lay untouched or were given over to grazing. Game, birds, wild foods, and other natural resources, like timber, were plentiful and readily available.

Leadership and governmental roles in these self-sufficient communities were simple and operated face-to-face. After the collapse of the Mycenaean system Greece most likely reverted to a government of local chiefs, similar to the type of organization that had existed in the Middle Bronze Age before the consolidation of power by a single chief. The graves and building remains from the eleventh and tenth centuries show little social differentiation. The chiefs and their families seem not to have lived much differently from the rest.

The Basileus

The Mycenaean Linear B tablets provide an important clue to the process of decentralization. As we saw in Chapter 1, there occurs on the tablets the title *pasireu*, which seems to have belonged to a minor official, the local representative of the *wanax*, who functioned as a kind of "mayor" of a town or village. The title *pasireu* survived into the Dark Age, written in the later Greek alphabet as *basileus*. In the Homeric society, however, the basileus is the political and military leader of a settlement and its adjacent land. It appears that when the Mycenaean kingdoms fell apart, their separate components—the villages, with their surrounding farmlands and pastures—continued to be headed by men called *basileis* (plural). The difference, of course, was that a basileus no longer reported to or carried out the instructions of a central wanax. This scenario is borne out by the fact that the title *wanax* does actually appear in Homer but is used only as an honorific equivalent of *basileus*, and as the title of Zeus, the supreme god, who is called "*(w)anax* of gods and men." Clearly, after the destructions of the palaces, no such figure as the wanax existed in real life, only the name and a vague memory of his exalted status.

The Greek word *basileus* is usually translated as "king" wherever it appears in literature, including in the *Iliad* and *Odyssey*. It would be misleading, however, to call the Dark Age leaders "kings," a title that conjures up in the modern mind visions of monarchs with autocratic powers. A more appropriate name for the Dark Age basileus is the anthropological term "chief," which suggests a man with far less power than a king. The basileus, nevertheless, was a man of great stature and importance in his community.

Evidence of an early Dark Age basileus was recently discovered at the site of Lefkandi on the island of Euboea. A bustling Mycenaean town, Lefkandi had declined during the collapse and then revived in the Submycenaean period, enjoying an exceptional prosperity (by Dark Age standards) until 700, when it was abandoned. In 1981, the excavators made a surprising discovery: the largest Dark Age building yet found, measuring 30 by 146 feet, constructed around 1000 BC. A burial beneath the floor of the main room held a bronze amphora containing the cremated remains of a man and beside it an iron sword, spearhead, and whetstone. Next to the amphora lay the skeleton of a woman, presumably the man's wife, buried with gold ornaments. Nearby was another burial containing the skeletons of four horses. Soon after the funeral the whole building was apparently deliberately demolished and covered over with a huge mound of earth and stones. Scholars remain puzzled about the building's function: Was it the couple's house or a deliberately designed massive tomb? In either case, the man who received this elaborate warrior's burial (and may have been given cult honors after his death), was plainly the basileus of Lefkandi and its surrounding area, a man who had been the focal point of the society in his life and was equally honored in death.

Recent excavations have revealed other early Dark Age chieftains and their societies. Especially noteworthy is the site of Nichoria, located in the southwest Peloponnesus, a poorer and less progressive region than Euboea, which had maintained steady contact with the Near East. Nichoria had been an important subsidiary town of the kingdom of Pylos and was abandoned around 1200, when the marauders came. It came back to life around 1050 as a much smaller village— actually several separate hamlets strung along the ridge top—whose population reached about two hundred early in the ninth century BC. Nichoria was fairly prosperous in a humble way, supporting itself by farming and herding, especially cattle.

In the main population cluster, located at the center of the ridge, archaeologists uncovered a large tenth-century building, about 35 feet long and 23 feet wide, consisting of one large room and a small porch (room 2). They identified it as the "village chieftain's house." Although much larger and better constructed than the ordinary houses on the ridge, it was the same shape and made of the same materials. Its floor was packed earth and its walls were of mud brick, supporting a steep thatched roof that extended over the shallow front porch. A remodeling early in the ninth century added a second, smaller room at the rear (room 3) and a large courtyard in front, lengthening the building to an impressive 52 feet. The house was abandoned in the late ninth century; but right next to it a new two-room house was erected, built even better and boasting a much longer courtyard. Around this time, however, the population of Nichoria was declining. Finally, the whole site was abandoned about 750 BC, perhaps the victim of Spartan aggression in Messenia.

The residences of Dark Age basileis reveal that they were important personages in their villages and the surrounding area. The construction and renovations of the chieftains' homes required the time and labor of a substantial number of persons, unlike the ordinary houses, which could be built by the occupants themselves. The chiefs' houses may also have had some communal functions. The excavators suggest that the chief's house at Nichoria, for example, served as the religious center of the settlement and perhaps as a communal storehouse. Yet, although the chiefs held the highest status in the community, it is clear that they lived in a style that was hardly different from that of their neighbors.

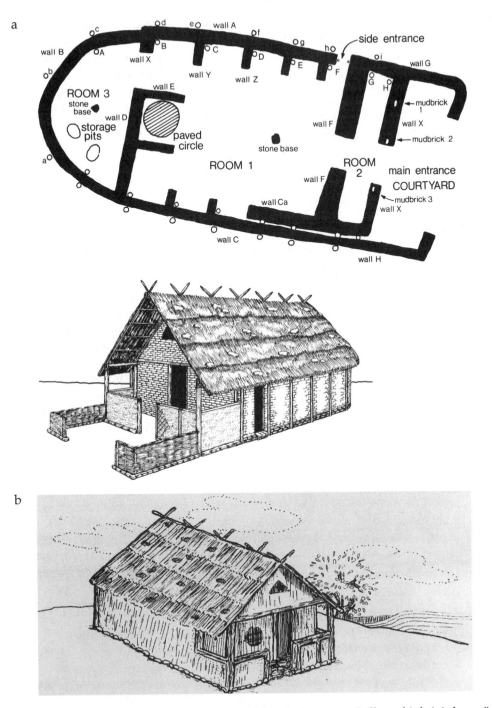

Figure 2.2a. Artist's plan and drawing of the ninth-century "village chieftain's house" at Nichoria. **Figure 2.2b.** Artist's conception of an "ordinary" Dark Age house.

Nichoria and other Dark Age sites also tell us that the economy, the government, and other social institutions underwent no basic changes during the Dark Age. New generations could expect to live the same kind of life as their parents, sharing the same beliefs, and under the same form of government. Such a static existence in small village communities was not a bad thing at all, for it created and preserved tried and true rules for social conduct. Throughout their history the Greeks would cling to their ancient traditions of right and wrong behavior, even amidst changing conditions. This persistent reference to the ancient ways was one of the binding forces of Hellenic culture.

REVIVAL (c. 900–750 BC)

Though social institutions remained constant, the pace of material progress quickened around 900 BC. As usual, vases found in graves provide the main index of change and development. The Protogeometric potters and painters of the tenth century were still very conservative and did not innovate or experiment much, but they continued to refine and perfect their techniques. However, around 900, as the late Protogeometric style evolves into the Geometric style, a new artistic and aesthetic spirit becomes evident. There is no dramatic break with the tradition, and in some regions the old style continues for some time. Nevertheless, a remarkable proliferation of geometric designs marks the Geometric as a distinctly new period.

The Geometric style (c. 900–700) is conventionally divided into three art-historical phases, Early (c. 900–850), Middle (c. 850–750), and Late (c. 750–700). In the Early Geometric period, the vase makers added new shapes and new decorative motifs to their repertoires. The circles and semicircles that had been the staple designs of the Protogeometric vases were largely replaced by more linear and angular motifs, such as the meander pattern (also called the Greek key design), zigzags, triangles, and cross-hatching, set into clearly defined zones and bands. The Middle Geometric potters display a growing command of increasingly elaborate linear decoration, gradually filling the entire surface of the vase. The vases become larger and more ambitious, show-off pieces for artists and costly trophies for buyers.

In the early eighth century, the vase painters began to depict living creatures once again, reviving a motif that had virtually disappeared after 1200. At first they drew only animals and birds, reproducing them cookie-cutter style on friezes across the vase. Human figures reappear around 760 to 750, and soon the pictorial elements begin to dominate, until representational drawing takes over most of the surface and geometric design recedes into the background. Late Geometric (c. 750–700) is linked to the past, but has unmistakably broken with it. Accordingly, Late Geometric vase painting and other cultural innovations of the "eighth-century renaissance" will be treated later in this chapter.

Other indications of material progress, consistent with the developments in the potter's art, become visible at the beginning of the Geometric period. Ninth-century Greek craftsmen were now producing luxury items like fine gold jewelry and ivory carvings for domestic consumption. This development attests not only to the revival of craft skills and a market for them, but also to a renewed availability of raw materials from abroad, including bronze, which begin to appear in larger quantities as a result of increasing trade with the Near East. These domestic luxury items, as well as imported ones, turn up with increasing frequency in ninth- and eighth-century burials. With very few exceptions, grave goods from before about 900 reveal little disparity in wealth or social status. In the ninth century, it is possible for the first time to speak of "rich" and "ostentatious" graves, although the distinctions of wealth are generally slight until the Late Geometric (c. 750–700).

Houses also were for the most part better built in the ninth century, reflecting the general rise in prosperity. But there were no major changes in building style and materials, and the top families were only a little more comfortably housed than the rest. There are still no signs of communal buildings. The earliest of these, the free-standing temple of a god, would not appear until about 800.

HOMER AND ORAL POETRY

The two great epic poems, the *Iliad* and the *Odyssey*, were not produced until the Late Geometric period, but they are introduced here because the texts as we have them are really the culmination of a long oral tradition going back centuries be-

Figure 2.3. Gold jewelry from the cremation grave of a wealthy Athenian woman, around 850 BC. In addition to the jewelry, she was buried with a large number of fine vases, bronze and iron pins, ivory seals, a faience necklace, and a large ceramic chest, surmounted with five model granaries, attesting to the agricultural wealth of her family.

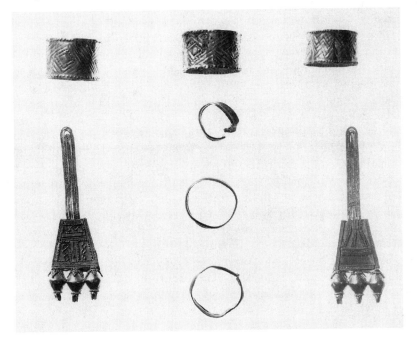

fore the eighth century. Epic poems are long narrative tales; they tell a story in verse and are sung or recited in front of an audience. The Homeric epics are the oldest known literature of Europe, though they are quite young compared with the epic poetry of the Near East, which goes back at least to the third millennium BC. Although the later Greeks revered Homer as their first and greatest poet, they knew nothing about him. Tradition had it that he was an Ionian, from Smyrna or Chios; some said that he was blind. And they gave widely different dates for his lifetime, most of them before 700 BC according to our reckoning of time.

Modern linguistic analysis of the Homeric poems places their composition between about 750 and 720, the *Iliad* several decades earlier than the *Odyssey*. The time differential has led many scholars to question whether the *Iliad* and the *Odyssey* were the work of a single poet or of two separate poets. The method of their composition has also been a matter of controversy. As early as the eighteenth century AD, suspicions had arisen that the poems were composed orally, and not written down, because so much of the narrative consists of frequently repeated combinations of stock phrases. But the composition of extremely long and complex poems without writing—the *Iliad* is around sixteen thousand lines and the *Odyssey* twelve thousand—seemed impossible. A theory thus arose that the poems as we now have them were "stitched" together centuries later, out of short "lays" or "ballads" that told about the deeds of olden heroes. The real authors of the *Iliad* and *Odyssey*, according to this theory, were the generations of anonymous, literate poet-editors who collected, expanded, and elaborated on the traditional oral songs.

A major shift in opinion occurred when it was shown that illiterate poets could in fact compose long poems that had the complexity and stylistic excellence of written poetry. In the early 1930s, a young classical scholar, Milman Parry, and his co-worker, Albert Lord, made phonograph records of illiterate Bosnian singer-poets singing a traditional type of south Slavic epic-heroic poetry. Comparing recordings of the same poems—some over 10,000 lines—made at different times, Parry and Lord discovered that no two performances were exactly the same. It turned out that the singer had not learned and memorized his poem, but was rather composing, or, more correctly, "recomposing" it as he went along. This was possible because the story content was traditional and was sung in a highly formalized style.

Parry concluded that the Homeric poems had been created in a similar manner. Homer, he believed, was the greatest in a long succession of oral singer-poets, who had learned the difficult craft of oral composition from the previous generation of poets, who in turn had learned it from their elders. In retelling the ancient stories, which were familiar to the audiences, Homer drew on an inherited stock of traditional "formulas" (fixed phrases, lines, and blocks of text) and "themes" (typical scenes, story patterns) that he had memorized and could vary as the occasion demanded. Over a lifetime of private rehearsals, "writing" the poetry in his mind, and public performances, Homer crafted and perfected the poems that bore his personal signature. The "oral-formulaic theory," as it is called, is now universally accepted and in fact has greatly influenced the worldwide study of other "oral literatures" of the past and present.

On the question of when the Homeric poems were committed to writing, and thus fossilized, so to speak, the prevailing view today is that they were written down very near the time of their composition. It was during this time that the art of writing returned to Greece. Lord argued that the illiterate Homer dictated his epics to persons who could write. Other scholars, however, believe that the poems as we have them were memorized and transmitted orally by professional reciters called "rhapsodes" for some generations before they were written down, perhaps as late as the sixth century. Still others maintain that Homer was trained in the oral tradition but had learned to write, and was therefore a writing poet. Whatever the actual role of writing in the final composition of the two great epics, it is agreed that they represent the culmination of a very long oral-epic tradition, which ceased to evolve with the advent of writing.

In the words of a Bosnian singer, epic poetry "is the song of the olden time, of the deeds of the great men of old and the heroes over the earth ." Such songs had been sung and resung in Greece continuously since the Bronze Age; in the intervening centuries, stories and themes from the heroic literatures of the ancient Near East also found their way into the slowly evolving Greek oral-epic tradition. For the Greeks of the Dark Age and later, the "olden time" was an Age of Heroes, a relatively brief period that encompassed a generation or two before, and one generation after, the Trojan War; this, in our time reckoning was approximately the thirteenth century BC.

The story of the Trojan War is a classically simple folk saga. Paris, the son of King Priam of Troy, seduced and brought back to Troy the beautiful Helen, the wife of Menelaus, ruler of the Spartans. To avenge the insult, Menelaus and his brother, Agamemnon, *anax* (*wanax*) of Mycenae, gathered a huge army of Achaean warriors, who sailed to Troy and destroyed the city after a ten-year siege. Whether such an expedition actually occurred is unimportant; for the Greeks themselves the Trojan War was the pivotal event of their early history.

The *Iliad* and *Odyssey* do not narrate the entire Trojan War. The *Iliad* compresses the action into about forty days in the tenth year of the War, and the *Odyssey* tells about the return home of one warrior-chief, Odysseus. The poems assume that the eighth-century audiences knew the rest of the plots and actions. In the seventh and into the sixth century, an "Epic Cycle" of separate, and shorter, poems was constructed around the two great poems, completing the story of Troy. These lesser epics, sometimes attributed to Homer himself, narrated the events leading up to the war, events during the war, including the "Sacking of Troy," and the "returns" of other Greek chiefs.

LATE DARK AGE (HOMERIC) SOCIETY

Not surprisingly, considering the vast remove in time, the Homeric poems preserve almost nothing about Late Bronze Age society. Nor do they reveal much about the poet's own time, the late eighth century. The poems do, however, provide a wealth of detail about Dark Age society a few generations earlier, somewhere around 800 BC. The time lag is not surprising. During the poet's lifetime, fundamental changes were taking place in the society, and these could not easily be fitted into the traditional narrative background that had evolved during the centuries of oral composition. The society depicted in the epics, therefore, must have been earlier than the time of their composition, yet within living memory of the poet and his audiences. Homeric society resembles both in its general structure and in many of its details the type of social organization that anthropologists call a "chiefdom." Such warrior societies have existed throughout the world and in all periods of history.

Homeric society is naturally a distortion of the late Dark Age society on which it was based. The oral poets were recreating an imaginary past world that was in every way better and grander than their contemporary world. For example, the Trojan leader Hector picks up, for use as a weapon, a stone

> which two men, the best in the land,
> could not easily lift from the ground onto a wagon,
> men such as mortals are today; but he brandished it lightly, all by
>   himself.
>
>   (Iliad *12.445–449)*

Nevertheless, aspects of that imagined world, especially its social institutions and ideologies, must have been based on the audiences' real-life experience in order for them to make sense of the action and to relate to the characters and their motivations. A modern analogy is science fiction, which has to reflect the reader's own world to some extent no matter how fantastic or surreal the setting and the plot. Similarly, the Homeric poems are full of sheer fantasy and exaggeration, yet studded with telltale signs of present-day reality. So, for example, the front courtyard of Odysseus' "splendid residence" contains a large pile of manure, as well as the family's geese and ewes at milking time. Inside, the floors are made of packed earth, and the great hall (*megaron*) is blackened with soot from the smoky central hearth. In fact, Odysseus' "palace" is far more like the house of the basileus of Dark Age Nichoria than the excavated palace of the king of Bronze Age Pylos.

The Homeric Chiefdoms

The geographical and political map of the Homeric world consists of distinct regions and peoples. For example, in the "Catalogue of the Ships" in the *Iliad* (2.484–759), which lists the contingents that made up the Greek army at Troy , the entry for the large region of Aetolia reads:

> Thoas, son of Andraemon led the Aetolians,
> those who dwelled in Pleuron and Olenos and Pylene
> and Chalcis by-the-sea, and rocky Calydon, ...
> and with him followed forty black ships.
>
>   (Iliad *2.638–644)*

Thoas is the "paramount" chief in Aetolia, superior in authority to the local chiefs of the villages listed here and the acknowledged leader of all who call themselves Aetolians. Elsewhere in the *Iliad* he is described as "Thoas, who in the whole of Pleuron and steep Calydon ruled over the Aetolians, and was honored like a god by the people" (*Iliad* 13.216–218). The "people" is the *dēmos* (the root of many English words such as demo-cracy, demo-graphics, and epi-demic). *Dēmos*, which on the Linear B tablets (in the form *damo*) apparently referred to a village community, signifies, from Homer on, both a territorial unit and the people who live in it. Thus, *dēmos* in this passage indicates both Aetolia, the region, and the Aetolians, the people.

The regional chiefdoms into which Homeric society was divided were simpler versions of the Mycenaean kingdoms from which they devolved. The essential difference was that the paramount chief, unlike the Bronze Age wanax, had only limited control over the local districts of the demos. The local chiefs, though subordinate to him, were essentially independent of him. One indication of the looseness of the power structure is that the paramount chief is called simply basileus, with no other title to distinguish him from the other basileis who rank below him. In fact, there are no other official titles of rank in Homer.

Chiefs and Followers

Because epic poetry concentrates almost exclusively on the activities of basileis and their families (largely ignoring the mass of the ordinary people), the *Iliad* and the *Odyssey* provide a fairly detailed description of chieftainship. As is common among chiefdom societies everywhere, the office and title of basileus pass from father to son. But inheritance alone is not enough; the young chief must also be competent to fulfill his role, which is to lead his people in war and peace. For the successor of the paramount basileus, there is an additional challenge—to secure the compliance of the local chiefs in the demos. A paramount basileus should have the capabilities of a man like Thoas, who was

> by far the best of the Aetolians, skilled with the throwing spear,
> and a good man in the close-in fighting; and in the assembly
>   few of the Achaeans
> surpassed him, whenever the young men competed in debate.
>   (Iliad *15.282–284*)

The two prime requisites of leadership, skill in battle and the ability to persuade, are encapsulated in the advice that the basileus Peleus gives to his young son Achilles as he sends him off to the Trojan War: "Be both a speaker of words and a doer of deeds." Above all, it is the deeds, "the works of war," that make a man the leader. In Homer, as in many chieftain societies worldwide, a chief's status is measured by the number of warriors who follow him. A chief who does not show himself a good warrior will find few who are willing to follow his lead. For example, in the Catalogue of the Ships, we are told that Nireus, the son of the basileus of the island of Syme, led only three ships to the Trojan War. Although he was the handsomest of the Greeks at Troy (next to Achilles), Nireus was "a weak man, and few people followed him" (*Iliad* 2.671–675). By contrast, Agamemnon was acknowledged as the leader of the entire Greek army at Troy, because, as the commander of one hundred ships from the region around Mycenae, "he led by far the most troops."

All basileis, both local chiefs and the paramount, have their own personal followings. The men who follow a chief are called by him and call each other *hetairoi* ("companions"), a word that conveys a deep feeling of mutual loyalty. Thus the "army" of a demos is composed of several individual hetairoi bands, each under the command of its own basileus, and all under the command of the paramount. However, the entire fighting force of the demos is mustered together under the paramount basileus only when there is an all-out war, usually for defense of the demos when an outside enemy has attacked in force. Otherwise, a local or a paramount chief is free to raise his own following and go on raiding expeditions against villages of another demos, either to even the score in some ongoing quarrel or just to steal or plunder their livestock, valuables, and women. Commonly, a chief recruits his followers with a large feast, showing that he is a generous leader and thereby binding his followers to him. For instance, Odysseus (posing as a warrior-leader from Crete), describes how he made a raiding expedition into Egypt. Having fitted out nine ships, he says, he gathered a following,

> and for six days my trusty companions (*hetairoi*)
> feasted, and I gave them many animal victims
> both to sacrifice to the gods and to make a feast for themselves,
> and on the seventh we got on board and set sail from broad Crete. . . .
> (Odyssey 14.247–252)

Raiding is a way of life in Homeric society. Booty raids not only enrich the raid-leader and his men, but also serve as a test of their manliness, skill, and courage, and thus bring honor and glory. Whether on a raid or in a war, the basileus is the one most severely tested, for he is literally the leader, stationing himself "among the front-fighters." The leader is obliged to risk his life fighting at the front of his army (a custom that persisted throughout ancient Greek history). In return for his leadership, the demos is under obligation to provide the basileus with honors and material gifts.

Document 2.1 Sarpedon, leader of the Lycian allies of the Trojans, addresses Glaucus, his close *hetairos* and second in comand of the Lycians, on the reciprocal obligations between chiefs and the people.

> Glaukos, why is it you and I are honored before others
> with pride of place, the choice meats and the filled wine cups
> in Lykia, and all the men look on us as if we were immortals,

and we are appointed a great piece of land by the banks of Xanthos,
good land, orchard and vineyard, and ploughland for the planting of
    wheat?
Therefore it is our duty in the forefront of the Lykians
to take our stand, and bear our part of the blazing of battle,
so that a man of the close-armoured Lykians may say of us:
"Indeed, these are no ignoble men who are lords of Lykia,
these *basileis* of ours, who feed on the fat sheep appointed
and drink the exquisite sweet wine, since indeed there is strength
of valour in them, since they fight in the forefront of the Lykians."

Iliad 12.310–321; translated by Richmond Lattimore, The Iliad of Homer.
Chicago: University of Chicago Press, 1951, p. 266.

Reciprocity—mutual and fair exchange—which governs all social relationships in the Homeric world, is the core of the leader-people relationship. The giving and the receiving should ideally balance one another. So, too, fairness is the rule in the apportionment of the spoils of war. Following a raid, the booty is gathered together. First the leader takes his share (and something extra as the leader's "prize") and, under his supervision, special rewards for valor are given out. The rest is then given to the men "to divide up, so that no one may go cheated of an equal share."

A leader who keeps more than he deserves or distributes prizes unfairly risks losing the respect of his followers. To a chief, being called "greedy" is almost as devastating an insult as being called "cowardly." In short, a basileus cannot afford not to appear generous and openhanded. Similarly, Homeric chiefs engage in a constant exchange of gifts and feasts with other chiefs and important men. This is both a way of showing off their wealth and a means to cement friendships, win new friends, and collect obligations through a display of generosity.

Despite the great authority given him by his position, a basileus has limited ability to coerce others to follow his lead. He is only a chief, not a king. Thus in the *Odyssey*, there are several occasions when Odysseus' hetairoi simply refuse to obey him. Once, when his followers decide to do exactly the opposite of what he has ordered them, Odysseus can only say that as "one man alone" he must abide by the will of the many. Odysseus' helplessness illustrates the fundamental fragility of leadership authority in this type of low-level chieftainship.

Rightful inheritance to the position of paramount basileus is not an absolute guarantee of succession. In a society in which performance is more important than descent, a weak successor will be challenged by rival basileis who wish to replace him as head chief. The problem of succession is addressed at length in the *Odyssey*. Odysseus, the paramount chief of Ithaca and its neighboring islands, has been gone for twenty years (ten at Troy, ten on his return home), and has long been presumed dead. Odysseus' aged father, Laertes, the previous chief, retired years ago to the countryside. Odysseus' son, Telemachus, who is barely 20 years old, with no experience of leadership and few supporters (his father's followers had gone to Troy with him), finds himself in a desperate situation. A group of young chiefs or sons of chiefs (mostly from the other islands of the chiefdom), are wooing Telemachus' mother, Penelope, presumed a widow. They are camped out in his courtyard, feasting on his livestock and seducing the slave girls. They mean to overthrow the lineage of Laertes, by allowing the one who succeeds in winning over Penelope to become paramount basileus. Marrying the widow of the dead chief would give a new leader some legitimacy. Even though the suitors agree that the chiefship belongs to Telemachus "by your paternal birthright," they have no scruples about taking it away from him.

The usurpers use force and the threat of force. When Telemachus calls an assembly of the people to complain about the outrage against his household, they threaten the few old men who stand up for the young heir, cow the rest of the Ithacans, and declare the assembly dissolved. Later they try to ambush and kill Telemachus himself. Like Odysseus, Penelope can be cunning and resourceful; she uses her guile to thwart the ambitions of the suitors. She holds the suitors at bay for several years, by saying that she will marry one of them only when she has completed a burial shroud for her father-in-law Laertes. Harboring a hope that Odysseus will return, she weaves by day, and at night secretly unravels the shroud. Eventually, Odysseus returns, kills the suitors, and assumes his rightful place as paramount basileus of Ithaca and the other islands. In most instances, however, weakened ruling dynasties would not have fared as well as the house and lineage of Laertes.

Government in the Late Dark Age

Governmental institutions in the Dark Age were few and simple, as Homer illustrates and the material remains of the late ninth and early eighth centuries corroborate. A council, called the *boulē*, was made up of the local chiefs and the paramount chief, in whose great hall (*megaron*) they met to formulate policy for the whole demos. The paramount basileus presided and had the determining voice in the discussions, but usually heeded the advice and counsel of the "elders," as the boule-members were called (though many were actually younger men). Their decision was presented at the assembly of the people, called the *agora* or "gathering," which comprised the men of fighting age and older. Sometimes in Homer, however, one or another of the chiefs or respected elders calls an assembly without consulting the other leaders. Then there is an open debate, which generally leads to an agreement. Although theoretically any man may address the assembly, customarily only the chiefs and other "outstanding men" speak out. At each proposal, the men of the demos make their will known by shouting, by muttering, or by remaining silent. In the end, if the assembly has been successful, the demos shouts its collective approval of the policy. The aim of the assembly is to achieve consensus, both among the leaders and between leaders and people.

In addition to his functions as the military and political leader, the basileus also had a religious and judicial role in the life of the community. His sole, but very important, religious duty was to preside at public sacrifices to the gods. When he prayed to the gods at a sacrifice he was the spokesman for the people, similar to the father sacrificing on behalf of his family. The basileus was not, however, one of the priests of the gods, nor did he claim to have a special personal relationship with the gods, although Homer firmly emphasizes that Zeus upholds and fosters the ruling authority of the office of basileus.

During the Dark Age, chiefs probably played a lesser role in judicial matters, because the judicial process was in an early stage of development. The only law was custom, that is, the community's traditions regarding right and wrong in particular situations. (A system of formal and written laws would not emerge until the seventh century.) Much of this custom-law involved procedures for settling differences privately. Even the most antisocial act, murder within the demos, was not a crime in the sense that it required arrest and trial of the alleged murderer by the society at large. It was the custom, rather, that the families of the killer and the victim should come to an agreement on a material "penalty" as compensation, thus avoiding a socially destabilizing feud between the families. The same procedure was followed for another sensitive offense, adultery. When the parties could not reach a private agreement, the dispute was brought before a court. Homer describes a dispute over the payment of the murder compensation, which is heard and decided by a group of "elders" (probably chiefs), one of whom will receive a reward of gold for speaking the "straightest judgement." The lawsuit takes place in an assembly, with the people pushing and shoving and shouting encouragement to one party or the other (*Iliad* 18.497–508). The council, assembly, and law court are all there is of government in Homer, but they were sufficient. They would remain the essential organs of government, in a more highly evolved form, in the later city-states.

Foreign Relations

In the Dark Age, "diplomatic" relations between one chiefdom and another were conducted by the chiefs themselves or by a trusted companion. As part of his training, Odysseus was sent at a young age to Messenia by his "father and the other elders" on an embassy to collect a "debt" owed to the Ithacans. This was a serious affair, for the Messenians had raided Ithaca and stolen three hundred sheep and their shepherds. If negotiations failed, the Ithacans would stage a revenge raid, and the bad feelings would likely escalate into an all-out war.

While he was in Messenia, young Odysseus stayed at the house of a "guest-friend" (*xenos*; plural *xenoi*). "Guest-friendship" (*xenia*) was a reciprocal relationship in which xenoi were pledged to offer one another protection, lodging, and assistance whenever they traveled to each other's demos. The relationship was handed down from generation to generation between the families of xenoi. While in Messenia, Odysseus stayed at the house of Ortilochus, an important man in his demos, though not the chief. Many years later, Odysseus' son Telemachus would stay overnight with the son of Ortilochus, on his way to visit Menelaus in Sparta and again on his return trip. The hospitality often included a lavish feast and sometimes musical entertainment. At the end of the visit, the host guest-friend gave his guest a valuable parting gift (e.g., a sword or a gold cup). The gift was the material token of their bond of close friendship, given to ensure that whenever he visited the demos of his friend, he would receive in return the same protection, hospitality, and a gift of at least the same worth.

Guest-friendship was an indispensable device for foreign relations in the Dark Age, for when a stranger came to another demos he had no rights and could be mistreated and even killed. The custom was particularly useful in sensitive situations. For example, when Agamemnon and Menelaus made a long visit to Ithaca to persuade Odysseus to join in the expedition against Troy, they did not stay with him but with a man named Melaneus, a guest-friend of Agamemnon. They used the hospitality of Melaneus, not because they did not have a friendly relationship with Odysseus, but because the delicate task of recruiting foreign allies required a neutral base. *Xenia* would continue, in a somewhat different form, as a means of diplomatic relations into the Archaic Age and beyond.

Social Values and Ethics

In all societies, the notions of good and bad, right and wrong, are largely determined by their own peculiar conditions of life. The codes of behavior for Homeric males center around war. The Greek adjective *agathos* ("good") when used of men in Homer, is almost always restricted to the qualities of bravery and skill in fighting and athletics. The opposite word, *kakos* ("bad"), means cowardly, or unskilled and useless in battle. In a society in which every ablebodied man fights to defend his community, all men are under constraint to behave bravely. The leaders are expected to be especially valiant, and in addition, to excel in public speaking and counsel.

Other traditional rules of conduct dictate that a "good man" should honor the gods, keep promises and oaths, and be loyal to friends and fellow warriors. He should exhibit self-control, be hospitable, and respect women and elders. Pity should be shown to beggars and suppliant strangers. It is proper to show pity even toward captured warriors and to refrain from defiling the corpses of the enemy. These gentler qualities are desirable, but they are not required; the sole criterion for being called agathos is good warriorship.

A warrior society is forced to breed into its future warriors a savage joy in the grim "works of Ares," a lust to annihilate the enemy. At the end of a poignant family scene in the *Iliad*, the Trojan hero Hector lifts up his baby son and prays to the gods that he may grow up to be a better warrior than his father and "bring back the bloody spoils of a dead enemy and make his mother's heart glad" (*Iliad* 6.479–481). Homeric Greeks are not only fierce in war but also savage in victory: they loot and burn captured villages, slaughter the male survivors including infants, and rape and enslave the women and girls.

A strong competitive spirit was an important part of the Greek male ethos. Homeric characters constantly compare themselves, or are compared with, one another. Men are driven to win and to be called *aristos* ("best"). One man is said to be "best of the Achaeans in bowmanship," while another "surpassed all the young men in running," or in spear throwing, or chariot racing, or speaking. This type of extracompetitive society is called agonistic, from the Greek word *agōn* ("contest," "struggle"). The instinct to compete and win permeates the society. A poor farmer is roused to work hard when he sees his neighbor getting rich, says Hesiod (c. 700); and "potter resents potter and carpenter resents carpenter, and beggar is jealous of beggar and poet of poet" (*Works and Days* 20–26).

The sole object of competing and striving is to win *timē* ("honor" and "respect"). *Timē* is always public recognition of one's skills and achievements. It always involves some visible mark of respect: the seat of honor and an extra share of meat at a feast, or an additional share of booty, or valuable prizes and gifts, including land. To modern readers, Homeric warrior-chiefs may appear overly greedy for material things, but their purpose in acquiring and possessing many animals and precious objects was mainly to increase their fame and glory. Not to be honored when honor is due, or worse, to be dishonored, are unbearable insults. Thus, when Agamemnon in the *Iliad* grievously dishonored Achilles by taking back the captive girl Briseis, a "prize of honor" awarded to Achilles by the army, a great quarrel arose between them that led to disaster for all the Greeks.

Adherence to the competitive ethic (summed up in the motto "always be the best and be preeminent over the others") spurred men on to accomplish great things and kept the quality of leadership high. On the other hand, the relentless pursuit of personal and family honor and obsession with avenging dishonor could cause enormous political instability. For better or worse, the Homeric codes of male behavior would endure throughout antiquity, and later generations of Greek writers would continue to look to the *Iliad* and *Odyssey* for models of right and wrong conduct.

Valuations of good and bad in respect to women and the behavior expected of them are determined by the male ethic. Within their communities, women are regarded with great respect by men. There is little trace in epic of the misogyny (from *miso-gynia*, "hatred of women") that often appears in later literature. In Homer, women are not reviled or treated contemptuously, and also appear to have more social freedom than those of later periods. Women go freely about the village and countryside and participate in festive and religious events. And though they have no political voice, women are nevertheless part of "public opinion." Those of high-status households join the company of their husbands and the other men in the great hall after supper and take part in the conversation. The wife of a chief, especially a paramount chief, is held in high esteem, and may even partake of her husband's authority, as does Arete, the wife of Alcinous, the basileus of the Phaeacians, in the *Odyssey*. Odysseus, disguised as a wandering beggar, flatters Penelope (who does not recognize her husband), saying that her "fame goes up to broad heaven, as of some blameless *basileus*."

The qualities that define a "good" woman in Homer are narrowly circumscribed by their domestic assignment as housewife and mother. They are honored for their beauty, skill and diligence in weaving, careful household management, and good practical sense. Like men, women are also compared with one another, though only within the few areas of excellence allowed them; for example, this one or that one, "surpassed her age-mates in beauty and work [i.e., weaving] and intelligence." They are expected to act modestly in public and in the company of men, and above all to be chaste. Although men are permitted to have concubines, adulterous women bring great disgrace and dishonor upon themselves and their families.

As in later Greece, women are under the strict control of their male relatives and husbands from birth to death. They are the most valuable prizes of raid and war, not only because of their intrinsic value—as workers or concubines, or as goods to be bartered or given away—but also because capturing an enemy's mother, wife, daughter, sister is the ultimate insult.

Document 2.2 In their meeting during a lull in the battle, Hector says these words to Andromache, his wife. Although the outcome of the war is still in doubt, both share a premonition that the Trojans will lose.

> For I know this thing well in my heart, and my mind knows it:
> there will come a day when sacred Ilion shall perish,
> and Priam, and the people of Priam of the strong ash spear.
> But it is not so much the pain to come of the Trojans
> that troubles me, not even of Priam the king nor Hekabe,
> nor the thought of my brothers who in their numbers and valour
> shall drop in the dust under the hands of men who hate them,
> as troubles me the thought of you, when some bronze-armoured
> Achaian leads you off, taking away your day of liberty,
> in tears; and in Argos you must work the loom of another,
> and carry water from the spring Messeis or Hypereia,
> all unwilling, but strong will be the necessity upon you;
> and some day seeing you shedding tears a man will say of you:
> "This is the wife of Hektor, who was ever the bravest fighter
> of the Trojans, breakers of horses, in the days when they fought
>   about Ilion."
> So one will speak of you; and for you it will be yet a fresh grief,
> to be widowed of such a man who could fight off the day of your
>   slavery.
> But may I be dead and the piled earth hide me under before I
> hear you crying and know by this that they drag you captive.

Iliad 6.447–465; translated by Richmond Lattimore, The Iliad of Homer.
Chicago: University of Chicago Press, 1951, p. 165.

Slavery

Slavery did not come under the heading of wrong for the Greeks. Enslavement was not even discussed as a moral issue until the late fifth century BC; and even though some expressed repugnance for it, the institution flourished in Greece throughout pagan antiquity and for centuries after the establishment of Christianity. The ancient Greek attitude toward slavery was simple. It was a terrible thing to become a slave but a good thing to own a slave. Slavery was a by-product of war and raid. One became a slave by being captured or kidnapped—human booty. Greeks did not breed slaves on a large scale, and indeed felt some qualms about enslaving other Greeks (although they did it), preferring to buy and sell non-Greeks. Eumaeus, Odysseus' swineherd, who had been kidnapped as a child by Phoenician traders and sold to Odysseus' father, sums up the degradation of slavery in a sentence: Zeus "takes away half of a man's worth when the day of enslavement comes upon him" (*Odyssey* 17.322–323).

Religion

By the eighth century, Greek religion had attained essentially the form it was to have throughout the rest of pagan antiquity. Yet little else is known about the evolution of religion after the collapse of the Mycenaean society except that some of the gods whose names appear on the Linear B tablets disappeared, and possibly one or two gods were added to the group of major gods. For example, Aphrodite, the Greek goddess of erotic love, may have been a post-Mycenaean import from the Near East, modeled on the Semitic love goddess Astarte/Ishtar; and one of Aphrodite's lovers, Adonis (Semitic *adon*, "lord"), is clearly Near Eastern. In the centuries after 700 the Greeks did adopt or assimilate a few other gods from the Near East and Egypt. There were also important later developments in religious ethics. In all essentials, however, Greek religion would remain for the next thousand years exactly as it was represented in Homer and Hesiod.

The two basic features of Homeric worship go back to the old Mycenaean-Minoan religion. These are polytheism, the worship of many gods and goddesses (singular *theos*; plural *theoi*); and the ritual ways of honoring the gods: with sacrifices and prayers, processions, music, dancing, and hymn singing. Like the other Mediterranean religions, Greek religion was formal, ritualistic, and communal, not private and meditative. But unlike some, it never developed an official set of doctrines or compulsory beliefs. Different and contradictory ideas about the gods coexisted comfortably in Greece.

Everything later Greeks understood about the origins of the world and of the gods they learned from late eighth-century epic poetry. The fifth-century historian Herodotus wrote

> Where each of the gods came from, whether they have always existed, what they look like—these things were unknown until only yesterday, so to speak, or the day before. . . . [Homer and Hesiod] are the ones who created a theogony for

the Greeks. They gave names to the gods, decided what their special skills were
and what honors they should be given, and described their appearance.

(Herodotus 2.53; Blanco 1992)

Hesiod's epic poem, titled *Theogony* ("the genealogy of the gods"), provided
the authoritative account of the beginnings of the universe and the history of the
gods up to the supremacy of Zeus and the other "Olympian" gods. According to
Hesiod, the Olympians were a third generation of gods, descended from the pri-
mal pair of cosmic divinities Gaia (Earth) and Ouranus (Sky). The story closely
parallels much older Mesopotamian accounts and is clearly influenced by them.

There were violent conflicts between each generation. Sky would not allow his
children to be born, and hid them within their mother Earth. Earth persuaded her
imprisoned son Cronus to cut off Ouranus' genitals with a sickle, freeing his
brothers and sisters, who made up the next generation of gods, the Titans. Cronus,
in his turn, tried to prevent his children by his Titan wife Rhea from coming into
being, by swallowing them as they were born. But Rhea deceived Cronus into
swallowing a stone instead of her last-born, Zeus, causing him to vomit up the
others. Then Zeus, with the help of the mighty thunderbolt and the powerful
monster sons of Ouranus, led his brothers and sisters in a violent ten-year war
against the Titans from their stronghold atop Mount Olympus. Successful in the
battle, the Olympians imprisoned the Titans deep in the earth. After overcoming
a final challenge by the monster Typhoeus, Olympian Zeus reigned forever over
the universe. After their victory, the gods divided up control over the universe.
Zeus received command of the heavens and the sky, Poseidon the seas, and
Hades the Underworld, where the souls of humans go when they die; and all the
Olympians shared control of their grandmother Earth and the creatures on Earth,
including humans.

The Olympian gods, therefore, were not the creators of the universe, but rather
the offspring of three and four generations of sexual unions, beginning with
Earth and Sky. As the descendants of the physical universe the gods embodied
the forces of nature; Zeus in effect *was* the sky and all its phenomena. But the
Greeks anthropomorphized their deities, portraying them as idealized men and
women with special powers to control and direct nature. Thus paintings and statues depict Zeus as a human holding or hurling the thunderbolt. All aspects of nature were endowed with human form; woods, mountains, sea, rivers, and springs
were inhabited by countless spirits, imagined as beautiful maidens or youths.
Even emotions and behaviors—fear, pity, hate, prayers, rumor, and so on—were
all perceived as divinities in human form, who, like the rest of the cosmos, had
come into being through procreation.

In their totality, the gods, nature spirits, and abstractions represent the whole
of being. The diversity of the supernatural realm offered the Greeks a satisfactory
way of ordering and explaining the baffling complexity of human experience,
from the vast mysterious universe of stars and planets, to the benign and hostile
world of nature, to the confusing inner world of the human psyche. The divine
world mirrors the human condition. So, for example, Ares, the god of war, is the

spirit of blood lust that enters a warrior and makes him eager to kill and destroy. Aphrodite, the goddess of love, is the irresistible force of sexual desire. Athena represents the sphere of practical wisdom (weaving, carpentry, metalworking, technology in general), while Apollo's wisdom extends to music, poetry, and philosophy. Artemis, like Athena, is a perpetual virgin, but whereas Athena is a friend and helper of warrior-heroes, Artemis shuns all contact with males, and lives in the forests as both hunter and protector of animals.

In Homer and in Hesiod, these powerful divinities look and think exactly like humans; their actions are just as unpredictable. But their infinitely superior powers and the fact that they are immortal and ageless and never subject to pain, unbridgeably set the gods apart from mortal beings. Mortals (*hoi thnētoi*, "the ones who die") are playthings of the gods (*hoi athanatoi*, "the deathless ones"), who squabble among themselves over the fate of this or that person or group. The complex intersection of the eternal divine and ephemeral mortality lay at the base of all later Greek philosophical and scientific speculation about the order and structure of the universe and the human condition.

The Greeks worshiped the gods out of awe for their power to do them good or harm. The gods demanded that their power be acknowledged through gift giving and other marks of respect. Mortals gave these willingly and in abundance because of their fundamental conviction that the gods were disposed to help and protect those who honored them, though realizing at the same time that capricious deities might do just the opposite. Every community had its special protecting god or gods and spared no expense or effort in honoring them in order to keep their favor. After the Dark Age, the Greek city-states would lavish on the gods gifts of public land, huge temples, expensive private dedications, festivals in their honor, and thousands of sacrificed animals.

In Homer, the gods insist on their proper honors but not much else. Their concern with morality as we now understand it is limited. Certain acts, such as incest or homicide, were thought to "pollute" the perpetrator, who must be ritually purified before being readmitted into the society. There were also dozens of other minor taboos (such as touching a corpse) that polluted for a few hours or days. But most deeds that are condemned by the major modern religions as sins against God, such as stealing, adultery, and rape, were not the concern of the gods. As far as interpersonal behavior is concerned, the gods in Homer primarily condemn only oath breaking and mistreating of strangers, suppliants, and beggars. Oaths, which were taken in the names of the witnessing gods, were especially important, because they sealed the contracts between individuals and between communities. A few times, however, the gods in Homer do show some concern for fairness and justice within the society. Thus, Zeus is said to send severe wind and rain storms against those "who make crooked decrees, using force, in the assembly, and drive out justice, heedless of watchfulness of the gods" (*Iliad* 16.384–388). Beginning with Hesiod, the idea of Zeus as the upholder of justice (*dikē*) would become an increasingly common theme in literature.

In many religions, earthly sorrow and suffering are eased by the promise of a paradise after death for those who have lived righteously. The Greeks did not have this consolation. Their conceptions of a personal afterlife remained vague and undeveloped throughout the Archaic and Classical periods. For most Greeks, existence in any meaningful sense ended when the soul (*psychē*) left the body and fluttered down to Hades. There is some punishment of sinners in Hades, but it is reserved for those who have insulted or tried to trick the gods. Later, however, through the influence of mystery cults (such as the worship of Demeter at Eleusis), and of philosophical speculation, ideas of a blissful afterlife for the morally good and eternal torment for the bad would become more highly developed.

Olympian religion was much more concerned with the here and now and propitiation of the gods for special favors through formal rituals. As in the Mycenaean Age, there were special priests and priestesses, who had care of the special prayers and rituals and sacred objects that made up the cult of a god. There was never, however, a professional priestly class or caste, set apart from the rest of the people, as in the Near East and Egypt. Greek priests and seers did not dress or live differently from other citizens; their official duties generally took up very little time and required little in the way of preparation and training. Priests and priestesses came almost exclusively from the upper ranks of society, and a large number of priesthoods were hereditary within a single lineage. Priesthoods increased the prestige of the leading families and thus buttressed their claim to leadership positions, but the office itself held little political authority or economic gain.

COMMUNITY, HOUSEHOLD, AND ECONOMY IN THE LATE DARK AGE

In 800 BC most Greek settlements were still quite small, containing a few dozen families. A handful of major settlements, such as Argos, Athens, Corinth, Knossos, and Sparta, probably held several hundred or more families. All the important sites and most of the smaller ones had been continuously occupied since the Bronze Age, for the obvious reason that they were good places for people to live. With their surrounding fields and pastures, they were for the most part economically self-sufficient.

The farmer's life and even the herdsman's life was village life. The isolated farmstead out in the countryside was rare in early Greece; farmers lived in the villages and walked out each morning to their plots, as they still do today in rural areas of Greece. Greek villages were enduring, close-knit communities. Families lived in them for innumerable generations, intermarrying with other families in the village and in other villages of the demos. The small village may be likened to an extended family, with the village chief as a sort of father. As we have seen, law was customary law; on the whole, public disapproval sufficed to deter antisocial behavior. Difficult disputes were resolved by the chief and the simple court of the village elders. Survival of the village depended upon cooperation among the families; they could not afford to let bad feeling between neighbors and relatives destroy the solidarity of the community. Social relationships were somewhat more complex in the larger settlements of several thousand inhabitants, but they were not qualitatively different.

The separate settlements within a territorial demos were likewise linked together by bonds of kinship and interdependence. Villages might quarrel with one another, and the inhabitants even come to blows, but they were unified against threat from outside. Odysseus describes how he and his men, on their way home from the Trojan War, attacked and pillaged a seacoast town of a people called the Cicones. Instead of sailing off immediately, as Odysseus ordered, the men stayed all night, feasting on the plundered cattle, sheep, and wine. But "in the meantime, the Cicones went and called the other Cicones, who were their neighbors . . . dwelling inland." The next morning these men from the neighboring villages counterattacked and killed a number of Odysseus' men before they could escape in their ships (*Odyssey* 9.39–61). Inside the boundary formed by the settlements that shared the demos name, a person or family could live and move safely. All the Cicones considered themselves akin to one another, as did Ithacans or Athenians: they all "belonged." Once outside the home territory one was "in the *dēmos* of others," in an alien country, so to speak, where the protection of tribal ties ended and one was a stranger, without rights. The largest social community that a Greek experienced was the demos.

The smallest, and the fundamental, social unit was the household (*oikos*). The oikos, not the individual, was the atom of Greek society. The household was the center of a person's existence; the overriding concern of every member was its preservation, economic independence, and social standing. The primary meaning of *oikos* is "house," which to the Greeks signified not only the dwelling itself but also the family, the land, the livestock, and all other property and goods, including slaves.

The ancient Greeks were monogamous, and the core of the oikos was the nuclear family of father, mother, and children. Greek society was patrilineal and patriarchal. The father was supreme in the household by custom and later by law. Descent was through the father, and on his death the property was divided equally among his sons. Although daughters did not inherit directly, they received a share of their parents' wealth as a wedding dowry. A new bride took up residence in the house of her husband; thus their children belonged to the husband's oikos, not to hers.

In Homeric society, the *oikoi* (plural) of the leading families—which are the only ones described—are residentially compact units. The five married sons of Nestor, basileus of the Pylians, continue to reside in the paternal oikos with their wives and children, occupying separate rooms set off from the main dwelling. Moreover, Nestor's married daughters also live in the family compound with their husbands. It is a common practice for a chief or important man to bring his daughter's husband into his household in contradiction of the normal custom. In this way, the daughter's birth family retains her labor, and also gains a man and the children. The clear purpose of these postnuptial residence customs in Dark Age Greece was to maximize the fighting force and the work force of the oikos. In later times, sons would normally leave the house and set up their own oikos after they married, and all daughters would become part of their husband's oikos.

Another common strategy for increasing manpower in Homeric society was for the oikos head to beget children by slave women even though this could cause friction in the house between husband and wife. (Laertes, Odysseus' father, did not sleep with the bought-slave Eurycleia—nursemaid to Odysseus and then to his son—and so "avoided his wife's anger.") Although the male children of slave women were inferior to the legitimate sons with respect to inheritance rights, they were otherwise full members of the family and were part of its fighting and work force. Illegitimate females had the same status as their legitimate half-sisters. For example, Priam married one of his daughters by a slave woman to a young warrior named Imbrius, son of a rich man. To fulfill his obligations as a son-in-law, Imbrius went to Troy when the war began, and "was outstanding among the Trojans and lived with Priam, who honored him equal to his own children" (*Iliad* 13.170–176). A chief also strengthened his oikos by recruiting nonkin (or distantly related) men as "retainers," who served the household in various capacities in peace and as fighters in war. Some of these became, in effect, adopted members of the family.

For the elite households of the Dark Age the aim was to have the largest possible number of members, either by birth, marriage, or affiliation. Males of fighting age were especially sought. Telemachus, Odysseus' son, was helpless against his mother's suitors because there were no kinsmen to back him up. As the only son of an only son, he had no brothers, brothers-in-law, uncles, or cousins; in addition, the family's retainers were gone off to war with his father.

All members of an oikos did a share of the work. The sons of basileis tended the flocks and herds, the main wealth of the family, and also did farm work and other household jobs. Odysseus, Homer tells us, built his and Penelope's bedroom and bed by "himself and no one else." The wives and daughters of basileis worked alongside the women slaves in the tasks of spinning and weaving, the most important domestic activities. The labor input of elite women in cloth production amounted to nearly a full-time occupation. The daughters did other tasks, such as fetching water from the communal fountain or washing clothes by the river. Penelope has a flock of geese that she takes care of personally.

Most of the labor of a wealthy oikos, however, was provided by female and male slaves (either bought or captured), and by hired workers called *thētes* (singular *thēs*), poor free men who did hard work for low pay. Poor free women, usually widows without close kinfolk, also worked for wages, as spinners and weavers or as nursemaids. Homer refers to this category of workers as those who labor "under necessity." The main economic resource for each of the families in a village or town was its ancestral plot of farmland called a *klēros* (plural *klēroi*). It is not known how these were originally acquired. Both Homer and early historical sources indicate that in brand new settlements, such as overseas colonies, the founder basileus distributed the *klēroi* among the new inhabitants on a more or less equal basis. Yet, however fair the original division of land may have been, inequities soon crept in. In Homer some families own "many *klēroi*," while others in the demos are "lotless men" (*aklēroi*). Although there is no way of determining the percentages of either the land-rich or the landless within the populations, most likely both groups were proportionally small. Before around 750, when land was becoming scarcer, it is highly probable that most families owned a kleros that gave them a sufficient living.

The minority without a kleros had to hire on as thetes, a galling life not only because of the hard work for very little pay (essentially their keep), but also because of the indignity of working for another man's family, a condition that all Greeks abhorred. To express the dismalness of existence in Hades, the ghost of Achilles tells Odysseus that he would prefer the indignity of living as the hired hand (*thēs*) of "another man, a man without a *klēros*, who did not have much of a living, than to rule over all the dead who have perished" (*Odyssey* 11.489–491). A lotless man, whatever the reasons for his situation, would eke out a precarious existence on a poor patch of unclaimed marginal land, far from the deep-soiled plainlands and gentler slopes where the kleroi were located. After the eighth century, the shortage of available land would become widespread and would be a serious point of tension between the wealthy few and a growing mass of poor citizens.

The economies of ordinary and elite households in the Dark Age differed primarily in scale. The prominent oikoi had large work forces, whereas average households had only one or perhaps two slaves or hired hands to share the work load. High-ranking families also farmed proportionately more land, needed to feed their larger households and to supply bread and wine for the feasts they provided to friends, followers, and the community at large. A Homeric chief sometimes received a sizable piece of prime farmland, called a *temenos*, awarded to him by the people in recognition of his services to the community. The agricultural surpluses of the elite, however, would not have risen much above their own increased consumption needs, since at that time there was little opportunity for trade in foodstuff.

The major economic difference between rich and poor households seems to have been in the number of animals owned. Odysseus' chief swineherd, Eumaeus, gives an account of his master's "unspeakably great" livelihood:

> No twenty men together
> have so much wealth; and I will count it off for you.
> Twelve herds of cattle on the mainland; as many flocks of sheep,
> as many droves of swine, as many roving herds of goats,
> both strangers and his own herdsmen pasture them.
> And here roving herds of goats, eleven in all,
> graze in the backlands, and good men watch over them.
> (Odyssey 14.96–104)

To these fifty-nine flocks and herds we may add the thousand pigs that Eumaeus and five other swineherds managed on Ithaca. Such large numbers are perhaps epic exaggerations, but the reality need not have been so far off, in view of the very large amount of available grazing land. An ordinary farmer would have had a yoke of oxen for plowing, perhaps a mule; no doubt he pastured some sheep and goats for his family's wool, cheese, and manure. But his oikos, even with a slave or two, was too small to herd large numbers of animals or to build and maintain the many huts and pens required.

Only the elite could command the labor force for large-scale stock raising. As a consequence, their families enjoyed an abundance of the preferred protein from meat, as well as a large surplus of wool, hides, and fertilizer. In fact, it was probably woolen goods and leather, produced within the oikos, that paid for the imported metal goods and ornaments the Dark Age elites valued as "treasure" and used for gift exchanges among themselves. The main value, however, of livestock was as meat for feasts, something only the few could provide in quantity.

Animal wealth was therefore prestige wealth. The very sight of large herds roving the pastures and hillsides was evidence of the owner's rank and status. It was also proof of his prowess as a warrior, since the most prestigious way of acquiring animals (as well as treasure) was by raiding. There was a certain circularity in this animal economy. Chiefs slaughtered large numbers of their animals in order to recruit warriors for raids that were conducted primarily for the purpose of acquiring animals for slaughter. It was not efficient in purely economic terms, but, as in all archaic rank societies, the aim of acquiring wealth was not to keep it but to exchange it for influence and good reputation.

The fact that cattle are the regular measurement of the worth of other kinds of objects is proof of the high value placed on them in Homeric society. For example, the first prize in a wrestling contest is a large bronze tripod, "which the Achaeans valued at twelve cattle's worth" (*Iliad* 23.702–705). This does not mean, of course, that cows, bulls, and oxen were used as actual payment; rather, in an exchange of goods the transacting parties mentally converted the value of the objects involved into cattle as the standard of value, a practice common in premonetary societies. (In Latin, the root of the word for money, *pecunia*, is *pecus*, "livestock.")

Therefore, the archaeologically visible wealth in the tenth and ninth centuries—valuable small objects deposited in graves—does not begin to measure the true extent of elite wealth and its social power. Nevertheless, the economic and social gulf between the top stratum and the mass of small farmers was not nearly so wide in 800 as it had been in the Late Bronze Age. If anything, we would expect Homer to exaggerate the differences in the lifestyles of the chiefs and the ordinary folk, but instead he shows the elite living not that much more luxuriously.

Though the elite do have some things the others cannot afford, such as horses and chariots and precious metal items, most of the distinctions are merely relative—more of this, better of that. The daily lives of Homeric chiefs and their families are easier and more pleasant; they have more servants, and, most important, more leisure time. Yet, all in all, their way of life is more like than unlike the kind of life led by those in the average households. The Homeric poems and the material record concur that social class distinctions between the "nobles" and the "commoners" had not progressed very far in the course of the tenth and ninth centuries.

THE END OF THE DARK AGE (c. 750–700 BC)

It was in the eighth century that Greek society underwent rapid changes. Some of these, such as developments in art and culture, were the result of an acceleration of the existing patterns of growth. Other, deeper, changes reflect a radical break with the past, particularly in economic and political relationships. The rapid developments that mark the end of the Dark Age have earned it the title of "the eighth-century renaissance." The last half of the eighth century is also viewed by many as the beginning of the Archaic Age (c. 750–490 BC), the period in which the social and cultural movements that started early in the eighth century would reach maturity.

Population Growth, Land Shortage, and the Rise of a Landowning Aristocracy

A major factor of change was a widespread rise in population in the early eighth century, after centuries of very slow growth. There is some disagreement about the rate of population growth, but there is general concurrence that there were considerably more people in Greece in the late eighth century BC than at any time within the preceding four centuries. Population would continue to rise in most regions for the next two hundred years. The reason for this increase remains one of many unsolved questions of early Greek history. A sharp upturn in population after a long period of slow growth is not an uncommon historical phenomenon. Certainly the material and social conditions at the end of the ninth century were favorable for population increase.

The presence of many people where there had been but few a generation or two before was bound to have a great impact on Greek society. A popular theory is that population rise was related to a shift from a predominantly animal economy to a predominantly agricultural economy. To feed a growing population, land that had traditionally been pasture was converted to the production of grain, a much more effective use of land in terms of sustenance yield per acre. Extension of farmland was accompanied by more intensive methods of farming to increase yield and variety of crops. By the early seventh century, at any rate, an agrarian economy was in place, and it was dominated by an aristocracy of large landowners.

Later written sources do not mention how the class of large proprietors came into being, but it is not difficult to piece together what might have happened. It was most certainly the leading households that were most active in converting pastureland into agricultural land. Although grazing land was nominally open to all to use, in reality the chieftain families had long before appropriated the best for themselves, in particular the moist grassy meadows, where their cattle and horses grazed, which were potentially the finest grainlands. Generations of use had given them what amounted to exclusive grazing rights. No doubt this prior occupancy gave the leading families some legal right to plow and plant the traditional pasturelands. In any case, as arable land became more precious, the chiefs and other prominent family heads came to own a disproportionate amount of it. In the span of two or three generations they transformed themselves into large-scale farmers, with smaller flocks and herds. The rest of the population continued to live off their small to medium-size farm plots and few (perhaps now fewer) sheep and goats.

The growing disparity in land distribution began to have a severe effect as rising populations and the custom of dividing the kleros equally among sons made family plots smaller. One early sign of land hunger was the emigration, starting in the second half of the eighth century, of substantial numbers of people from mainland and island Greece into southern Italy and Sicily, beginning a long wave of colonization that would eventually plant scores of new Greek communities from Spain to the shores of the Black Sea and beyond. Trade and the profits that could be earned attracted some, but for most it was the promise of a good-sized kleros on good soil. Among these no doubt were landless men; more, however, were seeking a better livelihood than their land at home could give them.

Although scarcity of land was certainly the primary motivation for emigration, this scarcity must be put into perspective. Nowhere in eighth-century Greece did the population approach the carrying capacity of the land. In fact, the filling in of the countryside continued through the seventh and into the sixth century. The problem was not that there was no land, but rather that the most productive land was concentrated in the hands of a minority of the families. Sons whose inherited share of their paternal kleros was insufficient for a decent livelihood were forced either to seek marginal land in the demos or to emigrate overseas. Colonization and the tremendous impact it would have on the political, economic, and cultural development of the homeland during the seventh and sixth centuries will be discussed in the next chapter.

Trade and Commerce

Early colonization was connected to widening contacts with the Near East and western Europe. Long-distance seaborne trade, both among Greeks and between Greeks and foreigners, had been increasing slowly in the tenth and ninth centuries, but it expanded considerably in the eighth. The earliest evidence for serious Greek involvement in overseas trade is a settlement of Euboean Greeks, around 825, at an international trading post of Al Mina in northern Syria. A Greek trading colony was founded shortly after 800 at Pithecusae in southern Italy. By the early seventh century, Greeks had once again become important participants in the Aegean and in the wider Mediterranean trade, and were competing with the Phoenicians, who had long been the leading sea merchants in the Mediterranean.

As it had in the Late Bronze Age, the need for raw materials, especially metal, drove long-distance trade. Imports of copper and tin, iron, and gold increased considerably from the later eighth century on, as well as of rare and expensive materials such as ivory, amber, dyes, and objects made of these. In return, Greeks were exporting larger quantities of fine pottery and metalwork abroad and probably also fine woolen goods, cattle hides, and leather. Production of olive oil and wine for overseas markets would begin in the later seventh century, followed still later by exports of building stone and marble, for which Greece was famous, and silver, which was abundant in regions such as Attica and Thrace.

Trade at the local or regional level within Greece was largely contained within a few hundred square miles. Crafts goods would have consisted mainly of plain pottery and utilitarian metal manufactures, such as iron axes and spear points, as well as some locally made luxury items for the wealthy. A large variety of local produce would have been exchanged. Besides the staples of grain, wine, and olive oil, producers would have bartered honey, fruit, and cheeses; a cow or goat; a catch of fish; or a load of lumber. As with foreign trade, the primary means of transport was by sea. Hesiod, for example, assumes that a farmer will put part of his surplus production in a boat and sail a fair distance for "profit." Goods were also hauled on land, along rough wagon tracks or by steep mule and footpaths through rugged passes. In this way, local and regional economies were able to produce and to distribute by themselves all that was necessary to satisfy the wants and needs of ordinary people.

Farmers, craftsmen, sailors, shipbuilders and outfitters, and carters were among those who found new economic opportunities in the steady increase of commerce and trade in the eighth and seventh centuries. The main beneficiaries, however, were the big landholders, who could produce large surpluses for the market and could subsidize the costs and bear the losses of long sea voyages. For these wealthy families, costly foreign and domestic manufactures continued to be emblems of status, whose function was almost exclusively to impress and to be given away, just as in the ninth and earlier centuries. Gold cups and silver plates, bronze tripods, and horses were the ritual coinage of elite social relationships and would remain so even after the introduction of silver coins around 600.

The Alphabet and Writing

The increased contacts with the East were responsible for the most significant cultural achievement of the late Dark Age, the Greek alphabet. Greeks borrowed letters from the Phoenician alphabet, a northern Semitic script, to represent the consonant sounds of Greek. They used other Phoenician letters to represent the vowel sounds, which the Phoenician alphabet did not have, and thus created the first truly phonetic alphabet. Because the earliest material evidence for the Greek alphabet comes from the eighth century, it is generally believed that it was developed around 800. The reasons the Greeks decided to have a writing system at this time and not earlier are still debated. Some propose that the alphabet was adopted for the express purpose of writing down epic poetry, whereas others cling to the older explanation that it was first used for commercial and other utilitarian purposes. Either theory is plausible, although so far no specimen of eighth-century commercial writing has been found.

The earliest known examples of connected Greek words are bits of epic-type verse scratched on vases and dated to the second half of the eighth century. These graffiti do not prove that the alphabet was designed for preserving oral poetry, although they do show that the epics of Homer could have been written down at about the same time as their composition. Whatever the initial motive, once writing was established it was used to record not only poetry but many other things besides. The earliest specimen of the civic use of writing is a stone inscription of laws from Dreros in Crete, carved around 650 BC. Writing spread quickly throughout the Greek-speaking world, not as one standard alphabet but as numerous local scripts, with variations in letter form among neighboring locales. The Greek alphabet of twenty-four letters was a huge advance over the cumbersome Linear B syllabic system of eighty-seven signs. Because each letter represented a single spoken sound, it was fairly simple to learn to read and even to write Greek. Since reading and writing were accessible to all and fairly easily learned, literacy could not become an instrument of power and control by the rulers over the people, as it was in Egypt and other contemporary empires, where literacy was an arcane skill confined to an elite group of officials, priests, and scribes.

The impact of literacy on Greek cultural development was enormous. Many of the achievements for which the Greeks are most famous—history, drama, philosophy, mathematics, science, medicine, law, and scholarship—could not have evolved without writing. Later Greeks reverently preserved the writings of earlier Greeks and held constant dialogue with the minds of the past. Progress toward general literacy, however, was slow. Greece in the eighth and much of the seventh century was almost as completely oral-aural as it had been in the earlier Dark Age. In fact, only a small percentage of ancient Greeks would ever read or write to any great extent. Orality coexisted with literacy throughout Greek history; even in the Classical and Hellenistic periods, when literacy was most widespread, most information passed from mouth to ear.

Art and Architecture

Development in artistic expression, of which pottery is the best example, as usual, is another index of the creative energy of the Late Geometric period. The stylistic transition from Middle Geometric pottery (c. 850–750) to Late Geometric (c. 750–700) was smooth, but clearly represents a new direction in vase painting. As we have seen, aside from showing an occasional horse or a bird, or, even rarer, a human figure, Greek vases were essentially without images from the eleventh to the eighth century. Pictures of animals and humans suddenly became frequent after 800 BC. The major decorative innovation, however, was the reappearance, after an absence of four hundred years, of group scenes that told a kind of story, such as battles, shipwrecks, funerals, and chariot processions.

a

b

c

b

Figure 2.4a. Examples of graffiti on eighth-century vases. Inscription (c) reads: "I am the drinking cup of Nestor, good to drink from. Whoever drinks this cup, immediately the desire will seize him of beautiful-crowned Aphrodite." The readable portion of inscription (a) says: "He who, of all the dancers, now dances most gracefully" [? will win this pot?]. Inscription (b) simply identifies the owner: "I am the cup of Qoraqos." **Figure 2.4b.** Late Geometric vase, c. 740 BC, from Athens, on which example (a) was inscribed.

In Attic pottery, which had long been the style setter, this development occurred just as the Geometric style reached a peak of complexity. On a massive amphora from about 750 BC, commissioned as a grave marker for a wealthy woman, a scene of the woman lying in state occupies the prominent area of the belly of the monumental vase, while the rest of the surface is covered by a masterful composition of abstract geometric designs. The silhouette figures of the corpse and mourners are themselves geometric in execution, as are the bands of repeating, identical deer and birds on the neck (see Fig. 2.5). Yet it is clear even in this bravura display of the Geometric style that the picture is the focal element. Inevitably, static geometric shapes became mere decorative borders for the pictorial narrative, which soon covered most of the pottery surface. As the repertoire of subjects and scenes expanded, the figures of animals, humans, and objects became increasingly more naturalistic.

Another artistic innovation was the depiction of scenes from Greek legends, painted on vases and engraved on metalwork. These scenes inaugurated the rich and lasting tradition of pictorial narrative in painting and sculpture. The unrestrained exuberance (if not always excellence) of this new artistic spirit is also evident in the increase of distinctive regional, local, and even individual styles, as craftsmen from all over Greece experimented with, mixed, copied, adapted, and abandoned, in rapid succession both homegrown and imported styles and techniques. Near Eastern influence on art appears especially prominent from around 730 or 720 BC and for about a century thereafter. Like the borrowing of the alphabet, the "orientalizing period" of Greek art exemplifies the importance of Near Eastern models in the development of Greek culture. As in the case of writing, what the Greeks learned from the East they increasingly transformed into a distinctively Hellenic expression.

The monumental temple, which is the "signature" Greek architectural form, emerged in the eighth century. The earliest known examples from around 800 BC were small, with mud-brick walls, wooden columns, and thatched roofs, and looked very much like regular houses. A rectangular temple to Hera on the island of Samos, constructed a few decades later, was the first to make a clear distinction between divine and human houses. Although still made of the same materials as earlier models, it was several times larger: 100 feet long compared with 25 feet. When, sometime later in the century, a wooden colonnade or peristyle was built all around the long but narrow shell, the building assumed the form of the Greek temple as we know it. By 700 there were dozens of major and minor temples, built along similar lines, in all parts of the Greek world.

The appearance of large temples shows that people wanted to and were able to spend their wealth, time, and labor on projects that gave honor to the whole community. In Athens at this time, expensive votive offerings placed in the temples of the gods—most notably bronze tripods and cauldrons, figurines, and bronze dress pins—greatly exceed the amount of metal wealth found in upper-class burials. Giving to the community rather than expressing family pride in the traditional manner was a new way of conspicuous display by the elite; a pattern was established that was to hold throughout the life of the Greek city-state.

A number of the sanctuaries were located in the countryside away from the population centers. Many see this as a sign of growing civic unity, a deliberate

a

Figure 2.5a. Large Late Geometric grave amphora from the Dipylon cemetery at Athens. **Figure 2.5b.** The funeral scene from the same vase.

b

Figure 2.6. A small bronze statuette from the mid-eighth century BC, depicting a man and a centaur fighting; very possibly a representation of the myth of Heracles and the centaur Nessus.

strengthening of the religious bonds for the purpose of more firmly uniting the demos. Religious processions from the central town to the rural sanctuaries symbolically connected its inhabitants with the inhabitants of the outlying villages and hamlets. The temples at the borders of the territory also served to stake out the territory of the demos against any territorial claims from a neighboring demos.

Thick brick and stone defensive walls, another major architectural feature of Greek towns, first appear in Greek Asia Minor and the Aegean islands. Old Smyrna (later Izmir) had an impressive circuit wall by around 850; Iasus, down the coast in Caria, was walled before 800. A number of Cycladic island sites were also fortified in the ninth century. On the mainland, however, the earliest circuit walls date to a little before 700. The increasing numbers of defensive walls possibly indicate that all-out warfare between communities, as opposed to raiding expeditions, was growing more frequent, and also attest to the growing wealth and communal pride of the communities.

Panhellenism

The eighth century also saw the rise of religious sanctuaries and festivals that were not merely local but were "Panhellenic" (*pan* = "all"), attracting worshippers from all over the Greek world. Panhellenic shrines and festivals celebrated and reinforced the idea that Greeks everywhere belonged to a single cultural group sharing the same heritage, language, customs, and religion. The most famous early Panhellenic sanctuaries were those of Zeus and Hera at Olympia, of Apollo and Artemis at Delos, and the oracles (places of divine prophecy) at the shrines of Zeus at Dodona and of Apollo at Delphi. All these sites, as well as others, show evidence of intermittent cult activity from the Late Bronze Age on, but they emerged as Panhellenic centers only in the eighth century. Eventually they would become large complexes of temples, treasure houses (for the depositing of gifts), and holy precincts.

The worshipers who came to the Panhellenic festivals participated in common rituals and sacrifices to the gods, and at some sanctuaries they took part in athletic contests as well. The first and the most prestigious of these athletic games were those held every four years at the great festival of Zeus at Olympia, a rather remote site in northwestern Peloponnesus. The games were inaugurated, according to later Greek computations, in 776 BC. At first, Olympia and the Olympian games attracted contestants and visitors only from the vicinity, but by the end of the century costly dedications were being deposited in the sanctuaries of Zeus and Hera by Spartans, Athenians, Corinthians, and Argives. By the sixth century, contestants and spectators would be drawn from all over the Greek world.

The rise of Panhellenism coincided with increased contact with the Eastern world, which made the Greeks more conscious of the cultural differences between themselves and non-Greeks. When Homer describes the Carians, allies of the Trojans, he calls them *barbaro-phōnoi* ("strange-speaking"), indicating the odd sound of foreign languages to Greek ears. This is the first occurrence of the word *barbaros*, which the Greeks later employed as the general term for "foreigner." Contrast between Greeks and "barbarians" would be most strongly expressed in the early fifth century, when the Greeks united to fight against the Persian empire.

The Heroic Revival

Closely related to Panhellenism were activities, at both the local and national levels, that centered around the recovery of the world of the Bronze Age ancestors. Quite suddenly, around 750, Greeks everywhere began to express their connection to the heroic past in new and dramatic ways. Numerous ancient tombs (mostly Mycenaean) that had been ignored throughout the Dark Age began to receive votive offerings, an indication that their anonymous inhabitants were now worshiped as "heroes." Other kinds of hero cults came into being during the late eighth century. They were celebrated not at graves, but at new shrines set up in honor of legendary heroic figures, for example, the precincts sacred to Agamemnon at Mycenae and to Menelaus and Helen near Sparta. The impetus behind hero cults was the belief that the great men and women of the Heroic Age had power in death to protect and to help the people. Like gods, they were given animal sacrifices and other divine honors, though on a smaller scale.

Wealthy Greeks of the later eighth century also expressed an urge to connect with the past through heroic-style burials, most notably in Attica, Euboea, and

Cyprus. These burials somewhat resemble the funerals of heroes in epic poetry. As in the funeral of Patroclus (the close hetairos of Achilles) in the *Iliad*, the corpse was cremated and the bones put in a bronze urn; weapons were placed in the grave, and occasionally sacrificed horses. Also around this time vases depicting events from the Heroic Age begin to turn up in these graves. There is additional evidence from Athens that wealthy families had begun to group their graves in enclosures that not only held contemporary graves but also took in Mycenaean graves, as if to convert the inhabitants of the ancient burials into family ancestors. All this suggests that the leading families were proclaiming descent from the heroes of old.

*   *   *

As the eleventh to the eighth centuries come more clearly into view, it becomes increasingly apparent that the Dark Age was the cradle of the city-state society and culture that was to follow. The basic structures and institutions of later Greek society were firmly in place well before 800 BC. And so, the emergence of Greece, during the eighth century, from the Dark Age into the renaisssance of the Archaic period, which not so long ago was seen as a sudden and revolutionary phenomenon, appears now more like a rapid evolution in response to rapidly changing conditions. The swift transformation of the traditional chieftain government into the city-state government and the turbulent history of the early city-states are the subjects of the next chapter.

TRANSLATIONS

Blanco, Walter. 1992. *The Histories,* from *Herodotus: The Histories,* Walter Blanco and Jennifer Roberts, eds. New York: W.W. Norton.

Lattimore, Richmond. 1951. *The Iliad of Homer.* Chicago: University of Chicago Press.

Lattimore, Richmond. 1965. *The Odyssey of Homer.* New York: Harper & Row. Lattimore's translations are faithful to the original Greek, and capture the style and rhythm of the Greek epic in simple, straightforward English.

SUGGESTED READINGS

Burkert, Walter. 1985. *Greek Religion.* Cambridge, Mass.: Harvard University Press. A classic history of ancient Greek religion from the Minoan-Mycenaean Age to the Hellenistic period.

Coldstream, J. N. 1977. *Geometric Greece.* New York: St. Martin's Press. A comprehensive presentation and analysis of the archaeological evidence from 900 to 700 BC.

Edwards, Mark W. 1987. *Homer, Poet of the Iliad.* Baltimore and London: Johns Hopkins University Press. A reliable, up-to-date general treatment of Homeric poetry and the epic style, with commentaries on selected books of the *Iliad*.

Finley, Moses I. 1978. *The World of Odysseus.* 2nd ed. New York: Viking Press. First published in 1954, this book revolutionized the study of Dark Age society and institutions.

Hurwit, Jeffrey M. 1985. *The Art and Culture of Early Greece, 1100–480 B.C.* Ithaca, N.Y.: Cornell Univerity Press, chaps. 1–3. A highly readable and insighful discussion of Dark Age art in relation to the changing social scene. Chapters 4 to 6 are also recommended reading for art and culture in the Archaic period.

Lord, Albert Bates. 1991. *Epic Singers and Oral Tradition.* Ithaca, N.Y.: Cornell University Press. A collection of articles and papers (some not published before), offering an overview of oral-traditional epic songs and singers, spanning the long career of one of the founders of oral-formulaic theory.

Morris, Ian and Barry Powell, eds. 1997. *A New Companion to Homer.* Leiden: Brill. A valuable collection of thirty new articles, covering all areas of Homeric studies, literary and historical, written by specialists for a nonspecialist audience.

Snodgrass, A. M. 1971. *The Dark Age of Greece: An Archaeological Survey of the Eleventh to the Eighth Centuries.* Edinburgh: University of Edinburgh Press. Remains the standard treatment of the archaeological evidence for the whole of the Dark Age.

3

ARCHAIC GREECE
(c. 700–500 BC)

The seventh and sixth centuries belong to the period called the Archaic Age (c. 750–490 BC). During those two hundred years the pace of change and development accelerated rapidly, continuing and surpassing the progress made in the eighth century as Greece emerged from its Dark Age. Once rather neglected by historians as being merely the prelude to the glorious and tragic fifth and fourth centuries—the Classical period—the Archaic period is seen now as the decisive formative time of the intellectual, cultural, and political achievements of Greece's "Golden Age."

The city-state form of government, which came into being with the demographic and economic changes of the eighth century, grew to maturity during the seventh and sixth. A steady movement of overseas colonization, starting in the later eighth century and continuing into the sixth, spread the Greek language and culture across the lands of the Mediterranean and Black seas. Trade, helped by colonization, dispersed Greek goods far beyond the limits known to the Bronze Age traders. Literature and art flourished; new genres of artistic and intellectual expression were invented. The great Panhellenic shrines, festivals, and oracles grew in importance, further nourishing the ideal of the cultural unity of all Greeks even as the Greek world expanded to far distant shores. Within the Greek city-states, new ideas began to form, two of which would shape the history of the western world: a rational view of the universe, which eliminated supernatural causes for natural events and replaced them with scientific explanations, and the concept of democratic government, in which all members were equal under the laws and the laws were made by the people directly by majority rule.

The Archaic period also had its dark side. Wars of one demos against another became much more frequent, and warfare itself became much more lethal. Worse, civil strife within a demos became commonplace. The leaders, with their armed followers, continually quarreled and fought amongst themselves. Widening economic inequality caused much human misery and produced serious tensions between the few rich and the many poor, which occasionally erupted in actual class warfare. Political instability gave rise to a new type of leader, the "tyrant," whose rulership in turn led to further turmoil. All in all, however, the good outweighed the bad. For all its problems, the Archaic period was one of growing confidence and prosperity; by its end the Greek states had made progress toward solving their internal problems and their citizens were living together in relative harmony.

SOURCES FOR THE SEVENTH AND SIXTH CENTURIES

Even though we are separated from the Archaic Age by 2700 years, we can apprehend what was happening all across the Greek world as the eighth-century renaissance turned into the "Greek miracle," as it has been called, of the seventh and sixth centuries. For the first time we can speak of actual events, with dates and names, and even connect events into a coherent historical narrative. That is possible because beginning in the seventh century the Greeks produced copious amounts of texts written on papyrus (the "paper" of antiquity), which were laboriously copied and recopied by hand until the invention of the printing press in the fifteenth century AD.

Only a small fraction of what the ancient Greeks wrote has survived the centuries of selection and chance. That as much survived as it did (enough to fill several library shelves) is the ultimate testimony of the continuing value of Greek literature to the western world. The writings of the Archaic Age did not fare as well as the literature of the later periods. Other than the works of Homer and Hesiod, only bits and pieces of the volumes of poetry and philosophical treatises from the seventh and sixth centuries have come down to us. Some of the fragments are preserved as quotations in the extant writings of later Greeks, who greatly admired the poets and thinkers of the Archaic period. Other fragments come from papyri of the Hellenistic and Roman periods luckily preserved in the hot sands of Egypt. Though pitifully few, the precious remnants of Archaic literature provide valuable insights into contemporary life and thought during the seventh and sixth centuries.

Most of our information about the events of the period is found in the works of the later historians, who had some access to earlier writings and records. They wrote many years later, however, and their accounts are often untrustworthy because much of their knowledge was based on orally transmitted legends. Public and private inscriptions carved on stone and the images and letters on coins, which were first minted in the sixth century BC, supplement the evidence given by the ancient historians. The amount of inscriptional material, however, is small before the fifth century.

The archaeological evidence follows the upward trajectory begun in the Geometric period. There is a sizable increase in the number of manufactured items found, a natural result of the growth in population and wealth. Architectural finds are also much more numerous. Moreover, because the temples and other monumental buildings were now constructed entirely of stone, much more can be learned from their ruins. An important new source of evidence is sculpture: life-size and larger figures in stone and bronze.

By comparison with the Classical period, the evidence for the seventh and sixth centuries is in general rather meager. Despite the large gaps in our knowledge, however, it is possible to put together a reasonably clear picture of Greek society and culture in the early city-states.

THE FORMATION OF THE CITY-STATE (POLIS)

The city-state form of government came into existence during the eighth century. By the early seventh century dozens of Greek communities all across the Greek world, from Ionia in the east to Sicily and southern Italy in the west, had formed themselves into city-states. The *polis*, as the Greeks called it, served as the characteristic social and political organization for Greeks until at least the Roman period. As an ideal, the polis has had enormous significance in the history of later nations. The very words "political" and "politics" are derived directly from *polis*.

What is a city-state? A simplified definition is: a geographical area comprising a city and its adjacent territory, which together make up a single, self-governing political unit. The essential elements of the city-states were in place during the later Dark Age. The capital cities of what became city-states existed all through the Dark Age, and most of them had been the major centers of their regions during the Mycenaean period. The territorial community, the *dēmos*, appears fully evolved in the Homeric epics, and therefore the unitary concept of "the land" and "the people" must go back generations before Homer. Within the demos there was a collective identification—"the Ithacans," "the Pylians"—and a communal worship of the same gods. The two primary governmental organs of the city-state, the assembly of men of fighting age and the council of "elders," appear firmly established in the Homeric chiefdoms. All that was lacking to make the *dēmos*-communities of 800 BC into the *polis*-states of 700 BC were certain necessary formalities: formal political unification of the demos and the creation of a central government.

Political Unification (Synoecism)

In all city-states, from ancient Mesopotamia to Renaissance Europe, the capital city is the focal point of the state. The original meaning of the Greek word *polis* (plural *poleis*), was "town" or "city," and that is how it is used in the Homeric epics. To the Greeks of the city-state period, however, the polis comprised not only the capital city or town (*polis*) but its adjacent territory as well. All the members of that territory, both those who lived in the capital and those who lived in the countryside, were called *politai* (members of the *polis*) as if they all lived together in the *polis* (city).

Later Greeks referred to the process of political unification of states as *syn-oik-ismos*, which may be loosely translated as "coming to live together," or more literally, "having the *oikoi* together." "Synoecism," to use the anglicized term, was the process by which every town, village, and hamlet of a demos accepted a single political center. Whatever local autonomy they had formerly enjoyed, whatever freedom of action they had exercised separate from the capital and the other settlements, was given up. Moreover, they identified themselves by the name of the capital city. Thus, all those who lived in the territory of Attica, of which Athens was the capital city, referred to themselves (and were referred to by others) as "the Athenians," even if they lived 25 miles from the city of Athens.

Synoecism took different forms, depending on the size of the territory. Synoecism of a small demos made up of a single main town and its adjacent plain, holding a couple of subsidiary villages, was a very simple process. In those cases, *polis* (the state) and *polis* (the town) were almost identical entities. For example, the polis (city-state) of Sicyon occupied a small plains region (Sicyonia) of about 140 square miles, which even in the fifth century contained only a few villages in addition to the main town called Sicyon. Because everyone lived within a few miles of everyone else, and most of the few hundred families in the demos were interrelated, drawing them together as a single political unit was merely a matter of making formal the ancient ties of kinship and neighborliness and precisely defining the territorial boundaries of the demos. Most of the several hundred city-states that came into existence during the Archaic period were of the Sicyon variety, a single town and its small plain; the majority, in fact, were even smaller in territory than Sicyon.

Synoecism of the regional territories, those that contained several important towns and villages besides the central town, was a more complex process and is not well understood. Scholarly opinion is that the unification of the regional states was a drawn–out development, beginning possibly in the ninth century and crystallizing between about 750 and 700. Archaeology provides a hint of how religion may have been used to promote unity within regions. As we saw in Chapter 2, it is thought that during the eighth century temples and shrines to the gods and heroes of a regional demos were built in the countryside to connect the center symbolically to the outlying villages; religious processions from the main *polis* to the outer sanctuaries would have fostered and strengthened the sense of being a single nation.

In some regions, unification was voluntary and peaceful, as in Megaris under the leadership of Megara and of Corinthia under Corinth. There is evidence, however, that in other mainland regions intimidation and even force was used to integrate the towns and villages into a single polis. The original four villages of Sparta absorbed the village of Amyclae, 3 miles south, into the unified Spartan polis against its will, and reduced the more distant settlements of Laconia to a dependent status. Synoecism was also incomplete in some regions. Argos, for example, never fully succeeded in unifying the whole of the large region of Argolis, and a number of small, separate, independent city-states continued to exist in the plains outside of the Argive plain. Even within the plain of Argos itself some villages retained a good deal of local autonomy. Other regions were never united into a single polis. Although Thebes had been the principal settlement in the large fertile region of Boeotia since the Early Bronze Age, the Thebans controlled only their local area and had to deal on more or less equal terms with ten other district poleis.

As this brief sketch shows, there was no single model of synoecism. Each region experienced its own kind of city-state development which was determined by local factors that are hidden from us. The important fact is that by around 700 BC the permanent boundaries of the Greek poleis were pretty well established. Of course adjustments continued to be made here and there—a small polis absorbed by a larger neighboring polis—but the political map of 700 BC remained much the same throughout the Archaic period and beyond.

THE ETHNOS

The history of Greece between 700 and 400 BC was primarily the history of city-states, for they were the main makers of Greek history. There were huge areas of Greece, however, that had a different form of political organization. The Greek name for these regions was *ethnos*, variously translated as "tribe," "nation," or "people." An *ethnos* was a regional territory and people (a *dēmos*) without a single urban center or a central government or formal political union.

The city-state Greeks tended to regard the *ethnē* (plural) as politically and culturally backward. In fact, the *ethnē* of the seventh and even sixth centuries were at a stage very much like that of the regional *dēmoi* in the Dark Age. Each ethnos had a strong sense of being a single people occupying a specific territory. The people were united in worship of the gods of the ethnos. They had institutions for reaching common decisions and for acting as a unit. No single town, however, was the official capital of the ethnos; and, as in Homeric society, united action occurred infrequently, mostly in situations of common defense against an outside enemy. Within this general description, however, the ethne varied considerably. Boeotia, for example, was a single ethnic region with separate small city-states. It differed from the synoecized region of Attica in one significant way: all the inhabitants of all the towns and villages of Attica considered themselves "Athenians," whereas in Boeotia they identified themselves as "Thebans," or "Plataeans," or "Orchomenians" first, and only secondarily as "Boeotians."

What really mattered in ancient Greece was cohesive military force. The Athenians could call on the manpower of 1000 square miles, whereas the Thebans had only the men who lived in the city of Thebes and its few square miles of adjoining plainland. To be militarily powerful the Thebans had to form alliances with their neighboring poleis, who might or might not contribute troops to some military enterprise or see it through to to the end. The ethne of the Peloponnesus—Arcadia, Achaea, and Elis—were similarly divided into separate, small poleis and were similarly second-rank powers until they formed effective alliances among their constituent city-states.

A purer form of the ethnos existed north of the Peloponnesus. Those regions contained no large urban centers; the population lived mostly in small villages spread thinly across the territory. The districts were not synoecized into poleis, but rather each village was independent and autonomous. Even an ethnos of this type, however, had some kind of communal government through which it could take concerted action in times of national crisis. The fifth-century historian Thucydides gives a revealing glimpse of how well a large ethnos could respond as a unit. In 426 BC the Athenians, who were a great power at the time, were campaigning in central Greece. They were told that, "The *ethnos* of the Aetolians was indeed large and warlike, but as they lived in unwalled villages which were widely dispersed, and were also lightly armed, they could be easily crushed before they could gather their forces" (3.94.4; Blanco 1998, adapted). Counting on this fragmentation, the Athenians planned to attack and defeat the villages one by one. A few days into the campaign, however, Aetolian warriors assembled from every part of the territory and drove the Athenians out with heavy losses.

GOVERNMENT IN THE EARLY CITY-STATES

The steps that led to the establishment of a city-state were the work of the landowning aristocracy that arose in the eighth century. Political union could not have occurred unless the local *basileis*, the leaders of the districts, towns, and villages of the demos, wished it. The same small group became the planners and architects of the new central governments. The governmental structures of the individual city-states, as we first glimpse them in the early seventh century, differed in specifics, yet all followed a similar pattern: (1) The office of paramount *basileus* was either abolished completely or was greatly reduced in power. (2) The governing functions formerly exercised by the basileus were distributed among several officials. (3) The importance of the council of aristocratic "elders" increased, while that of the assembly of the people decreased. Of course, these decisions were not arrived at in a single year or even a single generation. The sources make it clear, however, that the process of determining which villages and districts were to be included in the polis and what kind of government it would have took no more than two or three generations.

For a unified polis to be strong and to compete successfully against other unified poleis it had to create a more powerful and more intrusive central government than it had possessed before unification. A more complex system of organization and social control was a necessary response to the new conditions of rapidly growing populations, greater exploitation of the land and resources, increasing productivity and wealth, expanding trade, and more complicated relationships with neighboring states. Especially pressing was the need for ways to mobilize manpower and resources efficiently for warfare, for as population increased and land became scarcer, poleis fought each other over territory, a more serious business than the raids and counterraids for animals and booty that characterized "war" in the Dark Age. Firm control from the center was therefore both necessary and good for a polis as a whole.

The central control, however, was in the hands of the large landowners who, like all dominant groups in human history, were highly motivated to preserve their economic and political power. The key decision made by the basileis was to eliminate the position of the paramount basileus and rule collectively. This was an easy matter, because the basileus had no power over the other chiefs. It was obvious to the collective aristocratic families why such a drastic action was necessary.

If a basileus were given formal headship over the united polis he would be a legitimate monarch ruling over a state, a leader with power, not the traditional "first among equals." The powerful families opted to retain their independent status by making a cooperative arrangement to subdivide the spheres of authority—administrative, military, religious, and judicial—among magistracies that were not hereditary and had limited terms of office. The later Greeks called this kind of government an oligarchy (*oligoi* = "few"). The ruling oligarchs referred to themselves as *aristoi*, the "best men"; hence the term "aristocracy." Although the terms *oligarchia* (oligarchy) and *aristokratia* (aristocracy) do not occur in literature or inscriptions before the fifth century, the idea that the few best were the fittest to rule was certainly promoted assiduously by the wealthy, well-born families who controlled the Archaic city-states.

Each of the city-states developed its own system of magistracies according to its own needs and circumstances. Larger states, such as Athens, required more officers, while small city-states needed few. As poleis grew in population and complexity, they added more officials, with more specialized functions, such as treasurers and supervisors of public works. By the end of the sixth century in Athens, for example, there were several dozen officeholders; by the end of the fifth the number had grown to around seven hundred. The number of major magistracies, however, remained small.

In general there was no hierarchy among the major offices, although many states did have a principal official who was regarded as the chief administrator. The commonest names for the chief officer were *archōn* (e.g., at Athens and elsewhere in central Greece) and *prytanis* (e.g., at Corinth and poleis in Ionia). Both are very general titles: *archōn* (like *archos*) means simply "leader" and *prytanis* means something like "presiding officer." A more specifically named early officer (e.g., at Athens and Megara) was the *polemarchos* ("war leader"). Many other city-states, especially the smaller ones, were governed by small boards or colleges of magistrates, who divided the functions of government among them without stipulating the specific duties. In most states, by the middle of the seventh century term of office was limited to a single year and could not be held again until a stipulated number of years had passed. These measures had the dual purpose of curbing the power of any single magistrate and of distributing honors among the whole of the aristocratic community.

The true center of power in the government of the early city-states, however, was not the magistracies and boards but the council. In the Archaic poleis the council had even more power than the *boulē* in Homeric society. The members were normally recruited from the highest magistrates, who entered the council after their terms of office. Membership in the council might be for a long term or even for life. The council thus had a natural supremacy over the archons and other magistrates who had limited terms and would hesitate to oppose the august body of prominent men whose ranks they wished some day to join. The aristocratic council met more frequently than in the prestate period and assumed for itself the task of making policies and drafting laws for the polis.

Corresponding to the increased power of the council, the limited power of the assembly of adult male citizens to influence policy was further reduced in the oligarchic city-state. Some states excluded the poorest citizens from membership in the assembly by imposing a property qualification. Some restricted the number of assembly meetings and the business to be brought before it, or they curtailed free discussion of the issues. The total sovereignty of the aristocratic council, however, was short-lived; as time went on the inclusiveness and authority of the assembly to decide policy increased. In fact, before the end of the sixth century, even in oligarchic city-states, the assembly had gained the ultimate decision-making power.

The Survival of Basileis in the Archaic Period

Although the position of paramount basileus ceased to exist in its traditional Dark Age form, it survived in other forms throughout the Archaic and Classical periods. Usually, the title of *basileus* was reserved for an annual magistrate or a member of a board of magistrates. The responsibilities of the basileus or board of basileis varied from state to state. In some states, the chief magistrate bore the title of *basileus*; a few appear to have been military officials, equivalent to the polemarch. The large majority, however, were in charge of religious matters and also had judicial duties, especially in cases having to do with religion, such as homicides (which polluted the community). The widespread designation of the title *basileus* for religious officials signals how great a reverence was still attached to the name; the Greeks felt a need to keep the very important religious sphere of polis life connected to the basileis of old, the ancestral heroes of the demos.

There were even exceptional cases of states, mostly of Dorian origin, keeping alive a form of the traditional chiefdom. In Argos, a dynasty of hereditary basileis retained authority into the seventh century, resisting the attempts of the aristocrats to establish oligarchic rule. One of them, Pheidon, using his position of traditional basileus as a springboard, managed to make himself into a tyrant with absolute powers.

The Spartans retained the chief system the longest, though in a unique form. In the Spartan system of government there were two hereditary, life-long basileis who ruled jointly, a custom that continued unbroken until the third century BC. Still, the powers of the Spartan basileis were far from absolute. They did retain considerable authority as military commanders; but to curb their power the Spartans chose an annual board of five magistrates, *ephoroi* ("overseers"), whose job it was to make sure that the basileis ruled lawfully and to prosecute them if they did not. Continuance of hereditary "kingships," though severely limited in power, is also attested for several other poleis, some of which lasted until the fifth century and beyond.

The power and authority of the basileus were also perpetuated through so-called royal clans. The Bacchiads of Corinth are a good example. A legendary Corinthian basileus named Bacchis founded a new line of chiefs called the Bacchiads, the "descendants of Bacchis." According to the tradition, the Bacchiad basileis ruled in succession for several generations until 747 BC, when the last of them was killed by his own kinsmen. These collectively took over the leadership of Corinth, retaining the family name "Bacchiads." The Bacchiads, said to number more than two hundred, chose one among them every year to be prytanis and distributed among themselves other offices as well. Their assertion of common descent from Bacchis was a pure fiction, but was very useful as a way of legitimizing their control of the government. In actuality, they were a narrow oligarchy of prominent, wealthy oikoi. To ensure their exclusivity as a "clan," the families married only among themselves. Their rule lasted three generations until 657, when they were overthrown by the tyrant Cypselus.

Similar "royal clans" appeared in many other poleis, especially in the eastern Aegean. Around the mid-eighth century, a small group of aristocratic families who called themselves the Penthilids took over the government of Mytilene, the main polis of Lesbos, and ruled for about a century. They derived their name and claim to rule from Penthilus, grandson of Agamemnon and son of Orestes, the mythical founder of Mytilene. In like manner, the Ionian polis of Miletus was ruled for a time by the Neleids, who claimed descent from Neleus, the father of Nestor of Pylos. In several other city-states the ruling families simply assigned themselves the generic name, "the Basilids," that is, "the descendants of the basileus." All these royal clans, which appropriated for themselves the authority and power of the basileis on the basis of their direct descent from them, were deeply resented by the other wealthy families. By the middle of the seventh century most of them had been displaced, either by a broader oligarchy or by a tyrant.

THE COLONIZING MOVEMENT

The emergence of the polis system in Greece coincided with the beginning of an extraordinary emigration of Greeks from the Aegean homeland. This emigration began about the middle of the eighth century BC and continued for over two centuries. When it ended around 500 BC the Greek world extended from eastern Spain in the west to Colchis in the east. As was pointed out in Chapter 2, the primary causes of this remarkable expansion were twofold: the search for sources of metal to satisfy the Greeks' growing need and the hope of acquiring the land required to live the life of a citizen in the new poleis, as opportunities for land at home dwindled.

The decision to found a colony was one of the earliest and most difficult political actions taken by a polis, and one that helped determine its future identity.

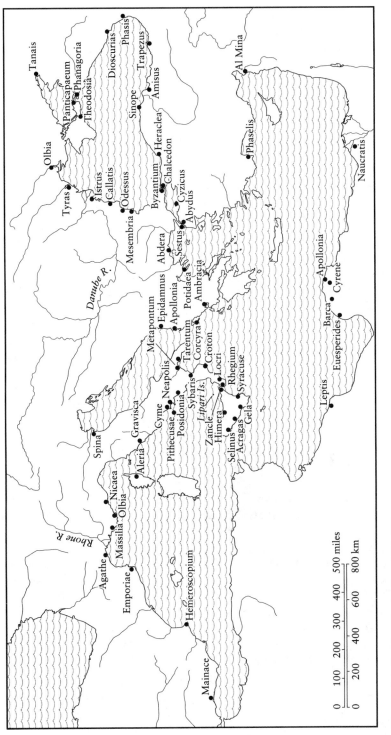

Figure 3.1 Greek colonization: 750–500 BC.

A mother city (*mētropolis*) had to choose a site for the colony, obtain divine approval for it, make plans for the new settlement, and choose its *oikistēs* (founder). Moreover, as the foundation oath for Cyrene reveals, the decision to found a colony involved the whole community and was backed by communal sanctions. Founding a colony also indirectly defined a metropolis' citizen body, since those who joined a colony gave up their citizenship in the mother-city.

<hr>

Document 3.1 Foundation Oath of Cyrene, Libya (late seventh century BC) Inscription from Cyrene containing the oath sworn by the Theraeans and the colonists of Cyrene.

Resolved by the Assembly. Since Apollo spontaneously told Battus and the Theraeans to found a colony in Cyrene, the Theraeans decided to dispatch Battus as the founder of the colony and *basileus*. The Theraeans shall sail as his comrades. They shall sail on equal terms; and one son shall be enrolled from each family. Those who sail shall be adults, and any free man from the Theraeans who wishes, may also sail.

If the colonists secure the settlement, any colonist who sails later to Libya shall have a share in the citizenship and honors. He also shall receive a lot from the unassigned land. But if they do not make the settlement secure, and the Theraeans cannot come to their aid and they suffer troubles for five years, the colonists may return without fear to Thera. They may return to their own property and become citizens of Thera.

If anyone is unwilling to sail when sent by the city, let him be subject to the death penalty and let his property be confiscated. Whoever receives or protects such a person—whether a father his son or a brother his brother—shall suffer the same punishment as the person who refused to sail. On these terms oaths were sworn by those remaining at Thera and those sailing to found the colony. They also cursed those who transgressed these conditions and did not abide by them, both those settling in Libya and those staying here.

They formed wax images and burned them while they uttered these curses, all of them together, men and women, boys and girls. The person who does not abide by these oaths, but transgresses, shall melt and flow away just as these images, he and his descendants and his property. But may there be many things and those good ones to those who abide by these oaths, both those sailing to Libya and those remaining in Thera, to themselves and their descendants.

Supplementum Epigraphicum Graecum 9.3;
translated by Stanley M. Burstein.

Once the decision to found a colony had been made, it was the oikist who was responsible for its success. Homer (*Odyssey* 6.7–10) clearly described his task: lead the colonists to their new home, lay out the colony's defenses, locate the sanctuaries of the gods, and assign house plots and farmland to the settlers. If the oikist fulfilled his duties wisely, he would become the ruler of a new polis and its guardian hero after his death. The colony itself would remain linked to its metropolis by bonds of kinship and cult symbolized by the fire the oikist brought from the metropolis' hearth to kindle the hearth of the new polis. So that the cults of the gods would be properly observed in the colony, priests and priestesses also migrated from the metropolis. Otherwise, however, the colony was a new and completely independent polis, as the Greek term for a colony, *apoikia*, indicates: a " home away [from their old home]" for the colonists.

Reconstruction of the history of the colonizing movement is difficult. The literary tradition concerning Greek colonization is encumbered with legends intended to connect various colonies to the Heroic Age and to establish divine sanction for their foundation. Stripped of these legendary accretions, the Greek sources preserve little more than a bare skeleton of dates of colonial foundations, names of founding cities, and, sometimes, of oikists as well.

Archaeology has made it possible for historians to overcome the limitations of the written sources by confirming the general chronology of colonial foundations, revealing the details of colonial city planning, and providing evidence for relations between the colonists and their non-Greek neighbors and the trade routes that linked the colonies to the Greek homeland. Archaeological evidence also indicates that the colonizing movement had two phases, each lasting a little over a century. The first began about the mid-eighth century BC and was directed to Italy and the western Mediterranean; the second started about a century later and was concentrated on the north Aegean and the Black Sea.

The pioneers in the colonization of Italy were Euboeans from Chalcis and Eretria, the same peoples who had helped maintain contact between Greece and the Near East during the Dark Age. Following routes that probably had been blazed by Phoenician traders, they founded their first settlement on the island of Pithecusae in the Bay of Naples in the early eighth century BC. Pithecusae conformed to the picture of an ideal colonial site described in the *Odyssey* (9.116–141): a deserted island, with "meadows, well-watered and soft; the grapevines would grow there endlessly; and there is level plowland . . . and the soil is deep and rich. There is also a harbor giving safe anchorage with no need for mooring cables or anchor stones. . . ." Pithecusae was also well located to exploit the iron deposits on the nearby island of Elba and to trade with the Italic populations of the mainland. The settlement grew rapidly, attracting settlers not only from the Aegean but even from Phoenicia. The Euboeans followed up their success at Pithecusae with additional settlements both on the Italian mainland at Cumae (757 BC), near modern Naples, and in northeastern Sicily, where they founded Naxus (734) Leontini (729), Catana (729), and Rhegium (712).

Meanwhile, Italy and Sicily also attracted the attention of the Dorian poleis of the Peloponnesus. Wracked by the problems of unequal distribution of land at home, these cities sought out sites for their colonies that had good agricultural potential. The Achaeans moved first, founding in the late eighth century Sybaris and Croton on the instep of Italy. Sparta quickly followed, establishing its only colony, Taras (712 BC) in the corner of the heel of the Italian peninsula. The Bacchiad rulers of Corinth also sought a solution to their internal problems in the west, founding Corcyra in the southern Adriatic Sea (c. 734 BC) and, most importantly, Syracuse (733), which would ultimately dominate the whole of southeastern Sicily and play a major role in the struggle for power in the central Mediterranean between Rome and Carthage.

Greek colonial activity in the Mediterranean was not limited to Italy and Sicily. Thera founded Cyrene in Libya in the late seventh century BC (c. 630), but it was the far west that offered the greatest possibilities. According to Herodotus, Greeks first learned of the opportunities offered by the western Mediterranean when a Samian merchant named Colaeus returned from the kingdom of Tartessus in southwestern Spain with a fabulously rich cargo. It was not Samos, however, but the west Anatolian city of Phocaea that took advantage of Colaeus' discovery, founding about 600 BC Massilia (modern Marseilles) at the mouth of the Rhone River.

Massilia quickly exploited its superb location, trading with the Celtic inhabitants of the upper Rhone valley and establishing a series of trading posts along the northeastern coast of Spain. By the early sixth century, however, opportunities for further Greek expansion in the central and western Mediterranean were disappearing. The powerful Phoenician colony of Carthage in modern Tunisia—probably founded in the late ninth century BC—also had ambitions in the region and established its own colonial empire in western Sicily, Corsica, Sardinia, and southern Spain. When the Carthaginians and their Etruscan allies forced the Phocaeans to evacuate their colony at Alalia on Corsica in the mid-sixth century BC, Greek colonization in the central and western Mediterranean came to an end.

As colonizing opportunities shrank in the Mediterranean, Greeks turned to the northeast for new areas to settle. Attracted by the rich fishing and agricultural wealth of the Hellespont and Black Sea region, various Ionian and Aeolian states founded colonies in the area. The most active of these was Miletus, credited by the ancient sources with seventy colonies, though the actual number was probably much smaller. Among Miletus' numerous colonies were such important cities as Cyzicus (675 BC) near the entrance of the Hellespont, Sinope (late seventh century) on the north coast of Anatolia, Olbia (c. 550) at the mouth of the Bug River in southwestern Ukraine, and Panticapaeum (c. 600) in the Crimea. Megara also colonized in this area, occupying the important sites of Byzantium and Chalcedon on both sides of the Dardanelles as well as founding the city of Heraclea Pontica (560 BC) in northwest Anatolia near one of the reputed entrances to Hades. Because they had no rivals in this area, unlike in the Mediterranean basin, the Greeks were able to establish new colonies throughout the Archaic and Classical periods until the Black Sea was almost entirely ringed by Greek poleis.

The colonizing movement is often viewed primarily as the story of the spread of Greek life and culture. Support for such reconstructions exists in the ancient sources. The new poleis proudly proclaimed their Greekness by building monumental temples, patronizing Panhellenic institutions such as the Delphic oracle and the Olympic games, and eagerly trying to keep abreast of cultural developments in the Aegean. The earliest examples of the Greek alphabet and hexameter verse in fact come from Pithecusae. Nevertheless, the creation of new poleis is only part of the story of Greek colonization.

Everywhere the small colonial expeditions settled, they encountered "barbarians," the non-Greek inhabitants of the shores of the Mediterranean and Black seas. A few cities, such as Syracuse, Byzantium, and Heraclea Pontica, ultimately succeeded in expelling or enslaving their non-Greek neighbors. Their local chroniclers later celebrated these victories with chauvinistic stories of how Greek cleverness overcame barbarian simplicity. Most colonies, however, were not so fortunate and had to find accommodations with their non-Greek neighbors, trading and intermarrying with them, and sometimes even sharing their territory. There were risks on both sides; Herodotus tells a tragic story of a Scythian king who married a Greek woman and became a devotee of Dionysus, only to be assassinated by his outraged subjects. More often, however, as the discovery of Greek manufactures in southern France and the spread of the Greek alphabet, art, and cults among the Etruscans indicate, the colonies became gateways through which the peoples of southern Europe and the Black Sea obtained access to the products and culture of the Mediterranean. Nor was the cultural exchange all in one direction, as cults such as those of the Thracian goddess Bendis and the divine musician Orpheus spread throughout the Aegean and beyond.

ECONOMIC AND SOCIAL DIVISIONS IN THE EARLY POLEIS

Those who left their homes to emigrate abroad in the late eighth century were chiefly lured by the prospect of the equal lot of farmland (*klēros*) promised to new settlers. The colonizing movement was both the sign of inequality in land ownership in Greece and a partial remedy. Not every family could emigrate, however, and meanwhile as population continued to grow land became scarcer. The result was a widening of the social and economic distance between the top families and the rest of the people.

The rich landowners cultivated an image of themselves as a true aristocracy, far superior to all the groups below them. They claimed exclusive entitlement to the term *hoi agathoi*, "the good," purely on the basis of their birth into illustrious and wealthy families, and labeled as *hoi kakoi*, "the bad," those who were not born into the landed nobility.This presumptuous arrogance was a large leap from the justified self-esteem of the warrior-chiefs whom the aristocrats boasted as their ancestors. For Homeric heroes, descent from great warriors, though a matter of pride, was not automatic proof of personal excellence, and they did not demand honors or privileges on that basis. Their claims to be called "good" (*agathos*) and "best" (*aristos*) were measured solely by their performance as warriors and leaders. In the same way, the term *kakos* also acquired social connotations in the seventh century. In Homer *kakos* had meant unskilled in warcraft or "cowardly"; in the aristocratic lexicon it referred to anyone who was not a member of the closed group of the wealthy and well-born. Similarly, they signaled their separateness from the rest of the community by narrowing the term *dēmos* from its inclusive usage as the "whole people" to mean the "masses" or the "poor," whom they also referred to disparagingly as *hoi polloi*, "the many."

The Rich, the Poor, and the Middle

The arrogance of the powerful aristocrats was rooted in their hereditary control of the land. The generations of aristocratic houses had inherited a disproportionate share of the total agricultural land in the demos and an even greater share of the good land. They became even richer through improved farming techniques that increased crop yields and through concentration on cash crops, such as wine and olive oil. Most significant for their profits was their ability to exploit the labor of the poorest farmers who were eking out a precarious existence on small plots of land or on marginal land. Some of those poor families rented land from the rich as sharecroppers in return for a portion of the harvest, while others mortgaged their land to the rich and were compelled to pay a stipulated amount of the crops as payment on the debt. Small farmers fell easily into debt. One bad year meant borrowing next year's seed from a wealthy neighbor; a run of lean years could put a family so deeply into debt that it lost its land. We may assume also that the number of *thētes*—those who contracted to work as hired hands in return for food, clothing, and shelter—increased considerably. The attitude of the landowning class toward those whom they exploited combined contempt, mistrust, and dislike.

Conjectures about the size of the noble class—defined as those whose landholdings provided them a leisured lifestyle—range between 12 and 20 percent of the families; for the lower class—those with insufficient land to support themselves—estimates are on the order of 20 to 30 percent. (Of course, the percentages would have varied from polis to polis.) These figures allow for at least 50 percent of the families to have been neither rich nor dependent upon the rich. The fourth-century philosopher Aristotle in his *Politics* calls this group "the middle" (*hoi mesoi*), the portion of the polis that was between "the very rich and the very poor," and possessed a moderate amount of wealth.

These three divisions were not monolithic, of course; within each there was a gradation of wealth and social rank. The small number of aristocratic households was dominated by a smaller number of families that were preeminent because of their nobler bloodlines and greater wealth: an aristocracy within an aristocracy. Moreover, the hierarchy was naturally subject to change; one family might rise into the ranks of the upper nobility while another might drop down into the lesser nobilty. Nevertheless, the propertied class as a whole remained clearly marked off from the groups below them. The agathoi protected and protracted their economic and social exclusiveness by marrying only within the group. The ideal was to maintain class solidarity and at least the facade of equality among the families.

Within the lowest group, gradations would have been only in the degree of abjectness. The chances for economic betterment for poor farmers were slight. The increase in trade, which rose steadily in the Archaic period, offered some opportunities for employment, but only as sailors and in other low-wage and low-status occupations. And the skilled crafts were mostly closed to the poor because crafts were family affairs and few apprenticeships were available to poor outsiders.

It was the middle group that had the greatest economic and social gradation. Some nonnoble oikoi shared in the rising prosperity of the Archaic Age and were fairly well off; at the other end of the scale were those barely keeping out of debt. The wealth differences, and therefore the social differences, between the extremes were large enough so that the top did not make marriages with the bottom. Accordingly, the whole group of independent farmers and craftsmen was not conscious of itself as a class with specific class interests as were the rich landowners. Upward mobility, though not impossible, was not easy. Aristocracies resist assaults on their exclusiveness; yet, if a commoner family became wealthy enough, it could marry into the nobility. The sixth-century aristocratic poet Theognis complains that although men take pains to make their animals "well-born" by careful breeding, a "good man" will not hesitate to marry the daughter of a "kakos man," if she brings with her a good dowry. "Wealth," he says, "corrupts a lineage" (*Theognidea* 183–192). Downward mobility, on the other hand, was much more common, as the precarious farmers slipped into dependence. The erosion of the independent farmer group in the seventh century became a serious problem within the city-states.

Citizenship

Although all the families of the three economic groups were citizens, they were far from equal in their rights as citizens in the early poleis. Citizenship, which the later Greeks defined as "having a share in the public life of the polis," was perceived as a graded status, fixed to a person's social and economic condition as well as to gender. While female citizens had important roles in the religious worship of the community, they were completely barred from participation in political, judicial, and military affairs. These were exclusively the domain of adult (over age 18) male citizens. Among the men, the share of civic responsibilities and rights—to vote and speak in the assembly, hold office, serve as judges, fight in the army—was divided unequally along mainly economic lines. In the early city-states, as we have seen, only the rich and wellborn possessed the full range of citizen privileges. Nonnoble citizens of moderate means were barred from holding office, and the poorest citizens had no vote in the assembly. The political history of the Archaic period is the struggle of the middle and lower classes to gain an equal share in the governance of their poleis. Full participation, however, would be achieved only in the democratic states; in oligarchic states the poorest members would remain second-class citizens.

Besides women, there were other categories of free persons living in a polis territory that were denied citizen rights, chiefly resident aliens and ex-slaves. And in some states (mainly Doric), whole villages and towns were regarded as nonmembers of the demos, and their members were given the status of half-citizens. We will have more to say about these *perioikoi* ("dwellers round about") in the next chapter. By far the largest groups of rightless inhabitants, however, were slaves and semislaves.

Slaves and Serfs

During the seventh century there was some increase in the number of chattel slaves (persons captured or bought and legally classed as property), but for the most part rich landlords used the labor of farmers who were in debt or otherwise obligated to them, which was in many respects economically better for the landlords than keeping multitudes of slaves. The real upsurge in slaveholding came in the sixth century when political reforms and measures in the city-states limited or abolished debt bondage, forcing the rich to use slave labor on their lands.

The Spartan "helots" provide an example of another category of agricultural laborers in Greece, whose status was characterized as "between free persons and slaves." The helots were the inhabitants of parts of Laconia and most of Messenia who were conquered by the Spartans in war and then made to work for the Spartan citizens as serfs on what had been their own land. (The importance of the helots to the Spartan way of life will be discussed in the next chapter.) Similar serflike groups existed in other Greek states, especially in the areas where the Doric dialect was spoken. The origins of these enserfed peoples is very obscure. One theory is that they were the people dwelling in the lands that were taken over by the Dorian immigrants in the early Dark Age. Because they were ethnically different from the newcomers, they could be treated as an inferior subclass, permanently stigmatized as "other." They were compelled to work the land as sharecroppers and provide other labor (including some military service), in return for which they were granted certain minimal protections, such as the right to marry and raise a family, and the guarantee that they would not be expelled from the land they farmed.

Thessaly also had a huge population of unfree agricultural workers called "the toilers," and, as we saw earlier, a few of the colonial city-states in the west and around the Black Sea reduced the nearby native populations to forced labor. It is not certain, however, whether other impoverished and exploited groups that we are told of were subjugated serfs or just the poorest class of citizens. That they were socially and economically inferior, however, is certain from the slang terms for them: "the naked ones" (Argos), "dusty-feet" (Epidaurus), "wearers of sheepskins" and "club-carriers" (Sicyon), "wearers of dog-skin helmets" (Corinth).

Resentment from Below and the Beginnings of Social Change

In the seventh century all the economic groups below the tightly closed circle of self-styled agathoi had reason to resent their power and arrogance. The families at the bottom of the economic ladder, both the dependent oikoi and those on the brink of impoverishment and debt, had the most reasons for hating the rich. They were not only struggling to make ends meet, they also had to endure the stigma (or the threat) of working for others, a condition Greeks equated with loss of freedom, that is, slavery. The slogan "redistribution of the land" became the rallying cry of the have-nots throughout Greece in the Archaic period.

The economically secure families—those that produced enough to live on and those producing enough and some extra—also had cause for resentment, even though they were not directly exploited. The best farmland was held by aristocratic households, who were successful in keeping it in their group. Most of the remaining decent farmland was also already taken. Their alternatives were to emigrate abroad, which many did, or to seek marginal land far from their villages. Yet, to make marginal land productive required extra travel time, labor, and equipment, resources that were much more available to the rich oikoi. The middle group also chafed at being shut out of positions of power and prestige by the oligarchy's lock on the magistracies, boards, and particularly the council, where the political decisions were formulated. The well-off farmers were just as liable to be cheated in the law courts as the poorer ones and were just as helpless against "crooked decisions." In the assembly, the one organ of government to which they were admitted, the people's voice carried little weight against the concentrated power of the rich.

Yet, in spite of the strength of the ruling oligarchs and the apparent weakness of the rest of the demos, the absolute domination by the former was destined to be short-lived. By the early sixth century, oligarchical rulership had broadened to include numerous families outside the exclusive club of hereditary agathoi, and in some states even broader governments were emerging that would eventually give political power to the mass of people, including the poor. The key element in the protest against aristocratic excess was the middle group of independent farmers, over whom the oligarchs had the least control. We are fortunate to have a very early spokesman for this group, Hesiod, who speaks to us about life and society in the emerging polis from the point of view of the ordinary citizen.

HESIOD: THE VIEW FROM BELOW

In addition to the *Theogony*, Hesiod is credited with another long epic poem (828 lines) about farming, called *Works and Days*. Unlike the Homeric epics, which were set in a distant Age of Heroes and told of the triumphs and tragedies of great warrior chiefs, the *Works and Days* was set in the present and told about ordinary people and their ordinary lives. In the *Iliad* and *Odyssey* common folk are visible only as part of the social background. They are given collective roles as the mass of soldiers or citizens in the assemblies or they appear in vignettes about farmers, housewives, shepherds, and craftsmen. These Hesiod puts in the foreground.

Hesiod also differs from Homer and the other epic poets in that he purports to be telling of his own experiences: "I, Hesiod." Many scholars maintain that the poet has adopted a *persona* or poetic character and that the details he provides about his own life are fictitious. Whether "Hesiod" was a real person and was giving his own autobiography matters little. No one doubts that his account of rural life in the early Archaic period is accurate.

Hesiod tells us that he and his brother Perses lived in the small Boeotian village of Askra (part of the polis of Thespiae 3 miles away), and when their father died a dispute arose over the division of the kleros. Perses defrauded Hesiod of a portion of the inheritance by bribing the judges (basileis). After the judgment, Hesiod intimates, Perses became a loafer and a spendthrift and reduced himself to such poverty that he found it necessary to go to his brother for help. Whether this is the literal truth or a fiction, such family situations must have been common.

The quarrel provides the pretext for the poem's form—a sermon to his erring brother. Sermonizing poetry, so different from that of the Homeric narrative, was clearly influenced by the ancient genre of Near Eastern "wisdom literature," which consisted of exhortations, instructions, and admonitions addressed to a son or other relative, or even to a king, and was spiced with stories and proverbs about right and wrong. Though Perses was ostensibly the one whom Hesiod was advising, the real audience was the whole group to which he and Perses belonged, namely the upper level of the independent farmers. At other points in the poem, however, he speaks on their behalf and directs his sermonizing to the ruling group, whom he calls *basileis*. This might have been their actual title as a board of magistrates or judges in the city-state of Thespiae, but it is more likely that Hesiod was using the term in the generic epic sense of the leaders of any community.

Hesiod addresses the basileis very sternly, not at all deferentially. He calls them "bribe-swallowing" basileis and accuses them straight out of habitually rendering their verdicts "with crooked judgments." He tells them that Zeus himself is watching over his daughter, Dike, "Justice," and avenges unjust acts against her committed by those in power. Thus, the basic civic moral that justice through law is the foundation of good government, appears already fully formed in Hesiod.

Document 3.2 Hesiod lectures the aristocrats.

> *Basileis*, give this verdict no little thought,
> for the immortals are ever present among men,
> and they see those who with crooked verdicts
> spurn divine retribution and grind down one another's lives.
> Upon this earth that nurtures many Zeus can levy
> thirty thousand deathless guardians of mortal men,
> who keep a watchful eye over verdicts and cruel acts
> as they rove the whole earth, clothed in mist.

Justice is a maiden and a daughter of Zeus;
the gods of Olympos respect her noble title,
and whenever men mistreat her through false charges
she rushes to sit at the feet of Zeus Kronion
and she denounces the designs of men who are not just,
so that the people pay for the reckless deeds and evil plans
of *basileis* whose slanted words twist her straight path.
Keep her commands, O gift-devouring *basileis*, and let
verdicts be straight; yes, lay your crooked ways aside!
He that wrongs another man wrongs, above all, himself,
and evil schemes bring more harm on those who plot them.
The eye of Zeus sees all, notices all;
it sees this, too, if it wishes, and knows exactly
what sort of host this *polis* is to justice.
As matters stand, may neither I nor my son
be just men in this world, because it is a bad thing
to be just if wrongdoers win the court decisions.
But I do not believe yet that Zeus's wisdom will allow this.

Works and Days 248–272; translated by Apostolos N. Athanassakis, Hesiod.
Baltimore and London: Johns Hopkins University Press, 1983, p. 73 (adapted).

The moralistic tone pervades the entire poem. Hesiod has a whole litany of proverbial do's and don'ts that we could find in any peasant society in the world. He counsels a strict reciprocity in all dealings. When you borrow from a neighbor, he says, "pay back fairly, the same amount, or more if you can, so that when you need something later you can count on him" (349–351).

At the core of Hesiod's moral program is the ethic of work, arduous manual labor:

Through work men grow wealthy and rich in flocks,
and by working they become much dearer to the gods.
Work is no disgrace; idleness is the disgrace.
And if you work, the idle man will soon envy you
as you grow rich, because fame and renown follow wealth.
(Works and Days 308–313)

Hesiod is asserting that through work the ordinary farmer may win the three prizes that in the Homeric epics could only be attained by heroes: wealth, the special favor of the gods, and glory. Thus unremitting toil in the farm fields becomes a virtue equivalent to great deeds on the battlefields. Of course, the prizes are pared down to suit the humble life of a rural village. To Hesiod and his neighbors wealth meant "having their granaries full of the sustenance of life" at harvest time and not having to borrow; renown was being admired and respected by all the folk in the village. This pragmatic and nonaristocratic system of values,

the motto of which was "work with work upon work," can be detected throughout the Archaic period.

As a social document of the peasant-farmer's values, the *Works and Days* also
allows us to appreciate class differences in outlook toward institutions such as
marriage. Among the upper class, marriage was primarily a means of establishing alliances and enhancing family prestige. Noble families often sought advantageous matches outside of their polis, and, as in Homer, suitors competed against
one another with expensive gifts and shows of manliness in athletic contests.
Aristocratic women, though they lived highly circumscribed lives, had a high status and were treated with great respect by the men. The different, much narrower
view, of the farmer class shows through in Hesiod's advice on marriage:

> Marry a virgin so that you can teach her proper habits,
> and especially marry one who lives near you;
> and check all around so that your marriage will not be a joke
> to your neighbors, for nothing is better for a man than a good wife
> and nothing more horrible than a bad one. . . .
>
> *(Works and Days 699–703)*

Prestige, though just as important as in an aristocratic marriage, is here confined
to the village and expressed in negative terms. It is not a wife who will bring him
advantageous connections that the farmer seeks, but one who will not cause him
to lose respect if she should turn out to be a glutton or lazy or unfaithful—typical faults that Hesiod attributes to women.

The misogyny expressed in Hesiod was a common attitude during the Archaic
period and continued throughout Greek antiquity. The best-known illustration of
this way of thinking is the myth of Pandora, the first woman, as it is told in both
the *Theogony* (571–612) and the *Works and Days* (60–105). Zeus, Hesiod says, commanded this "beautiful evil" to be created as a punishment for the crime of
Prometheus (one of the Titans) who stole fire from the gods and gave it to humans. Pandora opened the lid of a jar containing all the plagues and diseases of
the world and let them out. All womankind inherited Pandora's "shameless mind
and deceitful nature," her "lies and coaxing words." Women, the poet says, live
off men like the drones among the bees. "Do not let a woman wiggling her behind deceive you with her wheedling words. She is after your granary. The man
who trusts a woman trusts thieves" (*Works and Days* 373–375).

The members of Hesiod's economic class resembled the wealthy class in one
respect: they exploited the labor of others. The difference was that the ordinary
farmer had only a few workers and labored alongside them. Hesiod takes for
granted that the farmers he is addressing can afford to own at least one slave
woman or man, take on a hired hand (thes), and employ day workers at busy
times. The farmer keeps his eye on the bottom line. The day's food for a hired
plowman is carefully measured out—just enough to keep up his energy level. He
advises hiring a thes that has no oikos (he will work cheaper) and a childless female worker ("a worker with a child at her breast is a bother").

However much he railed against the wealthy and powerful, Hesiod, then, was not a "champion of the oppressed," as some historians have called him. Rather his was the voice of middle-class indignation. Underpinning all that he says is the firm belief that Zeus and the other gods will look favorably on those who are pious, hard working, and righteous and will punish in the end those who are not. A hundred years later in Athens another thunderous voice would be raised against the evil greed and violent actions of the aristocrats—this time not from below but from a member of the aristocracy, the statesman Solon, whose reforms would pave the way for Athenian democracy.

THE HOPLITE ARMY

Warfare took on a different character in the Archaic period. Between about 725 and 650 the Greeks made major changes in military equipment and tactics. Henceforth all Greek battles were fought by heavily armored foot soldiers called hoplites, arranged in a tightly packed formation called the phalanx. The phalanx, many now believe, evolved from an earlier looser type of mass formation. In this "protophalanx," as it is sometimes called, the fighting men were grouped in regular units arranged in straight rows or ranks. The protophalanx is depicted in the *Iliad*, though for dramatic effect the poet concentrates on encounters between individual warrior-heroes, largely ignoring the mass of soldiers who fought around them. This clouds our understanding of the actual deployment of the formation in battle. It appears, however, that the hostile ranks in Homer move into spear range, hurl their pair of short throwing spears, and then fight hand to hand with their long swords.

As the phalanx evolved, it became progressively more compact, with the soldiers lined up almost shoulder to shoulder and each rank almost treading on the heels of the one in front of it. Phalanx fighting was simple in the extreme: the two close-packed phalanxes charged at one another and collided. The more ranks the more effective the charge. In its developed form (by 650 at the latest), the phalanx was normally eight rows deep. Weapons and armor evolved in tandem with the compact phalanx, to make it more effective. The hoplite's main weapon was his long heavy spear, which he used as a thrusting weapon. After the initial collision, when there was no room to jab with the spear, the hoplite used his secondary weapon, a short slashing sword. In a hoplite battle the soldiers needed better protection than they had had earlier. Helmets, upper-body armor (breastplates), and shin-and-knee protectors (greaves), all of which had been used in earlier warfare, were redesigned to be thicker and stronger (bronze replaced other materials, such as padded linen) and to cover larger areas of the body.

The most innovative item of equipment was a new type of shield called the *hoplon*, after which the hoplite was named. Designed specifically for the phalanx formation, it was round, made of wood covered with a thin sheet of bronze. It was the hoplon that made the phalanx an effective fighting force. Larger than all previous round shields (about 3 feet in diameter), it was held by inserting the left arm through a central band and gripping a strap at the rim. The hoplon was large enough to cover the man on the left, allowing hoplites to fight shoulder to shoulder with half of their body protected by the next man's shield. Seen from the front, a phalanx presented nearly a solid wall of shields, helmeted heads, and spears.

A hoplite battle was a ferocious affair. At a signal from a trumpet, the phalanx advanced at a fast walk, sometimes at a trot; when they came close, the front ranks raised their spears, stabbing overhand at the enemy, aiming at vulnerable spots unprotected by armor. Meanwhile, the ranks behind literally shoved against those in front—the maneuver was called "the pushing"—using their weight to break the enemy's ranks. Enormous courage was required of every single warrior, for success depended on every man holding his place in the formation. To flee the fight brought the contempt of the whole demos; thus men as a rule stood their ground, "biting their lip with their teeth," as the Spartan poet Tyrtaeus (c. 650 BC) says.

The conditions of hoplite battle were awful. The equipment weighed about 70 pounds, almost half the weight of an average man. It was unbearably hot inside the armor; vision was restricted by the dust and the helmet; the noise was deafening. Everyone was spattered with blood; wounded men were trampled underfoot. Tyrtaeus describes an old hoplite "breathing out his brave spirit in the dust, holding his bloody genitals in his hands." The battles were fairly brief, however, seldom more than an hour. Casualties were relatively light for the losers as well as the victors, seldom over 15 percent. Once the enemy broke ranks and fled,

Figure 3.2. The earliest depiction of a hoplite battle; from a Corinthian vase (c. 640 BC).

there was not much pursuit, so that massacres of the defeated army were rare. Moreover, campaigns were short; usually, a single set battle ended the fighting for the summer. Both sides buried their dead and went back home to work their lands or practice their crafts, not to don their armor until the polis needed them again.

Not all citizens fought in the phalanx, however. Because hoplites had to furnish their own arms and armor, which were fairly expensive, the poorest men were disqualified and served instead as light-armed troops. Modern estimates of those who did qualify vary considerably. Given the importance of the phalanx to the survival of the polis, and taking into consideration that captured armor would be distributed and that items of equipment would be donated, a reasonable estimate is that at least half of the broad group of *mesoi* were able to serve. Thus 60 percent or more of a typical hoplite army would have come from the nonaristocratic families of the polis.

The Hoplite Army and the Polis

It is in the hoplite army that we most clearly observe the polis ideology that the citizen is the slave of the common good. The poems of Tyrtaeus of Sparta and Callinus of Ephesus, both from around the mid-seventh century, reveal a shift in values from the individual to the polis. Although Homeric warriors faced death willingly as the price of their glory, they nevertheless saw it as an unmitigated evil. In Tyrtaeus, dying in battle had acquired a positive value. "It is a noble thing for a good man to die, falling among the front ranks, fighting for his fatherland," he tells his fellow Spartans, and again, "Make life your enemy, and the black spirits of death dear as the rays of the sun." Bravery in battle was still the highest virtue, but it too had become a cooperative value—not the heroics of individual champions but simply keeping your place in the phalanx.

> This is the common good, for the *polis* and the whole *dēmos*,
>   when a man stands firm in the front ranks
> without flinching and puts disgraceful flight completely from his mind,
>   making his soul and spirit endure
> and with his words encourages the man stationed next to him.
>   (*Tyrtaeus fr. 12.15–19 West*)

Similarly, honor, glory, and fame are sought just as eagerly by the citizen-soldier as they were by the Homeric hero, but these could be earned only in service to the polis.

Distinctions of wealth and birth vanish in the ranks of the phalanx. Thus, Callinus says, though a man may have "immortal gods as his ancestors," he is despised by the demos if he flees the "thud of spears," while the stout-hearted man who dies in battle is mourned by both the "great and the small; in death he is missed by the whole people and in life he is treated as a demi-god" (i.e., as an epic hero). Tyrtaeus, too, shows how the hoplite ideal was eroding the Homeric notions of excellence that the aristocrats laid claim to as proof of their exclusive worth. In the elegy cited above, he lists all the things that the *agathoi* valued—skill in athletics, strength and beauty, great wealth, political power, eloquence in speaking—and says that he would not even mention in his poems a man that "had every kind of fame except a fighting spirit."

The reality of strict equality in the ranks, where aristocrats and nonaristocrats fought side by side, was making it increasingly difficult for the agathoi to maintain their exclusivity and their hold on political power. Already in Hesiod and Tyrtaeus we see the concomitant growth of an antielitist ideology that challenged elitist pretensions of natural superiority and substituted the leveling notion that nonaristocrats were equal to aristocrats off the field of battle as well as on. Throughout the Archaic and Classical periods the nonaristocratic hoplites would play a key role as the independent variable in the power relations within the city-state.

This class, comprising fairly well-off farmers and craftsmen, was the pivotal group in determining where a polis stood on the continuum from narrow oligarchies to full democracies. If they were content with an uneven distribution of power and agreed to or abetted the exploitation of the weak, oligarchical regimes reigned secure. If, on the other hand, they opposed the status quo and sympathized with the bottom half of the citizenry, the balance of power shifted from the elite to the mass. Because the well-off farmers tended toward conservatism, most Greek poleis in the Archaic and Classical periods were moderately oligarchical, granting citizen rights in accordance with economic status. But in those city-states where the upper level of the middle group came down firmly on the side of the poor, there was complete legal and political equality between the classes. The rapid swings from oligarchy to democracy (and vice versa) that occurred so frequently in the history of a polis are best explained by the shifts in attitude of the nonaristocratic hoplites. They also played a major role in the political phenomenon the Greeks called tyranny (*tyrannis*).

THE ARCHAIC AGE TYRANTS

Hardly had the aristocrats rid themselves of the position of basileus when a new type of one-man rule arose in the form of the *tyrannos* (tyrant). Between about 670 and 500 BC a great number of city-states throughout the Greek world went through a phase of tyranny. The words *tyrannos* and *tyrannis* were borrowed into the Greek language (perhaps from Lydia in Asia Minor) to describe a form of government for which the Greeks had no word: rule by a man who seizes control of the state by a coup and governs illegally. The Archaic Age tyrant was what we call today a dictator or strongman. At first the word *tyrannos* had no real negative connotation. It eventually came to mean a wicked and oppressive despot, in part because of propaganda spread by the aristocrats, who naturally hated the men who had overthrown their regimes, but also because later generations perceived that dictatorial rule by one man not accountable to the demos threatened the freedom of all. Yet there are ample indications that the nonaristocratic contemporaries of the early tyrants viewed them in a more favorable light. Unfortunately, only a few of the dozens of tyrants who grabbed power in their poleis are known in any detail. Still, we can see a general pattern in their rise and fall.

Tyrannies were short-lived. Although all the tyrants tried to form dynasties by passing on their rule to their sons, no tyranny lasted more than three generations and most collapsed after one or two. Despite aristocratic hate propaganda that described some tyrants as low-born, it appears that all were members of the aristocracy. For example, Pheidon of Argos was the hereditary basileus before he turned himself into a tyrannos. Not all tyrants, however, were from the top-ranked families. Cypselus of Corinth, for instance (c. 657–627), was marginalized within the "royal clan" of the Bacchiads, because his mother, a Bacchiad, had married outside the clan.

In addition to their membership in the elite, would-be tyrants were distinguished in their poleis for their individual achievements. Cypselus, prior to becoming a tyrant, had held the post of polemarch (military commander). Orthagoras of Sicyon (mid-seventh century) had also been polemarch and had compiled an outstanding battle record. Cylon of Athens, whose attempted coup in 632 failed, had won fame as a victor in the Olympic games.

Vicious infighting among the aristocratic families in the polis for honor and precedence was a major factor contributing to the emergence of the tyrants. Rivalry among the aristocrats, though it was channeled to some extent into competition for offices and control within the council, was particularly nasty in the seventh and sixth centuries because the struggles for power were waged among "clans" (*genos*; plural *genē*). Like the royal clan, an aristocratic *genos*—the word meant essentially a "lineage"—was composed of a preeminent family that extended the umbrella of fictive kinship over less prestigious noble oikoi, whose members supported the leader-family in its political ambitions. Disputes among these factions—gangs of hot-headed young aristocrats—frequently erupted in bouts of violence and bloodshed.

The Greeks called formal conflict between groups within the city-state *stasis* ("taking a stand"). Opposition of this sort was integral to the Greek political process of every period. The stasis between aristocratic factions in the Archaic period, however, was much more frequently violent than afterward (when the power of the gene had declined), and was highly disruptive of the society. Worse, because membership in a genos was hereditary, this kind of civil war could keep flaring up for generations. The intervention of a strongman who could stop, or at least check, the feuds of the noble families, though anathema to the nobles, was welcome to the rest of the people.

To climb to power these "renegade aristocrats," as some call them, needed resources and manpower. One potential source was disaffected aristocrats within the polis who were frozen out of the ruling circle. This band of followers might be supplemented by a mercenary force from outside the polis. Such aid was sometimes supplied by a friendly tyrant (for his abortive coup, Cylon received some troops from his father-in-law Theagenes, tyrant of Megara), or, in the case of many of the Ionian tyrants in the late sixth century, by the Persian empire. The best known tyrant, Peisistratus of Athens (who made three attempts before succeeding), availed himself of a variety of resources, including local bodyguards, mercenaries, and troops donated by powerful outsiders. His story will be told at greater length in Chapter 5.

No tyrant, however, no matter what his resources, could have succeeded without support of the citizens themselves, particularly the farmer-hoplites. There is no evidence that any tyrant came to power at the head of a hoplite army, but such active intervention would not have been necessary. An oligarchy could not have been overthrown if it had the loyalty of the nonaristocratic hoplites, whereas all that a would-be tyrant needed was their passive refusal to defend the nobles. Among the many reasons for the hoplites' disaffection with oligarchical rule, not the least was that the incessant infighting among the aristocratic families was harmful to the good order of the state. As for the lowest citizens, they naturally would have been very supportive of a coup against the group that was exploiting them.

That the tyrants were viewed as champions of the demos against the oligarchs was the judgment of all the later writers. Aristotle in the fourth century put it concisely:

> A tyrant is set up from among the *dēmos* and the multitude to oppose the notables so that the people may suffer no injustice from them. This is clear from the facts of history. For almost all the tyrants have arisen from being leaders of the people [*dēmagōgoi*; hence "demagogue"], so to speak, having gained their confidence by slandering the notables.
>
> (Politics 1310b 12–17; Rackham 1977, adapted)

The seizure of power was often followed by violence against the rich. Cypselus killed or banished many of the Bacchiad aristocrats and confiscated their lands (presumably some of it went to poorer Corinthians), and other tyrants did the same. Tyrants made laws to limit aristocratic power and privilege, including "sumptuary laws," which curbed aristocratic luxury and ostentation. They also protected the existing institutions; Aristotle said of the Orthagorid dynasty of Sicyon that "in many ways they were slaves to the laws."

Under tyranny, many poleis thrived and reached new heights. Extensive building and improvement projects—stone temples and other major buildings, harbors and fortifications, and urban amenities like the water supply, streets, and drainage systems—turned the capital towns into real cities (and also gave work to poor citizens).

Moreover, trade, commerce, and crafts were encouraged and supported under the tyrants. Pheidon, for example, standardized weights and measures for the Peloponnesus, an enormously important advance in the commercial economy of the area. And Cypselus' son and successor, Periander, built a stone trackway across the narrow Isthmus of Corinth (where a canal runs today) allowing ships and cargoes to be hauled between the Saronic and Corinthian gulfs. (It was still in use as late as 883 AD.) Tyrants also instituted new religious cults and festivals that celebrated and strengthened the unity of the polis, and they supported all cultural activities, competing to attract the best artists, architects, poets, and thinkers in Greece to stay at their city.

The sons of dictators are seldom as successful as their fathers. The Archaic tyrants had gained popular support for their takeover because of their personal charisma and achievements. Their sons, however, were heirs to a nonexistent office, and so were extremely vulnerable. A few succeeded on their own merits, but most found themselves resorting to increasingly "tyrannical" measures to repress opposition, which naturally exacerbated resentment against them. Tyrants were overthrown, and they and their families were exiled or killed. Usually, the aristocrats who had been banished by the tyrants returned and reestablished an oligarchy. Aristocratic rule was never the same, however, after a tyranny. The farmer-hoplites were no longer willing merely to vote for their leaders without being able to hold them accountable. Nor could the nobles now refuse their inclusion in the process of public decisons, or take away from the poor the benefits that the tyrants had bestowed on them to make their lives easier.

ART AND ARCHITECTURE

Many historians of art have maintained that Archaic art was superior even to that of the Classical period. There is no doubt at any rate that in art as well as in literature, philosophy, and science Archaic Greece experienced a burst of creative energy unsurpassed in any comparable time period of the ancient world.

Building on the achievements of the Late Geometric period, the craftsmen of the seventh and sixth centuries attained new heights of excellence in all the forms of visual art. With the development of the city-state, differences in style between the various poleis became more distinct. This is most evident in the pottery, which continues in the Archaic period to be the most ample source for measuring artistic evolution. The "orientalizing" tendencies of the eighth century reached a peak in the seventh, with a variety of new motifs borrowed from the Near East—floral designs and friezes of real and fantastic animals—replacing the earlier geometric patterns. The Corinthians were the most receptive to these influences and produced a very distinctive type of pottery.

Under the leadership of the tyrant Cypselus (c. 657–627), Corinth emerged as the leading commercial center of Greece and dominated the trade in finely painted pottery. Corinthian potters specialized in exquisitely decorated perfume flasks, 2 to 3 inches high, which they filled with scented olive oil and exported in huge quantities throughout the Greek world. They invented a new technique called "black figure," which permitted them to render minute details. The artist first painted a black silhouette on the reddish clay, and then with a sharp point he cut in the anatomical and decorative details, sometimes filling these in with red or white paint. Corinthian black figure was enormously popular, but as often happens, success led to mass production and inferior vases, on which their famous animal motifs were monotonously and carelessly repeated.

Soon Athenian potters mastered Corinthian techniques, and by 550 Athenian black-figure pottery, featuring a variety of new and larger vessels, had driven Corinthian vases from the export market. Around 530 the Athenians in turn invented a new style called "red figure," which reversed the black-figure technique. Here, the artist first drew outlines and then painted the backgound black, keeping the outline in the reddish color of the clay itself. He then painted the details in black with a fine brush. This allowed a more subtle and refined rendering of detail than the incised black-figure technique.

Seventh- and sixth-century vase paintings most commonly depicted episodes from mythology and the heroic sagas. In the later sixth century images from contemporary life were added, most of which focused on the activities of young upper-class males. Typically portrayed were athletics, horsemanship, and drinking parties (very rowdy), as well as school scenes, music lessons, and homosexual wooing. Women are represented less often than men. They appear either as servants and flute girls or as well-dressed upper-class women accompanied by their female slaves in a domestic setting. The Archaic potters were proud of their work, frequently signing their vases ("Aristonothos made me") and occasionally including a taunt to a rival potter.

Vase painting gives us some idea of a major artistic genre, large-scale representations of mythological and patriotic subjects painted on temples and other

Figure 3.3a. Two sides of an Athenian amphora (c. 525–520 BC) decorated in both the red-figure and the black-figure technique.

Figure 3.3b. A *symposion* ("drinking party") scene on an Athenian red-figure calyx krater (mixing bowl for wine and water), showing a man and a youth reclining on a couch, and a flute girl.

public buildings. Though the paintings are almost entirely lost to us, the artists who painted them were renowned beyond their poleis and their names were still remembered centuries later.

The artistic genre for which the ancient Greeks were most famous was monumental (life-size or larger) marble and bronze sculpture. This was an innovation of the Archaic period. Large bronze statues were first produced in the sixth century but did not became common until the fifth, after which they far outnumbered those made of marble and other stone. The first large marble statues appear around 650. Egypt was the source both of inspiration and technique.

The Greek statues were of two types, a naked *kouros* ("young male") and a clothed female (*korē*, "young maiden"). Throughout the Archaic period the figures retained the original rigid Egyptian stance, arms pressed against the sides, one foot stepping forward, but as time went on they became increasingly less blocklike. By about 500, the *kouroi* (plural) had come to resemble real youths, with precisely defined anatomical details and accurate bodily proportions. The *korai* (plural) had also become more natural looking. The body underneath the drapery was more clearly indicated and the facial features more distinctly female. In both types of statues Archaic elements were still notable, such as the blissful "archaic smile" and the highly conventionalized treatment of the hair, yet the statues clearly anticipate the Classical ideal of the human form. The kouroi and korai were set up by wealthy families either as grave monuments or as offerings to the sanctuary of a god or goddess. Because they normally bore an inscription with the dedicator's name, they were highly public advertisements of the family's status in the community.

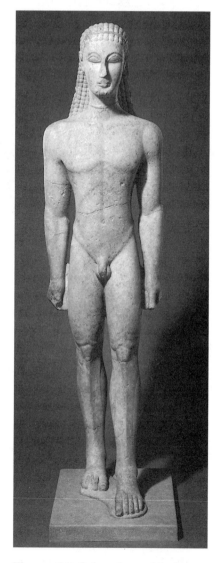

Figure 3.4 Statue of an Egyptian nobleman (early seventh century).

Figure 3.5 Colossal marble *kouros* from Attica (c. 600 BC). The statue imitates the stylized stance of Egyptian sculpture.

Another type of Archaic sculpture was reliefs depicting mythological scenes, carved on the triangular pediments and along the entablatures of late-sixth-century temples. Relief sculpture was increasingly successful at showing figures in movement and action. By contrast, the stylized free-standing kouroi and korai must have appeared rather old-fashioned by the end of the century.

In architecture, the temple continued to be the main focus. The small, modest prototypes of the early eighth century, as we have seen, had achieved monumental dimensions by its end. But the big step occurred around the middle of the seventh, when limestone and marble replaced mud brick and wood. Again, the Greek builders learned from the Egyptians the skills of quarrying, transporting, positioning, and dressing huge stone blocks. The temple plan, however, was a continuation of the Greek Geometric model, and most of the architectural features such as the low-pitched roof covered with terra-cotta tiles (replacing the

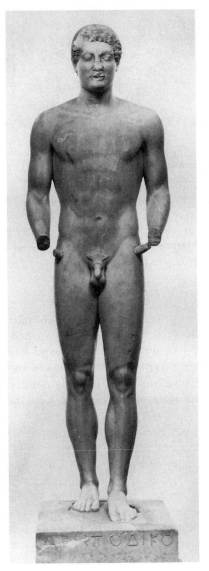

Figure 3.6. This marble *kouros* (c. 510–500 BC), was set atop the grave of Aristodikos in Attica; it shows the growth of naturalism in sculpture.

Figure 3.7. Late Archaic *korē* from the acropolis of Athens (c. 490), dedicated by Euthydikos.

Figure 3.8. Relief sculpture from the Siphnian Treasury at Delphi (c. 530–525) depicting the Battle of the Gods and the Giants. Apollo and Artemis are striding into battle (left) against the Giants (equipped as contemporary hoplites).

old thatched roof) were purely Greek. By the early sixth century the two main types or "orders" of columns, the Doric and the Ionic, were well established. Greek temples looked much as they would for the next five hundred years—but the extant structures are somewhat deceptive. Portions of the Greek temples and their sculptured reliefs, as well as standing marble statues, were actually painted in strong bright colors, presenting an impression quite unlike that given by the bare, gleaming stone we observe today.

During the sixth century other carefully built permanent structures appeared in the main cities. Most of these were built in and around the *agora,* "the gathering place," a large open space at or near the center of the city. The Dark Age agora had been only the place where the assembly met; in the Archaic period it became the marketplace and public space of the city and therefore of the whole city-state. Everyone gathered there to barter, exchange news and gossip, or conduct official business. By about 500 BC the agora contained one or more open colonnaded passageways called stoas, which provided shade and shelter and space for market stalls. Enhancing its dignity and importance were official buildings such as the council house and offices. Sanctuaries, fountain houses, and public monuments also graced the agora. In addition to the agora, Archaic poleis contained open spaces, with specified functions: the *gymnasion*, where men exercised, and the *palaistra,* a wrestling ground.

The agora and other public spaces would not receive numerous or splendid public buildings until the fifth and fourth centuries. Nevertheless, by about 550 all the capital poleis (except Sparta) merited the title of true urban centers. An aerial view of Corinth or Athens or any other major center would have revealed

Figure 3.9 Plan of the Athenian *agora* as it looked at the end of the Archaic period (c. 500 BC), showing the earliest public buildings (after J. Travlos 1974).

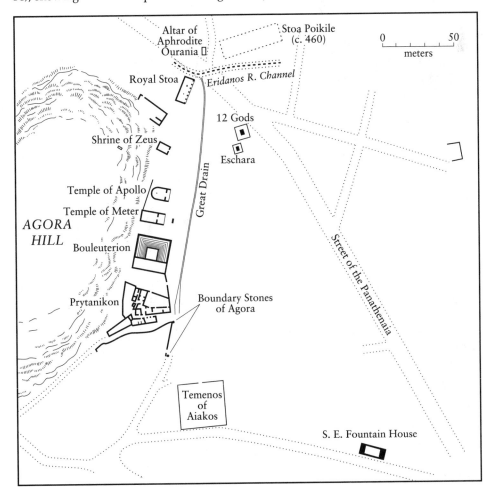

a dense concentration of buildings, most of them private houses, connected in blocks along narrow streets, broken up by patches of garden plots. The houses were larger than those of the Dark Age—three or four rooms rather than one or two—but still quite modest. Even the homes and furnishings of the elites, including the tyrants, remained unpretentious throughout the Archaic and most of the Classical period.

The modesty of private homes and the relative modesty even of secular civic buildings underscores the basic fact that efforts toward architectural and sculptural distinction in ancient Greece were directed primarily toward sanctuaries: the gods received the lion's share of a city-state's surplus wealth, both at home and in the panhellenic sanctuaries.

LYRIC POETRY

In literary expression, as well, the Archaic period was one of innovation. Archaic poetry is markedly different from the poetry of Homer and Hesiod. Many poets did continue to compose lengthy epic narratives (the so-called Epic Cycle of heroic sagas and the Homeric hymns described in Chapter 2 are examples). But the most original Archaic poets chose not to follow in the giant footsteps of Homer, already canonized as the supreme poet of all time by the early seventh century. They turned their talents instead to other genres of poetry, which we lump together under the rubric of "lyric poetry."

The roots of lyric poetry extend far back in time to folk songs created for specific occasions such as harvests, weddings, funerals, and coming-of-age rituals, or to hymns, fables, drinking songs, and love songs—everything, in other words, that pertained to communal and private life. With the advent of literacy such poems could be preserved and circulated; poets could attain not merely local but Panhellenic fame, by competing with their more carefully crafted songs composed and polished in writing.

Each of the several genres commonly grouped under the name "lyric" had its own metrical pattern, subject matter, occasion, tone (elevated and serious or low and scurrilous), and musical accompaniment. Like epic poetry, lyric poetry was "song" and was presented in performance. Some types were accompanied by the lyre (*lyra*; hence the name "lyric"), others by a flutelike instrument. And some were simply recited or chanted without musical accompaniment.

A major distinction was made between solo songs and songs performed by a chorus of young men or women, who sang and danced to the music of the lyre. Choral poetry and some kinds of solo poetry were presented before large public audiences at festivals, whereas others were performed in small private gatherings, usually a drinking party (*symposion*). Unlike the Archaic epics, which often ran to six or seven thousand lines, lyric poems were short—from a few lines to several hundred lines (in the case of choral songs).

Most lyric poetry was personal, sometimes extremely so, in subject and tone. The poets sang about drinking, friends and enemies, sexual love, old age and death, politics, war, and morality. The poet's tone could vary from lighthearted to bitter to contemplative. As we saw earlier with Hesiod, "personal" need not mean "autobiographical." Yet the lyric poets went far beyond Hesiod in revealing their own (or their persona's) emotional and mental states. They therefore not only give us rare insights into feelings about private matters but also, because private life and polis life were so closely intertwined, they reflect sentiments and attitudes about their society. Further, the poetry presents (from a strictly male point of view) the social attitudes of both the elite and the middle strata. Although we have fragments from about two dozen lyric poets of this period, we can sample only a few of them here. Three major lyric poets, Simonides, Bacchylides, and Pindar, whose careers were mainly in the fifth century, will be discussed in Chapter 6.

Some Lyric Poets and Their Social Attitudes

Archilochus of Paros (early seventh century) was particularly known for his mordant wit, which he often directed against the old heroic ideal. According to tradition, Archilochus was the son of a nobleman and a slave mother. Like other lyric poets, his voice is highly personal and passionate. His poems are about drinking and carousing, his sexual adventures, the pain of losing comrades in shipwrecks, hatred of his enemies, the uncertainties of life—in alternating tones of tenderness and cruelty, deep seriousness and obscene levity. He stresses his twofold role: soldier of fortune as well as inspired poet. "I am the squire of the lord of war, Enyalios [another name for Ares], and I understand the lovely gift of the Muses" (fr. 1 West). And again, "In my spear is my kneaded barley bread, in my spear my Ismarian wine. I drink leaning on my spear" (fr. 2 West).

Where Tyrtaeus and Callinus transvalue the epic-heroic conventions, Archilochus pokes fun at them. The Spartans found the following mock complaint so outrageous that they forbade the recitation of Archilochus' poetry at Sparta.

> Well, some Thracian is enjoying the shield which I left—I
>   didn't want to, and it was a perfectly good one—beside a bush.
> But I saved myself. What do I care about that shield?
>   To hell with it; I'll get another one just as good.
>
> *(fr. 5 West)*

This is not the boast of a Homeric hero. The irony and the humor lie in the incongruity between the poet's cynical stance and the Homeric ideal. Archilochus also uses humor to puncture the pretentiousness of the aristocratic equation of physical beauty and manly excellence.

I don't like a general who is big and walks with a swagger,
or who glories in his curly hair and shaves off his moustache.
Give me a man who's little, bandy-legged,
feet firm on the ground, full of heart.

(fr. 114 West)

The ostentatious display of luxury by the aristocrats was another thing that met with the censure of poets who reflected the sentiments of the ordinary yeoman farmers. For example, the Ionian philosophical poet Xenophanes (c. 550 BC) criticized the upper class of his native Colophon who went to the assembly in their all-purple cloaks, "glorying in their well-dressed long hair, drenched with the perfume of elaborate scents" (fr. 3 West). An earlier contemporary, Asius of Samos, registered similar displeasure at the elites who swept into the precinct of Hera in their snow-white robes, their long hair tied up in golden clasps and fancy bracelets on their arms.

At the same time as it deplores ostentation, the popular poetry promotes the practical wisdom and commonsense values held by the ordinary citizen of moderate means. A collection of homespun maxims from the first half of the sixth century, attributed to Phocylides of Miletus, is made up of sayings such as, "Many things are best in the middle; I want to be middle (*mesos*) in the *polis*"; and "What good is noble birth for those who lack grace in words and counsel?" In a similar vein, Xenophanes devalues the aristocratic pursuit of honor and prestige through athletic competition (only the wealthy could afford to compete), asserting that it is "small joy for the *polis*" when athletes win at the Olympic games, "for these things do not fatten the treasury of the *polis*" (fr. 2 West).

Perhaps the most colorful representative of the nonelite perspective was Hipponax of Ephesus (sixth century), who adopted the persona of an urban hustler, always broke and engaging in drunken brawls and escapades. Hipponax wrote in a vernacular full of street slang and obscenity, savagely lampooning his enemies and making fun of himself and his poverty. "Ploutos (the god of wealth)," he says, "never came to my house—for he's quite blind—and said to me, 'Hipponax, I'm giving you thirty minas of silver, and lots else besides.' No, he's too feeble-witted" (fr. 36 West).

Other poets present the world from an elitist perspective. Their poems are directed to an audience that had wealth and leisure. Most of this poetry was composed specifically for recitation at *symposia*, male drinking parties, which were an exclusively aristocratic form of entertainment. Symposiastic poetry, as it is called, covered a range of subjects, from the lofty (patriotic songs and retellings of ancient myths) to the playful (riddles and jokes). Partisan politics was a favorite topic. The commonest themes, however, were personal musings on the pleasures of wine and love (both heterosexual and homosexual) and the sad necessity that these joys must fade with old age.

Typical is this short poem by the seventh-century Ionian poet Mimnermus (from Smyrna or Colophon).

What life is there apart from Golden Aphrodite?
    What joy can there be? May I die when I
No longer care for secret love and tender gifts
    and bed, the alluring blossoms of youth for men
and women too. And when miserable old age
    comes on that makes a man both ugly and useless,
then troublesome worries forever wear and tear at his wits,
    nor can he enjoy the sight of the suns' rays.
Boys find him hateful, women contemptible.
    So sorrowful a thing has the god made old age.
                            (fr. 1 West; Fowler 1992, adapted)

Another Ionian poet was Anacreon of Teos (mid-sixth century), who was invited to Samos by the tyrant Polycrates, and after Polycrates' murder joined the court of the Peisistratid tyrants of Athens. The consummate aristocratic court poet, he particularly celebrates the pleasures of wine and love. For Anacreon these are the proper topics for symposia, not the worn themes of war and bloodshed:

I don't like the man who, while drinking wine besides the full mixing bowl,
    talks about quarrels and warfare with its tears,
but rather one who mingles the Muses' and Aphrodite's splendid gifts
    together and so keeps the charms of festivity in mind.
                            (Elegy 2; Miller 1996)

Similar in style and tone to Anacreon was his contemporary Ibycus, from Rhegium in Italy, who also spent years at Polycrates' court. Some of Ibycus' poems are long choral narratives in lyric meters, on traditional epic and mythological themes. Most of his extant work, however, is homoerotic poetry, full of sensuous imagery. In one poem, Eros ("Love") comes like the north wind from Thrace, and with "parching madness, dark and fearless, shakes me to the bottom of my heart with his might" (fr. 286 Page). In another poem, on falling in love again, he compares himself to an old champion racehorse that unwillingly drags his chariot to the contest (fr. 386 Page).

Mytilene, the dominant polis of Lesbos, produced two prominent poets, Sappho and Alcaeus, at the end of the seventh century. Both were from leading aristocratic families. Sappho is the only known woman poet from the Archaic period, in fact, one of the few in all ancient Greek literature (women were not encouraged to write). Her poetry was greatly admired throughout antiquity—she was hailed as the "tenth Muse." Unfortunately, very little of Sappho's poetry has survived. Most of what we have is solo songs, highly personal in tone, whose main theme is erotic love between women. It appears that Sappho was the leader of a close-knit circle of young upper-class women in Lesbos (hence the nineteenth-century euphemism "lesbian"), who shared their lives for a brief period before marriage. Sappho also wrote weddings songs (*epithalamia*) performed by choruses of young girls.

Document 3.3 Nine "books" (i.e., papyrus rolls) of Sappho's poetry were collected in the Alexandrian period, of which only one complete poem survives, along with several substantial portions of poems and a number of very short fragments. Here is a selection of shorter fragments.

> "I simply wish to die."
> Weeping she left me
> and said this too:
> "We've suffered terribly
> Sappho I leave you against my will."
> I answered, go happily
> and remember me,
> you know how we cared for you,
> if not, let me remind you
> . . . the lovely times we shared . . . (fr. 94 L-P)
>
> I have a beautiful child, her form
> like a golden flower, beloved Kleis,
> whom I would not trade for all of Lydia
> or lovely. . . . (fr. 132 L-P)
>
> Evening Star who gathers everything
> shining dawn scattered—
> you bring the sheep and the goats,
> you bring the child back to its mother. (fr. 104 L-P)
>
> The sweet apple reddens on a high branch
> high upon highest, missed by the applepickers:
> no, they didn't miss, so much as couldn't touch. (fr. 105 L-P)
>
> I loved you Atthis once long ago . . .
> You seemed to me a small child and without charm. (fr. 49 L-P)
>
> Atthis, for you the thought of me has become hateful,
> and you fly off to Andromeda. (fr. 131 L-P)

Translated by Diane J. Rayor, Sappho's Lyre. *Berkeley: University of California Press, 1991, pp. 60, 72, 74, 68.*

All the noble families of Lesbos, during the lifetimes of Sappho and Alcaeus, were embroiled in vicious power struggles. It would have been unthinkable for Sappho, a woman, to write of this stasis in her polis. Alcaeus, however, puts us in the center of the complicated intrigues, the political deals and betrayals, and the partisan hatreds and violence, which he relates in great detail. Alcaeus' venom was directed primarily at another aristocrat named Pittacus, a bitter enemy who had been a former ally. Predictably, Alcaeus levels at Pittacus the worst insults an aristocrat could muster: "base-born" (*kakopatridēs*; literally "son of a *kakos* father") and "tyrant" (he had been elected by the people to serve as a temporary dictator to end the incessant aristocratic feuding). Alcaeus is best known for this invective poetry, but the other symposiastic themes such as love, legend, and wine occupied his verses just as much. Indeed, he stresses that love, wine, and the pleasures of the drinking party offered him and his companions welcome repose from factional strife.

The fourteen hundred lines of poetry that have been attributed to Theognis of Megara (c. 550 BC) are probably a later compilation of poems written by many different authors, dating from the late seventh to the early fifth century. This anthology, called the *Theognidea*, includes the usual aristocratic themes; but it goes further in revealing the class prejudices and antagonisms of the elite toward the lower classes. The collection reads like a moral handbook for aristocrats, praising the values of the well-born agathoi and vilifying the base-born kakoi, who are represented as incapable of any sort of excellence. This intensified contempt is the reaction of a frustrated aristocracy, who realized that they were losing their status and privilege while a significant number of nonelites were making economic and political gains.

Conveyed again and again in verses such as these (addressed to the young lover of "Theognis") is a sense of helplessness mingled with bitter resentment at the intolerable reversal of station:

> Cyrnus, those who were *agathoi* once are now *kakoi*, and those who were *kakoi* before are now *agathoi*. Who could bear seeing this, the *agathoi* dishonored and the *kakoi* getting honor?
>
> *(Theognidea 1109–1112)*

Although aristocrats would continue to proclaim their innate superiority, the movement toward political leveling that had begun in the seventh century was essentially completed by the early decades of the fifth.

PHILOSOPHY AND SCIENCE

Like lyric poetry, philosophy (literally "the love of wisdom") arose with the awakening of the Greek world in the Archaic period. The earliest Greek philosophers, some of whom were the first to write in prose, are called the Presocratics to distinguish them from the disciples of Socrates who lived in Athens in the Classical period. The Presocratics are also clearly differentiated from the Socratics in that the former concentrated their attention on the structure and development of the physical universe while the latter were more interested in ethics, in the role human beings play in relationship to one another and to the larger society.

Cosmos: The Visible Sky

Because they did not have telescopes, the Greeks knew only the stars and the five planets they could see with the naked eye. But they were much more familiar with the night sky than most city dwellers are nowadays. Since there were no streetlights, smog, or tall buildings, their nights were filled with stars. They named the planets and constellations after their gods and characters in their myths, like Orion the hunter and the girls he pursued and never caught, the Pleiades. In the *Works and Days* Hesiod's agricultural calendar is addressed to farmers who learned when it was time to perform their seasonal chores by the position of the constellations. When Greeks sailed, they plotted their location by the position of celestial objects.

In the Archaic period, colonization, travel, and the development of trade and commerce spurred the growth of astronomical thinking. Contact with other civilizations in Asia, especially Babylonia, where astronomical records of phenomena such as eclipses had been kept for centuries from as early as 1600 BC, showed there was some regularity and predictability in the movements of the stars and planets.

The Search for Origins

Unlike the Babylonian recordkeepers, early Greek astronomers tried to find explanations for the celestial motions. They attempted to develop scientific models that not only would explain what had been observed but would predict future observations. Then as now, the same scientists who were interested in understanding the universe searched for its origins. Then as now, the search often took as its first axiom that at the beginning there was only one substance, or very few, out of which all matter evolved.

The earliest Greek scientists we know of lived in Miletus in the sixth century. Their thoughts have been transmitted to us because they were quoted by later Greek philosophers and scientists such as Aristotle. The Milesians were the first to abandon supernatural or religious explanations for natural phenomena and instead to seek purely physical causes. Thales, traditionally the first of the three great Milesians, was able to predict a solar eclipse and the solstices, thereby demonstrating that occultation of the sun and the length of days were not determined by divine whim. He also believed that the single origin of matter was water (for it could be transformed into both gas and solid forms), and that the earth was flat and floated on water. In contrast, his fellow Milesian, Anaximander, called the original principle "The Boundless," or "The Indefinite"; this limitless entity contained all matter, including such opposites as wet and dry and cold and hot. He postulated that the earliest creatures arose from slime warmed by the sun's heat, and he was also the first Greek to draw a geographical map. Another Milesian, Anaximenes, thought that everything had evolved from air: it became fire when it was rarefied, could change to wind and cloud, and when condensed was transformed into solid substances. Like Thales, Anaximenes believed that the earth was flat, but he thought that it floated on air.

Pythagoras, one of the most influential cosmologists, is familiar to us because of his discovery of the theorem that bears his name. He was born in Samos, but left around 531 BC because of the tyranny of Polycrates. Pythagoras settled in southern Italy and lived with a group of disciples. The original Pythagoreans and their successors followed strict rules in their daily lives. Women were included in the Pythagorean communities and were imbued with the philosophical doctrines that regulated the conduct of daily life. For example, the Pythagoreans observed many food taboos. They were strict vegetarians, for they believed in transmigration of the soul. Nevertheless, they were interested in worldly matters like politics and geometry. Geometry (literally "taking the measure of the earth") was a theoretical and practical science of special importance in the ancient world where land was the most valuable commodity: the founding of new cities included the careful measurement of land into plots of equal size and its distribution to colonists.

Pythagoras believed that arithmetic also held the key to understanding the universe. He postulated that the earth was a sphere in the center of a series of hollow spheres. The stars were fixed on the outer spherical shell, and the planets on smaller shells within. Each day the stellar sphere rotated from east to west while the planetary spheres rotated from west to east at various rates. Their movement created a sound, but since the sound is always with us, we are unable to hear it. The Pythagorean theory of the musical harmony of the heavenly spheres is an example of an attempt to find, or even to impose, an aesthetically pleasing mathematical explanation for the movement of celestial bodies. More than a century later Plato, who was much influenced by Pythagoreanism, also sought to explain the universe in terms of arithmetical abstractions and asserted that all celestial bodies move at the same rate in a circular path.

Document 3.4

Mortals made their gods, and furnished them
with their own body, voice, and garments.

If a horse or lion or a slow ox
had agile hands for paint and sculpture,
the horse would make his god a horse,
the ox would sculpt an ox.

Our gods have flat noses and black skins
say the Ethiopians. The Thracians say
our gods have red hair and hazel eyes.

Xenophanes fr. 12–14 Diehl; translated by Willis Barnstone, Greek Lyric
Poetry. *New York: Schocken, 1972, p. 131 adapted.*

Like Pythagoras, Xenophanes of Colophon (c. 550 BC) moved from the eastern Mediterranean to Magna Graecia where he traveled about as an exile. Fragments of his poems criticizing conventional religious and ethical beliefs are extant. Xenophanes' ideas about the development of the cosmos were based on personal observation. For example, when he noticed fossil imprints of marine life and seaweed in three different locations inland, he theorized that they were produced long ago when the earth was covered with the mud produced by a mixture of seawater and earth. An important characteristic of early Greek science is that ideas circulated widely through the writing of books. Because the city-states were nontheocratic, the early philosophers could freely criticize each other's theories. Heraclitus, who lived in Ephesus in the second half of the sixth century, was a fierce critic of Pythagoras and Xenophanes. Rejecting Pythagoras' world view that emphasized regularity and order, Heraclitus maintained that everything was constantly changing like a river: you can not step into the same river twice. The world consists not of one or more material substances but of processes governed by a principle Heraclitus calls "logos": a rational principle or statement that people must understand in order to understand the world in which they live. The world is not what it appears to be. The same idea was at the core of Parmenides' philosophy. He lived in the Greek colony Elea in southern Italy and wrote a poem in which he tried to analyze what it means to say that something is or exists. According to Parmenides, all you can say and think is that "being"exists but that "nonbeing" does not exist. Change is logically impossible because if something changes it is no longer the same and does not exist. For the rest of antiquity Greek philosophy struggled with these questions: What do we mean when we say that something exists, and what is the relationship between the world as we experience it and what it "really" is?

Some of the speculations of the Presocratics appear to be uncannily consistent with the hypotheses of modern cosmology. As we nowadays search distant planets for signs of life "as we know it" and delude ourselves that earth is the center of our galaxy when we view the pageant of the stars overhead, we can better understand the anthropocentric and geocentric arrogance of the Greeks and appreciate these early scientists who had no tools for exploration except their own intelligence.

RELATIONS BETWEEN STATES

With the emergence of the city-state, the external problem of coexistence became much more complicated and difficult than it had been in the prestate period. Despite many gaps in the historical record, it is evident that periodic warfare between neighboring states was common everywhere during the seventh and sixth centuries. As we shall see, solutions were sought to alleviate the tensions among states, and these were partially successful.

There were several reasons for the heightened tensions. As states began to run out of unoccupied land, they attempted to extend their boundaries. This caused disputes, usually over borderlands that had not required strict definition when populations were still small. Moreover, existing tensions between poleis in the motherland were extended to their colonies and were complicated by increasing trading competition. As a result, enmities were formed between city-states hundreds of miles apart. Relations were apt to be further strained because of the transference to the colonies of ancient antagonisms between large ethnic-linguistic groupings, especially the Ionians and Dorians. Legendary grievances going back to the Heroic Age frequently provided convenient pretexts for starting a quarrel.

On the mainland, where the impact of land scarcity was felt first, territorial wars began as early as the late eighth century. At that time, Chalcis and Eretria in Euboea fought over possession of the rich Lelantos River plain that lay between them. In the Lelantine War, as it is called, both sides were said to have had allies from much further away, a possible indication that it involved rival colonial networks.

How complex interstate relations could be is most clearly seen in the Peloponnesus, which contained three of the major Greek city-states—Sparta, Argos, and Corinth. After their conquest of Messenia in the late eighth century, the Spartans turned their attention to their other neighbors, the ethnos of Arcadia and the polis of Argos. In Arcadia they had little success; in Argos they did gain territory but against fierce resistance. They were badly beaten by the Argives, under the command of Pheidon, in a battle at Hysiae in the Argolis in 669. (It has been suggested that the Argive victory encouraged the revolt of the helotized Messenians in the Second Messenian War.) The Argives in the meantime were trying to expand their own land holdings and influence within the Peloponnesus, particularly in the Corinthian sphere; the Corinthians were doing the same to their smaller neighbor states of Megara and Sicyon. The two most powerful states, Argos and Sparta, continued to fight over territory until 547, when Sparta made its last big land gain at Argos' expense, a large disputed border area east of the Parnon range. Thereafter Spartan policy was to forego conquest and use diplomacy and alliances as a means of keeping their acknowledged supremacy in the Peloponnesus.

Diplomacy and Alliances

It was only in the sixth century that Greek states began in earnest to establish formal mechanisms designed to avoid war and promote cooperation and understanding among themselves. Almost all of these cooperative institutions had had their genesis in the prestate period, but they were refined and regularized during the later Archaic Age.

At the same time that formal means were being instituted, diplomatic relations were still being conducted much as they had been in the Dark Age, through personal relationships among the leading men. This was especially so in the tyrannies. Tyrants conducted foreign policy as sovereigns, making pacts of friendship or marriage alliances with other tyrants or with the top aristocrats. For example, Periander (c. 627–587), who succeeded his father Cypselus as tyrant of Corinth, developed a political friendship with Thrasybulus, tyrant of Miletus, which ended an old enmity between the two poleis going back to the Lelantine War. Their pact aided Corinthian traders in Egypt and the Black Sea and Milesian traders in the West. Periander was also asked by Athens and Mytilene to arbitrate a dispute over control of Sigeum, an important way station on the route to the Black Sea.

Personal diplomacy became institutionalized in the form of "proxeny," whereby a resident of one city-state acted as a semiofficial representative of the interests of another. Proxeny was a formalized version of the Dark Age institution of "guest-friendship" (*xenia*), observed in Homer. As we saw in Chapter 2, when Agamemnon and Menelaus came to Ithaca to recruit Odysseus and his followers for the Trojan War, they stayed at the house of their *xenos*, or "guest-friend," at Ithaca while they conducted their embassy. In the Archaic version, when an Athenian, say, came to Corinth on some public or private business, the *proxenos* of the Athenians at Corinth would aid him in his mission.

Temporary military alliances between communities, both offensive and defensive, were as old as war. In the Archaic period they became more formal and longer lasting. States began to make written treaties, pledging friendship and nonaggression for a stipulated time. The earliest formal pact we know of is on an inscription dating to around 550, between the polis of Sybaris in southern Italy, its allies, and another polis. It reads: "The Sybarites and their allies and the Serdaioi made an agreement for friendship, faithful and without guile, for ever. Guarantors, Zeus, Apollo, and the other gods, and the *polis* of Poseidonia" (Meiggs and Lewis, 1989, p. 10).

There also came into existence several types of multistate alliances or leagues. One was the amphictyony or "associations of neighbors," in which several independent city-states cooperated to maintain and protect a common sanctuary of a god. These associations may have gone far back in time, although we know of them only from the sixth century on, when they had taken on a more political character than merely protecting the common sanctuary. Although an amphictyony did not prevent its members from warring against one another, at least it mitigated hostility. Member states might pledge, for example, not to destroy each other's cities or cut off their water supply.

It was also in the sixth century that *ethnē* began to form loose unions of their separate towns and villages for the purposes of foreign relations and warfare. These differed from the amphictyonies in that they had an overarching governing body for coordinating communal action. Nevertheless, the authority of central governments over the independent entities would remain relatively feeble until the creation in the fourth century of true "federal states."

One of the most successful federations in the Archaic period was that of the ethnos of Thessaly. As early as the seventh century this vast, rich northern region was loosely united for military action under the headship of a war leader, called either *archon* ("leader") or *tagos* ("military commander"). Thessalian unity allowed them to become the major power of northern Greece for a period of time in the sixth century, until the confederacy was weakened by quarrels among the local chiefs. The ethnos of the Phocians, under pressure from the unified Thessalians, quickly developed a federal union of their own in the sixth century, complete with their own federation coinage and army. Similarly, the need for some unity against both Thessalian and Athenian pressure at this time prompted the rival poleis of Boeotia to form a confederacy under the leadership of Thebes. This early Boeotian league, too, proved fractious and unstable, because of opposition by the other city-states to Theban hegemony.

The mid-sixth century also saw the first of the mega-alliances, the Peloponnesian League created by Sparta. The history of the fifth century would be shaped by the rivalry and then the hatred between the Spartans and the Athenians. They would conduct their wars and diplomatic skirmishes as the hegemons of two huge alliances, the Peloponnesian and Delian leagues respectively, which together comprised most of the Greek world.

PANHELLENIC INSTITUTIONS

The ease with which poets, thinkers, artists, and ideas moved from city to city across the wide expanse of Greek occupation is a token of how culturally unified the Greek world was even as it remained politically divided. The Panhellenic gatherings played a most important role in shaping the concept of the cultural unity of all Greeks.

All the Panhellenic sanctuaries increased greatly in popularity and prestige in the seventh and sixth centuries. Ever greater numbers of people came to worship, consult oracles, and participate in or attend musical and athletic competitions. The two biggest attractions were the sanctuaries of Zeus at Olympia and of Apollo at Delphi. By the end of the seventh century, the quadrennial games in honor of Zeus were drawing spectators and contestants to Olympia from the entire Greek world. Shortly thereafter three new Panhellenic games were instituted at other sanctuaries: the Pythian games for Apollo at Delphi (582 BC), the Isthmian games for Poseidon near Corinth (581), and the Nemean games for Zeus at Argos (573). The new games were integrated into the four-year Olympiad so as to form an athletic "circuit" (*periodos*). The festivals were staggered so that there would be one major game every year, two in alternate years, with the Olympics remaining the premier event.

Well before the inauguration of the Pythian games, the oracle of Apollo at Delphi was far famed, drawing both Greeks and non-Greeks from all over the Mediterranean world. For a fairly hefty cost in obligatory sacrifices an individual could consult Apollo for advice on personal matters (marriage, careers, voyages, divine favor, etc.). City-states also consulted the god, seeking his guidance and sanction on important questions such as colonizing, religion, and laws. Apollo's answers came through a priestess, called the Pythia, who became possessed by the god and in a trance uttered the messages she received from Apollo. These were put into coherent (though frequently ambiguous) form by "interpreters" (*prophētai*), who gave their responses in hexameter verse. Because so many tyrants, foreign kings, and aristocratic leaders consulted the oracle, the sanctuary became a storehouse of information about political conditions in the wide world.

The Panhellenic contests and rituals fostered the idea of Greekness, of sharing the same language, religion, customs, and values. Indeed, they had the avowed purpose of knitting together the Greeks in peaceful celebration. During the Olympic games, for example, a sacred truce banning war throughout the Greek world was declared for the month in which the games were held. On the other hand, the athletic contests, the *agōnes* (from which we derive agonistic and antagonist) were viewed as competitions not only between individuals but also between states, much as they are today. The sacred precincts themselves became places for poleis to boast of their wealth and achievements with dedications of statues and costly stone and marble "treasuries" in commemoration of contest winners or of military victories by the polis.

There were no team events, only individual contests. Thus, the games kept alive the ancient ideal of the individual hero: to be declared best (*aristos*) by gaining victory over a worthy opponent. The content and spirit of the Panhellenic games had changed little from the games described in the *Iliad*. The events still tested speed, strength, dexterity, and endurance, precisely the qualities desired in a Homeric warrior.

Of the several foot races the most prestigious was the short sprint, called the stade (*stadion*, hence stadium) a distance of about 210 yards; at Olympia the winner of the stade race was listed first in the summary of all victors. At the end of the sixth century a new race run by contestants in full armor was inaugurated, in recognition of hoplite fighting. Other standard events at the games were wrestling, boxing, and the *pankration*, a vicious combination of boxing and wrestling with no holds barred except biting and eye gouging. There was also a track-and-field event, the *pentathlon*, combining five contests: the stade, javelin and discus throws, the long jump, and wrestling. In addition there were equestrian events, the most spectacular of which was the four-horse chariot race, a contest dating back to the Late Bronze Age. The winner of the chariot races and the horse races was not the charioteer or the jockey but the wealthy horse owner.

Separate sets of contests were held for boys (under age 20) and for men. Women did not compete at the major games, nor probably were they permitted to attend as spectators, although later at Olympia there was a stade race for girls in honor of Hera. The prizes were just tokens of glory, wreaths of foliage: at Olympia olive leaves, at Pythia laurel, at Nemea wild celery, and at Isthmia pine. (Much more substantial prizes were offered at the several less prestigious Panhellenic games that sprang up during the sixth century at Athens, Thebes, and elsewhere.) On their return home, however, victors reaped lavish rewards: triumphal processions, civic honors, statues, and even prizes of money. At the Pythian games and a number of other festivals there were also competitions and prizes in choral and solo poetry and in musical performances.

*   *   *

At the beginning of the Archaic period (c. 750 BC) the Greeks were still a relatively isolated and economically backward people, organized politically into low-level chiefdoms. By the late sixth century they had a culturally advanced state-society that spread across the entire Mediterranean zone and were major players in the complex international market economy.

The supreme political achievement of the Archaic Age Greeks was the polis, which in the course of the period evolved from narrow oligarchy to tyranny to a more broadly based polity in which the majority of its members participated in its governance. Because the people and not just the elite had a stake in the polis, the sense of loyalty and dedication to the "commonality of citizens," as Aristotle called the polis, was profound. It was this polis-citizen bond that made the Greek city-state unlike any other form of state in the ancient world. This fierce loyalty translated into a deep conviction that no persons from outside the state could be allowed to violate its independence.

Civic pride was the cement of the city-state and was largely responsible for the cultural flowering of the Archaic period. The Greeks' passion for autarchy, however, was a permanently divisive force, which in the second half of the fifth century would cause the poleis to exhaust themselves in the great Peloponnesian War between the Spartans and the Athenians and their allies. That would be the start of the slow decline of the polis as an autonomous political unit. But at the beginning of the fifth century, the Greek states were at the height of their prideful independence and had no inkling that their unyielding self-interest would drive them into such a calamitous war.

Yet, in a seeming paradox, the growing awareness during the Archaic period of a shared Greekness (what the historian Herodotus called *to hellēnikon*, "the Greek thing") also gave rise to a strong cultural identity and sense of kinship. The shining moment of Panhellenic solidarity would come in the early fifth century when the Greek poleis subordinated their individual loyalties to unite against the attempts of the Persian empire to conquer Greece. In the Persian wars (490–479) the Greeks would equate the freedom of their individual city-states with the "freedom of the Greeks" against the "slavery" of the Persian "tyrant."

The glow of Panhellenic unity would soon fade, however, and for the next century and a half the poleis and ethne of Greece would continue in their old ways, despite a growing realization among many observers that wars of Greeks against Greeks were tantamount to civil war within a city-state. For most of that period diplomatic and military activity would center on the two great powers of Sparta and Athens.

TRANSLATIONS

Barnstone, Willis. 1972. *Greek Lyric Poetry.* New York: Schocken.

Blanco, Walter. 1998. *The Peloponnesian War,* from *Thucydides: The Peloponnesian War,* Walter Blanco and Jennifer Roberts, eds. New York: W.W. Norton.

Fowler, Barbara Hughes. 1992. *Archaic Greek Poetry.* Madison: University of Wisconsin Press.

Meiggs, Russell and David Lewis. 1989. *A Selection of Greek Historical Inscriptions to the End of the Fifth Century BC*. Oxford: Clarendon Press.

Miller, Andrew M. 1996. *Greek Lyric*. Indianapolis: Hackett.

Rackham, H. 1977. *Aristotle: Politics*. Loeb Classical Library. Cambridge, Mass. and London: Harvard University Press.

SUGGESTED READINGS

Andrewes, A. 1956. *The Greek Tyrants*. New York: Harper & Row. Though written more than a generation ago, it remains the best introduction to the *tyrannoi*.

Boardman, John. 1974. *Athenian Black Figure Vases*. London: Oxford University Press.

Boardman, John. 1975. *Athenian Red Figure Vases: The Archaic Period*. London: Oxford University Press.

Boardman, John. 1978. *Greek Sculpture: The Archaic Period*. London: Oxford University Press. These three volumes make up a valuable set of handbooks on Greek art of the Archaic period, lavishly illustrated, with concise and informative commentary.

Easterling, P. E. and B. M. W. Knox (eds.). 1985. *The Cambridge History of Classical Literature. Volume I, Part 1: Early Greek Poetry*. Cambridge, Eng.: Cambridge University Press. Up-to-date articles on Hesiod and the lyric poets, with abundant bibliography.

Hanson, Victor Davis. 1995. *The Other Greeks: The Family Farm and the Agrarian Roots of Western Civilization*. New York: The Free Press. A wide-ranging, meticulously detailed study of the "yeoman" farmer-hoplite and his role in the formation of the city-state.

Mitchell, Lynette G. and P. J. Rhodes (eds.). 1997. *The Development of the Polis in Archaic Greece*. London and New York: Routledge. An up-to-date collection of articles on various aspects of the development of the Greek city-state.

Snodgrass, Anthony. 1980. *Archaic Greece. The Age of Experiment*. Berkeley and Los Angeles: University of California Press. The first major book on Archaic Greece written by an archaeologist, and an important reappraisal of the importance of the Archaic period to Greek history.

Starr, Chester G. 1977. *The Economic and Social Growth of Early Greece: 800–500 B.C.* New York: Oxford University Press. A comprehensive study of the economic and social evolution of the Greek city-states in the Archaic period, which pays special attention to the class divisions and tensions of the times.

Tandy, David W. and Walter C. Neale (eds.). 1996. *Hesiod's Works and Days. A Translation and Commentary for the Social Sciences*. Berkeley and Los Angeles: University of California Press. A specialized commentary incorporating the perspectives of sociologists, anthropologists, and social economists.

4

SPARTA

Admired in peace and dreaded in war, for much of the Archaic and Classical periods Sparta was the most powerful city in the Greek world. It was also different from other *poleis*. To be sure, the Spartans shared many basic institutions with other Greeks: their society was patriarchal and polytheistic, servile labor played a key role, and agriculture formed the basis of the economy. As elsewhere in Greece, law was revered and martial valor prized. Nonetheless, Sparta was unique in many important ways. No other Greek state ever defined its goals as clearly as Sparta or expended so much effort in trying to attain them. While the intrusion of the state into the lives of individuals was substantial in all Greek states, no state surpassed Sparta in the invasive role it played in the daily lives of its citizens. Spartans took enormous pride in their *polis*, and other Greeks were impressed by the rigorous patriotism and selflessness the Spartan system entailed. The Spartans' extreme denial of individuality fostered a powerful sense of belonging that other Greeks envied, and Sparta continues to cast an eerie spell over historians, philosophers, and political scientists even in an age that tends to recoil from totalitarianism.

SOURCES FOR SPARTAN HISTORY AND INSTITUTIONS

Despite the interest the Spartans sparked in their contemporaries, it is surprisingly difficult to write the history of Sparta and of its surrounding territory, Laconia. The problem is not lack of sources. Though unfortunately all the sources concentrate on upper-class and royal Spartiates and provide little information about the majority of the population of the territory of Laconia—the servile masses known as helots and the large disfranchised free class known as *perioikoi*—still the volume of ancient writing on Sparta is large. In the course of their narratives on Greek history, the two greatest Greek historians, Herodotus and Thucydides, reveal a great deal about Spartan history, but the bulk of our information comes from two authors who wrote works focusing specifically on Archaic and Classical Sparta: Xenophon and Plutarch.

Xenophon was born in Athens around 430 BC, and he knew the Spartans at first hand. With other young men Xenophon left Greece in 401 to serve as a mercenary in the army of Cyrus the Younger, pretender to the Persian throne. In the course of this expedition and subsequent campaigns in Asia he became acquainted with many Spartans including the king Agesilaus II, whom he came greatly to admire. In the late 390s, with Athens and Sparta at war, Xenophon was exiled by the Athenians for having favored the Spartans. Relocating in the Peloponnesus, he wrote a treatise called the *Spartan Constitution*. Since Xenophon was an eyewitness and knew many leading Spartans personally, his work is our best source for Spartan social, political, and military institutions, although his admiration of Spartan institutions as they were said to have been before his time may have influenced his account.

A similar enthusiasm marks the writings of Plutarch, who lived from 46 to 120 AD, a thousand years after the earliest events at Sparta that he describes. He was a Greek living in a Roman world, since by his day his native Boeotia had been incorporated into the Roman empire. Plutarch's writings on Sparta, more than those of any other ancient author, have shaped later views of Sparta, but Plutarch was a biographer and a philosopher of ethics, not a historian. His works on Sparta include five biographies: the lives of Lycurgus, Lysander, Agesilaus, Agis, and Cleomenes (the latter two combined in a single essay). The *Sayings of Spartans* and the *Sayings of Spartan Women* are also included among Plutarch's works. Despite the centuries that separated him from the people he depicted, Plutarch's work is of value since he visited Sparta and also read books that are now lost or survive only in fragments. Although his writings contain large quantities of information, Plutarch was influenced by histories written after the decline of Sparta and marked by nostalgia for a happier past, real or imagined.

The problem, therefore, is not so much the quantity of information about Sparta as the fact that our sources are tainted by their acceptance of an idealized image of Sparta that historians call the "Spartan mirage." This idea of Sparta was a vision of an egalitarian and orderly society characterized by selfless patriotism, superhuman tolerance for deprivation, and boundless courage in battle. (Such propaganda, which had an important core of truth, also won Sparta a position of leadership among the Greeks.) As Spartans did not write historical literature before the Hellenistic period, this view of Spartan invincibility must have been disseminated orally at first and in literature written by non-Spartans. Even Sparta's laws were preserved in memory rather than committed to writing. Except for some fragmentary lyric verse by the seventh-century poets Alcman and Tyrtaeus, our literary evidence for Sparta was created by outsiders who wrote well after many of the events they described and whose work was to some extent shaped by their enormous admiration for Sparta. In many ways the fictions that surrounded the Spartans are as interesting as the reality they sought to represent, but though fiction and reality are difficult to separate, they should not be confused.

Unfortunately, archaeological evidence has only limited ability to remedy the deficiencies of our written sources. In commenting on the need for historians not to be deceived by superficial impressions, the Athenian historian Thucydides observed that:

> If, for example, Sparta were to be deserted and only the temples and the foundations of the buildings remained, I imagine that people in the distant future would seriously doubt that Sparta's power ever approached its fame. . . . The Spartans never developed one metropolitan area or built lavish temples and buildings but rather live in scattered settlements in the old-fashioned Greek way.
>
> *(Thuc. 1.10; Blanco 1998)*

The calculated austerity of Spartan life meant that domestic dwellings were extremely simple, even by Greek standards. This is bad news for archaeologists. Furthermore, modern Sparta has not been the subject of extensive excavation as has Athens, where the efforts of scholars as well as haphazard finds due to the construction of subways and the expansion of the capital city of Greece have led to major discoveries. In Sparta, public construction was limited to a few government buildings, gymnasiums, and temples, and for our knowledge of most of these we are currently dependent less on excavations than on the descriptions of Pausanias, who wrote a guide to Greece in the second century AD. Inscriptions concerning public or private matters are likewise scarce. Even tombstones, which are ubiquitous in the rest of the Greek world, are rare; at Sparta only men who had died in battle or women who had died in childbirth were permitted to have inscribed epitaphs. Because lavish grave offerings were also forbidden, archaeologists have not unearthed the quantities of pottery, mirrors, weapons, and personal items that have been discovered in other parts of the Greek world and exploited in historical research. The only exception is a large number of votive offerings made of clay, amber, lead, bronze, gold, silver, and ivory dating from as early as the early seventh century and continuing through Roman times. These have been found at the site of the temple of Artemis Orthia ("Upright" or "Protector of the ordering of the life cycle"). Understandably, these rich finds from the earliest period of the sanctuary are important for the evaluation of Spartan culture, for they prove conclusively that in the early Archaic period the Spartans were on a par artistically and commercially with their neighbor states in the Peloponnesus. It was only later, in the course of the sixth century, that the famed Spartan austerity made art and other cultural refinements a very low priority.

The number of offerings to Artemis was enormous: over 100,000 separate items have been recovered. This material record is witness to the central role of her cult in religious and civic life. Ritual ceremonies enacted in the precinct of Artemis Orthia appear to have revolved around the passage of Spartan men and women through the key stages of their lives. Choruses of girls sang and danced at the presentation of a new robe for the statue of Artemis, an occasion that probably also celebrated the passage of their age group from girlhood to womanhood. Plaques depicting textiles may likewise have been dedicated at the time when women passed from one life stage to another. There were also dedications to Eileithyia, the spirit of childbirth and protector of young boys and girls. The many lead figurines of hoplite soldiers probably marked the graduation of young men to the status of warriors.

THE DARK AGE AND THE ARCHAIC PERIOD

Despite all these obstacles, painstaking research throughout the past two centuries has made it possible to trace the broad outlines of Spartan history. Laconia was an important center in the Bronze Age. Archaeological evidence indicates that there was a large settlement at Therapne east of the Eurotas, with shrines to King Menelaus and his wife Helen. Like much of the rest of Greece, Laconia experienced a sharp drop in population at the end of the Mycenaean period. Most of the settlements that had been inhabited during the second millennium BC were abandoned, and the popularity of cattle and sheep figurines as dedications in sanctuaries in the region suggest that stock raising became a mainstay of the local economy. Sometime in the tenth century BC Dorian newcomers entered the territory. By the eighth century BC trends similar to those documented elsewhere in Greece had begun to appear in Laconia as well. New villages were founded as population gradually increased, and four of those villages near the Eurotas River in the center of the Laconian plain united to form the city of Sparta. Early in the eighth century the town of Amyclae, 3 miles from the original four villages, was added to the city. Thus the Spartan polis was the city center plus the territory of the plain. Increased contacts with the rest of Greece were reflected in the emergence of a distinctive Spartan version of geometric art.

Like other early Greek poleis, Sparta (or Lacedaemon, as it was often called in antiquity) began to experience difficulties in satisfying its needs from its own territory. Sparta was located inland, with the nearest port, Gythium, 27 miles to the south. This atypical location encouraged the city to seek a novel solution to the need for land to feed a growing population, a solution that would determine the course of future Spartan development. Unlike other Archaic Greek cities, which repeatedly founded colonies overseas in an effort to alleviate the pressure on resources caused by population expansion, the Spartans founded only one colony, Taras in southern Italy. Instead of looking abroad for a solution to their difficulties, the Spartans sought a military answer to their problem through conquest of their neighbors, and by the end of the eighth century, they had gained control of the whole of the Laconian plain. The details of how this was accomplished are lost, but the results can be detected in the social structure of historical Sparta.

Helots and the Social Hierarchy

Sparta primarily needed to support its population. Consequently, to ensure control of the Laconian plain, its inhabitants were reduced to the status of helots, hereditary subjects of the Spartan state. The rest of the inhabitants of

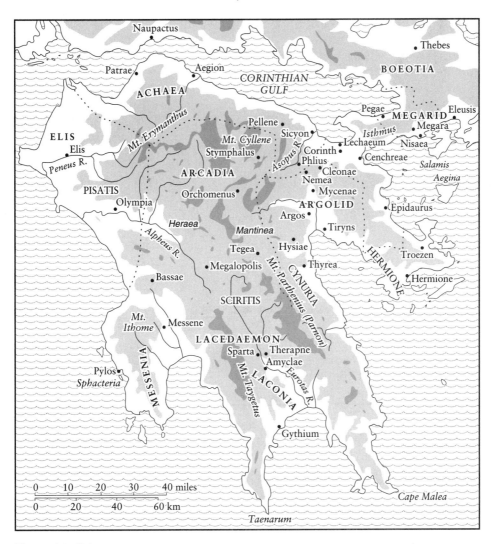

Figure 4.1. Peloponnesus.

Laconia, who occupied the area surrounding the city of Sparta, became *peri-oikoi* ("those who dwell around [Sparta]," or "neighbors"). Little was written about them in antiquity. Unlike the helots, who were in essence slaves, the perioikoi remained free. Despite the fact that they were obligated to serve in the Spartan army in their own units under a Spartan commander, and did so in large numbers, they were not permitted to participate in the Spartan government. They did enjoy some local autonomy, however, and in many ways lived like the majority of Greeks who were not Spartans, working as farmers, crafts-men, and merchants. Thus, despite their name, which implies that the perioikoi were peripheral, they constituted an essential part of the Spartan economic system.

Success only whetted Sparta's appetite for expansion, and this expansion in turn increased the institution of helotry significantly. As a result, early in the conquest of neighboring regions the helots outnumbered Spartan citizens by a ratio that may have been at least as high as seven to one. This phenomenon would play a dramatic role in the evolution of the Spartan way of life. As a result of the conquest of Laconia, the western reaches of Spartan territory abutted on those of another emerging Dorian state, Messenia. Dorian solidarity proved to be an ideal invoked by the Spartans only when it suited their interests. The Spartans coveted the fertile Messenian lowlands, and at some time in the third quarter of the eighth century they invaded Messenia, beginning what modern historians call the First Messenian War. The fighting centered around the formidable natural fortress of Mount Ithome in northern Messenia. The details of the war itself are lost. Tradition, however, made the war last twenty years and placed its conclusion about 720 BC. This dating is corroborated by the disappearance of Messenians from the Olympic victor list about that time. If the course of the First Messenian War is unclear, its results are not: Messenia became subject to Sparta. Like the Laconians, some of the Messenians became perioikoi, but most became helots, bound to their land and obliged to work it for their Spartan masters with no consolation but the promise that they would not be sold out of Messenia. The Spartan poet Tyrtaeus gloatingly described them as "burdened like asses, bringing to their masters under harsh compulsion one half . . . of the fruits of the land" (fr. 6 West).

The conquest of Laconia and Messenia made Sparta one of the largest of all Archaic Greek states, controlling an empire of over 3000 square miles (about three times the size of the Athenian state). Compared with Athens Sparta was never densely populated, and some centers of habitation were quite remote. Sparta was also one of the richest states. Spartan pottery and metalwork were among the finest in Greece. The beauty of Spartan women was widely celebrated, and Sparta's female choruses were famous. A vivid impression of the wealth and elegance of Spartan life is provided by a few surviving fragments of the works of the seventh-century-BC poet Alcman, whose hymns, written for choruses of unmarried Spartan girls to sing on ceremonial occasions, mention luxury items including racehorses, purple textiles, and gold jewelry in the shape of serpents.

> . . .
> For all the purple dye we have
> won't help at all,
> nor a dazzling serpent
> all of gold, nor Lydian cap, the pride
> of tender-glancing girls,
> nor even the locks of Nanno,
> nor god-like Areta,
> nor Thylakis, nor Kleesithera,

and no longer coming to Ainesimbrota's house will you say:
"if only Astaphis were mine,
or Philylla would look my way,
or Demareta, or lovely Vianthemis—
but Hagesichora wears me out with desire."
(fr. 1.65–78 Alcman; Bing and Cohen 1991)

Spartan prosperity, however, rested on insecure foundations. In the immediate aftermath of the First Messenian War, though civil unrest was probably a serious problem in the late eighth and early seventh centuries, civil war over the division of the conquered territory was avoided by exiling the dissidents, who founded Sparta's only colony, Taras. The growing desperation of the Messenians was a more serious threat. Greek political theorists considered it a mistake to enslave people in their own home territory, especially when the enslaved significantly outnumbered their masters, as the Messenians did the Spartans. Not surprisingly, the Messenians rebelled in the wake of a major Spartan military defeat by the Argives at the Battle of Hysiae in the early 660s BC.

As is true of the First Messenian War, little is known of the details of the Second Messenian War. The poems Tyrtaeus wrote celebrating Spartan courage in the war became Sparta's classics:

> Here is a man who proves himself to be valiant in war.
> With a sudden rush he turns to flight the rugged battalions
>   of the enemy, and sustains the beating waves of assault.
> And he who so falls among the champions and loses his sweet life,
>   so blessing with honor his city, his father, and all his people,
> with wounds in his chest, where the spear that he was facing has
>   transfixed
>   that massive guard of his shield, and gone through his breastplate
>   as well,
> why, such a man is lamented alike by the young and the elders,
>   and all his city goes into mourning and grieves for his loss.
> *(Tyrtaeus fr. 9 Diehl; Lattimore 1960)*

In the end Sparta prevailed, and the surviving Messenian rebels were exiled to Sicily. There they eventually gained control of the city of Zancle, which they renamed Messene. As for the rest of the Messenians, they had no choice but to resign themselves to the rigors of their former helot status.

The Second Messenian War had been a terrifying revelation of the potential risks of the helot system, and the possibility of a repetition haunted the imaginations of Spartans and their enemies. One certain way of avoiding such a catastrophe, abandoning Messenia, was unthinkable. Consequently, the Spartans were forced to find another way to preserve their domination over their helots and the prosperity it brought. The solution they found was drastic, and its implementation gradually transformed Sparta and eventually created the unique regimented society known to us from the Classical sources. Simply stated, the

Spartans realized that if all potential hoplites could be mobilized and trained to the highest degree of skill possible, Sparta would enjoy an overwhelming military advantage over its helots and other enemies. Therefore the Spartans reformed their institutions with a view toward achieving two goals: freeing male citizens of the five villages that constituted the polis of Sparta from all but military obligations, and socializing them to accept the extraordinary regimentation and discipline required of a Spartan soldier. Until the fourth century and the Hellenistic period, the Spartans were the only real professional soldiers. In effect they waged a perpetual war against the helots and were consequently always prepared to engage in other acts of aggression when necessary.

THE SPARTAN SYSTEM

Little is known about the actual development of the Spartan system. Greek historians followed Spartan tradition and ascribed its creation to Lycurgus, a shadowy figure who may or may not really have lived. Thucydides dates Lycurgus' reforms to the end of the ninth century BC; other Greek historians place him as early as the tenth. In that case, he would have lived before the conquest of Messenia and his reforms could not have been an attempt to deal with the problems that arose in the eighth and seventh centuries. Scholars today are agreed that many of the institutions whose creation Greeks credited to Lycurgus, such as men's dining groups, organization of the population by age cohorts, and the use of iron money, had, in fact, once existed in other Greek communities. They survived at Sparta because their place in Spartan life had been redefined to aid in the production of the ideal Spartan hoplite.

However this evolution occurred, the evidence indicates that the main features of the Spartan system were in place by the end of the seventh or the early sixth century BC. According to Plutarch, Lycurgus found the model for many of these features when he visited Crete. The Great Rhetra ("Statement"), said to have been given to Lycurgus by the Delphic oracle, was in existence early in the Archaic period, perhaps by the eighth or the beginning of the seventh century. This Rhetra— at least as preserved in Plutarch—deals only with military and political issues, such as the meetings and sovereignty of the citizens' assembly. The Rhetra includes the following provisions:

> After dedicating a temple to Zeus . . . and Athena . . . , forming *phylai* [tribes] and creating *obai* [divisions relating to the distinction between the five villages], and instituting a Gerousia of thirty including the kings, then hold an Apella from time to time. Thus bring in and set aside [proposals]. The people are to have the right to respond, and power. . . . But if the people speak crookedly, the elders and kings are to be setters-aside.

The Spartan regime may be called totalitarian, for it touched on almost every aspect of life, including those we in modern western society consider private: how to wear our hair, the choice of whether and when to marry, the conditions of conjugal intercourse, and the decision whether to rear a child.

The Education and Upbringing of Boys

As the poetry of Tyrtaeus made plain, the Spartan ideal for a man was to be skilled and courageous in battle, neither to run away nor surrender but to stand his ground and give up his life for his city. Training was designed to produce men who conformed to this pattern alone. The Spartan was liable for military service to the age of 60 and needed to stay fit; hence he never was trained for any other profession or way of life. The educational system, like much else that was unique to Sparta, received legitimacy from the insistence that it was created by Lycurgus.

The process of creating invincible warriors began at birth, for the state took upon itself the right to determine a new baby's viability. Whereas other Greek poleis left the choice to the father, at Sparta officials appointed by the government examined the newborns. The vitality of male infants and their potential as soldiers determined whether they would be raised, or abandoned in a place near Mount Taygetus designated for that purpose. (Female babies, apparently, were not subjected to official scrutiny, for their physical prowess did not directly affect the outcome of battles.) Fathers did not decide how to raise their sons. Rather, all boys received the same education under state supervision. Education in Sparta, as elsewhere, was organized by age groups: children, boys, youths (ephebes), young men, and adults. From the age of 7, boys left home to be trained in groups called herds according to principles designed to encourage conformity, obedience, group solidarity, and military skills.

The emphasis in the boys' education was not on reading, writing, and the liberal arts, but rather on practicing to endure hardships and to fend for themselves as would be necessary when they became hoplite soldiers. To toughen their feet, they went barefoot, and they often went naked as well. When they were 12, their hair was cut short. They never wore a tunic and were each allocated only one cloak yearly to wear in all kinds of weather. Unlike the rest of the Greeks, who made war only in the summer, the Spartans were perpetually at war with the helots and therefore needed to be prepared to fight year round. Magistrates called ephors ("overseers") inspected the boys daily and examined them in the nude every ten days. The boys slept in groups on rough mats that they had made themselves. To develop cunning and self-reliance, they were encouraged to supplement their food rations by stealing. Whipping awaited anyone who revealed his lack of skill by getting caught.

The harsh toughening process was ritually enacted at the altar of Artemis Orthia every year. One group of youths would try to steal cheese off the outdoor altar which was defended by a group of older youths with whips; blood was supposed to splatter on the altar. It is a sad irony of history that what began as a solemn test of manliness, witnessed only by the goddess and the community, attracted tourists in Roman times. The show was so popular that in the third century AD a stone theater was built in the sacred precinct. Sightseers could view the spectacle of Spartan youths exhibiting their legendary endurance of pain without flinching or crying out as they were brutally flogged, sometimes to death, in front of the altar, egged on by the priestess of Artemis holding a statue of the goddess. In old Sparta, competition was also encouraged in the form of athletic contests and other public displays of prowess, but a spirit of cooperation was considered essential as well, and it was instilled by forming groups of boys and creating rivalries between them.

These group activities served to identify the most talented among the youths and to prepare them to become leaders in the army. From the ages of 14 to 20 the ephebes performed their preliminary military service. At 20 they grew their hair long (unlike men in other parts of the Greek world) and shaved themselves in the distinctive Spartan style—a long beard and no moustache. Between ages 20 and 30 they were permitted to marry but had to continue to live with their army groups until the age of 30.

Acceptance into a *syssition* ("dining group," "messes") was an essential stage in reaching adulthood. The Spartan man ate his meals with about fifteen members of his army group, an experience that fostered the loyalty, solidarity, and cooperativeness essential to successful hoplite warfare. Each member of the syssition was obliged to contribute a fixed quantity of food and drink, but the wealthier soldiers could supplement the menu by providing such items as better grain than was required, or meat from animals they had hunted or sacrificed. The Spartan ideal of austerity dictated that the cuisine be nutritious and served in portions that were adequate but hardly generous. In some cases, small portions may have been a blessing. The staple of the common mess appears to have been a dish known as black broth. Composed of pork cooked in blood and seasoned with vinegar and salt, black broth was apparently an acquired taste, and the few foreigners who made their way to Sparta were repelled by it.

Figure 4.2. "Laconian Rider." Cup depicting rider on horseback, water birds, and a winged demon or figure of Victory.

The *syssitia* (plural) were in some ways analogous to the *symposia* ("drinking parties") enjoyed by Greeks elsewhere, but the fact that the Spartan was purposely schooled to drink in moderation points to an important difference. Though Greeks usually mixed their wine with water, helots were brought in and forced to consume undiluted wine and to perform vulgar and ridiculous songs and dances. Young Spartans, who were invited to the syssitia as part of their education, were encouraged to laugh at the spectacle of the drunken helots. The lesson was a double one: from this experience youths were expected to learn both to be wary of drinking to excess—for inebriation could lead to death in conditions of perpetual warfare—and to view the helots as pathetic creatures, patently inferior to the Spartan soldiery. In this way the older Spartans reinforced the young in their sense of a yawning gulf between themselves and the helots, and headed off any qualms about treating helots as subhuman.

Inevitably, the success rate in forging soldiers according to the prescribed mold was less than 100 percent. Though the harsh treatment of those perceived as cowards discouraged failure, the system did not work on everyone, and some boys failed to develop as expected. Since martial valor offered the sole path to the honor and respect of one's peers, life was wretched for boys who were unable to cope with the rigors of military life. When cowards were identified they were stigmatized and called "tremblers." Their ridiculous appearance announced their disgrace: they were obliged to wear cloaks with colored patches and to shave only half their beards. Mocked and humiliated in public, they were despised even by their own kinsmen, whom they were believed to have dishonored. They could not hold public office, nor was it likely that a woman would be given to them in marriage or that anyone would marry their sisters.

Becoming a Spartan Woman

Sparta's military ethos had implications for females as well as males. Just as boys were brought up to become brave fighters, girls were raised to bear stalwart soldiers-to-be. Spartans were the only Greek women whose upbringing was prescribed by the state and who were educated at state expense. Unlike other Greek females, who spent most of their time indoors and were regularly given less food than men, Spartan females exercised outside and were well nourished. Childbearing was their only social obligation. Though, like all Greek women, they did know how to weave, like Spartan men they were free from the obligation to engage in any form of domestic or money-making labor.

Specific lines of development were prescribed for Spartan girls much as they were for boys. The educational system for girls was also organized according to age classes. We are aware of fewer stages than marked the corresponding system we have described for boys; perhaps there really were fewer or, as is usually the case in the study of ancient history, perhaps we simply have less information about female activities. Girls were divided into the categories of children, young

Figure 4.3. Bronze statuette of a seminude Spartan girl running, wearing a racing dress (c. 500 BC).

girls, maidens who had reached puberty, and married women. Hairstyles distinguished maidens from the newly married women, for the latter (unlike adult women in other parts of the Greek world) wore their hair short. As with so much else in their way of life, Spartans ascribed the customary upbringing of Spartan girls to Lycurgus:

Document 4.1 Excerpt from Plutarch's *Life of Lygurgus* Plutarch's admiration for Sparta is revealed in his account of the institutions traditionally associated with Lycurgus.

First he toughened the girls physically by making them run and wrestle and throw the discus and javelin. Thereby their children in embryo would make a strong start in strong bodies and would develop better, while the women themselves would also bear their pregnancies with vigor and would meet the challenge of childbirth in a successful, relaxed way. He did away with prudery, sheltered upbringing, and effeminacy of any kind. He made young girls no less than young men grow used to walking nude in processions, as well as to dancing and singing at certain festivals with the young men present and looking on. On some occasions the girls would make fun of each of the young men, helpfully criticizing their mistakes. On other occasions they would rehearse in song the praises which they had composed about those meriting them, so that they filled the youngsters with a great sense of ambition and rivalry. . . .

There was nothing disreputable about the girls' nudity. It was altogether modest, and there was no hint of immorality. Instead it encouraged simple habits and an enthusiasm for physical fitness, as well as giving the female sex a taste of masculine gallantry, since it too was granted equal participation in both excellence and ambition. As a result the women came to talk as well as to think in the way that Leonidas' wife Gorgo is said to have done. For when some woman, evidently a foreigner, said to her "You Laconian women are the only ones who can rule men," she replied "That is because we are the only ones who give birth to men."

14–15; translated by R. Talbert Plutarch on Sparta. *New York: Penguin, 1988, pp. 24–26.*

As is the case in many warlike societies, the perpetual absence of men on military duty created a division of labor in which women managed domestic affairs. Aristotle, writing in the fourth century BC and considering some four hundred years of Spartan history, complained that for this reason Spartan women enjoyed altogether too much freedom, power, and prestige. The constitution of Lycurgus, he believed, was flawed from the start because only men conformed to it, while women escaped its regulations. He was convinced that Spartan women indulged in "every kind of luxury and intemperance," promoting greed and an attendant degeneration of the Spartan ideal of equality among male citizens. He also maintained that the Spartans' freedom to bequeath their land as they wished and the size of dowries led to two-fifths of the land in his own time having fallen into the hands of women; the truth of this statistic is impossible to determine. Yet it does seem to be the case that Spartan daughters received as dowries one-half the amount of their parents' property that their brothers received as inheritance. (In contrast, at Athens daughters received approximately one-sixth the amount that their brothers inherited.) Yet Aristotle no doubt exaggerates when he complains that Sparta was ruled by women, for they had no share in the government. Clearly, however, their ownership and control of property gave Spartan women far more authority than their counterparts in the rest of Greece.

Since Aristotle's strong convictions about the need for men to control women plainly played a role in shaping his perceptions of Spartan society, it is hard to know just what to make of his complaints. It is difficult to evaluate the status of women in antiquity, especially in the case of Sparta. Opinions vary according to whether one believes that Spartan women enjoyed a good life within a totalitarian, militaristic state.

Sex and Marriage

As elsewhere in Greece, marriages in Sparta might or might not entail a close emotional attachment between husband and wife. The Spartan requirement that married men continue to live in barracks until the age of 30 meant that young couples did not live together even in peacetime.

Nevertheless, heterosexual intercourse in marriage was essential to the production of Spartan warrior-citizens. Since women married at about the age of 18 and men before the age of 30, Spartan spouses were closer in age than their counterparts at Athens, where it was common for a 14-year-old girl to marry a 30-year-old man. Plutarch mentions that Spartan men were reluctant to marry and that the state provided incentives for marriage and the production of children. An array of unique wedding customs are attributed to the Spartans, including marriage by capture.

Document 4.2 Excerpt from Plutarch's *Life of Lycurgus* If we are to believe Plutarch, Spartan marriages often took on a strikingly clandestine character that seems bizarre by modern standards—and that plainly struck the ancients as worthy of comment. The custom, he writes,

was to capture women for marriage—not when they were slight or immature, but when they were in their prime and ripe for it. The so-called "bridesmaid" took charge of the captured girl. She first shaved her hair to the scalp, then dressed her in a man's cloak and sandals, and laid her down alone on a mattress in the dark. The bridegroom—who was not drunk and thus not impotent, but was sober as always—first had dinner in the messes, then would slip in, undo her belt, lift her and carry her to the bed. After spending only a short time with her, he would depart discreetly so as to sleep wherever he usually did along with the other young men. And this continued to be his practice thereafter: while spending the days with his contemporaries, and going to sleep with them, he would warily visit his bride in secret, ashamed and apprehensive in case someone in the house might notice him. His bride at the same time devised schemes and helped plan how they might meet each other unobserved at suitable moments. It was not just for a short period that young men would do this, but for long enough that some might even have children before they saw their own wives in daylight. Such intercourse was not only an exercise in self-control and moderation, but also meant that partners were fertile physically, always fresh for love, and ready for intercourse rather than being sated and pale from unrestricted sexual activity. Moreover some lingering glow of desire and affection was always left in both. . . .

14–15; translated by R. Talbert, Plutarch on Sparta.
New York: Penguin, 1988, pp. 24–26 (adapted).

In addition to the secret marriage, other reported customs include the random selection of spouses by cohorts of potential brides and bridegrooms groping in a dark room. In a system of aristocratic endogamy (i.e., marriage within the group), the haphazard selection of spouses is a symptom of equality, for one spouse is as good as the next. Since the sole purpose of marriage is reproduction, the secret, or trial, marriage permits the couple to find other spouses if their union proves to be infertile. If these customs were ever practiced, they apparently had died out by the Classical period. The absence of adultery at Sparta, however, continued to evoke comment among non-Spartans. Xenophon also mentions a combination of practices that satisfied both the private desires of individual women and men as well as the state's eugenic goals and insatiable need for citizens:

> It might happen, however, that an old man had a young wife; and he [i.e., Lycurgus] observed that old men keep a very jealous watch over their young wives. To meet these cases he instituted an entirely different system by requiring the elderly husband to introduce into his house some man whose physical and moral qualities he admired, in order to beget children. On the other hand, in case a man did not want to cohabit with his wife and nevertheless desired children of whom he could be proud, he made it lawful for him to choose a woman who was the mother of a fine family and of high birth, and if he obtained her husband's consent, to make her the mother of his children.
>
> He gave his sanction to many similar arrangements. For the wives want to take charge of two households, and the husbands want to get brothers for their sons, brothers who are members of the family and share in its influence, but claim no part of the property.
>
> *(Xenophon,* Spartan Constitution *1.7–10; Marchant 1971, adapted)*

Homosexuality and Pederasty

Ancient Greeks lacked the binary division modern society tends to impose between people who are considered homosexual and those who are viewed as heterosexual, and same-sex erotic relationships did not preclude their participants entering into heterosexual marriages, with which the homosexual relationship would often exist simultaneously. Ancient homosexuality differs from the modern version in several respects. The origins of many same-sex relationships lay in the educational system. Erotic relationships between members of the same sex were considered potentially educational for both women and men as long as the element of physical attraction was not primary. Single-sex education was the norm in the Greek world, and older men and women often functioned as "teachers" or informal guides to younger members of society. The disapproval that attaches today to romantic connections between teachers and students or between old and young would have puzzled the ancient Greeks, who viewed the erotic element in the teacher-pupil relationship as a constructive building block in the education and upbringing of the young. The attraction of teachers to their youthful, beautiful pupils was considered to have social utility, encouraging the enamored teacher to work hard at educating the student, who in turn was offered an inspiring role model in an older, wiser, more accomplished suitor. The pupils in question were generally in early adolescence. Their age would cause them today to be considered children and hence entirely unfit for the erotic attention of adults, but the Greeks saw things differently. This pattern of same-sex relationships was evident not only in the context of education but in life as a whole. How much physical sexual activity actually was involved is unclear, since many Greek intellectuals who left written records of social customs tended to be embarrassed about sex and were eager to stress the cerebral element in same-sex romantic connections. Xenophon, while making plain the frequency of homosexual relationships with a physical dimension, insisted that this was not accepted in Sparta. "I think I ought to say something about loving boys," he wrote,

> since this also has a bearing on education. In other Greek states man and boy live together like married people; elsewhere they become intimate with youths by giving them gifts. Some, on the other hand, entirely forbid suitors to talk with boys. The customs instituted by Lycurgus were the opposite of all these. If someone, being himself an honest man, admired a boy's soul and tried to make him a blameless friend and to associate with him, he approved, and believed in the excellence of this kind of education. But if it was clear that the attraction lay in the boy's body, he considered this most shameful. Thus he caused lovers to abstain from sexual intercourse with boys no less than parents abstain from their children and brothers from their sisters. I am not surprised, however, that some people refuse to believe this. For in many states the laws do not oppose desire for boys.
>
> (*Xenophon*, Spartan Constitution 2.12–13; Marchant 1971)

We know less about the homoerotic bonds between women, but Plutarch in his *Life of Lycurgus* reported that "sexual relationships of this type were so highly valued that respectable women would in fact have love affairs with unmarried girls," and the erotic element in the songs of female choruses (like the poem of Alcman quoted above), is not hidden.

For males and females alike, liaisons with members of the same sex provided much of the companionship, sexual pleasure, and sense of spiritual well-being that many people in modern Western society nowadays associate with marriage. Homosexuality was integrated into the system. The idealized model of the same-sex relationship involved an older person and an adolescent and consequently was time limited. With boys it was considered inappropriate to continue the relationship after the teenager's beard began to grow. Nevertheless, some relationships did develop between companions of the same age and endure throughout life.

DEMOGRAPHY AND THE SPARTAN ECONOMY

By their conquests of Laconia and Messenia, the Spartans created a situation where they never constituted more than a small fraction—perhaps a twentieth—of the total population of their territory. Hence, as is often the case with ruling aristocracies, their numbers were never deemed to be sufficient. Furthermore, unlike other Greek states, at the very start the lack of trade and colonization limited the growth of Sparta's population, for it had no colonies to which it might sometime in the future export a population that could no longer be supported at home. Xenophobia also restricted Sparta's numbers. Unlike the Athenians, for example, at no time did Spartans marry foreigners, nor did they recruit large numbers of new citizens of non-Spartan origin, though the desperation occasioned by the long war with Athens during the fifth century known as the Peloponnesian War did move them to take some exceptional measures. In this emergency, they allowed some non-Spartiate boys living in Sparta to be trained for service in the Spartan army, freed some helots for military service, and appointed perioikoi to some positions of command. Some of these practices continued after the end of the war and into the Hellenistic period when the population problem was even more acute.

Sparta's Shrinking Population

The Spartan lifestyle exacerbated the population decline. Sparta was the only Greek state in which male infanticide was institutionalized. Moreover, many deaths can be explained by the Spartan soldier's obligation to stand his ground and give his life for his country, rather than surrender when his situation was patently hopeless. This ideal was reinforced by peer pressure, epitomized by statements attributed to Spartan women such as that of the mother who told her son as she handed him his shield to come home "either with this or on this." (Spartan soldiers who were not buried on the battlefield were carried home on their shields.)

The reduction in the number of Spartans was gradual. In addition to the high rate of infant and juvenile mortality found throughout the ancient world, the Spartan problem was aggravated by their unusual marriage practices. Women married only several years after they became fertile; opportunities for conjugal intercourse were limited; husbands were continuously absent at war or sleeping with their army groups when wives were in their peak childbearing years; and both sexes engaged in a certain amount of homosexual, nonprocreative sex. As if these obstacles to maintaining the population were not sufficient, some women also declined to bear children. The risks of maternity were considered equal to those soldiers faced on the battlefield: as we have said, the only Spartans who earned the distinction of having their names inscribed on tombstones were those who had died in childbirth or in battle. Spartans, like other Greek women, probably had access to contraceptives including the use of herbs, douches of vinegar or water, and mechanical barriers made of wads of wool soaked in honey or olive oil. Control over fertility is often indicative of high status for women, and Aristotle may have been correct in contending that Spartan women controlled domestic matters, managing households that constituted a significant portion of the family's fortune.

Sparta's population problem was also accelerated at times by natural disaster, economic problems, and the emigration of men. There were nine thousand male Spartans in the Archaic period. In 479 there were eight thousand male citizens, five thousand of whom served at the battle of Plataea. There, according to

Herodotus, each Spartan hoplite was accompanied by seven helots who served as light armed forces and performed the menial jobs. Though these figures are probably not exact, they do give an idea of the proportion of Spartans to helots in the army. In 464 a devastating earthquake killed many Spartans. The entire co-hort of ephebes was among the fatalities. Early in the fourth century an unknown number of men left Sparta to serve as mercenaries in Asia Minor; some never returned. In 371 approximately seven hundred Spartans fought against Thebes at Leuctra, and of these four hundred perished. In 330 Aristotle reckoned the number of Spartans at one thousand. By 244 there were no more than seven hundred. By Roman times very few Spartans were left to perform their hoary rituals and tests of endurance for tourists. We have no information either on the absolute number of female Spartans or on their numbers relative to the number of males.

Helots and the Spartan System

The Spartan economic system was designed to enable citizens to devote all their time and energy to the defense and welfare of the polis. The state saw to it that they always had everything they needed as measured by a standard of austerity, not luxury. Though the perioikoi, who conducted business with the rest of the Greek world, used silver and gold coins, Spartans themselves were permitted to use only iron money: these small bars or spits made of iron had originally been used throughout Greece before the invention of coinage. The Spartans used iron until the end of the fifth century, when there was a vast influx of gold and silver after their victory in the Peloponnesian War.

The goal for men was economic equality, which was, in reality, a minimum income for all that would allow them to follow the Spartan way of life. The Spartans referred to themselves as *homoioi* ("peers," or "men of equal status"). As we shall see below, however, economic equality was an illusory ideal. When Messenia was conquered, the territory was divided up into nine thousand equal *klēroi* ("portions"). At birth, each boy was allocated a share of this land by the state, and a group or family of helots came with the land. The institution of helotry was inextricably tied up with the Spartan system, essential as it was to releasing Spartan men and women from the need to produce or purchase their own food.

The owner of each kleros was entitled to receive a specified amount of produce annually from the helots who worked it. The helots' burden seems to have varied over the centuries. Tyrtaeus describes them as sharecroppers, forced to give their masters half their yield, but Plutarch mentions a fixed rent of 70 bushels of barley for each Spartan man and 12 for his wife, in addition to oil and wine. Though they were not free, helots were not the same as slaves elsewhere in Greece. They belonged to the state, not to individuals. They lived in stable family groups on a farm assigned to them, and could not be sold abroad. Aside from the obligation to provide sustenance for the owner of the plot of land, to serve as auxiliaries in the army, and to mourn at the death of kings and magistrates, the helots had no specific obligations to their masters. They were permitted to sell excess crops in the market and to accumulate some money in that way.

So that they should never forget that they were enslaved, the helots were subjected to an annual beating. They were also obliged to wear a primitive and humiliating costume that identified them immediately, including animal skins and a leather cap. Submitting to the rule of others but living in their own territory, the helots did not lose their desire for freedom. The service they performed in the Spartan army, moreover, provided them with useful knowledge in their ongoing struggle against their masters. In 464 some of them took advantage of the earthquake that had devastated Sparta and staged a rebellion at Ithome that lasted ten years. In 455 the Spartans agreed to let the rebels depart on condition that they should never return to the Peloponnesus. The Athenians settled many of them at Naupactus, on the northern side of the Corinthian Gulf. Finally, in 369, Messenia regained its independence with the aid of Thebes and other Boeotian enemies of Sparta.

The system of helotry distinguished Sparta sharply from other Greek states, making it the only polis with an economic system totally dependent upon geographical and social distance between landowners and workers on the land. Despite the prevalence of slavery in the Greek world, nowhere else was the labor of the lowest class so essential to survival. In other states inhabitants were located at many points on a sliding scale of privilege; in Sparta, a clear line of demarcation separated haves from have-nots. As Plato's relative Critias observed, nowhere else were the free so free or the enslaved so enslaved. Furthermore, though agriculture remained the basis of the domestic economy throughout the Greek world, other sources of gaining a livelihood were customarily developed; at Sparta alone among major states agriculture remained the sole basis of the citizens' economy.

The Spartan system was a remarkably successful experiment in what is now called social engineering. To be sure, despite the ideology of equality among citizens that was associated with their polis, disparities of wealth did not disappear. Many Spartans had only their kleros to support them, whereas rich Spartans who owned additional land could afford, for example, to enter chariots in the Olympic games. Except for the members of the royal family and the tiny group elected to the Council of Elders, however, the role played by differential wealth in determining status and power was far smaller in Sparta than in other Greek poleis. The Spartans called themselves the "Men of Equal Status" for good reason. Rich or poor, they all had survived the same judgment at birth, they had endured the same training, and they wore the same uniform and fought side by side with the same weapons in the phalanx.

SPARTAN GOVERNMENT

Like Sparta's social and educational system, its government was much admired by contemporaries. It consisted of monarchical, oligarchical, and democratic elements: these constituted the kind of system political theorists like Aristotle called a mixed constitution. Spartan conservatism made for a reluctance to abandon traditional institutions like the monarchy and the council of elders when other

Greek poleis had abolished these institutions and had decreased the importance of hereditary power in government. As later on in the Roman republic, the various organs of government and shared offices were designed to serve as checks and balances to one another, minimizing the danger that the government would take too rapid, radical action.

Dual Kingship

The executive office was diluted by dividing it between two men. Two kings (*basileis*) served as the head of government. One each was drawn from the prominent families of the Agiads and the Eurypontids. This system probably reflects an effort to resolve the tensions that arose when the villages united to form the town of Sparta; perhaps these kings had originally been chiefs of the two most powerful villages. The succession was hereditary and usually passed to the oldest son born after the king's accession. When a king's marriage had not produced a son, the king was urged to take a second wife to help ensure the continuity of the male line. Despite these exceptions, and despite the report about wife sharing for reproductive purposes, the Spartans, like other Greeks, were monogamous. Nowhere was the value of the Spartan dual ideology of competition and cooperation more apparent than in the kingship. The two kings, who were both cooperative and competitive with one another, and who were equal in authority, served as a mutual check on the power of the monarchy. Sparta, moreover, was never without a leader, and thus avoided what the Greeks called "anarchy" (absence of leadership or of government).

Like the Dark Age basileis, the Spartan kings exercised military, religious, and judicial powers; in many ways their manner of rule resembled that of the Homeric chiefs. One king served as commander-in-chief of the armed forces, while the other supervised domestic matters at home and became in charge if his co-king was killed in action. (This division of labor came about when history taught the Spartans the harsh lesson that it was risky to send two kings out in command of a single campaign. Herodotus tells of the crisis that arose shortly before 500 BC, when King Demaratus changed his mind about attacking the Athenians and abandoned his co-king Cleomenes just as battle was about to be joined. For this reason the Spartans passed the law mandating that one king remain in Sparta while his colleague was away on campaign.)

The kings were not mere figureheads but were important leaders who contributed to the military effectiveness of the country. Considered descendants of Zeus through his son Heracles, the kings functioned as the chief priests and conducted all the public sacrifices in behalf of Sparta. Their interpretations of the sacrificial omens influenced their decisions in military matters. The royal compensation for fulfilling the office of priest included a supply of animals for a bimonthly sacrifice to Apollo and consequently the special favor of the god. The kings were given the skins of animals that were sacrificed, and double portions of the meat that was distributed. They did not consume the extra meat themselves, but gave it away as gifts, a practice that reflects the common Greek aristocratic system of demonstrating and consolidating one's power by showing signs of generosity. They were also expected to serve as moral exemplars. Thus, the courage and self-sacrifice of King Leonidas and his troops, who obeyed the command of the Spartans to fight at Thermopylae in 480 BC against all odds in the war against the Persians, became legendary and enhanced the image of the invincible Spartans, although many other Greeks fought bravely at the same battle.

Gerousia

The kings shared their judicial functions with the other members of the *gerousia*, the Council of Gerontes ("Elders"). In addition to the two kings, the gerousia was composed of twenty-eight men over the age of 60 who served for the rest of their lives. Sixty was also the age at which military service terminated. Though all male citizens were eligible, gerousia members were usually wealthy, influential men. Consequently, the gerousia constituted an aristocratic, oligarchic component. Election to the gerousia was the highest honor to which a Spartan could aspire. Candidates appeared in an order determined by lot. The winners were chosen by acclamation in the assembly. Those who received the loudest shouts were considered elected, a procedure Aristotle later criticized as "childish." The gerousia possessed the crucial right of legislative initiative: no bill could be brought before the assembly until it had first been discussed by the gerousia, and the gerousia could decline to accept a decision of the assembly by summarily declaring an adjournment. It also served as a criminal court for cases of homicide, treason, and other serious offenses that carried the penalty of disenfranchisement, exile, or death.

Ephors

Every year the Spartans elected five ephors by acclamation from candidates over the age of 30. The ephors ("overseers") supervised the kings and represented the principle of law, precious to the Spartans as it was to many Greeks. Since Spartan laws were unwritten, it was particularly useful to have officials whose role was to serve as judicial watchdogs. When the office of ephor came into being is unclear: it is not mentioned in the Great Rhetra.

The ephors took a monthly oath to uphold the office of the kings as long as they behaved in accordance with the laws, and they shared some of the kings' executive powers; but they were also empowered to impeach kings and depose them. Ephors monitored the kings in Sparta, and two of them always accompanied a king who was on campaign. The ephors presided over the gerousia and assembly, and dealt with foreign embassies. They also exercised judicial powers in civic matters and in cases involving perioikoi.

One ephor was always "eponymous," that is, his name was used at Sparta to signify the year. For example, Thucydides dates a treaty of 421 as follows: "The treaty is effective from the 27th day of the month of Artemisium at Sparta, when Pleistolas is an ephor; and at Athens from the 25th day of the month of Elaphebolium, when Alcaeus is an archon" (5.19). As a check on the ephors' power, they served for only one year, could not be reelected, and were subject to an audit by their successors. Thus, they were both a democratic and an oligarchic constituent of government.

The ephors exercised total control over the education of the young and enforced the iron discipline of Sparta. They were in charge of the *krypteia* ("secret police"), a force recruited from the young and designed to control the helots. This feature of government was unique to Sparta among Greek cities, though the Persian empire also had an elaborate spy system. Some of the most talented young men were sent out for a year to spy on the helots and were encouraged to kill any helots they caught, especially the best of them who might be most prone to rebel. The ephors declared war against the helots annually, thus making it possible for the Spartans to kill them without incurring the religious pollution that usually accompanied acts of homicide. Plutarch gives a vivid picture of the doings of the krypteia. The magistrates, he wrote,

> would despatch into the countryside in different directions the ones who appeared to be particularly intelligent; they were equipped with daggers and battle rations, but nothing else. By day they would disperse to obscure spots in order to hide and rest. At night they made their way to roads and murdered any helot whom they caught. Frequently, too, they made their way through the fields, killing the helots who stood out for their physique and strength.
>
> (*Plutarch*, Lycurgus 28; Talbert 1988)

Assembly

In terms of its membership, the assembly was the most democratic organ of Spartan government, for it included all male citizens over the age of 30. It met once a month at full moon, outdoors. Unlike the assembly that evolved at Athens, however, the Spartan assembly did not debate; citizens listened to a proposal made by the gerousia and simply voted to accept or reject it, without discussion. The Spartan was trained to obey his superiors and to conform, not to take sides in public debate. Lycurgus was said to have outlawed rhetoric teachers. This ethos gave rise to the English word "laconic" (derived from Laconia), which is used to describe a spare style of speech or someone who talks very little.

The Mixed Constitution of Ancient Sparta

Since antiquity, many political theorists have admired Sparta's government, believing it to confirm the basic principle that the best guarantee of stability lies in a blend of monarchic, oligarchic, and democratic elements. Certainly Sparta had kings, and the strong ideology of economic equality among male citizens fostered an egalitarian spirit. In reality, however, the oligarchic element considerably outweighed the other two. Power lay predominantly with the gerousia. As time went by, moreover, the five ephors also gained increasing power over the kings and frequently took the lead in framing foreign policy. Even if we discount the 95 percent or so of disfranchised residents of Laconia—perioikoi, helots, and Spartan women—the truth is that even within the subgroup of male citizens, participation in government was limited to a very small group of men, most of them rich.

SPARTA AND GREECE

In the sixth century, Sparta repeatedly became involved in the politics of other Greek states, often in order to suppress tyrannies. Philosophically, this hostility originated in an aversion to any government that was innovative and extraconstitutional. Tyrants, moreover, were generally supported by the poor, and in return for this support they expanded the nonagricultural economies of cities and adorned them with public works. This power structure and urban style of living were the precise inverse of the Spartan ethos, and it was understandable that the Spartans, who never developed an urban center, should look for allies in other states among men who were landed aristocrats like themselves. From time to time, of course, self-interest overrode principle: not long after helping the Athenians expel their tyrant Hippias in 510 BC, the Spartans tried unsuccessfully to set up another politician, Isagoras, as head of an oligarchy who would be friendly to them. (It was at this juncture that Demaratus abandoned Cleomenes.)

The Peloponnesian League

Until the Roman conquest of Greece, Sparta itself was never subject to the ongoing rule of non-Spartans. In the seventh century, Sparta tried to expand northward against Arcadia and Argos, with varying results. After the defeat of Argos in 546 BC, Sparta had become the most powerful state not only in the Peloponnesus, but in all Greece. With Peloponnesian states other than Messenia, Sparta adopted a policy of alliance, rather than conquest. Sparta had gradually assumed a position of leadership. Sparta's first important ally was nearby Elis; this alliance had been gained in return for supporting Elis's bid to gain control of the influential and lucrative Olympic games around 570. Eventually, around 510–500, "Sparta and its allies," or "the Peloponnesian League" as historians today call the Spartan alliance, was organized. The League included all the states in the Peloponnesus except Argos and Achaea, as well as key poleis that lay outside the Peloponnesus, such as Thebes. One of the first united actions of the League was its defeat of Argos at the Battle of Sepea in 494. Because Sparta depended on its hoplites, the membership of cities like Corinth, Aegina, and Sicyon, which had fleets, was of particular value to its defense. Such an alliance protected Sparta against foreign invaders who not only posed a threat to Sparta itself but might also foment rebellion amongst the helots. The purpose of the League was mutual protection. Each state pledged to contribute forces in case of war and swore an oath "to have the same friends and enemies, and to follow the Spartans wherever they lead." The League was not an empire, but an alliance; no tribute was paid except in wartime. Furthermore, Sparta did not dictate the policy of the League, and, for example, could not force the League to go to war if the allies were opposed to it.

The government of the League was bicameral, consisting of the assembly of Spartans and the congress of allies in which each state had one vote. Only Sparta could convene a meeting of the League and only Spartans served as commanders of its armed forces. Sparta's own reputation for distinction in military matters, along with the existence of the League—the most powerful military alliance in the Greek world in the early fifth century—made Sparta the natural leader of the Greeks in their war against the Persians. Foreigners, including Lydians, Scythians, and Greeks in Ionia sought the Spartans as allies in their struggles against the Persians. The League remained in existence until the 360s, when Corinth and other member states were obliged to quit it after Sparta's defeat by Thebes.

League members were bound by treaty only to Sparta, and they had no bonds with one another. Although they might rise to the occasion and band together for mutual defense in a crisis, as was the case when Persia invaded Greece shortly after 500 BC, in general Greek states had difficulty developing really warm ties. The states in the Peloponnesian League, consequently, were not especially concerned about one another's well being; the Spartans wanted assistance in the event of a helot uprising and backing in their ongoing quarrel with Argos, and the other states were interested in the guarantee of protection by Sparta. Just how much power League members other than Sparta really enjoyed depended largely on how much Sparta needed them. Thus for example Corinth was a cherished ally because of its fleet, and Corinthian rage at Athens would play a large role in the League's fateful decision to declare war on Athens in 432 BC.

HISTORICAL CHANGE IN SPARTA

Since there are no witnesses to the full operation of the Spartan community as described by Plutarch, and Xenophon states that the laws of Lycurgus were no longer enforced in his own time, we must admit the possibility that some features of the Lycurgan legislation were observed only briefly, or partially, or not at all. There are twentieth-century parallels for the failure of similar totalitarian dystopias or utopias. One reason it is difficult to trace historical development in Sparta is the Greeks' essentially negative view of change. Many Greeks shared the Spartan dislike of change and associated it not with progress but with decline. Consequently, much of what has come down to us about changes in Spartan society consists of laments about the falling off from the virtuous days of Lycurgus, alternating with the insistence that Sparta remained unchanged for centuries. Naturally, this sort of evidence is highly suspect. Modern historians follow the general model traced by Aristotle of drastic change over time in Spartan society, dating the "normalization," or loss of distinctiveness, to the later fifth century. Such a change may be observed in the public behavior of male Spartiates, but it is not at all clear that women's lives had been fundamentally altered, for, as Aristotle pointed out, women had never completely submitted to the Lycurgan system.

Some change, however, is plainly discernible. One area in which development is apparent is that of land tenure. Land was the most valuable commodity in the ancient world. Two systems of land tenure, a public one and a private one, existed in Sparta. When a man died, his kleros reverted to the state and then was allocated to another Spartan baby, who was not necessarily related to the previous owner. At the end of the fifth century or early in the fourth, a certain Epitadeus made a proposal to abolish the Lycurgan system regulating public property. Thenceforth a man could give his kleros and his house to anyone he wished, or bequeath them by testament. This change undermined the ideal of economic equality and eventually led to the concentration of great wealth in the hands of a minority. This shift created an impoverished underclass who failed to meet the economic requirements for full citizenship, for they could not make the necessary contribution to a syssition. They were no longer "Men of Equal Status" but known as "Inferiors."

By the Classical period (if not earlier), in addition to the land designated for distribution as kleroi, some land was held as private property. Though women had probably been excluded from the distribution of kleroi, they owned a larger portion of the private land than women in any other Greek city. Land came into women's possession as dowry and inheritance. It seems likely that before the free bequest of land was introduced, daughters automatically inherited half as much as sons. Some families, of course, had daughters but no sons. Sparta was always plagued by a lack of men, for men were continually lost in battle, left Sparta for mercenary service, or failed to meet the census requirements for full citizenship. Moreover, though male infanticide was systematically practiced, it seems unlikely that female babies were eliminated in this way. Plutarch, who supplies details about the official elimination of male infants, says nothing about girls, though his interest in the rearing of girls is noteworthy. If this deduction is correct, then these factors probably created a substantial imbalance in the sex ratio. A woman could inherit all her father's land, and many women became extremely wealthy by this means. Thus Aristotle's statement that in his day women owned two-fifths of the land of Sparta is credible.

THE SPARTAN MIRAGE

The admiration writers like Xenophon and Plutarch felt for Spartan society led them to exaggerate its monolithic nature, minimizing departures from ideals of equality and obscuring patterns of historical change. This perspective in turn made Sparta very attractive to subsequent thinkers, for whom a static society seemed to offer the stability lacking in a more dynamic state (such as democratic Athens). Luminaries of the Italian Renaissance like Niccolò Macchiavelli preferred seemingly stable Sparta to changeable Athens. The cult of Sparta reached its peak in the eighteenth century, which was an era, not coincidentally, when the popularity of Plutarch was at an all-time high. The philosopher and educational theorist Jean Jacques Rousseau rapturously labeled Sparta a "Republic of demi-Gods rather than of men," and many of the patriots caught up in the French Revolution modeled themselves self-consciously on the Spartans of antiquity, emulating their readiness to give their lives in a good cause.

The idealization of Sparta in modern political thought also owes much to Plato. Already in antiquity Sparta served as "the other" vis-à-vis Athens and its democracy, as intellectuals unsympathetic to Athens exaggerated the differences between the two societies. In their writings Sparta became a virtual utopia, a paradise of *eunomia*—a Greek word meaning "governed by good laws." The most dramatic instance of this concept is probably found in the blueprint for the utopian state in Plato's *Republic*, where many features of this idealized Sparta appear. They are evident, for example, in Plato's description of the life of his philosopher-rulers, the "guardians." Central to both social systems are commonality and totalitarian control. Women and men of the top class are given the same education, including physical training. The private family, with its emphasis on women's monogamy and the transmission of property to legitimate male heirs, is eliminated among Plato's guardians. Sexual intercourse

Figure 4.4. Hilaire Germain Edgar Degas' painting, "Young Spartans."

is guided solely by eugenic considerations. Female guardians will not have to perform domestic labor, for members of the lower classes perform the work usually accomplished by Greek women. Their only gender-related task is that of giving birth to children. Marriage is dispensed with, since the state educates all children. Private property and money are likewise outlawed to minimize the envy and class conflict that perpetually threatened to dissolve the fabric of Greek society.

*   *   *

The controversy about Sparta and its critics, both ancient and modern, continues to the present day. For the past 2400 years, historians and philosophers have put forward views that vary radically, though they are based on readings of precisely the same texts. Readers have widely differing reactions to the veritable fountain of anecdotes that has survived from antiquity embodying the underpinnings of the Spartan ethos. Several of these are collected in Plutarch's *Sayings of Spartan Women*. A Spartan mother burying her son, Plutarch reports, received condolences from an old woman who commented on her bad luck. "No, by the heavens," the mother replied, "but rather good luck, for I bore him so that he could die for Sparta, and this is precisely what has happened." Another woman, seeing her son coming toward her after a battle and hearing from him that everyone else had died, picked up a tile and, hurling it at him, struck him dead, saying "And so they sent you to tell us the bad news?"

The notion of a people whose response to stimuli is the very opposite of what human nature would seem to dictate has exercised quite a hold on the human imagination. As late as the twentieth century, critics of western capitalist society have idealized the Spartans as highly virtuous, patriotic people produced by a stable noncapitalistic society. In recent years, however, those who cherish individual freedom and social mobility have come to see in Sparta a forerunner of totalitarian regimes such as Nazi Germany, and in fact some Nazis did identify with Sparta. Furthermore the blueprint for twentieth-century Communism had many affinities with the Spartan utopia. Even today, however, the old idealization of Sparta has reappeared in the works of some feminist theorists, who have noted that the lives of women in aristocratic Sparta appear to have been more enjoyable and in many ways preferable to those of women in democratic Athens.

Although Athens was no more a typical Greek polis than was Sparta, examining Athens and Sparta together is a useful way of understanding the ancient Greek view of life. It is to Athens that we now turn.

TRANSLATIONS

Bing, Peter and Rip Cohen. 1991. *Games of Venus*. New York: Routledge.

Blanco, Walter. 1998. *The Peloponnesian War*, from *Thucydides: The Peloponnesian War*, Walter Blanco and Jennifer Roberts, eds. New York: W.W. Norton.

Lattimore, Richmond. 1960. *Greek Lyrics*. 2nd ed. Chicago: University of Chicago Press.

Marchant, E. C. 1971. *Xenophon in Seven Volumes, VII: Scripta Minora.* Loeb Classical Library. Cambridge, Mass. and London: Harvard University Press.

Talbert, R. 1988. *Plutarch on Sparta.* New York: Penguin.

SUGGESTED READINGS

Calame, Claude. 1997. *Choruses of Young Women in Ancient Greece: Their Morphology, Religious and Social Functions.* Translated by Janice Orion and Derek Collins. Lanham, Md: Rowman & Littlefield. From *Les choeurs de jeunes filles en Grèce archaïque.* 1977. Rome: Ateneo & Bizzarri. An influential study of Alcman's poems for female choruses including discussion of age groups and the educational purposes of the choruses.

Cartledge, P. A. 1979. *Sparta and Lakonia. A Regional History 1300–362 BC.* London, Henley, and Boston: Routledge. One of the standard surveys of Spartan political and military history.

Cartledge, P. A. and Antony Spawforth. 1989. *Hellenistic and Roman Sparta. A Tale of Two Cities.* London and New York: Routledge. Clearly written description of the social, political, and economic conditions of postclassical Sparta.

Dawkins, R. M. 1929. *The Sanctuary of Artemis Orthia at Sparta.* London: Society for the Promotion of Hellenic Studies. Description and photographs of the excavation and finds at the major Spartan sanctuary.

Oliva, P. 1971. *Sparta and Her Social Problems.* Amsterdam: Hakkert. Lengthy but interesting examination by a Czech scholar of major problems in Spartan history.

Page, Denys L. 1951, 1979. *Alcman. The Partheneion.* Oxford: Oxford University Press, 1951; repr. New York, Arno, 1979. A scholarly edition, essential for understanding this fragmentary poem.

Powell, A., ed. 1989. *Classical Sparta. Techniques Behind Her Success.* London and Norman, Okla.: University of Oklahoma Press. A collection of essays including Ephraim David, "Laughter in Spartan Society," and Stephen Hodkinson, "Inheritance, Marriage and Demography: Perspectives upon the Success and Decline of Classical Sparta."

Rawson, Elizabeth. 1969. *The Spartan Tradition in European Thought.* Oxford: Oxford University Press. The history of the idea of Sparta from Classical Greece through the Renaissance, Whig England, and Nazi Germany, with a short note on the United States.

5

THE GROWTH OF ATHENS
AND THE PERSIAN WARS

During the Archaic period, the Athenians struggled with the same problems that beset other city-states of Greece—factional quarrels among the aristocratic families, tension between the aristocrats and the people, and tyranny. By 500 BC, these problems had been largely resolved. The last tyrant had been expelled, Athens had a democratic government, and aristocratic stasis was largely confined to competition for office and persuading the democratic assembly. Because of their relative harmony, wealth, and great numbers, the Athenians had become the second most powerful Greek polis and were poised to play a major role in the great war that was about to begin. For while the Greek city-states were evolving, the Persian empire was growing into an ambitious power that would threaten to engulf the Hellenic world. A strong Athens would be vital to the defense of Greece against the invasions mounted by the Persian kings Darius and Xerxes.

SOURCES FOR EARLY ATHENS

Written sources for early Athenian history are almost as meager as they are for Sparta and the other Greek states. The first man to commit the history of Athens to writing seems to have been Hellanicus of Lesbos, who was born around 500 BC and was the earliest in a series of chroniclers known as Atthidographers, that is, people who wrote about Athens. (The other Atthidographers were Athenians, and they wrote during the fourth and third centuries BC.) To the surviving fragments of the Atthidographers we can add the valuable treatise, *The Athenian Constitution*, written by Aristotle (384–322 BC) or by one of his students, as well as Plutarch's lives of early figures such as Theseus and Solon, which made use of sources that are now lost. Aristotle, Plutarch, and other later authors also preserve substantial fragments of the poetry of Solon, the great Athenian statesman and lawgiver. Solon's poems, written around the beginning of the sixth century, constitute our earliest direct evidence for Athenian society at a crucial time in its development. The histories of Herodotus and Thucydides, though dealing mainly with fifth-century events, also contain some valuable information about early Athens.

ATHENS FROM THE BRONZE AGE
TO THE EARLY ARCHAIC AGE

Literary evidence and physical remains combine to show that during the Late Bronze Age Athens was the largest and most important settlement on the Attic peninsula and one of the major palace-centers of the Mycenaean world. It is probable that Athens was the premier power in Attica, exercising a loose control over the other fortified palace-centers in the region, which remained, however, largely independent of the wanax and his palace on the steep hill called the Acropolis. The tradition that the invasions at the end of the thirteenth century BC bypassed Athens is confirmed by archaeology. Perhaps the mountains that cut Attica off from central Greece—Mount Cithaeron, Mount Parnes, and others—discouraged the invaders who spread throughout the rest of southern Greece. As we saw in Chapter 1, the legends told that Attica served as the safe haven and point of departure to Ionia for refugees from southern Greece. If the story about the Achaean refugees is true (modern opinion is divided), they would have found in Attica the same collapse of the centralized ruling structure, drastic depopulation, and dispersal into small village communities as in the regions from which they had fled.

Recovery from the postinvasion slump is heralded by the appearance of Protogeometric pottery, apparently an Athenian invention, around 1050 BC. Athenian pottery would continue to set the style in Greece throughout the rest of the Dark Age. Dark Age Athens, though reduced to a cluster of villages around the Acropolis, continued without interruption as the central place of Attica. It is likely that by 900 BC, if not earlier, the basileus of Athens was the paramount basileus of the regional demos of Attica. The appearance of rich graves in the ninth century reveals a significant growth in wealth and overseas trade during the later Dark Age. The population around Athens rose sharply during the eighth century, and new settlements appeared throughout the sparsely populated countryside of Attica, perhaps through "internal colonization" from the plain of Athens.

Significantly, Athens did not take part in the overseas colonizing movement of the late eighth century. The synoecism of the towns and villages of Attica into a political unity under the leadership of Athens may have been a gradual process given the extent of Attica (roughly 1000 square miles)—beginning perhaps in the late ninth century, and completed around the middle of the eighth. The Athenians ascribed the unification of Attica to their greatest hero, Theseus, whom myth linked with his companion, the Dorian hero Heracles (later known to the Romans as Hercules). Theseus' adventures with Heracles, and his solo exploits, such as defeating the Minotaur in Crete and the Amazons (mythical women warriors from Asia) in Athens, were enshrined in Athenian art and literature. In the Athenian account of synoecism, Theseus, the basileus of Athens and paramount chief of Attica, created a political unity by proclamation, abolishing the governments of the other towns and villages and making a single government in Athens. Later on, the unification of Attica was celebrated in a festival called the Synoikia, believed to have been instituted by Theseus. Democratic propaganda also credited him with establishing an early form of democracy in the newly unified polis of the Athenians. In making Theseus the founder of the polis, the Athenians followed the common Greek practice of attributing important events of the preliterate period to some great figure from the legendary past. (The Spartans, as we saw, credited their laws and military and political institutions to the semimythical early lawgiver Lycurgus.) Yet the tradition that the formal unification was voluntary and cooperative was probably correct. For the inhabitants of Attica cherished a belief that they were autochthonous (i.e., sprung from the land), and thus had always lived in Attica, and shared a common kinship.

It is certain, at any rate, that by the end of the eighth century every town, village, and hamlet in Attica considered itself "Athenian," and there was never any attempt by any one of them to declare itself a separate polis, as happened in the Argolis and other regions. Nor was there ever in Attica, as in the Doric states, a subjugated population of helots, or communities with second-class citizenship, such as the perioikoi. The exercise of citizenship in a region as large as Attica presented difficulties of time and travel that citizens of smaller regional city-states did not encounter. For although any citizen of any Attic town could participate in the government of Athens on the same footing as residents of Athens itself, in reality people whose communities were closest to Athens would find it easier to vote than those who lived farther away. A farmer who lived, say, 10 miles out of town could expect to lose about three hours of his day walking into Athens and another three walking back, while a man whose home was 15 or 20 miles away would probably have to arrange to stay overnight. Although some people preferred the stimulation of living directly in Athens, most continued to live on the land that had been in their family for generations. When the Peloponnesian War began in 431 BC and Pericles urged the population of Attica to withdraw in its entirety within the walls of Athens, most people, Thucydides reports (2.16), were still accustomed to their lives in the country and found the move intensely painful.

The early government of the Athenian city-state was strictly aristocratic. Its beginnings, however, are very obscure. It was probably during the later eighth century that the chiefs of Attica replaced the position of paramount basileus with three civic officials who divided the leadership roles among themselves and were called collectively the archons, that is, "the leaders." In common with other city-states, the old title of *basileus* was retained; his official duties were to administer the cults of the polis and to judge lawsuits pertaining to cult property and other religious matters. The polemarch (*polemarchos*) commanded the Athenian army, which was composed of units from all over Attica. The leading office, which carried the most prestige and power, was that of the *archōn*, who had overall supervision of public affairs, including the duties of presiding over the council and the assembly and judging nonreligious cases. He was known as the eponymous archon, because he gave his name to the year: Athenians identified a given year as "the archonship of so-and-so." Subsequently (perhaps early in the seventh century), six judicial officials called *thesmothetai* ("layers down of the rules") were added, making up the governing body of the "nine archons." The nine archons were elected for a term of one year from candidates who came from the small circle of wealthy and well-known families known as the Eupatrids ("people with good fathers").

The archons did not rule alone. Rather they worked in concert with the council that met on the hill (*pagos*) sacred to the war god Ares and was called for that reason the Council of the Areopagus. Because former archons made up the membership of the council, sitting archons whose short terms in office would be followed by a lifetime of council membership would think twice before flouting its wishes. In addition, citizen males participated in the public assembly, but the precise role of the assembly in the government and the part that the ordinary men of the polis played in it are unknown; Aristotle in his *Politics* claimed that the assembly elected the archons (2.1274a1–2 and 15–17). What is clear is that policy was made primarily in the council by members of the aristocratic Eupatrid families.

Alongside these official state institutions were other forms of social organization that directed the lives of the citizens. In Attica, as in the rest of Greece, the basic social units—the individual households (*oikoi*)—were grouped into larger kinlike associations: tribes, phratries, and clans. Unfortunately, very little is known about them, especially in their early form. Our best evidence comes from Athens. Every citizen family in Attica belonged to one of four *phylai* ("tribes") and to another smaller group within their tribe, called a phratry ("brotherhood"). Since all the Ionian peoples had the same four tribes, it is assumed that these originated very early in the Dark Age. It is probable that in the early city-state they served as political and military divisions—each tribe, for example, being responsible for furnishing a contingent to the army. The phratry may originally have designated a "brotherhood of warriors," another name for the warrior bands led by Dark Age chieftains that we see in Homer. By the seventh century, however, the phratries had become quasi-official social groups concerned with matters of family and of descent. Membership in a phratry, for example, was the necessary proof that a man was a citizen of Athens; in cases of unintentional homicide, the members of the victim's phratry were obligated to support the family of the victim, or, if the victim had no family, to take the place of the family in pursuing the case. The "clans" (*genē*), as we saw in Chapter 3, were associations of several noble households dominated by a top *oikos* and claiming descent from a common ancestor. It is possible that some nonnoble families also belonged to a *genos*, as subordinate members. These aristocratic clans were politically very powerful in Archaic Athens. Many scholars believe that in the early city-state each of the phratries was in fact controlled by one or more gene. It was within this framework of oligarchic control of the polis that the events of the seventh and sixth century unfolded.

The Conspiracy of Cylon

Few specific events in early Athenian history leap out from the sparse records, but two dramatic developments punctuated the latter half of the seventh century, both plainly connected with unrest of some kind. In or around 632 BC, an Olympic victor named Cylon took advantage of his connection with Theagenes, the tyrant of nearby Megara (whose daughter he had married), to seize the Acropolis and attempt to become tyrant of Athens. Cylon and his backers—both Megarian and Athenian—soon found themselves besieged in the Acropolis by the determined hoplite farmers of Attica, and they decided to take refuge at the altar of Athena. Cylon and his brother escaped, but when his supporters saw that they were running out of food and water they surrendered to the nine archons on the promise that their lives would be spared. Not entirely confident that the archons would keep their promise, the conspirators tied a thread to the statue of Athena, so the story goes, and descended while holding onto it; in this way they hoped to retain the protection of the goddess. When the thread finally snapped, the archon Megacles and his supporters killed them. Many people believed that Megacles had committed sacrilege, and before long all members of his family group had been exiled, including dead relatives whose bodies were exhumed and cast beyond the Attic frontier.

Although Cylon's coup was unsuccessful and his political program remains unknown, the episode was to play an interesting role in future Athenian history because of the prominent family to which Megacles belonged. The Alcmaeonid *genos* would contribute important politicians to Athens, including Pericles, the most prominent Athenian statesman of the later fifth century. The demands—usually politically motivated—that surfaced periodically for the expulsion of all who belonged to the "cursed" clan could be counted on to send shock waves through the body politic. Plainly many people felt that the family shared responsibility for the action of one of its members—and that the state might be called to account by the gods for the impious act of an individual. This belief in group responsibility was characteristic of Greek thought, but although genuine religious feeling and fear of pollution probably played a large role in the original exile of the Alcmaeonids, subsequent attacks arose more from factional rivalries among Athens' aristocratic families than from sincere bursts of piety.

Draco and Early Athenian Law

Much more is known about the next drama, the formulation of a complex of laws by an otherwise unknown man named Draco around 620 BC. Because *drakōn* is Greek for "snake" and the Athenians worshipped a sacred snake on the Acropolis, it has periodically been suggested that the laws of "Draco" were in fact laws formulated by the priests on the Acropolis and promulgated on the authority of the local serpent. It seems more likely, however, that Draco was the name of a real person; if Britain can accommodate politicians named Mr. Fox, why deny Athens Mr. Snake?

Most of what is known about Draco's laws concerns homicide. Their thrust was to replace the family and kin with the state as the arbiter of justice in cases of both intentional and unintentional killings. (Whereas previously many Athenians viewed intentional and unintentional killings as identical with respect to the "blood guilt" they entailed, Draco distinguished between them.) Before Draco was commissioned (we are not sure just how) to overhaul the laws, bereaved family members customarily took it upon themselves to avenge the deaths of their slain relatives. Attica contained sanctuaries to which those believed responsible for a death could take refuge while arranging terms with the kinsmen of the slain. Frequently these terms entailed monetary compensation. Draco transferred the adjudication of these disagreements to the government; the next of kin could still prosecute, backed by his phratry, but it would be bodies of magistrates that would determine the appropriate outcome.

Most cases that came before Athenian judges did not concern homicide, and about Draco's other laws little is known except that they were severe, naming death as the penalty even for minor offenses that today would be classed as misdemeanors. The fourth-century Athenian orator Demades quipped that Draco's laws were written not in ink but in blood. What was significant about Draco's laws was their role in the process of developing the authority of the state at the expense of that of the family, a process that would continue for well over a century.

Just as Draco's laws limited the authority of the family, they also curtailed the opportunities of individual magistrates to shape their decisions in accord with their social and professional ties to particular litigants. Altogether, Draco resembled other early lawgivers in his desire to establish fixed principles of justice that would override the personal preferences of judges. Since judges all came from the wealthy families, Draco's system had something of an equalizing effect, although the rich have never entirely lost the advantages wealth affords in matters of law. The inequities that were causing unrest in Athens, however, were both economic and political, and reforms that focused entirely on the justice system could not soothe the tensions that seemed to be inviting tyranny. Besides, Draco's laws continued to permit enslavement for debt, a practice that by then had become a principal grievance of the poor.

THE REFORMS OF SOLON

The best evidence for the problems that were causing unrest in the seventh century is the legislation of Solon early in the sixth. Solon's reforms reveal his desire to strengthen the fragile agricultural base of the Athenian economy, grafting onto it a thriving commerce. The Athenians were predominantly farmers, but the defining characteristics of the Attic peninsula called for innovative strategies. The soil of Attica was simply too thin to raise enough grain to feed its increased population. The Athenians, consequently, grew what they could—olives, vines, figs, barley—and bartered it abroad for wheat. They also raised livestock for local consumption and for the production of milk and cheese. Olive oil was their most significant contribution to the market, and it was exported in beautiful vases made from the excellent clay of Attica. Its chief destination was what is now southern Russia around the Black Sea, the source of most of the wheat consumed in Attica. Just as in Roman times, Italy would be dependent for its grain on Sicily and then North Africa and Egypt, so the people of Attica depended on the Black Sea area. Athens fought fiercely to defend the routes that led to the Black Sea. The capture of Sigeum at the entrance to the Hellespont around 600 BC was Athens' first overseas venture, and it was by closing off that route that the Spartans finally ended the long Peloponnesian War of the fifth century. Selling oil, wine, and pottery was only one means of obtaining wheat. The Athenians also had at their disposal the silver they had found in the mines at Laurium in southeast Attica. Mount Pentelicum in the northeast provided an additional resource in the form of marble.

The Athenian state of 600, therefore, contained enormous potential in addition to a host of tensions: many poor sharecroppers were losing the struggle to survive, but there was much hope for the economy in a region with valuable natural resources and inhabited by people with many gifts including a talent for pottery. For a second time the Athenians staved off civil war by commissioning a respected individual to address the problems that threatened to spark violence. Perhaps in 594—though some scholars would put it some twenty years later— the Athenians empowered Solon, an aristocrat with a reputation for wisdom, to draw up laws that would develop this potential by alleviating the sufferings of the poor majority without entirely destroying the privileges of the rich minority. In economic terms, what the poor wanted was the abolition of debt and the redistribution of land; what they got was the abolition of debt slavery. It is harder to say what they wanted in the political arena. Probably Attica's poorer inhabitants were open to any number of strategies for loosening the stranglehold of the rich. Solon did in fact devise numerous innovative and effective ways of undermining the division of Attica into haves and have-nots. His reforms created a sliding scale of privilege that contained something for everyone and ensured that his work would not be rejected out of hand.

Solon composed numerous verses that still survive today and reveal something of the rationale for his work. Decrying both the selfishness of the rich and the leveling revolutionary inclinations of the poor, he frequently identified desire for wealth as a problematic force in human affairs and was quick to remind listeners (for early poets had more listeners than readers) of the transience of riches: "There are many bad rich men," he wrote, "while many good men are poor"; but, he went on, he would not exchange his virtue (*aretē*) for the riches of the wealthy, "for virtue endures, while wealth belongs now to one man, now to another" (cited in Plutarch, *Solon* 3). In his emphasis on the mutability of human affairs he looked ahead to the writings of the fifth-century historian Herodotus, who would use him as a mouthpiece for his own ideas. Although he urged justice for the peo-

ple, he was also committed to defending the rights of the elite both to their land
and to the lion's share of input into government:

> I gave the *dēmos* such privilege as is sufficient to them, neither adding nor taking
> away; and as for those who had power and were admired for their wealth, I also
> provided that they should not suffer undue wrong. I stood with a stout shield
> thrown over both parties, not allowing either one to prevail unjustly over the
> other.
>
> *(Cited in Plutarch,* Solon *18.4; Scott-Kilvert 1960, and in* The Athenian
> Constitution, *12)*

Solon's view of the demos as in effect a lobby, a special interest group similar to
that of the rich, reflected the orientation of early Greek political thinking. Later
in Greek history champions of democracy would identify the demos as all the
voters; antidemocrats, however, continued to identify the demos as the poor.

"In large things," Solon wrote about his endeavors, "it is hard to please everybody." His rueful lament that in trying to please everyone he pleased no one is
ironic in view of the cult that developed after his death, when he would become
the beloved George Washington of Classical Athens. Because politicians of all
stripes sought to co-opt him into their camps, Solon came in time to be credited
with a wide variety of programs: democrats and antidemocrats alike claimed him
as their ideological ancestor. Although the earliest surviving sources for Solon's
reforms—aside from his own poems—were written many generations after his
death, it is possible to reconstruct the outlines of his thoughtful and original programs.

Solon's first act was designed to address the sufferings of the poorest people
of Attica. These included sharecroppers who were called *hektēmoroi* ("sixth-
parters"), presumably because they owed a sixth of their produce to a wealthy
landowner to whom they were in debt, and also those who had fallen so deeply
in debt that they had become the slaves of their creditors. Solon not only made it
illegal for loans to be secured by anyone's property or person; he also freed those
who had already fallen into slavery through debt and canceled the debts of the
hektemoroi. This bold measure was known as the *seisachtheia*, the "shaking off of
burdens," and for many generations was commemorated by a festival of the same
name. To redress the evils perpetrated by debt slavery in the past, Solon tracked
down as many Athenians as he could who, because they could not pay their
debts, had been sold as slaves outside Attica. He then bought them back, setting
them up as free Athenians once more. None of this should be construed as an attack on slavery per se. Solon had no problem with Athenians enslaving non-
Athenians.

Solon's other economic measures were less dramatic but equally important.
Revising the weights and measures of Attica, he facilitated trade with other states
by switching from the Aeginetan standard to the Euboic. Thenceforth an Attic
coin would be worth half again as much. Seeing that the future of thin-soiled Attica would lie in oil and in crafts, he encouraged the cultivation of the olive and

made it illegal to export grain, which was needed at home. To attract craftspeople from other regions, moreover, Solon offered them citizenship if they would move to Attica and settle permanently there with their families. Since the Greek view of citizenship was a narrow one closely bound up with religious associations and membership in phratries, this measure was a radical one. (Later on, in the fifth century, when the state and the economy had undergone a long and successful process of development, the Athenians reversed Solon's liberal policy and reverted to restricting citizenship.) Solon was also credited with demanding that all sons be taught a trade; sons whose parents had neglected to instruct them in this regard he freed from any obligation to look after their mothers and fathers in old age. He was also said to have empowered the Council of the Areopagus to inquire into every man's means of supporting himself and to punish those who could show none. Solon's insistence that citizens earn their living makes a dramatic contrast with the Spartan ethos, which defined the citizen as a man whose only work was soldiering.

Easing the sufferings of the poor addressed only one source of tension. Solon had also to reckon with the outrage of the hoplite middle class, which resented the Eupatrid monopoly on privilege. His solution to this difficulty was to establish a constitution in which input into the political process was allotted in accord with income. Property classes that had been in being for some time were used to divide the citizens into tiers, with the addition of a special class at the very top. Classes were ranked according to agricultural wealth. The new class, the *pentakosiomedimnoi*, or "500-measure men," consisted of those whose estates produced at least 500 *medimnoi* ("bushels") of produce; any combination of oil, wine, or grain would do. Below them came the *hippeis* ("horsemen," since they were the men who could afford to keep a horse for the cavalry), whose income was between 300 and 499 medimnoi; followed by the *zeugitai*, men who could afford to own a team of oxen, with 200 to 299, and finally the *thētes*, poor people—some farmers and some landless workers—who produced fewer than 200 medimnoi. Members of the first class were eligible to fill the office of *tamias* ("state treasurer"); archonships and the other higher magistracies were restricted to members of the two upper classes; zeugitai could compete with the two higher classes to fill the lower offices; and the thetes could join the others in the assembly (the *ekklēsia*), which was to meet regularly. The zeugitai made enough of a living to purchase hoplite arms and constituted the majority of the phalanx. Most of the thetes served as light-armed troops or as sailors in the Athenian fleet. Three categories of persons were excluded from the system. Many residents of Attica were slaves, and many were the resident aliens called metics. About a third of the citizens, moreover, were women, for women's life expectancy was about ten years shorter than men's.

Citizen men from all classes could serve in the *hēliaia*, a body of prospective jurors. These people would serve in courts set up to receive appeals from the judicial decisions of the archons and try the cases of magistrates whom someone wished to accuse of misconduct in office. One of Solon's most revolutionary contributions to the Athenian justice system was his insistence that any male citizen—not just the victim or the victim's relatives—could bring an indictment if he believed a crime had been committed. Once the concern of families, justice was now the business of the community of male citizens as a whole.

Filled as it was with former archons, the Council of the Areopagus remained an aristocratic body unsympathetic to the concerns of the poor, and although magistrates were responsible to the people and could be prosecuted for malfeasance, members of the Areopagite Council could not. It seems likely that Solon created a counterweight in the form of the Council of Four Hundred, composed of one hundred men from each Athenian *phylē*. This body served a probouleutic function, that is, it prepared business for the assembly. This Council is evident in Athens not long after Solon's time, and it probably dates from his reforms.

Solon left Draco's homicide laws more or less as he found them, but he reduced the penalties for other crimes and decreed an amnesty to everyone who had been exiled for crimes other than homicide or attempted tyranny. It was probably under this amnesty that members of the notorious Alcmaeonid family returned to resume their involvement in factional politics. Like Draco, Solon was concerned that too much power in the hands of families was antithetical to the program of state building. It was probably for this reason that he made a law permitting men with no children (like himself) to bequeath their property as they wished; previously the property of a childless decedent would automatically revert to his relatives. (Despite Solon's law, juries frequently awarded property to families who contested wills.)

In general, Solon's numerous laws regarding sex and marriage reflect a strong sense of the state as a conglomeration of properly regulated oikoi whose orderliness was very much the concern of the government. Some of these laws seem aimed at giving men in government power over women in private life, but since Solon was concerned to undermine the power of the wealthiest aristocratic family groups, many of his more intrusive provisions such as the restrictions on women's behavior can probably be put down to his apprehension about the prestige of rich families rather than to direct interest in monitoring women's activities. Solon, Plutarch reports,

> made a law which regulated women's appearances in public, as well as their mourning and their festivals, and put an end to wild and disorderly behavior. When women went out of doors, they were not allowed to wear more than three cloaks, or to carry more than an obol's worth of food or drink, or a basket more than eighteen inches high, or to travel at night except in a wagon with a lamp in front of it.
>
> (Solon 21; Scott-Kilvert 1960)

These laws seem aimed at curbing the ostentation of the rich. Several of Solon's policies, however, had a significant impact on women's lives over many generations. Though he had abolished debt slavery and had forbidden fathers as a rule to sell their children into slavery, he made an exception for a man who discovered his unmarried daughter was not a virgin. At the same time he established state-owned brothels staffed by slaves, and his encouragement of immigration for commercial purposes had the effect of significantly increasing the number of prostitutes in Athens. The dichotomy between "respectable" women and sexually available ones would become an important building block of Athenian society.

Solon's work stands out across the ages as truly remarkable for its richness and creativity. Like the Lycurgus of Spartan imagination, with whom he would be compared throughout European history, Solon was given an unusual opportunity to think long and hard about what a community is. His laws established the principle that the Athenian state would be guided by all citizens working together. Indeed, in many respects he established the notion of citizenship itself. His law demanding that in a time of civil strife every man had to take a stand on one side or another demonstrates his determination to involve all male citizens in affairs of state, in fact to define a citizen as someone who is involved in public concerns. His laws also made plain that while the regulation of women's behavior was essential to a well-ordered society, nonetheless their role was to be confined to private life, thus excluding them effectively from the body politic.

Solon's laws were inscribed on wooden tablets called *axōnes* and put up in the agora where everyone could see them—though not everyone could read them, since literacy was not widespread in early sixth-century Greece. When the Athenians had agreed to keep his laws in effect for a hundred years and each archon had been compelled to swear that he would dedicate a gold statue at Delphi if ever he violated any of them, Solon left Attica and began traveling, partly from a desire to see the world and partly to forestall any attempts to persuade him to alter his legislation.

Solon was not a democrat nor did he intend that his reforms should alter the relationship among the classes in Athens. There was some justice, however, in the claims made in fifth- and fourth-century Athens that Solon was the father of the democracy. For by abolishing the hectemorage (sixth-part) system and debt slavery, Solon not only helped create the free peasantry that formed the basis of the democracy; he also established the distinction between freedom and slavery that was to be central to the Athenian concept of citizenship.

PEISISTRATUS AND HIS SONS

Solon's reforms alleviated considerable suffering in Attica. By intensifying the competition for political office, however, they probably played a role in fostering the civil strife that led to the tyranny of Peisistratus, which must be placed in the context of the tensions that survived Solon's labors—and of the spread of political thinking inevitable in an age of experiment. The inhabitants of sixth-century Attica were loosely divided into three factions known as the Men of the Plain, the Men of the Coast, and the Men of the Hill. Historians are still puzzled about exactly who comprised each group. It may be that the men of the plain were primarily large landowners while the men of the coast were fishermen and craftsmen and the poorer inhabitants of the Attic highlands made up the men of the hill; perhaps the city-dwellers were in this last group as well.

Peisistratus' Seizure of Power

Around 560, a successful coup was carried out by Peisistratus, a distant relative of Solon from northern Attica who had made a name for himself by capturing the port of Nisaea in nearby Megara earlier in the century. Peisistratus' backers included not only the Men of the Hill but also some of the poorer city-dwellers. Herodotus tells how Peisistratus wounded himself and his mules and then appeared in the agora demanding a bodyguard to protect himself from his made-up enemies. Back from his travels, so the story goes, Solon tried to warn the Athenians against being duped by his kinsman, but to no avail: packed with his supporters, the assembly voted Peisistratus his bodyguard, whereupon Peisistratus seized the Acropolis and with it the reins of government.

After about five years, the parties of the plain and the coast united against Peisistratus and drove him out, but when Megacles, the leader of the coastal party, quarreled not only with the party of the plain but also with his own faction, he decided to ally with Peisistratus and agreed to reestablish him in Athens provided he consent to marry his daughter. Herodotus marveled at the tale that was circulating in his day about how Peisistratus' return to Athens was accomplished. Peisistratus and Megacles, he reported,

> came up with what is far and away the most simpleminded plot to put him back in power that I have ever heard of, considering that from the very earliest times the Greeks have been distinguished from the barbarians by their intelligence and freedom from simpleminded foolishness—if, that is, these two actually did play this trick on the Athenians, who are said to be the foremost of the Greeks when it comes to brains.
>
> There was a woman in the village of Paeania whose name was Phya. She was tall—about five ten—and good-looking in other ways also. They decked this woman out in full battle gear, and after showing her how she should pose to seem the most beautiful, they put her in a chariot and drove toward the city with heralds sent running on ahead. As they approached the city, the criers, as ordered, shouted, "Athenians! Give a warm welcome to Peisistratus! Athena has honored him above all other men and is herself bringing him back to her own acropolis!" The heralds went from place to place saying this. Word immediately spread from village to village that Athena was bringing Peisistratus back, and even the city dwellers, in the belief that this woman was the goddess herself, worshiped a human being and welcomed Peisistratus.
>
> (The Histories *1.61: Blanco 1992*)

Whatever the truth of the tale, Peisistratus' alliance with his new father-in-law did not endure. By a previous marriage, Peisistratus had two grown sons. Not wishing to undermine their position by fathering any children with Megacles' daughter (whom in accord with Greek custom Herodotus declines to name), he had intercourse with his wife *ou kata nomon*—"not according to the accepted norm." (Herodotus is hard put to explain just how Megacles found out; he suggests that perhaps the bride's mother had asked her some pointed questions.) Outraged, Megacles made common cause with Peisistratus' enemies, and together they succeeded in driving him out a second time.

Peisistratus' next return to Athens was not as picturesque as his first. During the exile that lasted from about 555 to 546 BC, he put together a force of mercenary soldiers with wealth drawn from the gold and silver mines of Mount Pangaeus in northern Greece. Supported by the wealthy Lygdamis of Naxos and the cavalry of Eretria, he landed at Marathon and defeated the opposition in a battle at Pallene. He then governed Athens for over ten years until he died of natural causes in 527. Although Solon had not succeeded in sparing Athens from tyranny, his reforms played a large role in determining what form that tyranny would take. Solon's system continued to function while Peisistratus guided the city through a period of enormous growth and development. Though Peisistratus' regime has sometimes been described as a "law-abiding tyranny," it should be remembered that Peisistratus packed the archonships with his friends and relations, kept a standing force of mercenaries for his personal use, and held the children of potential opponents hostage. When the last of Peisistratus' sons was expelled in 510, the way lay open for the development of the democratic institutions that are still associated with the city of Athens. Although it might seem at first that the creation of a governing dynasty would roll back all the work Draco and Solon had done to undermine the power of families, in reality when the ascendancy of the Peisistratids had passed into history the development of democracy was served by the tyranny's equalizing effect: under the rule of a single family, all non-Peisistratids, rich and poor, found themselves in surprisingly similar circumstances.

Peisistratus' Policies

Strengthening the economy was a major focus of Peisistratus' program, and in this regard too he carried forward much of Solon's work, though this may not have been his intention. Like Solon, he was concerned about both agriculture and commerce. He offered land and loans to the needy. He encouraged the cultivation of the olive, and the growth of Athenian trade sparked by Solon's policies became yet more conspicuous under his regime. Already during the seventh century some Athenian pottery had found its way to the Black Sea and even to Italy and France, but quantities were quite small. During the first half of the sixth century, however, Athenian exports begin to show up in force throughout the Mediterranean and Aegean, and it is difficult to believe that this explosion was not due at least in part to Solon. Under Peisistratus fine Attic pottery traveled even farther than it had in Solon's day—to Ionia, Cyprus, and Syria in the east and as far west as Spain. Black-figure painting reached its apogee shortly after the middle of the century, and around 530 potters began to experiment with the more versatile red-figure style.

The growth of commerce went hand in hand with an ambitious foreign policy. Building a network of alliances in the central Aegean, Peisistratus installed his friend Lygdamis as tyrant at Naxos; Lygdamis in turn installed Polycrates in Samos. Sigeum, which at some point after its foundation had slipped from Athenian hands, was recaptured, and one of Peisistratus' sons was sent to govern it. Peisistratus also established a foothold in the Thracian Chersonese (the Gallipoli peninsula in western Turkey), sending Miltiades, who belonged to the rival Philaid clan, to establish Athenian power there. Under either Peisistratus or his sons, Athens issued the first of its silver coins, known as owls from the bird with whose image they were stamped. The owl symbolized the goddess of wisdom, Athena, and the Athenian owl immediately became the soundest currency in the Aegean.

In Athens, Peisistratus' public building projects served several ends at once. They provided jobs to people who badly needed them while at the same time focusing energy on the city as a cultural center. Replacing the private wells guarded by aristocrats with public fountain houses not only meant construction jobs for the short term but also signaled a long-term shift from private to public patronage. With expanded opportunities for jobs and housing in the city, more people could live in the city center; and those who lived in the urban area found it easier to vote. Under Peisistratus' regime the Athenians rebuilt the temple of Athena on the Acropolis and began a huge temple to Olympian Zeus which was left unfinished at his death and completed only seven centuries later by the Roman emperor Hadrian.

Peisistratus' support of the gods and the arts enhanced both his own reputation and that of the city of Athens. He commissioned a definitive edition of Homer's *Iliad* and *Odyssey* and made Homeric recitations a regular part of the Panathenaic festival, which was celebrated at Athens every four years in great pomp and annually on a smaller scale. Peisistratus also instituted new festivals, the greater and lesser Dionysia. State festivals such as the Dionysia and the Panathenaea were lavishly celebrated, and around 534 BC competition in tragic drama became part of the Dionysia. The worship of Dionysus flourished in Peisistratid

Figure 5.1. This silver coin worth four drachmas and thus known as the tetradrachm was minted at Athens shortly after Peisistratus' death. As if the image of Athena and her symbol the owl did not make the coin's origin plain, the first three letters of the word "Athens" also appear.

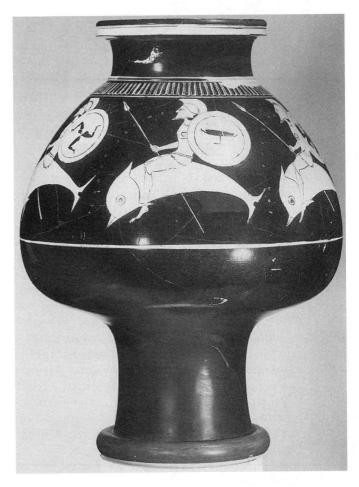

Figure 5.2. Detail of Attic red-figure *psyktēr* ("wine cooler") attributed to Oltos, Armed Warriors Riding on Dolphins, c. 520–510 BC. This vessel probably represents the chorus of an early theatrical production. It was made for use at the drinking party known as a symposion and, therefore, also depicts other wine vases as devices on the warriors' shields.

Athens, and dionysiac scenes of drinking and unrestrained merrymaking were popular subjects of vase painting. At the Dionysia, the god was honored by a choir of "satyrs" wearing goat skins and holding conversation with their leader in the form of a "goat song" or *trag-ōdia* that evolved into the great Attic "tragedies" of the fifth century. An expanded Panathenaic festival was celebrated with great fanfare, culminating in the great procession carrying to Athena's temple the robe woven for her by young Athenian women. Ironically the procession up the Acropolis at the Panathenaea would serve as the occasion for the murder of Peisistratus' son Hipparchus in 514.

The Collapse of the Tyranny

Patronage of the arts became still more conspicuous after Peisistratus' death in 527. The historian Thucydides believed that Peisistratus' son Hippias ruled alone, but he complains of many others who claimed that Hippias' brother Hipparchus was an equal partner in the government. In any event, Hippias and Hipparchus adorned their court with celebrated writers—Simonides of Ceos, whose choral odes were famous; the love poet Anacreon of Teos; and Lasus of Hermione, known for composing novel "hissless hymns," that is, poems in which the sound *s* was never heard. But the prestige of their glittering court did not keep the hereditary tyrants secure in their position. In 514, Hipparchus, so it seems, finding himself rejected in his romantic attentions to a young man by the name of Harmodius, slighted Harmodius' sister by forbidding her to carry a basket in the Panathenaic procession. Harmodius and his lover Aristogiton then formed a plot to murder both Hippias and Hipparchus on the day of the procession. When one of the conspirators was observed chatting with Hippias, the others, wrongly believing the plot had been betrayed, panicked and immediately killed Hipparchus. The results were devastating for Athens: a fundamentally benign government of two aristocrats now gave way to the overbearing and paranoid autocracy of Hippias.

What motivated Harmodius and Aristogiton's fellow conspirators we will never know, but we do know that the fall of Hippias four years later in 510 was in large measure the work of the exiled Alcmaeonids. Determined to return to Athens, they did everything in their power to foster good relations with Delphi, where the old sanctuary of Apollo had recently burned to the ground. The Alcmaeonids underwrote the contract to rebuild the temple, and in addition to honoring its terms also threw in a frontage of first-class Parian marble where the terms had called only for ordinary stone. After this, whenever the Spartans went to Delphi for advice about future projects they always received the response: "First free Athens." As the Spartans enjoyed their reputation as the enemy of tyranny, they were receptive to this suggestion, and in 510 King Cleomenes blockaded Hippias on the Acropolis. When Hippias' children were captured, the tyrant capitulated in order to get them back and departed with his family to Sigeum. A pillar was set up in the Acropolis recording the condemnation of the Peisistratids to *atimia* ("loss of civic rights").

The Athenians chose to remember the heroism of Harmodius and Aristogiton more vividly than the Spartan intervention. Drinking songs began making the rounds in aristocratic circles like the one that went

> I will carry my sword in a bough of myrtle
> The way Harmodius and Aristogiton did
> When they killed the tyrants
> And restored equal laws to Athens.

But the Spartan intervention of 510 had a price: Athens was compelled to join the Peloponnesian League, a development that would have important consequences for the future.

THE REFORMS OF CLEISTHENES

The Athenians did not have long to wait for the Spartans to intervene in their domestic affairs again. Predictably, the departure of the Peisistratids from Athens was followed by a resurgence of factional strife. The aristocrat Isagoras first gained the upper hand when he was elected archon in 508 BC. His popularity was due in part to his platform of revoking the citizenship of those whose ancestors had received it under Solon and Peisistratus. His rival Cleisthenes prudently opposed the plan, thus bringing the masses over to his side. Because Cleisthenes belonged to the Alcmaeonid clan, Isagoras, who had the backing of Sparta, dredged up the ancestral curse that had originated at the time of Cylon's conspiracy, and Cleisthenes withdrew from Athens. In his efforts to aid Isagoras, however,

Figure 5.3. The tyrannicides Harmodius and Aristogiton were commemorated in this statue of about 500 BC. It survives in this Roman copy.

Cleomenes was not able to repeat the success he had achieved on his last Athenian campaign, when he had helped to drive out Hippias. This time he overplayed his hand. Returning to Attica, he expelled seven hundred families pointed out to him by Isagoras and tried to establish an oligarchy. Now it was his turn to be blockaded in the Acropolis. The indignant Athenians rose up en masse, forced the capitulation of Cleomenes and Isagoras, and welcomed Cleisthenes and his supporters back to Athens. This would not be the last time that Athenian oligarchs allied themselves with Sparta.

Seeing clearly that the rivalries of the wealthy families could not continue without peril to the state, Cleisthenes resolved to overhaul the Athenian constitution in such a way as to break the power of rich families (other than his own) once and for all. His methods were ingenious. Abolishing for all practical purposes the four ancient Ionian phylai—they remained in existence for ceremonial purposes only—he established ten new tribes on an extraordinary basis. First he divided Attica into three geographical areas—the city, the shore, and the inland (overlapping only partially with the old divisions of the hill, the coast, and the plain.) He then subdivided each area into ten *trittyes*, or "thirds" (though actually they were thirtieths), composed of a number of the existing units known as demes—villages or townships of Attica. Since the demes were of unequal size—there were over a hundred in all—the number of demes in each trittys varied. He then took one trittys from each geographical area and put the three together to make a tribe: one tribe, in other words, would contain three trittyes, one from each of the three areas, made up of an irregular number of demes. To signal the weakening of family loyalties in favor of political ones, men were to begin identifying themselves by their demotic, that is, the name of their deme, rather than by their patronymic, the name of their father. It may be that Cleisthenes designed this shift in part to conceal the non-Athenian origins of some of his supporters, but its long-term purpose was to weaken the force of prestigious lineage in politics. Generations of tradition were not so easily cast aside, however, and the custom was employed only intermittently: we still think of Pericles as the son of Xanthippus and the historian Thucydides as the son of Olorus.

The new base of ten tribes sparked the creation of a new body, the Council (*boulē*) of Five Hundred, with fifty members chosen annually by lot from each of the ten tribes. Recognizing the principle of proportional representation, the fifty slots for the boule were distributed among the demes in accordance with the population of each. The use of the lot in determining the composition of each year's boule was a key democratic feature of the Cleisthenic system. The boule replaced the old Council of Four Hundred, taking over its "probouleutic" functions of preparing business for the *ekklēsia* (the assembly) and also managing financial and foreign affairs. Because five hundred was an unwieldy number, each tribe would be in charge for a tenth of the year. During its period of service the fifty presiding members of the council were called *prytaneis*, and the prytany came to be used as a measure of time, rather like a "month." The chair and secretary each changed every day.

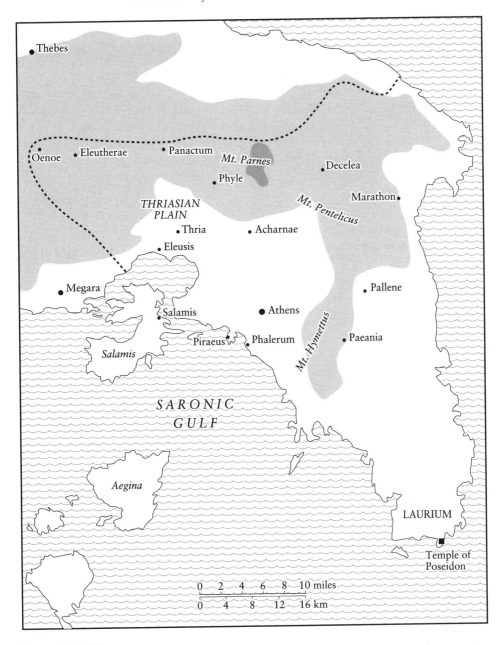

Figure 5.4. Attica.

The archons retained their administrative duties, but a new board of executives was created which—though Cleisthenes may not have anticipated it—would eventually surpass them in importance. The army was reorganized on the basis of the ten tribes, each tribe electing a *taxiarchos* (infantry commander), *hipparchos* (cavalry commander), and, most important, a *stratēgos*, or chief general. Unlike archons, *stratēgoi* could serve as many consecutive terms as they liked. In time the board of ten strategoi became the most prestigious executive body in Athens.

Because Cleisthenes was not granted extraordinary powers such as those with which Solon had been invested, his measures needed to be passed in the assembly. His reforms, consequently, were in themselves the product of democratic action. Around 500 BC a meeting place for the ekklesia was carved out of the rock on the hill called the Pnyx, and from then on the assembly met there on a regular basis and framed policy for the state.

The new Cleisthenic tribes were constituted on eminently artificial lines. It was their very artificiality that made them work, for tampering with the old ties of sentiment and obligation opened the door to framing a new network of alliances. Some noble families, however, remained in control of important (and profitable) cults such as that of Demeter and Persephone at Eleusis. Whether Cleisthenes actually steeled himself to break the power of his own family along with that of the other families is unclear; it should occasion no surprise that the Alcmaeonid power base seems to have survived his elaborate redistricting of Attica whereas those of other families were undermined.

THE RISE OF PERSIA

While the Greeks were struggling to create workable governments in their numerous small city-states, a rich and powerful state of a different character was taking shape to the east, where the Persians united the largest empire known to that time.

Sources for Persian History

The sources for Persian history are principally Persian and Greek, though there are some records in Elamitic, Akkadian, Aramaic, Egyptian, Hebrew, and Babylonian. The Persian sources include inscriptions written in Old Persian found in major archaeological sites such as Persepolis and Susa. In addition, scholars have been able to detect a Persian oral tradition glorifying the kings. Archaeological evidence includes monumental buildings with relief sculpture depicting historical events and seals picturing a wide range of activities yielding information on military, athletic, agricultural, and religious practices and often showing the flora and fauna of the empire. The historical sources emanating from Persia are, of course, biased in favor of the kings and their government. Inscriptions written in Old Persian are all official documents, and give a picture of prosperity, fertility, and security. The Greek sources include the historical writings of Herodotus and Xenophon. The works of the former, in particular, tend to stress differences between Greeks and Persians, between East and West. The Greek word for the Persians, and for all peoples who did not speak Greek, was *barbaroi*, for they seemed to be talking gibberish, saying "barbar, barbar." The Persians, however, should not be considered barbarians in the modern sense, for their political and artistic achievements were admirable by any standard.

Persia Before Darius

Like the Greeks, the Persians were originally an Indo-European people who came from the north. By the Dark Age they had occupied the territory now known as the Iranian plateau, a place rich in natural resources including gold, silver, copper, minerals, and semiprecious stones. Not much is known of Persian history before the seventh century BC. After a struggle for domination between the Persians and people related to them known as the Medes, the two groups came to be unified, perhaps under the king Cyaxares whose capital was at Ecbatana.

At a time when most Greek states had eliminated hereditary basileis from their governments and were wary of one-man rule, which they equated with tyranny, Persia was ruled by kings each of whom, with the exception of Darius, inherited his role directly from his father. Because the kings often had more than one wife, there was never a lack of candidates. At first the Persians were subject to the Medes, but around the middle of the sixth century Cyrus II of Persia (ruled 559–530 BC), a member of the Achaemenid family, took control and made Media the first of many satrapies (provinces) of the Persian empire. Henceforth the Persian dynasty known as the Achaemenids were to rule the Medes, though the Greeks considered Medes and Persians the same and described the act of favoring the Persians as "medizing."

Cyrus' conquest in 546 of the Lydian king Croesus brought Asia Minor into the empire and was one of the events that led ultimately to the war between the Greeks and Persians in the fifth century. Croesus had brought the Greek cities in Ionia under his domination in 560. His wealth was proverbial; the first coins, which were made of electrum, were said to have been minted in Lydia. Croesus' prosperous empire provided an Asian outlet on the Mediterranean and Hellespont that was indispensable for trade with the West. Herodotus portrays him as a phil-Hellene (a lover of things Greek), who enjoyed entertaining Greek philosophers such as Solon and who sought the advice of Greek oracles, sending envoys laden with gifts; but he also enjoys telling how Croesus' vanity and self-absorption led him to misconstrue what he was told. Pleased to hear from the oracle at Delphi that "if he made war on the Persians he would destroy a mighty empire," Croesus proceeded against Cyrus.

Apollo spoke the truth, of course, but Croesus had misunderstood. The great empire he destroyed was his own. In 546 BC Cyrus conquered Lydia, and the Lydian capital Sardis became the chief administrative center in Asia Minor for the Persians. Via the cities of Ionia, Cyrus' conquest brought about the first official contact between Greeks and Persians. Cyrus also conquered Babylonia, Assyria, Syria, and Palestine. These lands and their people were heterogeneous: differences between Greeks of various city-states pale in comparison with differences between parts of the Persian empire. The variety of languages, customs, laws, re-

ligions, and manner of waging war was vast. Cyrus' great achievement was that
he managed to unify the empire. Communication was facilitated by constructing
roads and creating a postal system staffed by royal messengers on horseback.
Herodotus reported that "Neither rain, nor snow, nor sleet, nor hail stays these
couriers from the swift completion of their appointed rounds" (8.98; Blanco 1992).
Cyrus also permitted his subjects to practice their own religions.

Cyrus was praised by Greek and Asian sources alike as a benevolent and talented ruler. Whereas the preceding Neo-Assyrian and Neo-Babylonian empires
had deported entire populations and had sown conquered territory with salt so
that it could never again become fertile, Cyrus' policies enhanced the prosperity
of his empire and the well-being of its inhabitants. Cyrus was hailed by the Jews
for allowing them to return from exile in Mesopotamia under the Babylonian captivity to Jerusalem and to rebuild their temple there and worship freely. The Old
Testament records the declaration of the Hebrew prophet Isaiah to the Jews:

> Thus says Yahweh to his anointed, to Cyrus whom he grasps by his
>   right hand,
> That he might subdue nations before him, and ungird the loins of
>   kings,
> To open doors before him, that gates shall not be closed:
> "I will go before you, and I will level the roads;
> I will shatter gates of bronze, and I will hew bars of iron to pieces.
> I will deliver buried treasures to you, and hidden riches. . . ."
>   (Isaiah II, 45:1–3)

Cyrus' son Cambyses succeeded him as king and reigned from 530 to 522 BC.
In 525, after fighting against an army that included Greek mercenaries, he added
Egypt to the empire. Always fascinated by the dangers attendant on wealth and
power, Herodotus takes care to depict his degeneration from a capable ruler into
a despotic madman.

The Achievements of Darius

Darius I seized power in 521 BC and reigned until 486. He created an administrative and financial structure that remained unchanged for two hundred years.
He centralized the government and moved the capital to Persepolis. The imperial buildings begun there were completed by his son, Xerxes. Building inscriptions record that Greeks were among the workmen drawn from all corners of
the empire to build the royal buildings. Darius facilitated travel for commercial
purposes in many ways, building a canal linking the Nile and the Red Sea. This
canal made the newly conquered territory of Egypt more prosperous than it had
been under native Egyptian rule. Darius was the first Persian king to mint his
own coins of silver and gold. The gold coins, Daric staters or "darics," demonstrated the king's talent at archery, a skill highly prized by the Persians, who,

Herodotus reported, were taught three things—to ride, to shoot straight, and to tell the truth.

The empire was divided into provinces or satrapies. These sometimes consisted of people of the same ethnicities or of those in a single region who had been conquered at the same time. Within each satrapy authority was divided between civil and military officials: the civil authority furnished supplies to the military and the military provided protection in return. Each province was obliged to pay an annual tribute to the king. The Persian monarchs wisely refrained from imposing a uniform system of administration throughout the empire and declined to uproot existing governors and procedures that functioned well. In some areas, for example Lydia, satraps governed fairly independently. Rebellions were discouraged through a system of spies known as the "Eyes and Ears of the King." Supreme political power was unified only in the person of the king. The king, as commander-in-chief, defended his subjects against intruders and in return they paid him taxes, gave him gifts, and paid him tribute. His income was stored in the royal treasury and much of it was lavished on monumental building projects. The labor of the subjects of the empire was exploited on a large scale through taxation, forced labor, and mandatory military service. The king exercised absolute authority and wielded the power of life and death over his subjects, who knelt or even lay prostrate in obeisance. Rather than envying the Persians for enjoying hundreds of years of peace, the Greeks pitied the subjects of the Persian king, considering them his slaves.

THE WARS BETWEEN GREECE AND PERSIA

Darius campaigned against the European Scyths and thus became the first Persian king to enter Europe. Although he failed to conquer Scythia, Thrace was subdued and became a satrapy. Darius' westward expeditions piqued his curiosity about the mainland Greeks, and a rebellion in his empire brought him into direct contact with them.

The Ionian Rebellion

In 499 BC revolt broke out among the Ionian Greeks. Discontent in Ionia was considerable; taxes had gone up when the Greek cities were transferred from Lydian to Persian hands, and the Greeks resented the system of puppet tyrants the Persians had imposed. Violence might not have erupted, however, had it not been for the ambition of Aristagoras, the tyrant of Miletus. Hoping to add Naxos to his domain, Aristagoras had persuaded the Persians to join him in a larger effort to subdue the whole chain of the Cyclades islands in the Aegean and perhaps move on to mainland Greece. When the plan failed, Aristagoras, noticing the restlessness of the Ionians, decided to recoup his failing fortunes by uniting them in revolt.

Figure 5.5. Delegations bringing tribute to Persepolis. The Persian king received a wide variety of goods from throughout the Near East in the form of tribute.

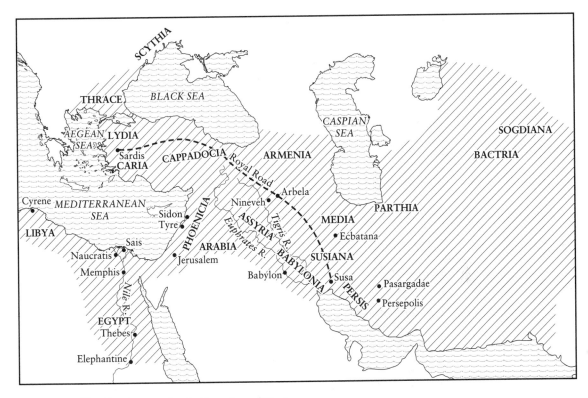

Figure 5.6. The Persian empire in the reign of Darius.

After resigning his tyranny and accepting a constitutional office instead, he set about overthrowing tyrants in the other Ionian cities. Most of this seems to have been accomplished without bloodshed, but the tyrant of Mytilene was so unpopular that he was stoned to death. The rebellious cities showed their unity by issuing coinage on a common standard. Herodotus' account of Aristagoras' attempts to gain support from King Cleomenes was geared to demonstrating the Spartan character as most Greeks imagined it—cautious, conservative, and leery of foreign adventures; the tale also illustrates the assertiveness of Spartan women and the respect in which they were held. Aristagoras, Herodotus maintains, carried with him a bronze map of the whole world—probably the work of the celebrated Milesian geographer Hecataeus. He pointed out to Cleomenes the people whose wealth would fall into Greek hands in the event of a victory and he exhorted the king to liberate the Greeks of Ionia. Capitalizing on the Spartans' dislike of foreign customs, he suggested that they could easily defeat men who fought in trousers and wore peaked caps on their heads, "so easy are they for the beating." Cleomenes asked for a couple of days in which to make up his mind. When the two days were up, Herodotus says,

Cleomenes asked Aristagoras how many days' journey it was from the Ionian sea to where the Great King [i. e., the king of Persia] was. In everything else Aristagoras was very clever and had tricked Cleomenes successfully, but here he tripped up. He ought not to have told the truth if he wanted to bring the Spartans into Asia. However, he did tell it, saying that the journey from the sea up to Susa was a matter of three months. Cleomenes cut off all the rest of the story that Aristagoras was set to give him about the journey and said, "My friend from Miletus, away with you from Sparta before the sun sets! There is no argument of such eloquence that you can use on the Lacedaemonians if you want to bring them three months' journey from the sea."

(The History 5.50; Grene 1987)

Not yet willing to abandon his quest, Aristagoras followed Cleomenes to his house, carrying with him the customary sign of supplication—an olive branch, covered with wool—and as he sat in Cleomenes' home as a suppliant he noticed young Gorgo, who was 8 or 9 years old, standing by her father. He asked that Cleomenes send his daughter away, but

Cleomenes bade him say whatever he liked and not to hold back because of the child. Then Aristagoras began with an opening promise of ten talents if the king would do what he asked. As Cleomenes refused, Aristagoras raised his bids, little by little, till he made an offer of fifty talents. At this the child cried out and said, "Father, this stranger will corrupt you if you do not take yourself away." Cleomenes was delighted by his daughter's advice and went into another room, and Aristagoras left Sparta altogether and never got another chance to give any more information about the journey from Ionia inland to the dwelling of the Great King.

(The History 5.51; Grene 1987)

The Athenians were more receptive to Aristagoras' designs. A more adventurous people than the Spartans, they were not constrained by fear of a slave rebellion in their absence. They were made nervous by the Persians' connection with Hippias, who had found his way to Persia, for they rightly feared that he was planning to return with Persian backing. Finally, access to grain and other resources in the Black Sea area was precious and deserving of protection. They agreed to send twenty ships; the Eretrians to the north were willing to send five.

The unsuccessful rebellion of the Ionian Greeks ended in a major naval defeat off the island of Lade near Miletus in 494 BC. Greek morale had fallen; the tyrants whom Aristagoras had expelled were spreading pro-Persian propaganda; and before the battle was over the Samians and Lesbians had deserted. Miletus was defeated, its women and children enslaved, and the men relocated to the mouth of the Tigris. In the course of the rebellion, however, the capital city of the western Persian empire, Sardis, was burnt, whether accidentally or on purpose.

Darius would not forget the burning of Sardis, but neither would the Greeks forget the annihilation of Miletus. Home of the philosophers Thales, Anaximander, and Anaximenes, and more recently of the geographer Hecataeus (who had warned Aristagoras of Persia's overwhelming superiority), Miletus had been one of the most cultured cities in the Greek world. When the poet Phrynichus produced a tragedy on its fall entitled *The Capture of Miletus*, the Athenians fined him one thousand drachmas for reminding them of their misfortune. The story of the Athenians' outrage reveals a growing sense of identity among the Ionians and perhaps among the Greeks more broadly. The Athenians had withdrawn from the rebellion in its early stages, after the burning of Sardis, so that Athenian soldiers had not been involved in the collapse of Miletus; yet they identified passionately with it in its final hour.

There was reason to believe that the fate of Miletus could soon be that of cities in mainland Greece. Under the leadership of a rising politician named Themistocles, who had just been elected archon, the Athenians began to fortify the three rocky harbors of Piraeus and convert them into a naval and commercial base. Unlike most Athenian politicians, Themistocles lacked family connections beyond those he had garnered by a prudent marriage, and unlike most previous politicians, who had drawn support from the leisured landowning class, he seems to have enjoyed the backing of those who made their living by trade. Acutely sensible to the Persian threat—Thucydides praised him for his ability to foresee what the future held (1.138)—Themistocles served Greece well at this critical time.

Darius' Invasion of Greece

Darius had been interested in Greece for some years before the Ionian rebellion, and the desire to avenge the burning of Sardis had added an additional spur to his ambition. In 492 BC he sent his son-in-law Mardonius west at the head of a large force. Though Mardonius successfully restored Persian prestige in northern Greece, conquering Thrace, Thasos, and Macedonia, the fleet was wrecked off Mount Athos on the Chalcidic peninsula, and Mardonius was forced to turn back. Darius promptly began mobilizing for another expedition, one that would sail straight across the Aegean, avoiding the treacherous promontories of the north. Mindful of the fate of Miletus, many Greek cities yielded to the demand of Darius' heralds for earth and water, the proverbial tokens of submission that signaled recognition of the king's supremacy on land and sea. The islanders felt they had little choice, and on the mainland Argos and Thebes went over to the Persians. Sparta and Athens, however, remained steadfast in their opposition.

Darius' first order of business was to punish Athens and Eretria for their role in the Ionian rebellion. In fact, it may have been the primary purpose of his expedition. In the summer of 490 his fleet arrived in Greece, commanded by his nephew Artaphernes and Datis, a Mede. The figure given by Herodotus of six hundred ships is probably exaggerated, but Datis and Artaphernes may have had twenty thousand men with them, one of whom was the aging Hippias, the exiled ruler of Athens whom they hoped to reinstall as both Athenian tyrant and Persian vassal. En route the Persians burnt the town and temples of Naxos, deport-

Figure 5.7. Herm of Themistocles. This Roman copy was probably modeled on a bronze statue of Themistocles erected about 460 BC. With its thick neck and coarse features, the head reflects the earliest known example of individual portraiture in Greek art. We should perhaps associate the unusual physiognomy with the tradition that Themistocles' mother was not Greek.

ing their captives; elsewhere they pressed men into service and seized children as hostages. After a siege of less than a week, Eretria was betrayed from within. The Persians burnt the Eretrians' temples in revenge for those destroyed at Sardis and deported the population in accordance with Darius' orders. (Several centuries later the peripatetic prophet of the Roman empire Apollonius of Tyana reported finding the descendants of the deported Eretrians at Ardericca in Cissia, still speaking their native Greek.) From Eretria the Persians moved down on Marathon in the old Peisistratid stomping ground of northern Attica.

The Athenian assembly immediately voted to dispatch their forces to Marathon, and a runner, Pheidippides (or perhaps Philippides) was sent to Sparta, covering, so the story went, fully 140 miles by the next day. The Spartans, however, could not take advantage of the speed with which the message was delivered, for, they explained to the breathless Pheidippides, they were celebrating a festival of Apollo, the Carnea, and were forbidden to march until the full moon. As the Spartans were deeply religious and no cowards in war, their explanation may have been sincere.

The Battle of Marathon

Herodotus' figures are probably erroneous, but it is likely that the Athenians were outnumbered, if not as outrageously as he suggests then at least by a factor of two to one. The Persians had the more versatile force, with cavalry, archers, and skirmishing troops, but the Athenian force consisting essentially of hoplites was more heavily armed. The most serious problem faced by the Athenians was the lack of a commander, for all decisions lay with the ten strategoi (the board of executives created by Cleisthenes) deliberating as a body. As some wanted to wait for the Spartan reinforcements expected after the full moon and others thought delay risky, there was danger that a deadlock in the Athenian camp would throw the victory to the Persians and Greece would be overrun. When the Athenians learned that some of the Persian troops and cavalry were missing and suspected that part of the Persian forces were heading for Phaleron, it seemed to several generals that the moment to strike had come, even though the moon was full and the Spartans could be expected shortly; any delay could be fatal. The strategos Miltiades seems to have played a key role in saving Greece.

A nephew of the Miltiades whom Peisistratus had dispatched to protect Athenian interests in the Chersonese (thus conveniently disposing of a potential rival), Miltiades the younger had inherited his uncle's power and had spent much of his life in the remote outpost. In part because he was a member of the prominent Philaid clan and indeed a distant relative of Peisistratus himself, he became the victim of Athenian factional politics on his return to Athens in 493 BC when he was prosecuted for alleged tyranny in the Chersonese. Since it is impossible to see why the Athenians would worry about one of their own citizens tyrannizing abroad, Herodotus is surely right to ascribe the trial to the machinations of Miltiades' enemies (6.104); alternative rumors ascribed the attack to Themistocles or the Alcmaeonids. In any event, Miltiades was acquitted and went on to take the lead in the Greek victory over Darius, persuading the polemarch Callimachus and several of the other strategoi to let him direct Athenian strategy. Herodotus offers a stirring rendition of his speech:

> Callimachus, it is up to you, *right now*, to enslave Athens or to make her free, and to leave for all future generations of humanity a memorial to yourself such as not even Harmodius and Aristogiton have left. *Right now*, Athens is in the most perilous moment of her history. Hippias has already shown her what she will suffer if she bows down to the Medes, but if this city survives, she can become the foremost city in all Greece. Now, I'll tell you just how this is possible, and how it is up to you—and only you—to determine the course of events. We ten generals are split right in two, with half saying fight and the other half not. If we don't fight now, I am afraid that a storm of civil strife will so shake the timber of the Athenian people that they will go over to the Medes. But if we fight now, before the cracks can show in some of the Athenians, and provided that the gods take no sides, why then we can survive this battle. All this depends on *you*. It hangs on your decision—*now*. If you vote with me, your fatherland will be free and your city will be first in all of Hellas, but if you choose the side of those who urge us not to fight, then the opposite of all the good I've spoken of will fall to you."
>
> (The Histories 6.109; Blanco 1992)

And so, early one morning in late September of 490, under Miltiades' command, the Athenians, flanked by some Plataeans, ran down the hill on which they had encamped, covering the mile or so that divided them from the Persians at double speed despite the weight of their hoplite armor. Aristides and Themistocles commanded their tribal contingents in the center, while Callimachus commanded on the right wing and the Plataeans held the left. Knowing they were outnumbered, the Athenians packed their wings as tightly as they could, concentrating as many men as possible on the outer ends of their formation, even though it meant leaving the center thin. Despite their numerical superiority the Persians were unable to withstand the disciplined and determined hoplites fighting in defense of their freedom. (The Greeks also had better armor and longer spears.) In the flight to their ships, many of the Persians were bogged down in the marshes.

Arriving too late to participate in the fighting, the Spartans visited the battlefield and surveyed the Persian corpses. Herodotus maintained that the Athenians lost 192 men, the Persians 6400. The Greek statistic is probably correct, for the names were inscribed on the battlefield; they included Callimachus. The dead were cremated where they had fallen, and a monument was subsequently erected on the site. Some Plataeans and some Athenian slaves also died, but their numbers are unknown. The playwright Aeschylus himself fought at Marathon. The epitaph he composed for himself makes no mention of his stupendous achievements as a tragic dramatist but speaks only of his service in this battle for freedom: "The glorious grove of Marathon," he wrote, "can tell of his valor—as can the long–haired Persian, who well remembers it." Throughout the next decades, the *Marathonomachoi*—men who had fought at Marathon—enjoyed singular prestige in Athens and came as time went by to represent the simple virtues of the older generation in an increasingly luxurious and complex society. About a quarter century after the battle it was memorialized in a painting in the Stoa Poikilē (painted portico) at the north end of the Athenian agora; Callimachus, Miltiades, Datis, and Artaphernes could all be identified, as well as Aeschylus' brother Cynegirus hanging onto the Persian ship, to which he clung intrepidly until his arm was cut off by an axe. Gods and heroes were present at the battle as well—Heracles, Athena, and Theseus, who many believed had offered phantom aid on the battlefield as Homeric gods had done at Troy.

Not all Greeks rejoiced in the defeat of Persia. A shield signal was apparently flashed from Athens after the battle advising the Persians that the city was prepared to surrender. Any connection between the Alcmaeonids and the signal was indignantly denied by Herodotus, who tended to favor the Alcmaeonids and seems to have used Alcmaeonid sources in his writing, but just such a connection was common gossip at the time. In any event, someone at Athens wished the Persians well. Over the years, accusations of Persian sympathies would dog aspiring Athenian politicians and offer an easy route to damaging a controversial figure's reputation.

Greek Leaders and Their Misadventures: Miltiades, Cleomenes, and Demaratus

Athenians held their leaders to high standards. Although the history of the fifth and fourth centuries would provide numerous examples of the exacting temperament of the demos, the earliest are among the most interesting. Shortly after the battle of Marathon, Miltiades was impeached in the assembly and condemned to pay a stiff fine. He died in disgrace before he could pay, and his son Cimon discharged the debt. The circumstances were curious. Because of his heroic standing after the victory of Marathon, the Athenians were agreeable to granting Miltiades ships on his promise that he would make them rich. When his attack on the island of Paros ended in failure and embarrassment—Herodotus claims the wound that eventually killed him was sustained while violating the sanctuary of Demeter—he was impeached at Athens and had to attend his trial on a stretcher, as his wound was beginning to gangrene. The Athenians considered putting him to death. Although it is impossible to know just how much the voters in the assembly had known about the object of Miltiades' expedition—security considerations would have argued against openly naming Paros, which had sided with the Persians during the war—what is clear is that the demos had developed the confidence to hold its leaders accountable. Throughout the decades that followed, interaction between the demos and its leaders would be characterized by a changing dynamic that helped define the nature of the democracy as it unfolded.

It was not only in Athens that political leaders tended to come to bad ends. Spartan kings had a habit of getting into difficulties as well. After winning a decisive victory over Sparta's inveterate enemy Argos at Sepeia, Cleomenes was accused by the Spartans of sparing the city as a consequence of bribes. A couple of years later, when he had enlisted the Delphic oracle in machinations to engineer the deposition of his fellow king Demaratus, further accusations of bribery followed. Cleomenes fled to Arcadia, where he stirred up the inhabitants against Sparta. Though the Spartans chose to pardon and recall him, he apparently lost his mind. If Herodotus' sources are correct, he perished horribly while displaying the Spartans' proverbial endurance of physical pain. When he came home, Herodotus maintains,

he was immediately seized by some frenzy of madness (even earlier he had been somewhat disturbed in his mind). When he met any of the Spartiates, he would strike at them in the face with his stick. For so doing, and because of his distraction, his relatives confined him in a pillory. But being so a prisoner, as soon as he saw his guard alone from the rest, he asked him for a knife. At first the guard refused to give him one, but the king kept threatening him with what he would do to him afterwards, until the guard, who was just one of the helots, finally gave him a knife. Cleomenes took the knife and started mutilating himself from the shins up. He cut the flesh lengthwise and went up from shins to thighs and from the thighs to the hip and the flanks, until he got to the belly. And he made mincemeat of the belly too and so died.

(The History 6.75; Grene 1987)

The exiled Demaratus fared better. As some of his conflict with Cleomenes had been over his sympathy with the pro-Persian party at Aegina, he found a warm welcome in Persia, served as an adviser in the wars with Greece, and was rewarded for his services with the grant of four cities in Asia Minor.

Athens After Marathon

The nature of political leadership in Athens changed shortly after the Battle of Marathon in a very specific manner. Events surrounding the campaign had impressed on the Athenians the importance of sound military leadership. Shortly afterward they signaled this awareness by a change in the method of selecting archons, who as primarily judicial officials had come to seem less important in comparison with the strategoi, who had life-and-death military responsibilities. In 487 they began choosing archons by lot from a large pool (perhaps a hundred men in total?) contributed by the various demes—the method already used for selecting members of the Council of Five Hundred. This shift ensured that men of ambition would stand not for the archonship, a nonrenewable office, but for the *stratēgia* (generalship). It also served gradually to undermine the status of the venerable Council of the Areopagus. Because it was composed of former archons, as time went by it came more and more to be filled by men who had been chosen by lot. It seems likely that the originator of this move was the feisty Themistocles. Not only was Themistocles hostile to the aristocratic ethos that granted special power and prestige to the Areopagites; as a man who had already served his archonship and was eligible to repeat only his generalship, he had a more immediate interest in enhancing the role of the strategoi at the archons' expense. Selection by lot was a procedure commonly associated with democracy in Greece. It worked to discourage the machinations of special interest groups and ensure that a significant proportion of the men eligible for each office would participate in politics, and it seemed to offer the gods a role in choosing officials. The Athenians were no fools, however. They subjected all would-be officeholders to an interrogation known as *dokimasia*, and they declined to employ the lot to select commanders for the state's armed forces. As a consequence, the generalship became the most prestigious office in the government, and the ten strategoi outranked all other Athenians in authority.

At the same time, the Athenians began deploying an unusual procedure for preventing any one individual from taking over the state, although the rapid disappearance of several of Themistocles' opponents serves as a reminder that the method was not foolproof. One of the innovations sometimes attributed to the reformer Cleisthenes was ostracism, a system whereby every spring the Athenians had the option of voting to send one of their fellow citizens into exile for ten years. The peculiar process took its name from the broken pieces of pottery known as *ostraka* on which the voters inscribed the name of the man they wanted to banish. No accusation was lodged; no shame attached to the departure; the exile's citizen rights and material possessions would be waiting for him upon his return. But the man who was identified as dangerous by receiving the most votes would be compelled to withdraw from Attica for a ten-year cooling-off period. Inevitably historians have wondered why, if this procedure was really developed by Cleisthenes, the first man to be exiled in this fashion—a Peisistratid named Hipparchus—was not ostracized until 487, fully twenty years after Cleisthenes' ascendancy. The answer may lie in the minimum of six thousand votes that the Athenians demanded be cast; perhaps the ostracism of Hipparchus was not the first attempted ostracism but just the first one in which the quorum was met, the first that "took." Perhaps, however, ostracism was simply invented later. It is probably no coincidence that the first man known to be ostracized bore such an unfortunate name; one common explanation of ostracism was that it was designed to ward off tyranny. Whenever ostracism was first devised, it should perhaps be seen as a means of replacing the expulsion of whole family groups, like the Alcmaeonids, with the less sweeping exile of a feared individual. Several prominent men were ostracized in the 480s—Megacles, leader of the Alcmaeonids, in 486; Xanthippus, the father of Pericles, in 484; and Themistocles' great rival Aristides, in 482.

What role Themistocles played in the first three ostracisms is a matter of speculation, but his conflict with Aristides is indisputable, and the ostracism of 482 compelled the Athenians to choose between two distinct policies. Civil war might be averted by the safety valve of ostracism, but the danger of another contest with Persia also had to be addressed. Darius raised taxes in the summer of 486, thus arousing suspicion that he was gathering resources to finance a new invasion of Greece. He would probably have some support in northern Greece—Thessaly, for example—and no doubt in the south as well. By this time the Persians were well

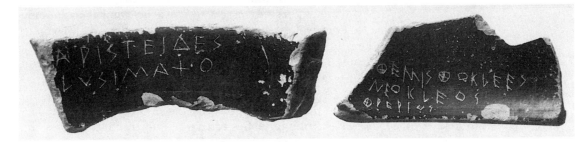

Figure 5.8. Numerous *ostraka* have been discovered in the Athenian agora. These bear the names of Artistides, son of Lysimachus, and Themistocles, son of Neocles.

aware how divided Greek cities were among themselves—they knew of the rivalry of Argos with Sparta, Aegina with Athens—and how racked by internal conflict. In the event, Thessaly, Locris, and all of Boeotia except Plataea and Thespiae would in fact give the requisite earth and water to the Persians after they learned Persian forces had crossed the Hellespont. Darius' project had to be delayed, however, because of a rebellion in Egypt sparked by the increase in taxes. In the fall of 486 BC he fell ill and died.

The Invasion of Xerxes and the Building of Triremes at Athens

Darius' son and successor, Xerxes (Cyrus' grandson on his mother's side) was at first ambivalent about carrying out the invasion, but by 484 BC he had made his decision, and the Greeks learned that ships were being built in large numbers throughout the ports of the extensive Persian empire from Egypt to the Black Sea. Engineers and laborers were dispatched to the Hellespont, where they bridged the crossing with boats, and to northern Greece where they cut a canal across Athos so that the shipwreck Mardonius had suffered in 492 could be avoided.

Fortuitously, at this very time the Athenians working the silver mines of Laurium in southeastern Attica for their modest yield hit upon an extraordinary lode of silver previously undiscovered. The new vein was so rich that it yielded well over 2 tons the first year alone. In Athens, voters were divided about what to do with it. Aristides led those who wanted to partition it among the citizens, but Themistocles advocated building ships. Well aware that gloomy prognostications of war with Persia were likely to make him unpopular, he reminded the Athenians of their constant warfare with the neighboring island of Aegina, which had just inflicted a serious setback on Piraeus trade by a major naval defeat. The ostracism of 482 decided the issue; Aristides left Athens, and the fleet that would save Greece was built. It is difficult to imagine how history might have turned out had the vote in that ostracism been different.

The ships the Athenians built with their windfall from Laurium were triremes, light, fast, maneuverable warships with three banks of oars. Although the first triremes had been built, probably in Corinth, as early as the seventh century, they were expensive vessels to construct, and it took some time for the trireme to replace older, less efficient models as the Greek warship par excellence. By the fifth century, however, the trireme had established itself as an indispensable tool of war. A long, slender vessel, the trireme was about nine times as long as it was wide, about 120 feet by 15 feet, and was powered by 170 rowers. Whereas Greek oared ships had originally been designed simply to transport soldiers to the theater of war, by the fifth century naval warfare had evolved to make ramming tactics crucial to success, and for this the trireme was ideal. It was triremes that would defeat the Persians, and the triremes would come from Athens. As the Athenian navy grew in power and

Figure 5.9. Photograph of a trireme at sea. Working in England and Greece, twentieth-century scholars and naval architects reconstructed the Athenian trireme of the Classical period.

prestige, the trireme came to be identified with Athens; in Aristophanes' play *The Birds*, an Athenian traveler, asked for his polis of origin, replies, "Where the fine triremes come from."

While the Athenians busied themselves constructing warships, Xerxes' heralds arrived in Greece seeking earth and water, and many states complied. Thessaly, Thebes, and Sparta's inveterate enemy Argos could not be counted on. Athens and the Peloponnesian League would have to take the lead, and in concert they called a congress of delegates at Corinth in 481 BC to plan the defense of Greece. There the thirty-one states that were determined to resist the Persians formed themselves into a league historians generally call the Hellenic League. In the crisis Aegina and Athens were reconciled and Aristides was recalled along with other Athenian exiles. The high command on both land and sea was conferred on Sparta. Troops would be sent north, though not so far north as to be in territory bound to go over to Persia, but the Greeks probably placed their greatest hope in their fleet. After an abortive expedition to Thessaly, they established their ground

193

forces at the pass of Thermopylae on the Malian Gulf while the fleet settled in at nearby Artemisium off northern Euboea. At the instigation of Themistocles, the Athenians probably voted to evacuate Attica and wait out the war on the island of Salamis and in nearby Troezen in the Peloponnesus. A third-century copy of the decree discovered on Troezen in 1959 is probably a reasonable facsimile of the original text:

> The Gods
> Resolved by the Council and People
> Themistocles, son of Neocles, of Phrearri, made the motion
> To entrust the city to Athena the Mistress of Athens and to all the other Gods to guard and defend from the Barbarian for the sake of the land. The Athenians themselves and the foreigners who live in Athens are to send their children and women to safety in Troezen, their protector being Pittheus, the founding hero of the land. They are to send the old men and their moveable possessions to safety on Salamis. The treasurers and priestesses are to remain on the Acropolis guarding the property of the gods.
>   All the other Athenians and foreigners of military age are to embark on the 200 ships that are ready and defend against the Barbarian for the sake of their own freedom and that of the rest of the Greeks along with the Lacedaemonians, the Corinthians, the Aeginetans, and all others who wish to share the danger.
>   *(Jameson 1970, p. 98)*

The information center of the Greek world, the Delphic oracle knew enough about Persian might to discourage resistance—the combined forces of the rich king contained many thousands of men, perhaps as many as a quarter million—and both the Spartans and the Athenians had received glum oracles. Themistocles argued that the "wooden wall" that Delphi conceded might save Athens was in fact the navy; Spartans were told that their only chance lay in the death of a king. The oracle may in part explain King Leonidas' tenacity in holding the Thermopylae pass against all odds. It is also true, however, that hard calculation called for a land operation, however unpromising, to buy time for Greece while the fleet off Artemisium could cripple the Persian navy. As luck would have it, a storm did much of the Greeks' work for them, and even before the indecisive fighting at Artemisium the Persians had lost many ships.

The Battle of Thermopylae

Leonidas marched into Thermopylae with about seven thousand men, a fairly small force; possibly the Spartans were ambivalent about taking a stand so far north. But for their dependence on the Athenian fleet, some of them might have been content to limit their defense to the Peloponnesus. The Phocian contingent, which was most familiar with the local terrain, was charged with defending the hidden road over the mountains against the chance that Xerxes would be lucky enough to find it. Lucky he was: a Greek traitor revealed the existence of the road

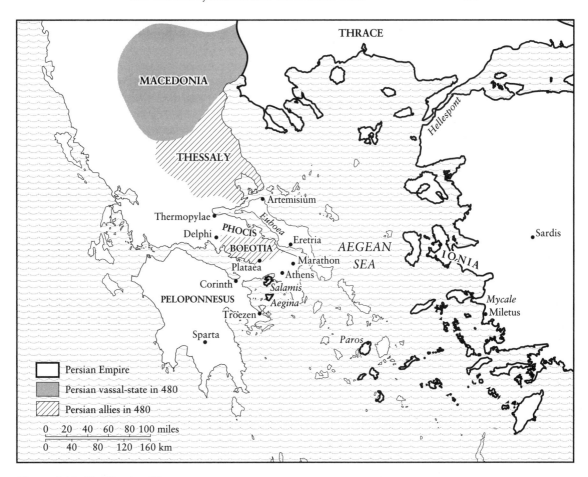

Figure 5.10. The Persian Wars.

and led Xerxes' commander Hydarnes up it with the crack troops known as the Immortals. For some reason Leonidas dismissed the bulk of his forces. He may have doubted their loyalty, or perhaps he knew his position was hopeless and wished to save as many soldiers as he could for future battles while still inflicting damage and delay on the enemy. Only the Thebans, Thespians, and three hundred Spartans remained. Leonidas and his men defended the pass heroically and fell fighting, having slain many "Immortals" including two brothers of Xerxes. On Xerxes' orders the body of Leonidas was decapitated and displayed on a cross.

The holding operation at Thermopylae not only bought time but went down in history as an extraordinary act of heroism. The defense of the Alamo in 1846 was commemorated as offering a modern parallel; German recruits in World War II were encouraged to emulate Leonidas' Spartans; and in the 'seventies the challenges of the futile war in Vietnam were captured in the film *Go Tell the Spartans*, which took its title from the epitaph composed for the Thermopylae dead attributed to Simonides:

> Go tell the Spartans, stranger passing by,
> That here, obeying their commands, we lie.

The Battle of Salamis

Their victory at Thermopylae opened central Greece to the Persians, whose confidence was boosted by the knowledge that they had killed a Spartan king. Swiftly they moved their land forces down on Athens. From Salamis just off the western coast of Attica, where the opposing fleets had taken up their position, the Athenians could see the smoke of the burning Acropolis all too easily, and those who had regarded the fortifications on the hill as the saving "wooden wall" touted by Delphi were forced to admit their mistake. Dissent racked the navy. Some of the Peloponnesians wanted to cut back to the isthmus, while the Athenians were determined to stay where they were and fight in the narrows. Xerxes was apparently tricked into taking action by a message from Themistocles, who purported to be on his side and urged immediate attack before the demoralized Greeks could disperse to their various homes. In reality, many Greeks were thinking of doing just that, and Xerxes' decision to attack was a foolish one. Herodotus, who came from Halicarnassus in Ionia, took delight in telling how Xerxes' prudent adviser Artemisia, queen of Halicarnassus, counseled him in vain against engaging battle when all the evidence suggested he could win by default. By arranging for the contest to be decided in the narrows, Themistocles maximized the chances that the lighter, more maneuverable Greek ships could worst the heavier Persian vessels. From his high perch on the shore Xerxes watched the course of the battle, in which the Greeks had the additional advantage that, as nearly all of them had grown up near water, they could swim; many of Xerxes' sailors could not. By sundown the Persians had lost two hundred ships and the battle. Rather than confront the foolishness of his decision to fight, Xerxes reacted to the defeat by executing his Phoenician captains for alleged cowardice in the battle, thus depriving himself of Phoenician naval support for the future.

Retreating with his navy to Persia in order to secure the Hellespont, Xerxes left Mardonius in Greece, where in the spring of 479 he faced the largest Greek army ever to have taken the field. Theban support bolstered the Persian cause, but it was insufficient to ensure victory. At the town of Plataea near the border between Attica and Boeotia, Mardonius ended his long years of service to Persia. Led by the Spartan Pausanias, nephew of Leonidas and regent for his infant son, the Greeks managed to win the hard fought battle, and in the fighting Mardonius fell. The Theban leaders who had "medized," that is, gone over to the Persians, were subsequently executed without trial. Around the same time—tradition claimed that it was the very same day as the battle at Plataea—the Greek fleet that had pursued the Persians eastward defeated their navy at the Battle of Mycale off the coast of Asia Minor, in part because the Ionian Greeks deserted from the Persian side.

The War Through Greek Eyes

Victors usually record the history of their triumphs. The vanquished reduce the same events to trivial, easily forgotten incidents. Until the work of Iranologists in the twentieth century following the decipherment of Old Persian in the nineteenth and the excavation of archaeological sites, our views of the Persian empire were shaped largely by Greek historical sources and by scholars who preferred the western, European democratic tradition to what they saw as "Oriental despotism." In other words, the sources have been overwhelmingly "Hellenocentric." Foremost among the ancient literary sources that established this perspective has been the *Histories* of Herodotus, who highlighted the unexpectedness of the Greek victory against all odds and searched for the causes in the fundamental institutions of Greek and Persian society and government. Although Herodotus portrays the early Achaemenids as virtuous and constructive, he depicts Xerxes as an impious madman who was responsible for initiating the decline of Persia. Xerxes' chief character flaw, in Herodotus' view, was *hybris* ("arrogance"). Like Croesus, Xerxes imagined himself on the same level as the gods. He dared to bridge the formidable Hellespont. Thus the gods were thought to have aided the Greeks in defeating Xerxes, and he was thought to have earned his humiliation. The playwright Aeschylus, who fought at Salamis as well as Marathon, also portrays Xerxes as responsible for the death of many noble Persians because of his folly. In 472 BC he produced a tragedy, *The Persians*, in which he reminded the Athenians of their role in defeating the Persians and celebrated the values for which they had fought—liberty as opposed to slavery, responsible democratic government as opposed to capricious autocracy and monarchy.

   The play also contains a vivid description of the battle itself. In reconstructing the events of the Persian wars, Plutarch's lives of Aristides and Themistocles are also of some value, dependent as they were on sources now lost to us. By far the bulk of our knowledge, however, comes from Herodotus' sweeping *Histories*. The first continuous extant prose narrative in the Greek language, Herodotus' work, rich in detail and resonant with many important themes, traced the conflict between East and West to before the Trojan War. The author's researches extended far in both time and space, dealing in depth with the consolidation of Persia, the growth of Greece, and even the customs of Egypt (which may originally have been contained in a separate work). Born of the marriage of Ionian inquisitiveness with the creativity of the Athenian enlightenment, Herodotus' *Histories* was only one reflection of the extraordinary burst of energy that erupted among the Greeks after their surprising victory over the wealthy and powerful empire that had sought to bring them into its orbit.

Document 5.1 The chorus from Aeschylus's *Persians* (472 BC)
Aeschylus took the occasion of his drama about Salamis to stress the differences
between eastern despotism and what he conceived as Greek freedom. Here the
chorus of Persian elders laments Persia's defeat by Greece:

> They throughout the Asian land
> No longer Persian laws obey,
> No longer lordly tribute yield,
> Exacted by necessity;
> Nor suffer rule as suppliants,
> To earth obeisance never make:
> Lost is the kingly power.—
> Nay, no longer is the tongue
> Imprisoned kept, but loose are men,
> When loose the yoke of power's bound,
> To bawl their liberty.
> But Ajax' isle, spilled with blood
> Its earth, and washed round by sea,
> Holds the remains of Persia.

*The Persians 584–596; translated by Seth Benardete, in David Grene and Rich-
mond Lattimore, eds.,* The Complete Greek Tragedies, *vol. 1, Aeschylus.
Chicago: University of Chicago Press, 1959.*

The Athenians later celebrated their triumph over the Persians in the relief
sculptures of the Parthenon, the temple built to honor their goddess Athena. The
reliefs on the four sides of the building showed battles: the gods against the giants; the Greeks against the Amazons; the Lapiths (a Greek people) against the
half-human, half-horse males known as Centaurs; and the Greeks against the Trojans, a reference to the struggle against the Persians, who also lived in the east.
Thus the Athenians elevated their victory to mythical status, perhaps becoming
guilty of hybris themselves.

*   *   *

Although Greek historical sources tend to depict Persian history as the gradual degeneration of the mighty empire established by Cyrus the Great, as we
shall see, the Persians were not decisively defeated by European forces until their
conquest by Alexander the Great (from 334–323 BC). They continued to play an
influential role in Greek politics, both in civic disputes and in rivalries between
Greek states, favoring now one side, now another, providing refuge for exiles and
soldiers of fortune including the Athenians Hippias, Themistocles, Alcibiades,
and Xenophon and the Spartans Demaratus, Pausanias, Lysander, and Agesilaus.

The Spartan victory in the Peloponnesian War of the late fifth century would have been impossible without Persian backing, and the relations of the poleis during the fourth century are impossible to understand without a watchful eye on Persian involvement in Greek affairs. Persia held special attractions for disaffected, greedy, or exiled Spartans, not only because it offered a luxurious way of life, but because of some similarities in social structure. Both Persia and Sparta were stable, hierarchical, class societies in which social mobility was virtually impossible. Both societies depended upon economic exploitation of vast numbers of people by the relatively few members of the upper class, who, in turn, were forced into a militaristic way of life in order to perpetuate the system. This way of life, however, was anathema to the volatile, mercurial Ionians.

The unanticipated success of the little city-states over the monolithic empire had little impact in Persia, but in Greece it would give birth to a civilization of extraordinary brilliance and originality. The unity the Persian empire had sparked, however, would prove short-lived, and its fragility would place limits on how long this civilization could endure.

TRANSLATIONS

Blanco, Walter. 1992. *The Histories,* from *Herodotus: The Histories,* Walter Blanco and Jennifer Roberts, eds. New York: W. W. Norton.

Grene, David. 1987. *The History: Herodotus.* Chicago: University of Chicago Press.

Jameson M., "A Decree of Themistocles from Troizen," Hesperia 29(1960) 200–201, modified by P. Green. 1970. *Xerxes at Salamis.* New York and London: Praeger.

Scott-Kilvert, Ian. 1960. *The Rise and Fall of Athens: Nine Greek Lives by Plutarch.* Harmondsworth, England: Penguin.

SUGGESTED READING

Bonner, R. J. and Gertrude Smith. 1968. *The Administration of Justice from Homer to Aristotle.* Reprinted New York: Greenwood Press. A classic study of the legal systems of ancient Greece.

Cook, J. M. *The Persian Empire.* 1983. London: J.M. Dent. A history that provides vital background in understanding fifth-century Persia.

Fornara, Charles. 1971. *Herodotus: An Interpretive Essay.* Oxford: Clarendon. A thoughtful study of the first surviving historian of Greece.

Forrest, W. G. 1966. *The Emergence of Greek Democracy.* New York and Toronto: McGraw-Hill. A lively and readable analysis of the governments of the Greek city-states.

Green, Peter. 1970. *Xerxes at Salamis.* New York and London: Praeger (also released as *The Year of Salamis*). A dramatic account of Xerxes' invasion by an eminent scholar who has done much to bring Greek history alive for the general reading public.

Hignett, Charles. 1963. *Xerxes' Invasion of Greece*. Oxford: Clarendon. An analysis of Greek and Persian strategy.

Lenardon, Robert. 1978. *The Saga of Themistocles*. London: Thames and Hudson. The life of the innovative and irreverent politician.

Stanton, G. R. 1990. *Athenian Politics c. 800–500 BC: A Sourcebook*. London and New York: Routledge. A very useful collection of sources that traces the evolution of the Athenian state.

6

THE RIVALRIES OF
THE GREEK CITY-STATES
AND THE GROWTH OF
ATHENIAN DEMOCRACY

In the struggle to prevent a Persian takeover of Greece, a powerful sense of Hellenic identity was forged. Eager to prevent a third invasion, a number of Greek states entered into an alliance, the Delian League, led by the Athenians, whose naval strength had been instrumental in winning the war. Because the Athenians controlled the League's treasury, the rise in Athens' prestige and self-assurance occasioned by the war was now compounded by a sharp increase in the city's wealth. Tribute from the League facilitated state pay for public service such as jury duty, thus expanding the number of men who could afford to participate in government. The fact that the lower-class citizens who rowed the triremes were becoming increasingly pivotal to the city's well-being also made it difficult for the rich and wellborn to maintain their traditional monopoly on political power. Democratic reforms consequently undermined the edge wealthy aristocrats enjoyed in politics, though nothing whatever was done to remove the civic disabilities of women or to abolish slavery. Indeed, Athens' imperial ventures probably increased the number of slaves in Attica, and the status of women seems to have declined with the growth of equality among citizen males.

During the decades that followed Xerxes' defeat, moreover, Athens became a major cultural center. Tourists came from all over Greece to observe the tragedies performed in honor of the god Dionysus, and some of the money Athens received to police the seas was diverted to the celebration of religious festivals and to the erection of magnificent public buildings such as the temple to Athena called the Parthenon; for the Greeks' deliverance from Persian autocracy the gods received ample thanks. The tragedians Aeschylus, Euripides, and Sophocles were all born in Athens, as was the comic dramatist Aristophanes, the sculptor Phidias, and the historian Thucydides. Many Greek thinkers like the historian Herodotus and the philosopher Anaxagoras came from elsewhere to enjoy—and enhance—what Athens had to offer.

Although it exerted a magnetic force on many of the artists and intellectuals of Greece, Athens was far from the only site that could boast major attractions. At Delphi, for example, donors grateful for deliverance from Persia set up splendid monuments and commissioned superb works of art. Olympia remained a vital religious center as well; the games were extended to five days, and after its completion in 456 participants could also worship at the imposing temple of Zeus. Democracies similar to that evolving at Athens developed in a number of places, most prominently Syracuse in Sicily, and throughout the Greek world intellectuals could be found bringing new ideas to birth. While Socrates was asking questions about justice and the human community in the streets of Athens, on the island of Cos Hippocrates was investigating medicine and the human body.

SOURCES FOR THE DECADES AFTER THE PERSIAN WARS

While Greek culture flourished throughout the Aegean, however, tensions between Athens and Sparta marred the scene. No Spartan writers of the Classical period have left us records of their view of the world or even of the history and habits of their country. For fourth-century Sparta the Athenian expatriate Xenophon provides considerable information, since his natural affinities were in many ways Spartan rather than Athenian and he lived for many years in the Peloponnesus after being exiled from Athens. Of course some of what he had to say about Spartan society is applicable to the fifth century as well. But in terms of foreign policy and domestic development, fifth-century Sparta remains an enigma whose story can be reconstructed only in part, using snatches from contemporary Athenians such as Thucydides or from much later writers like Plutarch. Even Plutarch with his penchant for biography did not write the lives of fifth-century Spartans (with the exception of Lysander, who spanned the fifth and fourth centuries), and much of what he has to say about Sparta is embedded in his lives of Athenian statesmen.

Sources for Athens are fuller. Though there is no detailed history of the decades that followed the defeat of Persia, a wealth of inscriptions survive that illuminate both domestic and foreign policy, and the sections dealing with this period in the first book of Thucydides' *History*, though sketchy, are enormously useful. Herodotus sheds light on the first months after the end of the Persian invasion. Some information can also be gleaned from the *Library of History* composed by Diodorus of Sicily, who lived shortly before the birth of Christ and made use of the fourth-century Greek historian Ephorus, whose work is now lost. Facts preserved in the work of Ephorus and of other lost historians who wrote during the fifth and fourth centuries and had marked biases sometimes pop up in Plutarch's lives of Athenian politicians. Plutarch wrote the lives of Themistocles, Aristides, Cimon, and Pericles.

Literary sources for day-to-day life and popular culture during the fifth century are meager indeed. Much of what we know has been inferred from the comedies of Aristophanes and the ancient commentaries on them by editors known as scholiasts. Art and archaeology also offer insights into how people lived and what they cherished; vase painting, for example, depicted not only mythological episodes but scenes from daily life. The organization of public and private space reveals a great deal about civic and family life. Much of what we know of customs and norms in the fifth century, however, has to be extrapolated from the rather richer evidence for the fourth. About the lives of women, slaves, and poor people we know much less than we would like. No Athenian woman, for example, has left us a written record of her thoughts or doings.

THE AFTERMATH OF THE PERSIAN WARS AND THE FOUNDATION OF THE DELIAN LEAGUE

We know from Herodotus that after their victory over the Persians at Plataea in 479 BC the Greek allies set up a monument at Delphi made of three intertwined bronze serpents. Centuries later the Roman emperor Constantine moved this important monument to Constantinople, where it still stands today prominently displayed in the central square called the Hippodrome in Istanbul. On its coils were inscribed the name of the thirty-one Greek states that had stood fast against the Persians. The Greeks agreed that Plataea should henceforth be considered sacred land, dedicated to Zeus the Liberator in gratitude for the victory over Persia.

First among the thirty-one states listed on the serpent column were Sparta and Athens. The role of the Athenian navy in beating back the Persians had radically altered the balance of power in Greece, and it was uncertain how the Spartans would accommodate this shift. Thucydides reports that when the Athenians began to rebuild the walls that the Persians had demolished, Sparta's allies, made nervous by the size of the Athenians' navy and by the daring they had shown during the war, pressured the Spartans to send an embassy to Athens to dissuade the Athenians from fortifying their city. Putting forward the bizarre argument that a walled city could be used as a base by the Persians should they return, the Spartans argued that no city outside the Peloponnesus should have walls, and indeed invited the Athenians to join them in razing the walls of any non-Peloponnesian city—in order to protect Greece more effectively against Persia. Not surprisingly, the Athenians found this line of reasoning unpersuasive, and work on the walls continued, with Themistocles reportedly deceiving the querulous Spartans with false denials until the fortifications were firmly in place.

The Continuing Persian Threat: Conflicts over Greek Leadership

As if the Athenians were not enjoying a sufficient rise in prestige after the role their navy had played in repelling the Persian invasion, developments in the Hellespont soon catapulted them to still greater heights. Despite the preponderance of Athenian ships, by custom a Spartan still commanded the fleet of the Hellenic League. While the League's fleet was at Byzantium in 478 seeking to consolidate Greek power in the east, the Greeks under his command began to complain bitterly about Pausanias, regent for Leonidas' underage son Pleistarchus. He conducted himself, they alleged, like an eastern potentate, dressing like a Persian and fortifying his position with a bodyguard of Medes and Egyptians. He was also accused of exchanging treacherous letters with King Xerxes. (Thucydides actually quotes the supposed text, but it is difficult to see how the letters would have been available to him or any other Greek.) Pausanias may have been guilty of treason or he may not; what is certain is that his lack of tact alienated the Greeks serving under him, particularly the Ionians, who had only recently been freed from the Persian king and were especially sensitive to the trappings of despotism. Having appealed to Athens to take over the leadership of the fleet, the Greeks were unmoved by the arrival of Dorcis, whom the Spartans had optimistically sent out to replace the disgraced Pausanias. In this way the leadership of the fleet passed into willing Athenian hands—a development many people in the allied states would come to regret.

Inevitably the Spartans were divided about this turn of events. To some no doubt the containment of Persia without undue Spartan exertion was an appealing prospect. Throughout Classical history, the underlying threat of a helot rebellion inhibited Spartan ambitions in the east. Others, however, were stung by the blow to Spartan prestige and found the Athenians' growing power ominous and unsettling.

In Athens, on the other hand, there was little cause for ambivalence. Because a shortage of fertile land made the Athenian economy dependent on grain from Ukraine, safeguarding the Hellespont and the northern Aegean from Persia was of supreme importance. In addition, the Athenians enjoyed a powerful sentimental attachment to their cousins the Ionian Greeks, and abandoning them to Persian rule would both feel bad and look bad. Athens, moreover, had seen its territory ravaged by the Persians, an experience Sparta had been spared. For all these reasons the Athenians considered it in their interest to assume leadership of the naval forces.

The Delian League

An alliance was consequently formed which, though it had no name at the time, later came to be called the Delian League because its treasury was originally located on the island of Delos in the Aegean. In 477 representatives from Athens and dozens of other states met at Delos and took oaths binding themselves into an organization designed to fight the Persians. The allied states entered into a treaty with Athens, which agreed in exchange for annual contributions in ships or money to lead the league in military operations against Persia while simultaneously respecting the internal autonomy of each polis in the alliance. Policy was to be established by a league assembly (in which each state had one vote regardless of its size). It would be executed, however, by an Athenian high command that would also control the treasury. Thus from the beginning, power in the league was concentrated in Athenian hands. The small size of Greek states is reflected in the number of poleis who enrolled in the alliance—probably about 150. Numerous states also declined to join, particularly those whose fear of the Athenians outweighed any apprehension about Persia, and those that decided to rely for their security on their membership in the Peloponnesian League. As was customary in Greek alliances, all states swore to have the same friends and enemies. The association, moreover, was conceived as permanent. Whereas the goals of the Peloponnesian League had never been defined, those of the Delian League were fairly clear—containment of Persia, the gathering of booty as compensation for damages done to Greece during the war, and simple revenge.

In view of the personality problems that had brought down Pausanias (and with him Spartan naval leadership), it was particularly fortunate for the Athenians that they had at their disposal a man as famous for his probity and affability as Aristides. It was he who was charged with assessing each state's appropriate contribution to the league treasury. Some of the larger states such as Lesbos, Samos, Chios, Naxos, and Thasos chose to make their contributions in ships; most preferred to pay cash directly to the temple of Apollo at Delos. As time passed, some of the bigger poleis converted to cash payments, and periodically the tribute assessment was revised. Funds were in the care of ten Athenian magistrates known as *hellēnotamiai* ("treasurers of the Greeks"). Although records of the tribute paid in the league's first years are lacking, it is possible to track the history of payments beginning in 454 through the compendium that survives today called the *Athenian Tribute Lists*, actually lists of the one-sixtieth of each contribution that was dedicated to the goddess Athena; these figures multiplied by 60 give the size of each state's contribution in a given year.

From Delian League to Athenian Empire

Though it was Themistocles' far-seeing naval policy that provided the base on which the Delian League was built, its heroes were his rivals, the revered Aristides and Miltiades' amiable son Cimon, who proved himself an estimable general. For over a quarter century—until Cimon's death in 450—the League fought against Persia and, under Cimon's leadership, expelled the Persians from Europe and made it impossible for them to establish naval bases in Ionia. In 476 Cimon set out with the League's navy for the northeast. His aims were to expel the Persians from all Thrace, banish troublesome pirates from the island of Scyros, and clear the route to the Hellespont of any obstacles. The fortress of Eion on the Strymon River was taken with little difficulty. The Athenians then moved against

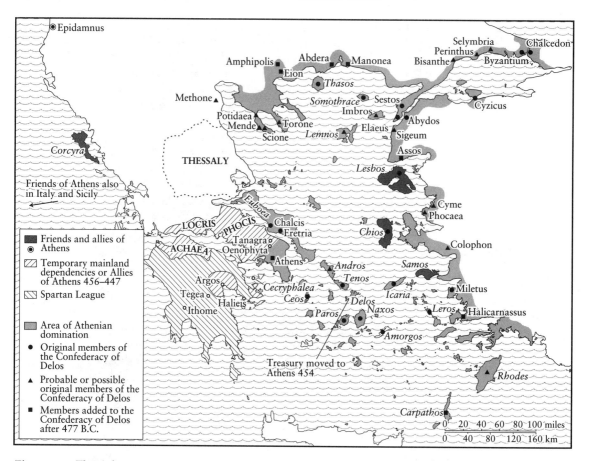

Figure 6.1. The Athenian empire at its height.

Scyros, a rocky island east of Euboea inhabited by pirates. Enslaving the pirates and their families, they established on the island the kind of colony that was known as a cleruchy. Unlike most Greek colonies, which were fully autonomous and independent of the mother city, cleruchies were in effect part of Athenian territory, for all their inhabitants (called cleruchs) retained their Athenian citizenship. Generally chosen by the government from among poor Athenians, each cleruch was granted a parcel of land (a *klēros*, hence the word "cleruch") adequate to maintain him in Solon's third class, that of the *zeugitai*, and hence qualify him for service as a hoplite infantryman. Cleruchies filled a double function: they provided an outlet for the disaffected and potentially dangerous poor, and they operated as garrisons in the empire to discourage rebellion from Athens.

While in Scyros Cimon also organized a search for the bones of King Theseus, who according to Greek tradition had died there, for the Delphic oracle had com-

Figure 6.2. Section of Athenian Tribute List inscription showing payments for 433–432 BC. The citizens of Mykonos, Andros, Siphnos, Syros, Styra, Eretria, Grynches, and Rheneia are listed here.

manded that the Athenians retrieve these remains and honor them as sacred relics. His triumphant announcement that he had indeed managed to find the king's remains won him enormous popularity in Athens. Plutarch tells the tale in his life of Theseus:

> [Cimon] caught sight of an eagle, at a place which had the appearance of a mound, pecking at the ground with its beak and tearing it up with its talons, and by some divine inspiration he concluded that they should dig at this place. There they found a coffin of a man of gigantic size and, lying beside it, a bronze spear and a sword. When Cimon brought these relics home on board his trireme, the Athenians were overjoyed and welcomed them with magnificent processions and sacrifices, as though the hero himself were returning to his city.
>
> (Theseus 36; Scott-Kilvert 1960)

Theseus became the object of a thriving hero cult, and from then on Cimon made a point of boasting of his connection to him whenever possible.

Shortly afterward the Athenians and their allies sailed against Carystus in southwestern Euboea, compelling the city to join the Delian League. Some time later when the island of Naxos decided to leave the League, the Athenians forcibly prevented its withdrawal. Defeated by the superior forces of the League, the Naxians saw their walls dismantled and their fleet confiscated. Henceforth their tribute would be paid in money, not ships. These two developments highlight the problematic nature of the Delian League. A strong case could be made—and was made—that since all Greek states benefited from the existence of the League, all should pay tribute and support its fleet. Against this argument, however, resentful poleis adduced their right to make their own determinations about the extent of the Persian peril.

Because the League's existence was justified only by the need for continued protection of Greece from the Persians, moreover, a problem would be created for the Athenians if Cimon and his navy did too good a job of squelching any designs Persia might have on Greece, for dramatic success in this endeavor would eliminate the need for an expensive anti-Persian alliance. Suspicions that the costly League might have outlived its usefulness mounted when around 467 the Persian forces were badly beaten by those of Cimon at the mouth of the Eurymedon River in southern Asia Minor. After destroying the two hundred Phoenician ships fighting on the Persian side, Cimon's men landed and defeated the Persian army; they then captured eighty ships that were coming from Cyprus as reinforcements. Cimon was now the hero of the hour, and his supporters in Athens were quick to identify his exploits at the Battle of the Eurymedon as yet another chapter in the conflict between East and West that had begun with the Trojan War—another contest that had culminated in a Greek victory in Asia.

Greek Leaders in Trouble Again: Themistocles and Pausanias

Though his stunning victory at the Eurymedon did much for Cimon's popularity in Athens, it also encouraged defections from the League. Cimon's success probably played a role in the revolt in 465 of the important island of Thasos, located just off Thrace, but economic considerations also contributed to tensions between the Thasians and the Athenians, for both hoped to control the mines of Thrace. After forcing the Thracian Chersonese into the League, Cimon had attempted to found a colony on the Strymon at a place known as Ennea Hodoi (The Nine Ways), an important link on the route to the mines on Mount Pangaeus and indeed to the Bosporus itself. The Thracians, however, set upon the colonists and killed them. The subsequent revolt of Thasos was quelled only after a siege of two years. When the Thasians finally surrendered to Cimon, they were compelled to yield the mines and their ships, paying tribute henceforth in cash—cash that could not be raised from the mines, which were now back in Athenian hands. Athenian activities in Thasos also gave rise to an interesting political trial in Athens. Despite his reputation for incorruptibility, Cimon was impeached by his enemies on the grounds that bribes from King Alexander of Macedon were responsible for his decision not to use his base in the north to invade Macedonia. Cimon was apparently acquitted, but one of the public prosecutors chosen to argue the case against the popular admiral was Pericles, a young man who would become the most distinguished statesman of Classical Athens.

The Athenians' refusal to permit states to remain aloof from the League, combined with the gradual conversion of tribute payments from ships to money, sent an increasingly clear message that Athens ruled the sea and was converting the naval alliance into an empire. Although Athenian leaders seem to have been largely of one mind about the merits of naval imperialism, however, they were divided about Athens' proper relationship to Sparta. These conflicts, moreover, were tied to disagreements about the further democratization of Athenian political life. Although sources for Athenian politics during these decades are sparse, some underlying fault lines are discernible: Themistocles encouraged competition with Sparta and the development of democracy, wheres Cimon favored Sparta and opposed any further democratization.

Sparta had helped Isagoras in his battle with Cleisthenes for the privilege of redefining the Athenian body politic, plotting to disband the *boulē* (the Council of Five Hundred) and entrust the government to an oligarchy of three hundred. But Sparta had also driven out the Peisistratids, and many Athenians viewed Sparta as their natural ally—Sparta, whose king Leonidas and his steadfast men-at-arms had bought time for Attica at Thermopylae, laying down their lives so that Greece might remain free. In both fact and memory, the union of Athens and Sparta had played an important part in the defeat of Persia (though naturally things looked different to Themistocles, whose chief involvement in the war was at Salamis, from which the Peloponnesians had sought to flee, abandoning Attica to its fate). The forces in Athens favoring warm relations with Sparta and opposing the increasingly democratic trend in the government were strong. So was Themistocles' personality: his sharp tongue and quickness to claim credit for his achievements played into the hands of his enemies, and it seems that he was ostracized around 471 BC. Probably he used his enforced absence from Athens to foment discontent and perhaps some democratization in the Peloponnesus, hoping to undermine the position of Sparta. In the 460s the Spartans and Athenians united against him: the Spartans provided evidence that purported to show that he and Pausanias were engaged in treasonable correspondence with the Persian king. In all likelihood Pausanias was guilty and Themistocles innocent, but when the Athenians recalled him from Argos to stand trial and he found no place in Greece that would harbor him, Themistocles fled to Xerxes' successor Artaxerxes. He died in Persia about ten years later, substantially outliving Pausanias, who was walled up by his enraged countrymen in a shrine in which he had taken refuge, and died of starvation.

Document 6.1 Thucydides recounts the story of Pausanias' death in his history of the Peloponnesian War. The ephors, he writes, intended to arrest Pausanias in the city:

The story continues that as Pausanias was about to be arrested on the street he saw the expression on the face of one of the ephors coming toward him and knew why they were coming, while another, sympathetic, ephor gave it away with a slight nod. He then escaped to safety by running to the Temple of the Goddess of the Brass House, the grounds of which were nearby. To avoid exposure to the weather, he went into a small building which formed a part of the temple and stayed there. The ephors were too late to catch him just then, but they afterward tore the roof off the building and, making sure that he was inside, they removed the doors, walled him in, encircled the place and proceeded to starve him to death. When they found out that he was about to die in that room, they started to lead him out of the temple while there was still some breath in him. As soon as he was out, he died.

The Peloponnesian War 1.134; translated by Walter Blanco, in Walter Blanco and Jennifer Roberts, eds., Thucydides: The Peloponnesian War. *New York: W.W. Norton, 1998.*

Further Conflicts at Athens: The Fall of Cimon and the Reforms of Ephialtes

Having rid themselves of a keen and colorful politician in Themistocles, the Athenians were left with the genial and gentlemanly Cimon. Themistocles and Cimon were opposites in every way. The conventional Cimon named his son Lacedaemonius while Themistocles cast his eyes farther westward and named his daughters Sybaris and Italia. Slow where Themistocles had been quick, and courteous where Themistocles had been insolent, Cimon was no intellectual, but he had a flair for generalship. Because of his military reputation, he continued to command a good deal of respect in the Athenian assembly even after the development of a calculating and determined coalition led by Ephialtes, whose purpose was to break with Sparta and further the growth of democracy.

For some years Ephialtes and his associates had been making attacks on individual members of the venerable and aristocratic Council of the Areopagus; Cimon's trial needs to be placed in this context. In 462, not long after Cimon's return from Thasos and impeachment by Pericles, matters came to a head. Two years earlier, when an earthquake in Sparta killed thousands of people and destroyed most houses, the helots had seized the moment and revolted. Unable to dislodge the rebels from their stronghold on Mount Ithome, the Spartans appealed for aid to the cities with which they were still technically allied by the terms of the Hellenic League formed in 481 for the defense of Greece during the Persian wars. The Athenians looked like promising associates, for they were reputed to be better than most at siege warfare, though standards of excellence in this branch of tactics were low in Classical Greece, where sieges were generally prolonged and tedious.

Sparta's request touched off a vigorous debate in the Athenian assembly. Cimon, it seems, defended the time-honored alliance between Athens and Sparta, imploring the Athenians "not to allow Greece to go lame, or their own city be deprived of its yoke-fellow," while Ephialtes exhorted his fellow citizens to "let

Sparta's pride be trampled underfoot" (Plutarch's *Cimon* 16.8; Scott-Kilvert 1960). Cimon carried the day, and he marched off to Sparta backed by four thousand hoplites. But something about the way the Athenian soldiers conducted themselves in Sparta sparked panic in the conservative and fundamentally xenophobic people they had come to help. Alone among the allies, the Athenians were sent home. Their abrupt dismissal imperiled what harmony had been achieved among the Greek states. Athens now made an alliance with Sparta's enemy Argos; Cimon, moreover, was ostracized for his miscalculation, leaving an open highway for Ephialtes and his associates. If the Spartans were alarmed by the Athenians' innovative and forward-looking ways of construing the world, they did a bad job of squelching these. The end of Cimon's ascendancy marked the beginning in Athens of full-blown democracy, taking democracy in the Greek sense of diffusing political power throughout the male citizen body, with no votes for women, no citizenship for immigrants, and slaves in abundance. Ironically, moreover, the naval ascendancy that Cimon had done so much to develop played a large role in fostering the democratic reforms he opposed. Cimon seems to have supported a moderate hoplite democracy, that is, government by those who could afford to provide their own weapons and armor. The success of his naval operations, however, underlined the increasing importance to the state of the men who rowed the triremes (some moderately poor, some indigent), a development that served to undermine the old-fashioned system of power following property and contributed to its replacement by a more broadly based form of government.

Ephialtes was able to seize on the discrediting of Cimon's policies by passing some significant democratic reforms. Though the details remain obscure, we know in a general sense that he substantially diminished the power and prestige of the ancient Council of the Areopagus. Time had already done some of Ephialtes' work for him: since the Areopagus consisted of ex-archons, it had been growing less and less aristocratic with each year that had passed since 486 when the Athenians had begun selecting archons by lot. Its members, however, held power for life, and the newer, poorer Areopagites may well have been co-opted into the value system of their aristocratic elders. At the instigation of Ephialtes, the assembly passed measures constricting the jurisdiction of this body, transferring many of its functions to the *boulē*, the *ekklēsia*, and the body of prospective jurors known as the *hēliaia*. Ephialtes was careful, however, to show respect for its venerable history and long traditions by leaving it with jurisdiction over homicide and some religious matters.

Shortly after these reforms were enacted, men who presumably disliked the turn the government was taking arranged for Ephialtes' assassination. With Ephialtes' death, his associate Pericles seems to have assumed leadership of the loosely organized political group to which we give the somewhat misleading term "party." With the exception of two years, Pericles remained the leading politician in Athens from roughly 461 to his death in 429, being elected repeatedly as one of the ten strategoi.

THE "FIRST" (UNDECLARED) PELOPONNESIAN WAR (460–445 BC)

Pericles took the lead in shaping Athenian policy throughout the decade during which Athens chose to wage war with both the Persian empire and the Peloponnesian League. Hostilities with Persia survived Cimon's ostracism, while tensions with Sparta and its allies escalated. The period from 460 to 445 BC is sometimes known as the First Peloponnesian War, an undeclared war between the Athenian and Spartan leagues that really consisted of a series of battles often punctuated by considerable intervals of peace. (The famous Peloponnesian War, which was fought fairly steadily for twenty-seven years from 431 to 404, was really the Second Peloponnesian War.) The fact that historians have labeled the war as "Peloponnesian" reflects the fact that the principal sources are Athenian; just as we know the Trojan War and the Persian wars from the Greek standpoint and do not normally call them the Greco-Trojan or Greco-Persian Wars, the Atheno-Spartan War has come to be known as the Peloponnesian War, though Thucydides himself called it the war of the Athenians and the Peloponnesians.

Athens' Conflicts with Its Neighbors

Athens' neighbor Megara played an important role in both Peloponnesian wars. Attica shared its western border with this small but pivotal polis that separated it from Corinth. A commercial state poor in agricultural resources, Megara was a trade rival of Athens. Megara's position made it vulnerable, but it also gave it power. Athens and Corinth did not always get along, and Corinth with its substantial navy was an indispensable ally of landlocked Sparta. The vacillations of Megara would have serious repercussions for all Greeks throughout the fifth century. Controlled by a prodemocratic faction, around the time of Ephialtes' death Megara decided to ally itself with Athens to obtain protection from the designs of Corinth. Alarmed by the Athenians' possession of the Megarian port of Pegae on the Corinthian Gulf, from which it was easy to sail to the west, the Corinthians became still more agitated at the upshot of the helot rebellion that had followed the earthquake in the Peloponnesus. For when the helots on Mount Ithome finally surrendered on condition that they be permitted to leave the Peloponnesus, the Athenians settled them at Naupactus near the mouth of the Gulf, on the northern shore. This bold action gave the Athenians yet another foothold for westward penetration and drove an additional wedge into the Corinthians' sphere of influence. With the two states locked in commercial rivalry, moves that promised to expand the territory easily accessible to Athenian shipping were bound to spark hostility in Corinth, and it was predictable that Corinth would seek the help of its powerful ally Sparta in conflicts with Athens. The tension between Athens and Corinth was bound to play a large role in determining the diplomatic relations of the Greek states, and it often led to outright war.

In 459 Corinth and Aegina combined against Athens. The Athenians not only repelled a Corinthian invasion of Megara but also built formidable walls, the so-called Long Walls, linking Athens to the port of Piraeus. This prudent strategy had the effect of making the whole town complex impossible to besiege by land, since supplies could always be brought in by boat. Around the same time they engaged Hippodamus, a native of Miletos who apparently wrote a treatise on town planning, to design the port area, which he laid out on a grid pattern similar to that of his home state in Ionia.

The Spartans' decision to enter the war against Athens in 457 did more harm to them than to their designated enemy. Fighting the Athenians in Boeotia, what the Spartans chiefly accomplished was to draw Athens into Boeotian affairs. By 456 the Athenians had come to control the whole region with the exception of Thebes, and Athenian influence (or pressure) had made democratic governments the norm in the Boeotian poleis. West of Boeotia, Phocis and Locris joined the Delian League, as did the vanquished island of Aegina, and Athens also gained two states on the Peloponnesus itself, Troezen on the east coast and Achaea on the Corinthian Gulf.

Figure 6.3. Aerial view of Piraeus.

Athenian Involvement in Egypt and the Transfer of the League Treasury to Athens

Athens' land empire now stood at its maximum extent. Determined to continue operations against Persia, Pericles persuaded the Athenians to send ships both to Cyprus, where they hoped to inflict damage on the Phoenician fleet, and to Egypt, which had rebelled from King Artaxerxes. The Egyptian campaign dragged on for years, ending in a wretched debacle in 453 when Artaxerxes' general Megabazus penned in the Athenians on the island of Prosopitis and besieged them for eighteen months. Ultimately Megabazus drained the channels around the island, leaving the ships high and dry, and marched across on foot to capture the Athenian sailors. Thucydides reports that nearly all the Athenians were killed. In addition, a relief force of fifty ships that arrived ignorant of the disaster was attacked by the Persian infantry and the Phoenician fleet, and only a small number of these ships escaped. Although the size of the original force is uncertain—Thucydides says two hundred ships, the Persian historian Ctesias only forty—still the loss in morale was enormous, surpassed only by the loss in life.

In 454, meanwhile, the Athenians transferred the treasury of the Delian League from the island of Delos, vulnerable to pirates and Persians alike, to Athens itself. Though their ostensible purpose was security, Delos was probably no more endangered than it had been previously, and the Athenians' decision to move the treasury was primarily a power play designed to demonstrate their supremacy. Historians therefore have taken 454 as a convenient date to stop referring to the Delian League and begin speaking of the Athenian empire, though in reality of course the transformation had been going on for some time.

A Brief Hiatus: Athens at Peace with Persia and Sparta

Returning from his ten years' exile in 451, Cimon seems to have come to an understanding with his rival Pericles; he would resume his efforts to make war on Persia and peace with Sparta but would not interfere with any domestic policies Pericles might wish to implement. In 451 Cimon negotiated a truce of five years between Athens and Sparta and abandoned Athens' alliance with Argos. Argos in turn signed a thirty-year treaty with Sparta; the expiration of this treaty in 420, eleven years after the beginning of the (Second) Peloponnesian War, would create a volatile situation in mainland Greece. When Cimon died campaigning in Cyprus in 450, the Athenians seem to have made peace with Persia. We do not, however, have the text of this agreement, the so-called Peace of Callias, named after Cimon's former brother-in-law, who was later said to have negotiated it. Because the only sources for the treaty date to the fourth century, some scholars have doubted its reality, while others place it considerably earlier or substantially later. What is certain is that Athens and Persia ceased fighting at this time, treaty or no treaty.

Peace with Sparta followed in 445 when the Athenian land empire collapsed virtually overnight. After sixteen years of imperialism within mainland Greece, the Athenians had lost hundreds of lives and had no more territory than they had possessed in 461 when fighting had begun. Just as the five-year truce between Athens and Sparta expired in 446, Euboea revolted, probably because of resentment at the cleruchies the Athenians were establishing there. While Athens was frantically trying to put down the Euboean rebellion, the Megarians took the occasion to defect, slaughtering their Athenian garrison. When Pericles returned from Euboea to Attica, the land had already been invaded by King Pleistoanax of Sparta. Delicate diplomacy and probably downright bribery as well enabled Pericles to persuade Pleistoanax to return home, but terror had been struck in the Athenians' hearts. Though in time Pericles himself subdued Euboea, Megara reverted to the Peloponnesian League, and Athenian influence in Boeotia crashed to a close as Thebes assumed leadership of an antidemocratic Boeotian League.

The Thirty Years' Peace

The peace the Athenians made with Sparta in 445 was optimistically named the Thirty Years' Peace, though it would not last even half that long. The Athenians had overextended themselves by fighting at the same time with the Persian empire and the Peloponnesian League, and their naked imperialism had also made them unpopular. They were in no position to dictate terms, and in fact the peace compelled them to surrender their whole land empire, retaining only Naupactus and Plataea. (Though they also held on to Aegina, this in fact violated the peace.) Their maritime empire, however, remained secure from Spartan interference, and the treaty also specified that neither state was to interfere with the allies of the other; neutrals were free to join either side; and disagreements were to be settled by arbitration. No allies were permitted to switch sides, and each hegemon was free to use force to resolve conflicts within its own alliance.

PERICLES AND THE GROWTH OF ATHENIAN DEMOCRACY

The guiding spirit of Athenian imperialism was Pericles, who owed his position at Athens in part to his repeated election to the post of strategos and in part to the high regard in which the Athenians held him. Though he always served concurrently with nine other strategoi every year, none of the other generals exercised a parallel influence in the ekklesia. It was the outdoor assembly meeting that made policy in fifth-century Athens, backed by the large juries of hundreds of citizens that were selected from the heliaia. Although Pericles occasionally campaigned—commanding, for example, the troops that regained rebellious Euboea—his skills lay primarily in formulating policy and in persuading members of the ekklesia to vote his proposals into law.

The Athenian Assemby

The assembly met in the open air on the hill known as the Pnyx—hot in summer, cold in winter, and often wet, but still a magnet for the many men of Attica who wished to play a role in determining the peninsula's future. In the early decades of the fifth century the assembly met only about a dozen times a year, but the number of meetings soon expanded, and in Pericles' time ten days rarely went by without at least one meeting. Assemblies that promised discussion of serious problems were likely to be attended by about six thousand—the quorum for certain important actions such as ostracism. This number was probably about an eighth or so of all adult citizen males in Attica during Pericles' career; when the population dropped later on, in part as a consequence of the ruinous Peloponnesian War of 431–404, the quorum of six thousand accounted for a higher proportion of the populace. During the first half of the fifth century, children with at least one Athenian parent would be enrolled in their demes as citizens at the age of 18, but in 451 Pericles persuaded the Athenians to limit citizenship to those whose parents were both Athenians. This was evidently an antiaristocratic measure aimed at affluent men who made marriage alliances with noble families from other states, following the example of Cleisthenes, for instance, whose wife was the daughter of the tyrant of Sicyon in mainland Greece. The citizenship law was not entirely retroactive, but probably children who had not yet reached the age of 18 were excluded from citizenship. Citizenship was important for girls as well as boys: though Athenian women could not vote or hold offices, they were now the only women who could bear Athenian children.

The consequences of this legislation were both wide and deep. Throughout Greece, the discouragement of marriage between citizens and aliens increased the jingoistic tendencies of the polis. The insistence that people marry citizens of their own state eliminated a powerful source of connectedness among poleis and fostered a sense of separateness that frequently led to war. Social problems were also created within the polis. Limited in their choice of marriage partners to Athenian women, married Athenian men frequently opened the door to domestic tensions by maintaining sexual relationships with the exotic "foreign" women whom they could not marry if they wanted civic rights for their sons and grandsons. A double irony awaited Pericles in his own family life: unhappy in his marriage, he divorced the mother of his legitimate children and lived instead with Aspasia, a highly intelligent immigrant from Miletus who was one of the most cultivated women of the century. When his legitimate sons died, he implored the assembly to confer citizenship on the son he had with Aspasia by a special decree. Admitted to citizenship, Pericles the younger served as strategos in 406 and was one of the six generals executed after they failed to pick up sailors in a storm off the Arginusae islands in Ionia.

The *prytaneis* alone—the fifty members of the boule whose turn it was to be in charge for the month—had the privilege of calling a meeting of the citizens' assembly, though sometimes they did so at the behest of the strategoi. Theoretically, no motion could be put at the assembly that had not been drafted by the boule and posted at least five days before the day of the meeting, but this restriction did not mean that only council members could frame legislation. Sometimes the boule's motion was deliberately couched in such vague terms that it was inevitable that some private citizen would reframe it at the assembly meeting; frequently amendments wound up revising an original motion beyond recognition. Besides, most people who burned to put motions could suggest them to some neighbor, relation, or friend of a friend who happened to be serving on the boule.

Those who attended the assembly might be lifelong advocates of certain policies and could well be followers of a popular politician, but they were not members of political parties as we know them today, for there was no such thing in Athens. Classical Greek even lacks a word for a political party; writers used expressions like "those around General So-and-So" to identify political groups. Even among those who elected to attend meetings of the assembly, the degree to which citizens chose to participate varied widely. As at gatherings of academic faculties today (or town meetings in New England), some never spoke, some spoke occasionally, a hard core of engaged citizens spoke frequently—and no doubt there were a few who seemed to speak incessantly. Generals had the privilege of speaking first, in order of age; among private citizens, originally those over age 50 took precedence over younger men. Some people spoke extemporaneously; others brought notes or even a text. Speakers had to be prepared for their remarks to be interrupted periodically by laughter, applause, or heckling of various sorts. Once the debate was concluded—assembly meetings rarely went past early afternoon, for some time had to be reserved before supper for the daily meeting of the boule—voting was conducted by show of hands.

Who attended the meetings of the assembly? Common sense would suggest that those who lived in the city center were more likely to turn up than those who lived far away, and no doubt the walk in from distant villages discouraged some citizens, especially on rainy days. Nonetheless it seems that people did take the trouble to make the trip when vital matters (like whether or not to go to war) were slated for discussion.

Athenian Officials

Athens had no president or prime minister; the generals exercised power in politics only by virtue of the esteem in which they were held. Until Pericles' death, men who lacked military reputations did not generally become distinguished politicians. The converse tended to be true as well—military heroes expected to be rewarded with political careers. In addition, though any man from the upper two classes of *pentakosiomedimnoi* ("500-measure men") and *hippeis* ("horsemen") might stand for office, the Athenians usually voted for fairly rich men from prominent families. All this changed after Pericles' death, when politics and the military began to diverge as careers and it became somewhat more customary for a man to be just a general or just a politician; concomitantly the government ceased to be dominated entirely by the scions of famous clans. Throughout Athenian history, however, wealth and lineage remained important factors, and generals continued to involve themselves in politics more than they do in many countries today.

The board of ten generals on which Pericles served was only one of many bodies the Athenians established. Including jobs entailed by the administration of the empire, there may have been as many as seven hundred official positions all told in Classical Athens, and most offices were held, like the strategia, by boards of several men, all serving one-year terms. Many, like the archons, were selected by lot. Most citizen males by the time they died had held some public office at one time or another, and a good number had held several. By diluting power in this way, Athenian voters believed they could inhibit the growth of an identifiable class of permanent officials (what we might call bureaucrats) with interests different from those of the populace at large. The interests of the disfranchised—of women, metics, and slaves—did not strike them as material to the body politic. The fruits of empire, fifth-century voters believed, were being shared by all.

The Judicial System and State Pay for State Service

In the absence of a chief executive, the Athenians considered sovereignty to be vested in the people. By the time of Pericles, they had come to call their form of government *dēmokratia*, a government in which the *kratos* ("power"), was in the hands of the *dēmos* ("the people"), by which they meant the male citizens in their capacity as voters in the assembly—and as jurors in the courts. The large size of Athenian juries—several hundred, sometimes as many as 1501—facilitated the legal fiction that a decision of a jury was a decision of the demos, and consequently there could be no appeal from a verdict in an Athenian courtroom. The Athenians were a notoriously litigious people. In Aristophanes' *Clouds*, a lively comedy whose depiction of Socrates contributed substantially to the hostility against the philosopher, one of Socrates' pupils points out Athens on a map to the crotchety Strepsiades, but Strepsiades is not persuaded. "What's that you're saying?" he asks; "I'm not convinced, since I don't see any courts in session." (208) The participation of large numbers of citizens in the judicial system was considered to be a hallmark of Athenian democracy.

To ensure that the privilege of serving on juries would be spread as widely throughout the citizen body as possible, not long after Ephialtes' death Pericles introduced a measure providing pay for jury service. It was a small amount, less than a day's wages for an average laborer, but not trivial, and no doubt this legislation bolstered Pericles' popularity at the polls. In time Athenians came to be paid for serving on the boule and even for attending the assembly; for many years during the fifth century magistrates were also paid for their time. As elsewhere in Greece, voters gained some free time as a consequence of the labor done by women and slaves, but even a citizen with a wife and a couple of slaves generally had to work hard to survive, and the sums men received for participating in government made a difference. Today it seems natural to compensate people for the time spent serving the community, and state pay for state service is now the norm. But many Athenians—mostly affluent men who could afford to serve without remuneration—viewed this system as a discreditable attempt on the part of democratic politicians to buy popularity and votes. In the aristocratic value system, it was acceptable for Cimon to court popularity by inviting passersby to pick fruit from his orchards and by holding banquets for the hungry at his home, but it was manipulative and underhanded of Pericles to introduce measures in the assembly providing for compensation to those who served the state.

Despite a variety of constitutional reforms and creative innovations designed to maximize popular participation in civic life, rich Athenians continued to enjoy substantial prestige. Democratic politicians cleverly harnessed the wealth of the elite into the service of the state by establishing a network of public services known as liturgies. Even though these politicians themselves belonged to the elite and hence were creating a system that would oblige them to spend their own money, they considered these liturgies to be good investments in public relations both for themselves and for democratic principles. Liturgies included major outlays such as maintaining a trireme and training its crew (the liturgy known as the trierarchy), leading and financing a delegation to a religious festival in another Greek state, paying and training a team of runners for the intertribal torch races at festivals within Athens, or offering a banquet to all members of one's tribe on the occasion of a religious festival. Some of the most elaborate (though not as expensive as the trierarchy, which remained the costliest liturgy) involved training choruses for performances at Attic festivals in honor of Athena or Dionysus. The fifteen members of a tragic chorus, the twenty-four members of a comic chorus, and the fifty members of a chorus that would recite the verses known as dithyrambs all needed to be selected, paid, and trained. Often the rehearsal period extended for months. The citizen who performed this liturgy might or might not know anything about sailing, running, or poetry; often he provided the funds and delegated the work to skilled experts. In addition to dozens of trierarchies, about a hundred civilian liturgies were performed each year. Everyone profited from this system. Those who lacked the means to offer such services benefited from the generosity of those who provided them, and the rich could garner tremendous prestige while simultaneously performing vital military, cultural, religious, and civic functions for the community. A competitive element also fostered excellence, for prizes at contests went to the victorious choregist as well as to the successful poet.

LITERATURE AND ART

In nearly every respect we know more about life in the bustling city of Athens than we do about how people lived in the other Greek poleis, but energy and talent were dispersed widely throughout the Greek world, and much of it went into literature and the arts. The word most commonly attached to the art and literature of the earlier fifth century is "grandeur." During this vigorous era of transition, talented poets, painters, architects, and sculptors carried the traditions of the sixth century throughout the wider Greek world, while in Athens the defeat of Persia was marked by innovations in tragic drama so striking as to constitute a new art form.

Lyric Poetry

Lyric was a necessary precursor of tragedy, and its practitioners were among the most distinguished writers of the fifth century. Simonides (c. 556–468 BC) is remembered chiefly as the unofficial poet laureate of the Persian wars. Born on the Ionian island of Ceos, he spent time at the court of Hipparchus in Athens, among the royal families of Thessaly, and in Sicily, where he was esteemed by the warring tyrants Hiero and Theron and was able to effect at least a brief peace between them. He was probably in Athens during the wars with Persia, and his epitaphs for the war dead (such as the one cited in Chapter 5) became to Greek literature what the Declaration of Independence and the Gettysburg Address are to Americans (only easier to remember, since they were in verse).

Sicilian tyrants were famed for their interest in culture, and Simonides' nephew Bacchylides, who was also a poet, accompanied him to Sicily. Bacchylides shared his uncle's interest in the genre known as epinician odes, that is, poems written *epi-nikē* ("upon [an athletic] victory"), and he composed a poem for Hiero's victory in the chariot race at the Olympics in 476. He had a gift for gripping narrative, and Hiero was drawn to his work, but the verdict of posterity went to his rival Pindar, who competed with him for the favor of the Sicilian rulers.

Born into an aristocratic family in Boeotia, Pindar traveled widely and enjoyed the patronage of the powerful throughout the Greek world; some of his most memorable poems honored his friends the Sicilian tyrants Hiero and Theron. Pindar's world view was diametrically opposed to that of democrats in Athens and elsewhere. Like Theognis, Pindar took it as axiomatic that merit was inherited. His many odes, rich in allusion and soaring in language, share a deeply held belief in an old-fashioned heroism—an excellence that takes as its starting point the assumption that men of worth spring from illustrious families that can trace their origins ultimately to divine ancestors. Writing numerous epinician odes, he was also disposed to connect physical prowess with all-around virtue. By connecting recent achievements with divine blood and tracing the ancestry of his subjects, he was able to elaborate his poems with powerful myths about gods and ancient heroes. His concern with the notion of excellence lent a lofty and inspirational quality to his verse, which was often quoted by Plato in his speculations about the highest human virtue.

Document 6.2 Excerpt from Pindar's sixth Nemean ode The occasion of this poem was the victory of Alkimidas of Aegina in the boys' wrestling contest at Nemea, perhaps in 465 BC. Characteristically, Pindar uses Alkimidas' success as a taking-off point for a discussion of larger issues.

> There is one race of men,
>   one race of gods.
>   Yet from one mother
>   we both take our breath.

The difference
  is in the allotment
of all power,
      for the one is nothing
while the bronze sky exists forever,
a sure abode.
      And yet, somehow,
  we resemble the immortals,
      whether in greatness of mind
        or nature, though we know not
      to what measure
day by day and in the watches of the night
      fate has written that we should run.
And now Alkimidas
    gives clear proof
      that the power
        born in the blood
      is like
    the fruit-bearing fields
that now, in alternation,
        yield mankind
yearly sustenance from the ground
and now, again, resting
      withhold their strength

  . . .

treading in the footprints of his father's father,
Praxidamas—
      for he, victorious at Olympia,
first brought the Aiakidai garlands from Alpheos;

  . . .

      come, Muse, direct
    upon this clan
the glorious breath of song—
    for when men have passed out of our midst
poems and legends
    convey their noble deeds. . . .

1–25; translated by Frank Nisetich, Pindar's Victory Songs. *Baltimore and*
London: Johns Hopkins University Press, 1980.

It is important that so much of Pindar's work has survived, not only because of the beauty of his verse but as a reminder of the diversity of highly developed cultures in all times and places. Since these poems celebrate the values and achievements of aristocrats, many modern readers coming to them assume they must have been written during the sixth century, before the rise of democracy in

Greece, but in fact they were not; Pindar died a few years before the outbreak of the Peloponnesian War, and his work was contemporary with that of Ephialtes and Pericles.

The Birth of Tragedy: Aeschylus

At least one poet who enjoyed the patronage of Hiero remained forever associated with his native polis. The Athenian tragedian Aeschylus (525–456) died in Sicily after a long life during which he wrote perhaps seventy plays. Unfortunately only a handful of these survive. After his death the Athenians paid homage to the greatness of his work by decreeing that the archon should grant a chorus to anyone who wanted to produce one of his plays. Aeschylus was the first of the famous tragedians of fifth-century Athens. Already in the time of Peisistratus Thespis had expanded the range of the choruses honoring Dionysus by adding an actor who could carry on a dialogue with the chorus; now Aeschylus added a second actor. This innovation made possible real conflict and moved tragedy beyond tableau into the realm of drama. At the same time, drama remained firmly grounded in poetry, and verse remained the vehicle for both tragedy and comedy throughout antiquity. The tragedy of Aeschylus retained a powerful anchor in the piercing beauty of the choruses, which celebrated the awesome power of the gods while also exploring the nature of the human condition. "Sing sorrow, sorrow," the chorus chants toward the opening of his play *Agamemnon*, "but good win out in the end":

> Zeus: whatever he may be, if this name
> pleases him in invocation,
> thus I call upon him.
> I have pondered everything
> yet I cannot find a way,
> only Zeus, to cast this dead weight of ignorance
> finally from out my brain.
> . . .
> Zeus, who guided men to think,
> who has laid it down that wisdom
> comes alone through suffering.
> Still there drips in sleep against the heart
> grief of memory; against
> our pleasure we are temperate.
> From the gods who sit in grandeur
> grace comes somehow violent.
>   (Agamemnon *160–66, 176–183; Lattimore 1959*)

Tragedy performed a central role in the spiritual and intellectual life of the polis. Wealthy citizens vied for honor and acclaim by undertaking the expense of training choruses, and during the festival of Dionysus in March actors and audience alike needed enormous stamina. Groups of actors performed four dramas in a day, and spectators had not only to follow the intricate poetry of the choruses but to turn up the next day and the day after that to compare the work of each playwright, to help determine who should receive the prize. A significant proportion of men—and perhaps women as well, though this is uncertain—attended the plays and no doubt continued among themselves a lively dialogue about the painful issues the dramas had raised. Even in eras of comparatively high literacy, ancient cultures remain oral to a considerable degree, and absorbing the complex imagery of Greek tragic choruses was not as difficult for people trained to listen and remember as it would be for most people today. Nonetheless, the popularity of performances that demanded serious intellectual work on the part of the audience tells us something about the richness of Greek culture. Over thirty tragedies have survived; what is missing, however, is any record (beyond the jokes in Aristophanes) of the discussions the performances must have inspired among friends and neighbors who had enjoyed this shared treasure of the community.

All parts in tragedy were played by men; masks facilitated the deception. They were shaped at the mouth rather like megaphones, and they made for good acoustics. To be sure, they discouraged the nuanced portrayal of personality. This was not, however, considered a great loss, for Greek tragedy was never intended to be naturalistic. Characters in Greek tragedy were not like characters in modern films or novels, whom one might expect to recognize walking down the street, or whose subtler traits might appear in one's friends or neighbors. They represented humankind in all its aspiration—and frailty. They are not easy to like or dislike, for they were not intended to be lifelike, flesh-and-blood individuals.

Nor was the material of tragedy anything one could call a slice of life. Tragedy was meant to be heroic and grand, far removed from the trivial and the mundane. Plots were generally taken from the rich myths of the Heroic Age, but as we have seen exceptions could be made for major events such as the Persian wars. (Even here, though, Aeschylus achieved a certain remoteness by setting the action of his *Persians* in faraway Asia, where people dressed exotically.) Formalities of several kinds limited the dramatist in his choice of material. No violence was permitted on stage, and all action had to take place within a twenty-four-hour period. Finally, the author had to contend with the challenge posed by the intricate meters of tragic verse.

The struggle of playwrights to mold drama within these constraints constituted a form of heroism in itself. Aeschylus' greatest surviving achievement is the trilogy known as the *Oresteia*, which treats the supreme difficulty of understanding and obtaining a just social and religious order. Apparently the sets of four dramas that playwrights entered in the competition generally involved three tragedies followed by a lighter work known as a satyr play, but the three tragedies did not need to treat the same theme, and frequently they didn't. In the case of the *Oresteia*, however, the three plays comprise one grand and complex drama, and this work is the only Attic trilogy that escaped destruction to be enjoyed today.

The Oresteia

The point of departure for the *Oresteia* was evidently Ephialtes' curtailment of the powers of the Areopagite Council, for the trilogy culminates in precisely the sort of trial that remained within the Council's purview—a murder trial. It seems likely that Aeschylus supported the reforms and chose this august drama as a vehicle by which to reassure conservative Athenians that the trying of homicide cases, the privilege with which Ephialtes had conspicuously not tampered, was in fact the ancient mission of this venerable body. In this way he could draw attention away from the significant limitations that had been placed on its jurisdiction. The material with which Aeschylus chose to convey his message was the familiar tale of the cursed house of the ancient hero Pelops and his descendant Agamemnon, commander-in-chief of the legendary expedition against Troy.

The first play, *Agamemnon*, portrays the Greek general's murder upon his victorious return from the Trojan War in a plot hatched by his faithless wife Clytemnestra and his cousin Aegisthus, who has become Clytemnestra's lover. Agamemnon's murder poses an agonizing dilemma for his children Orestes and Electra, for they are faced with a choice between killing their mother and allowing their father's death to go unavenged. Their pain and Orestes' eventual murder of Clytemnestra and Aegisthus form the subject matter of the second play, *The Libation Bearers*. As the play closes, Orestes finds himself pursued by the avenging earth goddesses known as the Furies. His suffering ends in the final play, *The Eumenides*. This play is set in Athens, where Orestes has taken refuge, hoping that a responsible government will afford him a fair trial. Athena's charge to the jury proclaims the glories of the Areopagus, the importance of justice, and the centrality of law.

Document 6.3 At the close of *The Eumenides*, the last play of Aeschylus' Oresteia trilogy, Aeschylus projects back onto Athena a blueprint for Athenian government, founded on principles of responsible government and trial by jury.

If it please you, men of Attica, hear my decree. . . .
Here is the Hill of Ares, here the Amazons encamped and built their shelters when they came in arms
for spite of Theseus, here they piled their rival towers
to rise, new city, and dare his city long ago,
and slew their beasts for Ares. So this rock is named
from then the Hill of Ares. Here the reverence
of citizens, their fear and kindred do-no-wrong
shall hold by day and in the blessing of night alike
all while the people do not muddy their own laws
with foul infusions. But if bright water you stain
with mud, you nevermore will find it fit to drink.

No anarchy, no rule of a single master. Thus
I advise my citizens to govern and to grace,
and not to cast fear utterly from your city. What
man who fears nothing at all is ever righteous? Such
be your just terrors, and you may deserve and have
salvation for your citadel, your land's defence,
such as is nowhere else found among men, neither
among the Scythians, nor the land that Pelops held.
I establish this tribunal. It shall be untouched
by money-making, grave but quick to wrath, watchful
to protect those who sleep, a sentry on the land.
These words I have unreeled are for my citizens,
advice into the future.

The Eumenides *681–708; translated by Richmond Lattimore in David Grene
and Richmond Lattimore, eds.,* The Complete Greek Tragedies. *Vol. 1,*
Aeschylus. *Chicago: University of Chicago Press, 1959.*

Athena breaks the deadlocked jury's tie, and her grounds are revealing. Following Apollo's proclamation that it is the male and not the female who is the true parent, and bearing in mind her own birth (fully developed from the head of her father Zeus), she decides that the claims of the father trump those of the mother, justifying Clytemnestra's death. Now tamed, the Furies are given a new name, the Eumenides (Kindly Ones). Plainly Aeschylus conceives the creation of responsible government in Athens as the antithesis not only of tyranny but also of a disordered chaotic universe in which emotional and female forces of vengeance were paramount. The new world will be governed by orderly, rational institutions planned and staffed by men, with vengeance replaced by justice.

The genre established by Aeschylus would become one of the defining art forms of Greek civilization. Tragic drama, as it evolved throughout Aeschylus' career and in the hands of his successors Sophocles and Euripides, was in many ways the hallmark of Athenian greatness. Through Shakespeare and other great tragedians of Europe, this remarkable testament to the heroic struggle against human limitations forms an important part of a legacy that has endured to our own time.

The Visual Arts

Greek painters and sculptors shared the tragedians' fascination with both the human and the divine. Throughout the decades of change and growth that mark the fifth century, both drama and the plastic arts reveal a powerful drive to organize the world in accord with harmony, balance, and proportion. During the fourth century, Plato, in the blueprint for the ideal society he described in his dialogue *The Republic*, would identify justice as the condition that obtained when all parts of the soul and state are in balance. The connections Plato posited between beauty and truth underlay much of the Greek view of the world throughout the Classical period.

Like tragedy, Greek painting and sculpture achieved what they did within the constraints posed by a variety of conventions. One popular vehicle for painting was the vase, which came in a wide variety of sizes and shapes, each affording distinctive challenges and opportunities. The smaller vessels called for particular ingenuity and skill. Bronze and marble, however, the customary materials for sculpture, were difficult to work with and did not lend themselves to naturalism. The two generations or so that followed the Persian wars mark a period of transition during which Greek artists begin to emancipate themselves from the canons of the Archaic period, as a spare austerity comes to distinguish Classical styles from those that had gone before. Some of the change may have had to do with a rejection of eastern influences in the wake of the bitter conflict with Persia; the ties with the Near East that were so conspicuous in Archaic styles now seem more tenuous. As tragedy became more dramatic with the addition of a second actor, so the visual arts grew less static during these decades, and action became important. Conveying a strong sense of movement in a still medium is no small achievement. Some of the most outstanding artists of these decades managed despite the constraints of their craft to build a sense of anticipation and excitement.

To be sure, the tranquility of Archaic sculpture persists in some of the work of this period. It is evident, for example, in the bronze charioteer dedicated at Delphi in the 470s by Hiero's brother Polyzalus after his victory in the chariot races at the Pythian games. The eerie stillness of the body and the garment that falls from it in perfect folds show precisely the discipline and self-control that Pindar celebrated in the aristocrats who carried off prizes in these events.

Probably the free-standing sculpture that conveys the most dramatic sense of movement to come was the so-called *diskobolos* ("discus thrower") of the Athenian sculptor Myron, who was known for his striking realism: admirers commented that a bronze cow of his on the Acropolis could easily be mistaken for the real thing. Though the bronze diskobolos Myron made around 460 does not survive, a variety of Roman copies enable us to appreciate the pent-up energy the athlete is about to unleash as he hurls his arm forward leaning into the throw.

The relief sculpture with which Greeks adorned their temples offered still greater opportunities for storytelling. Like tragedy, relief sculpture focused on mythological themes grounded in painful conflicts embroiling gods and mortals in tortuous scenarios. Tales involving animal-like figures also offered wonderful opportunities to visual artists. Thus the half-horse, half-human race of Centaurs figured in the sculptural programs of two of the most remarkable Greek temples of the fifth century, the Parthenon at Athens, to be discussed in Chapter 7, and the temple of Zeus at Olympia.

The temple of Zeus at Olympia was the first to be completed, between 470 and 456 BC, just when the dramas of Aeschylus were defining the Attic stage. Beginning in 1876, excavations brought to light remarkable sculptural groups on the portions of the temple known as the pediments—the elongated triangular spaces

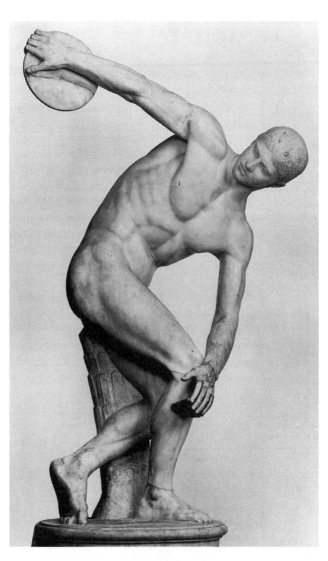

Figure 6.4. This bronze charioteer from the Delphi Museum (c. 475 BC) originally stood in the car of a four-horse chariot; it has survived because an earthquake cast it into an ancient drain.

Figure 6.5. Roman copy of the *diskobolos* or "discus thrower" by Myron. Scholars recognized Myron's statue as the model for the Roman copies because of a passage in the second-century-AD author Lucian, who describes the original work in detail.

that sat atop the columns and cried out for decoration. In the temple of Zeus, each pediment extended for over 80 feet from left to right and rose in the center to a height of 10 feet. Libon was the chief architect for the project, although plainly many artisans labored to create the elaborate sculptures. The west pediment celebrated the triumph of order and civilization over the animal-like barbarism represented by the Centaurs, who in their characteristic drunkenness had sought to

Figure 6.6a. Using surviving fragments, scholars have developed a number of different reconstructions for the sculptural composition of the east pediment of the temple of Zeus at Olympia (c. 460 BC) that tells the story of Pelops' chariot race. These two models are among the most recent.

Figure 6.6b. This marble statue of an elderly seer from the east pediment of the temple of Zeus at Olympia (third figure from right in the designs in 6.6a) is a dramatic blend of naturalistic and stylized elements.

disrupt the wedding of the hero Peirithoos to Deidameia only to find themselves worsted in the melee by Peirithoos and his friend Theseus. In the center of the relief stands a figure whom most scholars identify as Apollo upholding the principles of civility.

The east pediment portrayed a more complicated story—an episode in the life of Agamemnon's ancestor Pelops, who won his bride Hippodameia in a chariot race arranged by her father Oenomaus. It is no surprise that the circumstances surrounding this race should have been depicted on the temple at Olympia, since the event was associated with the beginning of the Olympic games. Motivated by a greater than normal attachment to his daughter, Oenomaus was accustomed to defeating her suitors in such races with the special equipment he had obtained from the god Ares. Hippodameia, however, fell in love with Pelops and arranged for the charioteer Myrtilus to sabotage her father's chariot by substituting wax linchpins for its metal ones. In the ensuing accident, Oenomaus was killed. Though Pelops won the race, married Hippodameia, and fathered several children, Myrtilus, who was also in love with Hippodameia, placed a curse on him that Greeks connected with the subsequent misfortunes of his descendants, including Agamemnon and his family. Numerous figures in the scene depicted on the temple have survived, including one of the most remarkable individuals depicted in relief sculpture, a pensive seer who even before the race has begun knows what is going to happen (Figure 6.6b).

Grave stelai also provided an important venue for relief sculpture. Although most commemorated the deaths of men, women and girls were depicted on their tombstones as well. One of the best preserved funerary reliefs of the fifth century offered a tender portrayal of a little girl holding her pet doves. This poignant reflection of the dead child makes clear that for all their preoccupation with war and civic engagement the Greeks could also feel private losses deeply.

Our insight into the private lives of the Greeks owes much to the scenes that appear on surviving vases. Unlike sculpture, painting was as likely to treat mundane scenes of daily activities as it was to portray deeds of epic proportions. In painting as in sculpture, we are often ignorant of the identity of the artist whose work stands before us. Painters are often known simply by the subject matter of their most memorable works or the places they were or can be found (e.g., the Pan painter, the Berlin painter). Greek wall painting of the Classical period has not survived to be placed beside the vivid frescoes of Egypt, Italy, or Bronze Age Crete; what we have are hundreds upon hundreds of vases. As in the Archaic period, these frequently took their subject matter from mythology, as in the fine vase in the Museum of Fine Arts in Boston depicting on one side the murder of Agamemnon and on the other that of Aegisthus.

Daily life, however, might also be represented, and scenes depicted on vases provide social historians with a wealth of information about how people spent their time at work and at play, showing women and men in a variety of activities; shoemakers, blacksmiths, agricultural workers, and other laborers are portrayed going about their tasks. We are indebted to vases for numerous scenes from women's lives and images of domestic space.

Figure 6.7. This marble grave relief, probably from Paros, dates from about 450 BC and stands today in the Metropolitan Museum of Art.

Like sculpture, vase painting of the earlier fifth century was focused on the human figure, to which the curving surfaces of the vessels lent a sense of movement and grace. Even more than in drama, the possibilities of facial expression are limited by the medium, and character portrayal is weak; we are often given a clear sense of what the dramatis personae of the vase are experiencing at the moment in time the artist has chosen to capture, but little understanding of who they have been over their lifetimes, what their driving anxieties or concerns. The figures on Greek vases are portrayed in action, not contemplation—they almost never appear to be posing for the artist—and we ask ourselves not only, "What are they thinking? What are they feeling?," but also, "What has just happened, and what will happen next?" But the focus always remains the human being. Landscapes are rarely developed in any substantive way, and though animals often appear as the companions of humans, they are rarely the center of attention as they had once been.

Figure 6.8. This Attic vase in the Boston Museum of Fine Arts was probably painted around 470 BC, shortly before the production of Aeschylus' *Oresteia*.

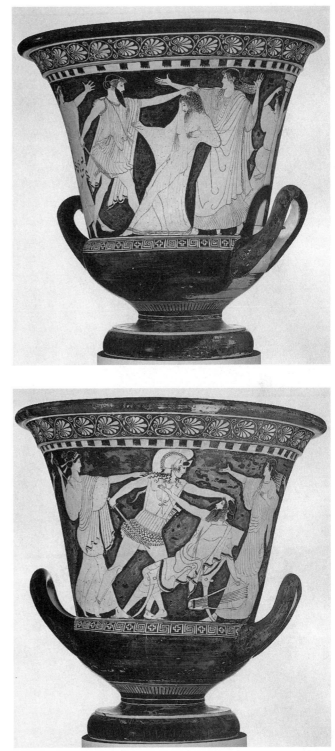

Figure 6.9. Vases frequently depicted craftspeople at work, such as this Attic black-figure neck amphora showing shoes being made and a blacksmith forging.

Although Greek wall painting has not survived the ravages of time, ancient critics suggest that facial expression was rather more varied in this medium, particularly after Cimon's friend Polygnotus of Thasos liberated it from traditional Archaic constraints—depicting, for example, open mouths and even teeth. Polygnotus was much admired in antiquity for the character portrayal in his vivid and complex murals—the Roman rhetorician Quintilian advised serious students of painting to begin with Polygnotus—but what we know of his work comes largely from descriptions by Pausanias, a traveler of the second century AD, whose *Description of Greece* is the principal source for many artworks that no longer survive today; Polygnotus' paintings are lost. The Roman polymath Pliny the Elder reported that Polygnotus was the first to portray women draped in transparent clothing, the "wet T-shirt" look.

Other painters active at Athens in the first half of the fifth century included Micon, who also seems to have enjoyed Cimon's patronage. Pliny the Elder records that Micon's daughter Timarete was also an artist and painted an image of Diana on a mural in Ephesus. Micon was one among several artists who were drawn to the theme of Theseus fighting the Amazons, placing it in the context of the ongoing conflict between West and East, Greek and alien. Theseus was also depicted around the same time fighting the mythical creatures known as Centaurs, who sported human torsos on the bodies of horses. The association of women with foreigners and animals and the notion that Greek male identity could and should be asserted by setting oneself against them would be repeated in Greek art and thought throughout the Classical period. Because Greek writers were often reticent in discussing women, visual images provide important clues to how women were thought of in ancient Greece. Vase paintings depict women of all social classes. Vases that were used at drinking parties for mixing and drinking wine frequently show prostitutes entertaining men. Some women are shown playing flutes, others are engaged in various stages of flirtation, and some scenes are frankly pornographic. Common prostitutes were often slaves. A woman of higher status who nevertheless mingled with men and received pay for her services was known as a *hetaira*. Such women were likely to be metics, either ex-slaves or freeborn, who—like male metics—gravitated to Athens because it was a commercial center. A few of these women, like Aspasia, the mistress of Pericles and the most famous hetaira of all, participated actively in the intellectual life of their male associates. In contrast, many paintings on vases used by respectable women depict wedding scenes, or women visiting tombs or sitting at home spinning wool or adorning themselves, often in the company of other women.

OIKOS AND POLIS

As in most cultures, the family was the primary locus of time and energy for women in Greece. We have much more information about family life in Athens than in any other Greek polis. The wide range of evidence includes not only vase painting but tomb sculpture and epitaphs, laws and courtroom speeches delivered in cases of family disputes, and portrayals of family life in comedy and tragedy. The material from drama, however, must be used with special caution. In any society, comedy, while revealing much about social norms, distorts for the sake of humor. Tragedy poses problems peculiar to Athens: though the authors were fifth-century Athenians, they show mythological characters and plots inherited from the Bronze Age, when values were different. All this material, moreover, was filtered through the imagination of the male poet. Sometimes the result seems misogynistic, as in Aeschylus' *Oresteia*; later in the fifth century authors like Sophocles and Euripides appear sympathetic to women's plight in Athenian society. One thing is clear: daring, outspoken women like Clytemnestra were not normally found in Classical Athens, where initiative (not to mention violence) was a male prerogative, and political power never shifted into female hands. We must always keep in mind that we have no idea what women were thinking. All the historical evidence from Classical Athens was created by men and (at least in the immediate sense) financed by them. So, for example, even vases designed for women's use and depicting women's daily activities were painted by men, then bought by men and given as gifts to women. Greek society was male dominated, in a word, "patriarchal."

The Greek polis comprised *oikoi* ("families," "estates," or "households"). The oikos was the primary unit of production, consumption, and reproduction. Citizens became members of the polis not directly as individuals, as they do in most modern states; rather, they first had to be accepted as members of an oikos.

Family Membership

When a baby was born in Attica the father decided whether to raise or expose it. He doubtless evaluated the newborn's health as well as the financial impact of raising another child. Most sons were raised, because male heirs were the normal means of perpetuating the lineage, and it was of great importance that families not die out. The offspring of a daughter was considered to belong to her husband's family, not her father's. As boys grew up, their labor was considered valuable. Moreover, they were expected to support their aged parents, bury them, and look after their tombs. At the scrutiny for public office known as the *dokimasia*, the areas investigated included proper treatment of parents and of the family tomb. In a state in which the government took minimal responsibility for those whom age or other infirmity prevented from working, proper bearing toward parents was crucial for the smooth functioning of society. Parents placed less value on girls, who lacked earning power and whose children would belong to a different family. Though the eldest child was normally raised regardless of its sex, some historians have conjectured that as many as 20 percent of newborn Athenian girls were abandoned in places like the local garbage dump. Slave dealers collected a few of the exposed infants and turned them over to wet nurses to be raised and sold as slaves. Most exposed infants, however, died, and exposure quickly became infanticide.

In Athens, after a baby boy was accepted as a member of his father's family he needed to be approved by his father's quasi- or pseudofamily: a boy inherited membership in his phratry ("brotherhood") and deme ("city ward or country village") from his father. Enrollment in the father's phratry was a desirable, if not essential, step toward becoming a full-fledged Athenian citizen. The father introduced and enrolled his baby in his phratry and vouched for him as being legitimate and his own, born of an Athenian mother.

Names

Names revealed family membership. Children were identified by their own names and patronymics; it was usual to name the first son after his paternal grandfather, and the second after his maternal grandfather. Because rules of etiquette required the suppression of respectable women's names, at least while they were living, the quantity of evidence available for the study of their names is far less than for men's names. Nevertheless, the data indicate that, like a boy, a girl was given a name that was derived from those in her father's family, skipping a generation. Thus the first daughter would be named after her paternal grandmother.

Demography and the Life Cycle

The average age at death in Classical Athens for adult females was 36.2 years and for adult males 45 years. The average woman bore 4.3 children, 2.7 of whom survived infancy. The death ratio for infants was 500 per 1000 adults. Athenian men married at approximately the age of 30 and women around the age of 15. Women were often widowed as a consequence of war, and the age difference heightened the likelihood of widowhood overtaking a woman before old age; men lost young wives in childbirth. Marriages could also be ended by divorce, which was not stigmatized unless some scandal were involved. Widowed and divorced people often remarried, and children of divorced parents generally lived with their fathers, to whose oikos they belonged. Only a minority of children reached adolescence living with both their natural parents; most had lost one or both parents at an early age and lived with distant relatives or in homes with a succession of stepparents and half-siblings. The intact nuclear family was the exception, not the rule.

Marriage

Marriage was the social institution that sustained the oikos, and its principal purpose was reproduction. At the time of betrothal the bride's father or other guardian declared in the presence of witnesses, "I give you my daughter to sow for the purpose of producing legitimate children." After the bridegroom agreed, "I take her," he and his fiancée's father agreed to the size of her dowry. For respectable girls there was no alternative to marriage, and the obligation to dower each daughter doubtless was a prime motivator in female infanticide.

Greeks could be married only to one spouse at a time, although there was a double standard for sexual conduct and husbands might have additional sexual

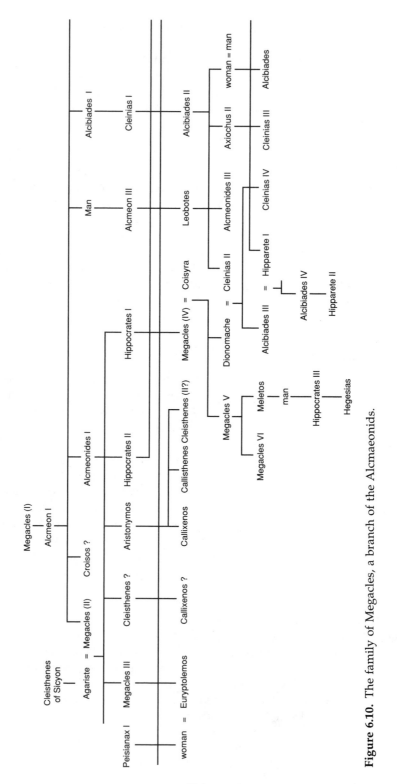

Figure 6.10. The family of Megacles, a branch of the Alcmaeonids.

partners of either gender. Marriages between close relatives such as first cousins or uncle and niece were common. In a family with no son, the obligation to perpetuate the oikos fell on a daughter, called an *epiklēros* (someone "attached to the estate," sometimes translated "heiress" for convenience, though she herself inherited nothing). The epikleros was required to marry the closest of her father's male relatives who was capable of procreation, usually her uncle or first cousin. If the two were married to other spouses, they had to divorce them. A son born of the union with the epikleros would be considered his grandfather's heir. Men without any children at all would try to adopt a male relative so that their lineage would not die out.

The wife's dowry plus the husband's contribution constituted the economic foundation of the oikos at the start of a marriage. At Athens dowries consisted of cash and movable property. The husband provided the land and the house with most of its contents. The ideal, at least for those who farmed their own land, was to furnish most of the basic necessities of life for the family without needing to

Figure 6.11. Detail of Attic red-figure *lebēs gamikos* ("wedding bowl") by the Washing Painter, last quarter of the fifth century. A bride displays a baby boy, the hoped-for result of her marriage. A standing woman toward the right is holding a *loutrophoros*, a wedding vase used for transporting water for the prenuptial bath. The woman on the far right holds a vase for perfumed ointment, or oil.

depend on purchasing supplies at the market. The division of labor was by gender: women's work was indoors and men's outdoors. The husband brought into the house agricultural products such as fruit, vegetables, grain, and raw wool, and the wife and domestic slaves transformed these products into textiles and edible food. Wives were also responsible for storing the household contents safely, so that there would always be enough to eat and wear, and even to sell if the family fell on hard times.

Document 6.4 The customary division of labor in the oikos is spelled out in Xenophon's Socratic dialogue the *Oeconomicus*, in which Socrates' friend Ischomachus explains to him how he taught his 14-year-old bride to manage the household.

He told me he said to her: "Wife, the gods seem to have shown much discernment in yoking together female and male, as we call them, so that the couple might constitute a partnership that is most beneficial to each of them. . . ."

"Those who intend to obtain produce to bring into the shelter need someone to work at the outdoor jobs. For plowing, sowing, planting, and herding is all work that is performed outdoors, and it is from these that our essential provisions are obtained. As soon as these are brought into the shelter, then someone else is needed to look after them and to perform the work that requires shelters. The nursing of newborn children requires shelters, and so does the preparation of bread from grain, and likewise, making clothing out of wool. Because both the indoor and the outdoor tasks require work and concern," he said, "I think the god, from the very beginning, designed the nature of women for the indoor work and concerns and the nature of man for the outdoor work. . . .

For the woman it is more honorable to remain indoors than to be outside; for the man it is more disgraceful to remain indoors than to attend to business outside.

. . . .

"And how did you arrange things for her, Ischomachus?"

"Well, I thought it was best to show her the possibilities of our house first. It is not elaborately decorated, Socrates, but the rooms are constructed in such a way that they will serve as the most convenient places to contain the things that will be kept in them. So the rooms themselves invited what was suitable for each of them. Thus the bedroom, because it was in the safest possible place, invited the most valuable bedding and furniture. The dry store rooms called for grain, the cool ones for wine, and the bright ones for those products and utensils which need light. I continued by showing her living rooms for the occupants, decorated so as to be cool in summer and warm in winter. I pointed out to her that the entire house has its facade facing south, so that it was obviously sunny in winter and shady in summer. I also showed her the women's quarters, separated from the men's quarters by a bolted door, so that nothing might be removed from them that should not be, and so that the slaves would not breed without our permission. For, generally, honest slaves become more loyal when they have produced children, but when bad ones mate, they become more troublesome."

Xenophon, Oeconomicus *7.18, 20–22, 30, 9.2–5; translated by Sarah B. Pomeroy,* Xenophon Oeconomicus, a Social and Historical Commentary. *Oxford: Clarendon Press, 1994, pp. 141, 143, 155.*

The fundamental division of domestic space was between men and women. Even in a small house with only two rooms, one upstairs and one on the ground floor, the upper room was normally the women's quarters and the lower room the men's. Entertainment took place in the men's quarters, and so a visitor to the Greek home would meet only male members of the family; when strangers were in the house women and girls would withdraw to the secluded parts of the home and not even be mentioned by name. The females in the household, both free and slave, slept in the women's quarters. They also produced textiles there, though in warm weather they might move their looms into an interior courtyard and work outdoors, protected by the surrounding walls.

Unless extreme poverty compelled them to work, citizen women rarely ventured far from the house except for festivals and funerals. In this way they avoided encounters with strange men who were not their relatives and who might compromise their respectability either by actual sexual contact or by the rumor of it. Only women in straitened circumstances would shop for groceries or household items themselves; wherever possible, slaves and husbands did the marketing and other errands that required leaving the immediate environs of the home.

The prevalence of slavery, in fact, shaped gender roles in a variety of ways. The availability of slaves even for families of fairly modest means was vital, for example, in perpetuating the social ideal of the virtuous woman who never left the house. Though some poor oikoi had to rely on the labor of family members, most oikoi had at least one or two female slaves. The division of labor among the very poor and among slaves was not so strictly gender based as it was for the middle and upper classes. Under the wife's supervision slaves performed domestic labor, working at food preparation, child care, and textile manufacture. They were also compelled to provide sexual services to their masters. There is some evidence that this practice caused strain in Greek households and that tactful husbands restricted their extramarital dalliances to locations outside their own homes.

Figure 6.12. Attic black-figure *lekythos*, sixth century, attributed to the Amasis Painter, showing textile production. Left: Woman spinning. Center: Women weaving at a vertical loom. Right: Woman weighing wool.

THE GREEK ECONOMY

The work of slaves did not always take place in the context of the oikos. The extent to which slaves were engaged in agricultural labor is controversial. Some scholars believe that large numbers of male slaves worked on farms, especially when a wealthy owner had large plots of land that were not contiguous but scattered about Attica. Others stress the grounding of the agricultural economy in the small family farm worked by the independent peasant farmer. Like women, slaves were a "muted group"; although they were numerous, their names and thoughts were not recorded, and few have left their mark on the historical record.

There is no doubt that large numbers of slaves were employed in the craft industries, some working for their owners and others rented out by them. Their jobs tended to be gender specific. Men worked in factories making swords, shields, furniture, pottery, and other items, while women often worked in textile-related industries. Inscriptions recording expenses incurred in construction on the Athenian Acropolis show that slaves were paid the same as free workers. Of course, the wages of slaves who were rented out were paid to their masters.

By no means all craftspeople were slaves; Aristotle in fact contended that most craftsmen were rich. Greeks whose economic status allowed them some choice shunned work that made them subject to the commands of another person, and this included most craft fields. Such a life, they believed, was demeaning to a free male citizen. Unlike farming, to which a certain nobility always attached, manual work performed indoors was despised by many wealthier Greeks and known by the name "banausic" labor, which means literally work performed over a hot furnace, and distinctions between skilled and unskilled labor were often ignored. It may be that the leisured classes disdained indoor work because of its connection with slaves and women. Litigants in Athenian courtrooms enjoyed making snide remarks about their opponents (or their opponents' relatives) ever having held any kind of job or even having run a business, and political theorists—who always came from the upper classes—contended often that strenuous indoor work ought to disqualify people from voting on the grounds that it damaged the mind as surely as it compromised the body. Most Greeks, however, had limited choices about how to support themselves and their families, and there is no reason to believe that those who worked for others or performed indoor manual labor were embarrassed about their professions. Some craftspeople, both citizens and metics, achieved high status as a consequence of their technical abilities and economic success. Tombstones frequently boasted of their occupants' craft skills; surviving examples include epitaphs of a woodcutter and a miner. As elsewhere, the ideology of literate elites was at odds with the daily practice of ordinary people.

The disdain with which some Greeks regarded paid labor did not prevent a great deal of work from getting done or a good bit of money from being made. Sometimes, however, revenue was the product of imperialism and other forms of exploitation. It might come as war booty (slaves included), or it could take the form of tribute. The size and wealth of the Athenian empire played a large role in defining the character of the fifth century. Without the tribute from subject allies it would have been difficult for the Athenians to initiate the system of state pay for state service and thus significantly expand the proportion of citizens able to participate in the business of government. Democracy was not entirely dependent on empire; the Athenians lost their empire in 404 BC but continued to have democratic government for several generations until their conquest by Philip of Macedon in 338 (and in many respects democracy persisted even after that). But it certainly seems to have received its impetus from the surplus funds generated by imperial tribute. The splendid buildings with which the Athenians began adorning the Acropolis shortly after relocating the treasury in Athens certainly owed their existence to imperial revenues; no empire, no Parthenon. In addition, the empire's maritime nature meant that it served as the organizing principle of Greek trade. The centrality of the Athenian empire to commercial life became abundantly plain in the late 430s when the Athenians banned Megarian merchants from trading in imperial ports, claiming they were simply making rules for their own sphere of influence as stipulated by the Thirty Years' Peace. The consequences of this move were fatal to Megarian trade, and outrage over this prohibition was one cause of the long Peloponnesian War of 431–404. Especially after the defeat of Aegina in 457, Athens' most formidable commercial rival was Corinth. Possessing ports both on the Saronic Gulf that divided Attica from the Peloponnesus and on the Corinthian Gulf to the northwest, the Corinthians hauled ships overland from the one harbor to the other and thus enjoyed a unique position in Greek commerce.

Agriculture and Trade

Before the nineteenth century AD most people in the world made their living by agriculture, and fifth-century Greeks were no exception. It was trade, however, that united the far-flung states that ringed the seas, and the routes over which material goods traveled also served as vital conduits for the exchange of ideas. Trade rivalries like that between Athens and Corinth accounted for a good deal of tension among Greek poleis. Most trade went by boat, land traffic being a slow and expensive business over rocky roads; the cost of carting heavy goods by land might well exceed the price of the goods themselves. Few roads were really suited for wheeled vehicles, and some parts of Greece (including Attica) lacked sufficient oxen to draw them. Boeotia, however, did a brisk business in transport, providing pack animals in large numbers.

Lacking sophisticated navigational instruments, Greek vessels avoided the open seas when possible, preferring to hug the shore. Mariners preferred to limit long voyages to spring and summer, though some determined speculators insisted on winter runs as well. Speeds, however, had increased considerably since Homeric times, and travel times had been cut in half or better. Merchant vessels as large as 250 tons ranged the ocean propelled by oars and sail, and Athenian determination cleared the waters of the piracy that had been such an important factor in Greek life; for this, at least, Athens' subject allies were grateful (though the pirates, presumably, were not). The widespread use of coinage, mostly silver, facilitated trade, and Athens pressured its allies to adopt its own currency. Litigation arising from sea trade was so widespread that the Athenians established a special court of *nautodikai*, or marine judges, to handle cases brought to Athens, but on the whole the embryonic state of international law offered little hope to victims of dishonest business practices.

The diversity of natural resources in the ancient world made trade a necessity; no polis had everything, and some poleis had very little indeed. Athenian commerce especially was driven largely by the need for grain to feed a large population. Grain might come from north or south. One crucial source was the Black Sea region, which also provided hides, cattle, fish, hemp, wax, chestnuts, iron, and slaves. For this the Athenians exchanged wine and oil, sometimes in decorated vases. These exports were themselves often resold elsewhere; the Phoenicians often sent Attic vases to Egypt, and a good deal of secondhand pottery from Athens has been discovered in Etruria in Italy. Italians also bought a good deal of Attic pottery firsthand. Another key granary lay in Egypt, where Attic olive oil was also traded for papyrus, ivory, glasswork, slaves, and exotic animals. Carthage provided textiles; Etruria fine bronzework and boots; Sicily pigs, cheese, and grain; Phoenicia purple dye and dates. Corinth exported its own wares as well as serving as an intermediary between east and west, sending out tiles and metalwork. Already in the fifth century it seems that some silks from China made their way to Greece via Scythian intermediaries. Arabia exported perfumes, and Persia carpets. Important sources of metals were identified early: Cyprus for copper, Spain for tin, Laconia as well as the Black Sea for iron, Thasos and Mount Pangaeus in northern Greece for gold. All these goods flowed throughout the Greek world, but most of all they flowed into Piraeus.

Throughout Greece, however, agriculture remained the most common source of income. Athens was by far the largest city, with a population that normally varied between 300,000 and 400,000. Most people in Attica who participated in political life were independent farmers who worked fairly small plots of land. Generally unaware of the value of rotating crops to maximize the productivity of the soil, farmers often allowed their land to lie fallow in alternate years, so the poorest were indeed quite poor; those who were doing a little better were able to buy a female slave or two to help out around the house. Some, of course, owned a great deal of land and did very well. Because only citizens could own land, even the neediest farmers took pride in their way of life.

Metics in Fifth-century Athens

Many rich residents of Athens, however, did not own land, since it was illegal for them to do so without special dispensation. These were the resident aliens known as metics, and they played a key role in the economy. Craftspeople and entrepreneurs who had come from all over the Greek world to conduct business in Athens, metics accounted for a significant proportion of the Athenian population. They could not vote or hold office; neither could their children or their children's children. They were forced to live in rented homes. But they suffered no social disabilities, and metic families mingled comfortably with families of citizens. A number of the central characters in Plato's works were metics, and the most famous Platonic dialogue, *The Republic*, was set at the home of the rich metic Cephalus, whom Pericles had invited to Athens from Syracuse. Citizens, metics, and slaves often worked side by side, sometimes for the same pay; a list of workers at one construction site included eighty-six laborers whose status can be determined—twenty-four citizens, forty-two metics, and twenty slaves. In a crisis, metics could be drafted into the armed forces.

Many of Athens' most distinguished intellectuals were metics, such as the philosopher Anaxagoras from Asia Minor and the rhetorician Gorgias from Sicily. Pericles' common-law wife Aspasia belonged to the metic class, and it was for this reason that he required a decree of the assembly to grant citizenship to their children. The inability of metic women to produce sons who could enjoy Athenian citizenship played a large role in shaping the contours of Athenian society, creating two classes of women available as long-term partners to citizen men— metic mistresses and citizen wives. (In addition, a variety of prostitutes, both slave and free, were available for briefer encounters, and owners enjoyed the privilege of sexual access to their slaves.) Most metic women, of course, were housewives married to metic men. Slaves who were granted their freedom became metics rather than citizens. Metics lived in many other poleis besides Athens, but almost nothing is known of metics in other parts of Greece.

*   *   *

The cultural achievements of sixth- and early fifth-century Greece were substantial, but the difficulties the city-states experienced in getting along with one another (and their aversion to uniting into a single political unit) would have a profound impact on the direction Greek civilization would take. The Thirty Years' Peace held a great deal of promise, but it was problematic in many ways. Dividing the Greek world openly into two spheres of influence—a Spartan land empire in mainland Greece and an Athenian naval one in the Aegean—was a dubious enterprise. From one standpoint, by drawing lines clearly the agreement seemed to hold out the hope of peace; but it also fostered a potentially dangerous bipolarity. The notion of submitting disputes to arbitration was all very civilized in the abstract, but with every state of any reputation allied with one side or the other, just who was going to act as mediator? No treaty, moreover, could change the fact that Megara still sat uneasily on the Attic border, or could diminish the commercial rivalry between Athens and Corinth. In 445 it was impossible to predict whether the peace would last.

TRANSLATIONS

Lattimore, Richmond. 1959. *Agamemnon*, from *The Complete Tragedies*, David Grene and Richmond Lattimore, eds. Vol. 1, *Aeschylus*. Chicago: University of Chicago Press.

Pomeroy, Sarah. 1994. *Xenophon Oeconomicus, a Social and Historical Commentary*. Oxford: Clarendon Press.

Scott-Kilvert, Ian. 1960. *The Rise and Fall of Athens: Nine Greek Lives by Plutarch*. Harmondsworth, England: Penguin.

SUGGESTED READINGS

Cohen, David. 1991. *Law, Sexuality, and Society: The Enforcement of Morals in Classical Athens*. Cambridge, Eng.: Cambridge University Press. What the framing and application of law reveal about sexual values and practices.

Ehrenberg, Victor. 1973. *From Solon to Socrates*. 2nd ed. London: Methuen. This remains a sensitive and thoughtful study of the evolution of Greek culture during the sixth and fifth centuries.

Fantham, Elaine, Helene Foley, Natalie Kampen, Sarah B. Pomeroy, and H. A. Shapiro. 1994. *Women in the Classical World: Image and Text*. New York and Oxford: Oxford University Press. An examination of the written and visual evidence for the lives of ancient women, placed within their historical and cultural context.

Hanson, Victor. 1989. *The Western Way of War: Infantry Battle in Classical Greece*. New York: Alfred A. Knopf. A gripping account of the experience of hoplite battle.

Hignett, Charles. 1952. *A History of the Athenian Constitution to the End of the Fifth Century B.C.* Oxford: Clarendon Press. A close study of the evolution of the constitution at Athens.

Just, Roger. 1989. *Women in Athenian Law and Life*. London and New York: Routledge. A study of how Athenian men sought to define and locate women.

Meiggs, Russell. 1972. *The Athenian Empire*. Oxford: Oxford University Press. A richly detailed examination of Athenian imperialism and the world that came under its sway.

Pollitt, Jerome J. 1972. *Art and Experience in Classical Greece*. Cambridge, Eng.: Cambridge University Press. A sensitive survey of Greek art that grounds it firmly in its historical context.

Pomeroy, Sarah B. 1998. *Families in Classical and Hellenistic Greece: Representations and Realities*. Oxford: Clarendon Press. An account of the Greek family as a productive, reproductive, and social unit.

7

GREECE ON THE EVE OF
THE PELOPONNESIAN WAR

Avoiding war was particularly important when the Greeks had such precious achievements to protect in so many areas. From Sicily to Anatolia, remarkable temples to the gods proclaimed the grandeur of Hellenic civilization under the open sky. Greek ships plied the seas in all directions, enabling men and women hundreds of miles away to exchange their wares and profit from a wide variety of resources and skills. Novel experiments in government were in progress. The same diversity that fostered the dynamic creativity of the Greeks, however, also fragmented their world. The world of the polis, moreover, was in many ways a narrow one. Despite the growth of what the Greeks called democracy, ultimately each polis was grounded in the rule of an elite of free men over everyone else; and the inability of the poleis to get along boded ill for the future of Greece. Inevitably, prospects for the future were clouded by intermittent suspicions that the peace between the Athenian and Spartan camps might not endure.

SOURCES FOR GREECE ON THE EVE OF THE WAR

The principal source for the decades that preceded the outbreak of the great war between Athens and Sparta is Thucydides' *History*. Thucydides served as a general in the war and wrote the history of the period from 479 to 411 BC, though his account of the years before 433 is not as detailed as his narrative of the war itself and the tensions that immediately preceded it. A good number of inscriptions survive, although nowhere near as many as we would like. Diodorus' *Library of History* remains useful. Though he was not a great historian and does not add to our understanding of the war when he is using Thucydides as his only source, Diodorus did sometimes draw information from other writers. Plutarch is helpful as well; biographies like that of Pericles incorporate a great deal of information from fifth- and fourth-century historians whose work is lost. All the intellectuals who have left records of their thoughts, from the historian Herodotus to the physician Hippocrates, have contributed to our understanding of how Greeks viewed their world at this fertile period in their cultural history. Finally, a great debt is owed to the visual artists who left us a wide array of pottery, sculpture, tombstones, and architecture. Unfortunately, however, Greek writers were hardly representative of the whole population. In many states artists worked at the behest of elites. To be sure, in some democratic poleis like Athens successful dramatic poets had to speak to the people, but it is important to remember that what we call history is in fact an image of the world reconstructed primarily from what seemed worthy of creation or transmission to the minds of that tiny fraction of the human race who were urban, literate males.

GREECE AFTER THE THIRTY YEARS' PEACE

In 445, right after the signing of the peace, many Greeks were optimistic, convinced that Athens and Sparta had put their differences behind them. The fact that their optimism was misplaced makes it hard for historians to avoid seeing the years before the Peloponnesian War of 431–404 as anything but a prelude to hostilities. Though it is important to try to understand events as they unfold rather than assessing them only in terms of their consequences, hindsight also has some value. Looking back from the vantage point of the war that followed, certain events of the 440s and 430s take on particular significance.

During this period the Athenians showed a marked interest in the west and in the northeast. Athens had multiple motives for accepting Megara into its alliance in 460, but the desire for access to the port of Pegae on the Corinthian Gulf was certainly one factor, and the settlement of the Messenians at Naupactus several years later provided a convenient stopping place for ships heading west. It was probably also in the 450s that Athens contracted an alliance with Egesta in northwest Sicily. Alliances with Rhegium in the toe of Italy and with another Sicilian city, Leontini, followed shortly afterward; it may be significant that tensions marked the relationship of Leontini with Syracuse, a colony and ally of Athens' trade rival Corinth. Commerce with the western Greeks played a key role in the Athenian economy. Large quantities of red-figure pottery were exported to Etruria, and Athenian ships returned from Italy laden with grain and cheese from Sicily and metalwork from the mainland. Gradually the Greek cities of Sicily adopted Athenian currency.

That Athens had a growing interest in the rich lands to the west is confirmed by Pericles' decision to found a colony in the instep of southern Italy in 443. Thurii, however, was to be no ordinary establishment, for the Athenians invited the other Greek states to share in founding a Panhellenic colony, thus demonstrating their commitment to a spirit of cooperation and goodwill. The colony was sent out under the guidance of Pericles' good friend Lampon the seer, whom many people believed to have a special relationships with the gods. Lampon obtained oracles regarding the city's founding from Delphi that could guide the colonists in selecting precisely the right site for the town. Laid out according to

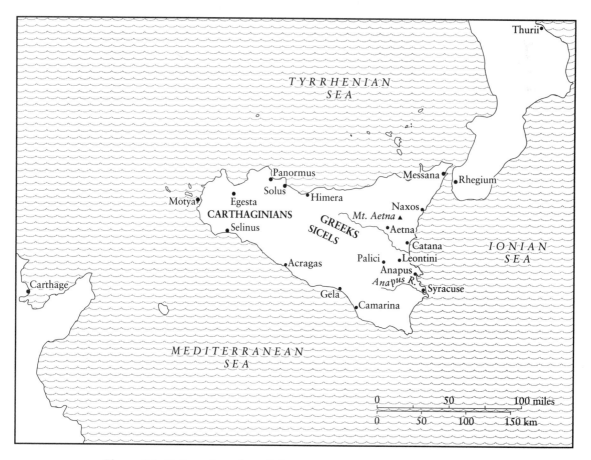

Figure 7.1. Sicily and southern Italy.

the plans of the same Hippodamus who had designed the Piraeus, Thurii became home to a number of non-Athenians including the historian Herodotus. Although the constitution of Thurii was democratic and the local coins were stamped with the head of Athena, the city adopted the laws of Zaleucus, an esteemed lawgiver from Locris, and when a disagreement led the colonists some years later to go to Delphi to ask to whom they belonged, the Delphic oracle claimed them for Apollo, not Athens.

Pericles' intentions for Thurii remain uncertain. Was his determination to cast the colony as Panhellenic a sincere disclaimer of Athenian meddling in the west, or was he simply hoping to head off Corinthian resentment by cloaking western imperialism in Panhellenism? In any event, the Attic element in the population was greatly diluted with the passing of time, and the Corinthians do not appear to have taken offense.

Athens' immediate interest, however, lay in the area around Thrace and the Black Sea region. From here the Athenians imported hides, dyes, and, more importantly, grain and timber, and the routes to this part of the world also gave access to the caravan route through the Ural Mountains to Central Asia and ultimately to the Chinese frontier, whence the West could expect furs, gold, and perhaps even silk. Around 445 the Athenians founded the Thracian colony of Brea, and some ten years later Pericles himself sailed with an Athenian squadron to the Black Sea.

While the Athenians were engaged in expanding their sphere of interest to the north and the west, an alarming revolt broke out in the east. In 440, Samos rebelled. Spreading to Byzantium, the uprising threw terror into the Athenians, for it seemed to threaten the very continuation of their Aegean empire. Years later, according to Thucydides, Greeks looked back and observed that Samos "had almost managed to wrest from the Athenians their control of the sea." (8.76.4) An oligarchy, Samos had quarreled with the democratic government the Athenians had recently established in neighboring Miletus, and the Milesians who complained to Athens were joined by some Samians who wished to overthrow their government. One of three privileged allies (along with Lesbos and Chios) who were still contributing ships rather than tribute money to the Athenian league, Samos took umbrage at the Athenian directive to submit the matter to arbitration, whereupon the Athenians sent forty ships to depose the government and replace it with a democracy. It was at this juncture that the Samian oligarchs seized control of the government by force and revolted from Athens. In this venture they were assisted by Pissuthnes, the satrap of Sardis.

The spread of the conflagration to Byzantium imperiled Athenian access to the Black Sea and raised the specter of a general revolt along the coast or even throughout the empire. The determined campaign that followed involved all ten of the Athenian strategoi and over 200 ships—160 from Athens and 55 from the remaining allies in the navy, Lesbos and Chios. The siege of Samos lasted nine months. When the city fell, the Athenians confiscated the Samian navy and established a democracy. A heavy indemnity was imposed and hostages taken. Plutarch reports that a local historian, Duris, claimed that Pericles bound the Samian commanders and marines to posts in the marketplace and left them there for ten days; he then gave orders that their heads be beaten in with clubs and their bodies tossed on the ground to rot (*Pericles* 28). Most scholars doubt the accuracy of this claim, but the existence of the story reflects the extreme bitterness of the feelings on both sides. About the subjugation of Byzantium we know nothing except that the Byzantines agreed to return to the empire.

Meanwhile Athens kept its gaze fixed on the northeast, planting a colony at a strategic point on the Strymon River by the border of Macedonia and Thrace. To the same site in a bend of the river where Cimon's would-be colonists had been murdered by angry Thracians some thirty years before, the Athenians sent the general Hagnon in 437 to found the colony of Amphipolis, so named because the river flowed around (*amphi*) the city on three sides. This time the colony flourished. In addition to protecting Athens' access to grain, timber, and minerals, Amphipolis helped the Athenians monitor activities in the recently organized kingdom of the Thracian Odrysians to the north and east as well as in Macedonia to the west. But the fact that the town drew much of its population from neighboring towns undermined its identification with Athens, and during the war with Sparta it failed to serve as a rallying point for Athenian loyalties in the north. Within less than fifteen years of its founding, Amphipolis was in Spartan hands.

We know next to nothing about how Spartans looked at the world during the years between the signing of the Thirty Years' Peace in 445 and their declaration of war on Athens in 432. The one tantalizing tidbit that leaps out from the pages of Thucydides is the Corinthians' claim that they dissuaded the Spartans from attacking Athens at the time of the Samian rebellion: "We did not cast the deciding vote against you," they report, "when Samos revolted from you, and when the Peloponnesians were evenly divided over whether to help them. We openly opposed it, saying that any city could punish its own allies." (1.40) If the story is true and not fabricated for the purpose of scoring points with the Athenians, then some Greeks who participated in meetings of the Peloponnesian League saw merit in attacking Athens in 440, and Spartans may well have been among them.

The Corinthians' claim also suggests that many, indeed most, people in Corinth were untroubled by the foundation of Thurii, or at least not so troubled that they wished to make war on Athens. The chances for peace, therefore, were probably still fairly reasonable during the early 430s. A series of interrelated crises later in the decade, however, brought the peace to an end, and in these crises Corinth played a large part.

THE BREAKDOWN OF THE PEACE

In the absence of a strong commitment to amicable coexistence, the terms of the Thirty Years' Peace contained within them the seeds of war. Arbitration was meaningless when all the major states were lined up on one side or another; rules made in one sphere of influence might well have an impact on the other; and some states enjoyed an ambiguous status, with one foot in each camp. On all these fronts the peace was vulnerable, as the events that began in 435 in a remote corner of the Greek world were to prove.

Trouble at Epidamnus

"The city of Epidamnus," Thucydides writes, "is on the right as you sail into the Ionic Gulf. Non-Greek speaking Taulantians—an Illyrian people—live nearby. The Corcyraeans colonized the city, although the *oikistēs*, summoned according to the ancient custom from the mother city, was a Corinthian" (1.24; Blanco, adapted). Plainly Thucydides assumes that readers may need to be told the location of this little-known town. In the Corcyrean colony of Epidamnus, he explains, a civil war broke out between the democrats and the oligarchs, moving the democrats to seek assistance from Corcyra. When their mother city turned them down for reasons we do not know, they were encouraged by Delphi to hand themselves over to their "grandmother" Corinth instead. Since colonies that established colonies of their own took an *oikistēs* (founder) from the original founding city, a Corinthian, Phalius, was the technical founder of Epidamnus, and the Corinthians agreed to assist the Epidamnian democrats, in part because of a long-standing feud with Corcyra. The Corcyreans, however, scored a conspicuous victory over the Corinthian fleet that sailed to the aid of Epidamnus. The appalled Corinthians set about building a more substantial fleet with which to humble Corcyra and retain their predominance in western waters.

The Alliance of Corcyra and Athens

Because the Corcyreans belonged to neither the Peloponnesian League nor the Athenian alliance, they had much to fear from the growing Corinthian navy. With the prospects of a Spartan alliance cut off by Sparta's relationship to Corinth, they determined to seek alliance with the Athenians, sending ambassadors to Athens in the summer of 433. Though the Thirty Years' Peace specified that neutrals might join either side, the Athenians were understandably nervous about allying with Corcyra, the enemy of the most powerful naval state in the Peloponnesian League; but they were even more apprehensive about what would happen if mighty Corinth defeated and absorbed Corcyra's substantial fleet. Better, they decided, to gain those ships for Athens, and so, after a debate that extended over two days, they voted to make an alliance with Corcyra. Presumably Pericles was one of those who argued in favor of the alliance. Though the Athenians sought to avoid provoking the Peloponnesians by making the alliance merely a defensive one, this technicality fooled nobody. It was plain that Corinth was about to attack Corcyra and that Athenians and Corinthians would soon be fighting.

It was probably in the slim hope of not provoking the Spartans that the Athenians sent only ten ships to Corcyra's assistance and chose as one of their commanders the son Cimon had named, of all things, Lacedaemonius. Their instructions, Thucydides writes, were to avoid battle with the Corinthians if at all possible, and to engage only if the Corinthians were actually on the point of landing on Corcyrean territory. In the late summer of 433, the Corinthians attacked the Corcyrean fleet of 110 ships off the island chain known as Sybota. The Peloponnesian force consisted of ninety Corinthian ships and sixty more supplied by Elis, Ambracia, Anactorium, Leucas, and—significantly—Athens' neighbor Megara. Though at first the Athenians hung back cautiously, when it was clear that the Corcyreans were getting the worst of it they began to give them increasing support. Thus, Thucydides points out, a situation inevitably came about in which Corinthians and Athenians were openly fighting with one another.

A misunderstanding rescued the Corcyreans from complete destruction. Toward evening, when the Corinthians had disabled over half the Corcyrean fleet and seemed to be on the verge of annihilating their own colony, the astonished Corcyrean sailors noticed that the Corinthian ships had suddenly begun to retreat. Investigation proved that they had sighted ships sailing up from the south and had conjectured that perhaps Athens had decided to aid Corcyra in full force.

They were only partially correct. The ships were indeed from Athens, where the Athenians, who were plainly divided about the expedition, had thought better of dispatching a mere ten ships and had decided to add twenty more. Most decidedly, however, it was not the entire Athenian armada that was approaching, and the Corinthians paid heavily for their moment of panic.

The Problem of Potidaea

Chances of a war between the Athenians and the Peloponnesians had now increased, and in the months following the Battle of Sybota Athens issued problematic decrees against two members of the Peloponnesian League. The city of Potidaea on the Chalcidic peninsula occupied two positions in the Greek world simultaneously: it was both a Corinthian colony and a member of the Athenian alliance. Because Greek colonies were fully autonomous, there was nothing illegal about this, but in a climate of escalating tensions, Potidaea's ambiguous identification was likely to be a source of strain. The potential difficulties were aggravated by the fact that Potidaea's relationship to its mother city was everything that Corcyra's was not. Corcyra was the proverbial bad colony, acting independently from Corinth in all things—excluding the Corinthians from the customary privileges at public festivals and boasting of its financial and military superiority to its mother city. Potidaea, on the other hand, was exceptionally attached to its mother city and even went so far as to accept its annual magistrates from Corinth. During the winter of 433–432, the Athenians ordered the Potidaeans to dismiss their Corinthian magistrates, reject any future officials from Corinth, tear down their seaward defenses, and give hostages. Their motives were probably mixed and included the desire to take vengeance on Corinth and fear of Corinthian interference in the Athenian sphere of influence. The proximity of Potidaea to Macedonia complicated an already difficult situation, for Macedonia was a valuable source of timber for shipbuilding—not only for Athenian ships but for Corinthian ones as well.

After unsuccessful attempts to negotiate with the Athenians, the Potidaeans sent envoys to the Peloponnesus. Thucydides reports that Corinthian envoys helped them extract a promise from at least some Spartans that Sparta could invade Attica if Potidaea were attacked. The first to involve themselves in the Potidaean affair, however, were not the Spartans but the Macedonians. Once an Athenian ally, Macedonia's king Perdiccas had been alienated by Athens' support of two relatives who challenged his right to the throne. Perdiccas not only encouraged the Spartans to move against Athens and urged the Corinthians to raise a revolt in Potidaea; he also persuaded the peoples of Chalcidice and Bottiaea to join with Potidaea in revolt against Athens. Athens then attacked Macedonia, while Corinth entered a secret alliance with the Bottiaean and Chalcidian states. Two thousand men called "volunteers"—some Corinthians, some Peloponnesian mercenaries—entered Potidaea. The Athenians defeated this force and laid siege to Potidaea. The siege would last for two years and cost the Athenians much in men and money.

Athenian Decrees Against Megara

Around the same time, the Athenians took action against Megara. Because Thucydides did not discuss the decrees relating to Megara in any detail, we understand much less about this third crisis than we do about the Corcyrean alliance and the conflict with Potidaea. The time frame is uncertain and the causes of the friction vague. Bordering poleis often quarreled. The Athenians accused the Megarians of harboring escaped slaves and of cultivating some sacred and undefined land that lay between Eleusis and Megara. They were probably angry too at the assistance Megara had given Corinth at the Battle of Sybota. At least one decree against Megara, passed probably in 432, excluded Megarian merchants from all ports of the Athenian empire. This decree enabled the Athenians to inflict considerable harm on a member of the Peloponnesian League without technically infringing the terms of the Thirty Years' Peace. Since there were few Greek ports outside the Athenian empire, their claim that they were simply regulating their own sphere of influence was disingenuous. Plainly the Megarian economy would be devastated by these economic sanctions, and the Athenians could hardly have expected the Spartans to sit idly by while their ally suffered so conspicuously.

Even more than the other actions taken by the Athenian assembly during the years that preceded the outbreak of the Peloponnesian War, the sanctions against Megara (and the subsequent refusal to revoke them) are associated with the name of Pericles. The plays of Aristophanes and Plutarch's biography of Pericles make it plain that some people considered the friction with Megara pivotal in bringing on the war and blamed Pericles for the outbreak of hostilities. Scattered references in Thucydides confirm this. In the autumn of 432 the Corinthians denounced the Athenians before the Spartan assembly. Though the Spartan king Archidamus urged caution and tried to convince his fellow Spartans to postpone taking any action until they could build up their resources for war, his arguments did not prevail, and the Spartans voted that the Athenians had violated the Thirty Years' Peace. They then summoned delegates from the Peloponnesian League who duly voted to go to war with Athens.

Last-Ditch Attempts to Avert War

Archidamus was an old family friend of Pericles, but he was by no means the only Spartan hesitant to fight Athens, and for several months after the formal decision for war had been taken the Spartans sent embassies to the Athenians demanding concessions that could preserve peaceful relations. These included "freeing the Greeks" (abandoning the empire), expelling any cursed Alcmaeonids in the city (Pericles was an Alcmaeonid on his mother's side), and rescinding the Megarian decree. The Athenians responded with demands of their own. They requested, for example, that the Spartans purify "the curse of the goddess of the Brass House," a reference to the impieties involved in the death by starvation decades earlier of Pausanias, who as we have seen had taken refuge in the goddess's temple. Though some of these exchanges involved nothing more than pious posturing, others were plainly sincere, particularly on Sparta's behalf. What these interchanges make clear are, first, that Pericles was firmly entrenched as the leader of the Athenians and as the framer of Athenian policy; second, that the Megarian decree was of considerable importance to the Spartans; and third, that both Athens and Sparta were split about the desirability of war. When negotiations had been going on for several months, the impatient Thebans forced ambivalent Sparta's hand by attacking Athens' ally Plataea. Because Plataea enjoyed a special position in Greece as the site of a great victory against Persia in 478, this assault was considered particularly heinous. Afterward nobody could question that the Peloponnesians and the Athenians were at war.

RESOURCES FOR WAR

Thus ended the period of a half century between the Persian and Peloponnesian wars to which Thucydides gave the name the Pentakontaetia ("the Fifty Years") (technically forty-seven years). In the jockeying for position that went on during the months leading up to the Theban attack on Plataea, the Spartans seem to have come out ahead. Though it was they who had declared war, the Greek world was inclined to see imperialist Athens as the aggressor—and some Athenians agreed, censuring Pericles for his combative stance and advocating the nullification of the Megarian decrees. Sparta did not keep as tight a hold on the members of the Peloponnesian League as did Athens on those of its empire. In a culture that prized autonomy as much as Greeks did, consequently, it was possible for Sparta to put itself forward in opposition to Athens as the champion of freedom—as the state that had never itself endured a tyrant and that opposed tyranny throughout Greece. When war broke out, Thucydides writes,

> Popular opinion shaped up in favor of the Spartans by far, especially since they had proclaimed that they were going to liberate Greece. Everywhere, city and citizen alike were eager, if at all possible, to join with them in word and deed, and everyone felt that any plan would come to a standstill if he himself could not take part in it. That is how angry most people were at Athens—some because they wanted to rid themselves of Athenian rule, and others because they were frightened lest they fall under that rule.
>
> (The Peloponnesian War 2.8; Blanco 1998)

Thucydides also lists the principal combatants at the time of the attack on Plataea in 431. On the Peloponnesian side were Corinth, Boeotia, Megara, Locris, Phocis, Ambracia, Leucas, Anactoria, and all states in the Peloponnesus itself except for Argos and Achaea (though in Achaea the state of Pellene did join the Spartans). Ranged on the Athenian side were an assortment of allies, some no doubt enthusiastic but many reluctant, expecting to gain nothing from the war and imagining that they would enjoy autonomy if Sparta could bring an end to Athens' imperial pretensions. (Those who believed this were mistaken. The Spartan hegemony that followed the war proved so distasteful that numerous states were eager to join the naval confederacy the Athenians established in the fourth century.) The Athenians' allies at the time war broke out were Chios, Lesbos, Plataea, Zacynthus, the Messenians of Naupactus, most of Acarnania, Corcyra, and some cities that paid tribute on the Carian coast (including the nearby Dorian cities), in Ionia, in the Hellespont, in Thrace, among the Cyclades (except for Melos and Thera), and among what Thucydides calls the islands that lie between the Peloponnesus and Crete toward the east.

The belligerents differed not only in temperament but also in the nature of their military strengths. The Athenians had a great deal more money than the Peloponnesians, and their navy was incomparably superior. Athens itself possessed over three hundred ships and could count on a hundred or so more from its allies Chios, Lesbos, and, of course, Corcyra. The Peloponnesians relied principally on the Corinthian navy and could not put many more than a hundred ships in the water. Their crews, moreover, could not compare in skill and experience with those of the Athenians. But the Peloponnesian infantry was formidable. An advancing phalanx of Spartan hoplites wearing their distinctive red tunics and sporting the dreaded "L" for Lacedaemon on their shields threw terror into Sparta's enemies. The combined infantry of the Peloponnesians outnumbered that of the Athenians. Moreover, a good number of their soldiers were Spartans who had spent their entire lives training for this war while helots and perioikoi attended to the other business of life. For these, the citizen farmer-soldiers of the average Greek state were a dubious match. Accordingly, Athens hoped to conduct as much of the war as possible at sea, while the Spartans would focus on the land. The Athenians were fighting essentially a defensive war, whose goal was to preserve the empire the Spartans sought to destroy. For Athens a stalemate would amount to victory. Sparta needed something more.

INTELLECTUAL LIFE IN FIFTH-CENTURY GREECE

As Pericles lay dying, Plutarch maintains, he spoke with pride of what he considered his greatest achievement—"that no living Athenian ever put on mourning because of me." The inaccuracy of this peculiar boast became increasingly clear with every passing year. The war Pericles had encouraged his fellow Athenians to fight with the Peloponnesian League would sap the strength of one of the most extraordinary civilizations the world has ever seen. Looking at the vibrant civilization of Greece in the middle of the fifth century, it would have been hard for anyone alive at the time to believe the horrors that lay ahead. Magnificent temples to the gods dotted the landscape, decked out with friezes that celebrated human and divine accomplishment. Ships plied the seas more or less unharried by pirates, transporting both raw materials like timber (to build more ships) and artifacts such as superb painted pottery. And throughout the Greek cities people had begun to explore new ideas about the universe and humanity's place in it.

Figure 7.2. Alliances at the outset of the Peloponnesian War.

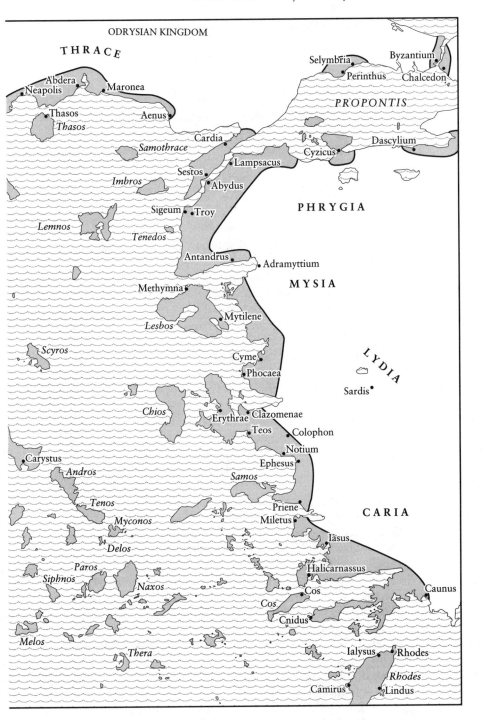

Speculating About the Natural World

Greeks of Hesiod's day had viewed the earliest state of the universe as a form-less void they called *chaos*. Out of chaos, they believed, the order of their own world had emerged—*kosmos*, a Greek word meaning both "order" and "beauty" (hence the word "cosmetics" for makeup, or "cosmetic" surgery to improve appearance). Mythology served the important function of grounding the growth of cosmos from chaos in various actions taken by the gods. The great contribution of the sixth-century Greek thinkers of Ionia had lain in their determination to abandon this mythological and religious framework and attempt instead to explain the world by material processes alone.

As we have seen in Chapter 3, the Ionian rationalists had focused on the natural world rather than on the values of the human community. Like those of Charles Darwin in the nineteenth century, however, their speculations raised inevitable questions about relations between gods and mortals, for they sought to enthrone human reason as the tool for understanding the universe and to replace divine plan (or caprice) with material forces. Anaxagoras from Clazomenae in Asia Minor (c. 500–428 BC) was one of many intellectuals who was drawn to the glittering city of Athens. There he became a trusted friend of Pericles, whom he served as a mentor for many years. Anaxagoras viewed material objects as composed of infinitely divisible particles and conceived of their organization as the work of a force he called *Nous* ("intellect"); from this came his nickname Nous ("the Brain"). The sun, he claimed, was not a deity but rather a white-hot stone a little larger than the Peloponnesus. When Pericles' political enemies sought to undermine his position in the 430s by bringing his known associates to trial, Anaxagoras provided an easy target and was forced to flee for his life.

The workings of the universe also intrigued other fifth-century thinkers throughout the breadth of the Greek world. Empedocles (c. 493–c. 433 BC), who lived in Acragas in Sicily, propounded a cosmogony based on the idea of four primary elements—earth, air, fire, and water. Physical substances, he argued, were produced when the twin forces of attraction and repulsion that he called "love" and "strife" acted upon these elements, combining them in various proportions. Maintaining that these combinations were randomly produced, Empedocles conjectured that monstrous forms had probably been created early in history but had perished through their failure to adapt.

An alternative view of how the world is made was put forward by Leucippus and Democritus. Like Anaxagoras, Leucippus, who seems to have been active around the middle of the fifth century, believed that matter was created of tiny particles, and his ideas were further developed by his pupil Democritus from Abdera in Thrace (c. 460–370 BC). In their view, moreover, the tiny particles were *atoma* ("uncuttable"). Ironically, then, the word for "atom," which has been split in our own age with such devastating consequences, originally meant "that which cannot be divided." In addition to atoms, so the theory had it, there was "void"; falling through void, atoms collided in a variety of ways to form visible matter. What determined the manner of these collisions was a little uncertain—Leucippus insisted it was necessity and not chance, though other atomists disagreed—but the atomic theorists agreed on one thing: whatever was active in shaping the form of matter was a natural force and no divine being.

Though they certainly looked around them for models and paradigms, thinkers like Anaxagoras, Empedocles, Leucippus, and Democritus were essentially philosophers, not scientists. A mix of observation and systematic thinking formed the basis of Greek medicine. Though prayer probably remained the most common Greek response to illness in antiquity, during the sixth century BC Greeks in Asia Minor began learning about anatomy from the observations Mesopotamians had made on animal entrails used in divination. By 500 BC, medical centers had been established on the island of Cos off the coast of Asia Minor and on the nearby peninsula of Cnidos. Some instruction also took place within the family; often the medical profession was passed down from father to son. Women were prohibited from practicing as doctors, but they frequently functioned as midwives.

Case studies formed the basis of the doctrines of Hippocrates of Cos (c. 460–c. 377 BC). The body of writings associated with Hippocrates' school included over a hundred works composed over a long period, and there is no way to know which of these might have been written by Hippocrates himself. Greeks did not develop many cures for diseases. The principal contribution of the Hippocratics lay not in any specific discoveries about medicine but rather in their commitment to seeking rational explanations of natural phenomena. Epilepsy, for example, had been labeled "the sacred disease" by the Greeks; in their treatise *On the Sacred Disease*, the Hippocratics took a different view, claiming that this notion was put forward by anxious charlatans who, "having no idea what to do and having nothing to offer the sick . . . labelled the disease sacred in order to conceal their ignorance." (*On the Sacred Disease* 2) Another treatise, *Airs, Waters, Places*, examined the impact of climate on health, laying the foundations for epidemiology.

The largest group of Hippocratic texts deals with gynecology. Along with the general devaluation of women in Greek culture, women's reticence about speaking to male physicians sometimes cut doctors off from information vital to understanding female reproductive processes. In the absence of real data concerning symptoms and sexual practices, where women were concerned speculation often substituted for the careful observation on which the Hippocratics prided themselves:

> If suffocation occurs suddenly, it will happen especially to women who do not have intercourse and to older women rather than to young ones, for their wombs are lighter. It usually occurs because of the following: when a woman is empty and works harder than in her previous experience, her womb, becoming heated from the hard work, turns because it is empty and light. There is, in fact, empty space for it to turn in because the belly is empty. Now when the womb turns, it hits the liver and they go together and strike against the abdomen—for the womb rushes and goes upwards towards the moisture, because it has been dried out by hard work, and the liver is, after all, moist. When the womb hits the liver, it produces sudden suffocation as it occupies the breathing passages around the belly.
> (Diseases of Women *1.7; Hanson 1975*)

THE LITERATURE OF THE FIFTH CENTURY

In the verbal realm, the principal achievements of the Athenians during this period lay in history and in tragedy. Dozens of tragedians were active in fifth-century Athens, though only the works of Aeschylus, Sophocles, and Euripides have survived, and of these only a fraction of their output—seven each of Aeschylus and Sophocles, and nineteen of Euripides. History was the less common genre, but the two works that survived in their entirety were remarkable in their scope and depth—Herodotus' history of the Persian wars and Thucydides' history of the Peloponnesian War. Between them, Herodotus and Thucydides enshrined in historical writing the model of the war monograph that has remained popular to this day.

Herodotus

Like Anaxagoras, Pericles' friends Herodotus and Sophocles also sought to challenge traditional ways of looking at the world. Born in Halicarnassus in Ionia, Herodotus was heir to all the traditions of Ionian rationalism and had a passionate curiosity about causes and origins. Why the Persians and the Greeks fought, what accounted for the Greek victory, how Darius came to rule Persia, where the Nile began, how the priestesses at Dodona came to be thought of as birds with human voices, where the Greeks got their gods—Herodotus used the Greek word *historia* ("inquiry") to describe his quest for understanding, and this word has given English and numerous romance languages their word for the investigation and analysis of the past: "history." He has set forth the results of his inquiry, he reports in the opening sentence of his work, "so that the actions of people shall not fade with time, so that the great and admirable monuments produced by both Greeks and barbarians shall not go unrenowned, and, among other things, to set forth the reasons why they waged war on each other" (*The Histories* 1.1; Blanco 1992).

Born probably shortly before Xerxes' invasion of Greece in 480, Herodotus was not old enough to remember the Persian wars, but he was able to interrogate informants of his parents' generation closely. His interests were not confined to a particular series of historical events; like his somewhat younger contemporary Thucydides, he was fascinated by what history revealed about human nature and the way the world works. What he learned from his study of history was that power goes to people's heads, and that the mighty rarely meditate on their condition with sufficient judiciousness and reflection—that rulers hear what they want to hear, and rush headlong to their own destruction.

This paradigm appears early in his history in his imaginative reconstruction of a conversation between Solon, the Athenian lawgiver, and Croesus, the fabulously wealthy king of Lydia who has given his name to the expression still current today, "rich as Croesus." During his travels, Herodotus maintains, Solon came to Croesus' palace, where the king made a point of having attendants give Solon a tour that would highlight Croesus' prosperity at every turn. Afterward, Croesus asked Solon if there was anyone in the world who struck him as particularly fortunate. Feigning innocence of Croesus' purpose in asking this question, Solon named a little-known Greek man who had died fighting for his city, leaving children behind him, and was buried with honors. When Croesus was dissatisfied with this response, Solon offered an alternative example. Two young Argives, he related, when their mother needed to attend a feast of Hera and the oxen had not yet returned from the field, yoked themselves to the family wagon and pulled it several miles to the temple. Amidst the great words of praise lavished upon the young men and on her for having such fine sons, their mother prayed to the goddess to bestow on her children whatever was best for humankind. Lying down to sleep in the temple, the youths never awoke, and the Argives dedicated statues to them at Delphi in commemoration of their excellence.

Resentful at not being named the most fortunate of men, Croesus spoke harshly to Solon, voicing his indignation at the notion that the Athenian should consider ordinary citizens more fortunate than a rich king like him. Solon in turn counseled him to think harder about what it means to be truly fortunate, cautioning him not to make facile judgments without waiting to see how things turn out in the end. "To me," he tells Croesus,

> it is clear that you are very rich, and clear that you are the king of many men; but the thing that you asked me I cannot say of you yet, until I hear that you have brought your life to an end well. For he that is greatly rich is not more blessed than he that has enough for the day unless fortune so attend upon him that he ends his life well, having all those fine things still with him. . . . One must look always at the end of everything—how it will come out finally. For to many the god has shown a glimpse of blessedness only to extirpate them in the end.
>
> (The History *1.32; Grene 1987*)

Croesus, however, does not listen. By carelessly misinterpreting a series of oracles, he loses his empire and comes to recognize Solon's wisdom.

It is not at all likely that Solon and Croesus really met. Solon's travels evidently preceded Croesus' accession to the throne around 560 BC. Herodotus has crafted this vignette to demonstrate the superiority of Greek over Persian ways of thinking—of the western dependence on the solid citizen over the eastern reverence for the powerful autocrat. Similar points are scored in Herodotus' characterization of the overconfident Xerxes. The implications of this are plain enough: for all their virtues, the Persians, like other eastern peoples, were dragged down by their habit of according immense power to a single individual, the king. Encouraging him in his childish self-confidence, they became slaves to someone who exaggerated his own importance not only vis-à-vis other mortals but, more dangerously still, in relation to the gods. In comparison, Greek civilization held all the promise that inhered in free institutions, in the rule of law, in respect for gods and the acceptance of human limitations.

In all this Herodotus was a typical Greek, but in other respects he sought to undermine knee-jerk assumptions he saw in the world around him—assumptions about the insignificance of non-Greek cultures and the low intellect of women. Greek men, in Herodotus' view, needed to think harder and longer about their place in the world. To assist them in this project, he included in his history many stories about the intelligence of clever queens (such as Queen Artemisia of his native Halicarnassus) and a detailed account of the accomplishments of the Egyptians, stressing the greater antiquity of Egyptian culture in relation to Greek and suggesting Egyptian origins for the Greek gods.

Sophocles

Herodotus' warnings about the vicissitudes of fortune and the impossibility of judging a man's life until it is over are echoed in *Oedipus Tyrannus*, the most famous play of antiquity. Here the poet Sophocles (c. 496–406 BC) presents to us the seeming good fortune of Oedipus, the highly intelligent and respected ruler of Thebes in the Heroic Age—only to show us his life disintegrating before our eyes. *Oedipus Tyrannus* was produced in the early years of the Peloponnesian War, but Sophocles had already made quite a name for himself during the 440s while Herodotus was in Athens, where the historian lived for several years after his travels and before moving to Thurii. Sophocles wrote over a hundred plays. Like Aeschylus and other tragic poets, Sophocles reworked the familiar plots of Greek mythology, with their emphasis on agonizing family discord, to express his view of the world. Just after Herodotus' departure for Thurii Sophocles produced the first of three surviving dramas about the unfortunate house of Oedipus, the legendary ruler of Thebes who was fated to kill his father and marry his mother.

In the first of Sophocles' Theban plays, *Antigone*, the playwright asks us to contemplate the painful tensions that arise in Oedipus' family after his death. One of his sons, Polynices, has died fighting to take the throne of Thebes from his brother; naturally Polynices' sister Antigone wishes to fulfill her religious obligation and bury his body. But their uncle Creon, now king of Thebes, forbids anyone to take up this project on the grounds that Polynices was a traitor. Like many characters in Greek tragedy, Antigone now finds herself confronted with a painful choice. She must decide whether to honor her obligation to her brother and to the gods, which means facing death herself, or to obey the laws of the state and keep herself safe. She is headstrong and defiant; Creon is rigid and insensitive.

Though Sophocles is a conventional Athenian in his respect for the gods and their power to guide human life, in other regards he challenged conventional mores. Antigone's situation paralleled that of the Athenian girl known as an *epiklēros*, a girl with no surviving brothers, and it is hard to doubt that Sophocles' sympathies lie with the fatherless, brotherless girl who experiences all the helplessness that fell upon Athenian women who lacked male protectors. Sophocles, as his other plays confirm, sympathized with the plight of Greek women. Creon, however, makes a good case for the importance of a law that makes no exceptions for family members, and as an Athenian democrat Sophocles certainly saw the need to uphold the rule of law. But is the decree of an autocrat really law, especially when the populace is on Antigone's side? Sophocles fully recognizes the complexity of the tortuous choices Antigone and Creon must make, and he sees in their confrontation proof of the wondrous complexity of humankind and the communities humans have struggled to develop.

Document 7.1 The soaring poetry of the chorus celebrates the achievements of the human race in a memorable passage.

> Many the wonders but nothing walks stranger than man.
> This thing crosses the sea in the winter's storm,
> making his path through the roaring waves.
> And she, the greatest of gods, the earth—
> ageless she is, and unwearied—he wears her away
> as the ploughs go up and down from year to year
> and his mules turn up the soil.
> Gay nations of birds he snares and leads,
> wild beast tribes and the salty brood of the sea,
> with the twisted mesh of his nets, this clever man.
> He controls with craft the beasts of the open air,
> walkers on hills. The horse with his shaggy mane
> he holds and harnesses, yoked about the neck,
> and the strong bull of the mountain.
> Language, and thought like the wind
> and the feelings that make the town,
> he has taught himself, and shelter against the cold,
> refuge from rain. He can always help himself.
> He faces no future helpless. There's only death
> that he cannot find an escape from. He has contrived
> refuge from illnesses once beyond all cure.
> Clever beyond all dreams
> the inventive craft that he has
> which may drive him one time or another to well or ill.

Excerpt from Sophocles' Antigone. *Antigone 11.332–368, translated by Elizabeth Wyckoff, in David Grene and Richmond Lattimore, eds.,* The Complete Greek Tragedies. *Chicago: University of Chicago Press, 1960, pp. 192–193.*

Like Herodotus, Sophocles combined profound reverence for the gods with a compelling interest in the human dimension of life. In his plays, dialogue—the talking back and forth of humans—was expanded at the expense of the chorus; he also added a third actor where Aeschylus had used only two (not counting silent actors, who appeared on the stage but did not speak).

Euripides

In the spring of 431 Athenians and foreign visitors gathered in the theater of Diony-sus to see Euripides' *Medea*. Plays by Euripides (c. 485–c. 406 BC) had been produced before, so the playwright was already known to the audience, but the subject matter for this drama was singularly shocking. Although the plots of Greek tragedy derived from familiar myths, Euripides enjoyed innovation, and there is some reason to be-lieve that the ending of the play came as a surprise to the enthralled onlookers.

The questions Sophocles posed about the society in which he lived seem tame compared with the more searching critiques of Greek values that appear in Eu-ripides' plays. In *Medea* Euripides used the tale of Jason, the celebrated leader of the Argonauts in their quest for the Golden Fleece, to undermine conventional views of what makes a hero. In his adventures Jason had acquired a wife—Medea, a sorceress from Colchis, at the far end of the Black Sea. He has such con-fidence in the excellence of the Greek way of life that even when he has decided to abandon Medea to marry a Corinthian princess, he boasts of the benefits he has conferred on her by rescuing her from a barbarian land and transplanting her to Greece. Predictably, these arguments do not sit well with a highly intelligent witch who has the advantage of a non-Greek perspective. The bitter laments of Medea enable the audience to see things differently as she details the constraints on her life as a woman in a Greek city:

> We women are the most unfortunate creatures.
> First, with an excess of wealth it is required
> For us to buy a husband, and take for our bodies
> A master; for not to take one is even worse.
> And now the question is serious whether we take
> A good or bad one; for there is no easy escape
> For a woman, nor can she say no to her marriage.
> (Medea 231–238; Warner 1959)

Jason's shameful rationalizations for his actions, moreover, raise serious ques-tions about a society that makes heroes of such men. Greek tragedies, however, were not morality plays, and when in the play's horrifying conclusion Medea de-cides to take vengeance on Jason by killing their children, even those in the au-dience who were sympathetic to her plight probably shifted their sympathy to the bereaved father. (In the same way, Sophocles' audience felt for the harsh Creon when his actions led to the death not only of Antigone but of his own wife and son as well.) *Medea* was only one of the plays in which Euripides explored the dynamics of the conflict between reason and passion—reason, which could justify Jason in deserting the wife who had risked her life for him in her youth, and passion, which could move a mother to kill her offspring. Inevitably the ag-onizing conflict that marked plays like *Antigone* struck a particularly resonant chord with the audience in *Medea*, which was produced just as war was breaking out between two very different states with opposing views of the world.

Thucydides

This war, which took thousands of lives, immortalized the name of the historian who told its story. Many intellectual currents of the fifth century flowed through Athens as Thucydides was coming to maturity and during the years when he composed his history of the long war in which he served. Some were plainly important to him, others apparently not. Clever speaking, careful observation, rational deduction, and a tragic view of the world can all be discerned in his history; unlike that of Herodotus, Sophocles, and Euripides, however, his writing shows no interest in women. Like many thinkers of the later fifth century, Thucydides construed the world as fundamentally human centered. Whereas Herodotus, born a generation earlier, had conceived history as an interaction of divine and human forces, both vitally important, Thucydides saw the actions of people as pretty much exclusively responsible for how things turn out. A similar progression can be seen in the extant tragedians: Sophocles was somewhat more concerned with the human factor than Aeschylus, who was more drawn to the role and nature of the gods, and Euripides in turn—despite considerable interest in religion—gave human nature center stage.

Almost nothing is known of Thucydides' life. Since he served as a general in 424, he must have been at least 30 in that year, and historians conjecture he was born around 460. He came from an aristocratic family with kinship ties to two of Pericles' best-known rivals, Cimon and Melesias' son Thucydides, but he had enormous admiration for Pericles. His opportunities for research took an unexpected turn when he was exiled after failing to keep the Spartans from taking Amphipolis. From then on he was able to gather a great deal of information from non-Athenian sources but could no longer attend meetings of the Athenian assembly. He lived long enough to see Athens lose the war. He claims to have begun writing as the war broke out, foreseeing its importance, and to have written up each year as it happened, but even if this is true in its outlines he certainly made some revisions based on hindsight; in Book 5, for example, dealing with the events of 421, he refers to the fall of Athens in 404 and identifies the length of the war as twenty-seven years.

Thucydides himself discusses his methodology at the outset of his history, stressing the lengths to which he went in his quest to determine the truth—and expressing impatience with those less committed to the search for knowledge. Most people, he complains, "expend very little effort on the search for truth, and prefer to turn to ready-made answers." His own approach will be different.

Document 7.2 Thucydides explains his methodology in his history of the Peloponnesian War, contrasting himself with less reliable reporters—including, it seems, Herodotus as well as rhetoricians given to virtuoso public displays.

One will not go wrong if he believes that the facts were such as I have related them, based on the evidence, and not as they are sung by the poets—who embellish and exaggerate them—or as they are strung together by pop-

ular historians with a view to making them not more truthful but more attractive to their audiences; and considering that we are dealing with ancient
history, whose unverified events have, over the course of time, made their
way into the incredible realms of mythology, one will find that these conclusions, derived as they are from the best known evidence, are accurate
enough. Even though people always think that the war they are fighting is
the greatest there ever was, and then return to marveling at ancient wars
once theirs have ended, it will be clear, after we examine the events themselves, that this actually was the greatest there has ever been.

As to the statements the participants made, either when they were about
to enter the war or after they were already in it, it has been difficult for me
and for those who reported to me to remember exactly what was said. I
have, therefore, written what I thought the speakers must have said given
the situations they were in, while keeping as close as possible to the consensus about what was actually said. As to the events of the war, I have not
written them down as I heard them from just anybody, nor as I thought
they must have occurred, but have consistently described what I myself saw
or have been able to learn from others after going over each event in as
much detail as possible. I have found this task to be extremely difficult,
since those who were present at these actions gave varying reports on the
same event, depending on their sympathies and their memories.

My narrative, perhaps, will seem less pleasing to some listeners because
it lacks an element of fiction. Those, however, who want to see things clearly
as they were, and, given human nature, as they will one day be again, more
or less, may find this book a useful basis for judgment. My work was composed not as a prizewinning exercise in elocution but as a possession for all
time.

> The Peloponnesian War *1.22; translated by Walter Blanco, in Walter Blanco*
> *and Jennifer Roberts, eds.,* The Peloponnesian War.
> *New York: W.W. Norton, 1998.*

Most twentieth-century readers have regarded Thucydides as the finest historian of the Greco-Roman world. This is reasonable. He is less disposed to see divine justice as a force in history than Herodotus, who had the luxury of writing
up a war which, in his view, the good guys won; the Peloponnesian War was a
war that everyone lost. He does not moralize like Plutarch. In comparison with
the famous historians of Rome, he is less jingoistic than Livy, and his partisanship is better concealed than that of Tacitus. He has often been described as the
world's first scientific historian, and his work has been cited for its objectivity.
This characterization rests on a misunderstanding of what the writing of history
really involves. History is not a science, and it cannot be objective, because it en-

tails humans writing about other humans. Every omission, every connection, requires a judgment call.

One example will illustrate the choices all historians must make. In analyzing the outbreak of the war, Thucydides downplayed the Megarian decree to a remarkable degree, saying almost nothing about it. He did this, presumably, either because he really believed the decree was unimportant or because he wished to deflect criticism from Pericles, who was commonly blamed for the decree and the war. It would be impossible to construe this decision as objective or scientific. The result of Thucydides' choice is that it is now very difficult for students of the past to reconstruct what really happened. If the Megarian decree really was unimportant, then presumably Thucydides did a good thing, but if he was wrong, then he did his readers a great disservice. There is no limit to the number of similar decisions that confront historians. Herodotus was more disposed to put everything in and let his readers sort it out, but one consequence of this decision is that he has been criticized for being less analytical than Thucydides.

CURRENTS IN GREEK THOUGHT AND EDUCATION

The convoluted arguments that help politicians who appear in Thucydides' narrative cloak ambition in fair-sounding words and the verses in which Euripides' Jason defends his action as calculated to improve his children's lives (won't it be wonderful for them to have royal stepsiblings?) show the influence of the itinerant intellectuals who gravitated to Athens during the second half of the fifth century, the men who came to be known as the sophists, from the Greek word *sophistēs*, which means something like "practitioner of wisdom." Unlike the philosophers who sought to understand the world, the sophists contented themselves with teaching eager, paying pupils how to get by in it. Many of the sophists were important, iconoclastic thinkers whose keen analysis pierced pretensions. Though their works do not survive except in fragments, it seems clear that they rejected facile assumptions about the connections between noble birth and true merit. Because of this, and because they enabled young men from newly rich families to learn to speak effectively, they aroused suspicion among Athens' entrenched elite.

Formal and Informal Education

The origins of the sophistic movement lie in the haphazard and informal nature of Greek education, in its literary and aristocratic bias, and in its ultimately superficial and stultifying nature. Since Homer's day, Greek children had learned primarily by watching the world around them and imitating respected elders. Few people in antiquity or the middle ages knew how to read, and "book learning" played a minor role in the educational system of Archaic Greece, where most formal education involved listening and reciting from memory. Girls were rarely sent to school. Neither were most boys. The problem was not simply that poverty usually compelled children to stay home and work on the farm; the fact is that Greek states did not provide public schools. Parents of the upper classes, however, paid for their sons to be instructed in what was called *mousikē*, a subject that included the memorization of poetry. Since ancient poems were sung, mousike also involved learning to play the stringed instrument known as the *lyra* hence our word "lyrics"—verses designed to accompany lyre playing—and of course our word "music" as well. Beginning in the sixth century, more and more children also learned to read and write. Vases from the sixth and fifth centuries show these skills being taught to boys and occasionally to girls as well: parents sometimes had daughters instructed in basic reading and writing skills in case they needed this knowledge to supervise household accounts or to manage temple properties if they became priestesses. Some instruction in math was also offered to children by private tutors and in schools, though not much was offered in the way of science. The curriculum included little of what we would call social studies, and the young were generally thrown back on family and friends for the answer to questions like, "How far is it to Sparta?" and "What kind of government do they have in Corinth?" By the time boys progressed to the age at which adolescents today would enter college, moreover, they had ceased to be students and had become soldiers and citizens.

Most education went on in less formal settings, however, and this sort of education would continue throughout life. In childhood, girls would absorb the norms of appropriate social behavior from their mothers and aunts, boys from their fathers and uncles. As in many societies, the upbringing of the two sexes was designed to cultivate very different skill sets for males and females. These differences were most pronounced in the upper classes, for poor children of both sexes were likely to learn farming and craft skills from parents. Among the elite, however, a sharp differentiation occurred in adolescence, for at this juncture girls married and reproduced. Their education in home management continued at the hands of older relatives, and probably older slaves as well, who had considerable experience of child rearing. In addition, husbands sometimes took it upon themselves to give their wives vocational training in household management. In the *Oeconomicus*, written in the fourth century in the form of a Socratic dialogue, Xenophon describes how a husband, Ischomachus, trained his young wife to be a successful estate manager:

> [Socrates] said, "I would very much like you to tell me, Ischomachus, whether you yourself trained your wife to become the sort of woman that she ought to be, or whether she already knew how to carry out her duties when you took her as your wife from her father and mother."
>
> "What could she have known when I took her as my wife, Socrates? She was not yet fifteen when she came to me, and had spent her previous years under careful supervision so that she might see and hear and speak as little as possible. Don't you think it was adequate if she came to me knowing only how to take

wool and produce a cloak, and had seen how spinning tasks are allocated to the slaves? And besides, she had been very well trained to control her appetites, Socrates," he said, "and I think that sort of training is most important for man and woman alike."

(Oeconomicus 7.4–5; Pomeroy 1994)

While teenaged girls might receive such instruction from their husbands, adolescent males were exposed to important influences of another kind. Books were expensive, and though literacy increased throughout the sixth and particularly the fifth century, learning still went on primarily in the interaction between two or more human beings, not in the interaction of a person with a written text. Relationships with somewhat older mentors formed a key element in the education of teenaged boys. Just as younger teachers today often serve as role models for adolescents, so young men in Greece offered examples of manhood to those who were just developing into men. The one-on-one nature of these friendships, however—untrammeled by any need for a teacher to be evenhanded with an entire class of students—combined with different attitudes to sexuality to produce a significantly different dynamic. The bond between a Greek male teenager and his adult mentor was often profoundly erotic. What we know about these relationships is somewhat compromised by a reticence about sex in the written sources and by the need many Greeks felt to stress the intellectual and spiritual bond at the expense of the sexual one. In his dialogue on love, the *Symposium*, Plato praises this bond for its value in the moral improvement of both the individual and society as a whole. "I would maintain," he writes,

> that there can be no greater benefit for a boy than to have a worthy lover from his earlier youth, nor for a lover than to have a worthy object for his affection. The principle which ought to guide the whole life of those who intend to live nobly cannot be implanted either by family or by position or by wealth or by anything else so effectively as by love. What principle? you ask. I mean the principle which inspires shame at what is disgraceful and ambition for what is noble; without these feelings neither a state nor an individual can accomplish anything great or fine.

(Symposium 178b; Hamilton 1951)

The bond between the older lover (the *erastēs*) and the younger beloved (the *eromenos*) shored up the stability of society by encouraging each generation (or half generation) to imitate the one that had gone before.

Finally, participation in the life of the city as a whole afforded an ongoing education to growing men, and to some extent to women as well, particularly those who served as priestesses. The poet Simonides put it well: *Polis andra didaskei* ("the polis teaches a man"). Only in mature life, however—by attendance, for example, at tragic dramas and the thoughtful discussions that no doubt followed in private gatherings—did this education entail any real questioning of conventional wisdom. In general, the purpose of Greek education was a blend of indoctrination and socialization calculated to foster the perpetuation of traditional values. Poetry was more likely to be memorized than analyzed, and despite the originality with which the Greeks are rightly credited, the culture did not as a whole prize innovation. What Greek youth was taught above all was to copy approved models.

All this changed when the sophists burst on the scene during the second half of the fifth century, sparking powerful tensions between the generations. Athens acted as a magnet for the philosophers and teachers of rhetoric who had sprung up throughout the Greek world as speculation about both the natural universe and the human community became increasingly popular among intellectuals. Democracy was grounded in skill in speaking and reasoning—in the ability to dissect and demolish the arguments of political opponents. The sophists offered to teach these skills. Sophists filled other needs as well, for they delighted in exploring tricky questions about the workings of the world. Not everyone had been satisfied by the conventional pieties about the awesome powers of the gods and the concomitant need to revere authorities of all kinds, and for the dissatisfied the sophists' speculations provided an opportunity to flex both their intellects and their rhetorical skills. No common belief system marked the thinking of the various sophists, but they shared an enthusiasm for the kind of exercises in argumentation that are central to much higher education today.

The Sophists

Like much of the education that had gone before, the instruction offered by sophists benefited only a fairly small class of affluent students who could afford to pay. What the sophists had to offer, however, differed sharply from earlier education, for the sophists questioned the notion that deferential emulation of one's elders and betters was the noblest of achievements. They challenged conventional beliefs in other ways as well. One object of their explorations was the notion of *nomos*.

Herodotus had shown in his history the centrality of nomos to society. The Greek word meant both "law" and "custom"; there were state-sanctioned nomoi forbidding burglary, but there were also social nomoi regarding what to wear at your wedding and religious nomoi about how to worship Apollo. In a society that had existed for centuries without written law, only a blurry line divided a legal nomos and a conventional nomos based on tradition. The two, however, began to diverge the harder people thought about the problem. Herodotus' *Histories* demonstrated two different sides of nomos. On the one hand, the Greeks had fought the Persians in order to live by nomos rather than at the whim of a despot. On the other hand, the multiplicity of nomoi in different cultures reveals a diversity that suggests that local customs are the product of tradition rather than of abstract, unchanging principles of right and wrong. To demonstrate the force of nomos, Herodotus tells the following tale:

> Darius . . . called together some of the Greeks who were in attendance on him and asked them what would they take to eat their dead fathers. They said that

no price in the world would make them do so. After that Darius summoned those of the Indians who are called Callatians, who *do* eat their parents, and, in the presence of the Greeks (who understood the conversation through an interpreter), asked them what price would make them burn their dead fathers with fire. They shouted aloud, "Don't mention such horrors!"

(The History 3.38; Grene 1987)

Each society, he concludes, considers its own customs to be best.

When this idea was assimilated to the speculations of the natural philosophers, an opposition evolved in many minds between the concept of *physis* ("nature"), and *nomos* ("convention"). The relationship between physis and nomos became central to Greek thought around Herodotus' time, for it carried powerful implications for the legitimacy of authority. If nomos was not the natural outgrowth of physis but actually existed in opposition to it, then the laws of the community were not necessarily to be obeyed, for they might have grown up randomly, endorsed by generations of unthinking traditionalists who had given no thought to their grounding in physis.

This concept of law varied conspicuously from the usual view that law ultimately came from the gods, and in fact the new ways of looking at the world had serious implications for relations between gods and mortals. One of the most renowned of the sophists who came to teach in Athens was Protagoras (c. 490–420 BC) of Abdera in northern Greece, who moved to Athens around 450 and spent most of the rest of his life there. He is best known for two sayings with religious implications. "Each individual person is the measure of all things—of things that are, that they are, and of things that are not, that they are not." Nobody, in other words, can tell you what is real or true—no state official, no parent, and no god. Another contention was still more provocative: it is impossible to know, Protagoras is said to have observed, "whether the gods exist, or how they might look if they do. Numerous obstacles stand in the way, such as the shortness of life and the difficulty of the subject matter."

Not all sophists had unconventional ideas about politics or society or religion. Plato represents Thrasymachus arguing that justice is nothing but the interest of the stronger, but Plato plainly did not like Thrasymachus. Xenophon reported that Hippias maintained that certain natural laws were common to all societies; if this is true, then Hippias did not see a conflict between nomos and physis. Some of what the sophists taught was simply practical knowledge that would be useful to an aspiring politician; they probably did tell you how far it was from Athens to Sparta and what sort of government ruled Corinth. Many sophists were highly esteemed in their birthplaces and in Athens, where they tended to wind up, but they also sparked hostility in many quarters. Their ideas about religion and authority seemed subversive, and people tended to associate them with thinkers like Anaxagoras who, after all, had said that the sun was not a divinity but rather an extremely hot stone. In fact, those who associated the sophists' speculations in moral and social philosophy with developments in scientific thought were on to something, for behind both lay the same commitment to open-minded, rational inquiry into basic structures, the same interest in the connection of appearance to reality, the same curiosity about the relationship between the eternal and the changing. Parmenides' contention that motion was illusory had something in common with the questions the sophist Antiphon raised about the validity of distinctions between aristocrat and commoner, Greek and barbarian, and his conclusion that all grew alike by nature. (Similarly Alcidamas argued that nature had made nobody a slave.)

More, however, lay behind the mistrust the sophists inspired. Some affluent Athenians were suspicious of people who took fees for anything, since inherited landed wealth was viewed as the most respectable form of income, followed by wealth earned by farming one's own land. Some of those who were less well off resented the sophists precisely because they could not afford to pay what the sophists charged. It was unclear, moreover, just what skill these people were teaching, and by what right they were charging their fees. It was easy to see how an experienced flute player could teach flute playing or how a gifted boxer could teach boxing, but it was harder to understand who was qualified to offer instruction in getting ahead in politics and in life. In many ways the sophists were the "consultants" of ancient Greece, inspiring many people to wonder grouchily (and enviously) just what they were selling that was making them so rich.

There was an answer, however, to the question, "Just what do these people teach, anyway?" That answer was rhetoric, and not everyone liked it. No parent who has ever gone head to head with a smart-alecky teenager can fail to sympathize with middle-aged Athenians who found themselves confounded at every turn by the smugness of a new generation that had studied the arts of argumentation from experienced masters. Concern that clever speaking was coming to substitute for serious thinking about right and wrong, moreover, was not limited to the stodgy and the stuffy. Euripides in his unsettling portrait of Jason in *Medea* and Thucydides in his representation of the dynamics of power politics show a painful awareness of the problems created when rhetoric is deployed to distract the listener from plain old-fashioned principles of fairness. Protagoras himself, who won respect as an honorable man even from the antisophistic Plato, was reputed to be the first person to write a treatise in the techniques of argument and to claim that he knew how to make "the weaker argument the stronger." Works ascribed to him included *Contradictions* and *The Knockdown Arguments*.

Another popular sophist was Alcidamas' teacher Gorgias (c. 485–c. 380 BC), a native of Leontini in Sicily who visited Athens in 427 on an embassy that sought to persuade the Athenians to become involved in Sicilian affairs. Gorgias' name is associated almost exclusively with rhetoric; it is unclear whether he thought much about philosophy. One of his more famous pieces was a rhetorical tour de force in which he defended Helen on a charge of causing the Trojan War by eloping with Paris. Gorgias lists three possible reasons for Helen's action, each of them worthy: "Either she did what she did because of the will of fortune and the plan of the gods and the decree of necessity, or she was seized by force, or persuaded by words," or, he later suggests, captured by love. All these possible explanations, he argues, exculpate Helen:

> If she left for the first reason, then any who blame her deserve blame themselves, for a human's anticipation cannot restrain a god's inclination. For by nature the stronger is not restrained by the weaker but the weaker is ruled and led by the stronger. . . .
> If she was forcibly abducted and unlawfully violated and unjustly assaulted, it is clear that her abductor, her assaulter, engaged in crime; but she who was abducted and assaulted encountered misfortune. . . . it is right to pity her but hate him.

He then takes the occasion of discussing persuasion to expatiate on the charms of fine speaking, arguing that

> If speech persuaded and deluded her mind, even against this it is not hard to defend her or free her from blame as follows: speech is a powerful master and achieves the most divine feats with the smallest and least evident body. It can stop fear, relieve pain, create joy, and increase pity. How this is so, I shall show; and I must demonstrate this to my audience to change their opinion. . . .

> How many men on how many subjects have persuaded and do persuade how many others by shaping a false speech! . . . The power of speech has the same effect on the disposition of the soul as the disposition of drugs on the nature of bodies. Just as different drugs draw forth different humors from the body—some putting a stop to disease, others to life—so too with words: some cause pain, others joy, some strike fear, some stir the audience to boldness, some benumb and bewitch the soul with evil persuasion.
> (Encomium of Helen; *Gagarin and Woodruff 1995*)

Many Greeks believed there was no limit to what sophists would use rhetoric to defend. The anonymous treatise known as *Dissoi Logoi* (Double Arguments) reveals the moral relativism that many associated with sophists. Can sickness ever be good? Certainly, if you are a doctor. But what about death? Death is good for undertakers and gravediggers. The author goes on to enumerate the many examples of cultural difference found in Herodotus in order to demonstrate that no act is intrinsically good or bad. A mental universe in which nothing was purely good or patently evil was not one in which all Greeks wished to dwell.

For all these reasons, the sophists drew to themselves a considerable amount of odium. They found themselves under attack not only in conversation but on the stage. In 423 Aristophanes produced the *Clouds*, in which the intellectuals of Athens—the "eggheads"—are derided as teaching a corrosive rhetoric that made a mockery of decent, sensible values. The man Aristophanes identifies as running the "think shop" was not, however, a sophist. Like some of Aristophanes' other characters, he was a real person, but not one who taught rhetoric or accepted fees.

He was Socrates, and the disposition to identify him with the sophists contributed in no small measure to his execution just after the end of the war.

THE PHYSICAL SPACE OF THE POLIS: ATHENS ON THE EVE OF WAR

The Greek world was both one and many: though common features tied the city-states together, each polis was unique in culture. As so often in attempts to recover the world of Classical Greece, however, the bulk of our knowledge about the development of the polis during the later decades of the fifth century comes from Athens. Even during the war, Athenian tragic dramatists continued to produce astonishing masterpieces. It was the war years that witnessed the birth of Attic comedy. Some of our best evidence about fifth-century Athens is physical in nature, for the revenues of empire helped to adorn the imperial city with splendid buildings, many of which still impress and intrigue visitors today.

The Acropolis

The structure most people associate with Classical Athens, the Parthenon, stood with other important buildings on the steep hill of the Acropolis, which had been fortified from earliest times. A hill was a distinct advantage to a city-state. Though most people today associate the word "acropolis" with the Acropolis of Athens, in fact it was a feature common to many poleis, which relied for protection on a fortified citadel from which one could see far into the distance; on a clear day the Acropolis of Athens was visible from the corresponding high point of Corinth, Acrocorinth. In Athens, the Acropolis was the spiritual focus of the polis. Because of its height and steeply sloped sides, this naturally fortified area had been the residence of early rulers and had always been home to the chief gods of the Athenians. The sixth-century tyrant Peisistratus, like Pericles later, initiated an ambitious building project on the Acropolis, for he understood not only that such work would provide steady employment to the restless urban poor, but also that a beautiful city would create still more jobs, foster patriotism among all citizens, and attract wealthy, talented metics. It would be, as Pericles would later say in the pages of Thucydides, "the school of Hellas." The Persian invasion of 480 destroyed the monuments and statues of Peisistratus's time. This rubble, in turn, was used as the foundation of the buildings constructed in Pericles' day on the Acropolis, largely financed by funds from the Delian League.

In the Classical period the two principal architectural styles or orders were the Doric and Ionic. (The ornate, flowery Corinthian capitals often used today did not become popular until Roman times.) Though both orders were used for the same building purposes, they differed in details such as the shape of the columns and of their bases and capitals and in the features of the entablature, or structure that supported the roof. The Ionic appears taller and more slender than the Doric. Architects strove to design buildings according to the principles of each order,

Figure 7.3. This model of the Acropolis in Pericles' day shows the Panathenaic procession proceeding through the front gates (Propylaea), which are flanked on the right (south) by the temple of Athena Nike (Victory). The largest building is the Parthenon. The Erechtheion is on the left (north) of the Parthenon.

rather than to invent new or highly individualized styles. The pleasure they took in their work was not the sort of delight one might take today in striking out in original and startling directions. Rather, Greek architects took from their work that special kind of satisfaction that comes from exercising creativity within the limits posed by an elaborate code of restraints.

The temple of Athena Parthenos ("the virgin") known as the Parthenon was a blend of Doric and Ionic elements. The rectangular structure with a ratio of eight columns on the front and back ends to seventeen on the sides was aesthetically pleasing. Athenian architects were well aware that from a distance the eye would perceive perfectly straight columns as thin in the middle and appearing to fall outward, and a perfectly horizontal foundation would appear to droop toward the center. Consequently they took pains to create optical illusions by subtle swelling (entasis) of the midportion of the columns, by tilting the columns toward the interior lest they seem to be falling outward, and by curving the middle of the floor and steps upward as though a wind were blowing under a rug.

Sculpture was an important feature of Greek architecture. The sculpture of the Parthenon depicted myths and history of Athena and Athens. The east pediment showed the birth of Athena while the west pediment illustrated the contest

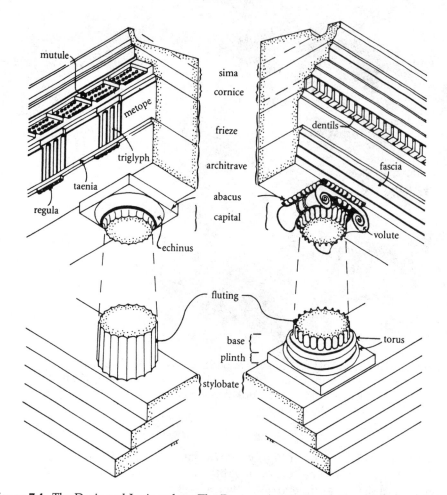

Figure 7.4. The Doric and Ionic orders. The Doric order (left) may be a direct translation into stone of building elements that were originally made of wood. The more complex capital of the Ionic order is in a spiraled form known as a volute.

between Athena and Poseidon over primacy in Athens. A sculpted frieze running around the top of the exterior wall of the cella or "inner shrine" showed human figures, horses, sacrificial animals, and the twelve Olympian gods. Probably the array of human figures and animals depicts the procession at the Greater Panathenaic festival that was held every four years and the presentation of a new dress for the goddess by young girls who had helped to weave it.

The temple was not a place where worshippers congregated, but rather the home of a divinity whose image was placed inside and a storehouse for the cult's belongings. Thus, within the cella of the Parthenon was a tall statue of Athena covered with ivory and gold. Locked in a back room were the goddess's possessions, among which were the treasury of the city of Athens and, after the middle

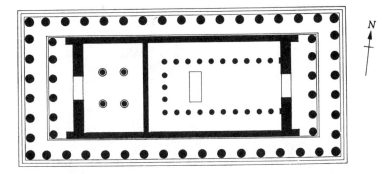

Figure 7.5. Ground plan of Parthenon showing exterior colonnade and cella (main room) within. The cult statue of Athena was kept in the cella and the state treasury was stored in the back room.

Figure 7.6. The Parthenon, built 447–438 BC, photographed in the twentieth century, seen from the east.

Figure 7.7. Parthenon east frieze, slab V, probably showing the presentation of the dress known as the peplos for Athena at the Panathenaea. A section of the continuous frieze running along the top of the exterior cella wall. Other portions show a cavalcade of horsemen, religious officials, sacrificial animals, and the Olympian gods.

of the fifth century, that of the Delian League as well. In front of the Parthenon on the west stood a huge bronze statue of Athena the Warrior who fights in the front (Promachos). The goddess was portrayed standing, with her left hand holding her shield and her right arm holding her spear. The statue was nearly 30 feet tall: sailors rounding Cape Sounion could see the welcome glint of sunlight off the tip of the spear. Like the statue inside the temple, it was the work of the sculptor Phidias, a friend of Pericles. Viewed by his contemporaries as the greatest sculptor of gods, Phidias also created a huge gold and ivory statue of Zeus at Olympia that was considered to be one of the seven wonders of the ancient world.

In contrast to the Doric, which was massive, solid, and plain, the Ionic order gave a slender, graceful, ornate impression. The Erechtheion, sacred to Poseidon Erechtheus, was the chief purely Ionic monument on the Acropolis. The sites of temples and shrines were selected because of their association with some legendary divine act that had occurred on the spot. The plan of the Erechtheion was irregular, complicated by a variety of religious constraints: it needed to enclose the mark of Poseidon's trident on Athenian soil and a salt well on the northern side; to shelter Athena's original olive tree that stood nearby on the west and to include her shrine in the eastern section; to cover the tomb of Athens' first king Cecrops under the southwest corner; and to house other venerable cult objects. The building consisted of three Ionic porches. The striking south porch that faced the Parthenon employed six figures of maidens, called Caryatids, to support the roof (instead of columns). The building was begun in 421, and because of the Peloponnesian War the decorations may never have been completed. Many other buildings, temples, statues, and votive offerings adorned the Acropolis. Though little remains of these monuments nowadays except the bare marble framework of the major ones, in antiquity they were much more colorful: some of the architectural and sculptural features were painted red and blue and were covered with gold leaf. Below the Acropolis, dramas were staged in honor of the god Dionysus. Spectators sat in the open air in a semicircle on the bare hillside watching the performances that took place below in the orchestra ("dancing place").

The structures that comprised Pericles' building program confirmed most Athenians in their support for the empire, for without the tribute pouring in from subject states such lavish public monuments would have been difficult to finance. They also enhanced Pericles' popularity, providing jobs as well as beautifying the

Figure 7.8. Using surviving descriptions of the statue of Athena, sculptor Alan LeQuire crafted this 43-foot replica for the life-size Parthenon replica in Centennial Park in Nashville, Tennessee.

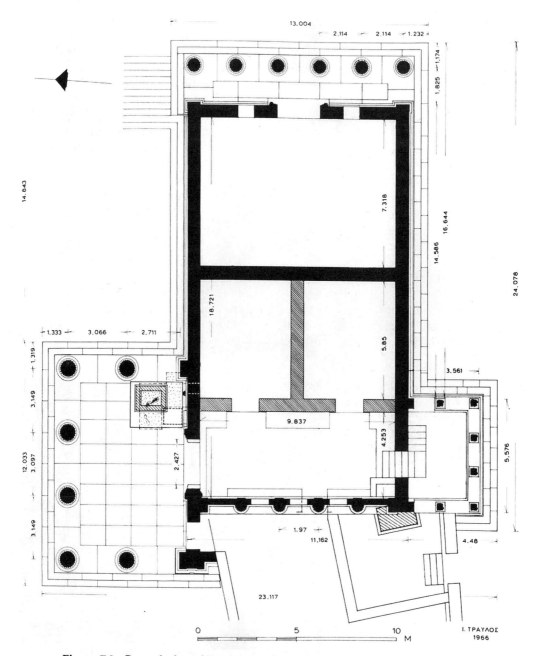

Figure 7.9. Ground plan of Erechtheion (421–406 BC). This graceful temple was sacred to Athena, Poseidon, and the legendary Athenian king Erechtheus. The complicated shape was the result of needing to skirt Athena's sacred olive tree and to enclose Poseidon's trident mark.

Figure 7.10. The Erechtheion, built 421–406 BC, photographed in the twentieth century, showing the Porch of the Maidens (Caryatids) that faces the Parthenon. Since this photograph was taken, the statues were moved indoors to protect them from pollution and were replaced with copies.

city. At the same time, they provided an opening for Pericles' enemies—personal rivals or those who disliked the march of democracy—to undermine him by calling into question the propriety of diverting League funds to the aesthetic improvement of the hegemonic city. The end result of this clash confirmed Pericles' power and prestige in Athens. When an ostracism was held in 443, the "winner" was the most vocal opponent of the building program—Thucydides, the son of Melesias (probably a relative of Thucydides the historian). Thucydides' departure left Pericles with no serious rival in Athenian politics.

The Agora

The *agora* was principally a center for secular human activity, though the gods, who were never excluded from human activities, also had their place. The agora served as a market, as a meeting place for the exchange of goods and of news, and as a focus of social, political, and judicial activities. Daily life for women was ideally indoors and for men outdoors. Men who stayed indoors were suspected of being effeminate and antisocial, and women who ventured outdoors were likely to have their chastity questioned. In the *Laws* Plato noted that the greatest good in the polis is that the citizens be known to each other, as the men (certainly not the women) would be if they saw one another every day in the agora. Aristotle distinguished human beings from other living creatures by their use of speech (though, again, women were placed in a different category and are characterized as ideally silent). Speaking was essential for the activities that took place in the agora.

Document 7.3 Aristotle in his *Politics* explored the nature of political association and of the polis.

From these considerations it is evident that the polis belongs to the class of things that exist by nature, and that man is by nature an animal intended to live in a polis. He who is without a polis, by reason of his own nature and not of some accident, is either a poor sort of being, or a being higher than man: he is like the man of whom Homer wrote in denunciation: "Clanless and lawless and hearthless is he." The man who is such by nature [i.e., unable to join in the society of a polis] at once plunges into a passion for war; he is in the position of a solitary advanced piece in a game of draughts.

The reason why man is a being meant for political association, in a higher degree than bees or other gregarious animals can ever associate, is evident. Nature, according to our theory, makes nothing in vain; and man alone of the animals is furnished with the faculty of language. The mere making of sounds serves to indicate pleasure and pain, and is thus a faculty that belongs to animals in general: their nature enables them to attain the point at which they have perceptions of pleasure and pain, and can signify those perceptions to one another. But language serves to declare what is advantageous and what is the reverse, and it therefore serves to declare what is just and what is unjust. It is the peculiarity of man, in comparison with the rest of the animal world, that he alone possesses a perception of good and evil, of the just and the unjust, and of other similar qualities; and it is association in [a common perception of] these things which makes a family and a polis.

We may now proceed to add that [though the individual and the family are prior in the order of time] the polis is prior in the order of nature to the family and the individual.

Politics 1253a 9–12, translated by Ernest Barker, The Politics of Aristotle. *Oxford: Oxford University Press, 1973.*

The Athenian agora was a large level space at the foot of the Acropolis on the road from the main city gate. The area was cluttered with public buildings of which the most easily identified is the round structure called the Tholos, which housed the *boulē* and where official weights and measures were stored. The agora was also the site of law courts, altars, shrines, statues, inscriptions, fountains, drains, and trophies of war. On the western border stood a Doric temple that was dedicated either to Hephaestus, the god of crafts, or to Theseus, a legendary hero and king of Athens. It has withstood the ravages of time far better than the Parthenon and is still in remarkably good condition. Roofed, multipurpose colonnades called stoas flanked the agora. Sandwiched between the permanent structures and within the stoas as well were shops, bankers' tables, booksellers, wholesale merchants, schools, and people buying and selling the necessities of life.

One important place in Athenian life was not a building: the hillside of the Pnyx where the assembly met towered above the city. Throughout the fifth century, citizens sat either on cushions or directly on the rocky ground that sloped from south to north, filling an area of 15,000 square feet. Around 400 BC the meeting place was evened out and enlarged, and benches seem to have been added. The adult male citizens of Attica gathered in all kinds of weather to listen to speeches and debates, to make motions, and to hold high officials to account. In voting (which was by show of hands) they not only took into consideration what they had heard on the Pnyx but also made use of all the information they had garnered in the agora.

Rural Life in Attica

The growth of the urban center was not at the expense of rural areas. Public buildings were also located away from the city center. Gymnasiums and stadiums that required plenty of level space were often found in the suburbs, which were cooler and shadier and closer to plentiful supplies of water than could be found in central Athens. Cult centers and rural agoras, as well as fortresses and other structures for defense, were scattered throughout Attica. It was an easy walk, moreover, from city to country.

Document 7.4 Plato depicts Socrates and Phaedrus enjoying a stroll through the countryside while discussing philosophy, rhetoric, and love.

SOCRATES.   My dear Phaedrus, where is it you're going, and where have you come from?

PHAEDRUS.   From Lysias, the son of Cephalus, Socrates; and I'm going for a walk outside the wall, because I spent a long time sitting there, since sun-up. I'm doing what your friend and mine, Acumenus, advises, and taking my walks along the country roads; he says that walking here is more refreshing than in the colonnades.

. . .

SOCRATES.   Let's turn off here and go along the Ilissus; then we'll sit down quietly wherever you think best.

PHAEDRUS.   It seems it's just as well I happened to be barefoot; you always are. So we can very easily go along the stream with our feet in the water; and it will not be unpleasant, particularly at this time of year and at this time of day.

SOCRATES.   So lead on, and keep a lookout for a place for us to sit down.

PHAEDRUS.   Well then, you see that very tall plane-tree?

SOCRATES.   I do indeed.

PHAEDRUS.   There's shade and a moderate breeze there, and grass to sit on, or lie on, if we like.

SOCRATES.   Please lead on.

PHAEDRUS.   Tell me, Socrates, wasn't it from somewhere just here that Boreas is said to have seized Oreithuia from the Ilissus?

SOCRATES.   Yes, so it's said.

PHAEDRUS.   Well, was it from here? The water of the stream certainly looks attractively pure and clear, and just right for young girls to play beside it.

SOCRATES.   No, it was from a place two or three stades lower down, where one crosses over to the district of Agra; and there somewhere there is an altar of Boreas.

Phaedrus 227A–229C; translated by C. J. Rowe, Plato: Phaedrus. *Warminster, England: Aris & Phillips, 1986.*

In the fifth century probably three-quarters of the citizens owned some rural property. Farming could be a part-time occupation that produced enough food to provide sustenance for a family. Many people still lived in villages, were loyal to their rural demes, and depended upon their family farms. Except for the spaces set aside for public activities, Athens was neither a beautiful city nor a comfortable one, and many propertied citizens were happy to leave it to artisans, to the urban poor, and to metics, who were not permitted to own land in Attica. The city had merely grown up in the Archaic and Classical periods without conforming to a town plan. Streets were irregular and narrow; housing in the city center was flimsy and sanitation poor. These problems were exacerbated when the entire population withdrew inside the city walls during the Peloponnesian War.

*   *   *

Thucydides, as we saw in Chapter 4, commented on the lavishness of Athens' monumental architecture and revealed his suspicion that its physical remains might lead observers to exaggerate its greatness vis-à-vis Sparta, where public space was filled by humbler structures. Certainly the substantial funds they collected in imperial tribute made it possible for the Athenians to deck out their city with edifices of unusual elegance, but the underlying principles governing the allocation of space obtained in other poleis as well. Throughout the Greek world from Ionia to Sicily stood bustling city centers adorned with temples, government buildings, and agoras; some, like Olympia, had special connections to religion, whereas others, like Corinth, were great ports. Some cities, like Thurii, were carefully laid out; most just sprang up little by little, with streets at odd angles making it easy to get lost. Everywhere, the city and its surrounding countryside were interdependent, and residents traveled back and forth comfortably between the two areas. Commerce and agriculture were both central to the functioning of each polis.

Although commerce entailed a good deal of specialized labor, throughout Greece one sort of work was diffused throughout the male population, and that was fighting. Except in Sparta, Greek men generally worked at the land (or, less often, in trade) in the winter and were available for military campaigns in the summer, serving in the infantry if they belonged to the propertied class or, in the case of poor men, rowing in the fleet. When fighting broke out between the Athenian and Spartan camps in 431, warfare began to claim an increasingly large share of people's time, energy, and worry. The ensuing social upheaval caused women to assume some responsibilities previously exercised by men. In time the comfortable division of the year into fighting and nonfighting seasons evaporated, and during the last decades of the fifth century Greece found itself consumed by a protracted and debilitating war of unprecedented scope. Fighting, always an important element in Greek civilization, now came to be the organizing principle of life in the city-states.

TRANSLATIONS

Blanco, Walter. 1992. *The Histories,* from *Herodotus: The Histories,* Walter Blanco and Jennifer Roberts, eds., New York: W.W. Norton.

Blanco, Walter. 1998. *The Peloponnesian War,* from *Thucydides: The Peloponnesian War,* Walter Blanco and Jennifer Roberts, eds. New York: W.W. Norton.

Gagarin, Michael and Paul Woodruff, eds. 1995. *Encomium of Helen*, in *Early Greek Political Thought from Homer to the Sophists*. Cambridge: Cambridge University Press.

Grene, David. 1987. *The History: Herodotus*. Chicago: University of Chicago Press.

Hamilton, Walter. 1951. *Plato: The Symposium*. Harmondsworth, England: Penguin.

Hanson, Ann. 1975. *Hippocrates: Diseases of Women*, in *Signs* 1.

Pomeroy, Sarah B. 1994. *Xenophon: Oeconomicus, A Social and Historical Commentary*. Oxford: Clarendon Press.

Warner, Rex. 1959. *Medea*, from *The Complete Greek Tragedies, Euripides I: Four Tragedies*, David Grene and Richmond Lattimore, eds. Chicago: University of Chicago Press.

SUGGESTED READINGS

Guthrie, W. K. C. 1971. *The Sophists*. Cambridge, Eng.: Cambridge University Press. A brilliant study of the issues regarding the sophistic movement, excerpted from the author's three-volume *History of Greek Philosophy*.

Harris, William V. 1989. *Ancient Literacy*. Cambridge, Mass.: Harvard University Press. A survey of the evidence for literacy and the lack of it in ancient Greece and Rome.

Hill, Ida Thallon. 1953. *The Ancient City of Athens: Its Topography and Monuments*. London: Methuen. A clearly written description with illustrations and plans of the architectural and sculpted antiquities at Athens, before the restorations that are now in progress began masking many of the major monuments.

Kagan, Donald. 1969. *The Outbreak of the Peloponnesian War*. Ithaca, N.Y.: Cornell University Press. The first installment in Kagan's four-volume history of the war.

Osborne, Robin. 1987. *Classical Landscape with Figures: The Ancient Greek City and Its Countryside*. London: G. Philip. An illustrated discussion of life in rural Greece, natural flora and agriculture, written by an author who plainly loves his subject.

McGregor, Malcolm. 1987. *The Athenians and Their Empire*. Vancouver: University of British Columbia Press. A history of the Athenians' dealings with their allies that takes a sympathetic view of imperialism.

Ste. Croix, G. E. M. de 1972. *The Origins of the Peloponnesian War*. Ithaca, N.Y.: Cornell University Press. An analysis of the available sources and an intensive study of the data concerning the Megarian decrees.

Vlastos, Gregory. 1991. *Socrates: Ironist and Moral Philosopher*. Ithaca, N.Y.: Cornell University Press. An attempt to capture the essence of the philosopher, by one of the foremost students of the Platonic dialogues.

Wycherley, R. E. 1979. *The Stones of Athens*. Princeton, N.J.: Princeton University Press. A detailed study of what the physical remains of Athens have to tell us about the city.

8

THE PELOPONNESIAN WAR

When war broke out between Athens and Sparta, few Greeks foresaw that it would be different from any war they had ever experienced or even imagined. The twenty-seven-year conflict cost thousands upon thousands of lives and proved a stern teacher. It enhanced many of the worst features of Greek society—competitiveness, jingoism, lack of compassion, and gross disregard for human life. At the same time, a number of extraordinary thinkers sought to focus attention on the problems people face in their attempts to live together: the writings of Thucydides, Sophocles, and Euripides showed vigor and spirit throughout the war years, and the comic dramatist Aristophanes continued to produce enchanting plays through three decades of fighting and for a generation afterward—though a biting sorrow is often evident beneath the madcap facade. The Peloponnesian War would alter the world the Greeks knew in many respects. Comfortable assumptions about the citizen-fighter and his role in the polis would break down, and conventional morality and piety would face many challenges. Much, however, would stay the same—the polis as a political unit, the primacy of agriculture, the rivalries of the city-states, and the worship of the Olympian gods. The trauma occasioned by the war and its aftermath was also strikingly fertile, for the war supplied the impetus for many of the social, political, and intellectual changes we identify with the fourth century and the period after the death of Alexander in 323 BC that we call the Hellenistic Age.

SOURCES FOR GREECE DURING THE PELOPONNESIAN WAR

Thucydides writes with such eloquence and certainty that historians have had to struggle hard to challenge his conclusions and strike out on their own paths. His *History* is our principal source for the war. Although Thucydides tried to write each year up as it happened, understandably he began to fall behind as the war progressed, and at the time of his death around 395 BC he had gotten only as far as 411. Rumor had it that his daughter preserved the unfinished manuscript and gave it to Xenophon to edit. Whatever the truth of this, Xenophon, who picked up where Thucydides left off and wrote the history of Greece down to 362 (in the work called the *Hellenica*), equaled Thucydides in neither analytical capacity nor narrative skill. Shortly after the war, however, Xenophon did have the advantage of friendship with leading Spartans including their king Agesilaus. In the course of the trek through Asia Minor that he described in the *Anabasis*, he certainly would have heard war stories of soldiers and officers from cities other than Athens. After he returned to Greece, moreover, he was exiled from Athens and was settled by Agesilaus in Scillus near Olympia. His sons were apparently educated according to the Spartan system; thus Xenophon certainly understood the Spartans' methods of training soldiers and waging war.

The workings of Athenian democracy were explored in a pamphlet called *The Constitution of the Athenians*, whose unknown author is sometimes called the Old Oligarch; he is also sometimes called pseudo-Xenophon, since before the twentieth century historians believed he really was Xenophon. Hostile to democracy, the essay makes an interesting contrast with the happier view of Athenian government and society set forth in the famous funeral oration for the war dead that Thucydides ascribed to Pericles, and it offers a keen analysis of the distinctive dynamic of naval imperialism and its relationship to Athenian government.

Diodorus and Plutarch continue to be useful. Diodorus' treatment of the war survives intact, and Plutarch wrote the lives of the Athenian politicians Nicias and Alcibiades and of the Spartan commander Lysander. The sources Diodorus and Plutarch used include the fourth-century historians Theopompus and Ephorus, as well as Timaeus, who lived around 300 BC, and Philistus, who had been a boy in Syracuse at the time of the Athenian siege. Speeches delivered in court— or at least written for such delivery—throw considerable light on the later years of the war. Andocides, who was implicated in the religious scandals of 415, described his subsequent imprisonment in his speech *On the Mysteries*. Lysias, who came from a wealthy metic family and knew Socrates, wrote a number of speeches early in the fourth century that touched on events during the war and its aftermath; one (*Against Andocides*) attacked Andocides, and another (*Against Eratosthenes*) detailed his own misfortunes at the hands of the "Thirty Tyrants" whom Sparta set up in Athens at the end of the war.

Although Sophocles produced *Oedipus Tyrannus* during the first years of the war and continued to write until his death in 406, the two playwrights who reveal most about what it was like to live in Athens during this war were the tragedian Euripides and the comic dramatist Aristophanes. Plays like Euripides' *Trojan Women* dealt with the sufferings occasioned by war through the vehicle of the Trojan War, and several of Aristophanes' wartime comedies made plain the immense deprivation of noncombatant men and women and their yearnings for peace. Some of the flavor of intellectual life in Athens can be gathered from Plato's and Xenophon's dialogues, which offer imaginative reconstructions of conversations Socrates held in Athens during the war with fellow Athenians, with metics, and with visiting luminaries such as the rhetorician Gorgias of Leontini, or the sophist Protagoras of Abdera.

Finally, inscriptions continue to shed light on the workings of the Athenian empire, and archaeological and topographical investigations have been of some use in illuminating particular military campaigns—that, for example, at Pylos on the west coast of the Peloponnesus in 425. On the whole, however, our ability fully to understand the war is compromised severely by the lack of authentic Spartan sources. The Spartans' aversion to writing literature has placed them at a great disadvantage in history. One consequence of their choice has been the fact that the Spartan-Athenian War derives the name by which it is known from the perspective of Sparta's enemy: though most of the battles were fought outside the Peloponnesus, for Athens it was the war against the Peloponnesians, and it has been known for centuries as the Peloponnesian War. The Spartans' decision not to record their own story about the war has made it necessary for us to reconstruct it for them, working entirely from non-Spartan sources and largely from the writings of Thucydides, who may—or may not—have enjoyed contacts at Sparta after (or even before) his exile. Spartans miraculously brought back to life in our own time might be very surprised to learn how their wartime strategies have been imagined.

THE ARCHIDAMIAN WAR (431–421 BC)

To many Greeks alive at the time, the decade of fighting that stretched from 431 to 421 seemed like a discrete entity in itself, and in fact this war has been given its own name—the Archidamian War, after the Spartan commander Archidamus. We owe the concept of a single Peloponnesian War extending from 431 to 404 to Thucydides. Another historian might have seen a continuous war extending from 460 to 404, or three wars—one from 460 to 446, one from 431 to 421, and another beginning somewhere between 418 and 415 and continuing to 404. Students of historiography (the writing of history) use the expression "colligation," that is, "tying together," to describe the way historians "create" an event or a process by linking together separate events in such a way that they form a coherent whole. Joining what others might construe differently, Thucydides, the earliest and most important source for the history of this period, has by colligation successfully persuaded most people of the reality of what is today commonly called "the" Peloponnesian War, the war of 431–404.

The Periclean Strategy and the Plague

Pericles devised an ingenious strategy for winning a war he conceived as essentially defensive, and it is a measure of his influence and eloquence that he was able to persuade his fellow Athenians to do something so conspicuously at odds with human nature. Harassing Peloponnesian territory with their navy, the Athenians declined to participate in hoplite battle with the enemy. At Pericles' instigation, the Athenian farmers abandoned their land, taking with them what few household goods could be loaded on wagons, and huddled with the city-dwellers

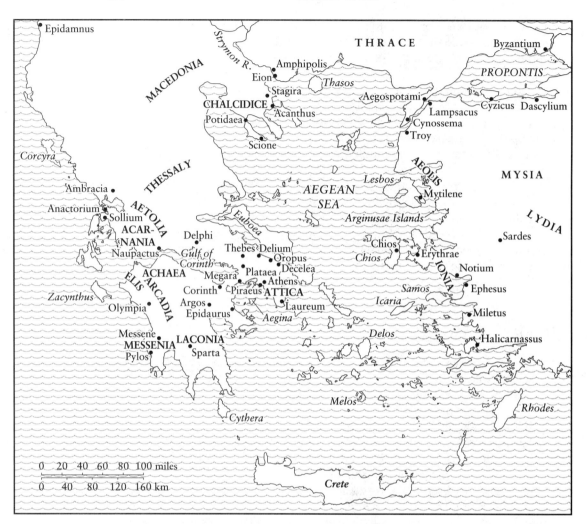

Figure 8.1. Theaters of operation during the Peloponnesian War.

inside the Long Walls that linked Athens to Piraeus. These walls, Pericles rightly perceived, made Athens in essence an island. Food and other necessary goods would continue to be imported by ship from throughout the empire. The enemy, Pericles calculated, would tire of ravaging the land when nobody came out to fight. Seeing that the superior training and numbers of their infantry would do them no good, they would soon sue for peace. The Spartans, meanwhile, conjectured that the Athenians would grow restive cooped up in the overcrowded city throughout the campaigning season and, seeing their land being ravaged, would be unable to tolerate the frustration. They foresaw one of two consequences: either the Athenians would seek peace or they would overrule Pericles and come out to fight. In foreseeing that the enemy would give up after a couple of years, both sides miscalculated badly, but there was nothing intrinsically foolish in their thinking.

It was with reluctance and apprehension that the Athenians abandoned their homes and the familiar temples nearby, and when the farmers arrived in Athens only a few were able to find shelter with friends or relatives. Most had to seek out empty space in the city or bunk down in temples and shrines. Some wound up spending summers in the towers along the walls. Fortunately, the Athenians thought, the war would not last too long; but of course the Spartans knew this was just what they were thinking.

The first year of the war was relatively uneventful. The Athenian fleet busied itself around the Peloponnesus. Archidamus moved on Attica with his troops, but nobody came out to meet them, so they had to content themselves with cutting down olive trees. In the fall, when the Peloponnesians had gone home, the Athenian army ravaged the territory of Megara (something they continued to do annually for several years). Though this year saw few casualties, by tradition the Athenians held a public funeral for those who had died in the war. This much we know: Pericles was chosen to offer the eulogy. How closely the stirring paean to Athens that appears in Thucydides' history approximates what Pericles actually said is another question. We have no other versions of this speech. It could represent Thucydides' accurate recollection of what was said, or a faulty recollection, or a composition of his own; and even if Pericles said these things, his speech could have been written by someone else. In any event, the speech we have focuses not on the dead themselves but on the city of Athens and the way of life it represents—a way of life that is defined as the antithesis of everything Spartan.

The organizing principle of the speech reveals much about Greek views of the state, for Pericles assumes that a wise form of government provides the cornerstone for the good life in all its manifestations. In this he is in complete agreement with the political theorists of the fourth century, Plato and Aristotle. Though they disliked democracy, they certainly shared Pericles' conviction that the *politeia* (a kind of government or "constitution") a state chooses will have the widest ramifications for the nature of its citizens and the spirit of its communal life.

The speech has a markedly defensive tone. Its purpose seems to be to counter suggestions that an easygoing polis such as Athens, with its love of words, of ideas, and of beauty, could not compete successfully in war with a highly regulated, militarized society like Sparta, where words are despised as a hindrance to action, people have little choice about how they live their lives, and anxious secrecy is the order of the day. "We love nobility without ostentation," Pericles says,

> and we have a virile love of knowledge. Furthermore, wealth is for us something to use, not something to brag about. And as to poverty, there is no shame in admitting to it—the real shame is in not taking action to escape from it. Finally, while there are those who manage both the city and their own private affairs,

there are others, who though wrapped up in their work, nevertheless have a thorough knowledge of public affairs. . . . For we are the only people who regard a man who takes no interest in politics to be leading not a quiet life but a useless one. We are also the only ones who either make the governmental decisions or at least frame the issues correctly, because we do not think that action is hampered by public discourse but by not learning enough in advance, through discourse, about what action we need to take.

*   *   *

To sum up, I tell you that this city, taken all in all, is the school of Greece, and as far as I am concerned, any man among us will exhibit a more fully developed personality than men elsewhere and will be able to take care of himself more gracefully and with the quickest of wit.

(*The Peloponnesian War* 2.40–41; Blanco 1998)

Pericles' concluding charge to the women of Athens sat oddly on the lips of a man who lived with a companion far more visible and renowned than many of his fellow politicians:

And since I must also make some mention of womanly virtue to those who will now be widows, I will define it in this brief admonition: your greatest fame consists in being no worse than your natures, and in having the least possible reputation among males for good or ill.

(2.45; Blanco 1998)

This is certainly striking advice in a society as loquacious as the one Thucydides depicts in Athens. It is posited on a notion of woman as in every way the opposite of political man, in whose mind reputation (as Plato would soon lament) counted for practically everything.

The next year saw two entirely predictable events and one unexpected development. The invasion of Attica by the allied forces of the Peloponnesian League and the harassment of the Peloponnesian coast by the Athenian navy were becoming routine, but nobody could have foreseen the horrific plague that attacked the population of Athens. Its origin is unknown, as is its precise nature—typhus, probably, or perhaps smallpox or measles—but it spread rapidly in the crowded, unsanitary environment of a city packed to capacity and beyond. Probably about a third of the populace died. Thucydides, who himself fell ill but recovered, took pains to record everything he could about the course and symptoms of the illness so that it would be possible for readers to recognize the disorder should it ever reappear.

In many ways Thucydides' meticulous account of the disease and its behavior is a microcosm of his history as a whole, revealing his passionate interest in chronicling events that seem to him to have broad significance, reflecting as they do patterns in events. Beginning with a detailed account of the symptoms of the disease—the oral bleeding, the bad breath, the painful vomiting, the burning skin, the insomnia, the memory loss, the often fatal diarrhea—he goes on to describe the way in which people reacted to the disease. Those who recovered from the illness, sensing that they were now proof against it, not only nursed the sick but "in the jubilance of the moment held the vain belief that they would never die from any other disease in the future, either." Most, however, took a darker view of life, as the overwhelming catastrophe seemed to obviate the necessity for observing customary moral and religious norms. The disease, Thucydides wrote, "initiated a more general lawlessness in the city" as people

> decided to go for instant gratifications that tended to sensuality because they re-garded themselves and their property as equally short-lived. No one was willing to persevere in received ideas about "the good" because they were uncertain whether they would die before achieving it. Whatever was pleasurable, and whatever contributed to pleasure, wherever it came from, that was now the good and the useful. Fear of the gods? The laws of man? No one held back, conclud-ing that as to the gods, it made no difference whether you worshipped or not since they saw that all alike were dying; and as to breaking the law, no one ex-pected to live long enough to go to court and pay his penalty. The far more ter-rible verdict which had already been delivered against them was hanging over their heads—so it was only natural to enjoy life a little before it came down.
> (The Peloponnesian War 2.53; Blanco 1998)

Demoralized by the plague and frustrated by being forbidden to march out and offer battle, some Athenians tried to open negotiations for peace with the Spartans. Pericles mustered one last effort to persuade them to abandon this pro-ject. In a tough speech markedly less idealistic than the funeral oration, he argued that though the empire might be a tyranny and might have been wrong to ac-quire, still the Athenians, having a tiger by the tail, would put themselves in great danger by letting it go. Though embassies to Sparta did cease, the citizenry voted to depose Pericles (bringing forward some charge against him, as was common in Athens when politicians had ceased to please their constituency) and indeed to fine him. Nothing much happened when Pericles was out of office except the long-awaited surrender of Potidaea. Finding that other leaders conducted the war no better, the Athenians returned Pericles to office at the next elections. Then he caught the plague and died.

Cleon and Diodotus:
The Revolt of Mytilene (428–427 BC)

One motive for decrees excluding the Megarians from Athenian ports had prob-ably been Pericles' desire to bring on a war, if there had to be one, while he was still there to conduct it; at the time the decrees were passed, he was about 60. With Pericles gone and the war still raging, the Athenians needed to reassess the merits of his strategy and to choose other leaders. At first they stuck to the plan of avoiding infantry combat, but in time they ventured forth and met the Pelo-

Figure 8.2. This image of Pericles by his younger contemporary Cresilas survives in a Roman copy of the head of a bronze original. Pericles was rumored to have worn a helmet in order to conceal the deformed shape of his head, which made him resemble the tyrant Peisistratus.

ponnesians on the battlefield, with mixed success. No one man replaced Pericles as the unquestioned leader of the Athenian people, but one of the most popular of the new politicians was Cleon (d. 422 BC).

Hated by Thucydides and pilloried by Aristophanes, Cleon has come before the tribunal of history at a desperate disadvantage. The 420s saw a change in the character of Athenian government. Though no formal distinctions divided rich from poor or separated social classes, still until the war Athenians had felt most comfortable with political power in the hands of men from old, wealthy families—men like Cimon and Pericles. Now this ceased to be true. Richer men still had the advantage in elections for the generalship, but increasingly men whose fathers and grandfathers had recently made money in business began to compete successfully with those whose families had been living off their land holdings for generations. New words, moreover, crept into discussions of Athenian politics: *dēmagōgos* and its relative *dēmagōgia*, which first appears in the surviving literature in Aristophanes' *Knights*, produced in 424 BC. Literally a "leader of the people"—surely there is nothing wrong in that—in the hands of class-conscious critics the word *dēmagōgos* came to signal a calculating politician who manipulated the voters for his own ends rather than letting himself be guided by patriotism and principle. In reality, however, there is no way to be sure of people's motives, and sometimes the word just betrays the class prejudice of the writer using it.

Thucydides described Pericles as leading the Athenian people rather than being led by them. Did this mean Pericles was a demagogue too?

Foremost among the men who came to be identified as demagogues was Cleon. Deliberately cultivating an antiaristocratic persona, Cleon was the brash and outspoken owner of a successful tannery. He was the first of several leading politicians at Athens who commanded respect in the assembly without having held the generalship. Before Cleon, politicians had always exercised the *stratēgia* even if, like Pericles, they had not greatly distinguished themselves in the field. Cleon, however, who was a talented public speaker, had become influential already in Pericles' lifetime and was probably the most powerful politician in Athens during the years after his death (though he never attained Pericles' stature or exercised comparable authority).

By 428, when the war had been going on for three years, it looked as if Athens might win. Though the siege of Potidaea had been costly, at least it was over. The Athenian admiral Phormio had won some naval victories in the northwest, damaging Corinthian trade. The Spartans destroyed Plataea, but they were squeamish about invading Attica in 429 because of the plague, and they were disappointed in their hopes of aid from Sicily or Persia. Perhaps they would give up. In 428, however, the Spartans received some very good news. Four of the five cities on the island of Lesbos were revolting from the Athenian empire. Led by Mytilene, the revolt was particularly unexpected since, along with Chios, Lesbos was one of the two remaining so-called autonomous members of the empire, that is, a member that provided its own ships for the navy rather than being assessed in tribute money.

The uprising evoked the important revolt of Samos in 440, which had spread to Byzantium. The Athenian alliance appeared to be coming apart at the seams, and the Spartans were happy to grant the Mytilenaeans' request for alliance and assistance. The promised aid, however, never materialized; the Spartans were not yet ready for decisive naval action. The next year the Athenian siege achieved its aim: the Mytilenaeans surrendered. The discussion in the Athenian assembly about what to do with the capitulated rebels first brings Cleon alive in the pages of Thucydides. The Athenians initially voted to put all the men in Mytilene to death and to sell the women and children into slavery, and they dispatched a boat to bring the news to the general in command on the island, Paches. The next day, however, some people at least had second thoughts, and a debate ensued. Cleon shows a cocky self-assurance in the dismissive way he addresses his audience: "I, for my part," he begins, "have often noticed before that democracies cannot rule over others, but I see it especially now in these regrets of yours about Mytilene . . ." (3.37). Deriding the Athenians for their openness and flexibility, he advocates a policy of harsh consistency. Bad laws that stay the same, he insists, are better than good ones that change. His studied anti-intellectualism contrasts pointedly with the praise of deliberation and debate in Pericles' funeral oration delivered three years earlier: ordinary people, Cleon says, "run their cities far better than intelligent ones, for these want to seem wiser than the laws and to top whatever nonsense is said in public assemblies. . . . They are the downfall of cities because of this sort of thing" (3.37; Blanco 1998). In other respects, however, Cleon for all his crassness is plainly Pericles' heir. "You don't understand," he says, "that you hold your empire as a tyranny and that your subjects are schemers who are governed unwillingly" (3.37). Compare Pericles in his last speech: "You hold your empire like a tyranny by now. Taking it is thought to have been criminal; letting it go would be extremely dangerous" (2.63; Blanco 1998).

Diodotus, who is otherwise unknown, spoke against proceeding with the original plan, making a marvelous argument grounded in human psychology. Deterrence, he contended, was not as effective as commonly believed, because people who undertake risky ventures do so in the expectation that they will succeed, not fail. Furthermore, he argued, there was no merit in killing people even when they had surrendered, for to do so removed any incentive for surrender in future rebellions. He then made a key observation about the dynamics of the empire. "So far," he maintained,

> the populace in all of the cities is well-inclined toward you. Either they do not join in rebellion with the oligarchs, or, if they are forced to do so, they quickly turn against them. Thus, when you go to war you have the populace of the city you are attacking on your side.
>
> (The Peloponnesian War 3.47; *Blanco 1998*)

Though some might debate the accuracy of Diodotus' contention, it certainly makes us think twice about Thucydides' claim that the Athenian empire was universally detested in the subject cities.

Diodotus won the day, and a second boat was sent out to overtake the first. Envoys from Mytilene provided extra rations for the rowers and promised a large reward if they arrived in time. As it happened, the rowers on the original boat had been in no hurry to announce impending doom, and the second boat managed to arrive just as the death sentence was being announced. Instead of putting all the men to death and enslaving all the women and children, the Athenians executed the ringleaders of the revolt—who apparently amounted to over a thousand men.

The War Continues

Meanwhile misery and death prevailed elsewhere in Greece as well. Frustrated in their attempts to unite Boeotia under Theban leadership as Athens had united Attica, the Thebans hated the Plataeans because of their friendship with Athens. In 427 they persuaded the Spartans to destroy Plataea, killing those who had not managed to escape to Athens. At the same time a particularly vicious civil war broke out in Corcyra. This conflict was so bloody and impassioned that both sexes took part, women throwing tiles as the women of Plataea had done in trying to prevent a Theban takeover in 431. As Thucydides points out, the war raging throughout Greece intensified the long-standing tensions between the ordinary citizens, who resented the wealth of the elite, and the aristocrats, who considered a lavish lifestyle to be their birthright, for the former could expect help from Athens and the latter from Sparta. The result was *stasis* ("civil strife") more frequent and ferocious than ever before. Thucydides describes the agony that ensued when the democratic party gained the upper hand and, as allies of the demos, the Athenians under their admiral Eurymedon made no move to curtail the butchery. To avoid death at the hands of the democrats, some oligarchic partisans

> hanged themselves from trees. Others killed themselves in any way they could. Eurymedon remained at Corcyra for seven days with his sixty ships, during which the Corcyraeans ceaselessly slaughtered those among them whom they thought to be enemies. . . . One saw every imaginable kind of death, and everything that is likely to take place in situations like this did, in fact, take place—and even more. For example, fathers killed their sons; people were dragged from the temples and slaughtered in front of them; some were even walled up in the temple of Dionysus and left to die."
>
> (The Peloponnesian War *3.81; Blanco 1998*)

While operating in the west, the Athenians sailed to Sicily with a variety of motives—to assist their allies there against the encroachments of Syracuse, to cut off the export of grain to the Peloponnesus, and to explore the possibility of bringing Sicily into the empire. Their designs, however, were foiled by the charismatic Syracusan leader Hermocrates, who persuaded the Sicilians to patch up their differences in the face of a possible Athenian invasion. Disappointed that they had not managed to get more of a foothold on the island, the Athenians promptly deposed and fined Eurymedon, reserving the punishment of exile for the other two strategoi who had participated in the expedition. Meanwhile the general Demosthenes (not to be confused with the fourth-century orator by the same name) experienced a disastrous failure followed by great success around the Ambracian Gulf. It was Demosthenes who conceived a project that dramatically altered the balance of the war and would have brought it to an end had the Athenians not rejected Spartan peace overtures. Bad weather off the western Peloponnesus helped Demosthenes persuade his colleagues to put into shore at Pylos. The legendary home of Nestor, this promontory combined with the narrow island of Sphacteria to enclose a body of water known today as the Bay of Navarino. There Demosthenes and his men built a fort.

Fearing that Sphacteria might fall into Athenian hands, the Spartans recalled the army that was ravaging Attica and positioned 420 hoplites on the island. When the Athenians defeated the Spartans in naval combat, effectively marooning the hoplites on Sphacteria, the Spartan government panicked and sent envoys to Athens to plead for an armistice. So limited was the number of Spartans that their government was willing to do anything to get those hoplites back—even make a peace that took no account of their allies' interests. On the advice of Cleon, the Athenians refused, whether out of overconfidence or because they feared the fallout from a hasty peace that ultimately excluded key players like Corinth and Thebes.

Figure 8.3. Pylos and Sphacteria as they appear today.

The Spartans, then, remained on Sphacteria, and when Cleon made disparaging remarks about the failure of Athens' generals to capture them, he took for his particular target the respected strategos Nicias. A wealthy and religious man, Nicias had impressed many Athenians by the lavish sums he spent on religious festivals, and his base of support lay with Athens' richer and more conservative voters—the sort of men who despised Cleon. Pointing his finger at Nicias, Thucydides reports, Cleon "said scornfully that if the generals were real men they could easily set out with an armada and capture the troops on the island. If he were in command, he continued, that was what he would do" (4.27; Blanco 1998). Nicias promptly suggested that Cleon himself be given a special commission to go to Pylos and get hold of the stranded hoplites. Against the expectation of upper-class Athenians, the inexperienced Cleon worked well with Demosthenes, and to the astonishment of all Greeks of all social classes, the Spartan soldiers surrendered rather than fight to the death. As 128 of the Peloponnesians had been killed in the fighting, the Athenians now had 292 bargaining chips with which to negotiate an end to the war. Of these the most valuable were the 120 full-blooded Spartiates, "equals." Seeing their position strengthened by the possession of hostages, the Athenians resolved to keep fighting rather than to make peace. This was probably a mistake, for any peace that Sparta made in order to regain its men was likely to alienate its allies and foster the disintegration of the Peloponnesian League.

The presence of Spartan hostages at Athens put an end to the annual invasions of Attica, but the war did not end. Now, growing in confidence because they had compelled Spartan hoplites to lay down their arms, the Athenians occupied the Megarian port of Nisaea and seized the island of Cythera off Laconia. These were both essentially naval operations that Pericles would doubtless have approved, but the Athenians also began experimenting with substantial departures from Pericles' strategy, sending out infantry to face the enemy in battle. A sound defeat by the Boeotians at Delium in 424 dampened the high spirits sparked by the success at Pylos; the philosopher Socrates, fighting in the ranks, might well have been killed had he not been rescued by his admirer, the young Alcibiades. Athenian losses farther north added strength to the Spartan cause even while Spartan soldiers remained captive in Athens. For the Spartans had discovered what they had previously lacked, at least since the loss of Archidamus around 427: a charismatic general. As talented an orator as he was a strategist, Brasidas by his campaigns in Chalcidice very nearly won the war for Sparta, just as Demosthenes and Cleon had nearly won it for Athens at Pylos.

Brasidas and Chalcidice (424–422 BC)

Athens' hold on Chalcidice had always been fragile, and no doubt the increase in the tribute assessment the Athenians had voted in 425 intensified discontent there as elsewhere. When some Chalcidic towns requested Spartan aid and were joined in their appeal by Athens' on-again, off-again ally Perdiccas of Macedonia, the Spartans promptly dispatched the dynamic Brasidas. Once in Chalcidice, Brasidas was able to persuade the towns of Acanthus, Stagirus, and Argilus of Sparta's sincerity as a liberator and to induce them to revolt from Athens, promis-

Figure 8.4. This bronze shield found in the Athenian *agora* was inscribed as booty taken from Pylos.

ing that Sparta would not interfere with their governments. (His eloquence was great, but Thucydides stresses that fear of the Spartan presence was also a factor in these revolts.)

Though Brasidas had accomplished much for Sparta, the greatest prize lay ahead. Gaining possession of Amphipolis would require a little more effort, but this cherished Athenian stronghold was Brasidas' principal target, and in fact he brought it over to the Spartan side in less than twenty-four hours. Horrified by this loss, the Athenians banished one of their generals who had been offshore at Thasos when the catastrophe occurred: the historian Thucydides. The events of that snowy December night in the north played a large role in determining just what form Thucydides' history of the war, already begun earlier, would take. Just as they cut off the opportunity for hearing speeches delivered in the assembly and for picking up the latest scuttlebutt in the agora, they also ensured that Thucydides, freed from civic responsibilities and perhaps more trusted by foreigners now that he was on the outs with the home government, would have more reliable non-Athenian sources. Thucydides seems to know a great deal about Brasidas' thinking, for example; perhaps the two men got to know each other.

The following spring (423) the Athenians and the Spartans signed a year's armistice that was respected in most parts of Greece. Trouble continued in Chalcidice, where the city of Scione revolted to Sparta, probably before learning of the truce. When the armistice expired in 422, it was in Chalcidice that fighting resumed. There Cleon, now a regularly elected general, met Brasidas in battle at Amphipolis, deciding not to wait for reinforcements from Perdiccas, who had returned to the Athenian fold. Greek generals fought in the front lines, and in the fighting both Cleon and Brasidas were killed.

The Peace of Nicias and the *Peace* of Aristophanes (421 BC)

The door to peace was opened by the deaths of the men Aristophanes called the pestles who were grinding down the mortar of war. Athens and Sparta had both had enough. Agriculture in Attica had been horribly disrupted and with it the trade between city and countryside that was the foundation of polis life, and the Athenians were unsettled by the patent unrest throughout their sphere of influence in the north. Sparta was nervous about continuing its war with Athens when the Spartan-Argive truce of thirty years was on the verge of expiring. A number of Spartan soldiers had died in captivity in Athens, and the Spartans were extremely eager to recover the survivors. Both sides were disturbed by the degree to which they had been compelled to hire mercenaries to keep the war going; it seemed like a bad precedent, and it was also costly. The other key players on the diplomatic scene, however—Corinth, Megara, and Boeotia—had somewhat less to gain from peace in general (although they had also experienced devastation during the war), and nothing to gain from the particular peace on which the Athenians and Spartans agreed. In fact, they refused to sign it. The highly problematic agreement known as the Peace of Nicias (named for the principal Athenian negotiator, Cleon's old rival) was essentially a victory for Athens.

Countless men and women throughout the Greek world had no doubt longed increasingly for peace during the ten years of the Archidamian War, but, as is often the case, we know most about the situation in Athens, from which the bulk of our written sources originate. In 425, Aristophanes had presented his *Acharnians*. Comic dramas were produced twice a year in Athens, both times at festivals of the god Dionysus. As at tragic competitions, several dramatists presented plays, but though we know the names of other comedians and fragments of their work remain, no whole plays by any hand other than Aristophanes' have survived. Obscene and boisterous, Aristophanes' plays also manifest a tender love of the countryside, a nostalgia for a simpler time, and a sober commitment to peace. Though Aristophanes' comic genius was unique, his values must have been congenial to the community; the decision whether to grant a chorus for training lay with the city magistrates, and of course prizes were awarded by citizen judges.

The *Acharnians* had presented as its hero a certain Dicaeopolis ("the man of the just city"), a grumpy farmer from the deme of Acharnae north of Athens. Dicaeopolis' spleen was directed not at the invading enemy but rather at the Athenian politicians who were determined to continue the war. Acharnae had been ravaged annually by the Peloponnesians, and Dicaeopolis, disappointed in his hope of a general peace, decided to make his own private peace with Sparta. Now in 421, with an end to the war in sight, Aristophanes wrote his *Peace*; by the time it was presented, the treaty was close to becoming a reality. Here, parodying a lost play by Euripides, Aristophanes shows his protagonist Trygaeus riding on a huge dung beetle to the house of Zeus (accomplished on stage by a crane) to inquire why Zeus is destroying Greece by war. There he learns from Hermes that the gods have been alienated by the two sides' childish squabbling. The audience cannot have been entirely comfortable with Hermes' evenhanded allotment of blame. The gods, he says,

> were frequently for peace.
> But you guys wanted war. Laconians,
> when once they got a little piece of luck,
> would say, "By God, those Atticans will pay!"
> Or if it seemed that luck was on your side,
> and then the Spartans came about a peace,
> at once you'd cry: "We're being taken in!
> Athena! Zeus! we can't agree to this!
> If we hang on to Pylos, they'll come back. . . ."
> (*Peace 211–219*)

He then explains that War has imprisoned Peace in a cave and, having obtained a huge mortar in which to grind down all the Greek cities, has sent his slave Tumult in search of pestles. Tumult, however, has learned that Athens and Sparta have recently lost their pestles—Cleon and Brasidas. Perhaps, then, there is some hope of setting Peace free.

Trygaeus finally persuades Hermes to help him organize the rescue of Peace. This is no mean task, since it is difficult to get all the Greeks to pull together on the necessary ropes even with divine assistance, but in time their efforts are successful. The blessings Peace will bring are celebrated in terms that reflect the concerns of the Athenian farmers in the audience:

> Trygaeus: Fellow farmers! Stop and listen! Can you hear these
>   wondrous words?
>   No more spears, men, no more javelins, no more fighting
>   with our swords!
>   We've got peace with all its gifts now, we can trade in all
>   that arming
>   For a happy, happy song as we march home to do some
>   farming.
> Chorus: What a day, not just for farmers but for anyone worthwhile:
>   What a yearned-for, hoped-for vision! See how joyously I
>   smile
>   As I think about how soon I'll see the vines upon my land;
>   And the fig-trees that I planted as a youth with my own hand!
>   (Peace *551–558*)

The terms of the real-life peace were to be observed for fifty years. Athens was to keep the empire with which it had entered the war; the treaty contained the expression "the Athenians and their allies." Sparta was to return Amphipolis, while Athens would abandon Pylos and Cythera and release all prisoners of war. Though at tremendous cost in money and human lives, the Athenian war goal had been met: the Spartans had failed to destroy the empire. Without even trying, the Athenians had done much to weaken the Peloponnesian League. After a grueling war of ten years Sparta had suffered loss of life and loss of prestige, and now she was about to lose her allies as well.

Angry that no substantial damage had been done to the Athenian empire and that two cities on the west coast, Sollium and Anactorium, remained in Athenian hands, Corinth refused to sign the peace. Megara would not sign an agreement that allowed the Athenians to retain Nisaea—as the Spartans should have foreseen. The Boeotians, furious at the order to relinquish the border fortress of Panactum to the Athenians, not only declined to sign the treaty but demolished Panactum sooner than give it back. The disintegration of the Peloponnesian League might have proven helpful to the Athenians had the terms of the limited Athenian-Spartan peace been respected. When Argos decided not to renew its treaty with Sparta and Sparta responded by nervously signing a fifty-year alliance with Athens, the position of the Athenians seemed quite enviable. But Sparta, as it proved, exaggerated its ability to control even its weakest allies. The Amphipolitans, for example, had buried Brasidas with honors and come to revere him as their founder, extinguishing the memory of the Athenian Hagnon who had previously enjoyed that status, and they refused to return to the Athenian empire. In retaliation, the Athenians held on to Pylos. The chance for a productive alliance between the two most powerful states in Greece was lost. Probably this was a lucky thing for Sparta's erstwhile allies. Though Athens and Sparta did not attack one another directly, the years that followed were very tense, and Thucydides viewed the Peace of Nicias as a false peace, a troubled interlude before the resumption of hostilities.

BETWEEN PEACE AND WAR

Events were to prove that the thousands who had died in the Archidamian War had given their lives for nothing. The short-lived peace not only failed to solve the problems of previous years; it also compromised the hopes of the future. The sense that the Spartans betrayed them in failing to honor the terms of the Peace of Nicias was probably a key factor in the Athenians' aversion to making another negotiated peace with their rival. Though the Athenians and Spartans who desired peace wanted it very badly indeed, they had to contend with formidable countervailing forces.

Effectively excluded from the peace of 421, Sparta's most powerful allies posed a serious threat to peace in Greece. Danger also came from individuals within the hegemonic states. Two ephors, Cleobulus and Xenares, schemed with the Corinthians and Boeotians to bring Argos over to the Spartan side and set the stage for continuing the war. In Athens, the ambitions of one memorable Athenian had a powerful impact on the course of events. As a rule, it is dangerous to accord too large a role to high-profile individuals in shaping the course of history. At times, however, a particular person does seem to bear an extraordinary share of the responsibility for the way things turn out. Such was the case with the flashy Athenian aristocrat Alcibiades. Strategos for the first time in 420, Alcibiades had little prospect of making a name for himself in a tranquil world. His future glory was contingent on the disintegration of the fragile peace. To Alcibiades, even more than to the average Greek aristocrat, a life without glory was barely worth the name.

Alcibiades, Renegade Aristocrat

Alcibiades had been 3 when his father died, and he was raised in the home of his relative Pericles. Handsome, witty, athletic, charming, and sensuous, he was eagerly courted by lovers of both sexes. His rakish personality and flamboyant lifestyle were conducive to anecdote, and Plutarch tells several stories illustrating the opposition between the responsibility of Pericles and the irresponsibility of his irreverent ward. One day, it seems, when Alcibiades had grown up and wished to speak to Pericles, he

> went to his house, but was told Pericles could not receive him, as he was considering how to present his accounts to the people. "Would it not be better," asked Alcibiades as he came away, "if he considered how to avoid presenting accounts to the people at all?"
>
> (Alcibiades 7; Scott-Kilvert 1960)

Alcibiades never did like rules. His passions included his teacher Socrates, the breeding and racing of horses, and indeed competition in all its forms, on and off the track. His wealthy family (whose genealogy we have diagrammed in Chapter 6, Figure 6.10) had connections abroad, and despite his relationship to Pericles, his grandfather had been the Spartan *proxenos* at Athens—the man charged with representing Spartan interests in his home state. To the family connections that were his by birth, he added a marriage connection; his wife Hipparete, daughter of Hipponicus, belonged to one of the most prominent families in Athens.

At first it appeared that Alcibiades' interest in reactivating the war would come to nothing. Although Elis and Mantinea joined the alliance Athens had formed with Argos, Sparta managed to defeat the new grouping in battle, scoring a decisive victory in Mantinea in 418 BC, and also succeeded in mending fences with its disaffected allies Boeotia and Corinth, thus in effect restoring the Peloponnesian League. Meanwhile tensions ran high among the various would-be leaders in Athens. An ostracism might have decided the rivalry of Alcibiades and Nicias, the hawk and the dove, but the two men seem to have panicked and mobilized their supporters to turn on a third man, Hyperbolus, instead.

A politician from the rising business class, like Cleon, Hyperbolus appears to have been an effective speaker who shared Cleon's imperialistic policies, but otherwise little is known about him. In retrospect, the Athenians were upset by the way the voting had gone, and they never again held an ostracism. The fact that ostracism was in reality something of an honor is underlined by Plutarch's claim that it was Hyperbolus' unworthiness that sparked this decision; a contemporary comic poet apparently quipped, "The man, indeed, deserved the fate, but not the fate the man." At this distance, it is impossible to determine whether the Athenians' distress at the outcome of the ostracism resulted from Hyperbolus' political insignificance or his social origins; those who had been ostracized earlier in the century came from aristocratic families. In any event, the Athenians now turned to a different, less peculiar strategy for ensuring democratic control on government. Around this time they begin utilizing the *graphē paranomōn* ("indictment for illegal proposals") to punish politicians who brought forward proposals in conflict with existing laws. Like ostracism, however, this procedure was often used politically—a development that is not surprising, since, without a written constitution or bill of rights, only a highly subjective judgment could determine what new laws were and were not in harmony with the old.

The Destruction of Melos (416 BC)

The years that followed were marked by conflict in Athens and chaos in the Peloponnesus. Argos switched alliances more than once, and both Alcibiades and Nicias had sufficient support to be elected two of the strategoi for 417–416. A disturbing Athenian naval expedition stands out from these troubled years, memorialized in some of the most frequently read pages in Thucydides. In 416, probably at the instigation of Alcibiades, the Athenians decided to bring the little island of Melos under their control. The only island in the Cyclades that had stood aloof from their alliance, Melos had technically remained neutral in the previous war but had given Sparta a small sum for the war effort. A Spartan colony, Melos definitely leaned to the Peloponnesian side, but Athens and Sparta were not really at war any longer, and Melos was of no strategic significance. It is unclear what Athens had to gain by subjugating Melos besides the satisfaction of making an example of the uncooperative Melians, but for whatever reason, Athenian ships were dispatched to Melos to order its inhabitants to enter their alliance. Hope of Spartan assistance moved the Melians to turn Athens down. Spartan aid did not materialize, and as punishment for their recalcitrance, the Athenians killed all the Melian men and sold all the women and children into slavery.

To treat an enemy this way was not unheard of in Greece; this is precisely what the Athenians had done to the inhabitants of rebellious Scione in 421. But the Melians were not the Athenians' enemies. The episode plainly made a deep impression on Thucydides, who chose to include in his history a chilling rendition of the conversation between the Melians and the Athenians—the only sustained dialogue in his work. Melos was a tiny island in a remote locale. How did Thucydides know what was said there in such detail? He didn't. The set piece known as the "Melian Dialogue" shows us Thucydides experimenting with an art form closer to drama than to history.

Thucydides was not the only Athenian alive at the time who used his verbal talents to showcase the horrors of war and to explore its corrosive effect on morality. The following spring (415 BC) Euripides confronted the Athenians with his anguished *Trojan Women*. No one could seriously doubt that this exquisitely painful drama, ostensibly set in Troy in the aftermath of the city's fall, was designed to illustrate the dreadfulness of war in general and the current war in particular. The specter of the enslavement of the wives and sisters and daughters of the Trojan heroes and the execution of the young Astyanax, Hector's son, thrown to his death from the city walls, was all too evocative of recent developments: many of those sitting in the audience had themselves done the killing at Melos. It also proved prophetic of events yet to come.

THE INVASION OF SICILY (415–413 BC)

While a small number of men met daily to practice singing the unsettling choruses in Euripides' sobering drama, a large number busied themselves preparing for the largest military expedition in Athens' history. In the winter of 416–415 temptation had appeared to the Athenian assembly in the form of ambassadors from the Sicilian city of Egesta, an old ally. Their request for assistance against their neighbor Selinus provided a springboard for warmongers like Alcibiades. In a war with Egesta, Selinus could count on the backing of Syracuse, the most powerful city in Sicily—and a Corinthian colony. The expansion of Syracusan power in Sicily augured well for Athens' enemies, and the Egestans' request piqued the interest of men who yearned for new adventures. Pericles had warned the Athenians that attempts to expand their empire would undermine their chances of winning the war, but Pericles was long dead and his strategy had died with him. When Alcibiades advocated full support for Egesta and Nicias argued with equal passion against involvement in Sicily, the Athenians resolved on a peculiar compromise. Alcibiades would indeed be sent west with a large force, but he would be accompanied by two other strategoi—Lamachus, an experienced general, and Nicias himself, whose presence they hoped would serve as a check on Alcibiades' rashness.

Just about everything that could have gone wrong with the Sicilian enterprise did. The idea that Nicias' prudence would counter Alcibiades' impulsive nature was singularly wrongheaded. Shortly before the expedition was to sail, moreover, a bizarre nocturnal escapade in Athens sparked a scandal of extraordinary proportions that spilled over from religion to politics. Outside Athenian homes and temples stood religious images known as herms—stone pillars bearing images of the face and erect phallus of the god Hermes. They were meant to bring good luck and protection from danger. One morning not long before the expedition was to set sail, the Athenians awoke to find that nearly all these herms had been vandalized.

Cultural differences make it hard for us fully to understand why Athenians reacted to this sacrilegious prank with utter terror and became convinced that a plot was afoot to overthrow the government, but this is exactly what happened. Though many were punished, responsibility for the project has never been determined. It may have been the work of one or more of the organizations known as *hetaireiai*. Drinking clubs composed of upper-class young men, often with oligarchic leanings, hetaireiai involved themselves in a variety of social and political activities. To democrats they seemed sinister and potentially treasonous.

Not surprisingly, fingers were pointed at Alcibiades, precisely the sort of irreverent individual who would set his drinking companions on such an enterprise whether they belonged to a hetaireia or not. Fuel was added to the flames by accusations that Alcibiades had staged a burlesque mocking the mystery rites celebrated at Eleusis, violating their secrecy by parodying them in front of the uninitiated. Since he had solid support among the adventurous sailors bound for Sicily, Alcibiades wisely demanded that he be tried at once, before the fleet left. Instead his opponents waited to bring charges until the expedition had sailed.

The fleet the Athenians dispatched for Sicily was entirely out of proportion to the size or importance of its intended objective. It consisted of 134 triremes with 130 supply boats, a total of over 25,000 men. Dozens of merchant vessels decided to accompany the navy, hoping for profits. Both citizens and foreigners crowded the shore ogling the armada, which Thucydides says was the most expensive any Greek city had launched until that day. A trumpet proclaimed silence, and a herald recited the prayers. On every deck both officers and marines offered libations to the gods in vessels of gold and silver. The crews raised the paean, and when the libations were finished, put out to sea, sailing first in single file and then racing one another as far as Aegina. From there they hastened to Corcyra to rendezvous with the rest of their allies.

Of the many who sailed for Sicily few returned. The Athenians received less support from the cities of Sicily and southern Italy than they had expected, and even the eager Egestans turned out not to have the resources they had claimed. Envoys dispatched to Egesta, it proved, had been duped into believing the city was rich when in fact it was poor. Thucydides tells how the various Egestans received the crews of the Athenian ships in their homes, rounding up as many gold and silver cups as they could find in town and in the neighboring cities and presenting them at parties as if they belonged to the household:

> They all used the same goblets, for the most part, and they showed so much of it everywhere that it absolutely awed the Athenian crewmen, who, when they returned to Athens, spread the news about the great wealth they had seen. Those who had been deceived in turn misled others, and they were all held responsible by the troops when word got out that Egesta did not have any money.
> (The Peloponnesian War 6.46; Blanco 1998)

The three generals, moreover, were unable to agree on a plan of action. Nicias wanted to head for Selinus, settle its quarrel with Egesta, and then consider returning home. Alcibiades preferred to build up alliances with other Sicilian cities. Lamachus' plan was probably the best—an immediate attack on Syracuse before the city could fully mobilize itself and recover from its terror at the Athenians' arrival on the island. Lacking support for his good proposal, Lamachus threw his backing to Alcibiades' plan. The generals then frittered away nearly a year in minor enterprises, but Alcibiades did not spend much of this year in Sicily. After his departure from Athens, his enemies had lodged formal charges against him for sacrilege, and one of Athens' two official state triremes, the Salaminia, was dispatched to Sicily to bring him home. Permitted to follow the Salaminia in his own ship, Alcibiades escaped to Thurii and thence to the Peloponnesus, where he defected to Sparta and set about advising Athens' old enemy of the best ways to undermine it. When in the winter of 415–414 envoys from Syracuse and Corinth came to seek Spartan aid for the Sicilian campaign, Alcibiades warned the Spartans that the Athenians were planning to conquer Sicily and Italy, attack Carthage, and then go after the Peloponnesus. The dispatch of a Spartan general to Sicily, he suggested, might be necessary if the Spartans wanted to prevent an Athenian takeover of the entire Greek world.

Meanwhile Nicias and Lamachus had occupied the plateau known as Epipolae west of Syracuse and had begun building a north-south wall with the idea in mind of blockading the city. In the fighting that ensued with the resisting Syra-

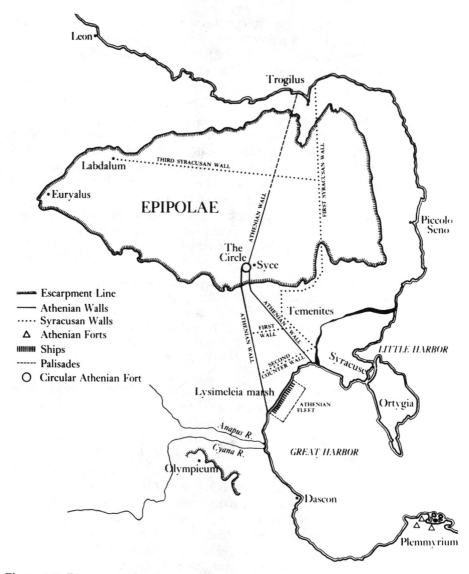

Figure 8.5. Diagram of Syracuse and Epipolae.

cusans, however, Lamachus was killed, leaving Nicias in sole command. Nicias at first handled the situation well, successfully moving the Athenian fleet into Syracuse's harbor and creating a real possibility of blockading the city, but the Spartans were determined to prevent an Athenian takeover of Sicily. Though the numbers of the full-blooded Spartiate caste had dropped, talent was not lacking, and the reinforcements that arrived in Syracuse were led by Gylippus, a gifted commander from the new class known as *mothakes*—sometimes the offspring of a Spartan father and helot mother, sometimes the sons of impoverished Spartans who no longer had the means to contribute to the common meals and thus maintain their status in the corps of "equals." The arrival of Gylippus with reinforcements changed the situation dramatically. Gylippus scaled the Epipolae heights via a pass that the Athenians had carelessly left unguarded—the same pass they themselves had used a few months before. The Syracusans, moreover, built a counter-wall that destroyed Athenian chances for a blockade.

Nicias was now suffering acutely from kidney disease and asked the Athenians to recall him. They refused. Convinced the situation was hopeless, he tried to dissuade them from continuing their efforts in Sicily by a long letter to the assembly maintaining that only a force as large as the original expedition could have any chance of success. To his horror, the Athenians sent Demosthenes out at the head of the proposed reinforcements. When he arrived with the second fleet and promptly suffered a serious reverse on the Epipolae heights, Demosthenes advocated immediate withdrawal. Afraid to move without orders from the assembly, Nicias at first insisted on remaining. When he realized that Gylippus had gathered still additional forces from throughout Sicily and had also received further reinforcements from the Peloponnesus, he changed his mind. At that point, however, religious anxiety once more intruded into the secular sphere. When everything was ready for the Athenians' departure, Thucydides related,

> and just as they were about to sail, there was an eclipse of the moon, which happened to be full. The event made most of the Athenians feel uneasy, and they urged their generals to stay; and Nicias, who was too inclined to believe in the interpretation of omens and that sort of thing, refused even to discuss a move until after they had stayed for "three times nine days," as their seers decreed. This was the reason the Athenians stayed on after all their delays!
>
> (The Peloponnesian War 7.50; *Blanco 1998*)

On learning that the Athenians had been planning to leave, the Syracusans attacked the Athenian fleet and blocked the exit from the harbor. A fierce battle ensued, with some two hundred ships rammed together in a tight space. The din made it impossible to hear the calls of the coxswains.

Unable to make their escape by sea, the Athenians resolved to depart overland, abandoning their sick and wounded. About 40,000 men set out on the dismal trek, the Syracusans hot on their heels. Nicias and Demosthenes became separated; the Syracusans caught up first with Demosthenes, who surrendered in the hope of saving his soldiers' lives. The Syracusans then overtook Nicias' army.

Document 8.1 Thucydides is at his narrative best in portraying the final collapse of the Athenian effort in Sicily.

The Athenians pushed on to the Assinarus river, all the while being devastated by the spears, arrows and stones coming from everywhere and by the hordes of cavalry and other troops. They thought that if they could just get across the river, things would be a little easier for them. They were desperate to stop the pain, to drink some water. When they got to the river, they broke ranks and ran into it, every man struggling to make the brutal crossing first as the enemy bore down. Driven to cross all together, they fell onto one another and trampled each other down. Some were killed immediately by their own spears; others got tangled up in their equipment and with each other and sank into the river. Syracusans positioned on the other bank, which was steep, hurled down spears at the Athenians, most of whom were jumbled together ravenously drinking from the nearly dry riverbed. The Peloponnesians went down into the river after them and did most of the killing there; and though it quickly became fouled, the Athenians nonetheless fought among themselves to gulp the muddy water clotted with blood.

Finally, with dead bodies heaped atop each other in the riverbed, and the army decimated, some in the river and others—such as got across—by the cavalry, Nicias surrendered himself to Gylippus, trusting him more than the Syracusans. He told Gylippus and the Spartans to do with him what they wanted, but to stop slaughtering his men. After this, Gylippus ordered his troops to take prisoners, whereupon the surviving men were brought in alive, except for the large number who had been hidden by individual Syracusan soldiers. They also sent a search party out after the three hundred who had broken through the sentries by night and captured them. . . . A large number, of course, were killed, for there was a great slaughter at the river, greater than any which occurred in the whole war.

(The Peloponnesian War 7.84–85; *translated by Walter Blanco, in Walter Blanco and Jennifer Roberts, eds.,* Thucydides: The Peloponnesian War. *New York: W. W. Norton, 1998.*

The triumphant Syracusans celebrated their victory by presenting Apollo with lavish offerings at Delphi. The Athenians, on the other hand, had lost tens of thousands of men and accomplished nothing. For them, the outcome of the campaign was so horrific that they at first refused to believe the appalling news. Plutarch claims that word of the disaster first reached Athens by way of a hapless man who had reported it matter of factly to a barber in Piraeus as if it were common knowlege: the agitated barber promptly ran the 5 miles to Athens, where he repeated the tale. He was in the very process of being tortured as a troublemaker when messengers arrived to confirm the astonishing story. As Thucydides was later to write, "All was lost. Ships. Men. Everything" (7.87).

The war party at Athens had not been crazy to believe the Athenians could bring Sicily under their control. With better management, the campaign might have succeeded. But the Athenians' ambivalence about the project and about individual leaders proved fatal. Though the mutilation of the herms could not have been predicted, the mistrust inspired by Alcibiades' well-known irreverence and recklessness was a terrible—and foreseeable—liability to the war party. Nicias' timidity was in large part a feature of his personality, and he bears a great deal of responsibility for the expedition's miserable end. His fear of acting without authorization from the assembly, however, was exacerbated by the Athenians' impeachment of several unsuccessful generals in the 420s—the three generals who had failed in the first expedition to Sicily, and the historian Thucydides himself. Although the bad judgment shown by Nicias had little to do with the form of government in operation at Athens, aristocrats who had never liked democracy found in the failure of the Sicilian invasion an opening for their oligarchic programs, and antidemocratic agitation was not long in getting off the ground.

THE WAR IN THE AEGEAN AND THE OLIGARCHIC COUP AT ATHENS (413–411 BC)

By their defeat at Syracuse the Athenians stunned the Greek world as much as they had by their victory at Marathon. The myth of naval superiority that had held the Delian League together was shattered. Athens' fighting force was vastly smaller than it had been in 431. Money was in short supply; previously one trierarch had been appointed for each ship, but soon after the disaster in Sicily the Athenians introduced the syntrierarchy, allowing two men to share the expense. For Athenian subjects, suddenly revolt became not merely an option but a powerful temptation. Might not making friends with Sparta when it seemed poised on the brink of victory prove more prudent than waiting for events to take their course? Alcibiades cruised the seas on Sparta's behalf, fomenting rebellion wherever he could. Meanwhile in Attica some twenty thousand slaves deserted to the Spartan king Agis, who at Alcibiades' instigation had established himself in a fort at Decelea in northeast Attica. The disappearance of the slaves from the mines prevented the continued tapping of the silver veins, and the strength of the encampment at Decelea interfered gravely with Athenian agriculture. Now the Spartans could ravage Attica all year, killing farm animals as they went and keeping Athens in a perpetual state of siege. Seeing success well within their grasp, the invigorated Spartans set about building a new naval force of a hundred triremes and began negotiating for Persian support.

Incredibly, it took Sparta eight years to bring Athens to its knees—eight years during which the Athenians, crippled by devastating losses in Sicily, survived the loss of the huge island of Euboea off the Attica coast and an oligarchic coup in the city. The history of these eight years is crowded with shifting alliances, plots and counterplots, murders and lies. Within Athens, lines between democrats and oligarchs appear blurred as key players in the political arena move back and forth between the parties, and a new creature appears, the "moderate"—a politician whose motives for keeping one foot in each camp are often impossible to determine: sincere patriotism becomes increasingly difficult to distinguish from unprincipled time-serving. Spartans are divided as to how seemly it might be to barter the Ionians' freedom in exchange for Persian gold. Persians cannot decide which side, if any, to support. Alcibiades remains a wild card, cagily shifting position to suit the rapidly altering international situation—and to keep himself safe from the wrath of Agis, whose wife he appears to have seduced in a moment of imprudence. The fortunes of battle swing wildly back and forth. In 413 Athens seemed to be finished; by 410 the Spartans sue for peace. Athens wins a stunning victory in 406 only to lose the war by 404 (really by 405).

Civil Strife in Athens

The burst of Peloponnesian energy that erupted in the wake of Athens' defeat in Sicily was short-lived. The Spartans soon reverted to their natural sluggishness. Their lukewarm efforts would have come to little had it not been for the dynamic energy of Alcibiades and for the tensions that erupted in Athens, setting the hoplite infantry and the aristocratic elite against the thetes who manned the fleet.

For nearly a century after the clash between Cleisthenes and Isagoras, Athens had been free from the danger of civil war. The debacle in Sicily, however, gave an opening to would-be oligarchs who wanted to reconstitute the government on less democratic lines. The first rumblings of discontent were mild, though ominous: in 413 BC the Athenians placed decision-making in the hands of ten older men called *probouloi*. Despite the undemocratic nature of such a board, however, the individual probouloi were men of impeccable democratic credentials; one was the playwright Sophocles. The Athenians now tapped the emergency reserve funds they had been storing on the Acropolis since the beginning of the war and used it to rebuild the fleet and train new crews. With the new ships they were able to prevent the secession of Chios from the empire and win a few victories on the coast of Asia Minor.

Unrest continued, however, as men of oligarchic inclinations played on the Athenians' anxieties about the failure of their democratic leaders to bring the war to a successful conclusion. The machinations of Alcibiades provided a catalyst for a more substantial change in the government. Alcibiades had rendered signal service to Sparta in encouraging rebellions in a number of cities including Erythrae, Rhodes, Ephesus, Chios, and Miletus. Having fallen foul of Agis, however— whether because of the alleged affair with his wife or for some other reason—he had begun to plot a return to Athens. The entry of Persia into the equation provided the springboard he needed. In the years that followed the Athenian defeat in Sicily, Persian policy toward Greece was determined not primarily by the king, Darius II, but by the coastal satraps—Pharnabazus (the satrap of Dascylium) in the north, and Tissaphernes (the satrap of Sardis) in the south.

Tissaphernes in particular had a lively interest in Greek affairs, and indeed in Greek culture as a whole. At first he leaned toward Sparta, and in fact negotiated a series of treaties with Sparta in which the Spartans, uncomfortably but unmistakably, agreed to sell out the freedom of the Greek cities of Ionia in exchange for Persian gold. Thus died the Spartans' claim to be the liberators of Greece. Sparking Persia's interest (however vacillating) in their cause was pretty much Sparta's only achievement during these years, and even this the Spartans owed in good

Figure 8.6. This Greeklike coin struck by Tissaphernes reveals his desire to be identified with Greek culture.

part to Alcibiades. Not long afterward, however, Alcibiades persuaded Tissaphernes that it might be better for Persia to let Athens and Sparta wear each other down. When Tissaphernes' support for the Spartan cause began to waver, Alcibiades sent word to Athens that he had it in his power to bring the Persians into the war on the Athenian side—but that their support would be contingent on replacing the democracy with an oligarchy. His support, of course, would be contingent on his recall.

That Alcibiades really believed he could persuade Tissaphernes to pour money into the Athenian treasury is unlikely, though not impossible. In the event, he couldn't, but by the time it became clear that the Persian support he had promised was illusory, the wheels had been set in motion for a change in government and Alcibiades' return. It is an index of how deeply the long war had shaken the Athenians that in 411 the assembly, some members intimidated and others just demoralized, voted itself out of existence and placed the safety of the state in the hands of a new, provisional Council of four hundred, which, it was understood, would soon give way to a larger body of five thousand. Despite the way the war had undermined confidence in the democratic government, this vote was made possible only by the absence of the fleet, based now at Samos; for sailors, who were generally poor men, could be counted on to oppose any reforms that had the effect of limiting the franchise to property owners.

Experiments in Oligarchy

Neither of the reformers' notions was entirely new. Solon was believed by many people to have created a Council of four hundred—certainly such a body dated from approximately his time—and the five thousand were thought to correspond to the hoplite class. Sailors were right to be alarmed by such projects. What was really at issue here was the disfranchisement of the lowest class in the Solonic census, the thetes. The notion of "hoplite democracy" had been Cimon's ideal, and he was not alone. From this moment many Athenians of anti-democratic tendencies began to make use of a new watchword, "the ancestral constitution," that

is, a democracy limited to landowners, which they insisted was more traditionally Athenian than the upstart democracy that included the poor men who served
as rowers in the fleet. This issue, which had seemed to be settled in 508 with
Cleisthenes' victory over Isagoras, was now once again on the floor.

As was often the case in antiquity, Athenian revolutionaries cast their program
as a return to an earlier time. The probouloi had been older men; the two whose
identities are known to us were Pericles' associate Hagnon, who was in his 50s,
and the playwright Sophocles, who was over 80. If old men made good advisers,
dead men were even better; and so those discontent with democracy called frequently on the names of Solon, Draco, and Cleisthenes, claiming to be restoring
a more authentic Athenian government than the one that had operated during
their own lifetimes. Under the oligarchy of 411, consequently, the clock was
turned back and pay was abolished for most state offices. Though this did serve
the purpose of concentrating money on the war effort, it also effectively limited
participation in government to those who could afford to spend time in nonre-
munerated labor. Carrying arms and flanked by an additional 120 men, the Four
Hundred also entered the Bouleuterion where the council met, paid the councilors the balance of what was owing to them, and dismissed them. Their own
despotic rule was also made easier by the ominous suspension of the graphe
paranomon, the indictment for illegal proposals.

There were now two Athenian governments—the oligarchy of the Four Hundred in the city and the democratic fleet stationed at Samos, which functioned as
the assembly. Considering themselves the real government of Athens, the sailors
on Samos deposed the incumbent generals and appointed new ones, including
the trierarch Thrasybulus, a champion of the democracy. Those who had always
suspected Alcibiades of designs on the democratic constitution proved to have
much justice on their side. Not only had he suggested constitutional innovation
directly; indirectly he had also brought it about by fomenting rebellions in the
east that kept the democratic fleet away from Athens. His support, however, did
not come entirely from antidemocratic quarters. Thrasybulus was just one of the
democrats who backed him, and soon after his arrival on Samos Alcibiades too
was elected general.

Back in Athens the Four Hundred were undermined by two powerful divisions in their camp. Some wanted to prosecute the war vigorously, but others
with different plans prevailed and sent an embassy to Sparta seeking peace at
any price. In addition, some fully expected the implementation of the government of the Five Thousand while others understood that it was nothing but a
fiction calculated to bring about the abdication of the assembly. Meanwhile rumors circulated among the fleet at Samos that the Four Hundred were exercising a reign of terror, that no wife or child was safe from their outrage. At this
juncture, it appears, Alcibiades rose to statesmanlike heights and dissuaded the
furious sailors from sailing to Athens to overthrow the Four Hundred. Their departure would have left the east at the mercy of Athens' many enemies, and
their intervention at Athens proved unnecessary, as the Four Hundred were
self-destructing anyway.

The belief that Athens' foreign affairs would do better under oligarchic guidance suffered serious setbacks when the peace with Sparta failed to materialize—and Euboea successfully revolted from the Athenian empire. The hoplites whom the Four Hundred had set to fortifying the promontory of Eetionia at Piraeus mutinied, and the Five Thousand were promptly installed. They then recalled Athens' exiles, including Alcibiades, and governed Athens for eight months, from September 411 to June 410. Not a great deal is known about their government, though they seem to have limited the franchise to the hoplite class (cutting out the thetes who manned the triremes). Thucydides, who was frequently impatient with democracy, praised the government of the Five Thousand as a laudable blending of democratic and oligarchic elements.

The vigor the Athenians showed in rebuilding their fleet and carrying on the war despite acute domestic conflict was remarkable. After a victory at Cynossema, the Athenians, led by Alcibiades, scored a still more striking one at Cyzicus, where the Spartans lost their admiral-in-chief, Mindarus. The battle is memorable for the "laconic" dispatch the Athenians intercepted on its way to Sparta afterward: "Ships lost; Mindarus dead; men starving; can't figure out what to do." (It is also memorable as the first major encounter of the war not described by Thucydides: Thucydides' account breaks off shortly after Cynossema. From this point on the principal sources are Xenophon and Diodorus.) The victories in the east had been won by the cooperation of the Five Thousand in Athens and the fleet at Samos, and in June the democracy was formally restored at Athens. A number of the leaders of the Five Thousand remained powerful under the democracy. Among these was Hagnon's son Theramenes, who seemed to find a place for himself in any group. Animosity and suspicion were not entirely gone, however, and as one of its first official acts the restored democracy administered a loyalty oath, requiring each citizen to swear: "I will do my best to kill by word and by deed, by my vote and by my hand, anyone who overthrows the Athenian democracy, holds office under an undemocratic regime, or seeks to establish a tyranny either for himself or for someone else. If anyone else kills such a person, I will consider him clean in the eyes of gods and spirits" (Andocides, *On the Mysteries*, 97).

The Spartans sought peace from the restored democracy, but only on the basis of the status quo. That the Athenians had regained their confidence is indexed by their refusal. In this decision Cleophon played a large part. A good financial planner, he played a key role in framing policy at this time and was responsible for the conversion of temple properties into money, which was distributed to the most needy in the amount of two obols a day. In retrospect, many Athenians must have regretted their rejection of the Spartan offer, but at the time it did look as if they might win back their lost possessions.

The Last Years of War (407–404 BC)

In 407, however, the union of two powerful men dramatically altered the situation in the Aegean. Alcibiades was not the only Greek with charm. The new chief admiral of the Spartan navy, Lysander, was a *mothax* like Gylippus, but far more ambitious. He had managed to win the heart (and presumably the body as well) of young Agesilaus, half-brother to Agis. This remarkable coup presaged an illustrious future, and indeed there were rumors that Lysander was plotting to make the Spartan monarchy elective. Darius, meanwhile, recalled the two coastal satraps and replaced them with his son Cyrus, granting him large powers to help Sparta end the war. Though not the elder son, Cyrus hoped to become king of Persia, and he accepted his new responsibilities with enthusiasm. Lysander and Cyrus shared a profoundly ambitious temperament, and the two became fast friends. Ultimately, their association spelled doom for Athens.

In 407 Alcibiades, having raised a hundred talents for Athens by looting the coast of Caria, decided it might finally be safe to return home. It was an extraordinary circumstance—a man with so many friends that he was repeatedly elected to the board of generals but with so many enemies that he feared to set foot on Attic soil. Even after his ship had sailed into Piraeus in June, he stood motionless on the deck surveying the huge crowd that had assembled on the shore until he saw a party of his friends waiting to escort him. Only then did he disembark. Shortly afterward, in the hopes of boosting the Athenians' spirits while at the same time dispelling the suspicions of impiety that still attached to him, he led the state procession to Eleusis, daring to go by land: since the occupation of Decelea the Athenians had nervously conducted the procession by sea. In autumn he sailed east in command of one hundred ships, invested with full powers to direct the war with Sparta.

His ascendancy, however, was remarkably brief. Within a matter of months, the Athenians lost twenty-two ships to Lysander at a naval engagement off Notium, where Alcibiades had left his personal pilot Antiochus in charge with orders under no circumstances to engage the Spartans. Antiochus, a friend of Alcibiades, probably had no business in a position of such authority, since he was not a trierarch, and Alcibiades had not acquitted himself well; but the strength of the Athenian reaction attests to the continuing agitation of his enemies. Alcibiades' career at Athens was finished. It is certain that he was not reelected to the strategia, and it is likely that he was actually deposed before his term was out. Rumors circulated that he had fortified a castle in the Gallipoli peninsula as a refuge in case of emergency. Now that the emergency had materialized, he promptly withdrew to this very fortress. He never saw Athens again.

That spring the Athenians offered freedom to slaves who would join the navy that was about to set out for the area of Lesbos. There they scored an impressive victory in a huge naval battle off the Arginusae islands, sinking fully seventy-five Peloponnesian ships. Some twenty thousand Greeks lost their lives. Among these was the Spartans' chief admiral Callicratidas, another mothax who had taken over from Lysander, since the annual office was nonrenewable. A noble and generous young patriot, Callicratidas represented the best elements in Sparta—those willing to risk their lives to prevent the imperialist Athenians from tyrannizing over the weak, and committed to doing it without Persian help—where Lysander represented the worst. Callicratidas always fought bravely despite his dislike of

Sparta's growing imperialism, and he retained the loyalty of his men in the face of Lysander's constant machinations against him. His loss boded ill for the future of the Greek world.

The aftermath of the battle witnessed a bizarre frenzy of self-destruction. Though the Athenians were heartened by their victory at Arginusae, they knew that their admiral Conon and his fleet were blockaded at Mytilene. While the Athenian strategoi were debating whether to set about retrieving the sailors in the water or to sail to Mytilene to rescue Conon's force, a sudden storm came up that made rescue impossible. When news of the casualties reached Athens, people began anxiously to cast blame on one another. The generals blamed the trierarchs Theramenes and Thrasybulus, and the trierarchs blamed the generals. Whether the men in the water were dead or alive is uncertain, but for Greeks the recovery even of bodies was important, since the souls of those left unburied would wander eternally in Hades, unable to find a resting place. The eight generals in command were summoned home for trial, and six chose to return. In violation of customary procedure—and over the protests of the philosopher Socrates, whose turn it happened to be to chair the assembly meeting that day—the generals were tried on a single slate, condemned, and executed. Ironically, after the death of his legitimate sons, Pericles had implored the Athenians to confer citizenship on his sons by Aspasia, and Pericles the Younger was among the generals executed.

The Final Battle

Again, the Spartans offered peace on the basis of the status quo (though they were willing to evacuate Decelea); again, the Athenians followed Cleophon's advice and declined. Time, however, was running out, as was the pool of talented commanders—and of money. It seemed that the next major battle would be Athens' last stand, and in fact it was. Late in the summer of 405 Lysander, making good use of the subsidies he had obtained from his friend Cyrus, stormed the city of Lampsacus in the Hellespont with a fleet of some two hundred ships and established a base there. In August the Athenian generals Conon and Philocles stationed their fleet 2 miles across the channel at Aegospotami. Alcibiades, seeing that the Athenians' position was highly vulnerable, descended from his fortress and advised them to move, but they disregarded his cautions. After the fleets had been in these positions for five days, Lysander gave the signal for attack when the Athenian crews had gone ashore to gather provisions. The Spartans captured 171 ships, and their infantry overwhelmed the camp. Understandably, the Athenians' carelessness gave rise to rumors of treachery. Only a handful of Athenian vessels escaped, one of them the official state trireme the Paralus, another commanded by Conon. Remembering the fate of the victors of Arginusae, Conon took refuge in Cyprus and did not return to Athens until he had engineered a victory over the Spartans at Cnidus in 394, ten years after the end of the war.

Lysander then called a meeting of the allies to solicit their thoughts about the proper treatment of the prisoners. The speeches made about the Athenians, Xenophon reports, were many and bitter,

> both with regard to all the crimes they had committed in the past and about the decree which they had passed to the effect that, if they won the naval action, they could cut off the right hand of every man taken alive; there was also the fact that, after capturing two triremes, one from Corinth and one from Andros, they had thrown every man in the crews overboard. It was Philocles, the Athenian general, who had all these men killed. Many other such stories were told, and in the end it was decided that all the prisoners who were Athenian should be put to death with the one exception of Adimantus. He had been the only man in the Assembly who opposed the decree for cutting off the hands of prisoners. He was also, it should be said, accused by some people of having betrayed the fleet. As for Philocles, who had thrown the Andrians and Corinthians overboard, Lysander first asked him this question: 'What do you deserve for having been the first to act like a criminal toward your fellow-Greeks?' He then had his throat cut.
>
> (Hellenica 2.1.31–32; Warner 1979)

The Spartan victory at Aegospotami had cut off Athens from its principal source of grain; to make sure there would be no slip-ups, Lysander also decreed death as the penalty for anyone caught bringing grain to Athens. Lysander knew that the war was now over, and the Athenians would know it soon enough, for the Paralus was en route to Piraeus with the dismal tidings. The ship arrived at night, and as the news was reported, Xenophon relates, "one man passed it on to another, and a sound of wailing arose and extended first from Piraeus, then along the Long Walls until it reached the city. That night no one slept. They mourned for the lost, but more still for their own fate" (2.2.1; Warner). Late in the fall Lysander sailed victorious for Piraeus. Along the way he accepted the surrender of Athens' former allies and replaced their democracies with oligarchic governments beholden to Sparta. He also ensured still further stress on the Athenians' dwindling food supply by encouraging Athenian garrisons to return home. Samos persisted in its loyalty to Athens, in recognition of which the Athenians uncharacteristically granted the Samians citizenship. Agis, whose occupation of Decelea had played its desired part in the starvation of the city, moved down to the walls of Athens, where he was joined by Pausanias, his co-king. Miserable and terrified, the Athenians were at a loss for what to do. "They could see no future for themselves," Xenophon wrote, "except to suffer what they had made others suffer, people of small states whom they had injured not in retaliation for anything they had done but out of the arrogance of power and for no reason except that they were in the Spartan alliance" (2.2.10).

The mutability of fortune had been a commonplace in Greek literature, and the Athenians gathered in the theater in 415 had been given the opportunity to contemplate the cruelty of war's chances in Euripides' *Trojan Women*. Of those who prosper, the Trojan queen Hecuba had suggested, "consider no-one blest until he's dead" (509–510). This notion so reminiscent of Solon's warning to Croesus

in Herodotus' cautionary tale was developed later in the play, as Hecuba under-
lines the foolishness of those who believe prosperity is secure:

> like someone who's gone mad, in changing moods
> fortune leaps wildly, now this way, now that:
> nobody ever prospers all the time.
>
> (Trojan Women *1204–1206)*

In the end, Athens was spared. The Thebans, Corinthians, and other Spartan allies advocated doing to Athens precisely what had been done to Melos—killing
all the adult men and selling all the women and children into slavery. The Spartans declined, pleading Athens' noble service to Greece during the Persian wars.
The brutality of Lysander's temperament makes it more likely that the real motive was fear of the power vacuum into which Corinth or—more likely—Thebes
could be counted on to rush.

The Athenians' first offers to Sparta involved joining the Peloponnesian League
if only they could keep the Long Walls and Piraeus, and on the motion of
Cleophon a decree was passed forbidding anyone to so much as propose agree-
ing to dismantle the walls. Early in the spring, however—by which time many
had died of starvation and Cleophon had been executed on a trumped-up charge
brought by oligarchs—the Athenians agreed to a treaty negotiated by Theramenes
on the Spartans' terms: Athens would not only become Sparta's ally but would
agree to the destruction of the Long Walls and the fortifications of Piraeus and
would surrender all but a dozen ships. Exiles would also be recalled; these were
largely men of oligarchic sympathies. The walls were pulled down, Xenophon
says, to the merry accompaniment of flutes, for "it was thought that this day was
the beginning of freedom for Greece" (2.2.23; Warner). The Spartans' actions,
however, presaged ill for freedom. The willingness to sell out the Ionians to Persia and the establishment of pro-Spartan oligarchies in cities formerly in the
Athenian empire were bad signs, and worse was to come.

FALLOUT FROM THE LONG WAR

As we have seen, it sometimes happened that men who did not belong to the entrenched aristocracy became wealthy through industry—Cleon, for example, whose
family owned a tannery. It was also true, however, that the tendency to keep land
in the family constricted social mobility in Greece, limiting opportunities for improving one's lot in life. The frustrations of the poor resulted in frequent stasis,
with the poor likely to favor democracy and the rich oligarchy, although there were
always some aristocrats among the partisans of democracy, men like Pericles and
Cleisthenes at Athens. The natural disposition of Greek city-states to factionalism
and civil strife had been intensified during the war. Predictably, his interest in human nature and the drive to power focused Thucydides' interest on this development, which he encapsulated in his description of events occurring early in the war.

༼ 𝕡𝕡 ༽

Document 8.2 In one of the most memorable passages in his *History*, Thucydides took the occasion of the bloody events at Corcyra in the 420s to comment on the way the three decades of war intensified conflict within the polis.

Later, virtually all of Greece was in a frenzy, with dissension everywhere, and the leaders of the people trying to bring in the Athenians, and the oligarchs, the Spartans. In peacetime, there would have been neither pretext nor inclination for inviting their intervention; but in war, where alliances are at one and the same time a way to hurt your enemies and gain something for yourself, inducements came easily to those who wanted radical change. Events struck these strife-torn cities as they always do and always will for so long as human nature remains the same, hard and fast with more or less violence, quickly changing shape as change keeps pace with happenstance. In times of peace and prosperity, both cities and individuals can have lofty ideals because they have not fallen before the force of overwhelming necessity. War, which robs the ease of every day, is a harsh teacher and absorbs most people's passions in the here and now.

*   *   *

The cause of all this was power pursued for the sake of greed and personal ambition, which led in turn to the entrenchment of a zealous partisanship. The leadership in the cities on both sides advanced high-sounding phrases like "The equality of free men before the law," or "A prudent aristocracy," but while serving the public interest in their speeches, they created a spoils system. Struggling with one another for supremacy in every way they could, they kept committing the most horrible crimes and escalated to ever greater revenges, never to promote justice and the best interests of the city, but—constantly setting the limit at whatever best pleased each side at any given moment—they were always prepared to glut their partisanship by either rigging votes or by seizing power with their bare hands. Thus, neither side observed the rules of piety: they were more respected for the high words with which they got away with performing their base actions. As for the citizens who tried to be neutral, they were killed by both sides either because they did not join in the fighting or out of envy because they were managing to survive.

(The Peloponnesian War *3.82, translated by Walter Blanco, in Walter Blanco and Jennifer Roberts, eds.,* Thucydides: The Peloponnesian War. *New York: W. W. Norton, 1998).*

༼ 𝕡𝕡 ༽

Of the hegemons, only one had remained immune to this disease. A unique state, Sparta managed throughout the war to confine internal bloodshed to the usual suppression of helots (or at least to keep word of murderous civil conflict from leaking beyond the Peloponnesus). Throughout the war, it remained for many Greeks a model of stable government. Athens, however, was not free from civil strife. From Cimon to Theramenes, selected Athenian politicians had always had serious reservations about democracy, and the democracy's failure in the theater of war always carried with it the danger of an oligarchic coup. The take-over of 411 had been short-lived, but Lysander's victory in 404 would spark a second and far bloodier episode.

The Thirty Tyrants (404–403 BC)

Throughout the Aegean Lysander set up "decarchies," that is, boards of ten pro-Spartan officials designed to ensure that Athens' former allies were now governed in accordance with oligarchic principles and served Spartan interests. Ten men would not be enough for Athens; the intimidated assembly had no choice but to accede to Lysander's request and ratify a new government to be run by a board of thirty (the Thirty). Athenian citizens, these thirty were sympathetic to Sparta and willing to sacrifice democratic principles, but they were not all committed oligarchs. Theramenes, who was among them, became a controversial figure not only among Athenians of the fourth century but also among modern historians. His propensity for landing on his feet in any crisis has suggested to some that he was a flexible man who saw merit in a variety of regimes, whereas others have seen him as an unprincipled time-server. The most prominent of those who came to be known as the Thirty Tyrants, however, left no doubt as to his political convictions. Plato's relative Critias was a chilling figure—a pupil of Socrates, a brilliant intellectual, an avowed atheist, a passionate antidemocrat, a long-time admirer of the Spartan constitution, and, as events were to show, a man who would order murders by the hundreds without a qualm. Banished at the instigation of Cleophon after the fall of the Four Hundred, to which he had belonged, Critias was now back with a vengeance.

A letter written by Plato (or by someone using Plato's name as a pseudonym) describes the philosopher's joy at the accession of thoughtful intellectuals who wanted to reform the constitution along Spartan lines, and the author of the Aristotelian *Athenian Constitution* echoes the view that the beginning of the new regime seemed full of promise:

> At the outset, therefore, they were engaged in . . . . removing the blackmailers and the persons who consorted undesirably with the people to curry favor and were evil-doers and scoundrels; and the state was delighted at these measures, thinking that they were acting with the best intentions.
>
> ([Aristotle], The Athenian Constitution 35.3; Rackham 1961)

But soon afterward, he goes on,

> when they got a firmer hold on the state, they kept their hands off none of the citizens, but put to death those of outstanding wealth or birth or reputation, intending to put that source of danger out of the way, and also desiring to plunder their estates; and by the end of a brief interval of time they had made away with not less than fifteen hundred.
>
> (The Athenian Constitution 35.4; Rackham 1961)

The Thirty did not establish the "ancestral constitution," although they did abolish the organs of democratic government such as the popular courts and appointed a new boule of five hundred antidemocrats. To protect themselves from a popular uprising, they requested from Lysander seven hundred soldiers and a Spartan "harmost" (garrison commander) similar to those Sparta had established in states throughout the Aegean it had "liberated" from Athenian hegemony. They also surrounded themselves with three hundred whip-bearers and set up a board of ten to keep an eye on the Piraeus, rightly considered a hotbed of democratic radicalism.

The execution of enemies began. Under protest from the alarmed Theramenes, Critias and his clique agreed to broaden the oligarchy by establishing a citizen roll of Three Thousand whose members would be entitled to trial by the boule. The consequence of this, however, was the opposite of what Theramenes intended. Now it appeared to the Thirty that the existence of this protected Three Thousand gave them carte blanche in treating all others as they wished, and a bloodbath commenced. Not all victims were citizens who could possibly have been conceived as political enemies; many were wealthy metics whose property the Thirty coveted.

Understandably, so many Athenians were appalled—and frightened—that the Thirty came to fear that Theramenes might organize a resistance movement, and they summoned him for trial in the boule—a "trial" at which young oligarchs with concealed daggers had been stationed by prearrangement. When it appeared that Theramenes' impassioned defense of moderate government had moved the councilors, Critias struck his name from the roll of the Three Thousand, thereby obviating the need for a trial. Dragged off to prison from the altar where he had taken refuge, Theramenes was executed by being forced to drink hemlock, the poison later used to execute Socrates. Heroic at least in his final hours, Theramenes went out in style and not without irony, toasting Critias' health with the last drops.

Ultimately the Thirty were undone by their own abandon. By forbidding those not on the list of the Three Thousand to enter Athens and confiscating many of their farms, they created a dangerous body of exiles. Though Sparta had forbidden neighboring states to receive refugees from the Thirty, the murderous conduct of the Athenian oligarchy had alienated many Greeks from Sparta, and neither Thebes nor Megara was disposed to turn away Athenians fleeing the brutal Spartan-backed oligarchy. It was in Thebes that the Athenian exiles mounted their campaign to regain their city, making their move in January of 403. Led by Thrasybulus, seventy of the exiles seized Phyle, a stronghold on Mount Parnes on the Athenian side of the Attic/Boeotian boundary. There they waited until their numbers rose to seven hundred; in spring they moved down to Piraeus, joining the dissidents there and establishing themselves on the hill of Munychia. Critias and his men attempted to dislodge them in an uphill charge, and in the attempt Critias died.

Thrasybulus' call for peace and union between the two camps was rejected by the oligarchs, who expected Spartan aid. In Sparta, however, the murderous arrogance of Lysander and his associates was making many powerful men nervous, including the kings Agis and Pausanias. Marching into Attica, Pausanias took the lead and masterminded not only the reconciliation of the various Athenian parties but also the temporary eclipse of Lysander. Under his aegis the Athenians agreed on the first recorded amnesty in history. Under its terms, only the Thirty and their chief officers could be brought to justice for crimes committed before 403; all others were compelled to renounce the many bitter grievances that had accumulated. In September Thrasybulus led his men unopposed to the Acropolis, where they sacrificed to Athena in gratitude for the salvation of the city and their own safe return. The work of reestablishing the democracy then began.

The Trial of Socrates (399 BC)

The Athenians came close to respecting the terms of the amnesty upon which they had agreed. Nonetheless, decades of war followed by months of terror under the Thirty had taken a heavy toll, and there was no lack of people eager to assign blame for Athens' problems. The colorful Socrates had annoyed jealous parents whose young sons had lionized him, and though the Athenians were averse to breaking the amnesty law, some were open to bending it. Raw from the devastating war and frustrated by the change they saw in the world around them, three Athenians—Anytus, Meletus, and Lycon—zeroed in on this eccentric old philosopher who haunted the public spaces of Athens confuting the careless in argument. Socrates (470–399 BC) had been quick to identify the drawbacks of democracy, and he had also been the teacher of (at least) two men who in different ways had harmed Athens: Alcibiades and Critias. The amnesty prevented his accusers from charging Socrates with inciting his pupils to treason, so instead they brought a three-pronged accusation of a kind somewhat unusual in Athens. Socrates, they claimed, did not believe in the gods of the state; he taught new gods; and he corrupted the young.

Though this sort of charge was unusual at Athens, precedents were not lacking. Greek states had no constitutional principles separating church and state or protecting free speech. Because of his naturalistic explanation of the universe and his sophisticated conception of divinity as *Nous*, Anaxagoras had been forced to leave Athens to avoid possible execution for atheism. This accusation, however, which was lodged at the same time as Aspasia's trial for impiety, was plainly political in its motivation. The same must be said about the trial of Socrates, though no doubt the ironic manner that charmed some and infuriated others played a role as well.

Since Socrates never wrote anything, we are dependent for our conception of him on the dialogues of his admirers Plato and Xenophon. Plato's pupil Aristotle observed about Socrates that the two things one could be certain of attributing to him were inductive reasoning and universal definition. We can be sure of a few other things. Socrates, an Athenian citizen, performed conventional civic services in Athens, fighting as a hoplite at Potidaea, Delium, and Amphipolis in the Peloponnesian War and serving as president of the assembly on the day of the Arginusae trial in 406. His avocation was discussing interesting philosophical questions with young men, questions that focused on the best way for humans to think and live; at least in his mature years, he was not particularly excited by natural science. He believed that the best way to develop ideas was in the give and take of conversation, and that the best way to educate people was to ask them a series of questions leading in a particular direction (now named for him "the Socratic method"). However painful it might be to find oneself the object of injustice, he was firmly convinced that doing wrong oneself was the only real misfortune that could befall a person. He had a keen wit and an engaging personality, and pupils flocked to him eagerly, though he had nothing that could be called a school. He was not a sophist; he became poor through his refusal to charge fees, and his goal was to inculcate moral excellence, which he viewed as the particular excellence of a human being. Like the sophists, however, he used clever arguments and subjected conventional notions to rational analysis, and like them he disrupted the customary bond that placed education in the context of the family, wounding Athenian parents whose sons preferred his company to theirs—and who gave his ideas greater credence. Whom, Socrates asks Meletus in Xenophon's rendition of his defense speech, do I corrupt? "By God," Meletus replies, "I know some—those you've persuaded to obey you rather than their parents." (Xenophon, *Apology of Socrates* 20) It is not peculiar, therefore, that he was mistaken for a sophist, or that the sophists' shady reputation should have rubbed off on him. He was parodied in Aristophanes' *Clouds*, which showed him carried across the sky in a crane in a flaky educational establishment known as a "think shop."

He also spoke sharply about democracy. Whether it is fair to say that he opposed it and would have liked to see a different regime instituted at Athens is another question. Socrates enjoyed puncturing illusions, and it may be that had he lived under a monarchy or an oligarchy, those would have been the governments he spent his time undermining. But if anything can safely be gathered from Plato's dialogues, then Socrates was troubled by the notion of amateur government, in which anyone's opinion counted for as much as the next man's and in which a volatile assembly was swayed this way and that by rhetorical displays. Most people, he pointed out, aren't terribly thoughtful or analytical, so why should "most people," that is, the majority, make the life and death decisions that affect the polis?

This is a question any advocate of democracy must ask, and Socrates' insistence on asking it need not be taken as implying that he wanted decisions made by a minority. Combined with his association with Alcibiades and Critias, however, his pointed remarks about the foibles of democracy seemed downright unpatriotic, and he could easily enough be cast as a purveyor of dangerous ideas.

By Athenian custom, Socrates' trial took only one day. It is intolerably painful for most readers of Plato's *Apology of Socrates* to believe that the words written down by Plato were not actually spoken at Socrates' trial. Perhaps they were, and perhaps they weren't; Xenophon's account of Socrates' speech, also called the *Apology*, is less inspiring and much thinner. (The Greek word *apology* does not connote "apologizing" in the modern sense but rather means a refutation.) Plato's rendition contains the famous dictum that "the unexamined life is not worth living" and constitutes an extraordinarily moving paean to intellectual freedom and the life of the mind. Shunning the strategy that he identifies as standard procedure in an Athenian courtroom—weeping, pleading, parading his children in front of the jury—Socrates, according to Plato, took the position that the best defense was a strong offense. Using the question and answer method for which he was famous and which had apparently gotten him into trouble, he demolished his accusers by demonstrating the inconsistencies in their allegations and then went on to explain in poignant detail the great service provided to the state by his relentless probing. His service to the state, he argues, is precious and irreplaceable. It is, literally, a godsend:

> Know that if you kill me, I being such a man as I say I am, you will not injure me so much as yourselves; for neither Meletus nor Anytus could injure me; that would be impossible, for I believe it is not the gods' will that a better man be injured by a worse . . . . For if you put me to death, you will not easily find another, who, to use a rather absurd figure, attaches himself to the city as a gadfly to a horse, which, though large and well bred, is sluggish on account of his size and needs to be aroused by stinging. I think the god fastened me upon the city in some such capacity, and I go about arousing, and urging and reproaching each one of you, constantly alighting upon you everywhere the whole day long. Such another is not likely to come to you, gentlemen; but if you take my advice, you will spare me. But you, perhaps, might be angry, like people awakened from a nap, and might slap me, as Anytus advises, and easily kill me; then you would pass the rest of your lives in slumber, unless the god, in his care for you, should send someone else to sting you.
>
> (*Apology 30C–31A; Fowler 1966, adapted*)

Socrates persuaded nearly half the jury of 501 Athenian citizens; he seems to have lost his case by about thirty votes. Meletus, the principal accuser, had proposed the penalty of death. Athenian procedure called for convicted defendants to recommend an alternative penalty, and it seems clear that Socrates' accusers expected him to propose exile—and would have been quite content to see him leave town. Instead, he provoked the jury by suggesting rather that the Athenians should provide him with free meals for the rest of his life as their benefactor, just as they did for Olympic victors. Xenophon ascribed this strategy to Socrates' wish to end a satisfying life before the sad realities of old age overtook him; it is also possible that Socrates was testing the jury to see if they understood who he really was and what he really provided to Athens. A number of those who had wanted him acquitted had a change of heart and voted for the death penalty. Socrates was then executed by one of the customary Athenian methods, being ordered to down a poisonous draft of hemlock.

At his trial, if we are to believe Plato, Socrates prophesied that the Athenians would bring great odium on themselves for killing him. He was right. Throughout subsequent history, the execution of Socrates is the most serious charge that has been brought by the critics of Athenian democracy. Socrates' death also made a deep impression on his brightest disciples, young aristocrats like Xenophon and Plato. Though Xenophon's works are little read today, they were very popular in ancient Rome and during the Renaissance. The dialogues Plato began soon after his teacher's death, in which Socrates served as a mouthpiece for his own thinking, became the foundation of western philosophy. In this way the strains occasioned by the Peloponnesian War played a dramatic role in the history of ideas.

THE WAR IN RETROSPECT

There was nothing inevitable about the Spartans' ultimate victory in the war. Darius of Persia died in 404. Had the Athenians not been so careless at Aegospotami, the withdrawal of Persian support that would probably have attended on Darius' death would gravely have compromised the Spartans' chances of winning the war. On the other hand, the Spartans—although not as quickly as prudence would have dictated—did in time learn a vital lesson about the centrality of naval power. The anonymous treatise written sometime during the later fifth century by the so-called Old Oligarch (once confused with Xenophon) had judged sea power superior to power on land. The Athenians, the author argued, did well to sacrifice the development of their infantry to that of their navy. For it is possible, he wrote,

> for small subject cities on the mainland to unite and form a single army, but in a sea empire it is not possible for those who are islanders to combine their forces, for the sea divides them, and their rulers control the sea. . . . Further, it is possible for the rulers of the sea to do what land powers cannot always do; they can ravage the land of more powerful states. They can sail along the coast to an area where the enemy forces are few or non-existent, and if the enemy approach they can embark and sail away; in this way they get into less difficulty than those operating on land. Then again, the rulers of the sea can sail as far as you like from their own land, but land powers cannot make lengthy expeditions from their own territory, for marching is slow, and it is not possible to take provisions for a long period when travelling on foot. Also, a land force must march through friendly territory or win a passage by force, but a naval force can disembark where it is stronger and not do so where it is not, but sail on until it reaches friendly territory or a less powerful state.
>
> ([Pseudo-Xenophon] The Constitution of Athenians 3–4; Moore 1975)

When Sparta became a sea power, the Athenians lost this advantage, lost the war, and lost their empire.

The economic consequences of the war were grave. Except in Sparta proper, where helots continued to till the land and no foreign force dared invade, agriculture suffered terribly. The redoubled labor of women and slaves was insufficient fully to compensate for the death or absence of farmers on long campaigns far from home, and a good deal of territory (in Attica on the Athenian side and Megara on the Peloponnesian, for example) was regularly ravaged by the enemy.

Livestock and farming implements were destroyed. Vines took several years of nurture before they would produce a rich crop of grapes, and damage wrought by the destruction of olive trees was even longer lasting: though cuttings carefully grafted onto damaged trees or stumps might produce enough olives for a small family in five or ten years, newly planted trees generally took about fifteen years to produce a salable crop. Commerce by land and sea was disrupted; cities like Corinth suffered immensely.

Unlike the overseas wars of the Roman republic, which enriched the few while impoverishing the many, the Peloponnesian War hurt everyone. Throughout Greece poverty pushed a significant number of men beneath the hoplite census. Some men took service as mercenaries, an increasingly popular profession. As usually happens in wartime, many women were forced to work outside the home. Population also dropped in many parts of the Greek world, and the loss of thousands upon thousands of soldiers and sailors left many women without husbands. In the play named for her and produced in 411, Aristophanes' protagonist Lysistrata, who has organized the wives of Greece in a sex strike to force an end to the fighting, is scandalized when a magistrate complains about uppity behavior on the part of women "who bore no share in the war":

> None, you hopeless hypocrite?
> The quota we bear is double. First, we delivered our sons
> to fill out the front lines in Sicily. . . .
> Next, the best years of our lives were levied. Top-level strategy
> attached our joy, and we sleep alone.
> But it's not the matrons
> like us who matter. I mourn for the virgins, bedded in single
> blessedness, with nothing to do but grow old.

Men, the Commissioner protests,

> *have* been known

to age, as well as women.

No, Lysistrata replies,

> not as well as—better.
> A man, an absolute antique, comes back from the war, and he's
> barely
> doddered into town before he's married the veriest nymphet.
> But a woman's season is brief; it slips, and she'll have no husband,
> but sit out her life groping at omens—and finding no men.
>> (Lysistrata, *pp. 587–589, 591–597; Parker 1964*)

In Athens alone, as many as fifty thousand people probably died of the plague, many of them doing so before they could reproduce. War casualties seem to have included at least five thousand hoplite soldiers and twelve thousand sailors (including some three thousand executed by Lysander after Aegospotami), and the Thirty Tyrants of 404–403 apparently killed some fifteen hundred citizens, perhaps many more. Probably the number of adult male citizens in 403 was half what it had been in 431. Some cities, like Melos and Scione, had been virtually annihilated. In Sparta, absolute numbers dropped less sharply, but the various classes began to redefine themselves, as the ranks of commanders as well as soldiers were swelled not only by distinguished mothakes but also by helot fighters rewarded with freedom and land and known as *neodamōdeis* ("new citizens").

The long war also undermined what one scholar has called the "Polis-citizen axis." Whether Thucydides was right to identify a single war as lasting from 431 to 404 remains an open question, perhaps one that can never be resolved: where one war stops and another begins may be a subject more for philosophers than for diplomatic historians. But he was correct to envision something unprecedented about these decades of conflict. For until this time Greek warfare had observed almost courtly rules of play. When winter came, fighting ceased; using citizens for fighting in farming season violated both decorum and common sense. There was a time to plow and a time to fight, and it was not the same time. Previously in Greek history important conflicts and even so-called wars could be decided by brief hoplite encounters on level ground. The growth of Athenian naval power had begun to change this, but never before the Peloponnesian War had fighting become the central fact of life in both hot and cold weather. The Battle of Delium took place in winter, as did the climactic naval battle in the Syracusan harbor. Thucydides lost Amphipolis to Brasidas in the snow. Brasidas, moreover, had with him seven hundred helots and numerous mercenaries. The use of mercenaries and the periodic emergency enfranchisement of helots and slaves—there were one thousand neodamodeis in Sparta by 421 and probably at least fifteen hundred by the end of the war—blurred the lines that had traditionally divided citizens from noncitizens and eroded the concept of the citizen-soldier and the citizen-sailor, and the frequency of bloody civil strife eroded the concept of the polis itself. Aristophanes' Trygaeus at the doorstep of Zeus was not the only Greek to inquire how it could be that the gods would allow Greece to be consumed by a war of this scope. At the same time, however, the shattering of faith fostered a questioning spirit that opened the door to the reflections of Socrates, Xenophon, and Plato. The Peloponnesian War transformed the Greek world, but it did not destroy it.

TRANSLATIONS

Blanco, Walter. 1998. *The Peloponnesian War*, from Walter Blanco and Jennifer Roberts, eds. *Thucydides: The Peloponnesian War*, New York: W.W. Norton.

Fowler, H. N. 1966. *The Apology of Socrates* in *Plato: Euthyphro, Apology, Crito, Phaedo, Phaedrus*. Loeb Classical Library. Cambridge, Mass. and London: Harvard University Press.

Moore, J. M. 1975. *The Constitution of the Athenians Ascribed to Xenophon the Orator* in *Aristotle and Xenophon on Democracy and Oligarchy*. Berkeley: University of California Press.

Parker, Douglass. 1964. *Lysistrata*. New York and Scarsborough, Ontario: Mentor.

Rackham, H. 1961. *Aristotle: The Athenian Constitution*, in *The Athenian Constitution; The Eudemian Ethics; On Virtues and Vices*. Loeb Classical Library. Cambridge, Mass. and London: Harvard University Press.

Scott-Kilvert, Ian. 1960. *The Rise and Fall of Athens: Nine Greek Lives by Plutarch.* Harmondsworth, England: Penguin.

Warner, Rex. 1979. *Xenophon: A History of My Times [The Hellenica].* Harmondsworth, England: Penguin.

SUGGESTED READINGS

Connor, W. Robert. 1992. *The New Politicians of Fifth Century Athens.* Indianapolis: Hackett. A nuanced but highly readable examination of the changing dynamics of Athenian political life in the fifth century.

De Romilly, Jacqueline. 1988. *Thucydides and Athenian Imperialism.* Trans. P. Thody. Reprinted Salem, N.H.: Ayer Co. Publishers. A classic study of Thucydides and the empire.

Ehrenberg, Victor. 1974. *The People of Aristophanes.* Reprinted New York: Barnes & Noble. A study of the sociology and economics of the Athenian state based on a close examination of data in Aristophanes' comedies.

Green, Peter. 1970. *Armada from Athens.* London: Hodder and Stoughton. A spirited account of the Athenian invasion of Sicily by a distinguished ancient historian.

Hansen, Mogens Herman. 1995. *The Trial of Socrates from the Athenian Point of View.* Copenhagen: The Royal Danish Academy of Sciences and Letters. Discussion of the sources, a reconstruction of the trial, and an investigation of the political background of the prosecution.

Hornblower, Simon. 1986. *Thucydides.* Baltimore: Johns Hopkins University Press. A penetrating study of the "historian's historian."

Kagan, Donald. 1974, 1981, 1987. *The Archidamian War (1974), The Peace of Nicias and the Sicilian Expedition (1981),* and *The Fall of the Athenian Empire (1987).* Ithaca, N.Y.: Cornell University Press. These three volumes offer a detailed analysis of the war's military and diplomatic history.

Loraux, Nicole. 1986. *The Invention of Athens: The Funeral Oration in the Classical City.* Trans. Alan Sheridan. Cambridge, Mass., and London: Harvard University Press. An examination of the key role of the Athenian funeral oration in shaping ideals of civic life and defining what Athens was all about.

Meiggs, Russell. 1972. *The Athenian Empire.* Oxford: Oxford University Press. A history of Athens' relationship with its allies from the inception of the Delian League to the end of the Peloponnesian War, with chapters on the judgments made on the empire in both the fifth and fourth centuries and a chart recording tribute payments for the years 453 to 420.

Strauss, Barry. 1993. *Fathers and Sons in Athens: Ideology and Society in the Era of the Peloponnesian War.* Princeton, N.J.: Princeton University Press. A sensitive analysis of Athenian society during the last decades of the fifth century that grounds conflict in intergenerational tension.

9

THE CRISIS OF THE POLIS AND THE AGE OF SHIFTING HEGEMONIES

The long Peloponnesian War wrought changes in the Greek world so far-reaching that it is impossible to imagine the course of history without it. To be sure, fourth-century Greeks continued to farm and weave and fight, and the politically aware polis remained the primary unit of government for several generations. Years of futile warfare, however, accompanied by economic difficulties and attendant civil strife led many people to question their relationship to the world around them. Already around the middle of the fifth century Greek thinkers had begun to ask key questions about the human community. What was the purpose of civic life? Why had people come together in communities in the first place? Were the laws of the polis in accord with nature or in conflict with it? Why were some people free and others slaves? How were Greeks different from non-Greeks? Should Greeks war with other Greeks and enslave them when victorious?

To these questions others came to be added. Why should some have so much more than others? Did the autonomous city-state provide the best way of life? Did the exclusion of women from decision-making go without saying? Was warfare worth the sacrifices it entailed? A smaller group debated larger questions— the nature of justice, of piety, of courage, of love. Though many of these concerns had engaged fifth-century minds, the postwar generations were more prone to this kind of questioning and less confident that they lived in the best of all possible worlds. New genres took the place of the old as the search for meaning in life moved forward on different paths: whereas the painful issues of human existence had been explored during the fifth century in tragedy and history, fourth-century thinkers developed the philosophical dialogue and treatise.

While many Greeks were subjecting their traditional values to scrutiny, others perpetuated the squabbles of the fifth century. The Peloponnesian War had solved nothing. In many poleis the economic problems arising from the war exacerbated existing class tensions and sparked bloody civil conflict, though the Athenian democracy remained remarkably free of stasis. Interpolis warfare continued to be the order of the day, and civil strife—often very bloody—was extremely common. The eager involvement of Persia heightened an already chaotic situation. When an extraordinary individual arose to the north in the form of Philip of Macedon, the inability of the Greeks to work together productively had dramatic consequences, and the autonomous polis ceased to be the defining political institution of the Greek world.

SOURCES FOR FOURTH-CENTURY GREECE

In almost all respects the sources for the political history of the fourth century are richer than for the fifth. A wealth of inscriptions sheds light on both international relations and domestic policy, and Aristophanes' *Ecclesiazusae* (*Women in Congress*) and *Plutus* (*Wealth*) provide valuable information about Athens' troubles in the generation after Aegospotami. Plutarch's biographies of the Spartans Lysander and Agesilaus and of the Theban Pelopidas survive; unfortunately the life of Epaminondas is lost. Much can be gleaned from the vast body of miscellany gathered together in the collection known as Plutarch's *Moralia*, though some material has crept in from other authors.

Attic oratory provides a vital window into the lives and thought patterns of fourth-century Athenians. Unfortunately no comparable body of texts has survived from any other polis. Dozens of speeches written for delivery in Athens— sometimes to the courts, sometimes to the assembly—reveal the political, social, and economic situation in the city. Numerous speeches have been preserved under the name of the metic Lysias, though some of them may really be by others. The speech Andocides gave when he served as ambassador during the Corinthian War is very useful. Of the many speeches attributed to Isocrates, about half of the twenty-one that survive were composed during the period between the end of the Peloponnesian War and the rise of Macedon. Those written later, moreover (Isocrates lived to be 98 and continued writing until his death in 338 BC), also contain useful perspectives on the previous decades. Indeed, orators active primarily after the accession of Philip of Macedon in 359 provide some of our most precious information about the half century after the end of the Peloponnesian War. Most prominent among these is Demosthenes (384–322 BC), dozens of whose speeches survive. (He is of course a different person from the fifth-century general by the same name who was executed in Sicily.) Even the speeches that seem to have been wrongly attributed to Demosthenes comprise a valuable compendium of detail about Greek law.

Speeches, however, must be used with even more caution than is generally exercised with sources. Though a priceless index to the values of the community, and dotted with allusions to historical events, they aimed at persuasion, not truth, and the so-called information they contain must be regarded with some skepticism. There were no professional lawyers in Athens, moreover; those who had to appear in court simply hired trained rhetoricians to write speeches for them. Not surprisingly, the laws embedded in these rhetorical displays were often quoted partially or inaccurately, since the speech writers could not be held to account for their misrepresentations. Even as late as the fourth century, Greek culture retained a thick overlay of orality, and the notion of verification by reference to documents was not so firmly entrenched as it is today.

No history of the fourth century survives that can match that of Herodotus or Thucydides in either painstaking research or depth of analysis. One gifted historian wrote during the fourth century, but his work is almost entirely lost; a little on the Peloponnesian War and on the years 397 to 395 is all that survives of the writer known as the Oxyrhynchus historian because the fragments of his work were found amidst other papyri at the Egyptian village of Oxyrhynchus. Only fragments survive of Ephorus, Theopompus, and the Sicilian Philistus, though Ephorus was apparently the principal source for Diodorus' account of this period, and much of Philistus' work (greatly admired in antiquity) found its way into Diodorus' account of affairs in his native Sicily. In the absence of fuller contemporary sources, therefore, we are thrown back chiefly on Xenophon.

A lively and innovative writer, Xenophon had a hardy partiality for Sparta even at its more disgraceful moments that sometimes mars the account he gives of Greek history in his *Hellenica*. We are nonetheless indebted to his narrative for much information that would otherwise have been lost; the same is true of his encomiastic biography *Agesilaus*. His *Ways and Means* provides valuable insight into Athens' economic difficulties in the fourth century. The *Anabasis*, the account of his experiences with fellow mercenaries in Persia, is an incomparable eyewitness source for Greco-Persian interaction. The *Cyropaedia*, a historical romance based on the life of Cyrus the Great, tells us a great deal about Greek perceptions of Persia. Various dialogues in which Socrates appears reveal a good deal about the values of Xenophon's social class, and may even tell us a bit about Socrates.

Socrates, like Jesus, expressed himself in speech and wrote nothing. Most of Plato's work consists of conversations Plato has imaginatively "reconstructed," in which someone he calls Socrates leads one or more young men to a greater understanding of some subject. Aristotle was still more prolific. Ancient estimates of Aristotle's prodigious output ranged from four hundred to one thousand different works. Though many are lost and some are thought to be the work of his students, the Aristotelian corpus fills several volumes.

POSTWAR GREECE AND THE STRUGGLE FOR HEGEMONY

There had been nothing inevitable about Sparta's victory in the Peloponnesian War. The Athenians might well have won had events turned out just a little differently. Consequently the poleis of Greece watched Sparta's self-aggrandizement warily. The economic situation of the Greek cities, though it varied from one polis to the next, seemed to favor war. On the one hand, the long years of fighting at the end of the fifth century had harmed the economy of many Greek states sufficiently to create a desire for both booty and revenge; at the same time, however, the postwar poleis showed remarkable resilience, and within less than ten years from the end of the Peloponnesian War, the economy had rebounded sufficiently for people to contemplate new military undertakings. The economy, in short, was bad enough for many people to want war and good enough for them to consider it. It was not long after the war that the hostility of the Greek states found a focus, and that focus was Sparta.

Spartans were noble in death but insufferable in victory. Plutarch, as we have seen, enjoyed reporting the disappointment Spartan mothers professed if a son made the mistake of surviving a battle, and Xenophon told of the heroic fortitude of the Spartans in hearing of their resounding defeat at the hands of the Thebans in 371: the next day, he wrote, "you could see those whose relatives had been killed going about in public looking bright and happy, while as for those whose relatives had been reported living, there were not many of them to be seen, and those who were to be seen were walking about looking gloomy and sorry for themselves" (*Hellenica* 6.4.16; Warner 1966). The protocol for dealing with victory, however, was more elusive. Though at first their hoplites continued to do well on the battlefield, a graceless diplomacy regularly led the Spartans to lose the peace after winning the war. In time, Sparta's aggressive foreign policy would spark a counterattack that would also end the myth of Spartan invincibility on the battlefield.

Jubilant after bringing Athens to its knees in 404, Sparta housed significant imperialist factions supporting the aggressive policies of Lysander and King Agesilaus. In 395 Sparta's alienated allies combined against it. The resulting war ended in 387, but continuing high-handed behavior on Sparta's part caused existing resentments to fester. In 377 Agesilaus' provocative policies resulted both in the formation of a new Athenian naval confederacy and in the alliance of Athens and Thebes. By 371 Thebes was strong enough to defeat Sparta on the battlefield, and the years that followed saw the Thebans cripple Sparta still further by the liberation of Messenia. The Thebans' ascendancy died, however, when their charismatic leader Epaminondas was killed in battle, and revolts during the 360s and 350s gradually weakened the Athenian confederacy. The resulting vacuum would be filled by Macedon under the resolute leadership of Philip.

The New Imperialists of Sparta

Though details about their collapse are lacking, the murderous decarchies Lysander established in the wake of Aegospotami seem to have been short-lived. Sparta's interference in the domestic affairs of its allies, however, continued. Just as the imperialist Athenians had always preferred democracies in allied states, so the Spartans of the postwar period sought to establish oligarchies wherever possible—by military intervention if necessary. Alarmed by this proclivity, the Thebans declined to help their Spartan allies when King Agis II marched on Elis around 400 in order to compel the democratic government there to grant independence to the outlying cities in its control. Bad feeling increased when Agis died and Lysander engineered the succession of the king's brother, his friend Agesilaus. When Agesilaus, planning to invade Asia, tried to lend legitimacy to his crusade by sacrificing at Aulis, just as Agamemnon had done en route to Troy, the Boeotian cavalry was dispatched to stand in his way. Agesilaus never forgot the insult, and he lived a long time. The next decades saw frequent warfare between Sparta and Thebes.

The genesis of Agesilaus' journey to Asia is significant in a number of respects. Sparta's relations with Persia began to deteriorate when Lysander's ally Cyrus the Younger became enmeshed in a quarrel over the succession. When his brother Artaxerxes succeeded Darius II in 404, Cyrus mounted a rebellion for which he engaged thirteen thousand Greek mercenaries. Though Cyrus' army was successful at the pivotal battle of Cunaxa near Babylon in 401, in the hour of victory Cyrus caught sight of his brother and, losing control, attempted to kill him. He was promptly cut down in the ensuing melee. This untoward development left his Greek soldiers in an extraordinarily vulnerable situation, deep in the heart of a huge empire whose king they had just attempted to overthrow. Their circumstances deteriorated still further when the Spartan Clearchus and the other Greek generals, having been hospitably received by the satrap Tissaphernes, were treacherously murdered.

In desperate straits they elected new leaders, one of whom was Xenophon the Athenian. Acting as a mobile polis under this new leadership, they managed to complete the arduous march back to the sea and sail back to their homes in Greece. Xenophon's lively account of their adventures in this "march up-country" (*Anabasis*) survives intact and has provided entertainment and excitement for generations of intermediate Greek students (as well as anthropologists and zoologists). Xenophon's contemporaries, however, found news of the Greeks' experience in Asia to be more than entertaining. It was also profoundly instructive. What it taught was that the Persian empire was by no means as formidable an adversary as Greeks had imagined. In time, this knowledge would issue in the campaigns of Alexander, campaigns that would transform the civilizations of Greece, Egypt, and western Asia. In the short run, it prompted Agesilaus to invade Asia. With Cyrus dead, prospects for friendship with Persia had waned. Now there would be war instead.

While Agesilaus and his men fought in Asia Minor, the Spartans continued to alienate their allies in mainland Greece by intervention in domestic affairs, marching on Messenian Naupactus, for example, and Heraclea Trachinia near Thermopylae. When nearly a decade had passed since the end of the Peloponnesian War and the economies of the mainland states had managed a partial recovery, Sparta's longtime allies Thebes and Corinth were open to allying with their old enemy Athens against Sparta. At this juncture one Timocrates of Rhodes appeared in Greece bearing gold from the Persian king: eager to get Agesilaus off his back, Artaxerxes was prepared to disburse this money to those who would make war on Sparta.

The Corinthian War (395–387 BC)

The war that ensued was known as the Corinthian War, since much of the fighting took place in the area of the isthmus. It pitted Sparta against a coalition of Athens, Thebes, Corinth, and Argos. The first consequence of this futile war was the death of Lysander, who was killed fighting at its outset. The Persians then got their wish: Sparta recalled Agesilaus from Asia. Meanwhile the Persian navy commanded by the satrap Pharnabazus and the Athenian admiral Conon won a decisive victory over Sparta at Cnidus (394 BC) in southwest Asia Minor. Feeling secure at last from the odium that had attached to all who had been present at Aegospotami, Conon now returned to Athens and played a large part in re-building the Long Walls there. In this project he was assisted by Persian ships and money.

Loss of life in the ongoing war was considerable. About four thousand men were killed fighting by the Nemea River in the northeast Peloponnesus in 394, the largest hoplite battle Greeks had ever fought. Eventually the Spartans persuaded the Persians to ally with them by offering, once more, to abandon the Greeks of Asia Minor to Persian domination. Peace negotiations initiated in 392 failed, however, and fighting continued.

To the hoplite warfare of these years was added a crucial new element—a variety of lightly armed troops including archers, slingers, and javelin throwers. A particularly useful brand of javelin thrower was the man known as the peltast, named for the small round wicker shield he carried, the Thracian *peltē*. Enjoying a mobility unthinkable for the hoplites with their heavy shields and armor, peltasts and other lightly armed soldiers expanded the possibilities of warfare. They could be deployed to forage for supplies, to seize and defend passes, to ambush enemy troops, and to ravage enemy territory. They also played key roles in what were basically hoplite confrontations, for harassment at a distance by javelin-throwing peltasts made it difficult for the heavily armed enemy hoplites to retreat. A hardy band of peltasts backing up a hoplite force could easily turn the tide of battle.

Perhaps because of their history of success at hoplite warfare, the Spartans never really learned to make use of light-armed troops—and this despite a harsh lesson administered in 390, when harassment by peltasts in the command of the Athenian Iphicrates enabled the Athenians to destroy an entire Spartan regiment at the Corinthian port of Lechaeum. The Spartan commander, Xenophon reports,

> ordered the infantry in the age groups 20 to 30 to charge and drive off their attackers. However, they were hoplites pursuing peltasts at the distance of a javelin's throw, and they failed to catch anyone, since Iphicrates had ordered his men to fall back before the hoplites came to close quarters. But when the Spartans, in loose order because each man had been running at his own speed, turned back again from the pursuit, Iphicrates' men wheeled round, some hurling their javelins again from in front while others ran up along the flank, shooting at the side unprotected by the shields. . . . Then, as things were going very badly, [the Spartan commander] ordered another pursuit, this time with the men of the age

groups 20 to 35. But in falling back from this pursuit even more men were killed than before. . . .

After a while, Xenophon continues, the Spartans were

> at their wits' end, suffering as they were and being destroyed without being able to do anything about it; and now when, in addition to all this, they saw the hoplites bearing down on them, they broke and ran. Some plunged into the sea. . . .
> (Hellenica 4.5.15–18; Warner 1966)

This remarkable achievement stunned the Greek world. It also made the reputation of Iphicrates. Subsequently elected on numerous occasions to the *stratēgia*, Iphicrates became one of Athens' best-known generals. In time he introduced longer swords and light, comfortable boots that came to be called Iphicratides.

Mercenary service and the popularity of light armed troops frequently went hand in hand: the lesser cost of the light wicker shield made service as a peltast more appealing to the impoverished landless men who chose to support themselves as soldiers of fortune. Like mercenaries, lightly armed soldiers had been used throughout the later fifth century. Having learned of their potential from his painful experiences with the Aetolians, Demosthenes had made sure to deploy them at Pylos and Sphacteria, where they were crucial to the Athenians' success. As in so many areas, what appear as distinguishing characteristics of the fourth century in fact had their roots in the Peloponnesian War.

In 387 the exhausted Greeks agreed to a peace negotiated in Persia. This agreement was the first of several fourth-century attempts at what Diodorus, following Ephorus, called a *koinē eirenē* ("common peace"), a peace applicable to all poleis and whose overriding principle was that of autonomy. Throughout the fourth century, intellectuals and politicians expressed longing for such a peace. The form this particular peace took, however, was calculated to drive home to the Greeks the Persian king's clout in Hellenic affairs. The text appears in Xenophon's *Hellenica*:

> I, King Artaxerxes, regard the following arrangements as just: 1. The cities in Asia and, among the islands, Clazomenae and Cyprus should belong to me. 2. The other Greek cities, big and small, should be left to govern themselves, except for Lemnus, Imbros and Scyros, which should belong to Athens, as in the past. And if either of the two parties refuses to accept peace on these terms, I, together with those who will accept this peace, will make war on that party both by land and by sea, with ships and with money.
> (Hellenica 5.1.31; Warner 1966)

Negotiations nearly broke down over the thorny question of the Boeotian League. When the Thebans wanted to ratify the treaty on behalf of all Boeotia, Agesilaus demanded that they swear to leave all the Boeotian cities autonomous. Meeting resistance, he began mobilizing forces to invade Boeotia. In the face of a Spartan attack, the Thebans grudgingly agreed to Agesilaus' terms. Future developments would show, however, that their ambitions had not subsided.

Greece After the King's Peace

The governing principle of the King's Peace was autonomy. Ironically, Sparta as Persia's ally was cast as the guarantor of this peace despite the fact that it was Spartan disregard for the autonomy of other Greek states that had sparked the war in the first place. In the guise of enforcing autonomy, Sparta promptly set about using force and threats of force to dismantle a variety of existing arrangements in Greece. Since the long-standing Boeotian League was dominated by Thebes, its disintegration had given Agesilaus particular pleasure. During the war Corinth and Argos had undertaken a curious experiment in "isopolity" whereby citizenship and its privileges were shared by both states in a novel form of union. Sparta demanded its dissolution. When Phlius declined to change its government in response to Spartan pressure, it was besieged and ultimately forced to replace its government with that of pro-Spartan exiles. Mantinea, composed of five villages, was compelled to tear down its fortifications and dissolve itself into the five original communities.

All this was as nothing, however, to Sparta's seizure of the city of Thebes. During the 380s the Thebans were divided between a pro-Spartan faction led by Leontiades and a pro-Athenian group led by Ismenias, and in 382 Leontiades persuaded the Spartan commander Phoebidas to occupy the Theban acropolis called the Cadmea and install a pro-Spartan government. Phoebidas' actions sparked outrage throughout Greece. Though the Spartans brought Phoebidas to trial, Agesilaus argued for his acquittal on the grounds that the only criterion for judging Phoebidas' behavior should be its usefulness to Sparta. Phoebidas got off with a small fine, and the Spartan garrison remained on the Cadmea. Equally shocking to Greeks was the trial at Thebes of Ismenias, whom the pro-Spartan government executed on charges of conspiring with Persia and accepting Persian money. Sparta's own record of collaboration with Persia made this turn of events particularly scandalous.

In 379 seven of the partisans of Ismenias who had taken refuge in Athens slipped unnoticed into Boeotia and, linking up with fellow conspirators there, were brought to the magistrates disguised as women who had been supplied for their delectation. Drawing their weapons, they easily overpowered and killed the oligarchs; proceeding to the house of Leontiades they killed him as well. The next day two Athenian generals and their regiments appeared, probably as volunteers, and helped the Theban patriots expel the Spartan garrison on the Cadmea.

The Spartans promptly sent out their young king Cleombrotus at the head of an expedition. Though he was unable to do anything about the situation in Thebes, his campaign had important consequences. Alarmed by the Spartan military presence, the Athenians brought the two generals who had helped the Thebans retake their city to trial, executing the one who turned up for his hearing and exiling the other. Though the generals' assistance to the Thebans had probably been of an unofficial nature, still it was reprehensible for the Athenians to punish them in this way for implementing a policy the Athenian state surely approved.

The trial of the generals contrasted not only with the light sentence meted out to Phoebidas in Sparta a few years before but also with a mockery of a trial that followed a few months later. In 378 Sphodrias, the harmost (governor) whom Cleombrotus had left behind in Boeotia, decided that a night march could bring him to Piraeus by dawn, and he plotted to seize the port for Sparta. He miscalculated: a night march brought him as far as the Thriasian plain near Eleusis. His plan to seize Piraeus came to nothing, and the Athenians were furious. Immediately they seized some Spartan envoys who happened to be at Athens, but they released them when the envoys assured them that Sphodrias had acted without authorization and would surely be executed at Sparta. Nothing of the kind happened. Sphodrias' son and Agesilaus' son were lovers, and Agesilaus engineered Sphodrias' acquittal.

Sparta, Athens, and Thebes

Enraged at Sparta's failure to punish Sphodrias and deeply sorry they had let the Spartan envoys go, the Athenians now allied with the Thebans for mutual protection against Sparta. They also moved forward with their plans to establish the new naval league that historians call the Second Athenian Confederacy, plans that had probably begun to take shape even before the Sphodrias fiasco. Learning from history, the Athenians conceived the new league along lines very different from the old one. The decree proposed by Aristoteles setting up the league included in its preamble the statement that the assembly was taking this action "so that the Spartans may allow the Greeks to live in peace, free and autonomous, with all their territory secure" and so that the peace of 387 "may remain in force forever." All allies, the decree proclaimed, "will remain independent and autonomous, enjoying the form of government they wish, admitting no garrisons or magistrates and paying no tribute." Athenians were prohibited from acquiring property in allied territory. The total number of states in the alliance was somewhere between sixty and seventy. League members came from all over the Aegean and western Greece. They included about thirty-five former members of the Delian League, a noteworthy development that must be thrown in with the other evidence for the popularity of Athens' first experiment in league leadership.

League policy was to be controlled by two bodies of equal weight, the Athenian assembly (*ekklēsia*) and the assembly of the allies (*synedrion*). All proposals required the approval of both bodies. Thus each assembly had the power to veto measures approved only by the other. Each state, however, sent only one delegate to the synedrion, with the result that Athens could garner quite a number of votes in support of its policies by intimidating the tiniest poleis. The Athenians also retained control over military operations. Finally, though the decree of Aris-

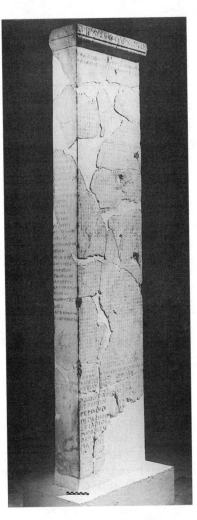

Figure 9.1. The Decree of Aristoteles, 377 BC. The names of the cities that joined the alliance were inscribed on the same stone as the decree. As new states joined, their names were added.

toteles specified no tribute, a system of *syntaxeis* ("contributions") was established to finance league operations. These syntaxeis did not occasion the same bitterness as the tribute assessments of the Delian League, but allies did not always meet their obligations, thus causing financial problems for the league and revealing some ambivalence on the part of its members.

Under the Athenian general Chabrias, the confederacy promptly won an important naval victory over the Spartans at Naxos. Operating in the Aegean and Thrace under Chabrias and in the west under Timotheus, the fleet brought several new states into the confederacy. The Spartans, whom these events had made quite anxious, were further alarmed by the growth of a powerful state in the north, where Jason of Pherae was succeeding in his efforts to unite Thessaly and revive the old title of *tagos* (dictator of all Thessaly), uniting the Thessalians under one leader for the first time since the sixth century. Athens, on the other hand, though enjoying victories at sea, found naval operations costly, and saw merit in ending the fighting. In 375 Sparta, Athens, and Thebes signed a "Common Peace" that acknowledged the existence of the Athenians' new league. Fighting, however, soon broke out again and continued until another attempt at a common peace was made in 371.

This time the ambitions of Thebes sank the peace negotiations. The status of Thebes in the Boeotian League had varied over the years, and the Thebans were now stronger than ever. In the 370s they had enjoyed the energetic leadership of two intimate friends, Epaminondas and Pelopidas. Both had been involved in the liberation of the Cadmea in 379 (Pelopidas more than Epaminondas), and each was often elected to serve on the board of eleven "Boeotarchs" who governed the region. Pelopidas excelled primarily in generalship, Epaminondas in charismatic political leadership. As the Boeotarch representing Thebes in 371, Epaminondas walked out of the peace congress in Sparta when Agesilaus would not let him sign the treaty on behalf of all Boeotia.

This power play did not sit well with the Spartans. King Cleombrotus invaded Boeotia with ten thousand men—about nine thousand hoplites plus cavalry. Epaminondas and Pelopidas met him on the plain of Leuctra with an army of six thousand hoplites and one thousand cavalry. Innovative Theban tactics proved decisive despite the Spartans' superior numbers. It was traditional for Thebans to fight in an unusually deep formation; at Delium in 424, for example, they had fought twenty-five deep. Now, however, Epaminondas packed his left wing (normally the weaker side of a Greek formation) fully fifty shields deep. He also advanced in an oblique line so as to hold back the center and right wing while overpowering the enemy with the left at the point where he could expect Cleombrotus to be. The cutting edge of the Theban line was provided by the elite corps known as the Sacred Band, 150 pairs of select hoplites. Plato was probably thinking of the Sacred Band when he wrote that if "one could contrive that a state or an army should entirely consist of lovers and loved, it would be impossible for it to have a better organization than that which it would then enjoy through their avoidance of all dishonour and their mutual emulation; moreover, a handful of such men, fighting side by side, would defeat practically the whole world" (*Symposium* 178–179; Hamilton). Plutarch analyzed the dynamic in his life of Pelopidas: "a band cemented by friendship grounded upon love is never to be broken, and invincible; since the lovers, ashamed to be base in sight of their beloved, and the beloved before their lovers, willingly rush into danger for the relief of one another" (*Pelopidas* 18; Dryden, rev. Clough). The Sacred Band and the novel tactics of Epaminondas carried the day, and of the seven hundred Spartans present— the bulk of the army consisted of Spartan allies—fully four hundred were killed, Cleombrotus among them. The remainder of the Spartan army withdrew, the legend of Spartan supremacy in hoplite warfare forever shattered.

The loss of life at Leuctra was critical to the future of interpolis relations in Greece, for there now remained only about a thousand Spartan hoplites. When the Spartans' weakness became apparent to their allies, the Peloponnesus began seething with sedition. Democratic revolutions in many cities led to banishments and executions, and a league was formed consisting of Mantinea, Tegea, and the communities of southern and central Arcadia. Inevitably Sparta opposed the new federation, but it received the support not only of Thebes but of the various states it had managed to gather under its leadership: when Epaminondas arrived in the Peloponnesus his army amounted to at least forty thousand men. Though this force was unable to take the city of Sparta, it ravaged Laconia, something that had never happened previously. Most important, it succeeded in the liberation of Messenia. Helots were now citizens, and the new capital of Messene was founded on Mount Ithome. Epaminondas also founded a new capital for the Arcadian League, Megalopolis. This new foundation became the meeting place of the Council of Fifty that represented the communities of the league in proportion to their population, and of the Assembly of Ten Thousand, in which all league citizens could participate. This development indexed a growing interest in experimenting with amicable federations. (So did the founding of the Second Athenian Confederacy, though its professed egalitarianism seems to have broken down over the years.)

Within a few years and with comparatively little loss of life, Thebes under Epaminondas and Pelopidas managed to accomplish what generations of Athenians could not, fight and die as they might. Sparta was finished as an international power. Jason of Pherae, a dangerous ally with serious aspirations of his own, was assassinated in 370. The remaining threat to Theban expansion was the Athenian navy. Epaminondas built a fleet and capitalized on growing restlessness in the Athenian league to bring some of Athens' allies over to his side, but the cost and labor of supporting a navy was ultimately unmanageable, and the Thebans found themselves overextended. Pelopidas was killed fighting in Thessaly. Fearing the collapse of the Boeotian League, the Thebans marched against restive Orchomenos and destroyed it, killing the men and enslaving the women and children.

For all his personal magnetism, Epaminondas seemed to have no plan for Greece beyond replacing Athenian and Spartan imperialism with Theban imperialism. His support in the Peloponnesus was waning: a number of Arcadian communities allied with Achaea, Elis, Athens, and Sparta against Thebes. Marching south, Epaminondas tried to take Sparta by surprise by a night march but failed. Finally he met the alliance on the plain of Mantinea (362 BC). Deploying the same strategy as at Leuctra and outnumbering the enemy by some ten thousand men, the Thebans were victorious, but Epaminondas himself was killed and with his dying breath counseled his countrymen to make peace. Ultimately Thebes gained nothing by its decade of military ascendancy. It had failed to inspire loyalty or unify Greece in any productive way. Though the liberation of Messenia was certainly pleasant for the Messenians and offers a certain satisfaction to the enemies of slavery in all times and places, by knocking out Sparta as a military power Epaminondas performed a great service to Philip of Macedon, the future conqueror of Greece, something for which not all Greeks would ultimately be grateful.

Disaffection in the Second Athenian Confederacy

In his naval operations Epaminondas took advantage of growing unrest in the Athenian alliance. Ambiguities in the evidence have left historians divided as to just how honorably the Athenians adhered to the fair-sounding principles set out in the decree of Aristoteles. It seems likely that at the very least the passing of time fostered erosion. Some cleruchies appear to have been established in violation of the prohibition against Athenians' owning property in allied territory. Particularly under their embarrassingly violent and ungovernable general Chares, the Athenians did sometimes intervene in domestic affairs. The fourth-century historian Theopompus was quick to observe sarcastically that the use of the word *syntaxeis* ("contributions") clothed the old tribute in a euphemism that fooled nobody. Resentment grew when the Athenians diverted league funds to operations that benefited Athens alone, such as the constant operations in the area around Amphipolis, where the struggle for precious natural resources continued.

Revolts from the league, however, were frequently connected with outside agitators—Epaminondas, for one, who dealt the Athenians a serious blow by detaching Byzantium, and subsequently Mausolus. Technically a satrap of the Persian king, in fact Mausolus operated as an independent ruler of the mountainous region of Caria in southwest Asia Minor that lay south of the Maeander River. The Carians claimed to be indigenous, but by Mausolus' day they were Hellenized, for the area included the Greek cities of Cnidus and, most importantly, Halicarnassus, the home of Herodotus. Mausolus' decision to move his capital to Halicarnassus from the Carian city of Mylasa probably signaled his identification with Hellenism; Greek sculptors worked on the huge tomb that he was constructing for himself (the Mausoleum, whence our English word) and that his wife Artemisia finished after his death. Eager to develop Caria's maritime capabilities, Mausolus saw the Athenian league as a serious obstacle to his ambitions. The island of Cos, which blocked the harbor at Halicarnassus, was a member of the league. A substantial Athenian cleruchy, moreover, stood on nearby Samos. Mausolus' solution was to encourage the unrest he had noticed among oligarchs in allied states governed by democracies. In 357, after receiving promises of Carian backing, Rhodes, Cos, and Chios revolted from Athens. So apparently did Byzantium, though there is some question whether the Byzantines had ever really returned to the Athenian alliance since they had defected to Epaminondas in the 360s.

All Athens' most prominent generals were sent east to squelch this uprising, which is generally known as the Social War from the Latin word for ally, *socius* (the same root that appears in "associate" and "society"). Chares and Chabrias went first, but Chabrias was promptly killed trying to force his way into the harbor at Chios. Iphicrates and Timotheus were dispatched the following year and together with Chares prepared to meet the rebel fleet off the little island of Embata that stood between Chios and the mainland. When Timotheus and Iphicrates declined to engage battle because of bad weather, Chares attacked anyway. Without the backing of his colleagues, he suffered substantial losses, and he later accused Iphicrates and Timotheus of treason at the "exit hearings" known as *euthynai* that all Athenian officials had to undergo upon leaving office. Iphicrates was acquitted, but Timotheus was fined such a large sum that he was forced to go into exile since he could not pay it, and he died soon afterward.

Late in 355 or early in 354 Athens made peace, in part because of irate threats from the new Persian king Artaxerxes III, who had succeeded Artaxerxes II in 358. Chares was recalled and the independence of Byzantium, Chios, Rhodes, and Cos was recognized. Soon Lesbos and several other states also broke away from the confederation. The sanitized Delian League had not endured more than a generation. Though the Athenian confederacy continued to exist, it was severely crippled. In the end, Philip was the beneficiary of Mausolus' agitation, as he was of the failed Theban imperialism that had broken the power and prestige of Sparta.

LAW AND DEMOCRACY IN ATHENS

The body that tried Timotheus and Iphicrates when Chares accused them may have been the assembly, but it could just as well have been one of the people's courts known as dicasteries (*dikastēria*). The people's courts were central to the Athenian democracy. Athenian society was notoriously litigious, and in the hands of unscrupulous politicians court cases often became tools of factional strife. Trials of impeached officials—strategoi in particular—were frequently of a political nature, for impeachment at Athens was often used as a forum for a debate on foreign policy. Since decrees proposed in the assembly could be challenged by the *graphē paranomōn* ("indictment for illegal proposals"), it can be argued that in fourth-century Athens the dicasteries rather than the ekklesia were the ultimate arbiters of policy. In the absence of a supreme court or a body of jurisconsults, dicasteries were also the arbiters of law. Courts were also used, of course, in the adjudication of private lawsuits and criminal cases with no political ramifications.

The Functioning of Dicasteries

All male citizens over the age of 30 were eligible to serve on dicasteries, and dicasts (jurors) were chosen each year by lot from those who volunteered. As we saw in Chapter 6, to ensure that the composition of the courts would reflect the voters of Athens, Pericles had instituted pay for jury service. The three obols a day, or half the average wage of a laborer, doubtless attracted the poor, who could not earn three obols another way, as well as comfortably retired older men who enjoyed the opportunity to sit with their fellow citizens in situations that often offered spellbinding entertainment. Perhaps, then, it was not as representative as Pericles had hoped. The number of dicasts allocated to a given case varied usually from 201 to 501 (odd numbers prevented a tie), although a larger body might be used for high-profile trials of a political nature, and some important political trials were held in the assembly itself. Large juries were designed in part to involve large numbers of citizens in decision-making, in part to discourage bribery. Further obstacles to bribery included an elaborate mechanism to select juries by lot and the custom of choosing them at the last possible moment before the trial. Small plaques, each inscribed with a dicast's name, were inserted into a *klērotērion*, an allotment device that distributed the names haphazardly among the daily juries. Voting was by secret ballot. Each dicast was given two pebbles or bronze discs, one of which had a hole punched through it; a herald would proclaim that "the pebble with the hole is a vote for the prosecutor, and the whole pebble a vote for the defendant." To cast his vote he would throw the one he wanted to be counted into a copper receptacle and discard the other pebble into the wooden one.

As the case of Socrates reveals, the dicasts also determined the penalty. Precedents were not binding, so each jury was sovereign. The decision of an Athenian jury was final. There could be no appeal to a higher court or to the people, for an Athenian dicastery was both the highest court and the people. Consequently dicasts functioned as judges as well as jurors.

Murder and the Courts

The earliest known laws in Athens and those that remained unchanged for the longest time concerned homicide. Since the Greeks believed that murder offended the gods, there were religious sanctions against homicide, and anyone

Figure 9.2a. This fragment remains to give us some idea of the functioning of the kleroterion or allotment device that assigned jurors to dicasteries.

who killed another person outside of wartime was considered polluted. At the same time a pressing religious and social obligation lay upon the male next-of-kin to avenge a death by killing the perpetrator, even if an act of homicide had been involuntary, say, as the result of a hunting accident. In accordance with basic principles of vendettas that operate across many societies, therefore, one homicide could evolve into an unending series of retaliations. The Athenians claimed to have founded the first law court in the world when Agamemnon's son Orestes came to Athens from Argos seeking absolution for the murder of his mother, whom he had killed in order to avenge his slain father. The Bronze Age myth that Aeschylus had fleshed out in his *Oresteia* had offered the playwright an opportunity to explain how law had come to replace family feud in just such a case. The court of the Areopagus in Athens adjudicated the case, marking the historic transfer of jurisdiction from the family to the state.

A personal element, however, remained, for accusations of homicide had to be brought by family members. Thus, while the murder of a slave by his or her master might be illegal, prosecution was unlikely in the absence of a citizen relative who could bring charges. Throughout Athenian history, self-help remained a central principle in law. (It also extended to helping friends and relations in a wide variety of instances. Citizens were expected to show both friendship and civic-mindedness by bringing cases on behalf of others who were wronged, such as orphans or girls of marriageable age without dowries.)

Besides the Areopagus there were four additional venues for murder trials. The court of the Palladion was used for unpremeditated killings, the Delphinion for justifiable ones (i.e., homicides committed in self-defense, or by a man who discovered someone in the very act of having intercourse with his wife, mother, sister, or daughter). The Prytaneion handled cases of unidentified murderers and cases in which an animal or an object such as a falling roof tile had caused a death. Finally, those who were already sentenced to exile for homicide and were on trial for an additional murder had to plead their cases on a boat off the coast of Phreatto to avoid polluting the land of Attica.

Conduct of Cases

The seriousness of the charges dictated the amount of time allocated to a trial, and the minutes were measured out by a water clock. The conduct of cases differed from those in modern western courts in that the Greeks relied heavily on the testimony of witnesses not only as to the facts but also as to the character of the defendant. It was customary for witnesses to testify to the virtues of the accused and the public services he had performed—or to the calamities his family would experience if he was convicted. Though rules of time were stringently observed, rules of evidence were few, and defendants themselves were not discouraged from speechifying about their past services to the polis or from parading their vulnerable children before the jury. Even after the advent of writing, Greeks remained somewhat suspicious of texts, and jurors usually trusted the testimony given by witnesses under oath more than written evidence; they under-

Figure 9.2b. In this *klepsydra,* or "water clock," water drained from the upper vessel to the lower one. It took several minutes for a vessel to empty. Ten vessels were allocated for cases involving large sums of money.

stood that a document such as a will could be forged. Slaves were often the optimal witnesses, for they were ubiquitous and often obliged to assist their owners in illicit activities. Theoretically, the testimony of slaves was admissible only if it had been given under torture, but we are uncertain how often such torture was actually inflicted. Following a guilty verdict, prosecutor and defendant proposed alternate penalties, as in the case of Socrates, and the jury decided between the two. The principle of self-help also meant that in private, or civil, cases the prosecutor had to execute the judgment himself. When the orator Demosthenes succeeded in convincing a jury that his guardians had dissipated the fortune his father had left, it was his own responsibility to try to collect the missing funds and property.

Politics in the Courts

With a few notable exceptions such as the trial of Socrates, on the whole the Athenians observed the amnesty of 403. In significant measure the remarkable stability of fourth-century Athens was the legacy of Critias and his companions, for the Thirty had disgraced the name of oligarchy in such a thoroughgoing way that nobody dared hint at its revival. Previously oligarchy and tyranny had been distinct concepts. Now, however, they had come to be indissolubly linked in most Athenian minds, a development that guaranteed the health of the democracy.

Still, a variety of policy and factional disputes gave rise to political and quasi-political trials. A large proportion of Athenian public officials found themselves in court at some point in their lives as either accusers or defendants. This had been true in the fifth century, when Miltiades, Aristides, Themistocles, Cimon, Pericles, Alcibiades, and a host of less famous officials found themselves impeached or ostracized, and it remained the case in the fourth with a few differences: not all important public figures served as general, and the graphe paranomon had replaced ostracism as a weapon that could be used against those who happened to hold no office. Some trials took place in front of regular dicasteries, other in front of the demos assembled in the ekklesia. Factors that gave rise to such trials included genuine suspicion of incompetence or treason, factional disputes, and self-protective behavior of various kinds. In the fourth century as in the fifth, moreover, important men might bring accusations. Iphicrates was involved in accusations against Timotheus; Timotheus and Iphicrates were impeached by Chares.

The Athenian Democracy in the Fourth Century

The survival of so many speeches and inscriptions from the fourth century enables us to see Athenian democracy in action more vividly in this period than was possible for the fifth century. In some ways the democracy changed after the restoration of 403, particularly in the constitution of various ad hoc boards of *nomothetai* ("creators of laws") to approve and review legislation. The fundamental principles, however, remained the same. All free adult males had a theoretically equal right to participate in government regardless of differential prestige and economic standing. Women and slaves were excluded, and it was difficult for resident aliens or their children to become citizens. Only men with two citizen parents could vote. Wealth and illustrious ancestry were distinct advantages in seeking public office. Boasting of your benefactions to the state was a good strategy if you needed to defend yourself in court, which was often the case in this litigious society. Although Solon's four classes were never formally abolished, it is clear that at least by the middle of the fourth century public offices were open to men of all groups. Many thetes and zeugitai were selected for offices chosen by lot, such as service on the boule. Thus participation in government was widely diffused throughout the community of citizen males.

Jokes in Aristophanes' plays reveal a change in the dynamics of assembly attendance. The *Acharnians* (425 BC) alludes to the habit of roping citizens in with a cord covered with red paint that would smear the clothes of the recalcitrant, but when women dress as men and pack the assembly in the *Ecclesiazusae* (392 BC) until a quorum is reached, the real men of Athens complain that they arrived too late to get their pay. The carrot replaced the stick shortly before 400, when a salary of three obols was instituted for attendance at the assembly. By Aristotle's time it had been raised to a drachma (six obols) for an ordinary assembly and a drachma and a half for the *kyria ekklēsia*, that is, the principal assembly of a prytany. At the level of assembly attendance, then, the government of the fourth century was somewhat more democratic than the fifth, for a higher number could afford to take time away from work, though it remained the case that attending meetings was easier for those who lived close by and those who worked for themselves. The large number of political issues ultimately decided in the courts was another democratic element.

As in the courts, where even criminal cases depended on volunteer prosecutors to set them in motion, the voluntary principle played a key role in the assembly. In the absence of organized political parties, concerned citizens took it upon themselves to initiate legislation. No well-defined group of officeholders saw itself—or was seen by others—as clearly marked off from the rest of the populace. By "politicians" people simply meant those who most enjoyed making proposals in the assembly and giving speeches in their support. The importance of oratory and debate to the functioning of the democratic system is attested in the Greek word that comes closest to our word "politician": *rhētōr*. Since *rhētores* shared common interests and habits, no doubt people were comfortable identifying a particular citizen they might see walking down the street as "one of the rhetores," but it is important to remember that there was no official "board of rhetores" to which such men belonged. Today it would be peculiar to identify someone who did not hold public office as a politician, but the Athenians saw nothing strange about it. It was precisely because of the power private citizens could gain through skillful oratory that the Athenians made sure to have the graphe paranomon on the books to ensure the accountability even of those who took part in public affairs without holding office. Those convicted of proposing something illegal were generally fined; three convictions deprived a citizen of the right to make further proposals.

The frustrations of Athens' imperialist ventures, the exacerbation of class tensions, and the rise of individualism all played a role in the creation of a new phenomenon at Athens: a large class of wealthy men who chose not to involve themselves in politics. Though this is common enough today, when even among the elite participation in national affairs tends to be limited to a small fraction, this development was noteworthy in fourth-century Athens, for during the previous century men from affluent families normally had chosen to stand for the high offices they considered appropriate to their status. Now after the ruinous Peloponnesian War the quietism some had always chosen became more widespread. The Athenian system, however, still guaranteed that civic responsibility would be shared by a large group—the hundreds who sat on the boule (still a one-year term), the thousands who served as dicasts and attended meetings of the ekklesia, and the hundreds who sat for a day in a new body that was periodically constituted to inspect and pass laws, the nomothetai. Socrates was certainly onto something important in the ideology of Athenian democracy when he complained that it meant government by amateurs: because many Greeks were somewhat suspicious of professionalism and considered it incompatible with good breeding, Athenian democracy was run largely by people who devoted only a fraction of their time to politics. It is important to remember, however, that the ignorant and untalented were discouraged from involving themselves in public affairs by the Athenians' relentless use of the machinery of accountability against anyone who chose to mount the speaker's platform, let alone hold a state office;

and the principles of selection by lot and frequent rotation in office meant a good deal of hands-on training in the business of government.

THE FOURTH-CENTURY POLIS

Although the bulk of our evidence comes from Athens, most Greeks, of course, lived in other states. In the fourth century as in the fifth, some Greek poleis were governed by democracies, others by oligarchies that varied in their narrowness. As had always been the case in Greece, uneven distribution of wealth fostered ever-present tensions that threatened constantly to erupt and disturb the tenuous concord that united citizens, and changes of constitution were frequent. Although warfare remained a fact of life, many people were sick of it and had come to question its efficacy in improving their lives. While some poorer citizens continued to welcome war for the pay it offered to rowers in the fleet, those who had land or commerce to protect were hesitant. No longer did war seem to promise either the tangible rewards of booty or the intangible ones of glory and prestige. The ideal of the citizen-soldier was wearing thin, and an increasing share of the fighting was conducted by mercenaries from outside. Agriculture remained the basis of the economy, but the devastation of the land during the Peloponnesian War had fostered a drift to the cities. By throwing people together, this development heightened the awareness of economic inequality and sharpened class bitterness. Plato and his pupil Aristotle both took it for granted that a polis consisted in reality of two cities, one of the many poor and one of the few rich. The division of citizens into haves and have-nots that had always marked Greek states was exacerbated in the fourth century by the increased poverty of the have-nots, bringing latent tensions to the surface where they could no longer be ignored.

Stasis

Where the economy was most prosperous and families from the lower classes had the best chance of remaining above the poverty level, stasis might be avoided, as was the case in democratic Athens, the stablest state of the fourth century. Many poleis with large concentrations of poor people, however, were consumed with civil strife; Xenophon's *Hellenica* mentions over thirty instances. Bloodshed was common, and religious pieties were often ignored. In 392 Corinthian democrats violated the sanctity of temples by murdering oligarchs who had taken refuge there. Diodorus reports revolutions in Corinth, Sicyon, and Phlius and Xenophon recorded serious tensions in Tegea, Phlius, Sicyon, Pellene, and Elis. Diodorus, who shared the antidemocratic orientation of most ancient writers, took a certain satisfaction in relating the torture and murder of the elite by Argive democrats in 371, when class tensions erupted with violence exceptional even by Greek standards. After the execution of twelve hundred influential men, Diodorus contends,

the populace did not spare the demagogues themselves. For because of the magnitude of the calamity the demagogues were afraid that some unforeseen turn of
fortune might overtake them and therefore desisted from their accusation,
whereas the mob, now thinking that they had been left in the lurch by them, were
angry at this and put to death all the demagogues. So these men received the
punishment which fitted their crimes as if some divinity were visiting its just resentment upon them, and the people, eased of their mad rage, were restored to
their senses.

(Library of History 15.58.4; Sherman 1952)

Internal strife was exacerbated by tensions among poleis. Thus for example a
certain Euphron gained power at Sicyon by playing on anti-Spartan feeling in the
Peloponnesus: "He told the Argives and the Arcadians," Xenophon writes, "that
if the men of the wealthy classes remained in control of Sicyon, quite obviously
the city would, at the first opportunity, go over to Sparta again. 'But if,' he said,
'a democratic government is set up, you can be sure that the city will remain loyal
to you'" (Hellenica 7.1.44; Warner 1979). Outside help was valuable in stasis. In
Elis, Xenophon reports, while the Eleans were at war with the Arcadians, the democrats enlisted the Arcadians' help in seizing the acropolis. Assistance might
also come from the large pool of available mercenaries, such as those who helped
Euphron regain power in Sicyon.

Both Athens and Sparta used the prevailing discord and demoralization to
good rhetorical effect in arguing for their own hegemony. Those who would reject Athenian hegemony in favor of the "autonomy" guaranteed by the King's
Peace, Isocrates argued, should think again:

> For who would desire a condition of things where pirates command the seas and
> mercenaries occupy our cities; where fellow-countrymen, instead of waging war
> in defence of their territories against strangers, are fighting within their own
> walls against each other; where more cities have been captured in war than be-
> fore we made the peace; and where revolutions follow so thickly upon each other
> that those who are at home in their own countries are more dejected than those
> who have been punished with exile?

(Panegyricus 116–117; Norlin 1966)

Document 9.1 Isocrates puts similar arguments about Spartan hegemony in
the mouth of Archidamus III, the son of Agesilaus. Even allowing for a considerable degree of rhetorical exaggeration, the picture of life in the Peloponnesus is
sobering.

Not only the people of the Peloponnesus in general but even the ad-
herents of democracy, whom we consider to be especially unfriendly to us,
are already yearning for our protection. For by revolting from us they have
gained nothing of what they anticipated; on the contrary, they have got just

the opposite of freedom . . . ; and the war of factions, of whose existence in other territories they used to know only by report, they now see waged almost every day in their own states. They have been so levelled by their misfortunes that no man can discern who among them are the most wretched; for not one of their states is unscathed, not one but has neigh- bours ready to do it injury. . . . They feel such distrust and such hatred of one another that they fear their fellow-citizens more than the enemy; in- stead of preserving the spirit of accord [*homonoia*] and mutual helpfulness which they enjoyed under our rule, they have become so unsocial that those who own property had rather throw their possessions into the sea than lend aid to the needy, while those who are in poorer circumstances would less gladly find a treasure than seize the possessions of the rich; having ceased sacrificing victims at the altars they slaughter one another there instead; and more people are in exile now from a single city than before from the whole of the Peloponnesus.

> *Archidamus 64–67; translated by George Norlin, in* Isocrates *vol. 1. London and Cambridge, Mass.: Harvard University Press, 1966, p. 387.*

Beginning late in the fifth century, Greek intellectuals had begun calling for *homonoia* ("concord") among citizens, but the frequency with which the appeal was made reveals the discordant reality: in fact the slogan caught on during the contentious days of the Peloponnesian War. In praising the rule of law, Socrates had insisted in the pages of Xenophon's *Memorabilia* that throughout Greece homonoia was advocated by the "best men" (the *aristoi*). Aristotle, however, took a darker and more realistic view. In some states of his own day, he wrote in the *Politics*, the oligarchs in charge take an oath to be hostile to the demos and "plot whatever evil possible against the people" (1310a).

Not all poleis were constantly torn apart by stasis and debilitated by interpo- lis wars. Since the principal cause of internal weakness and vulnerability to out- side attack was the frustrations of the poor, prosperity might act as a powerful deterrent. Megara with its brisk woolen trade flourished throughout the fourth century, and civil strife was rare. The progress of the economy was facilitated by peace with other poleis: the alliance between Corinth and Athens during the Corinthan War eliminated Megara's pivotal position in interpolis diplomacy, and the Megarians seem to have preserved their neutrality throughout that war. Megarian woolens found eager markets throughout Greece. Sheep grazed in abundance, and large numbers of slaves, probably mostly female, turned out well-made and inexpensive garments. The private homes of Megara were known for their elegance, and a variety of monuments decorated the city. The Athenian sculptor Praxiteles (370–329 BC) produced numerous statues of the gods for the sanctuaries of Artemis and Apollo and the temple of Aphrodite. Scopas, who contributed to the Mausoleum in Caria, also worked in Megara. Exactly what kind of government fourth-century Megara enjoyed is uncertain—Plato praised it but did not describe it—but it seems at least to have been fairly stable. Megara was not, however, entirely immune to the endemic stasis of the fourth century, for Diodorus reports an abortive uprising in the 370s.

Marginalized Workers in the Economy

The economy of each polis was different, but throughout Greece prestige attached to some kinds of work more than to others. Because social prejudices favored self-sufficiency through farming, or making money by selling the produce of one's land, free citizens tended to avoid involvement in commerce and banking, turning over these activities to metics and slaves. Such workers became important in the fourth century and often made considerable fortunes, for one phenomenon that distinguished the polis of the fourth century from that of the fifth was the rise of banking.

Bank owners trusted slaves to manage the daily operations of banks independently and even to travel with large sums of cash. Such slaves were highly skilled, usually literate, and very valuable. A slave who managed a bank could be completely responsible for his master's property. Therefore, a master might write a will freeing his bank manager on condition that he marry his widow and manage his bank in behalf of his minor children. Manumitted slaves became metics. Some of these metics, including a certain Pasio and Phormio, were among the wealthiest Athenians of the fourth century. In gratitude for their generous benefactions to the state, Athens rewarded them with citizenship. Thus slaves in banking might experience rapid social mobility.

The stigma that attached to working for someone else was greater for women than for men; few women chose to work outside the home unless compelled to do so by poverty. In the fourth century as in the fifth, however, some women did work at service jobs outside their homes. Slave women were sometimes rented out by their owners, and former slaves, metics, and even citizen-women in straitened financial circumstances worked at a variety of jobs. Some hired themselves out as nurses for other women's children; some sold goods in the marketplace; and older women often served as hired mourners at funerals. Although unacceptable for citizen-women, prostitution was probably the work done most frequently by women outside the home. Some were put to work when they were still children. In Corinth, Nicarete, a former slave, purchased young girls from slaveholders and trained them for their work:

> Nicarete, who was the freedwoman of Charisius of Elis and the wife of his cook Hippias, bought seven girls when they were small children. She was an astute judge of natural beauty in little girls and furthermore she understood how to bring them up and train them skillfully, for she made this her profession and got her livelihood from the girls. She used to address them as daughters, implying that they were free women, so that she might extract the largest fees from those who wished to get close to them. When she had reaped the profit of the youth-

ful prime of each, she sold all seven of them: Anteia, Stratola, Aristocleia, Metaneira, Phila, Isthmias, and this Neaera here . . .

Neaera . . . was working with her body, although she was still very young, for she had not yet reached puberty.

(Pseudo-Demosthenes, 59.18–20; Murray 1936)

Neaera's further adventures are also detailed in this speech, which is included in the corpus of Demosthenes although it was almost certainly written by someone else. Two of Neaera's clients purchased her from Nicarete to be their slave. But when these men were about to marry, they offered Neaera the opportunity to buy her freedom. Neaera borrowed her purchase price from former clients, and repaid them from her earnings as a free prostitute. Her attempt at social mobility was quashed, however, when she moved to Athens, married a certain Stephanus, and pretended to be an Athenian citizen. Apollodorus, an enemy of Stephanus (who had brought against him one indictment for an illegal proposal and another for murder), brought her to trial for false assumption of citizen rights. He also charged Stephanus with living with a non-Athenian woman as though she were his wife, and with giving Neaera's daughter in marriage to an Athenian citizen as being his own daughter born from a citizen-woman.

PHILOSOPHY AND THE POLIS

The changing political situation in the Greek world helped shape Greek thought in each new generation, and the problems of the fourth-century polis were no exception. Philosophy evolved with the polis and survived it when Philip of Macedon brought the freedom of the independent city-states to an end in 338 BC. The Greek word *philosophos* means "a lover of wisdom," and for many years before Plato and Aristotle founded their famous schools in Athens, Greek thinkers had taken delight in searching for the underlying principles that shaped the cosmos and determined the life humans made in it. Democritus contended that he would "rather find the explanation for a single phenomenon than gain the kingdom of Persia." The truly prosperous man, Empedocles said, is one who enjoys the riches of a divine intelligence. Philosophers came in many shapes. Thinkers like Thales and Anaximander focused on the natural world. Others like Herodotus and Thucydides used the writing of history as a vehicle for their ideas about the human condition, while still others expressed them through dramas as did Aeschylus, Sophocles, and Euripides. In time, Plato would write dialogues and Aristotle treatises. These innovative thinkers explored the areas that still make up philosophy today—ethics, logic, epistemology (the philosophy of knowledge), metaphysics (the science of being), aesthetics, theology, philosophy of science, and social and political theory. It was in the realm of social and political theory that philosophy was most closely tied to the polis. Because most surviving texts of political theory were composed in democratic Athens, one might imagine that they praised democracy. In fact, the opposite is true: the principal texts of Greek political theory were the work of intellectuals who were intensely critical of democratic government. Indeed, modern political scientists have observed that political theory—literally, "looking at the city-state"—was invented to show why democracy could not possibly work. It is the workings of democracy itself that reveal the ideology behind it.

Democracy and Political Theory

The Old Oligarch had defended Athenian democracy with biting irony as a beautifully efficient way of guaranteeing the suppression of one class by another, but no surviving text treats the dynamics of democracy in a positive way. Reconstructing the theory behind democracy from written texts requires assembling patches from a variety of sources that engage the issue only obliquely. Thucydides' version of Pericles' funeral oration gives us a sense of what the Athenians at any rate prized in their government. At Athens, Pericles says, worth is assessed in terms of ability, not wealth or class. Athenians consider remaining aloof from politics a vice, not a virtue. They view debate as an aid to constructive action, not a hindrance.

Just as Thucydides, who was not particularly sympathetic to democracy, included Pericles' speech in his history, so Plato, one of democracy's sharpest critics, included a statement of democratic ideology in his dialogue *Protagoras*. There the famous sophist tells a quaint myth in support of his thesis that all people possess the rudiments of civic-mindedness. In earliest times, Protagoras says, people were unable to live together constructively in cities because of their lack of *politikē technē*, the skill of forming and managing a polis. Seeing this and fearing the destruction of the species, Zeus sent Hermes to bring *aidōs* ("shame") and *dikē* ("justice") to mortals. When Hermes asked Zeus whether these should be distributed to a select few, as was the case with the arts of medicine and other techniques, or to everyone, Zeus ordered him to give some to everybody, since "cities cannot be formed if only a few share in these skills as they do in the other arts." (322D) It is for this reason, Protagoras says, that when the Athenians come together to make decisions that require the sense of justice that goes into political wisdom "they take advice from everybody, since it is held that for states to exist everyone must partake of this excellence" (322E–323E). Because the politike techne is diffused throughout the community, Protagoras concludes, the Athenians do right to welcome political advice from anyone who is moved to give it. Nowhere does he suggest that everyone is equally skilled in civics, but everyone, he argues, has at least a little.

Further clues are provided in the dozens of orations surviving from the fourth century, which praise freedom of speech, liberty, equality before the law, and the rule of law. Our best clue to the theory of democracy, however, is its practice. The Athenian democracy itself reveals what most men in Athens believed about government: they believed in a democracy of male citizens that required active participation on the part of these citizens, guaranteed by frequent rotation in office, and they believed that the average man was qualified to make political decisions, as evidenced by the use of the lot and the taking of important decisions in the assembly by majority vote. They believed in trial by jury, and they feared the corruption that inhered in small groups more than the mob psychology that threatened large ones. They believed that the people had the right to call its officials to account with regularity and on the slightest pretext. They believed in capital punishment for a wide variety of offenses including military incompetence and the seduction of the wives, daughters, and sisters of citizens. They believed that the stability of the state was so crucial that it was reasonable to exile a man for ten years under the system known as ostracism even if he had done nothing to break the law. They believed in slavery and patriarchy. They believed that the control of women's sexuality was essential to the smooth functioning of the community and that the sequestration of women and girls was a good step in this direction. We know all this not because they wrote it down but because of how they chose to run their government and live their lives.

We know also that Greeks who did not live under democratic governments believed in the rule of law, which appears as a persistent leitmotiv in the literature of the fifth and fourth centuries. Its prominence begins with the efforts of Herodotus and Aeschylus to define and celebrate what it means to be Greek; for them living under law played a key role in shaping that identity. Euripides also connected law with democracy in his *Suppliants*, where he defined Athens even under Theseus as a place where

> Our city is not subject to one man.
> No, it is free, for here the people rule.

> *(404–406)*

Under a tyranny, one man governs, keeping the law in his private hands, and there is no equality:

> But when the laws are written down, the weak
> Enjoy the same protection as the rich.

> *(434–435)*

Although many Athenans identified their democratic constitution with the rule of law, Greek intellectuals sometimes saw things differently. Plato frequently identified democracy with tyranny, and his pupil Aristotle complained that the decrees of a democratic assembly were no different from the edicts of the tyrant.

Plato

It is certainly a tribute to Athenian democracy that it produced its own most astute critics. An aristocrat from one of Athens' most distinguished families and a relative of the oligarch Critias, Plato became a disciple of Socrates and was profoundly shaken by his death. The loss of his mentor, however, only heightened his creative powers. Over his lifetime Plato composed numerous dialogues, in most of which the principal part is played by a character he identifies as Socrates. What is beauty? What is piety? What is justice? What is love? These questions were explored in Plato's Socratic dialogues. As Plato's thinking evolved with the passing of time, this "Socrates" had less and less in common with the historical Socrates and came to serve as a vehicle for Plato's own ideas.

Chief among these was the theory of Forms. Plato's belief in Forms was connected to his passion for definitions, for both depend on a conviction that disparate acts and items can nonetheless be classified in categories—that beautiful objects and acts and ideas, for example, all have something in common. In Plato's view, they all partake of the ideal Form of beauty. While a beautiful sunset might seem different from a beautiful mathematical proof or a beautiful young athlete, in fact what ties them together is more enduring than what sets them apart. Similarly with the various seats that are mundane representations of the ideal Form of chair, or the various pale things that are earthly examples of the ideal Form of whiteness.

The relationship of appearance to reality in Plato's world view can perhaps be best grasped in the context of mathematics. A ring or a princely diadem or the perimeter of a hoplite shield might seem to the casual observer to be circles, but they are not circles in the same sense that the locus of all points in a given plane equidistant from a given point is a circle. They only look like circles; if you were to put them under a magnifying glass you would see that they were not circles at all, merely objects vaguely circular in appearance precisely because they bring to mind the Form of the circle. Only the circle depicted in the mathematical definition is a circle. Some people might say that these concrete objects are real circles whereas the geometrical concept is imaginary, but Plato was not one of these people. For Plato, only the concept is real. The tangible objects are debased copies, feeble imitations of the ideal Form. Plato, in other words, was an idealist and a dualist. He believed in an opposition between the physical world of appearances, which are deceptive, and the intellectual universe of ideas, which represent reality. The first is tawdry and serves only to distract people from ultimate truth; the second is noble, and to contemplate it ennobling.

In many ways Plato was a revolutionary. The close connection between appearance and reality was fundamental to Greek civilization. If you are rich and handsome, most of his contemporaries believed, then probably you are also good; if you are poor and ugly, probably you are bad as well. If everyone admires you, then all is right with the world; if you are despised, then you have no reason to go on. For most Greek men, reputation, power, and material success were central to happiness. Like Socrates before him, who preferred being right to being alive, Plato identified values that were more important than being well liked or envied. In his dialogue on government and education, *The Republic*, he raised a key question about justice. Let us say, he proposed, that you had a magic ring that would make you invisible. Would you practice justice, or would you take the opportunity to grab as much power and wealth as you could, practicing injustice in the happy expectation of getting away with it?

As usual, Plato does not appear in this dialogue. His brothers Glaucon and Adeimantus, however, do, and they are quick to point out the customary Greek view that only convention, *nomos*, holds people back from committing injustice. The behavior that the man-made *nomoi* of punishment and disgrace discourage, however, is encouraged by *physis*, the natural instinct that urges people to take whatever they can get away with taking. This was the drive that Thucydides' Athenians at Melos had identified as the customary engine of human conduct: people, they had argued, "are always forced by the law of nature to dominate everyone they can" (5.105; Blanco). This sort of thing, Glaucon and Adeimantus say, is what the average person believes. It is up to Socrates to show that justice is in fact good for people.

This is a large task, and Socrates decides to shift gears and explore justice in the state in order to discover justice in the individual writ large. In the course of this exploration, he spins out threads that are even more revolutionary. The subject of the dialogue becomes an ideal state of Plato's imagining. It is a state divided into three classes, corresponding to Plato's conception of the tripartite nature of the soul. At the top are the guardians, who represent reason. Their supreme rationality, inculcated by years of education, qualifies them to govern. After them come the auxiliaries, who are characterized by a spirited temperament which suits them for the duties of soldiers. Last come the majority, who correspond to desire in the soul: they are not especially bright or brave and live only to satisfy their own material yearnings. They will do all the jobs in the state other than governing and fighting. Initially a tricky myth will assign people to classes, and then the three groups will reproduce themselves biologically. On those occasions when a child seems to have been born into the wrong class, it will be transferred, but Plato seems to have great faith in heredity, for he plainly expects such cases to be rare.

The only classes that require much education are the top two, and the education and lives of the guardians soon become the focus of Plato's attention. They will study for many years, approaching the understanding of the Forms by applying themselves to mathematics. Surprisingly, the guardians will be of both genders, and Plato advocates a unisex education for them.

Document 9.2 Though on the whole, Socrates argues, women are inferior to men in all skills besides weaving and cooking, nonetheless there will always be individual women who are more skilled than individual men. When Glaucon agrees, Socrates launches into his plan for having guardians of both sexes (though he always speaks of guardians and their wives, never guardians and their husbands).

Soc.   To conclude, then, there is no occupation concerned with the management of social affairs which belongs either to woman or to man, as such. Natural gifts are to be found here and there in both creatures alike; and every occupation is open to both, so far as their natures are concerned, though woman is for all purposes the weaker.

Glau.   Certainly.

Soc.   Is that a reason for making over all occupations to men only?

Glau.   Of course not.

Soc.   No, because one woman may have a natural gift for medicine or for music, another may not.

Glau.   Surely.

Soc.   Is it not also true that a woman may, or may not, be warlike or athletic?

Glau.   I think so.

Soc.   And again, one may love knowledge, another hate it; one may be high-spirited, another spiritless?

Glau.   True again.

Soc.   It follows that one woman will be fitted by nature to be a Guardian, another will not; because these were the qualities for which we selected our men Guardians. So for the purpose of keeping watch over the commonwealth, woman has the same nature as man, save in so far as she is weaker.

Glau.   So it appears.

Soc.   It follows that women of this type must be selected to share the life and duties of Guardians with men of the same type, since they are competent and of a like nature, and the same natures must be allowed the same pursuits.

Glau.   Yes.

Soc.   We come round, then, to our former position, that there is nothing contrary to nature in giving our Guardians' wives the same training for mind and body. The practice we proposed to establish was not impossible or visionary, since it was in accordance with nature. Rather, the contrary practice which now prevails turns out to be unnatural.

Glau.   So it appears.

Soc.   Well, we set out to inquire whether the plan we proposed was feasible and also the best. That it is feasible is now agreed; we must next settle whether it is the best.

Glau.   Obviously.

Soc.   Now, for the purpose of producing a woman fit to be a Guardian, we shall not have one education for men and another for women, precisely because the nature to be taken in hand is the same.

Glau.   True.

The Republic *455; translated by F. M. Cornford,* The Republic of Plato. *London and New York: Oxford University Press, 1945.*

The guardians' lives will be unusual in many respects. The acquisitive principle that guides most people's activities will be alien to them, for Plato envisions a communistic regime within the guardian class; private property, though it exists for the other two classes, will be abolished for the top group. Nor will they have spouses in the conventional sense of the word. In short, they will have no oikoi—

something that makes them eminently un-Athenian. Though they will not live in households, however, the guardians must reproduce in order to perpetuate the system. An elaborate mathematical scheme will dictate temporary couplings. (Plato was deeply influenced by the Pythagoreans, and he found in mathematics not only the embodiment of perfect abstraction but elements of mysticism as well.) Once born of these short-term "marriages," however, children will be mixed in with all the other children conceived around the same time and raised in common nurseries. Thus no parent will know his or her own child and vice versa.

Like other utopias, Plato's is designed to demonstrate the shortcomings of real states. Whether he ever planned or even wished to see his Republic established is uncertain. What is clear is his dislike of the existing governments in Greece, and particularly of democracy. Tyranny and oligarchy are easiest to dismiss; nobody should have to live by the whims of a power-hungry autocrat, and money is no measure of merit. Democracy is harder to dispose of, but living under a government he did not like galvanized Plato into a vehement attack on a system he categorized as "an agreeable form of anarchy" marked by "an equality of a peculiar kind for equals and unequals alike" (558C; Cornford 1945). The debunking of the so-called equality of democracy was common to the thinking of fourth-century intellectuals. Aristotle and Isocrates shared Plato's preference for what they labeled "proportional" or "geometric" equality. It was the ratio between merit and privilege, they argued, that ought to remain constant. Such a system was far more equitable, they believed, than the "arithmetic" equality of democracy that accorded equal privilege to people of unequal merit. For Plato, giving equal political power to all alike was no different from giving all students the same grade regardless of their performance on papers and exams.

Good government, Plato concluded, will never come into being until philosophers and rulers are one and the same. To help bring this about, Plato founded a school he called the Academy because of its location by the groves of the ancient Greek hero Academus. There men studied for years to achieve an enlightenment which, in Plato's view, would qualify them to participate in government—but which he acknowledged would in fact drive a wedge between them and their unenlightened fellow citizens. Former students at the Academy included many famous philosophers, astronomers, mathematicians, and even scientists. The presence of scientists at the Academy is a testament to its breadth, for Plato himself was not drawn to science. How could he be, when he believed that only the eternal mattered—that the forms were the ultimate and only reality? Science deals with change and with motion. Like Parmenides, Plato conceived reality as unchanging and unchangeable. Without a mechanism for explaining change, Plato's idealist philosophy was antithetical to science.

Aristotle

It was Plato's star pupil Aristotle who founded the great institution of scientific learning at Athens, the Lyceum. His father had been a court physician in Macedon, and he had been trained in scientific observation from his youth. He was never happier than in the meticulous observation and classification of species. Scholars in all disciplines, but especially perhaps biologists, will recognize the delight he took in connecting the particular to the general, and in observing nature at work in all its perfection: even in the animals that are not attractive to the senses, he wrote, "the craftsmanship of nature provides extraordinary pleasures to those who are able to recognize the causes in things and who have a natural inclination to philosophy" (*On the Parts of Animals* 645a 7ff). Certainly Aristotle thrived in the constantly changing world of nature, while Plato was happiest contemplating the eternal truths of mathematics. For Aristotle, the dynamic power of change accounted for a great deal of the excitement of mental life. And not only this: it was movement toward a particular end—teleology, from the Greek *telos* meaning "end" or "goal"—that he saw as the guiding force behind life. A prime mover, he argued, shaped the universe in accord with his ends. Only the prime mover was not itself moved. Loosely speaking, the prime mover was what most people would call God. Aristotle's philosophy was very popular in Europe during the Middle Ages, when Thomas Aquinas (1225–1274 AD) adapted it to Christian theology.

That Aristotle was a less eccentric person than Plato. Though he came from the Ionian city of Stagira in northern Greece and hence did not belong in Athens the same way the blue-blooded Plato did, he was more firmly grounded in the customary relations of Greek society than Plato, who apparently never married or had children. He lived with two successive women, his wife Pythias and then, after Pythias' death, his concubine Herpyllis; he had a daughter and a son. After Plato's death in 347, when Aristotle had studied at the Academy for nearly twenty years, he left Athens and took up residence in Assos in Asia Minor. Several years later he returned to Macedon, where Philip had summoned him to serve as tutor to the young prince Alexander. Back in Athens in 335, he established his own school, the Lyceum. He and his students conversed there while strolling through the colonnaded walks (*peripatoi*, which gave his followers the name "peripatetics" by which they are still known today). When he was accused of impiety in the burst of anti-Macedonian feeling that erupted after news of Alexander's death arrived in Athens, Aristotle left Attica. Looking back somberly at the trial of Socrates, he observed that he did not want the Athenians to sin a second time against philosophy. He died the following year, in 322.

That Aristotle loved science while Plato loved mathematics reveals a profound difference between the two men and their ways of engaging with the world of ideas. Live things excited Aristotle and inspired in him the desire to categorize them. The same urge would lead him to classify all the political arrangements familiar in his day in his famous work of political theory, the *Politics*. Where Plato had used reason as virtually his only tool in the quest for understanding, Aristotle placed tremendous importance on observation. His stay in northwest Asia Minor and the adjacent islands was particularly rewarding to him because of the opportunity it afforded him to study the lagoon of Pyrrha on Lesbos, which teemed with life. Though reason was not his only tool, he was the founder of the discipline of logic. To Aristotle we owe the articulation of the fundamental principle of the syllogism—the principle that tells us that if A yields B and B yields C, then A by itself must yield C. If Sneaky is a cat and all cats are mammals, then Sneaky must be a mammal. Since the Parthenon is in Athens and Athens is in Attica, then the Parthenon must be in Attica.

Whereas Plato had developed a framework for discussing politics so theoretical that scholars are often puzzled as to what real states he might have had in mind, Aristotle approached the question of the human community by amassing and analyzing a tremendous amount of data. In this project he was assisted by his students at the Lyceum, where 158 essays on constitutions of various poleis were drawn up. That all these have disappeared except for *The Athenian Constitution* is an incalculable loss to the study of Greek history. Aristotle was fascinated by issues surrounding government. His principal work of political theory is his *Politics*, which remained a cherished handbook throughout the medieval, Renaissance, and early modern periods.

In his conception of the universe at large, Aristotle differed with Plato on a key point—the existence of Forms. To Aristotle, as to the average person, Forms were not real. Only the combination of form and matter created something real. Plato, Aristotle thought, had failed, like Parmenides, to account for change. Aristotle also rejected the broad level of generalization at which Plato operated. In their views of the human community, however, the two men were quite similar. Both saw the polis as more than a practical arrangement for the exchange of goods and mutual protection; for them human existence and the existence of the polis were coterminous. (The lack of a state structure would make a fully human existence impossible, but a structure larger than the polis seemed unimaginable. Aristotle identified the largest possible size for the state at ten thousand citizens, the number who could be addressed by a speaker at one time.) Aristotle is famous for having said "man is a political animal." What he actually said is that people are animals whose nature it is to live in a polis. Only in a polis could individuals realize their social natures and grow through the sharing of ideas. This growth, however, was limited to a few people of intellectual gifts who belonged to a social class that guaranteed them leisure for contemplation. Powerful obstacles prevented the poor from participating in politics—especially the nonfarming poor, who did "banausic" labor, arduous jobs that compromised the mind along with the body. The best state, he concludes, will not make common laborers citizens, for citizens must have adequate property to ensure sufficient leisure for goodness and political activity. So much for democracy.

Both the blue-blooded Athenian aristocrat and Athens' most famous metic, then, were intensely class-conscious. Aristotle's political philosophy, however, differed from Plato's in two key respects. First, Aristotle believed in collective wisdom: a mass of people who are individually unwise, he argues, may surpass the wisdom of the few best men, just as potluck dinners may prove to be tastier than those hosted by a single individual. The masses, he claims, can be perfectly good judges of music and poetry, since "some appreciate one thing, some another, and taken together they appreciate everything" (*Politics* 1281b). For this reason, he is open to a compromise similar to that of Solon: poor people in his ideal state would be allowed to choose officials and hold them to account, but not to hold office. Second, Aristotle had such a powerful belief in natural hierarchies—free over slave, Greek over non-Greek, adult over child, male over female—that he recurred with some frequency to the theme of the inferiority of women to men.

Whereas Plato's utopia entailed a unisex education aimed at producing guardian men and women who would govern together, Aristotle was a staunch supporter of patriarchy, which he believed had a solid basis in women's biological inadequacy. Women, he maintained, had colder bodies than men. For this reason, though they were able to provide matter for embryos, only men could provide the soul. In the womb, embryos that stopped short of full development for lack of heat became female. Thus women were literally half-baked. From this came the inferior strength he identified in a variety of species. The female, he contended, "is, so to speak, a deformed male" (*Generation of Animals* 737a). At times, as was the case with the Hippocratics, Aristotle's powers of observation deserted him when women were their subject. The twentieth-century philosopher Bertrand Russell quipped that Aristotle would not have claimed that women had fewer teeth than men if he had allowed his wife to open her mouth.

For all their differences, Plato and Aristotle shared a passionate conviction that the goal of philosophy was to enable selected people to pursue enlightenment in a republic of virtuous citizens. The state for them meant the polis, and it was central to the good life. Their thinking contrasts strikingly with that of most moderns, who are more likely to see the state as designed to grant individuals the freedom to pursue their private goals, particularly their economic ones. Though Plato and Aristotle were both intensely critical of democracy, they shared with the Athenian democrats an eminently Greek belief in the active nature of the polis. So far from an artificial institution whose chief goal was to redistribute goods and prevent crime, the polis was conceived by its residents as a force for the moral and spiritual improvement of its citizens. For this force to operate properly, citizens had to engage eagerly in political life; participation was a duty, not a right. The problems of the fourth century, however, raised serious questions about whether the polis as traditionally conceived was adequate to serve people's needs.

Signs of Despair: Flirting with Monarchy

Aware that his ideal republic would not be realized in his lifetime, Plato framed a second-best state in his late dialogue *The Laws*. Toward the end of his life, however, he also toyed with the notion that rule by a particularly wise individual might be preferable to government by even the best laws. Laws, after all, are inflexible and cannot easily be adapted to individuals. In his dialogue *The Statesman*, Plato gave a blank check to the man of extraordinary wisdom. Such men, he writes,

> whether they rule over willing or unwilling subjects, with or without written laws, and whether they are rich or poor, must, according to our present opinion, be supposed to exercise their rule in accordance with some art or science. . . .

And whether they purge the state for its good by killing or banishing some of the citizens, or make it smaller by sending out colonies somewhere, as bees swarm from the hive, or bring in citizens from elsewhere to make it larger, so long as they act in accordance with science and justice and preserve and benefit it by making it better than it was, so far as is possible, that must at that time and by such characteristics be declared to be the only right form of government.

(The Statesman *293; Fowler 1925*)

Although this notion was the predictable consequence of Plato's own conviction that knowledge is absolute in nature, it can also be seen as a natural outgrowth of the particular strains of the fourth century. As draining interpolis wars and economic difficulties dragged on and on, some people with world views very different from Plato's began to question whether in fact the rule of law would solve the problems of the polis. What if an exceptional individual were to arise with an extraordinary gift for knowing what was right? Perhaps it would be easier to find and educate one such person than to round up many, or even a few.

The notion that one gifted man could make an improvement in the life of Greece is apparent in the writings of Plato's contemporaries Xenophon and Isocrates. Each man had something in common with Plato: Xenophon shared Plato's admiration for their teacher Socrates, and Isocrates had his own school. The two men were very different from one another: Xenophon was a man of action, a soldier and adventurer who enjoyed writing about horsemanship and hunting, whereas Isocrates was too nervous to feel comfortable speaking in public even though he made his living teaching oratory and writing speeches. Both men, however, were intrigued by the possibilities of a kind of political leadership few Greeks of the fifth century would have dared praise. For different reasons, both were drawn to monarchy.

The concept of a wise monarch ruling by law, which appears in Xenophon's encomium on his friend Agesilaus, also plays an important role in his *Cyropaedia* (*The Education of Cyrus*), a historical romance set in an imaginary, sentimentalized Persia. In one of their many heartwarming conversations, Cyrus' mother assures him that Persia is superior to Media in that "among the Persians what is just is defined as what is equal" (*Cyropaedia* 1.3.18). His father the Persian king, she boasts, is always the first to carry out the orders of the state and accept what has been decreed, for "his standard is not his own inclination but rather the law" (1.3.18). This, she says, is what distinguishes kingship from tyranny.

The happy egalitarian Persia of the *Cyropaedia* is a far cry from the despotism set up by Aeschylus and Herodotus as a foil to Greek freedom. Xenophon's image of monarchy would have seemed incongruous (and probably treasonous) in the fifth century, when oligarchy and democracy always provided the poles of the debate. Greeks knew where one man ruled: Persia. The invasions of Darius and Xerxes left Greeks with a strong feeling that to be themselves they needed to live under some form of nonmonarchic government. By the fourth century, despite the overbearing conduct of Artaxerxes, it seemed more likely that the next invasion would go from west to east. Now memories of the Persian menace served primarily to stir thoughts of revenge, not to shape Greek identity. The world had changed, and increasingly people began to question whether a still more radical shift was not called for.

Isocrates proposed just such a change. His view of monarchy also had to do with Persia, but in an entirely different way. Convinced that the manly and intelligent Greek race had a natural right (and an economic need) to rule over slavish and effeminate barbarians, Isocrates yearned for a man who would unite the Greeks in a holy war against Persian degenerates. Such a project would unify the Greeks by turning their aggression outward against a common foe, would enthrone the master race in its appropriate position in world politics, and would improve the economic condition of Greece by taking from Persia: "Try to picture to yourselves," he suggests to his fellow Greeks in his *Panegyricus* of 380, "what vast prosperity we should attain if we should turn the war which now involves ourselves against the people of the continent, and bring the prosperity of Asia across to Europe" (*Panegyricus* 187–188; Norlin)

It was this practical concern that prompted him to cast about for a strongman who could save Greece. He considered such disparate personalities as Jason of Pherae, *tagos* of Thessaly; Dionysius I, the tyrant of Syracuse; and Archidamus III of Sparta. The fact that both Jason and Dionysius owed their power to mercenaries reveals the price he was willing to see Greece pay for unification. When Jason and Dionysius died and Archidamus proved to have more local concerns, Isocrates turned to Philip and the rising power of Macedon to put the program of the *Panegyricus* in motion. Isocrates did not imagine a Macedonian empire over Greece but rather a league of old-fashioned poleis united under a determined leader. When Macedonia did unite Greece in the year of Isocrates' death, the terms were very different from what he had envisioned. Nonetheless, the hope of a Panhellenic crusade against Persia kept him going until the age of nearly 100. After Philip's conquest of Greece in 338 Isocrates wrote to the Macedonian king assuring him that

> a glory unsurpassable and worthy of your past deeds will be yours when you compel the barbarians . . . to be serfs of the Greeks, and when you shall force the king who is now called Great to do whatever you say. For then there will be nothing left for you except to become a god.
>
> (To Philip II 5)

A Real-life Experiment: Dionysius I of Syracuse

An embryonic experiment in uniting Greece under a charismatic leader had already taken place in the west before Philip acceded to the throne of Macedon. Isocrates was not the only person who had once thought Dionysius of Syracuse might be destined for greatness. Dionysius thought so too. Had his successors inherited his energy and determination, the empire Dionysius created in Italy, Sicily, and beyond might have changed the Greek world much as the conquests of Macedon did later in the century. In the event, however, those who came after him lacked his talents and his luck, and in the end all his hard work was re-warded with oblivion. Almost nobody remembers Dionysius, except perhaps as the tyrant caricatured in Cicero who had his daughters shave him because he did not trust barbers. In time, he did not trust his daughters either, and he asked them to forgo the razor and remove his beard by singeing it with heated walnut shells.

Although in some ways his regime evokes that of Peisistratus in sixth-century Athens, Dionysius was very much a product of his time, for his power was firmly grounded in that quintessential fourth-century phenomenon, the mercenary army. Carthaginian invasions provided a springboard for his ambitions. De-nouncing his fellow generals for their failure in dealing with the invaders, he per-suaded the Syracusans to dismiss his colleagues and place him in sole charge. When a staged assassination attempt (after the manner of Peisistratus) gave cre-dence to the need for a bodyguard, he set himself up as a de facto tyrant (405 BC), using a variety of titles such as *basileus* and archon of Sicily. As in Peisistratid Athens, much of the day-to-day machinery of democracy continued to function, but Dionysius always had the last word, and his regime was far bloodier than that of his Athenian predecessor. Whatever he called himself, Dionysius owed his power to a mercenary force that numbered somewhere between ten and twenty thousand men and effected his restoration whenever popular uprisings ousted him from his office. Dionysius remained in power for thirty-eight years until his death in 367, leading the Sicilians in a series of Carthaginian wars with mixed success. Though he was never able entirely to rid Sicily of Carthaginians, he did succeed in uniting much of the island under his rule. He did not hesitate to make alliances with non-Greek peoples in Europe who were attacking Hellenic cities. His alliance with the Lucanians who lived in the Italian interior facilitated his conquest of many coastal Greek cities in southern Italy, and his Gallic allies en-abled him to ravage the coast of western Italy, establish a naval base on Corsica, and occupy the island of Elba. He also took part in the politics of the Greek home-land, usually siding with Sparta but trying to maintain good relations with Syra-cuse's old enemy Athens whenever possible. The Athenians granted him hon-orary citizenship shortly before his death.

Just as he did not scruple to ally with Lucanians and Gauls, Dionysius happily incorporated Sicel and Italian mercenaries into his army, believing that the ad-mixture of non-Greeks would invigorate his fighting force. Naturally he also wished to see as many people as possible indebted to him for their positions. While some were bitter because of his constant conscriptions of labor to build walls that made Syracuse the best fortified city in Europe and to construct a navy of over three hundred ships, others were grateful that he had given them citi-zenship or freed them from slavery. For every slave he freed, however, another free person was seized and sold, for substantial revenue was required to main-tain the mercenaries in the style they demanded. Whole populations were also forcibly relocated to Syracuse from Italy and other parts of Sicily.

Dionysius was the most remarkable military innovator of his day. His ad-vances were most conspicuous in the arena of siege warfare. As we have seen from the course of the Peloponnesian War, Greek sieges normally ended when hunger forced surrender. Dionysius, however, anticipated Alexander the Great in his ability to take cities by storm, making use of the new device known as the *gastraphetēs* (or "bellyshooter" because of the way its operator used his stomach to activate it). In essence a huge composite bow, the gastraphetes was cocked by a soldier who rested his stomach in a groove and pushed the instrument to maximum extension by pressing forward on it. This device could hurl a projectile about 250 yards. Along with wheeled six-storey siege towers with flying bridges, the gastraphetes seems to have been to good effect in Dionysius' siege of Motya, a key Carthaginian stronghold in Sicily that he destroyed in 397. (Greek inhabitants who had remained loyal to Carthage were crucified.) With the addition of artillery to light and heavy infantry and cavalry, Dionysius' army was the most complex in organization and equipment of any fighting force in Greece down to his time.

Document 9.3 Diodorus of Sicily, who often spoke harshly of Dionysius, nonetheless admired his energy and determination. He recounted in his *Library of History* the eagerness with which workmen vied to make the best contributions to the war effort. His account also stressed the force of Dionysius' personality.

After collecting many skilled workmen, he divided them into groups in accordance with their skills, and appointed over them the most conspicuous citizens, offering great bounties to any who created a supply of arms. As for the armour, he distributed among them models of each kind, because he had gathered his mercenaries from many nations; for he was eager to have every one of his soldiers armed with the weapons of his people, conceiving that by such armour his army would, for this very reason, cause great consternation, and that in battle all of his soldiers would fight to best effect in armour to which they were accustomed. And since the Syracusans enthusiastically supported the policy of Dionysius, it came to pass that rivalry rose high to manufacture the arms. . . .

In fact the catapult was invented at this time in Syracuse, since the ablest skilled workmen had been gathered from everywhere into one place. The high wages as well as the numerous prizes offered the workmen who were judged to be the best stimulated their zeal. And over and above these factors, Dionysius circulated daily among the workers, conversed with them in kindly fashion, and rewarded the most zealous with gifts and invited them to his table. Consequently the workmen brought unsurpassable devotion to the devising of many missiles and engines of war that were strange and capable of rendering great service. He also began the construction of quadriremes and quinqueremes, being the first to think of the construction of such ships. . . . With so many arms and ships under construction at one place the beholder was filled with utter wonder at the sight.

Library of History 14.41.4–43.1; translated by C. L. Sherman in Diodorus of Sicily, *vol. VII, Loeb Classical Library, Cambridge, Mass. and London : Harvard University Press, 1954.*

Dionysius envisioned himself as the founder of a dynasty, and he made a public display of the tyrant's freedom from conventional restraints by marrying two women in a single ceremony. In so doing he borrowed considerable trouble for the future. Upon his death, Dionysius II, the son of one wife, found himself in charge but saddled with an official adviser in the person of Dion, the other wife's brother. The two men had radically different temperaments, and they fought for years. Plato, who had met Dion during a stay in Sicily in the 380s, wound up in the middle when Dion twice invited him back to Sicily in the hope that Dionysius II could be improved by the study of philosophy. The attempt was not successful; Plato returned to Athens, and Dion was assassinated in 354.

The burgeoning of an imperial tyranny in the west must be seen in the context of the rising individualism of the fourth century, a phenomenon also visible in Athens in the withdrawal of many affluent citizens from politics to follow private pursuits and in the independent ventures many Athenian generals undertook as mercenaries. Iphicrates married the daughter of the Odrysian king Cotys and spent many years fighting on Cotys' behalf. (What did he do when Cotys attacked Athens' bases in the Chersonese and elsewhere?) The pull that the drive to power exerted on talented individuals is evident in literature as well as life. Plato's dialogue *Gorgias* depicts Socrates in conversation with a brash youth Plato calls Callicles. For Callicles, conventional pieties must be cast aside when they inhibit men of exceptional abilities (such as, presumably, himself). "The man who is to live rightly," he argues, "should let his appetites grow as large as possible and not restrain them, and when these are as large as possible, he must have the power to serve them, because of his bravery and wisdom, and to fill them up with whatever he has an appetite for at any time" (*Gorgias* 491e–492a; Irwin 1979). People of average abilities, Callicles says, being unable to do this, praise temperance and justice to conceal their own impotence. Dionysius, whom Plato had known in Sicily, would probably have agreed. So would Aristotle's employer Philip of Macedon.

*   *   *

The fourth century BC witnessed an explosion of creative energy in many areas. Philosophy, biology, political theory, mathematics, and military science all made significant advances. Where all this fertility was leading is unclear. Solid foundations were established for intellectual traditions that lived and grew for centuries; many of them still flourish in altered—or unaltered—forms. The knowledge generated did not, however, offer salvation to Greece. The increasing specialization of the fourth century led to a division between generals and politicians that resulted in more professional military skills. Consequently generals in the fourth century were better than those of the fifth. Their weapons and machinery were more versatile and sophisticated. New ways of thinking also led to specialized monographs like Xenophon's treatises on the art of horsemanship and the skills necessary for a successful cavalry commander, and the *Siegecraft* of the author known as Aeneas Tacticus. No good, however, came of these improvements. Greeks simply expanded the repertoire of available methods for killing.

The great texts of Greek political theory continue to be read today. The insight they afforded, however, seems to have had little real-life application in their own day. Plato's students never did take over Athenian government, and Aristotle's influence on his pupil Alexander seems to have been negligible. Identifying those who are likely to govern best is always a challenge, and it contributes little to point out the imprudence of according sovereign power to a power-hungry tyrant, a clique of rich men, or an angry mob. It is precisely because wealth and birth have historically been the criteria for inclusion in the elite that democracy has become a popular alternative to oligarchy. It is one thing to advocate an aristocracy of intellect and another to design practical machinery for establishing one. It was a central tenet of Greek intellectuals that most people lacked capacity for growth. Plato and Aristotle worked on the assumption that the secret to reforming government was in nurturing the tiny minority that had this capacity. Their goal was basically to design a constitution that minimized the power prudence must accord to the mindless masses who might otherwise rise up and slaughter their betters.

To say that the polis ultimately failed because it lacked a truly democratic ideology would nonetheless be ridiculous on several counts. First, mighty empires have flourished for long periods without any democratic ideology whatsoever. Second, we know from the vigor and stability of fourth-century Athens that democracy was alive and well, albeit not in the minds of Greece's intellectuals. Third, the polis did not entirely fail. The collapse of polis ideology before the Macedonian onslaught was certainly noticeable in states like Athens and Sparta that had once enjoyed the privilege of framing their own foreign policies. Smaller poleis, however, had long been accustomed to eking out what dignity they could in the shadow of greater powers. The bustling city in fact remained the core of Greek civilization for centuries to come.

TRANSLATIONS

Blanco, Walter and Jennifer Roberts. 1998. *Thucydides: The Peloponnesian War.* New York: W.W. Norton.

Cornford, F. M. 1945. *The Republic of Plato.* London and New York: Oxford University Press.

Dryden, John. n.d. *Pelopidas* in *Plutarch's Lives,* rev. A. H. Clough. New York: Modern Library.

Fowler, H. N. 1925. *The Statesman,* from *Plato: The Statesman, Philebus,* H. N. Fowler, and W. R. Lamb, eds. Loeb Classical Library. Cambridge, Mass. and London: Harvard University Press.

Hamilton, Walter. 1951. *Plato: The Symposium.* Harmondsworth, England: Penguin.

Irwin, Terence. 1979. *Plato: Gorgias.* Oxford: Oxford University Press.

Murray, A. T. 1936. Pseudo-Demosthenes, *Against Neaera,* from *Demosthenes.* Vol. VI. Loeb Classical Library. Cambridge, Mass. and London: Harvard University Press.

Norlin, George. 1966. *Archidamus* and *Panegyricus,* from *Isocrates.* Vol. I. Loeb Classical Library. Cambridge, Mass. and London: Harvard University Press.

Oldfather, C. H. and C. L. Sherman, 1952, 1954. *Diodorus of Sicily.* Vol. VI, VII. Loeb Classical Library. Cambridge, Mass. and London: Harvard University Press.

Warner, Rex. 1979. *Xenophon: A History of My Times* [*The Hellenica*]. Harmondsworth, England: Penguin.

SUGGESTED READING

Bryant, Joseph. 1996. *Moral Codes and Social Structure in Ancient Greece.* Albany: State University of New York Press. The connection between values and social organization from the Archaic period through the Hellenistic Age.

Cartledge, Paul. 1987. *Agesilaos and the Crisis of Sparta.* Baltimore: Johns Hopkins University Press. A close study of fourth-century Sparta.

Caven, Brian. 1990. *Dionysius I: War-Lord of Sicily.* New Haven, Conn.: Yale University Press. A readable examination of the sources for Dionysius' rule that seeks to present him in a more favorable light than has been customary.

Field, G. C. 1967. *Plato and His Contemporaries.* 3rd ed. London: Methuen. The intellectual and historical context of Plato's work.

Grene, Marjorie. 1963. *A Portrait of Aristotle.* Chicago: University of Chicago Press. A lively summary of Aristotle's thought that grounds his world view in his enthusiasm for biology.

Hansen, Mogens H. 1991. *The Athenian Democracy in the Age of Demosthenes.* Oxford and Cambridge, Mass.: Basil Blackwell. An engaging analytical study of Athenian democracy that is crammed with useful facts.

Hunter, Virginia. 1994. *Policing Athens. Social Control in the Attic Lawsuits, 430–320 B.C.* Princeton, N.J.: Princeton University Press. An examination of social control and conflict resolution in Athens, with emphasis on the social matrix and special emphasis on gender relations, slavery, and the role of gossip.

Ober, Josiah. 1989. *Mass and Elite in Democratic Athens: Rhetoric, Ideology, and the Power of the People.* Princeton, N.J.: Princeton University Press. A sociopolitical study of fourth-century Athens that uses the findings of modern social scientists to shed light on the ideology of the democracy as revealed in the work of the orators.

Sage, Michael, ed. 1996. *Warfare in Ancient Greece: A Sourcebook*. London and New York: Routledge. A collection of passages relating to Greek warfare, tied together by thoughtful and detailed commentary that includes critical readings of the sources themselves.

Sinclair, T. A. 1968. *A History of Greek Political Thought*. 2nd ed. Cleveland and New York: Meridian. A thought-provoking analysis of Greek political thinking from Homer through the Roman conquest.

Todd, S. C. 1993. *The Shape of Athenian Law*. Oxford: Oxford University Press. A detailed and analytical study of Athenian law dealing with both procedure and substance.

Tritle, Lawrence, ed. 1997. *The Greek World in the Fourth Century: From the Fall of the Athenian Empire to the Successors of Alexander*. London and New York: Routledge. A collection of essays on the problems of the fourth century, including chapters on Thebes, the Greeks of Asia Minor, and the states of western Greece.

Wood, Ellen Meiksins. 1988. *Peasant-Citizen and Slave: The Foundations of Athenian Democracy* London and New York: Verso. The relationship between agrarian labor and democracy in Classical Athens.

10

PHILIP II AND THE RISE
OF MACEDON

It is one of the great paradoxes of ancient history that the Greek poleis were able to maintain their independence until almost the last third of the fourth century BC. Their tiny size and constant quarrels made their escape from Persian conquest in the early fifth century BC appear almost miraculous, even in antiquity. It was not surprising when the threat of foreign conquest returned a little over a century later. What was surprising was the source of the threat: not the mighty Persian empire, feared by the Greeks for almost two centuries, but the hitherto insignificant kingdom of Macedon located north of Greece in southeastern Europe.

The success of Macedon in conquering the Greek states was due in part to the internal divisions and economic strains that inhibited the evolution of a consistent policy in Athens, in part to the mutual mistrust that stood in the way of an effective united front on the part of the leading poleis—Athens, Sparta, and Thebes. A large part was played as well by the longing many Greeks felt for a radical cure for the ills of Hellas—monarchy, perhaps, and even a crusade such as a monarch could mount against Persia. Credit however must also be given to the unique military and diplomatic gifts of the man who became king of Macedon in 359 BC. A man of exceptional talents and indefatigable determination, Philip II has fascinated historians of antiquity for over two thousand years and continues to do so today.

SOURCES FOR MACEDONIAN HISTORY

Reconstructing the history of Macedon before the reign of Philip II is difficult. The lack of sources that bedevils much of Greek history is an obvious part of the problem. We know the names of several historians who wrote histories of Macedon in antiquity, but only meager fragments of their works survive. The most important of these works was the fifty-eight-book-long *Philippica* of Theopompus of Chios (fourth century BC). A few manuscripts of Theopompus' history were still extant in Constantinople in the ninth century AD, but they disappeared soon thereafter. Nevertheless, much of the content of these works survives in general histories such as those by Diodorus of Sicily (first century BC) and Justin (second century AD).

The biographer Plutarch, the geographer Strabo, and several Athenian orators, including Aeschines, Hyperides, and especially Demosthenes, also preserve important evidence. In addition, archaeological discoveries constantly supplement the evidence of the literary sources. In recent decades, for example, archaeologists have revealed the remains of the early Macedonian capital of Aegae and the adjacent royal cemetery, the important sanctuary of Zeus at Dion, and an Archaic Age cemetery rich in spectacular gold jewelry at Sindos. The combination of literary and archaeological sources has made it possible for historians to reconstruct the history of Macedon in greater detail than ever before.

This reconstruction is complicated by the threefold biases of the available sources. First and foremost, ancient historians treated Macedonian history prior to Alexander the Great as a mere prologue to Alexander's spectacular reign. Second, many sources originate in Athens and, not surprisingly, view Macedonian actions almost entirely in terms of their putative effects on Athenian interests. The fiercely partisan political conflicts of mid-fourth-century Athens only exacerbate this tendency in some of the most important sources. Finally, the authors of most of our sources were strongly influenced by the fourth-century debate concerning the Greek or barbarian character of the Macedonians. As a result, constructing a chronicle of early Macedonian history is relatively easy, but viewing that history from a Macedonian perspective is not. Only recently have historians attempted to study the history of Macedon from a Macedonian point of view instead of reproducing the orientation of the ancient sources by treating it as an appendix to Greek history.

EARLY MACEDONIA

According to the historian Herodotus, Perdiccas, the first king of Macedon, was promised the land illuminated by the sun as his kingdom. The reality was different. For most of the Archaic and early Classical periods of Greek history, the kings of Macedon ruled a chronically unstable kingdom that was often a state more in name than in fact. Sandwiched between Thessaly on the south, Thrace and the Chalcidian League on the east, Paeonia on the north, and Illyria and Epirus on the west, Macedonian kings had to struggle hard to fend off foreign enemies. At the same time, they strove hard to assert their preeminence over the local dynasts, who ruled the various regions that made up the kingdom of Macedon.

Macedonia's geography rendered their struggle even more difficult. Ancient Macedonia consisted of two distinct geographical regions: Lower Macedonia, the great alluvial plain created by the Haliacmon and Axius rivers as they flowed down to the Gulf of Therma; and Upper Macedonia, the horseshoe of rugged uplands and mountains that stretched northwestward toward Illyria and Epirus and was drained by the same two great rivers. The plains of Lower Macedonia formed the heart of the kingdom of Macedon and supported a large agricultural population. Its mountainous hinterlands not only held extensive forests and rich mineral deposits but also sheltered various tribes who jealously guarded their freedom from the control of the lowland Macedonian kings. Uniting these two regions under the authority of the king of Macedon was the essential precondition for the growth and expansion of Macedonian power.

MACEDONIAN SOCIETY AND KINGSHIP

Were the Macedonians Greek? This question is the most contentious issue in Macedonian historiography. In contemporary Balkan politics, conflicting claims to the territory of ancient Macedonia have made the question of the "Greekness" of the ancient Macedonians a burning issue. Modern nationalists may be confident of their answers, but sufficient evidence to settle the issue one way or another is lacking. Thus, although the sources are clear that Greeks could not understand spoken "Macedonian," no texts written in Macedonian survive. Linguists cannot even determine whether Macedonian was an archaic dialect of Greek or another language altogether. Nevertheless, one fact is undisputed: in antiquity neither Macedonians nor Greeks considered the Macedonians to be Greek. Greeks viewed the Macedonians as barbarians like their Thracian and Illyrian neighbors. An exception was made only for the members of the ruling Argead house, who claimed to be the descendants of immigrants from Argos.

More important, although Macedonian kings encouraged the Hellenization of the Macedonian nobility, Macedonian and Greek culture had little in common. While most people in Greece lived by agriculture, still the cities were the core of what was most distinctive in Greek civilization. City life in Macedonia, on the other hand, was limited to a few Greek colonies on the coast of the Gulf of Therma. The few large settlements in the interior of Macedon, such as Aegae and Pella, were dynastic centers without civic institutions. The vast majority of Macedonians were small farmers or seminomadic pastoralists, who lived in scattered villages and owed their primary allegiance to Macedonian aristocrats. Other distinctions divided the two cultures as well. The Macedonian elite, for example, was polygamous, whereas the Greeks were monogamous. The Macedonians' love of unmixed wine and their preference for tumulus burial instead of simple cremation or interment were other significant if less remarkable differences.

The history of the Macedonian monarchy is as much about the efforts of Macedonian kings to tame their turbulent nobility as it is about their efforts to expand their territory. The lifestyle of the Macedonian nobility had more in common with that of Homeric heroes than with that of Classical Greeks. War and hunting were the only suitable activities for a Macedonian noble. Killing was a way of life. Before being recognized as an adult, a young man had to spear a boar without the

Figure 10.1. Macedonia and its neighbors.

aid of a net and kill an enemy. Heavy drinking, fierce competition for preference at the royal court, and struggles over the favors of young men and women all generated violent feuds.

The monarchy was the central institution of Macedonian society. Like Louis XIV of France, the Macedonian kings were autocrats who could well say "I am the state." Although earlier theories held that their powers were limited by an army assembly invested with the right to elect the king and try cases of treason, it is now clear that these hypotheses are groundless. The army might acclaim a new king and witness trials of nobles, but the king and his advisers always made the final decisions. The king made all appointments, all grants of land and privilege, and all responses to petitions. The king alone represented Macedon in foreign affairs. Treaties and alliances were made with him personally, and foreign allies pledged their support to him and his family without reference to the Macedonian people. The king even decided the royal succession. Macedonian kings were polygamous, and, provided only that the new king was an Argead, a king could designate any son by any wife as his successor.

Nevertheless, such a bald summary of the powers of the Macedonian kings is potentially misleading. There were no constitutional limitations on the king's powers, but there were extraconstitutional limits on how these prerogatives were exercised. Greek political theorists usually equated monarchy and tyranny, because they considered the supreme importance of the ruler's personality in public and private spheres alike to be the distinguishing feature of both. This was especially true of Macedon, where no impersonal bureaucracy buffered the king from his subjects. The kings of Macedon spent their lives in the midst of their companions—Macedonian nobles who formed their personal entourage. The kings chose their closest advisers and the members of their bodyguard from these companions. In war, the companions served in an elite cavalry unit personally commanded by the king. It is not surprising, therefore, that Macedonian kings sat on insecure thrones. Only two of Philip II's predecessors died natural deaths. One, Archelaus, was murdered by a disgruntled homosexual lover. The rest died in battle or fell victim to conspiracies.

The Predecessors of Philip II

Philip II was the beneficiary of almost two centuries of patient state building by his Argead predecessors. In view of the decisive role that Philip II and his son Alexander would play in the destruction of the Persian empire, it is ironic that this state-building process began in the late sixth century BC with Amyntas I's alliance with Persia. The alliance was sealed by the marriage of a Macedonian princess to a high Persian official and lasted for over three decades. The Macedonians proved to be loyal allies. During the Persian invasion of Greece in 480 BC, Amyntas' son and successor, Alexander I, personally led the Macedonian contingents against the Greeks. Not surprisingly, after the Persian defeat Alexander I encouraged the spread of stories testifying to his covert support of the Greek cause during the invasion.

Persian rule brought Macedon great advantages, even if later Macedonian tradition attempted to conceal the extent of their collaboration with Persia. Shielded from attack by Thracians and Paeonians by Persian power, Macedon flourished. As a result, Amyntas' successors, Alexander I, Perdiccas II, and Archelaus, were able to take advantage of the Persian defeat and expulsion from Europe in the 470s and extend their territory northwestward to incorporate the highlands of Upper Macedon and eastward to encompass the rich silver-mining area between the Axius and Strymon rivers. By the end of the fifth century, Macedon was the strongest kingdom in the region.

Macedon's growing power and its extensive natural resources attracted the attention of Athens and other Greek cities. Macedonian grain helped sustain many of Athens' allies and subjects, and Macedonian timber was critical to the survival of Athens' fleet. For their part, the fifth-century Macedonian kings used their newfound wealth to pursue their twin goals of winning recognition for themselves as Greeks and Hellenizing the life of the royal court. The first steps were taken by Alexander I. Although he may not actually have competed in the Olympic games, Alexander did support Greeks and Greek culture, offering sanctuary to Mycenaean refugees after the destruction of Mycenae by Argos in 462 and commissioning a poem in his honor from the great Theban poet, Pindar.

Alexander I's successors continued his policy of Hellenization. Archelaus was especially active in this regard, creating a new capital at Pella and establishing a festival in honor of Zeus at Dion in emulation of the festival of Zeus at Olympia. Archelaus also supported Greek artists and writers extensively. Greek craftsmen helped build his new capital at Pella, and probably also the system of fortresses and roads that he had constructed. Even Euripides, the last of the great Athenian tragedians, visited Macedon and wrote his last two tragedies at Archelaus' court. One, the lost *Archelaus*, celebrated his host's alleged Argive ancestry. The other, the *Bacchae*, offered a terrifying and unforgettable evocation of the power of Dionysus—a god particularly at home in Macedon, where excessive use of alcohol often resulted in violence and tragedy. As a result of the actions of the fifth-century kings, the Macedonian court gradually became the principal cultural center in Macedon and the focus of the social life of the Macedonian aristocracy.

Growing commercial and cultural ties could not avert tension between Macedon and Athens. Macedonian expansion into southern Thrace threatened both Athens' control of its north Aegean allies and its desire to secure the rich gold mines of Mount Pangaeus. Athens responded to Macedonian advances by allying itself with Macedon's Thracian rivals and covertly supporting various Macedonian pretenders. For his part, Perdiccas II protected his predecessor's gains by alternately supporting Athens and Sparta during the Peloponnesian War in a diplomatic dance that made his name a byword for treachery among contemporary Athenian writers.

Nevertheless, the achievements of the three great fifth-century kings were short-lived. When Philip II came to power in 360, Macedon was faced by the most severe crisis in its short history. Chronic instability had left the kingdom vulnerable to threats from both Greek and non-Greek enemies. Eight kings ruled Macedon between 400 and 360 BC. Finally, in 360, Philip's brother, Perdiccas III, was killed in battle with the Illyrians. In addition to the king, four thousand Macedonian troops and numerous members of the Macedonian aristocracy died in the battle. Macedon's enemies quickly took advantage of this unprecedented debacle and the chaos that resulted from it. The Illyrians and Paeonians prepared invasions, while the Athenians and Thracians offered their support for insurrections in favor of pretenders to the Macedonian throne. The kingdom seemed on the verge of collapse.

THE REIGN OF PHILIP II

Philip II was born about 382 BC, the last son of Amyntas III and his Illyrian wife Eurydice. Little is known about his early life. According to Plutarch, his mother Eurydice learned to read in order to educate her children. Whatever chance Philip had for education, however, was ended by the turbulent politics of Macedon in the 370s. An unsuccessful attempt by his brother Alexander II to weaken Theban influence in Thessaly led to Philip's spending the years 369 to 367 as a hostage in Thebes. His exile was not all loss. Philip's enforced residence in Thebes, scarcely two years after its victory at Leuctra made it the greatest power in Greece, gave him an insight into Greek politics and military tactics that would later prove invaluable.

Figure 10.2. This miniature ivory head of Philip II was discovered at Vergina. The damage to his right eye caused by a catapult bolt is clearly indicated.

Philip's return to Macedon in 367 coincided with the descent of the kingdom into chaos. Three kings ruled Macedon during the middle and late 360s: Ptolemy of Alorus, Pausanias, and Philip's brother Perdiccas III. The instability encouraged Macedon's enemies and apparently foreclosed any hope for a quick restoration of order to Macedonian affairs. It also provided Philip with an unexpected opportunity. The crisis created by Perdiccas' death demanded a ruler capable of taking decisive action. That ruler could only be Philip, since he was the sole surviving adult Argead. Philip quickly assumed control of the government, and by 357 at the latest he had supplanted his infant nephew Amyntas to become king of Macedon.

When Philip took power in 360, his chances of survival seemed slim. Macedon was threatened by formidable enemies on all sides. Worse yet, pretenders challenged his right to the throne. Seuthes II, the powerful king of the Thracians, supported the claims of three of Philip's half-brothers. The Athenians, still hoping to regain their long-lost colony of Amphipolis, backed the claims of Argaeus, a pretender who had briefly ruled Macedon in the 380s before being expelled by Philip's father, Amyntas II.

In the next two years the situation had changed dramatically. Through astute diplomacy, Philip persuaded the Thracians and Athenians to abandon the Macedonian pretenders they had been supporting. Free to concentrate all his forces against his other enemies, Philip quickly defeated both the Paeonians and Illyrians and regained control of western and northwestern Macedonia. Philip's brilliant use of diplomacy to prepare the way for his decisive military victories over the Paeonians and Illyrians in 358 set the pattern for the rest of his reign.

Success followed success during the remainder of the decade. An alliance with the Molossians in Epirus, who also had long suffered from Illyrian attacks, completed the pacification of Macedon's western frontier and freed Philip to turn his attentions to the east. In quick succession, Philip seized the Greek cities along the coast of the Gulf of Therma and in southwestern Thrace, together with the rich gold-mining region of Mount Pangaeus. The same mines provided Philip with the financial resources—one thousand talents a year, according to Diodorus—required to carry out his various plans during the remainder of his reign.

In less than a decade, Philip had freed Macedon from the enemies that had threatened its survival since the sixth century. His military and diplomatic successes in the 350s were accompanied by far-reaching reforms, giving the kingdom unprecedented military strength and political cohesion.

The Reforms of Philip II

Philip II's rise to power coincided with a revolution in military tactics and weaponry that ended the Greek hoplite's dominance of the battlefield. By introducing these innovations to Macedon, Philip transformed it almost overnight into the preeminent military power in southeastern Europe. Some of his innovations were technological. Dionysius I of Syracuse had first demonstrated the potential of the catapult at the siege of Motya in 397. It was Philip, however, who realized that potential by introducing new and more powerful torsion catapults powered by energy stored in tightly twisted ropes. Combined with the creation of an elite corps of military engineers, these new weapons enabled Philip successfully to besiege fortified cities such as Amphipolis. At the same time, the skirmishing and scouting abilities of his army were enhanced by special units of light armed infantry and cavalry recruited from his non-Macedonian subjects and allies.

Document 10.1 Alexander's Speech at Opis (324 BC) In this speech the Roman historian Arrian has Alexander adduce the changes Philip II brought to Macedonia in an effort to quell the mutiny of his troops at Opis in 324.

In the first place, as is reasonable, I shall begin my speech from my father Philip. For he found you vagabonds and destitute of means, most of you clad in hides, feeding a few sheep up the mountain sides, for the protection of which you had to fight with small success against Illyrians, Triballians, and the border Thracians. Instead of the hides he gave you cloaks to wear, and from the mountains he led you down into the plains, and made you capable of fighting the neighboring barbarians, so that you were no longer compelled to preserve yourselves by trusting rather to the inaccessible strongholds than to your own valor. He made you colonists of cities, which he adorned with useful laws and customs; and from being slaves and subjects, he made you rulers over those very barbarians by whom you yourselves, as well as your property, were previously liable to be carried off or ravaged. He also added the greater part of Thrace to Macedonia, and by seizing the most conveniently situated places on the sea-coast, he spread abundance over the land from commerce, and made the working of the mines a secure employment. He made you rulers over the Thessalians, of whom you had formerly been in mortal fear; and by humbling the nation of the Phocians, he rendered the avenue into Greece broad and easy for you, instead of being narrow and difficult. The Athenians and Thebans, who were always lying in wait to attack Macedonia, he humbled to such a degree . . . that . . . those states in their turn procure security to themselves by our assistance.

Arrian, Anabasis Alexandri 7.9, *translated by E. J. Chinnock.* Arrian's Anabasis of Alexander and Indica. *London and New York: G. Bell & Sons, 1893.*

Philip's most important military reform was the reorganization of the Macedonian infantry. Philip created a new uniformly equipped phalanx to replace the old undisciplined militia that had served Macedonian kings so poorly in the past. As in the old general levy, the six divisions of the new phalanx were recruited from each of Macedon's traditional territorial divisions, but they were equipped

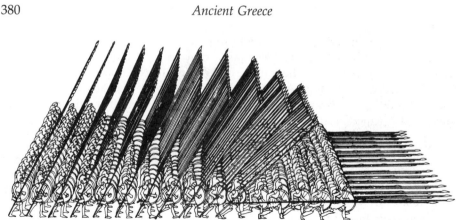

Figure 10.3. The Macedonian phalanx.

with new weapons and assigned a new role in battle. Each member of the phalanx wore a metal helmet and carried a small shield and a short sword. His principal weapon, however, was an enormous pike that could be as much as 18 feet
long, allowing the soldier to strike a blow before his enemies could close and use
their shorter weapons.

In this way, Philip deprived his Greek opponents of their chief tactical advantage: the ability to concentrate hoplites in close formation against an enemy and
destroy him. As a result, the mere presence of the new phalanx in a battle forced
Philip's enemies to modify their tactics to cope with this unusual formation. The
tactical opportunities thus created could then be exploited by the companion cavalry, which would deal a decisive blow to an enemy force already confused by
the phalanx and the elite guard units protecting its flanks.

Philip's reforms were not limited to reorganization of the Macedonian army.
He also took steps to strengthen the bonds between the army, its leaders, and the
king. He freely shared his men's hardships and dangers, as his many wounds (including the loss of an eye) attested. He conferred a new title on the common soldiers, *Pezhetairoi* ("Foot Companions"), suggesting that they too, like the nobles,
were the king's personal companions. A generation later, the rage of Alexander's
soldiers at the thought of sharing their cherished new status with the conquered
Persians clearly demonstrated the powerful bond Philip had forged with his soldiers.

Philip also made important changes in the nature of the bond between the king
and the Macedonian nobility. Perdiccas III's disastrous defeat had caused the
deaths of many Macedonian noblemen. Philip used the opportunity thus created
to recruit new members for the royal companions, chosen from the Greeks and
non-Greeks who flocked to Macedon in search of opportunity and wealth. He
also created opportunities for members of the old nobility, who received commands in Philip's new model army. Their sons also became members of a new
institution, the royal pages. The pages personally served the king and were educated at court. From them Philip recruited his future officers. But at the same time

the royal pages also served a second purpose: they were hostages for the good behavior of their families.

Theopompus, the moralizing contemporary historian of Philip's reign, sarcastically characterized Philip's expanded corps of companions as composed of men more suited to be "courtesans" than "courtiers." Nevertheless, their personal loyalty to Philip was strong, and for good reason. Philip's victories gave him unprecedented resources in land and treasure, and he used them to reward his followers liberally. Philip's ability to attract and reward loyal supporters was enhanced by land reclamation projects, such as the draining of marshland in Lower Macedonia, combined with the foundation of colonies such as Philippi. As a result, Philip possessed what no previous Macedonian king had ever had before: an extensive and loyal base of support for his policies at home and abroad.

Philip Becomes a Force in Greece

Macedonian kings had long feared the potential danger posed by a united Thessaly, with its large population and its strong military tradition. Philip's predecessors had sought unsuccessfully to avert that threat. They repeatedly supported Larisa against Jason and Alexander—Pherae's ambitious tyrants—and their Theban allies. Jason, in fact, nearly reduced Philip's father Amyntas III to the status of a vassal in the late 370s, and, as we have already seen, Alexander II's unsuccessful Thessalian campaign in 369 resulted in Philip's Theban exile.

Not surprisingly, developments in Thessaly in the mid-350s led Philip also to intervene in the tangled politics of Macedon's southern neighbor. The primary cause was the conclusion of an alliance between Phocis and Macedon's old enemy Pherae. Phocis had suddenly emerged in the mid-350s as one of the major powers in central and northern Greece. The union of Pherae and Phocis threatened the interests of both Larisa and Thebes (Phocis' bitter enemy), and forced them to invite Philip's intervention. Philip initially underestimated the seriousness of the threat posed by the alliance of Pherae and Phocis. He was disabused by two defeats inflicted by Phocian forces in 353—the most serious he suffered in his entire reign—and he returned to Thessaly with overwhelming force the following year, crushing the Phocians at the Battle of the Crocus Field.

This battle transformed Philip's relationship to Thessaly and the rest of Greece. In the immediate aftermath of Philip's victory, Pherae was seized, and its last tyrant fled into exile. Finally freed of the Pheraean threat, the Thessalian League met and appointed Philip *archōn* ("commander-in-chief") of Thessaly, effectively uniting Thessaly and Macedon in the person of Philip. The union of Thessaly and Macedon virtually doubled the military forces at Philip's disposal and brought the first decade of his reign to a successful conclusion. It also allowed Philip to expand his influence deep into central Greece.

While Philip was busy extending Macedonian influence in Thessaly, central Greece was convulsed by the conflict historians call the Third Sacred War. Behind the outbreak of the war was Thebes' attempt to consolidate its hegemony in central Greece. Exploiting a favorable majority on the council of the Delphic Amphictyony, Thebes arranged to have Phocis severely fined in 357 for cultivating land sacred to Apollo. Phocis' response was unexpected.

Phocis had long been Thebes' chief rival for preeminence in central Greece. Thebes had exploited its victory at Leuctra in 371 to force Phocis to sign a treaty recognizing Theban suzerainty. Phocis' acceptance of Theban suzerainty had been grudging at best, and in 357 the Phocians made a desperate effort to regain their independence. Instead of submitting to Theban blackmail, they seized control of Delphi and used the treasures of Apollo to recruit a powerful mercenary army. Although the sacrilege outraged Greek opinion, Thebes' attempt to form a united front against Phocis was frustrated by Athenian and Spartan hostility to further expansion of Theban power. As a result, the Phocians quickly brought almost the whole region from the Gulf of Corinth to Thessaly under their sway.

Frustrated at their inability to defeat the Phocians, Thebes and its Thessalian allies appealed to Philip, the new leader of Thessaly, to come to Delphi's aid. Hostilities in Thrace as well as with Athens and Olynthus in the north Aegean prevented Philip from taking action against Phocis for several years. In 347 he finally intervened on the side of Thebes in the Sacred War. Although Macedonian intervention tipped the scales against Phocis, increasing Theban power was not in Philip's interest. Philip, therefore, played a double game. At the same time that he supported Thebes militarily, he also opened negotiations with Phocis over possible surrender terms.

The traditional penalty for sacrilege such as the Phocians had committed against Delphi was the execution of all males of military age. With that dire threat hanging over their heads, the Phocians quickly accepted Philip's offer and surrendered in the summer of 346. As Philip had promised, the terms imposed by the Delphic Amphictyony on Phocis proved to be relatively mild. Phocian cities were broken up into their constituent villages. The Phocians undertook to pay back the treasure they had taken from Delphi at a rate of sixty talents per year. Most important, Phocis' votes in the Delphic Amphictyony were transferred to Philip, who henceforth, thanks to his control of Thessaly, enjoyed a voting majority on the Amphictyonic Council.

As a result of his timely intervention in the Sacred War, Philip had won for himself an important role in Delphic affairs. Just how significant a position he now occupied was made clear to all Greeks in 346 when he became the first Macedonian king to be granted the honor of presiding over the Pythian games supervised by the Amphictyony. Philip's spectacular success in the Sacred War also temporarily halted the growing hostility between Macedon and Athens.

Philip, Athens, and the Peace of Philocrates

Because of the Athenians' vested interest in Chalcidice, their tense relations with Philip dated back to the beginning of his reign. In 359, Philip had induced Athens to withdraw its support from his rival, Argaeus, by promising to restore Amphipolis to its authority. The Athenians quickly learned, however, that their trust in Philip's promises had been misplaced. Philip needed Amphipolitan land to reward his supporters; moreover, its strategic location near the mouth of the Strymon River made the city too significant to turn over to Athens. Two years later, in 357, Philip himself occupied Amphipolis after a brief siege. The rapidity with which Philip's new siege engines broke through Amphipolis' defenses gave the Greeks a vivid demonstration of the effectiveness of his new engineering corps.

Relations worsened a year later when Philip also captured Athens' principal remaining Macedonian allies, Pydna and Methone, as well as Potidaea. In so doing, he eliminated the main centers of Athenian influence in the Chalcidice and on the coasts of the Gulf of Therma. Though many Athenians wanted to fight Philip, and in fact the city declared war, circumstances prevented Athens from mounting serious military operations in the north Aegean.

Athens' slow recovery from the economic devastation caused by the Peloponnesian War restrained the ambitions of all fourth-century Athenian politicians. Financial resources had to be carefully husbanded. Early in the 350s this meant that Athens ignored Philip's actions in northern Greece to focus its efforts on coping with the threat to the Second Athenian League caused by the outbreak of the Social War in 357. Athenian foreign policy was further constrained by an important political innovation of the 350s.

Until this time, surpluses from the annual government budgets had been channeled into a fund normally devoted to military expenditures. Eubulus (c. 405–c. 335 BC), however, the leading politician of this era, persuaded the Athenians to pass a law assigning all surplus instead to what is known as the Theoric Fund; he himself served as one of the commissioners of the Fund. Some of this Fund was to be used for projects such as repairing roads and fortifications. The rest was earmarked for distribution to Athenian citizens at religious festivals; the Fund received its name from the "theatrical" performances that played a key role in these celebrations.

By mitigating the poverty of Athens' neediest citizens, this arrangement reduced tensions between rich and poor. For good reason, the orator Demades called it "the glue of the democracy." The Theoric Fund also, of course, encouraged a pacifist foreign policy. Before, the poorer classes might expect to benefit from war, during which they would be paid to row in the fleet, whereas those who had more were sometimes inclined to protect what they had by voting against military involvements. After the establishment of the Theoric Fund, however, this changed, since the outbreak of war would require that funds be redirected to military operations, and the level of the populace's benefits would be reduced.

Eubulus' keen interest in finances had dramatic results. Under his stewardship, Athenian revenues rose from 130 talents to 400, enabling Athens to construct new triremes and improve the docks and fortifications. Work at the neglected silver mines at Laurium was renewed and new inducements lured additional metics to Attica. The wealth of individual citizens grew with that of the state. This situation makes it easy to understand why for most of the decade the Athenians confined their response to Philip's actions to desultory raids into Macedonian territory that were little more than nuisances. Only the threat of pos-

Figure 10.4. Polyeuctus' posthumous portrait of Demosthenes was erected in the Athenian *agora* in 280 BC and survives in this Roman copy. It shows the orator as gaunt, worried, and thoughtful. (Note: The position of the hands is reproduced incorrectly in this copy.)

sible direct military intervention by Philip in central Greece induced them to take stronger action.

With a Macedonian invasion of Attica seemingly imminent, the Athenians dispatched a large expeditionary force in 352 to occupy Thermopylae, to block the Macedonian advance. The motion was made by a close associate of Eubulus. In such a crisis, concern for Athens' security clearly overrode any scruples Eubulus and his supporters may have had about dipping into the Theoric Fund. Otherwise, however, Athens failed utterly to hinder the Macedonian king's growing influence in northern and central Greece.

Athens' actions in the early 340s were similarly ineffective. When Olynthus, increasingly suspicious of Philip's growing power, abandoned its alliance with the Macedonian king and sought to make peace with Athens, Philip turned on his former ally. Athens' response to Olynthus' desperate appeals for help were too little, and too late. The Athenians could only watch in dismay when, in 348, Philip captured the city, razed it, and carried off its citizens to become slaves in Macedon. Worse, he dismantled the Chalcidic League, Macedon's only potential Greek rival in the north Aegean.

Athens' restraint in the face of Philip's growing power was prudent. Nevertheless, its inability to regain Amphipolis or to aid its erstwhile allies was humiliating. Not surprisingly, proponents of a more aggressive Athenian policy toward Macedon became more insistent in their demands.

The most prominent of these politicians was Demosthenes. The most famous orator of the Greek world, Demosthenes acquired such a reputation for eloquence that the Roman statesman Cicero named his speeches against Mark Antony "Philippics" after the orations in which Demosthenes had sought to rouse the Athenians against Philip. Demosthenes had entered politics initially as a supporter of Eubulus. By 351, however, he had become disenchanted with Eubulus' policies and consequently began to forge a new political identity for himself. In the famous *First Philippic*, Demosthenes revealed his new views by vigorously attacking Philip and berating the Athenians for their sluggish response to the danger he posed to Athens. Simultaneously, he urged the Athenians to vote for the establishment and support of a strong naval force to conduct the desired war. Demosthenes continued to advocate resistance to Philip in subsequent years. Still, even he recognized that the fall of Olynthus, combined with Philip's triumph in the Sacred War and the defection of the vital Athenian naval base of Euboea, made peace imperative if Athens was to avoid total disaster.

The Athenian politician Philocrates negotiated peace with Philip in the summer of 346. The process of negotiating the treaty and securing its approval by the Athenian assembly was both complex and contentious. Because the Peace of Philocrates quickly collapsed amidst bitter dispute over the responsibility for its negotiation, much remains unclear about the details of the diplomacy that produced it. The terms of the treaty, however, allow no doubt about its meaning. Faced with the unpalatable alternatives of continuing the war with Macedon or accepting the humiliating terms offered by Philip, Athens chose the latter. Athens publicly renounced its long-cherished claim to Amphipolis, accepted the exclusion of its Phocian and Thracian allies from the protection of the treaty, and agreed that the city and the remnants of the Second Athenian League would become permanent allies of Philip and his descendants. Athens' impotence in the face of growing Macedonian power and influence in Greece was now revealed for all to see.

The Aftermath of the Peace of Philocrates

By signing the Peace of Philocrates, the Athenians recognized Philip's preeminence in northern and central Greece. Nevertheless, Philip's diplomatic triumph was short-lived. Athens' support for the treaty had been the result of the fear of war with Macedon and its consequences. It was therefore no surprise that support dissipated as soon as the threat of war receded. Philip's treatment of Phocis, moreover, not only angered and embarrassed the Athenians; it also cast doubt on the credibility of the ambassadors such as Philocrates and Eubulus' ally the orator Aeschines. Along with Philocrates, Aeschines had persuaded the Athenian assembly that no harm would come to the Phocians as a result of their exclusion from the Peace. When Phocis surrendered to him, however, Philip, as already mentioned, destroyed the towns of Phocis and resettled their inhabitants in separate villages. The Amphictyonic Council transferred to Philip the two votes at their meetings that had previously belonged to the Phocians. The Athenians and Spartans were so angry at the Council's decision that they declined to send their customary deputations to the Pythian games. Aeschines, however, was in attendance, apparently as Philip's guest.

Philip's critics in Athens steadily undermined the Peace of Philocrates and the men associated with it, using the destruction of Phocis to point out the dishonesty of Philip and the questionable competence and integrity of his Athenian supporters. Philip's proposals to strengthen the peace were rebuffed. Indeed, Athens once again demanded that he return Amphipolis. Philocrates, the principal architect of the peace, was indicted for bribery and fled into exile to escape execution. Demosthenes, another of the ten ambassadors who had been sent to negotiate with Philip, nervously sought to protect his position by also impeaching his fellow envoy Aeschines on a charge of accepting bribes.

Aeschines' open partisanship for Philip even after the destruction of Phocis was foolish, and it seems clear that he had accepted gifts from the Macedonian king. Though it was not necessarily a crime in Athens for politicians to receive presents from a foreign head of state unless it could be demonstrated that these gifts led them into unpatriotic acts, the case against Aeschines looks fairly strong. It is a testimony to the power of his allies that when the case finally came to trial in 343 he was acquitted, though by a very small margin. In his corner was not only Eubulus, the most prominent politician in Athens and a staunch advocate of peace, but the strategos Phocion (c. 402/401–318 BC). A biting denigrator of democracy who was elected to the strategia more often than any other man (forty-five times between 371 and 318), Phocion was favorable to Macedon and in fact was executed for his Macedonian sympathies in 318. In addition to harboring many Macedonian partisans among its own citizens, moreover, Athens openly supported or sheltered enemies of Philip from other states.

Only Philip's need for peace in Greece during his Thracian campaign in 342 prevented him from taking strong action against Athens. Philip finally declared war in 340, when Athens in alliance with several other Greek states and Persia frustrated his siege of the Hellespontine city of Perinthus. Athens responded with its own declaration of war.

The actual outbreak of hostilities was delayed for another year. First, Philip unsuccessfully besieged Byzantium; then, he campaigned against the Scythians, who ruled the Dobruja in modern Romania and threatened Macedonian control of Thrace. Nevertheless, he was still able to give Athens a sharp reminder of the potential consequences of war with Macedon. Athens depended for much of its food on grain imported from the Black Sea, so that when Philip seized the whole Black Sea grain fleet in 340, panic broke out in the city.

Philip's long-awaited opportunity to strike directly at Athens finally came in 339, when the Delphic Amphictyony invited him to lead a sacred war against the city of Amphissa, just south of Delphi. He quickly accepted the invitation, and by the end of the year he and his army were securely ensconced in Phocis, within easy striking distance of Athens.

In one of the most famous passages in Greek literature, Demosthenes proudly recalled that only he had the courage to address the assembly, when news reached Athens of Philip's presence in Phocis.

> At dawn the next day the Prytaneis called the Council to the Chamber, and citizens moved into the Assembly. . . . The Council appeared, announced the news they had received, and brought forward their informant to repeat it. The herald then voiced the question "Who desires to speak?" No one moved. The question was repeated several times without a man standing up, though all the strategoi were there, all the orators, and the voice of Athens called for a word to save her. . . . I came forward and addressed the Assembly.
>
> (On the Crown, *pp. 169–172; Saunders 1975*)

The Athenians' despair was understandable. Demosthenes' efforts to form a grand Greek alliance against Macedon had only limited success. Only Corinth, Megara, and Messenia, together with a number of other cities in the northern and western Peloponnesus, had heeded Demosthenes' appeal. Sparta, still bitter about the Thebans' liberation of Messenia three decades earlier, remained aloof from the alliance. Throughout history, the Athenians have been censured for failing to respond quickly and vigorously to the growing Macedonian threat, but it is important to remember the role played in the final confrontation by the Spartans' refusal to stand by their fellow Greeks. When battle was finally joined in late summer 338 at Chaeronea in Boeotia, only the levies of Athens and Thebes and the Boeotian League and a few Peloponnesian units faced Philip.

A monumental stone lion still gazes over the plain of Chaeronea, marking the site of this pivotal battle in world history. Otherwise little is known about the battle itself beyond two facts: Greek casualties were heavy, and the decisive blow was struck by the companion cavalry led by Philip's 18-year-old son and heir, Alexander. A thousand Athenians were killed and another two thousand cap-

Figure 10.5. This burial monument marks the graves of 254 Thebans buried at the site of the battle of Chaeronea.

tured; the Thebans' cherished Sacred Band was slaughtered to a man. Philip's triumph over his Greek foes was complete. Whether Philip had planned all along to conquer Greece is unknown. After his victory at Chaeronea, however, any resistance to his authority in Greece would have been futile. All that remained to be determined was the form Macedonian domination of Greece would take.

MACEDONIAN DOMINATION OF GREECE

According to the historian Diodorus, a drunken Philip celebrated his victory by mocking the Greek dead until an Athenian prisoner, the politician Demades, sobered him up with the remark that his conduct ill befitted a great king. Whether the story is true or not, Philip's decisions after Chaeronea reflected careful thought. Exactly when Philip decided to attack Persia is uncertain, but his actions in the aftermath of the battle make it clear that the decision had already been made by the early 330s.

Philip's immediate concern was how to deal with his two principal enemies. The Thebans were treated with exemplary harshness. As Thebes had a long record of collaboration with Persia and was Macedon's chief rival for power in central and northern Greece, Philip took advantage of his victory to break the city's power. Theban and other Boeotian prisoners were released only after payment of a heavy ransom. Thebes' political leaders were either executed or exiled. A Macedonian garrison was installed on the Cadmea, the city's acropolis. Finally, Thebes was stripped of its traditional position of leadership in the Boeotian League.

Philip's treatment of Athens was dramatically different. Athenian support was essential to the long-term pacification of Greece. A difficult siege would be required to capture the city, and in the meantime, its fleet could seriously interfere with his projected Persian campaign. Consequently, Athens escaped significant punishment despite its leading role in the war. Athenian prisoners were returned without ransom, and the bodies of the Athenian dead were escorted back to the city by an honor guard led by Alexander and Antipater, Philip's most trusted general. Nor did Philip object when Demosthenes, his most implacable opponent, delivered the funeral oration over the dead of Chaeronea.

Philip's actions were well received. Few Greeks regretted the humiliation of Thebes, whose arbitrary behavior in the decades since the Battle of Leuctra had bred widespread resentment. Athens, for its part, responded to Philip's unexpected leniency by showering the city's former enemies with honors. Antipater and Alexander were made Athenian citizens and a cult was established in Philip's honor in one of the city's gymnasia. Needless to say, Athenian suspicion of Philip's intentions or those of his supporters at Athens did not disappear: a law passed in 337 promised severe penalties for anyone who conspired to overthrow the democracy and establish a tyranny. Some, however, welcomed Macedon as a force in Athenian politics. After Chaeronea as before, all shades of opinion thrived in the city along with a variety of sentiments toward Philip ranging from reverence to hatred.

Officially, however, relations were amicable. Antipater and Alexander were not the only Macedonian subjects to benefit from the thaw in relations between Philip and Athens. Athenian inscriptions demonstrate that contact between Athens and the Macedonian court became increasingly common in the years after the Battle of Chaeronea. One of those who took advantage of the new relationship between Athens and Macedon was the philosopher Aristotle. A close friend of Antipater and the former tutor of Alexander, Aristotle returned to Athens in 335 and remained there until 322, when renewed anti-Macedonian sentiment forced him to flee to Euboea. There he died the same year.

The school that Aristotle founded at Athens, the Lyceum, became the model for the great research institutions of the Hellenistic period. Philip, however, had no such elevated goals in mind when he so dramatically dispatched Antipater and Alexander to Athens in 337. His immediate purpose was to avoid a difficult siege and win Athens' acquiescence in his plans for Greece, and his calculated generosity largely succeeded in achieving those goals. Athens offered no further resistance to Macedonian preeminence in Greece. More important, the Athenians agreed to send representatives to the general meeting of Greek states at Corinth that Philip called in the summer of 337 BC, where Philip revealed his plans for the future.

The Corinthian League

Except for the Spartans, who refused to attend, all the major Greek states sent representatives to Corinth to learn Philip's plans. No account of what transpired at Corinth survives, but the main points of Philip's proposals are known. The centerpiece of the new order was an alliance, traditionally referred to as the Corinthian League, but which Philip called simply "the Greeks." The purpose of the alliance was twofold: to maintain a common peace in Greece and to retaliate against the Persians for the invasion of 480 BC and other acts of aggression against Greeks. To achieve those ends, the council (*synedrion*) of the alliance was empowered to pass decrees binding on member states, to arbitrate disputes between them, and to try individuals accused of betraying the goals and policies of the alliance. Member states of the alliance also received pledges of mutual nonaggression and promises of support against attack or subversion of their governments. Not surprisingly, Philip's proposals were approved by the delegates, and he was appointed *hēgemōn*, ("leader") of the alliance and commander of the war of revenge against the Persians.

Document 10.2 Oath of Members of the League of Corinth

(338–337 BC) Fragment of an Athenian inscription recording the oath sworn by the Athenians when they ratified the treaty establishing the League of Corinth.

Oath. I swear by Zeus, Earth, Sun, Poseidon, Athena, Ares, and all the gods and goddesses. I will abide by the peace, and I will not break the agreements with Philip the Macedonian, nor will I take up arms with hostile intent against any one of those who abide by the oaths either by land or by sea. I will not seize in war by any device or stratagem any city or fort or harbor belonging to those who share the peace, nor will I suppress the kingdom of Philip or of his descendants or the constitutions in force among any of those [who share the peace], when they swore the oaths concerning the peace. I will not commit any act that contravenes the agreements nor will I permit any other to do so. If any one breaks the agreements, I will assist those who have been wronged in accordance with their requests and I will fight against those who break the common peace just as the common council and the leader (*hēgemōn*) decide. . . .

Inscriptiones Graecae 2.236.

Historians have long recognized that the primary purpose of the League of Corinth was to legitimize Philip's domination of Greece, and it did so in a way that was all the more effective because it reflected important trends in contemporary Greek thought. Ever since the end of the Peloponnesian War, Greek politicians and thinkers, dismayed by chronic political and social unrest, had sought ways to end the constant warfare that plagued fourth-century Greece. In works like the *Republic* and the *Laws*, Plato and other philosophers offered utopian visions of ideal cities free of stasis that they themselves knew could not be realized. More pragmatic thinkers sought to redefine the place of war in Greek life. They denounced wars between Greeks as civil wars, while insisting that wars against barbarians were inherently just or even desirable as a way of reducing internal tensions in Greece. These ideas were embodied in the repeated attempts to establish "common peaces," such as the King's Peace and its various successors, that are so characteristic of fourth-century Greek diplomacy.

The most prominent of the just-war theorists was the Athenian educator Isocrates. Isocrates was almost 100 years old when the Battle of Chaeronea occurred. Throughout his long career as a speech writer and teacher of rhetoric, he had brooded on Greece's chronic social problems. His proposed solution, as we have seen in Chapter 9, was conquering a portion of the Persian empire, providing a place to which economically deprived and potentially dangerous segments of Greek society could emigrate. He had appealed in vain to various Greek rulers, including Dionysius I of Syracuse and Jason of Pherae, to forcibly unite Greece and lead it in a crusade against Persia. Philip must have seemed Isocrates' last chance to see his dream realized. Unfortunately, we do not know how Philip responded when he invited him to lead such a crusade after his victory at the Battle of Chaeronea, but by uniting in the League of Corinth the ideas of a "common peace" and a crusade against Persia Philip was exploiting ideas that had deep roots in fourth-century BC Greece.

The Death of Philip II

The Corinthian League's approval of Philip's plan for a Persian war was well timed. The early 330s were a time of severe crisis for the Persian empire. The able but ruthless king Artaxerxes III (358–338 BC) had struggled throughout his reign to rebuild Persian power, and by the late 340s his efforts had been crowned with success. He ended the satrapal rebellions that had disrupted the reign of his father Artaxerxes II (405–359 BC), reestablished Persian authority in Phoenicia and Asia Minor, and even reconquered Egypt, which had been independent since the end of the fifth century.

Artaxerxes' power rivaled that of his great sixth- and fifth-century ancestors. Demosthenes and other enemies of Philip looked to the Persian king for assistance against Macedon. But disaster struck almost as soon as Persia had reemerged as a significant factor in the affairs of the eastern Mediterranean basin. In 338, an ambitious eunuch named Bagoas assassinated Artaxerxes III and precipitated a succession crisis that lasted for almost two years. Only after a relative of Artaxerxes succeeded in killing the treacherous eunuch and himself ascended the throne of Persia as Darius III did the crisis end and a semblance of stability return.

In 336, Philip quickly took advantage of the chaos at the heart of the Persian empire by sending an expeditionary force across the Hellespont, commanded by his trusted general Parmenion. As the Macedonian army moved southward down the west coast of Anatolia, Philip's supporters in various Greek cities revolted and overthrew their pro-Persian tyrants. At Eresus on Lesbos, the new government signaled its adhesion to the Macedonian cause by establishing a cult to Zeus Philippios; at Ephesus Philip's supporters had a statue of the king placed in the temple of Artemis. The successes achieved by Parmenion and his expeditionary force in 336 augured well for the main campaign Philip was to lead the following year.

Before that campaign could take place, however, fate intervened. In the summer of 336, Philip was assassinated at Aegae by a member of his own bodyguard named Pausanias. His assassination was the climax of the turbulence that had marked his personal life during the last years of his reign, resulting from his seventh marriage in 338. For most of his reign Philip's queen had been his fourth wife, the Epirote princess Olympias, who bore his designated heir, Alexander. His other marriages to Thessalian, Thracian, Illyrian, and even Scythian brides had served diplomatic ends without threatening Olympias' position at court. Philip's seventh marriage was different. For the first time, Philip took a Macedonian bride, a young woman named Cleopatra, and allied himself to a powerful Macedonian noble family.

Scholars have been unable to explain Philip's final marriage. Ancient writers saw it as the result of a disastrous infatuation with a younger woman. Some modern scholars have suggested that Philip may have hoped that the new marriage might result in additional sons to strengthen his family's hold on the throne. Whatever Philip's plans may have been, the dramatic consequences of his marriage quickly became evident. In short order both Olympias and Alexander fell from favor and fled into exile, amidst talk that Philip intended to supplant his son with a "Macedonian" heir.

As it turned out, the threat to Alexander's position ended almost as suddenly as it had begun. In 337 Cleopatra bore Philip a daughter named Europa. The child's name bore witness to Philip's understandable pride in his accomplishments, but a woman could not succeed to the Macedonian throne. Without a new son to replace Alexander as heir, Philip had no choice but to reconcile with him. A mutual friend, Demaratus of Corinth, effected the rapprochement. Although Olympias remained in exile in Epirus, Alexander returned to Pella and resumed his place at court. The crisis over the succession had ended, it seemed, without serious consequences.

Indirectly, however, Philip's ill-advised marriage to Cleopatra proved to be his undoing. The union inevitably embroiled Philip in the enmities of her family, and one of them involved his assassin, Pausanias. According to Aristotle, Pausanias killed Philip because he had been abused by Cleopatra's uncle Attalus and Philip had done nothing about it. The details are preserved by Diodorus, who makes it clear that the abuse had been extreme. Attalus' servants had raped Pausanias. The motive for this atrocious act was revenge for the death of a young relative of Attalus, whom Pausanias had slandered because Philip had chosen the latter as his lover. Unwilling to endanger his alliance with his new queen's family, Philip sought to palliate Pausanias' grievance by promoting him to the coveted rank of royal bodyguard.

Philip's efforts to mollify the young man were conspicuously unsuccessful, and the wedding of Philip's daughter Cleopatra gave Pausanias an opportunity for vengeance. The climax of the wedding festivities was a splendid procession led by Philip. As the procession entered the theater at Aegae, Pausanias rushed forward and stabbed Philip to death before the startled eyes of the guests who had come from all over the Macedonian empire to witness the king's triumph. So ended the reign of the most controversial of all Macedonian kings.

*   *   *

Could Greek union and resolve have prevented the Macedonian takeover? Twentieth-century historians have sometimes compared Philip with Hitler, casting Demosthenes in the role of Winston Churchill (a construct deeply flattering to Demosthenes, whose efforts failed conspicuously). Whether or not the analogy has validity, it raises the question whether Philip's success was not contingent on Greek vacillation and appeasement—and on the collusion of pro-Macedonian factions in the poleis: it is important to remember Phocion's long-standing affection for Macedon. This question seems ultimately unanswerable, for history is not a laboratory science, and we have no way of replaying the fourth century BC with a healthier, richer, and less divided Greece. What is clear is that Philip II was a remarkable man.

Since antiquity, historians have had difficulty assessing Philip and his achievements. Polybius was bewildered by the opening of Theopompus of Chios' great history of Philip. It began with the observation that "Europe had never produced a man like Philip" and then went on to catalogue Philip's "crimes and follies," including his unbridled sexuality and drunkenness, his betrayal of his friends and allies, and his destruction of Greek cities. As so often in such matters, the problem is partly one of perspective. Polybius wrote two centuries after Philip's death and found it difficult to sympathize with Theopompus, a fourth-century Greek who had viewed Philip primarily as a foreign, malignant force in Greek affairs and not as the founder of Macedonian greatness.

Which point of view is correct? In fact, both have merit. It is impossible to deny that in many ways Philip's influence on contemporary Greek affairs was negative. The destruction of cities such as Amphipolis, Methone, Stagira, and Olynthus is well documented. Nevertheless, Philip was first and foremost king of Macedon. His primary concern was the welfare of Macedon, not that of Greece. In that regard he succeeded. In the twenty-four years of his reign, Philip transformed Macedon from a kingdom on the verge of dissolution to a unified state, ruling an empire that extended from the Danube to southern Greece. Whether his plans to extend Macedonian power into Asia were as grandiose as those carried out later by Alexander cannot be known. Nevertheless, it is clear that without Philip's legacy of a united, powerful Macedon the achievements of Alexander and his successors would have been impossible.

TRANSLATIONS

Chinnock, Edward James. 1893. *Arrian's Anabasis of Alexander and Indica.* London and New York: G. Bell & Sons.

Saunders, A. N. W. 1975. *Demosthenes and Aeschines.* Harmondsworth, England, Penguin.

SUGGESTED READING

Adcock, F. E. 1957. *The Greek and Macedonian Art of War.* Berkeley and Los Angeles: University of California Press. Lucid introduction to Greek and Macedonian ideas of war.

Andronicos, Manolis. 1984. *Vergina: The Royal Tombs.* Trans. Louise Turner. Athens: Ekdotike Athenon. Beautifully illustrated account of the discovery of the Macedonian royal cemetery at Vergina.

Borza, Eugene N. 1990. *In the Shadow of Olympus: The Emergence of Macedon.* Princeton, N.J.: Princeton University Press. Insightful history of the kingdom of Macedon from its origin to the reign of Philip II.

Cawkwell, George. 1978. *Philip of Macedon.* London: Faber & Faber. Perceptive biography of Philip from a Greek viewpoint.

Ellis, J. R. 1976. *Philip II and Macedonian Imperialism.* London: Thames and Hudson. Lucid treatment of Philip's reign from a Macedonian viewpoint.

Martin, Thomas R. 1985. *Sovereignty and Coinage in Classical Greece.* Princeton, N.J.: Princeton University Press. Important study of the numismatic evidence for Macedonian relations with Thessaly.

Sealey, Raphael. 1993. *Demosthenes and His Time: A Study in Defeat.* New York: Oxford University Press. Important revisionist biography of the Athenian statesman.

11

ALEXANDER THE GREAT

Rarely has an epoch-making reign begun in such uncertainty as that of Alexander the Great. In his reign of almost two and a half decades, Alexander's father, Philip II, had transformed Macedon into a strong, centralized monarchy. Philip's military reforms had made Macedon the premier military power in the region, controlling an empire that stretched from the Danube River in the north to Thessaly in the south. By creating the League of Corinth, Philip had extended Macedonian influence deep into southern Greece and gained the public support of his Greek subjects and allies for his projected invasion of Asia. Philip's assassination on the eve of his departure to join his forces in the east threatened to ruin not only his Asian adventure, but all of his achievements.

Like his father's, Alexander's reign began with a succession crisis. Alexander III was only 20 years old at the time of his father's death in the summer of 336 BC. Omens were later said to have forecast his rule. His mother, Olympias, who had much to gain in securing the succession for her son, claimed to have dreamed that lightning struck her womb. The great temple of Artemis at Ephesus was believed to have been destroyed by fire on the day Alexander was born. Although Philip had offspring from several of his wives, Alexander was clearly treated as his father's heir for most of Philip's reign.

Philip and Olympias groomed Alexander carefully for the role he would ultimately play. A series of Greek tutors who included Aristotle provided him with the education in Greek literature and culture that Philip had lacked. From them Alexander gained his lifelong love of Homer and his determination to equal or excel the exploits of his legendary ancestors, Heracles and Achilles.

Alexander's practical training in kingship was not neglected. He governed Macedon in Philip's absence and suppressed a Thracian rebellion. Like his father, Alexander founded a city named after himself in Thrace. Finally, he took part in Philip's campaigns, even commanding the companion cavalry in the decisive Battle of Chaeronea that established Macedonian rule in Greece in 338 BC. Nevertheless, Alexander's succession was not assured. He was isolated at court at the time of Philip's death. Olympias and Alexander's friends and advisers remained in exile. Not surprisingly, rumors quickly spread after Philip's assassination that

Alexander had encouraged the assassin and that Olympias even had mourned him.

There was also talk of other possible successors. The most important of these potential rivals was Philip's nephew, ward, and son-in-law, the former king, Amyntas IV. Only timely intervention by Antipater, one of Philip's most senior

Figure 11.1. Alexander's campaign.

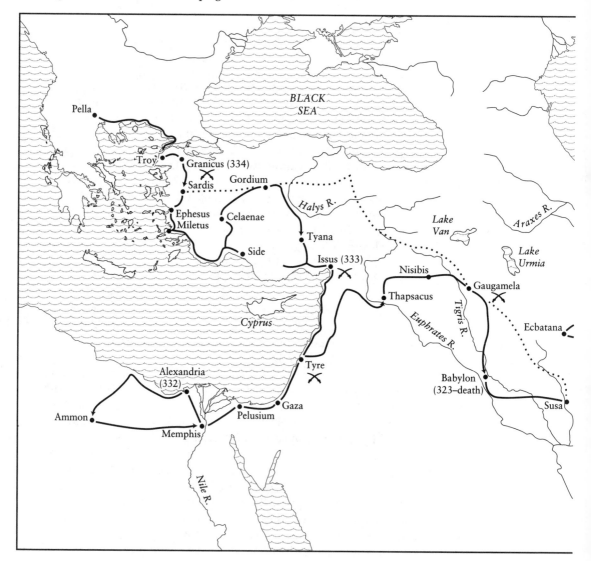

generals, saved the succession for Alexander. Antipater's presentation of Alexander to the Macedonian troops at Aegae for the traditional acclamation as king, combined with the death of the assassin Pausanias and the rapid condemnation and execution of his alleged fellow conspirators, secured the throne for the young prince. It also changed the history of western Asia.

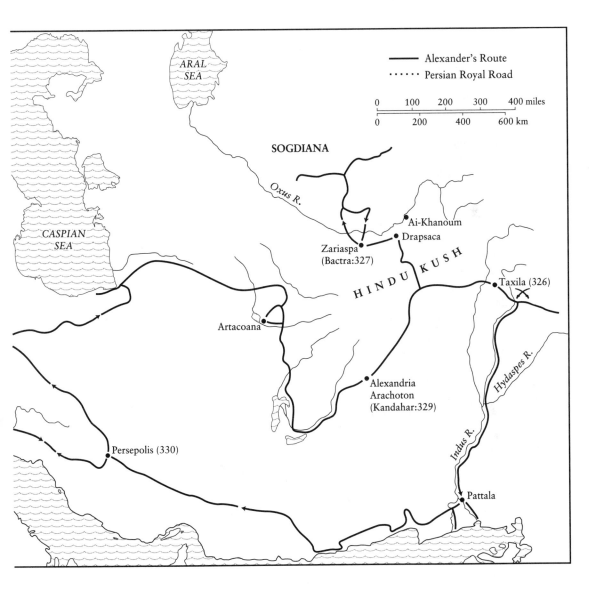

SOURCES FOR THE REIGN OF ALEXANDER

The English poet Chaucer (d. 1400) wrote in *The Monk's Tale* (lines 641–643) that "the storie of Alisaundre is so commune,/ that every wight that hath discrecioun/ hath herd somewhat or al of his fortune." For most of the Middle Ages, the most widely read nonreligious book in the Old World was a romantic biography of Alexander (the so-called *Alexander Romance*) that freely mingled history with fiction. The popularity of his remarkable story has continued to the present, inspiring films and novels. A selective bibliography of works dealing with Alexander contained the titles of almost seven hundred studies published between 1700 and 1970, and dozens of new explorations of his reign have appeared every year since. Despite this vast outpouring of scholarship, interpretations of Alexander's character and goals differ widely. Historians have cast Alexander in many roles: as the chief agent in the spread of Hellenism, as an idealistic believer in the unity of mankind, as an Aryan superman, and, more recently, as a brutal conqueror without constructive plans for the future of his empire. The reasons for this lack of agreement on even the most basic issues of Alexander's biography among Greek historians are clear: the limitations of the available sources for his life and reign and historians' difficulty in transcending their own historical context. Although archaeology has revealed much about the times in which Alexander lived, including the discovery of unlooted tombs that may belong to his father and son, historians must still rely on the evidence contained in Greek and Latin literature for the essential details of his life and career.

The ancient evidence concerning Alexander originally was varied and extensive. Alexander himself actively promoted the development of literature about himself and his achievements. In addition to engineers and other technical experts, his entourage included an official historian (a nephew of Aristotle named Callisthenes) as well as poets and scholars who were to celebrate his conquests and describe the discoveries made during his campaign. In the two generations following his death, the literary tradition concerning Alexander was enriched by the publication of numerous works—both ephemera such as political pamphlets and substantial histories of his reign written by participants in his expedition including the admiral Nearchus, the Cynic philosopher Onesicritus, and the later king of Egypt, Ptolemy I. The treatment of Alexander's reign in these works ranged from official *apologiai* (i.e., "defenses against criticism") to heroic adventure story. Unfortunately, none of the histories by Alexander's contemporaries survives in its original form. Our limited knowledge of their contents is based on the collection and intensive analysis by modern scholars of the few extant quotations, summaries, or allusions to them found in later writers.

The recent publication of cuneiform texts concerning Alexander holds out the hope of the discovery of new sources that would provide a much needed Asian perspective on the Macedonian conquest. Modern historians reconstruct Alexander's life from the five extant biographies of Alexander, namely, those contained in the universal histories of Diodorus (first century BC) and Pompeius Trogus (first century BC), the latter extant only in the form of an abridgment prepared in the second century AD by an otherwise unknown writer named Justin; the *History of Alexander* by Quintus Curtius Rufus (first century AD); Plutarch's *Life of Alexander* (second century AD); and the *Anabasis of Alexander* by Arrian (second century AD). These biographies were all written between three hundred and five hundred years after the king's death and reflect the interests and ideas of the early Roman empire, a period very different from that in which Alexander lived. Their value depends, therefore, on the fact that they drew their information from the now lost works of Alexander's contemporaries. As no infallible method of evaluating the relative merits of each of the five late biographies has yet been devised, the variation in modern assessments of Alexander results in large part from the differing judgments of scholars concerning the weight to be assigned to their evidence. On one matter, however, all biographers of Alexander, ancient and modern, agree: Alexander's personal actions were of decisive importance in shaping the remarkable events of his reign.

CONSOLIDATING POWER

Alexander's personal role was never more important than in the critical first year of his reign. The support of Philip's senior commanders had been indispensable in securing the succession for Alexander. In the aftermath of his accession, they urged the young king to proceed cautiously, consolidating his base in Macedon and using diplomacy to conciliate Macedon's northern subjects and allies, even at the risk of losing influence in Greece. Such caution was not to Alexander's taste, and not for the last time he rejected the advice of the Macedonian old guard in favor of decisive action.

Greece first claimed Alexander's attention. Immediately after conducting his father's funeral, Alexander made a sudden and dramatic appearance there. Anti-Macedonian politicians at Athens and Thebes quickly abandoned plans to exploit a presumed weakness in Macedon in the wake of Philip's assassination and to free Greece from continued Macedonian rule. Alexander was confirmed in Philip's former positions as *archōn* of Thessaly and *hēgemōn* of the Corinthian League, and Greek support for the war against Persia was reaffirmed. After a brief stay in Macedon following his return from Greece, Alexander waged an even more wide-ranging northern campaign in the spring of 335, intended to impress on the Thracians and Illyrians that Philip's death would bring no easing of the Macedonian yoke.

Alexander's first major campaign extended as far north as the banks of the Danube. Only sketchy accounts of the course of events survive, but it is clear that Alexander achieved his principal goals in the north. His main target was the Triballi, who had humiliated Philip in 339 during his return march to Macedon after his victory over the Scythians. The Triballi's attempt to hold a key pass against Alexander failed, thanks to the discipline of his Macedonian troops, who quickly cleared a path for the wagons their enemies sent careening down the mountain in the hope of breaking their line. Triballian resistance collapsed shortly thereafter when Alexander defeated their main forces and then launched an amphibi-ous assault on an island where the Triballi had placed their women and children for safety. Alexander's dramatic raid in force across the Danube into the territory of the Getae gained the submission of the remaining Thracian tribes. Alexander also concluded a treaty of friendship with a group of Gauls, the vanguard of a migration that was greatly to affect southeastern Europe and Anatolia in the early Hellenistic period.

Having secured his northern frontier, Alexander turned southwestward into Illyria to deal with Philip II's old enemy, King Cleitus. Alexander received the first of his many battle wounds during this phase of the campaign. Only his in-tuitive understanding of the psychological impact that a display of Macedonian close order drill would have on the Illyrians enabled him to extricate his army from a potentially disastrous trap. He inflicted a decisive defeat on Cleitus that finally ended the Illyrian threat to Macedon's western frontier that had loomed over so many of his predecessors.

Alexander's long absence in the north sparked rumors of his death in Greece. Hope was mother to the fact. Demosthenes even introduced a supposed eyewit-ness of Alexander's death to the Athenian assembly. Confident of Athenian aid, the Thebans rose in revolt, besieging the city's Macedonian garrison on the Cad-meia, the acropolis of Thebes, and inviting other Greek states to join them in the struggle for freedom. Forced marches by Alexander, who had been informed of the events unfolding in Greece, brought him and his army under the walls of Thebes before the rebellion could spread. The Athenians, who had voted military aid for Thebes, now hesitated. The Spartans, who had failed so stunningly to help at Chaeronea, also held back. When the Thebans nonetheless spurned Alexan-der's demand for surrender, the city was stormed and sacked. Alexander ordered that Thebes' Boeotian neighbors decide the ultimate fate of the city and its sur-viving citizens. All too mindful of past efforts by Thebes to subdue them, they decided that Thebes should be destroyed and the remaining Thebans sold into slavery. Alexander carried out the decree, sparing from destruction only Thebes' temples and the descendants and house of its illustrious poet, Pindar.

The destruction of Thebes was remembered for centuries as one of the great atrocities of Greek history. Alexander himself was said later to have given spe-cial consideration to personal requests by Thebans. For the moment, his calcu-lated use of terror achieved its purpose. As news of the destruction of Thebes spread, active resistance to Macedonian rule ceased throughout Greece. For the second time in a little over a year, the Corinthian League acknowledged Alexan-der as its hegemon and affirmed its support for his policies. Now that the exam-ple of Thebes' horrible fate had sapped Greek resolve, Alexander could afford to adopt a more moderate stance, abandoning his demands for the surrender of anti-Macedonian leaders at Athens and elsewhere in Greece.

Similarly ruthless methods were also used to neutralize potential opposition in Macedon. Measures such as freeing Macedonians from all personal obligations except military service won Alexander popularity among his subjects, while po-tential rivals were eliminated. The sources conceal the full extent of the purge because they emphasize instead the brutal and unauthorized murder of Philip II's last wife Cleopatra and her daughter by Olympias during Alexander's absence in Greece in 336 BC. In fact, the male members of Cleopatra's family, who had hoped to profit from her position as Philip's queen, were also wiped out. Furthermore, Amyntas IV, Alexander's only legitimate rival for the throne, was assassinated. Those of their supporters who could escape fled to their only possible refuge, Persia, leaving Alexander as the unchallenged ruler of Macedon.

Invasion of Asia

In the spring of 334 BC, with his position in Macedon finally secure, Alexander led his forces across the Hellespont to Asia. His formidable army was fully 37,000 strong. Its core consisted of the 12,000 Macedonian troops who formed the phalanx. They were supplemented by 3000 hypaspists ("royal guards") and 1800 companion cavalry. In addition to his Macedonian troops his army included special light-armed units from Illyria and Thrace and almost 9000 allied Greek infantry and cavalry. A fleet of almost two hundred ships provided by Alexander's Greek allies supported his troops and maintained his communications with Europe.

Alexander's first actions in Asia were bold, even theatrical. He was the first Macedonian to land on Asian soil, leaping ashore and casting his spear into the land to claim all that he conquered as territory won by the spear. He then went to the traditional site of Troy, where he sacrificed to Athena, asked pardon of the

Figure 11.2. Leonine hair adds to his ferocity in this portrait of Alexander as hero-king. Roman marble copy after the head of an original statute of about 330 BC. Inscribed "Alexandros, son of Philip, of Macedon."

ancient Trojan king Priam for invading Asia, and paid homage to Achilles, who he believed was one of his ancestors.

The symbolism suited the leader of the Greek crusade, but serious problems lay behind all the bravado. To maintain his authority in Macedon and Greece, Alexander had been compelled to leave almost half his Macedonian troops behind in Europe with Antipater. In Asia everything won by Philip's advance guard in 336 had been lost to a vigorous Persian counteroffensive except for the bridgehead at Abydus. Worse yet, Alexander had sufficient funds for only a brief campaign; and his friends did not yet hold important positions in the government and army. In Macedon, Antipater governed as regent in his name. Alexander's second-in-command in Asia was Parmenion, a close friend of Antipater, and until Philip's death, an ally of Cleopatra's family. Moreover, Parmenion's relatives held key commands in the army's critical cavalry units. Alexander needed a quick victory to achieve the goals of his campaign and ensure his freedom from the domination of the Macedonian aristocrats who had made him king. Fortunately for him, the Persians proved to be "convenient enemies."

The Battle of Granicus (334 BC)

The vast size of the Persian empire meant that mobilization of its main forces to confront a threat on a remote frontier was always slow. In the meantime, local satraps had to rely on the limited forces stationed in their territories to cope with the initial phases of an invasion. In such circumstances, satraps normally used a defensive strategy that aimed at controlling key strong points while denying the enemy use of local resources until the Great King could mobilize the empire's financial and military forces, and bring them to bear on the invader. Such a strategy was in fact proposed by Memnon, the Rhodian general who had defended Asia Minor against Parmenion's forces the year before. The Anatolian satraps, however, were jealous of Memnon's high standing with Darius and unwilling to risk having to justify the losses in revenue and the destruction of royal lands that such a strategy would entail. Instead they chose a bolder course, deciding to confront Alexander directly in battle in the hope of killing him.

The strategy almost worked. The Persians met Alexander at the River Granicus, the modern Koçabas, in northwest Anatolia. Their position was strong. Their cavalry was stationed along the riverbank itself to prevent the Macedonians from successfully crossing the river; their infantry, including several thousand Greek mercenary troops, were posted behind them as support. The details of the battle itself are unclear. Alexander apparently overruled Parmenion's suggestion that he wait until the next day to attack in order to allow his soldiers to recover from their march. Instead, he ordered an immediate attack. The fighting was hard, and disaster was barely averted.

The Persians nearly succeeded in killing Alexander, who stood out clearly in the flamboyant "armor of Achilles" that he had taken from the temple of Athena at Troy. The king was saved from certain death only by the daring action of Cleitus the Black, the brother of Alexander's nurse: at a crucial moment Cleitus sliced off the arm of a Persian noble who was about to deal a fatal blow to an already dazed Alexander. Because the Persians had staked everything on killing Alexander, the failure of their plan brought disaster. Trapped between the Macedonians and their own infantry, the bulk of the Persian cavalry was slaughtered. The Persian infantry, which had taken no part in the battle, fled and abandoned the Greek mercenaries who formed the core of the Persian army. Since many of these were exiled enemies of Macedonian rule in Greece, it is not surprising that Alexander ordered all but two thousand of them massacred as traitors to the Greek cause. The survivors were sent to Macedonia to work in chains. Alexander boldly announced his victory to the Greek world by sending to Athens three hundred suits of Persian armor as a dedication to Athena with the inscription: "From Alexander, the son of Philip, and the Greeks, except the Spartans." His barbed reference to the Spartans highlighted their refusal to join the League of Corinth and share in the Panhellenic crusade against Persia that he was leading.

Alexander's decisive victory at the Granicus changed the character of the war. Their defeat deprived the Persians of a principal advantage: no longer could they mount an effective defense in Anatolia while exploiting their naval superiority and financial resources to harass Alexander's communications with Macedon and foment rebellion in Greece. With most of the Persian commanders dead and much of their best cavalry and Greek mercenaries lost, the Persian position in Anatolia disintegrated. Although the Phoenician fleet freely cruised the Aegean, the Greeks as a whole refused to commit themselves to the Persian cause. Alexander's forces, meanwhile, swept south along the west coast of Anatolia. Fierce resistance by the Persian garrisons at Miletus and Halicarnassus slowed the Macedonian advance but could not stop it. In quick succession the satrapies of Lydia, Caria, and Lycia fell to Alexander. By the spring of 333, Alexander had reached Gordium, the capital of the ancient kingdom of Phrygia, near modern Ancyra in central Anatolia. In less than a year, Isocrates' once seemingly impossible dream of severing Anatolia from the Persian empire had been realized.

The first year of the campaign also exposed the unresolved conflict inherent in Alexander's position as hegemon of the League of Corinth and leader of the Greek crusade, and king of Macedon. As hegemon he was required to respect Greek opinion and the commitments he and Philip had made to the League of Corinth. Consequently, he punished the Greek mercenaries after the Battle of the Granicus and turned deposed pro-Persian tyrants over to the council of the League of Corinth for trial. As king of Macedon, however, conquered territory was his to do with as he saw fit, and increasingly his interests as king overrode his obligations to the League and his concern for Greek opinion.

Greek Reaction

Alexander made his supremacy clear immediately after his victory at the Granicus. He told representatives of Greek and non-Greek cities that had surrendered to him to obey their new Macedonian satrap and pay to him the same tribute they had paid to the Persians. Alexander retained the existing pattern of satrapal government elsewhere in Anatolia. When it became clear that his previous severity had only stiffened the resolve of Greek mercenaries in Persian service to fight, he eased the terms for surrender offered to them. Similarly, active support for democracy in the Greek cities of Asia became royal policy only when democratic factions offered their support to the Macedonian forces. Cities so liberated, however, found their new freedom hedged about with restraints. They were free of the obligation to pay "tribute" to the Persians, but they now had to make financial "contributions" to the Macedonian military effort and were severely punished if they objected. Moreover, as a series of inscriptions from Chios and other Asian cities reveal, Alexander freely intervened in the internal affairs of the Greek cities of Asia whenever he thought it necessary.

The development of his relations with his new non-Greek subjects was similar. Befitting his position as the hegemon of the League of Corinth, the first new satraps Alexander appointed were Macedonians. In the course of the campaign, however, Alexander took steps to win local support. In Caria, he entrusted the civil administration of the area to Queen Ada, who adopted him as her son and heir. At the same time, control of military affairs remained in the hands of a Macedonian garrison commander responsible to himself.

Alexander pursued the same policy elsewhere in Anatolia, appointing Persian satraps for Cappadocia and Armenia. Although circumstances prevented these latter appointments from becoming effective, the policy was clear. Non-Greek leaders who recognized Alexander could expect royal favor and promotion. Although Isocrates had dreamed of a new greater Greece in Anatolia, the true situation was more accurately reflected in the symbolism of Alexander's dramatic severing of the "Gordian knot." According to a famous legend, rule over Asia was promised to whomever loosed the complex knot that connected the drawpole to the wagon the first Midas had ridden when he became king of Phrygia. While he was at Gordium, Alexander fulfilled the prophecy by slashing through the knot with his sword, allowing no doubt that a new king had arisen in Asia.

Document 11.1   Letter of Alexander to the Chians (334 BC) The tension between Alexander's claim to have "freed" the Greek cities of Asia and the reality of Macedonian power is particularly clear in this letter of instructions concerning the reform of the city's government that Alexander wrote to the citizens of Chios:

All the exiles from Chios are to return and the government at Chios is to be a democracy. Law drafters are to be chosen who shall draft and correct the laws, in order that nothing may be contrary to the democracy or to the return of the exiles. The laws that have been corrected or drafted are to be referred to Alexander. The Chians are to provide twenty fully manned triremes at their own expense. These are to sail as long as the other fleet of the Greeks sails with us. Those who betrayed the city to the barbarians and have escaped are to be exiled from all the cities that share in the peace and are to be liable to arrest according to the decree of the Greeks. Those, who have been captured, however, are to be brought back and judged in the *synedrion* ("council") of the Greeks. Any dispute which may develop between those who have returned and those in the city is to be judged before us. Until the Chians are reconciled to one another, there is to be a garrison among them from king Alexander. The garrison is to be of sufficient strength; and the Chians are to support it.

Translated by A. J. Heisserer, Alexander the Great and the Greeks: The Epigraphic Evidence. *Norman: University of Oklahoma Press, 1980, pp. 80–81.*

A severe fever that brought Alexander to the brink of death delayed the departure of the Macedonian army from Anatolia until the summer of 333. The ancient biographies, with their concern for Alexander's heroic stature, focus on his steadfast trust in his personal physician in the face of Parmenion's warning that he had been bribed by the Persians. More important, Alexander's brush with death revealed to everyone his unique importance to the expedition. Without an heir and with no plausible available alternative king, Alexander was indispensable. Only he held the army together and gave its actions force and direction. The army's dependence on Alexander and the power it gave him would only increase as the army's march carried it further and further away from Macedon.

The Battle of Issus (333 BC)

After recovering from his illness, Alexander made a characteristically bold decision. Instead of moving to confront the forces of Darius III directly in Mesopotamia, as the young Persian prince Cyrus had done in his revolt against his brother Artaxerxes II almost seventy years earlier, Alexander directed his forces toward the coastal regions of Syria, Palestine, and, ultimately, Egypt. Behind this decision lay a risky calculation. Having disbanded most of his Greek fleet almost a year earlier, Alexander hoped to end Persian naval operations in the Aegean by depriving the Persian fleet of its Syrian and Phoenician bases.

The strategy was daring and almost resulted in catastrophe. Alexander marched south along the Syrian coast during the late summer and fall of 333. At the same time, Darius III, who had completed the mobilization of the Persian empire's main forces, moved northwestward from Babylon along the Euphrates River in the hope of catching Alexander before he succeeded in leaving Anatolia. At one point, the two armies, marching in opposite directions, passed each other at a distance of less than a hundred miles. On learning Alexander's location, Darius wheeled his army around the northern end of the Amanus Mountains and hastened southward to take the Macedonian forces in the rear. Having brilliantly cut Alexander's communications with Anatolia and his Macedonian base, however, Darius yielded the initiative to Alexander by allowing him to choose the battlefield. Alexander chose to meet the Persians at Issus in northern Syria in a narrow coastal plain confined between the Amanus Mountains on the east and the sea on the west. By preventing Darius from fully deploying his forces, this choice of battleground neutralized the significant numerical superiority the Persians enjoyed over Alexander's Macedonians.

When Alexander entered the plain of Issus he found the Persian forces posted along the north side of the river Payas, the modern Pinarus. Darius had stationed his cavalry on both wings while he, his royal guard, and his remaining Greek mercenaries occupied the center of the Persian line. Alexander, for his part, drew up his Macedonians in the unbalanced line that had by now become traditional. Parmenion commanded the phalanx and most of the infantry on the left wing; Alexander placed the bulk of the cavalry on the right wing under his personal command.

The official historian, Callisthenes, whose account is the ultimate source of the several extant narratives of the Battle of Issus, treated it as a Homeric contest between Alexander and Darius III, but we do know the main outlines of the battle.

Figure 11.3. Plan of the Battle of Issus.

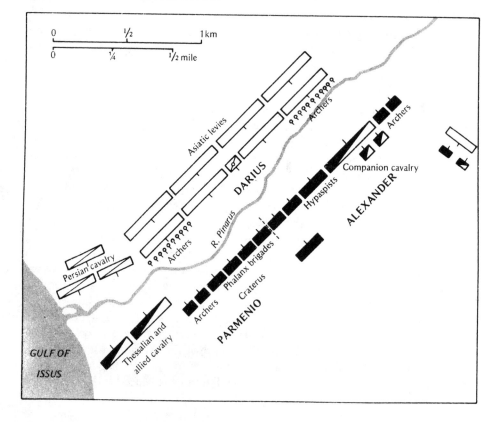

The Macedonian left suffered severely from the Persian assault, until a direct attack by Alexander and his cavalry units on the center of the Persian line forced Darius to abandon his army and flee. This moment was brilliantly depicted in a famous painting of the late fourth century BC, a copy of which appears in a mosaic that was discovered at Pompeii and is now preserved in the Naples Museum. The flight of Darius turned the defeat of the Persian army into a fearful rout. Years later Ptolemy I recounted in his history of Alexander how his units had crossed streams on the piled up bodies of Darius' dead soldiers while pursuing the fleeing Persian forces.

Alexander's victory at Issus was a fundamental turning point in his campaign. Darius III was in headlong flight. Most of the core of the Persian forces had been destroyed. The royal treasure stored at Damascus quickly fell into Alexander's hands and put an end to the financial problems that had threatened his plans since their inception. In his haste to escape, moreover, Darius had abandoned his family, which, in accordance with Persian custom, had accompanied him during the campaign. The Great King's mother, wife, daughters, and son and heir to the Persian throne were now all Alexander's prisoners.

Alexander had not merely defeated the Great King: he had humiliated him. This humiliation continued, as Alexander summarily rejected Darius' written of-

Figure 11.4. This mosaic from Pompeii is believed to be a late Hellenistic or Roman copy of a fourth-century-BC painting depicting the Battle of Issus.

fer of friendship and alliance in exchange for his family's return. He also accorded the Persian royal family the protection and public deference to which their former station entitled them, but which they had lost when Darius deserted them. The symbolism was clear and unambiguous: henceforth Alexander and not Darius was the arbiter of the fate of the Achaemenids.

The significance of Alexander's victory was equally great for the Greeks. After Issus all hope of Persian aid against Macedonian rule had to be abandoned. Not surprisingly, the rest of Greece remained passive when Antipater crushed a Spartan rebellion in 331 BC. Finally, and most important, the road to Egypt lay open to the Macedonian army. With the expulsion of Persian power from the shores of the Mediterranean, even the conquest of the empire itself suddenly seemed possible.

FROM ISSUS TO EGYPT: CONQUEST OF THE EASTERN MEDITERRANEAN (332–331 BC)

While Darius fled eastward, Alexander resumed his march south along the coast of Syria. Without hope of Persian support, the majority of the Syrian and Phoenician coastal cities surrendered, successfully concluding Alexander's plan to defeat the Persian fleet by depriving it of its bases. The situation is less clear with regard to the peoples of the interior of Syria and Palestine, but the surrender of the Samaritans in northern Judaea suggests that they also quickly came to terms with Alexander.

Only at Tyre and Gaza did Alexander meet with resistance, and his response was characteristically vigorous. When the Tyrians, trusting to the strength of their island fortress, rejected Alexander's request to enter the city and sacrifice to his ancestor Heracles in the guise of their chief god Melqart, he laid siege to the city. Rightly seeing in the Tyrians' refusal a rejection of his authority, Alexander pressed the siege of Tyre for almost eight months. The city fell in August 332 and suffered the same brutal fate as Thebes: slaughter of most of the male population and sale of the surviving women and children. The decision by Gaza's Persian governor, a eunuch named Batis, to maintain his loyalty to Darius in the face of Alexander's demand for surrender resulted in a similar unhappy fate for his city two months later. The fall of Gaza removed the final barrier between Alexander and the greatest prize of the first phase of his Asian adventure: Egypt.

Alexander in Egypt

Alexander's stay in Egypt dramatically altered his view of himself, but the conquest of Egypt itself was somewhat anticlimactic. Isolated in the midst of a restive population and without hope of aid from Darius, Mazaces, the last Persian satrap of Egypt, surrendered his satrapy without a fight.

Unlike most of the other peoples of the ancient Near East, the Egyptians had never accepted Persian rule. The fifth and fourth centuries BC had been marked by repeated Egyptian rebellions and severe Persian repression; the last episode was only a few years before Alexander's invasion. Not surprisingly, therefore, the Egyptians welcomed Alexander and his Macedonians during their march through the Delta to the ancient capital of Memphis, where he celebrated his victory by holding Greek-style games and sacrificing to Zeus. At the same time, Alexander sought to conciliate the Egyptians by publicly honoring the Apis bull, the living incarnation of Ptah, chief god of Memphis, and other Egyptian deities. Alexander doubtless accomplished much during the six months he spent in Egypt, but the sources concentrate on only two episodes: his consultation of the famous oracle of Zeus-Ammon and the establishment of Alexandria, the first and greatest of his foundations.

The oracle of Zeus-Ammon, about 300 miles west of the Nile in the oasis of Siwah in the Libyan desert, was one of the three principal oracles patronized by the Greeks. Because of its impact on Alexander's conception of himself, the ancient sources suitably embellished the tale of his visit to Siwah with miracle and romance. Unseasonable rains provided his party with water, and sacred animals, such as snakes or crows, guided them when they became lost. Unfortunately, Alexander revealed neither his motives for consulting the oracle nor its reply to him. Ancient and modern historians have proposed widely differing explanations for his visit: he may have hoped to equal his legendary ancestor Heracles, who was reputed to have visited the oracle; or to have desired to surpass the Persian king Cambyses, who had failed to conquer the oasis; or he may simply have sought divine approval for the new city he was already planning to found in Egypt.

Whatever Alexander's original motives may have been, all the ancient accounts agree that the decisive moment of his visit was when the chief priest of the oracle greeted him as Son of Ammon. Through the process historians call syncretism ("the unification of religious beliefs"), Greeks equated Ammon with Zeus. The Greeks, therefore, understood that Alexander was presenting himself as a Son of Zeus. Whether or not the priest was merely according Alexander the welcome traditionally granted a king of Egypt, Alexander clearly took it as a divine sign that, as his mother had always claimed, there was something more than mortal about his birth.

Alexander had probably selected the fishing village of Rhakotis near the western tip of the Delta as the site for his new city during his trip to Siwah, but the actual foundation of Alexandria was delayed until his return from the oracle in April 331. The strong Homeric associations of the site played an important role in his choice of Rhakotis. Less than a mile offshore was the island of Pharos, which Homer had mentioned in the *Odyssey*. The site was also ideal for a great commercial center, with Pharos creating a sheltered anchorage for ships and the nearby Lake Canopus affording ready access to the Nile and the interior of Egypt. Understandably, the sources depict Alexandria as marked out for greatness at its inception. They tell how birds consumed the sacred flour with which Alexander was marking its boundaries, thereby indicating that the city would have abundant resources and nourish people from all over the world.

The foundation of Alexandria was Alexander's last major act in Egypt. Assessment of the full significance of Alexander's conduct in Egypt is difficult. Historians have assumed that Egyptians considered him their liberator from Persian tyranny and that he acted accordingly. Support for this view was thought to be provided by the honor Alexander paid to Egyptian gods and the fact that he was crowned Pharaoh. They have also suggested that he hoped to avoid the hostility aroused by the sacrilegious outrages supposedly committed by the Persian kings Cambyses and Artaxerxes III Ochus.

Consideration of Alexander's actions in Egypt as a whole indicates significant continuity between his policies in Egypt and those he followed in the territories conquered earlier in the campaign. This is particularly clear with regard to Alexandria, which was founded as a Greek polis with citizenship limited to Greeks and Macedonians. Alexander's organization of Egypt itself likewise followed the model he had used in Anatolia. Thus, although he did not appoint a single satrap for all of Egypt, Alexander retained much of the Persian organization of Egypt including the requirement that Egyptians pay tribute. Natives, both Egyptians and Greek, exercised only civil authority. Military power remained in the hands of Macedonian officers.

Only in one area was there significant change, but that area was the most important of all: Alexander's self-image. The revelation of his divine parentage at Siwah struck a responsive chord in Alexander. It confirmed his sense of his own uniqueness and heightened his personal identification with his heroic ancestors Heracles and Achilles. Henceforth, although Alexander never renounced Philip as his earthly father, his unshakable belief in his connection to his divine father Ammon would be the linchpin of his personality. His belief in his divine descent also opened a rift between him and the older Macedonians. They could not accept Alexander's view of his special tie to a "barbarian" god and the implied slight to Philip, the king they believed responsible for Macedonian greatness.

FROM ALEXANDRIA TO PERSEPOLIS: THE KING OF ASIA (331–330 BC)

A few weeks after the foundation of Alexandria, Alexander left Egypt, intent on seeking a final and decisive confrontation with Darius III. While Alexander marched north toward the Euphrates River, Darius made one last desperate effort to avoid battle, offering Alexander marriage to his eldest daughter, cession of all territory west of the Euphrates River, and an enormous ransom for his family. Darius' offer was unprecedented. It involved division of the empire, surrender of several of its richest satrapies, and permanent exclusion of Persian power from the shores of the Mediterranean.

Parmenion probably spoke for most of the army when he advised Alexander to accept Darius' proposal. Alexander, however, would have none of it, curtly observing that he would accept it too if he were Parmenion! Faced with Alexander's

Figure 11.5. Representation of Alexander as Pharaoh before Ammon-Ra and Khonsu-Thoth in the Bark shrine at Luxor temple at Thebes. Ca. 330–325 BC.

refusal, Darius had no choice except to hastily gather together another army to face the Macedonians. The two armies finally met on October 1, 331 BC, at Gaugamela, just south of Mosul in northeastern Iraq. Thanks to the capture of the Persian headquarters after the battle, which gave Alexander's historians a unique insight into Persian plans, the Battle of Gaugamela is the best documented of all battles in ancient Greek history.

The Battle of Gaugamela (331 BC)

Learning from his defeat at Issus the previous year, Darius carefully chose a battlefield that suited the peculiar strengths and weaknesses of his army. Deprived of almost all its Greek mercenaries and other units drawn from the western portions of the empire, Darius' new army was composed primarily of levies drawn from Persia and the eastern portions of his empire. This meant that his forces were more cohesive than most Persian armies and particularly strong in cavalry, but weak in first-line infantry. Darius hoped that the broad plain of Gaugemela would allow him to exploit his superiority in cavalry to outflank and ultimately envelop Alexander's Macedonians, while relying on shock and terror weapons such as scythed chariots and elephants to compensate for his lack of good infantry.

These hopes were disappointed. Alexander employed a modified version of the tactics that had worked so well at Issus. He stationed the bulk of his infantry under the command of Parmenion on his left wing and posted his best cavalry units under his personal command on his right wing. A strong force of allied Greek infantry was held in reserve to prevent the Persian cavalry from encircling his forces and attacking them from the rear. Although the fighting was fierce, particularly on the left wing, where the Macedonian phalanx was hard pressed, the battle ended as at Issus, when the attack of Alexander and the companion cavalry on the center of the Persian army forced Darius to abandon his forces and flee the battlefield.

Alexander's victory was marred only by his failure to capture Darius. The sources characteristically blamed this failure on Parmenion, who was reported to have recalled Alexander from his pursuit of the Persian king in order to rescue the Macedonian left wing. Otherwise, however, the heartland of the Persian empire was now Alexander's for the taking. With justification his troops saluted him as king of Asia. In rapid succession, the three westernmost capitals of the Persian empire (Babylon, Susa, and Persepolis) fell to Alexander, while Darius and his immediate entourage sought refuge in eastern Iran.

Alexander's treatment of his three great prizes differed sharply. Alexander entered Babylon in triumph in mid-October, 331. Cuneiform texts leave no doubt that, as in Egypt, he actively sought to conciliate the local population and especially the influential Babylonian priesthood. His troops were ordered to respect property during the march to Babylon. During his stay in the city Alexander offered sacrifice to its chief god Marduk and ordered the reconstruction of Marduk's great ziggurat, Esagila, which the Persians had destroyed a century and a

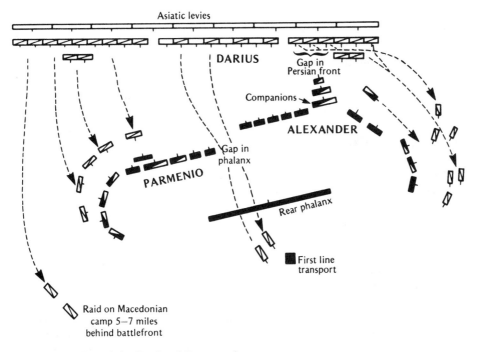

Figure 11.6. Plan of the Battle of Gaugamela.

half earlier as punishment for a Babylonian rebellion. Mazaeus, the Persian satrap of Babylonia, had played a key role in the surrender of Babylon, and Alexander rewarded him appropriately by confirming him in his former position. As he had done in Egypt, however, Alexander strove to ensure Mazaeus' loyalty by assigning command of the Babylonian garrison to one of his own officers, a Greek from Amphipolis named Apollodorus. In like manner Abuleites, who surrendered Susa to Alexander with its royal palace and treasure intact, was reappointed Satrap of Susiana. Far different, however, was the fate of Persepolis, the third of the Persian capitals to fall into Alexander's hands, and its citizens.

The Destruction of Persepolis

In deciding the fate of Persepolis, Alexander could not consider expediency alone, as he had done with regard to Babylon and Susa. Persepolis was the spiritual center of the Persian empire. The central events and rituals of Persian rule, including the new year's festival and the ceremonial presentation of their tribute to the Great King by the subjects of the empire, all took place there. It was also at Persepolis that Greek ambassadors had been required to abase themselves before Persian kings since the reign of Darius I. Persepolis was therefore identified with Persian rule in the eyes of Greeks and Persians alike, and its treatment would send a clear message to both peoples. The message Alexander chose to send was one of vengeance for the destruction of the temples of Athens during the Persian wars a century and a half earlier. On the eve of Alexander's departure from Persepolis in April, 330 BC, the Macedonians torched the city's palaces.

The sources heightened the sense of "poetic justice" in the destruction of Persepolis by assigning credit for the burning of the city to an Athenian, the courtesan Thaïs, who was said to have suggested it to Alexander and his friends during a drunken revel. Thaïs may have inspired the actual burning of Persepolis, but there are clear signs that Alexander already had decided four months earlier that the city was to be destroyed at the time of its capture. Despite its surrender, Persepolis suffered all the same rigors of a sack as had Thebes and Tyre. Modern excavations have also revealed that its palaces were completely stripped of their treasures, the accumulated wealth of two centuries of Persian imperial rule, before they were set on fire. With the flames rising over the ruins of Persepolis Alexander unmistakably signaled the triumphant end of the Greek crusade.

THE HIGH ROAD TO INDIA: ALEXANDER IN CENTRAL ASIA

As Alexander watched Persepolis burn, he could not have anticipated that the next four years would be the most difficult of the campaign. At first, his good fortune seemed to continue unabated. News of the end of the Spartan rebellion had already reached him before he left Persepolis. Meanwhile, Darius had fled eastward from Media, leaving Ecbatana, the last of the Persian capitals, to fall into Alexander's hands with its treasures intact. Having secured Persia and Media, the historical heartland of the Persian empire, Alexander liquidated the last traces of the Greek crusade by discharging his remaining Greek troops. All that was needed to complete his victory was to capture Darius III himself and put an end to the long line of Achaemenid rulers.

The Death of Darius (330 BC)

Leaving Parmenion behind at Ecbatana to secure his communications with the west, Alexander raced toward the Caspian Gates, the gateway to the eastern satrapies. He hoped to intercept Darius before he could reach Bactria, roughly modern Afghanistan, and continue resistance from there. Before Alexander could overtake the fleeing Great King, news reached him that a cabal of eastern satraps headed by Bessus, the satrap of Bactria, had arrested and then assassinated Darius III in July, 330 BC. Worse yet, Bessus had escaped to Bactria, where he had assumed the throne of Persia as Artaxerxes IV.

The assassination of Darius III changed the dynamics of the campaign. As the sack of Persepolis clearly indicated, Alexander had hitherto acted in Persia as the avenger of past Persian misdeeds. It was a stance that was popular with Greeks but hardly calculated to foster Persian acceptance of the new regime. Darius' assassination gave Alexander the opportunity to escape from this dilemma. Upon learning of Darius' death Alexander immediately assumed the role of his successor and defender of Achaemenid legitimacy against the regicides. To symbolize his new role Alexander adopted a new style of dress that combined elements from both Macedonian and Persian royal style. Darius' body was brought back to Persia and buried with full royal honors at the royal cemetery at Naksh-i Rustam. A rumor even began to spread that Darius' last wish had been that Alexander avenge him.

Alexander's strategy was clever and effective. While Persian nobles and even some surviving members of the Achaemenid house joined Alexander, Bessus alienated potential supporters by relying on a scorched-earth defense to halt Alexander's advance instead of attempting to confront him directly. As a result, resistance melted away as Alexander moved further and further into eastern Iran. Finally, in the spring of 329, Bessus' fellow regicides, fearful for their own survival, seized Bessus and surrendered him to Alexander in exchange for a pardon and confirmation in their offices, much as they had betrayed Darius III a few months earlier. Alexander remained true to his new role as the successor of the Achaemenids. Bessus was turned over to Alexander's Persian supporters for trial and execution as a regicide.

The Struggle for Bactria and Sogdiana (330–327 BC)

Alexander's ignorance of conditions in eastern Iran almost cost him everything he had gained through his astute dynastic policy. By misunderstanding the close ties that connected the peoples of eastern Iran with the nomadic Scythian tribes of the central Asian steppe, Alexander ignited a rebellion that quickly spread throughout much of Sogdiana and Bactria when he tried to establish a controlled border between Sogdiana and Scythia at the Jaxartes River. The revolt was marked by atrocities on both sides. It was led by a guerrilla commander of genius, Spitamenes, a Sogdian noble and former regicide, who betrayed Alexander as readily as he had previously betrayed Darius III and Bessus. The revolt lasted almost three years and ended with the murder of Spitamenes by his Scythian allies in the spring of 327. By the time it was over, Alexander had suffered some of the worst military defeats of the entire campaign and had been forced to develop a whole new approach to the control of conquered territory.

Alexander replaced Iranian satraps with Greek and Macedonian officials. He also settled Greek mercenaries and superannuated veterans in a series of military colonies established at strategic sites throughout Sogdiana and Bactria. Most important, the crisis in central Asia starkly revealed the growing tensions in the army and even within Alexander's court itself.

Macedonian Unrest

No Greek or Macedonian army had ever campaigned for so long or so far away from home, and Alexander's soldiers became ever more reluctant to go on as their march led them deeper into Asia. It had taken all of Alexander's persuasive powers to dissuade his troops from going home as soon as they learned of Darius' death. The miseries of the subsequent struggle against Spitamenes in the forbidding environment of Sogdiana and Bactria only increased their frustration and longing for home. More worrisome to his officers was Alexander's gradual abandonment of the traditionally informal Macedonian style of kingship and the growing prominence of Iranians and Iranian practices at his court. The most dramatic example of the trend was Alexander's marriage in the spring of 327 to Roxane, the daughter of a powerful Sogdian noble. The advantages of the marriage were obvious: Alexander gained an important ally in Bactria and Sogdiana. Nevertheless, the fact remained that Alexander's queen and the potential mother of his successor was not a Macedonian or even a Greek but an Iranian!

Tension at court was increased still further by Alexander's unsuccessful demand for the ritual prostration known as *proskynēsis* on the part of all members of his court. Both ancient and modern thinkers have seen a connection between Alexander's attempt to impose proskynesis on his court and his claim to be son of Ammon, but they disagree as to his intentions. According to Arrian, Alexander desired that people recognize his divine descent:

> The fact is that the report prevails that Alexander desired people actually to do him obeisance, from the underlying idea that his father was Ammon and not Philip, and as he was now expressing his admiration for the ways of the Persians and Medes, both in his change of dress and in addition by the altered arrangements for his attendance, and that even as to obeisance there was no lack of flatterers to give him his wish.
>
> (Anabasis; *Brunt 1976*)

Plutarch, on the other hand, thought that Alexander hoped to use proskynesis as a means of dominating his eastern subjects:

> In general, he bore himself haughtily towards the Barbarians, and like one fully persuaded of his divine birth and parentage, but with the Greeks it was within limits and somewhat rarely that he assumed his own divinity. However, in writing to the Athenians concerning Samos, he said: "I cannot have given you that free and illustrious city; for you received it from him who was then your master and was called my father," meaning Philip. At a later time, however, when he had been hit by an arrow and was suffering great pain, he said: "This, my friends, that flows here, is blood and not Ichor, such as flows from the veins of the blessed gods." . . . From what has been said, then, it is clear that Alexander himself was not foolishly affected or puffed up by the belief in his divinity, but used it for the subjugation of others.
>
> (Life of Alexander; *Perrin 1919, adapted*)

Most modern scholars adopt a view similar to that of Plutarch, especially since it is clear that Persians viewed proskynesis primarily as an affirmation of the hierarchical order of society. Whatever his intentions may have been, however, Alexander underestimated the resistance his plans would encounter. Greeks and Macedonians saw proskynesis as a recognition of divinity and an unwelcome reminder of past Persian arrogance. They tolerated its performance by Persians at Alexander's court, but bitterly resented his effort to make them also perform it. It is not surprising, therefore, that the sources for the first time refer to open resistance to Alexander's policies and even conspiracies against his life during his stay in central Asia.

The first sign of trouble appeared late in 330 and involved one of Alexander's senior commanders. Philotas, the commander of the Companion Cavalry and son of Parmenion, was executed after failing to inform Alexander of an alleged plot to kill him. Philotas' guilt has been debated since antiquity. Some scholars even suggest that Philotas was the victim of a plot devised by Alexander. Whether the charges against Philotas were true or not, Alexander henceforth took seriously the possibility of conspiracies against him and acted accordingly. Philotas' father Parmenion was assassinated, and one of his bodyguards, who was suspected of complicity in the plot, was cashiered. Alexander of Lyncestis, a son-in-law of Antipater (Alexander's regent in Macedon), had been held under arrest since the beginning of the campaign; now he was executed in order to remove a potential focus for rebellion. Alexander also instituted censorship of his soldiers' and officers' correspondence.

These measures muted the rancor at court, but as later events revealed, they did not eliminate discontent. The most dramatic incident was Alexander's drunken murder in autumn 328 of Cleitus the Black, who had saved his life at the Granicus and had just been appointed satrap of Bactria and Sogdiana. Cleitus' offense was criticizing Alexander's efforts to accommodate the Persians and his unwillingness to recognize the contribution of his officers and soldiers to his successes. More seriously, Alexander barely escaped assassination six months later by a group of his own pages, who claimed at their trial that they hoped to free the Macedonians from Alexander's growing tyranny. As the case of Philotas had revealed, Alexander was implacable in the face of disloyalty by members of his personal entourage. The pages were summarily tried and sentenced to death. Callisthenes, Alexander's official historian and the pages' tutor, whose public opposition to proskynesis was neither forgotten nor forgiven, was arrested and later died under mysterious circumstances.

By the summer of 327 Alexander could consider Sogdiana and Bactria secure. Spitamenes was dead and open resistance to Macedonian rule had ended. Before that happy outcome, the years of hard fighting and suffering had resulted in major changes. Most obvious were the changes in the army. Forced to cope with a mobile and resourceful enemy and cut off from European reinforcements, Alexander reorganized his army to allow greater flexibility in its use. In particular, he extensively recruited Iranian units to supplement his steadily dwindling supply of Macedonian and Greek troops.

Document 11.2 Plutarch's Account of the Murder of Cleitus the Black in 328 BC The rift that opened between Alexander and his Macedonian officers and soldiers during his campaigns in central Asia is particularly clear in Plutarch's vivid account of the murder of Cleitus the Black at a dinner party in Bactria:

After the company had drunk a good deal somebody began to sing the verses of a man named Pranichus . . . , which had been written to humiliate and make fun of some Macedonian commanders who had recently been defeated by the barbarians. The older members of the party took offense at this and showed their resentment of both the poet and the singer, but Alexander and those sitting near him listened with obvious pleasure and told the man to continue. Thereupon Cleitus . . . became angrier than ever and shouted that it was not right for Macedonians to be insulted in the presence of barbarians and enemies. . . . Alexander retorted that if Cleitus was trying to disguise cowardice as misfortune, he must be pleading his own case. At this Cleitus sprang to his feet and shouted back, "Yes, it was my cowardice that saved your life, you who call yourself the son of the gods, when you were turning your back to Spithridates' sword. And it is the blood of these Macedonians and their wounds which made you so great that you disown your father Philip and claim to be the son of Ammon!" These words made Alexander furious. "You scum," he cried out, "do you think that you can keep on speaking of me like this, and stir up trouble among the Macedonians and not pay for it?" "Oh, but we Macedonians do pay for it," Cleitus retorted. "Just think of the rewards we get for all our efforts. It's the dead ones who are happy, because they never lived to see Macedonians being beaten with Median rods, or begging the Persians for an audience with our own king." *The argument between Alexander and Cleitus became more heated, and Cleitus' friends hustled him out of the dining area.* But soon afterwards he came in by another door, and, as he did so, recited in a loud and contemptuous voice this line from Euripides' *Andromache* (line 683): "Alas, what evil customs reign in Greece." At this Alexander seized a spear from one of his guards, faced Cleitus as he was drawing aside the curtain of the doorway, and ran him through.

Plutarch, Life of Alexander *50–51, translated by Ian Scott-Kilvert* The Age of Alexander. *(London: Penguin Books, 1973, pp. 307–308).*

Equally important changes occurred in Alexander's court. The Macedonian "old guard" had largely disappeared in the purges that resulted from the period's various conspiracies and tumults, leaving preeminent men personally tied to Alexander such as Perdiccas, Craterus, Lysimachus, and Ptolemy. These men would play critical roles in the turbulent events that followed Alexander's death.

Finally, the relationship between Alexander and his soldiers had altered in a subtle but significant way. Their loyalty remained unchallenged, but, as events in India were to demonstrate, Alexander would never again be able to count on their unquestioning obedience after the strains of the central Asian campaign.

INDIA AND THE END OF THE DREAM

When Alexander crossed the Hindu Kush mountains in the summer of 327 BC, he believed he was approaching the end of the inhabited world. For Greeks and Persians alike, India was the land of the Indus River, essentially modern Pakistan. Aristotle believed that beyond India there was a great desert and then ocean, which supposedly was visible from the peaks of the Hindu Kush Mountains. Although Darius I had conquered India and briefly made it a part of the Persian empire, Persian rule had long since ended when Alexander entered the region. He would be campaigning in a mysterious land that Dionysus, Heracles, and the legendary Assyrian queen Semiramis all had failed to conquer, a land where fact and fiction co-existed, where cannibals and monstrous men and animals lived, where cloth grew on trees, and ants mined gold. What Alexander actually found was almost as remarkable: a vast subcontinent occupied by a complex network of peoples and states, who viewed Alexander as a new piece to be played in their complex political chess game.

It was virtually a new world that Alexander and his army entered in the summer of 327 BC. Nor can he have remained long in doubt about conditions in India. As the Macedonian army passed along the famous route through the Khyber Pass to the plain of the Indus River in the summer and fall of 327, it

Figure 11.7. The Greek view of the inhabited world.

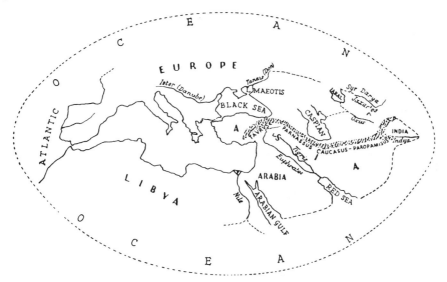

encountered some of the fiercest resistance in the campaign. Opposition ended only when the army reached the city of Taxila, whose ruler, called Taxiles, had already solicited Alexander's aid while he was still in central Asia. Taxila was one of the principal centers of Indian religious thought. Throughout antiquity Greek and Roman moralists continued to be fascinated by Alexander's sojourn there and his meeting with a group of "naked philosophers"—ascetic Indian holy men, one of whom, Calanus, even joined his expedition.

Taxiles had sought Alexander's aid against his eastern neighbors, Abisares, the ruler of Kashmir, and especially Porus, whose kingdom included all the territory between the Jhelum and Chenab rivers. When Abisares offered his submission, Alexander moved against Porus in early 326.

The Battle of the Hydaspes (326 BC)

The two armies met at the Hydaspes River, the modern Jhelum. There Alexander found that Porus had established a strong defensive position, using his infantry and his two hundred elephants to form a living wall along the east bank of the river. Solving this difficult military problem took all of Alexander's tactical skills

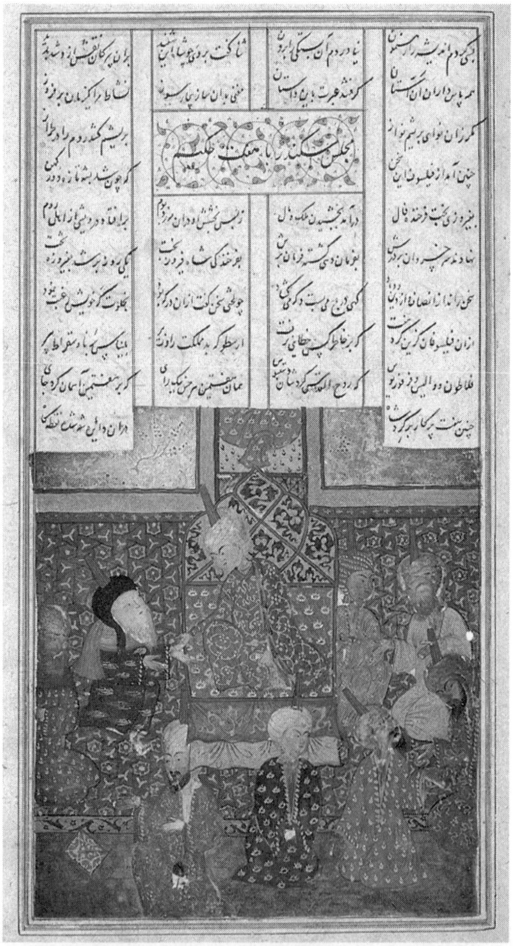

Figure 11.8. In this image in an Islamic manuscript Alexander is depicted wearing Indian costume with philosophers in India.

and involved a daring secret crossing of the flooded river. In the end, however, the outcome was the same as that of his earlier battles: the total destruction of his enemy's forces. Much to the displeasure of Taxiles and his other Indian allies, Alexander did not exploit his victory to destroy Porus. Instead, impressed by the nobility of his defeated opponent, who asked only to be treated "like a king," Alexander restored his kingdom to Porus and even added new territories to it.

Although Alexander did not realize it at the time, the confrontation at the Hydaspes was to be his last pitched battle. As the army marched further eastward through the Punjab, morale dropped steadily. The crisis came when Alexander reached the river Hyphasis, the modern Beas. Exhausted by the stresses of fighting and marching during the endless rains of the summer monsoon, terrified by rumors of yet another great river valley occupied by great kingdoms possessing thousands of war elephants, and doubtful that they would ever return home, the army mutinied. This time not even Alexander's formidable powers of verbal and moral persuasion could convince his soldiers to go on. Ultimately, Alexander yielded, defeated by his own army, and agreed to return to the Indus, where he had already ordered the construction of a great fleet.

The End of the Campaign

Alexander did not announce his long-range aims to his contemporaries. From antiquity to the present, therefore, historians have speculated about his goals. After he had defeated Darius, avenged the Persian wars, and taken control of the Persian empire and its vast treasures, why did he continue to push ever eastward? Did he have a master plan for world conquest when he left Macedonia, or did his ambitions grow with each new success? Unfortunately, no definitive answer is

Figure 11.9. Silver five-shekel coin from Babylonia (c. 326–323 BC). Obverse: Alexander attacking Porus on his elephant. Reverse: Alexander holding scepter and thunderbolt, attributes of Zeus.

possible. Whatever Alexander's ultimate intentions may have been, the resistance of his army forced him to adopt a more modest goal: the conquest of the entire Indus River valley to its mouth.

From early winter 326 to midsummer 325, Alexander's army moved steadily southward against heavy resistance. The tale of slaughter told in the ancient sources is unparalleled elsewhere in the campaign. Alexander himself received a near fatal wound, leading his increasingly reluctant troops in storming a city of the Malli. Finally, in July 325, the army reached the mouth of the Indus and the ocean. On an island near the mouth of the Indus Alexander made offerings to gods for whom his father Ammon had ordered sacrifices; then he sailed out onto the Indian Ocean to pray to Poseidon for a safe voyage to Babylonia. Alexander's seemingly endless eastward advance was at an end, and the preparations for the journey home had begun.

Results of the Indian Campaign

Alexander's invasion was the first major incursion into India from the west since the reign of Darius I almost two centuries earlier. Like that of his Persian predecessor, Alexander's campaign resulted in a flood of new information about the Indian subcontinent and its peoples. Also like the Persians, the Macedonians were to remain only briefly in India. Within little more than a decade after Alexander's death, most traces of his campaign and its results had disappeared from the Indian landscape and even Indian consciousness. Indian culture knows only the romantic Alexander of medieval legend, not the Alexander of Greek history.

The ephemeral character of Alexander's achievements in India has led some historians to suggest that he lost interest in the area once his army prevented him from extending his conquests to the Ganges Valley, but this is to confuse results with intentions. Alexander's political arrangements suggest that he intended to maintain control of his Indian conquests after his return to the west. Three Macedonian satraps supported by strong detachments of mercenary troops governed the Indus Valley from its northern approaches to the sea. Local rulers such as Taxiles, who had demonstrated their loyalty, retained their thrones but were placed under the supervision of one of the Macedonian satraps. Three new Greek cities were founded at strategic locations in the northern satrapy, and several foundations were also planned for the other satrapies. Finally, the Macedonian eastern flank was protected by the expanded kingdom of Alexander's ally, King Porus. Alexander had planned carefully for his Indian domain, but the resources available to his agents proved inadequate to maintain Macedonian rule in this remote part of his empire.

RETURN TO THE WEST

Alexander left India for Persia in late August 325. He intended to lead his army through Gedrosia, an arid region in southwestern Pakistan. His purpose was to establish supply depots for his fleet, which was to follow the time-honored route along the north coast of the Indian Ocean from the mouth of the Indus River to the Persian Gulf. Nearchus, the commander of Alexander's fleet and one of his closest friends, later claimed that Alexander, ever the competitor, was also determined to surpass Semiramis and Cyrus II of Persia, who were said to have lost their armies in Gedrosia. For almost two months, Alexander's men struggled through the arid wastes of Gedrosia. Including the wives and children the soldiers had acquired in the course of their campaigns and the camp followers that had attached to the group, possibly as many as eighty thousand souls comprised what was virtually a moving city. Before the army finally reached Carmania and safety, thousands died, including most of the soldiers' families, who were swept away together with the bulk of their possessions in a flash flood. Only news of the safe arrival of the fleet at the head of the Persian Gulf sometime in December 325 after a difficult and adventure-filled voyage that included encounters with whales and exploration of a "haunted" island lessened Alexander's sense of having barely escaped total disaster.

Reorganization of the Empire

Alexander's return from India sparked turmoil throughout his vast empire. In short order, eight satraps and generals—both Macedonians and Iranians—were deposed and executed. One of Alexander's oldest friends, the royal treasurer, Harpalus, fled to Athens with a huge fortune looted from the king's funds and a private army of six thousand mercenaries. The ancient sources argued that the upheaval was caused by the deterioration of Alexander's character. Modern admirers cite his outrage at the reports of corruption and oppression by his officials while he was away. The truth is more complex. Some victims of the king's wrath, such as the governors of the satrapies along his line of march through Gedrosia, clearly were scapegoats for a disaster that was largely of Alexander's own making. Others were victims of court politics and jealousies, but as the Roman historian Curtius Rufus (10.1.7) perceptively noted, most were guilty of the one unforgivable crime: they had assumed Alexander would not survive and had begun to exploit his empire for their own personal benefit.

Alexander's actions were not limited to punishing overly ambitious and corrupt subordinates. He also attempted to prevent similar problems in the future. All satraps were ordered to disband immediately their mercenary forces. When the security of his Asian realm was threatened by roving bands of embittered cashiered soldiers, a further order was sent to the cities of European Greece requiring them to permit their exiles to return home. Fully twenty thousand exiles are said to have heard Aristotle's son-in-law Nicanor read the royal decree at Olympia in the summer of 324 BC. The problems of reintegrating them into the life of their various cities were to cause turmoil in Greece for years to come, sparking a last desperate attempt by the Greek cities to free themselves from Macedonian rule immediately after Alexander's death.

"Unification of Mankind"

Almost as serious a threat to Alexander was posed by the dismay and suspicion of his veteran Macedonian troops at the changes in their relationship to their king. In the early spring of 324 Alexander celebrated the conquest of India in grand style. Decorations were distributed to officers of the army and fleet. The climax of the celebration was a grand marriage ceremony in which Alexander himself took two Persian wives, daughters respectively of Artaxerxes III and Darius III. Ninety of his principal officers took noble Persian and Median wives. Gifts were distributed to ten thousand of his soldiers who had followed Alexander's example and married Asian women, and their debts were paid by the king.

The good feelings quickly dissipated when Alexander introduced into the army thirty thousand young Iranian troops trained to fight in Macedonian style, whom he referred to as his "Successors." Their name suggested that they were eventually to replace his Macedonians. It is not surprising, therefore, that when Alexander announced at Opis in the summer of 324 that he intended to discharge and send home veterans who were too old or too ill to fight, the army mutinied. The soldiers demanded that the king discharge them all and sarcastically urged that he henceforth rely on his father Ammon. Only after Alexander reassured them that his Macedonians were his only true "companions" did the mutiny subside.

The victory of his veterans was only symbolic. Although Macedonians occupied seats of honor at a great banquet Alexander held at Opis to celebrate the end of the mutiny, he remained steadfast in carrying out his original plans. He discharged the veterans shortly thereafter and sent them back to Macedon, while retaining the children produced by their marriages to Asian women with him as the nucleus of a new generation of soldiers loyal only to himself. In the meantime, the integration of Iranian units into the army continued.

Death in Babylon

The final year of Alexander's reign was full of activity and unfulfilled plans. It began with a personal tragedy. In November 324, Hephaestion, Alexander's most intimate friend, drank himself to death. The grief-stricken king executed Hephaestion's doctor and ordered a monstrous zigguratlike monument to Hephaestion to be built at Babylon. When he believed he had received approval from Ammon, he ordered the Greek cities to grant his dead friend heroic honors. It may also have been at this time that Alexander issued another decree demanding that the Greeks worship him as a god.

Alexander further assuaged his grief with a winter campaign in the Zagros Mountains before returning to Babylon in the spring of 323. There he received a series of delegations bearing congratulations and petitions from the Greeks and other peoples of the Mediterranean. He also began to formulate plans for his next major project, the conquest of the Arabians, who, he claimed, had not sent an embassy to honor him. But omens of his impending death were already being bruited about. In desperation, the Babylonian priests even revived the ancient substitute-king ritual: a criminal was seated on the king's throne dressed in the royal regalia, then executed in the hope of averting the doom threatening the king.

This frantic effort was to no avail. On May 29, Alexander fell ill at a party hosted by one of his officers. After suffering from fever and delirium for almost two weeks, he died on June 10, 323 BC. Legend would later claim that he was the victim of a plot concocted by Aristotle and Antipater, whom he had decided to replace as his regent in Europe. More likely, his body, exhausted by the strain of constant campaigning and numerous wounds, was unable to fight off a disease, possibly malaria, that he contracted during his final sojourn at Babylon. He was almost 33 years old.

*   *   *

On learning of Alexander's death the Athenian politician Demades remarked that he "could not be dead because the whole world would stink from the stench of his corpse." Alexander had roused strong passions during his life and continued to do so after his death. He had conducted the longest and most far-reaching military campaign in Greek history, and in so doing he had changed forever the world the Greeks and Macedonians knew. From the Mediterranean to India, Eurasia had been linked together and would remain so until the end of antiquity. The cities he established in Egypt and central Asia provided the foundations for a significant Greek presence in those areas.

Since antiquity, scholars have disagreed about Alexander's plans for the future of his empire. A clear tendency toward increasing autocracy can be detected over the course of Alexander's reign, culminating in actions such as the decrees ordering the return of exiles and his own deification. No clear evidence exists that might reveal how Alexander envisioned the final form of that autocracy or the roles he expected the various peoples of his empire to play in it. In part, of course, this is because Alexander did not expect to die when he did. There is, however, a more fundamental reason. When he heard that Alexander had completed most of his conquests by the age of 32 and was perplexed about what he should do with the rest of his life, the Roman emperor Augustus is said to have expressed surprise that Alexander did not consider governing his empire a greater challenge than conquering it. Not surprisingly, his papers contained only schemes for grandiose monuments and future campaigns, not plans for the governance of his empire.

In a very real sense, therefore, Alexander's greatest achievement was negative. He destroyed the Persian empire, thereby liquidating a state system that governed relations in the Near and Middle East for over two centuries. He also ended the role of the Greek states as significant players in the politics of the eastern Mediterranean basin. His successors, however, and not Alexander himself, would shape the new political order that would replace the Persian empire and provide the framework for social and cultural relations in much of western Asia for the rest of antiquity.

TRANSLATIONS

Brunt, P. A. 1976. *Arrian: Anabasis of Alexander*. Vol. I. Loeb Classical Library. Cambridge, Mass. and London: Harvard University Press.

Perrin, Bernadotte. 1919. *Plutarch's Lives*. Vol. VII. Loeb Classical Library. Cambridge, Mass. and London: Harvard University Press.

SUGGESTED READING

Bosworth, A. B. 1988. *Conquest and Empire: The Reign of Alexander the Great*. Cambridge, Eng.: Cambridge University Press. Unsentimental and clearly written political and military history of Alexander's reign.

Bosworth, A. B. 1996. *Alexander and the East: The Tragedy of Triumph*. Oxford: The Clarendon Press. A revealing study of Alexander's Indian campaign and its treatment by ancient and modern historians.

Engels, Donald W. 1978. *Alexander the Great and the Logistics of the Macedonian Army*. Berkeley and Los Angeles: University of California Press. An illuminating account of the practical problems of supplying Alexander's army during its long campaign.

Holt, Frank L. 1989. *Alexander the Great and Bactria*. Leiden: E. J. Brill. Lucid account of Alexander's central Asian campaign and its significance for the establishment of Greek culture in Bactria.

Stewart, Andrew. 1993. *Faces of Power. Alexander's Image and Hellenistic Politics*. Berkeley and Los Angeles: University of California Press. Detailed study of the development and use of the best-known royal portrait image in antiquity.

Wheeler, Mortimer. 1968. *Flames over Persepolis: Turning-Point in History*. New York: Reynal and Company. Illuminating survey of the archaeological evidence for Alexander's campaign.

12

ALEXANDER'S SUCCESSORS AND THE COSMOPOLIS

Alexander's conquests changed forever the world the Greeks knew. From citizens of minuscule city-states on the fringes of the Persian empire, the Greeks had become partners in the rule of a vast territory that stretched from the Mediterranean to the borders of India. This enormous "cosmopolis" (literally, "a city-state comprising the world") was unified by the use of Greek as the common language of government and culture and by the creation of islands of Greek culture in settlements scattered throughout this broad area. The cosmopolis served as a huge arena for the military and political struggles of Alexander's successors. Against this bloody backdrop, ordinary people, both Greeks and their subjects, attempted to retain traditional values while making innovations that enabled them to live in a world that was vastly different from that of their grandparents.

The Macedonian conquest ended the Greek world known today as Classical. Classical Greece certainly set standards in a number of areas, such as sculpture, architecture, philosophy, and political theory, that continue to shape the direction of western culture even today. The modern world, however, is sharply different from the narrow and intensely political universe of the polis; in many respects its closest affiliation is with the era we call Hellenistic.

A NEW WORLD

The Hellenistic period spans the three centuries from the death of Alexander in 323 BC to the death of Cleopatra VII of Egypt in 30 BC. This period witnessed the attempts of people from different cultures to build communities in ways that would have been unthinkable in the age of the purely Hellenic polis. In many ways, the challenges of the Hellenistic age anticipated those faced by modern imperial powers. Moreover, in the large multiethnic Hellenistic states the average man was no longer as intensely invested in politics as he had been in, say, Classical Athens. Private life occupied a larger share of people's energy. Schools of thought like Stoicism, Epicureanism, Cynicism, and Skepticism addressed the same feelings of stress and anxiety that trouble men and women today. Whereas the philosophies of Plato and Aristotle were designed for affluent men who could expect to participate in the government of their poleis, the philosophies that developed during the Hellenistic Age spoke to a broader spectrum of the human community. In the visual arts, the Classical preoccupation with the beautiful

Figure 12.1. This old market woman survives in a Roman marble copy of an original of the third- or second-century BC.

young male diminished and the sculptural repertoire expanded to include such groups as the elderly, children, women, non-Greeks, and even the deformed.

SOURCES FOR THE HELLENISTIC PERIOD

Like Alexander's conquests, his empire's collapse generated an extensive historical literature, much of it written by participants in the events. The most important were two great histories that covered the whole period from the death of Alexander to the last conflict of his successors in the late 280s BC. One was written by Hieronymus of Cardia, a diplomat and courtier who served several of Alexander's successors, and the other by Duris, a student of the philosopher Theophrastus and tyrant of the large island of Samos. The written evidence that once existed was not limited to general histories. City and regional histories; biographies of rulers, intellectuals, and artists; descriptions of the lands conquered by Alexander; political pamphlets; and even collections of inscriptions were all composed during the two generations following Alexander's death.

Unfortunately, virtually all of this extensive body of evidence has disappeared, and the reason is clear. The modern view of the Hellenistic period as one of the formative eras of history was not shared by the Greeks of late antiquity, who decided what books would be copied and thus would survive into the Middle Ages. In their opinion, these centuries were a time of foreign rule and humiliation that contrasted unfavorably with the Classical period, when Greece was independent and triumphant over its enemies. Their medieval successors, the Byzantines, were likewise uninterested in the history of the Hellenistic period, but for a different reason. Since they viewed themselves as Christians and Romans, their interest in Hellenistic history was limited to the story of Roman expansion in the east and the fate of the Jews in the intertestamental period. As a result, interest in and copies of the works of the Hellenistic historians steadily declined. In the end, only one detailed account of the three centuries that followed the death of Alexander the Great survived into the Byzantine period—that contained in Books 21 to 40 of the *Library of History* of Diodorus of Sicily—and the last manuscript of Diodorus' work that included those books was destroyed during the Turkish sack of Constantinople in 1453 AD.

For much of Hellenistic history, therefore, modern historians are forced to cobble together their narrative of events from disparate, fragmentary, and often intractable sources. Fortunately, the situation is less desperate with regard to the critical half-century after Alexander's death, when the fate of his empire was decided. Diodorus' account of the last two decades of the fourth century BC survives intact. When his narrative fails, historians still can draw on a variety of sources that include Plutarch's lives of Demetrius and Pyrrhus, Justin's epitome of the *Philippica* of Pompeius Trogus, and a number of inscriptions to reconstruct the history of the next quarter of a century. Historians are far better served, however, with regard to sources for everyday life and administrative and economic history.

For most writing the Greeks and the other peoples of the ancient Mediterranean world used papyrus, flat sheets woven from strips cut from the papyrus reed. Because of dampness elsewhere, documents written on this material have survived in large numbers only in Egypt. There archaeologists have discovered documents written in several languages, including Greek, Latin, Egyptian, and Aramaic. These documents illuminate all aspects of the lives of the inhabitants of Hellenistic Egypt. They include private letters, wills, marriage contracts, leases and other financial documents, and even elementary school texts. Papyri also often provide our main evidence for activities of the government of Alexander's successors, the Ptolemies, including tax collection, religious affairs, and legal proceedings. This rich documentation gives us unique snapshots of the Ptolemaic government at work, from the royal court to the smallest Egyptian village.

Papyri have also preserved long-lost works of Greek literature, many of which survive only in fragmentary copies discovered in the ruins of Greek towns in Egypt. Thus, some of Sappho's poetry and Aristotle's *Constitution of Athens*, so important for the history of the Athenian democracy, survive only because Greeks living in Egypt had their own copies of these texts. Likewise, the plays of the Athenian playwright Menander and the "Lock of Berenice" of the Alexandrian poet Callimachus are extant only in papyrus copies. The vast number of papyri that have been discovered in the Egyptian countryside testify to both the use of the Greek language and the spread of Greek culture, one of the most enduring results of Alexander's conquests. Equally important, not all papyri are written in Greek. Scholars have just begun to study in detail the numerous Demotic (vernacular Egyptian) papyri, which show that, despite the influx of Greeks, the Egyptian way of life, legal system, and religious institutions all endured and even flourished in the Hellenistic period.

Figure 12.2. Letter to Zenon complaining about ill treatment: . . . to Zenon, greeting. You do well if you keep your health. I too am well. You know that you left me in Syria with Krotos and I did everything that was ordered in respect to the camels and was blameless toward you. When you sent an order to give me pay, he gave nothing of what you ordered. When I asked repeatedly that he give me what you ordered and Krotos gave me nothing, but kept telling me to remove myself, I held out for a long time waiting for you; but when I was in want of necessities and could get nothing anywhere, I was compelled to run away into Syria so that I might not perish of hunger. So I wrote you that you might know that Krotos was the cause of it. When you sent me again to Philadelphia to Jason, although I do everything that is ordered, for nine months now he gives me nothing of what you ordered me to have, neither oil nor grain, except at two month periods, when he pays the clothing (allowances). And I am in difficulty both summer and winter. And he orders me to accept ordinary wine for salary. Well, they have treated me with scorn because I am a "barbarian." I beg you therefore, if it seems good to you, to give them orders that I am to obtain what is owing and that in future they pay me in full, in order that I may not perish of hunger because I do not know how to act like a Greek. You, therefore, kindly cause a change in attitude toward me. I pray to all the gods and to the guardian divinity of the King that you remain and come to us so that you may yourself see that I am blameless. Farewell.

Business Papers of the Third Century B.C. Dealing with Palestine and Egypt, Vol. 2, eds. W. L. Westermann, C. W. Keyes, and H. Liebesny [New York: Columbia University Press, 1940] NR. 66.

THE STRUGGLE FOR THE SUCCESSION

Alexander's reign began and ended with a crisis over the succession to the Macedonian throne. When Alexander died suddenly in the summer of 323 BC, Macedonian power extended from Macedon to India. The Persian empire, which had dominated the Near and Middle East for over two centuries, had disappeared, but no new political structure had emerged to replace it. Only Alexander's charismatic personality held his vast realm together. His sudden death removed that focus of loyalty. Survival of the empire required that a new king be chosen quickly, but there was no obvious heir. Alexander had married late in his reign

and none of his wives had produced a child at the time of his death, although Roxane was pregnant. Of Alexander's own immediate family, only his mentally deficient half-brother Arrhidaeus survived. A regency, therefore, was inevitable. The question was who would lead the regency and for whom would he be regent?

Speculation was rife among the Macedonians at Babylon about Alexander's wishes concerning the succession, but all that was known for certain was that on his deathbed he had given his signet ring to his chief minister, Perdiccas. Not surprisingly, Perdiccas took the initiative, proposing that no decision be made until Roxane's child was born. Alexander's bodyguards and the cavalry supported Perdiccas' proposal. The Macedonian infantry was not so supportive. Faced with continuing uncertainty about the succession and enraged at the idea of a half-Iranian heir should Roxane bear a son, they mutinied and demanded that Arrhidaeus be recognized as their new king.

For an instant, civil war threatened between the Macedonian infantry and cavalry, only to be averted at the last moment by a bizarre compromise. It was decided that Roxane's child, if it were male, and Arrhidaeus would be joint kings! With their demand for a Macedonian king satisfied, the infantry abandoned its rebellion and watched passively while Perdiccas seized and summarily executed its erstwhile leaders. When Roxane gave birth to a son shortly thereafter, he and Arrhidaeus were proclaimed kings under the names of Alexander IV and Philip III. The crisis, it seemed, had ended almost as suddenly as it had begun. Events were to prove, however, that Alexander had spoken the truth when he said that he foresaw great "funeral games" over his corpse.

The struggle for Alexander's empire—the funeral games he had foreseen—lasted, in fact, for almost half a century. The hope of maintaining his vast empire intact proved to be a seductive will-o'-the-wisp. Repeated efforts by Alexander's "Successors" to hold the empire together were frustrated by coalitions of their rivals. When the last of them finally died in 280 BC, the vision of a single great empire occupying the whole area from the Mediterranean to India had disappeared. In its place were the first glimmerings of a new political system that would be dominated by three kingdoms ruled by Macedonian dynasties: the Ptolemies, whose realm included Egypt, Palestine, Libya, and Cyprus; the Seleucids, whose territories included much of the Near and Middle East; and the Antigonids, who ruled Macedon and northern Greece. This arrangement formed the framework for political and social life in Egypt and western Asia for over two centuries. It also facilitated a vibrant culture that provided the basis for much of the cultural life of later antiquity and the middle ages.

THE REGENCY OF PERDICCAS

The vast extent of the Hellenistic world and the inadequacies of the sources give its history a kaleidoscopic quality that makes synthesis difficult. The sources leave no doubt, however, that more was at stake at Babylon during the turbulent summer of 323 than merely determining the identity of Alexander's successor. Decisions also had to be made concerning the goals of the new imperial government. Conquest and expansion characterized Alexander's reign, and there were no signs of any change in policy. Quite the contrary: even during his final illness, Alexander was still making plans for his projected invasion of Arabia. After his death, the regent Perdiccas claimed that he found among the king's papers plans for even more grandiose schemes, including the conquest of Carthage and the construction of a tomb for Philip II equal in size to the great pyramid of Khufu at Gizeh in Egypt.

A decision had to be made concerning the status of all these projects, and Perdiccas had no doubt as to what that decision should be. He laid before an assembly of the Macedonian army held at Babylon the most extravagant and ambitious of Alexander's plans and asked for the soldiers' opinion. Exhausted by years of arduous campaigning and fearful that they would never see Macedon again, the soldiers responded as Perdiccas expected, demanding that Alexander's final plans be abandoned. The fantastic career of conquest that had begun with Alexander's crossing of the Hellespont a decade earlier was over. The phase of imperial expansion had ended. The time for consolidation of Macedonian rule and enjoyment of the fruits of victory had arrived, or so the soldiers thought.

With the question of the succession settled, Perdiccas moved quickly to give form to the regency. The first order of business was reallocating the satrapies of the empire. The sources anachronistically highlight the satrapies assigned to the men who would dominate the events of the next few decades: Cappadocia to Eumenes, Egypt to Ptolemy, Thrace to Lysimachus, and much of western Anatolia to Antigonus the One-Eyed. Cappadocia, however, had yet to be conquered. Egypt was held by the notoriously corrupt usurper Cleomenes of Naucratis, while the satrapy of Thrace was vacant and much of its territory had been lost in a Thracian rebellion. This is not surprising. In the wake of the crisis at Babylon, Perdiccas needed to avoid alienating the powerful Macedonian satraps in Asia to survive, and such appointments met this need.

The same cautious and conciliatory approach can also be detected in Perdiccas' plans for the organization of the regency itself. Three men were to govern the empire in the name of the kings: Antipater, Alexander's strategos in Europe; Craterus, the most prominent field commander in the last years of Alexander's reign and his intended successor to Antipater in Europe, who became *prostatēs* (protector) of the kings; and, of course, Perdiccas himself. The potential disruption of Macedonian unity threatened by Alexander's plan to supersede Antipater in Europe was avoided, and Perdiccas' two most powerful potential enemies were transformed into allies in the joint governance of the empire. Antipater, for his part, responded in traditional Macedonian fashion, seeking to cement the new alliance by arranging to marry two of his daughters to Perdiccas and Craterus.

Hardly had the regency been formed than Perdiccas' position began to crumble. Revolts broke out at both the eastern and western ends of the empire. Alexander's Asian subjects had remained passive spectators of the crisis that had followed his death; not so the Greeks. The Greek settlers and garrisons in central

Asia were the first to revolt. Bactria was to become home to a remarkable Greek kingdom that would exert a significant influence on the cultures of central Asia and India. The glories of Bactrian Hellenism, however, lay in the future. In 323 the Greek settlers and garrison troops left there by Alexander saw it as a place of bitter exile, and on learning of his death 23,000 of them mutinied and set out on the long march home. Perdiccas' response was prompt and decisive. Pithon, one of the Royal Bodyguards, intercepted the rebels and crushed them, forcing the survivors to return to their posts in Bactria. Almost simultaneously with the revolt in Bactria, the European Greeks rose in an even more serious rebellion that briefly seemed to threaten the very survival of Macedonian rule in Greece.

Like the revolt of the Bactrian Greeks, the roots of the European uprising lay in the last years of Alexander's reign. Alexander's decree of 324, ordering the return home of Greek exiles, threatened the governments of many Greek cities with social and political upheaval, as large numbers of erstwhile citizens came home and demanded the return of their property. At the same time, his order that his satraps disband their mercenary forces had created a "buyer's market" in trained soldiers ready to fight for anyone who would pay them. The leaders of the revolt were Athens and Aetolia, the two states whose interests were most threatened by the exiles decree. A decade of financial reforms designed and implemented by the conservative aristocrat Lycurgus had restored Athens' fiscal and naval strength. With newfound financial resources, Athens hired a mercenary army and launched the strongest naval force mobilized by the city since the Peloponnesian War.

Victory initially seemed to be almost within the Greeks' grasp. Caught by surprise and outnumbered by his Greek enemies, Antipater was forced to take refuge in the Thessalian city of Lamia, from which the revolt gets its name, the Lamian War (323–322 BC). While the Greek forces besieged Lamia, the Athenian fleet dominated the Aegean. But then events turned inexorably against the Greeks. The Athenian general Leosthenes, the man responsible for building the allies' mercenary army, was killed in battle, and the Athenian fleet was decisively defeated near the island of Amorgos. Meanwhile, the arrival of Macedonian reinforcements from Asia enabled Antipater to escape from Lamia and then to crush the forces of the Greek rebels at Crannon in Thessaly in 322. Unlike the Bactrian Greeks, the European Greeks would have no glorious future to compensate them for the failure of their revolt. Antipater intended that there should be no further revolts. The League of Corinth was dissolved and with it the last traces of the fiction, so carefully fostered by Philip II and Alexander, that the Greeks were allies and not Macedonian subjects.

Not surprisingly, the heaviest punishment fell on the prime instigator of the revolt: Athens. Demosthenes and the other leading anti-Macedonian politicians were hunted down and executed, or they committed suicide. The pillars of the Athenian democracy—selection of officials by lot, pay for office, and the enfranchisement of all Athenians—were abolished. Twelve thousand Athenians, over half the citizen body, failed to meet the new financial requirements for citizenship and were disfranchised. For the first time in almost a century, Athens was ruled by an oligarchy beholden to a foreign government, and maintained in power by a foreign garrison.

The Death of Perdiccas

Unlike the Athenians, the Aetolians escaped Antipater's wrath, as disturbing news concerning Perdiccas' activities forced Antipater and his allies to turn their attention to Asia. While Antipater and Craterus were occupied with the Lamian War, Perdiccas was unsuccessfully struggling to impose his authority on the satraps in Asia. In 322 BC, Antigonus the One-Eyed, the satrap of Phrygia, first defied the regent's order to help Eumenes take control of his satrapy of Cappadocia and then fled to Macedon. Worse, Antigonus brought to Macedon the disconcerting news that Perdiccas was negotiating with Olympias to marry Cleopatra, Alexander's sister, despite his promise to wed one of Antipater's daughters. Antigonus' news outraged Antipater and split the regency. The spark that ignited the first of the wars of Alexander's successors, however, was lit by Ptolemy, who intercepted the elaborate funeral cortege that was bringing Alexander's body to Macedon for burial and diverted it to Egypt. In so doing, Ptolemy may have thought that he was only following Alexander's wishes, since there is evidence that Alexander desired to be buried at Siwah near the sanctuary of his divine father, Ammon. Still, Perdiccas could not ignore so direct and humiliating an affront to his authority. In 321, therefore, he moved against Ptolemy in force, only to have his invasion of Egypt thwarted when Ptolemy opened the dikes that held in the Nile and flooded the eastern delta, drowning thousands of Perdiccas' soldiers in the process. In war, as in everything else, timing is all important. Perdiccas' officers, demoralized by defeat and seduced by Ptolemy's promises, assassinated him. Soon after the death of Perdiccas a messenger brought the news that Craterus had been killed, and that Perdiccas' ally Eumenes had defeated in Anatolia the force sent with him by Antipater to support Ptolemy.

Shortly after Perdiccas' death, the victors met at Triparadeisus in Syria to reorganize the regency. Their actions were few but significant. Antipater replaced Perdiccas as regent for the kings, and the satrapies were reassigned yet again. Some satraps such as Ptolemy and Lysimachus were too entrenched in their positions to be touched. Perdiccas' relatives and allies among the satraps, however, were replaced by men uncompromised by ties with the former regent, such as Seleucus, who received Babylon as his satrapy. The heaviest blow was reserved for Eumenes, the only Greek among the major satraps and Perdiccas' closest ally; he was condemned to death. At the same time, Antipater rewarded Antigonus the One-Eyed for alerting him to Perdiccas' ambitions with the position of strategos in Asia. He also assigned Antigonus the task of hunting down Eumenes and Perdiccas' other surviving supporters. With the reorganization of the government complete, Antipater returned to Macedon with the two kings. For the first time since Alexander had crossed into Asia over a decade earlier, a king would occupy the royal palace at Pella.

At first glance, little had changed at Triparadeisus. The empire was still intact. Argead rule continued in the persons of Philip III and Alexander IV. Only the identity of their regent and of some of the satraps seemed to have changed. Nevertheless, the appearance of continuity was deceptive. Macedonian loyalty to Argead rule might still be firm, but the Macedonian aristocracy's deep-seated hostility to royal power burst forth again after Alexander's death. Perdiccas had failed to reimpose royal authority. Antipater, who was old and had, moreover, been deeply suspicious of Alexander's growing autocracy, was unlikely even to try. Moreover, by taking the kings back to Macedon with him, Antipater had made clear that Macedon was central in his view of the empire, while at the same time he eliminated whatever restraint the presence of the kings had imposed on the Asian satraps. The person best situated to exploit the new situation was Antigonus the One-Eyed, whose position as strategos in Asia gave him full control of all royal forces and resources in Asia and complete liberty to use them as he thought best.

THE PRIMACY OF ANTIGONUS THE ONE-EYED

Antigonus' rise to preeminence in Asia was rapid. In a little over a year he succeeded in suppressing Perdiccas' remaining allies in Anatolia, driving Eumenes from his satrapy of Cappadocia and besieging him in the fortress of Nora in central Anatolia. The decisions made at Triparadeisus seemed on the verge of being implemented, when Antipater's sudden death in 319 BC precipitated a new round of conflict among Alexander's successors. Antipater's son Cassander refused to accept his father's choice of Polyperchon as regent for the two kings and fled to Antigonus. Antigonus, Cassander, Ptolemy, and Lysimachus quickly formed a grand alliance against the new regent.

The struggle lasted for three years and ended with the complete collapse of the royal cause in both Europe and Asia. When it became clear that Cassander was winning, Polyperchon turned in desperation to Olympias for help. In the absence of competent male Argeads, the surviving female Argeads increasingly embodied the charisma of Philip II and Alexander in the eyes of the Macedonians. Olympias' entry into the fray energized Polyperchon's cause, but it did so at the cost of splitting the dual kingship. Her single-minded passion for the cause of her grandson Alexander IV forced Eurydice, the daughter of Amyntas IV and queen of Philip III, to recognize Cassander's claim to be regent for her husband, but to no avail. In 317 the two queens finally commanded opposing armies in a battle, where Olympias first crushed her rival, Eurydice, and then ordered the execution of both her and Philip III.

Olympias' triumph, however, was brief. Six months later she suffered the same fate as Eurydice, leaving her grandson and Macedon in the hands of Cassander. Outwardly, Cassander claimed only to be regent for Alexander IV, but the reality was different. Cassander was the new ruler of Macedon, and he quickly consolidated his power. The child-king and his mother Roxane were confined under house arrest in Amphipolis, never to be seen in public again. Meanwhile, Cassander himself sought to legitimize his hold on power by marrying Alexander's half-sister Thessalonice.

Cassander's first acts left no doubt about the nature of the new order in Macedon and Greece. Macedonian tradition gave kings the prerogative of founding cities named after themselves or members of their families, and Cassander founded two such cities. One was named Thessalonice after his new queen and the other, on the site of Olynthus, was called Cassandrea after himself. In addition, he ordered the restoration of Thebes, the city whose destruction had marked the beginning of Alexander's dominance in Greece. The regime of Alexander the Great and his family was over; that of his successors had begun.

A similar fate befell the royal cause in Asia. Although Alexander's former secretary Eumenes unexpectedly proved to be a brilliant tactician, his military skills were ultimately insufficient to save him. Isolated from Europe, Eumenes received only grudging support from the Asian satraps, who despised him as a Greek upstart. Nevertheless, he managed to avoid defeat for three years before his own soldiers betrayed him in 316 to Antigonus, who ordered the immediate execution of his resourceful foe.

As in Europe, so in Asia—a victory won in the name of the heirs of Alexander resulted instead in the usurpation of Argead rule. With Eumenes dead, Antigonus replaced his supporters among the eastern satraps with men loyal to himself. Seleucus thought it best to abandon Babylon and flee to Ptolemy. Although officially only strategos in Asia for Alexander IV, Antigonus, in fact, controlled the child-king's vast Asian territories as securely as Cassander did his European ones.

The "Freedom" of the Greeks

Antigonus' emergence as the dominant power in Asia also destabilized the alliance that had brought down the regency and made renewal of war inevitable. The new alignment of forces was quickly revealed. On his return to Phoenicia in 315, Antigonus was greeted by an ultimatum from his allies, demanding that he share all the treasure and territories that he had captured. Not surprisingly, Antigonus rejected their ultimatum and countered with an ultimatum of his own demanding that his rivals recognize the principle that all Greek states should be free and self-governing. As both ancient and modern historians have recognized, these rival ultimatums were essentially propaganda intended to seize the diplomatic high ground and woo Macedonian support while both sides prepared for war. Antigonus' invocation of the principle of Greek freedom, however, was addressed to a different audience: the Greeks.

Antigonus' assertion of the principle of Greek freedom has been the subject of much discussion. Scholars have rightly pointed out that Antigonus never freed the Greek cities under his control and have concluded, therefore, that his support of Greek freedom was only propaganda. It was propaganda, however, that Antigonus had good reason to believe would have a strong resonance in Greece.

The Greeks were fiercely devoted to the independence of their poleis, and the Macedonian kings had found no way to solve the problem of reconciling the Greeks' hunger for independence with maintaining control of the cities located in their territories. After the Lamian War, Antipater's and Cassander's new policy of controlling the Greek cities directly through puppet governments backed by resident garrisons made the issue particularly contentious. The result was inevitable: increasing resentment of Macedonian rule. Already in 319, Athens had rebelled in response to an earlier promise by Polyperchon to restore democracy and freedom to the Greeks. Antigonus hoped that his declaration of his support for Greek freedom would have a similar effect among Cassander's other embittered Greek subjects when he launched his projected invasion of Macedon.

Although Antigonus continued making preparations for war throughout 314 and 313, his invasion of Macedon never materialized. Antigonus faced the same tactical problem that Perdiccas had almost a decade earlier: attacking one enemy while simultaneously defending against another in his rear. As before, the effort failed. Before Antigonus could cross to Europe to confront Cassander, Ptolemy inflicted a massive defeat on his son Demetrius, who had been guarding his father's southern flank, at Gaza in 312 BC. Ptolemy completed the debacle by helping Seleucus return to Babylon the same year, where he immediately began to incite defections among the eastern satraps. With his southern and eastern fronts in ruins, Antigonus had no choice except to make peace with his former allies, which he did in 311.

The Peace of 311 BC represented Antigonus' admission that temporarily, at least, his ambitious plans to gain control of all of Alexander's empire had failed. The terms of the treaty itself reveal the magnitude of the failure: Cassander to remain as strategos in Europe until Alexander IV came of age, Antigonus to continue as strategos over all Asia, Ptolemy and Lysimachus to retain their satrapies, and the Greek cities to be free. In return for a pledge to support the principle of Greek freedom that neither he nor his rivals intended to fulfill, Antigonus had retracted all the substantive demands he had made against his enemies at Tyre and agreed to the continuation of the division of the empire as it had existed at the beginning of the war.

Document 12.1 Letter of Antigonus the One-Eyed to Scepsis (311 BC)

The importance of the theme of the "Freedom of the Greeks" in the wars of Alexander's successors is reflected in this letter sent by Antigonus the One-Eyed to the citizens of Scepsis in northwest Anatolia shortly after the conclusion of the Peace of 311 BC and preserved in an inscription discovered at Scepsis.

. . . we exercised zeal for the liberty of the Greeks, making for this reason no small concessions and distributing money besides. To further this we sent out together Aeschylus and Demarchus. As long as there was agreement on this we participated in the conference on the Hellespont, and if certain men had not interfered the matter should then have been settled. Now also, when Cassander and Ptolemy were conferring about a truce and when

Pepalaus and Aristodemus had come to us on the subject, although we saw that some of the demands of Cassander were rather burdensome, still as there was agreement concerning the Greeks we thought it necessary to overlook this in order that the main issue might be settled as soon as possible. We should have considered it a fine thing if all had been arranged for the Greeks as we wished, but because the negotiation would have been rather long and in a delay sometimes many unexpected things happen, and because we were anxious that the question of the Greeks should be settled in our life-time, we thought it necessary not to let details endanger the settlement of the principal issue. What zeal we have shown in these matters will I think be evident to you and to all others from the settlement itself. After the arrangements with Cassander and Lysimachus had been completed, to conclude which they had sent Pepalaus with full authority, Ptolemy sent envoys to us asking that a truce be made with him also and that he be included in the same treaty. We saw that it was no small thing to give up part of an ambition for which we had taken no little trouble and incurred much expense, and that too when an agreement had been reached with Cassander and Lysimachus and when the remaining task was easier. Nevertheless, because . . . we saw that you and our other allies were burdened by the war and its expenses, we thought it was well to yield and to make the truce with him also. We sent Aristodemus and Aeschylus and Hegesias to draw up the agreement. They have now returned with the pledges, and the representative of Ptolemy, Aristobulus, has come to receive them from us. We have provided in the treaty that all the Greeks are to swear to aid each other in preserving their freedom and autonomy, thinking that while we lived in all human expectation these would be protected, but that afterwards freedom would remain more certainly secure for all the Greeks if both they and the men in power are bound by oaths. For them to swear also to help to guard the terms of the treaty which we have made with each other, seems to us neither discreditable nor disadvantageous for the Greeks; therefore it seems to me best for you to take the oath which we have sent. In the future also we shall try to provide both for you and for the other Greeks whatever advantage we have in our power. . . . Farewell.

Orientis Graeci Inscriptiones Selectae *(ed. W. Dittenberger, 2 vols., Leipzig: S. Hirzel 1903–1905, Nr. 5) translated by C. B. Welles*, Royal Correspondence in the Hellenistic Period. London: *Yale University Press* 1934, pp. 4–5.

Antigonus' Last Gamble

The Peace of 311 was not a true peace, merely a truce in the struggle between Antigonus and his enemies that both sides used to rebuild their strength. After an unsuccessful attempt to expel Seleucus (who had not been included in the truce) from Babylon, Antigonus was compelled to make peace with him in 308. He then turned his attention to the west, where he tried to exploit the divisions between Cassander and Ptolemy. In 307 Demetrius, Antigonus' son, intervened in Greece at the head of a strong expeditionary force with a mandate "to free all the cities of Greece."

Success was immediate. Demetrius drove Demetrius of Phalerum, whom Cassander had appointed governor of Athens in 317, into exile in Egypt and restored democratic government in Athens. With his base in Greece secure, Demetrius crossed to Cyprus in 306, where he quickly began to undermine Ptolemy's hold on the island, focusing on the city of Salamis on the southeast coast of the island. The siege of Salamis was the first of the epic sieges that would later gain for Demetrius the sobriquet Poliorcetes ("the Besieger"). The fall of Salamis and the rest of Cyprus left the whole island in Antigonid hands. Demetrius finally had his revenge for his humiliation at the hands of Ptolemy at Gaza six years earlier. More important, possession of Cyprus gave Antigonus and Demetrius an invaluable base from which their fleet could dominate the whole of the eastern Mediterranean basin.

Demetrius' successes radically transformed the political world of the late fourth century BC. Previously none of Alexander's successors had dared to put aside the fiction that he was anything but a deputy of the murdered child-king Alexander IV. In Egypt and Asia, documents even continued to be dated by the years of the reign of Alexander IV for almost half a decade after his death! When the news of Demetrius' victory in Cyprus reached Antigonus and his troops in Syria, however, all this changed: the soldiers acclaimed Demetrius and Antigonus as kings of Macedonia. The crowning of Antigonus and Demetrius announced a new reality: the replacement of the Argeads by a new royal dynasty.

The basis of Antigonus' and Demetrius' claim to be kings and the nature of their kingdom are evident. Like the heroes of Homeric epic, Macedonian kings were first and foremost military leaders, and the sources leave no doubt that it was the glory of Demetrius' decisive victory at Salamis that justified the acclamation of his father and himself as king. Macedonian kings ruled subjects, not territories. Antigonus and Demetrius, therefore, did not claim to be kings of Alexander's empire or any other territory but to be kings pure and simple. The extent of their realm would be determined not by geography but by history, that is, by their success in subduing their rivals.

The elation of Antigonus and Demetrius proved short-lived. Instead of intimidating their rivals, their assumption of the royal title had the opposite effect. Within a year Cassander, Lysimachus, Ptolemy, and Seleucus also had assumed the title "King," thereby denying any claim by Antigonus and Demetrius to sovereignty over their territories. Nor was their defiance purely symbolic. In 305 BC Ptolemy beat off an attempted invasion of Egypt by Antigonus' forces. A year later he joined with Cassander and Lysimachus to help foil the second and most famous of Demetrius' great sieges, his year-long effort to subdue the city of Rhodes, a close ally of Ptolemy and the only significant remaining independent Greek naval power in the eastern Mediterranean. Antigonus' and Demetrius' regal pretensions and aggressive actions had reunited their enemies, setting the stage for a final renewal of the struggle for control of Alexander's legacy that had been interrupted by the Peace of 311.

As he had done before, Antigonus opened his final campaign for supremacy among Alexander's successors by attacking Cassander's holdings in Greece. In 303 BC, Demetrius quickly seized Corinth and much of the northern Peloponnesus, and began to organize a new federal league along the lines of the League of Corinth that Philip II had established almost four decades earlier. Before Demetrius and his father could complete their plans, however, Cassander mounted a strong counterattack by sending Lysimachus to Anatolia. Throughout much of 302 BC, Lysimachus evaded Antigonus' best efforts to capture him, until Seleucus linked up with him in the winter of 301. Facing what was clearly to be the decisive battle of his long career, Antigonus recalled Demetrius from Greece. Over 100,000 men confronted each other in the spring of 301 at Ipsus in central Phrygia, and this time Antigonus' tactical brilliance failed him. At the end of the battle, the 80-year-old veteran of the wars of Philip II and Alexander lay dead on the field, trampled to death under the feet of Seleucus' war elephants, while his son Demetrius was in headlong flight, their dreams of empire in ruins.

BIRTH PANGS OF THE NEW ORDER (301–276 BC)

Like the death of Perdiccas, that of Antigonus the One-Eyed was followed by the division of his territories in Asia among his enemies. Since Cassander had long since abandoned any interest in extending his power outside Europe, it was his allies Lysimachus and Seleucus who profited from Antigonus' demise. To Lysimachus fell all of Anatolia north of the Taurus Mountains. The kingdom that resulted from this development was enormous, extending from the Danube River in the northwest to the borders of Armenia in the east. Seleucus, for his part, added to his vast holdings in Babylonia and Iran the remainder of Antigonus' territories in western Asia, essentially the coastal regions of southern Anatolia, Syria, and Mesopotamia.

New Alliances

The division of western Asia into two such massive contiguous states was bound to shift the focus of Macedonian interest westward as tension developed along their mutual borders, and so it would have—except for an unforeseen development. The original plan for the campaign that led to the Battle of Ipsus envisaged a three-pronged offensive against Antigonus, with Ptolemy joining Lysimachus and Seleucus for the decisive confrontation. Ptolemy advanced only as far as southern Syria and then returned to Egypt. Before returning to Egypt, however, he occupied the territories along his line of march: Judaea, Phoenicia, and southern Syria. He also strengthened his position by allying himself with Seleucus' northern neighbor, Lysimachus. The alliance was concluded in 298 BC in traditional Macedonian fashion, with an exchange of brides that was rich in future consequences. Lysimachus married Ptolemy's daughter Arsinoe, and Ptolemy's younger son, the future Ptolemy II, married Lysimachus' similarly named daughter.

Irony is woven deep into the fabric of history. Confronted by the alliance of Ptolemy and Lysimachus, Seleucus sought an ally of his own and found an unlikely one in Demetrius, the son of Antigonus the One-Eyed, who had escaped from the field of Ipsus and now ruled a "kingdom" comprising his father's fleet and a handful of cities in western Anatolia, the Aegean, and Greece, including the key ports of Ephesus and Corinth. Once again war seemed imminent between rival alliances of Alexander's successors, but this time the outbreak of fighting was deferred for over a decade.

Building New Kingdoms and Cities

The prolonged conflict with Antigonus had forced his rivals to put off their plans for the development of their own kingdoms. Freed from this concern by his death, they devoted themselves to local affairs during the 290s. Thus Lysimachus struggled with limited success to secure his northern frontier against the Getae, who lived across the Danube, while simultaneously founding or reorganizing several major cities in western Anatolia. The most important of these cities was Ephesus, which he moved to a new site closer to the sea and renamed Arsinoea after his new wife or, perhaps, his daughter of the same name. As we shall see, Ptolemy also built on a large scale in this period, transforming Alexandria into a worthy capital for his kingdom. The greatest builder of the period, however, was Seleucus, who founded numerous cities and military settlements in Syria, including his new capital of Antioch, which he built on the site of Antigonus the One-Eyed's name city of Antigoneia near the mouth of the Orontes River.

As thousands of Greeks emigrated to Egypt and the Near and Middle East, the new cities grew and prospered. Ultimately, Alexandria and Antioch supported populations numbering in the hundreds of thousands and boasting splendid public buildings and amenities unknown to the cities of old Greece. Little is known of Hellenistic Antioch and Alexandria, although the recent discovery of extensive archaeological remains under the waters of Alexandria harbor promises finally to reveal some of the glory of ancient Alexandria. In the meantime, an idea of their splendor and prosperity can be gained from the site of Ai Khanum, probably Alexandria on the Oxus, in northern Afghanistan, where French archaeologists have discovered a large city with broad streets, elegant mansions, and all the public buildings essential to a Greek polis: monumental temples, a gymnasium, a theater, and an agora. The preoccupation with domestic affairs that occupied much of the decade after the death of Antigonus was ended, however, by the actions of his son Demetrius.

The Final Struggle

Unlike the other successors of Alexander, Demetrius Poliorcetes (the Besieger) possessed a "kingdom" without a territorial base, and he spent most of the 290s trying to remedy that deficiency. In 295 he occupied Athens, and a year later his efforts were finally crowned with success when he seized control of Macedon from the feuding sons of Cassander.

Demetrius' success, however, was short-lived. While the other kings might have acquiesced in his rule of Macedon, Demetrius saw Macedon only as a base from which to launch one last effort to gain power in Asia. Before he could complete his preparations for his invasion of Asia, his rivals struck. While Ptolemy supported yet another Athenian revolt, Lysimachus joined with Pyrrhus, the king of Epirus, to occupy Macedon and to force Demetrius into prematurely launching his Asian campaign in 286. The result was inevitable. Badly outnumbered and ill, Demetrius had little choice except to resign himself to his fate and surrender to the joint forces of Seleucus and Lysimachus. In 283, this most flamboyant of Alexander's successors died while confined under house arrest near Antioch.

Demetrius' conquerors did not long survive him. A bitter succession crisis, in which Lysimachus executed his own eldest son Agathocles, split the Thracian monarch's court. Agathocles' supporters fled to Seleucus and urged him to support their cause, thereby setting the stage for the resumption of the struggle for control of Alexander's empire between the last of his generals. The forces of the two aging monarchs—both were over 80—met in early 281 at Corupedium (the "Field of Crows"), in Phrygia. At the end of the battle, Lysimachus lay dead on the field and Seleucus, it seemed, finally had achieved the dream that had haunted Perdiccas and Antigonus the One-Eyed and his son: the reunion of the European and Asian portions of Alexander's empire.

The role of chance can never be ignored in history. Within a year Seleucus was dead, assassinated by an exiled son of Ptolemy, Ptolemy Ceraunus ("The Thunderbolt"), to whom he had given sanctuary. The Thunderbolt's moment of glory also passed quickly. A little over a year later, in 279, he was also dead, killed trying to stem the invasion of Macedon by bands of migrating Gauls. A Celtic people, whose migration from their west European home had begun in the early fourth century BC, the Gauls took advantage of the chaos in Macedon caused by the death of Lysimachus and overran Macedon and northern Greece as far south as Delphi.

Despite its horrors, the Gallic eruption was only an isolated episode in the history of European Greece, but it was one that had significant consequences. Although the Gauls soon transferred their terror to Anatolia, two of their raiding parties suffered humiliating defeats at Delphi and Lysimacheia at the hands of the Aetolians and Antigonus Gonatas ("Knockknees"), the son of Demetrius, who had maintained a precarious hold on the few remaining Antigonid possessions in Greece since his father's death almost a decade earlier. Their victories over the Gauls transformed the position of both the Aetolians and Antigonus, legitimizing the emergence of the former as the preeminent power in central Greece and the protector of Delphi and the latter as king of Macedon. The final pieces of the new political system that had so gradually and painfully emerged from the wreckage of Alexander's empire had fallen into place.

Figure 12.3. The Hellenistic world.

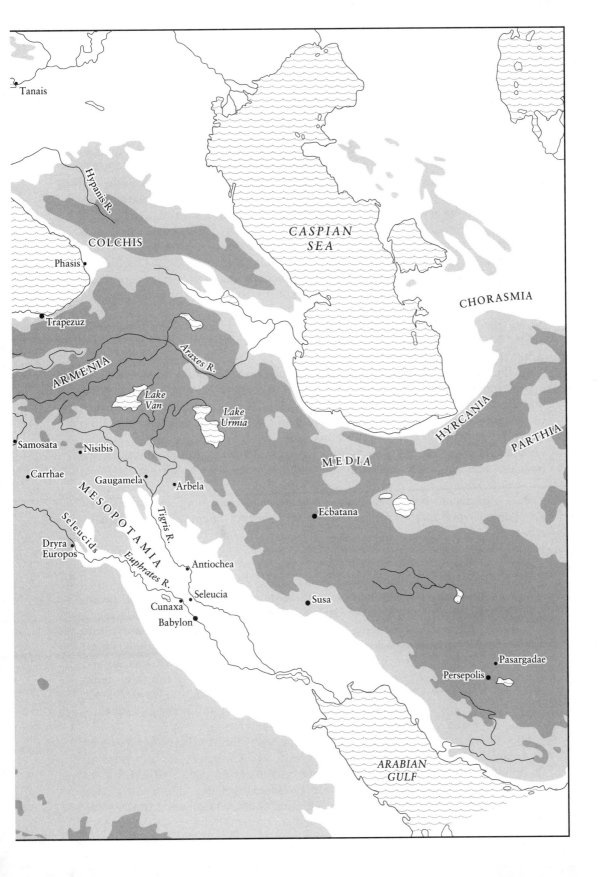

Tanais

COLCHIS

Phasis

Trapezuz

Hypanis R.

CASPIAN
SEA

CHORASMIA

Araxes R.

ARMENIA

*Lake
Van*

*Lake
Urmia*

Samosata

Nisibis

Carrhae

Gaugamela

Arbela

MEDIA

HYRCANIA

PARTHIA

MESOPOTAMIA

Tigris R.

Ecbatana

Seleucids

Dryra
Europos

Antiochea

Euphrates R.

Seleucia

Cunaxa

Babylon

Susa

Pasargadae

Persepolis

*ARABIAN
GULF*

THE PLACE OF THE POLIS IN THE COSMOPOLIS

Although the emergence of the new Macedonian kingdoms changed the character and shape of the world the Greeks knew, one aspect of Greek life remained largely unchanged: the polis continued to form the basic framework for the life of most Greeks. Old poleis such as Athens, Syracuse, and Ephesus grew and prospered. At the same time, the incidence of war between poleis actually declined, and the peaceful settlement of international disputes through arbitration became almost routine. Even the notorious particularism of the classical polis was partially overcome by the Aetolian and Achaean leagues. They succeeded in building strong federal states that could deal with Macedon and the other Macedonian kingdoms on a roughly equal basis by expanding their membership to include cities outside their traditional homes in central Greece and the northern Peloponnesus. Unlike the polarizing Athenian and Spartan leagues of the Classical era, the federal leagues of the Hellenistic Age were invoked as inspiring models by later aspirants to federalism such as the intellectuals of revolutionary America in the eighteenth century.

At the same time, political trends that had appeared already in the fourth century BC intensified in the centuries following the death of Alexander. While nominal democracy became the norm in Greek cities, democracy itself lost much of its meaning, coming to signify little more than the absence of tyranny. In reality, the role of average citizens in government steadily dwindled, and aristocratic oligarchies managed affairs from behind the scenes. Although numerous inscriptions documenting their generosity and public service attest to the patriotism of these new leaders, such core institutions of polis life as popular assemblies and elected councils inevitably declined, as poleis came to rely more and more on the assistance of such men to rescue them from recurrent financial and diplomatic crises.

Athens and Sparta

As usual, Athens and Sparta were exceptions to the prevailing political trends. Although its democracy was never fully restored, Athens continued to be the cultural center of Greece and prospered. The tone of Hellenistic Athenian culture differed greatly from that of the fifth- and fourth-century city. The change is most obvious in drama, the principal Athenian literary form. The grand tragedies and biting political comedies of the Classical era were replaced by a lighter genre known as New Comedy. The gentle, amiable plays of Menander (344–c. 292 BC), which reflect the new political order and the interests of its upper-class audience, are our chief surviving representatives of this literary genre.

Menander had been a pupil of Theophrastus, head of the Lyceum after the death of Aristotle. He was also a friend of Demetrius of Phalerum, another pupil of Theophrastus, whom Cassander appointed as governor of Athens in 317. Historians are disposed to believe that Menander's plays provide reliable historical evidence: a scholar in Alexandria wrote, "O Menander and O life, which one of you has imitated the other?" All Menander's plays are contemporary and depict a Greek world populated by swaggering mercenaries in search of plunder and romance, impoverished citizens who live next door to extremely wealthy people, courtesans and pimps, spendthrift youths, and respectable young women whose only appropriate destiny is marriage. Menander's characters are completely wrapped up in their private worlds, as though weary of war and political upheaval.

Slaves are ubiquitous in New Comedy, and in fact when Demetrius conducted a census in Athens there were 21,000 citizens, 10,000 metics, and 400,000 slaves (including those who worked in the mines). Even if the figures for slaves are exaggerated, still the ratio of slaves to free is likely to have been unusually high. The quarter century of campaigns had certainly reduced many people to slavery. Entrepreneurial slave dealers also took advantage of the habit of exposing unwanted newborns. The abandonment of infants, especially females, was an acceptable means of coping with the insecurity of life in the Hellenistic period. Infant exposure forms the theme of several of Menander's plots (though literature ascribed abandoned babies happier destinies than those that awaited them in real life). Significantly, the chief divinity in New Comedy is Tyche ("Fortune"), a fitting emblem of this chaotic era.

Figure 12.4. Fortune (*Tychē*), personified as a goddess wearing a crown representing city walls, was a common theme in Hellenistic sculpture. This Roman bronze statuette reflects the lost statue of the Tyche of the city of Antioch by Eutychides.

The altered temper of the times was evident also in new developments in the realm of philosophy. Though they had much to say to ordinary men and women, and continue to be studied today with interest by people of varied social and economic backgrounds, Classical philosophers like Plato and Aristotle directed their teachings to affluent men of leisure who were interested in improving their political activities in the autonomous poleis. Hellenistic philosophies, on the other hand, were designed to help people cope with a world over which they had little control.

Like the establishments of Plato and Aristotle, two of the most important schools of Hellenistic thought flowered in Athens. These were Stoicism and Epicureanism. Born in Citium in Cyprus, Zeno (335–263 BC), the founder of Stoicism, was a friend of Antigonus Gonatas and spent many years in Athens, where he lectured on the terrace known as the Stoa Poikilē ("Painted Porch"). For this reason his followers received the name of Stoics (i.e., "Porchers").

Zeno's philosophy reflected the realities of the new political order. According to Zeno, the earth stood at the center of the universe with Zeus its prime mover. Just as cosmic motions never changed and Zeus remained king of the gods, so monarchy was the divinely ordered system of government. Revolution, consequently, violated the natural organization of the world, whereas patriotism and public service harmonized with the cosmic order. Serenity, the Stoics believed, was impossible without the confidence that one had fulfilled one's duties to others, and Stoicism entailed a large dose of humanitarianism.

Zeno urged his followers to attain an inner tranquillity that was proof not only against agonizing pain—hence our word "stoical"—but against excessive pleasure as well. He did not, however, advocate withdrawal from the social and political realm as did some of his contemporaries. Instead, he encouraged Stoics to uphold justice—but not to engage in any serious attempts at reform. Thus, while in principle Stoics considered slaves just as free as their owners, they made no attempt to abolish slavery. It was considered enough for slaves to be made aware that, deep inside, they enjoyed no more or less freedom than their masters and mistresses, who might be themselves "slaves" to greed or lust. Because they rejected excessive pleasure, moreover, Stoics embraced sex only for purposes of procreation. Their acceptance of a hierarchical sociopolitical order and their rejection of sexual pleasure are two important arenas in which Stoicism anticipated the teachings of early Christianity.

In keeping with their belief in an orderly universe, Stoics believed that life was rational and could be planned. A very different position was taken by Epicurus (341–270 BC), a native of Samos who moved to Athens, where he established in his home a school called The Garden. Epicurus even included women among his students. Adopting the atomic theory first put forward by Leucippus and Democritus, he rejected the determinism of the early atomists. Though he agreed that atoms fell in straight lines from the sky, he added a new element. Epicurus argued that the multiplicity of substances in the universe arose from periodic swerves in the atoms' paths, causing them to collide at a variety of angles. Like the domains continually carved out and altered by Alexander's successors, the entire universe combined by chance, and would perish and regenerate by chance as well.

This construction left little room for the gods, and in fact Epicurus contended that though the gods must exist since people saw their images in dreams, they had no interest in humans. In the Epicurean system, the gods lived serene, untroubled lives, indifferent to such staples of Greek religious and social life as prayers, offerings, and rituals. (The good news was that the horrific punishments associated with the underworld were fictions; the bad news was that nobody on Olympus was interested in listening to complaints, offering solace, or avenging injustices.) After death, the atoms that had comprised the soul and body of each person merely dissolved.

In the absence of eternal rewards and punishments, Epicurus viewed happiness on earth as the purpose of life, thus winning for himself the name of history's first humanist philosopher. He defined happiness as the attainment of *ataraxia*, an untroubled state free from excessive pleasure and pain, much like the serenity advocated by Zeno. Unlike Zeno, however, Epicurus advocated withdrawal from a wide variety of activities that might bring pain, both the risky quest for love or money (which the Stoics would also see as problematic) and participation in politics (which the Stoics praised). For Epicureans, anything that might threaten ataraxia was to be avoided. Though in modern parlance the label "Epicurean" connotes indulgence in pleasure, particularly in the pleasures of fine dining, Epicurus actually counseled moderation in food and drink in order to avoid indigestion and hangovers. Unlike the Stoics, Epicureans approved of sex as long as it did not entail falling in love with all the attendant pitfalls.

Despite their substantial differences over sex and politics, Stoics and Epicureans shared a common goal: attaining tranquillity in a turbulent world. A similar aim characterized two other schools of thought that evolved around the same time, Cynicism and Skepticism. The principal theorist of the Cynic movement was Diogenes of Sinope (c. 400–325 BC), who encouraged his followers to become self-sufficient by shedding the trappings of civilization for the naturalness of animals. Denying that humans had needs different from those of other mammals, Diogenes scandalized contemporaries and earned himself the name of the Cynic ("dog," "*kuōn*" in Greek) by brazenly maintaining that people should follow instincts just as animals do—urinating or masturbating in public, for example. The heirs to the Cynics' rejection of civilized norms were the Skeptics, who also shared the Epicureans' disillusionment with public life. Skepticism, associated with the name of Pyrrhon of Elis (c. 365–275 BC), became popular around 200 BC. Stressing the impossibility of certain knowledge, Skeptics urged people to withdraw from the world around them. The quest for truth, after all, was hopeless, as was the quest for power. Today, the words "skeptical" and "cynical" are linked when we talk about people who are not easily persuaded. In this respect the philosophies we associate with the Hellenistic world (though Cynicism began in the fourth century) contrast sharply with those of Plato and Aristotle, who really believed that knowledge was possible and could be gained through education.

While Athens continued to serve as a magnet for intellectuals, it is significant that the center of philosophical speculation in the Hellenistic era shifted not only away from Athens but also away from mainland Greece in general. The best-known Stoic thinkers, for example, came from places like Cyprus and Syria, while Tarsus, Alexandria, and Rhodes became the most famous Stoic university towns. In time Stoicism took root firmly in the Roman empire, where it anchored the minds and souls of many men and women seeking to cope with the decadence and autocracy of the imperial government.

Almost as remarkable was the fate of Sparta. After a century long decline that saw the number of Spartiates dwindle to fewer than a thousand and tensions between rich and poor become acute, two reformer kings, Agis IV (262–241 BC) and Cleomenes III (260–219 BC), revitalized Sparta's "Lycurgan" institutions. Debts were canceled, land was redistributed, and the traditional Spartan educational system, the *agōgē*, was reestablished. For a brief while, Sparta became the Stoic model state. The Stoic notion that individual suffering is part of some great natural scheme and should be borne without lamentation struck a responsive chord in Spartans, and the idea that austerity was preferable to self-indulgence reverberated with Spartan ideals as well. For a few years Spartan arms were invincible and the city seemed on the verge of dominating the Peloponnesus again. Greek intellectuals trumpeted once more the virtues of the Lycurgan system. Their dreams of Greek renewal were shattered when the joint forces of Macedon and the Achaean League crushed the Spartans at Sellasia in 222 BC. As the fate of Sparta revealed, not even the strongest polis could resist indefinitely the power of the Macedonian kingdoms that strove to subdue them or to use them as pawns in their own diplomatic and military struggles.

THE MACEDONIAN KINGDOMS

Greek literature, with its polis bias, contains little information about the organization and day-to-day operation of the Macedonian kingdoms that dominated the Hellenistic political world. Fortunately, the discovery by archaeologists of extensive nonliterary evidence in the form of inscriptions and especially papyri has enabled historians to remedy this deficiency. More than a century of intensive study of these new sources has demonstrated that the Hellenistic kingdoms were conquest states whose organization was based on two fundamental principles: first, that as spear-won land, the kingdom and its population belonged to the king; and second, that the conduct of the king's business and the performance of the king's work took precedence over all other considerations. These two principles were common to all the Macedonian kingdoms. Their operation is clearest, however, in the case of Ptolemaic Egypt, where the rich papyrological evidence has provided scholars with a detailed view of the government and society of a major Hellenistic kingdom.

The Case of Egypt

The basis of Egypt's wealth was its agricultural land. Like the Pharaohs before them, the Ptolemies claimed ownership of all Egypt. Nevertheless, for practical purposes the Ptolemaic government divided Egyptian land into two broad categories: royal land for basic agricultural production and "released land." The latter category was further divided into four subcategories: cleruchic land, used to provide land grants to soldiers; gift land, used to reward government officials; temple land, used to provide economic support for Egypt's numerous temples; and private land, used for individual house and garden plots. The nonagricultural sectors of the economy were also tightly organized. Major economic activities such as textile, papyrus, and oil production were state monopolies, intended to generate the maximum revenue for the king from fees and taxes. Foreign competition for the profits of Egyptian commerce was minimized by strict currency controls and limitations on imports. An extensive administration headquartered in Alexandria supervised the entire system. Its agents—Greek at the upper levels and Egyptian at the lower ones—could be found in even the most remote village. To ensure that the king's work was done, that taxes were paid, and that the all-important irrigation system functioned properly, every adult from peasant to immigrant soldier was registered according to place of residence and economic function. Finally, the king and, eventually, also the queen presided over the whole system with all the powers of autocrats whose every word was law. The supremacy of the royal family over all levels of society was symbolized by the institution of an official cult of the living ruler and his ancestors. Monarchs encouraged belief in their own divinity as a way of legitimizing their use of absolute power, while subjects enjoyed participating in ruler cults as a means of demonstrating patriotism, loyalty, and gratitude. In recognition of their belief in monotheism and of their support of the regime, only the Jews were formally excused from these observances.

Ptolemy II used both sculpture and coinage to announce the apotheoses of members of his family. In ruler cults men generally represented themselves as Dionysus or Heracles, while females were portrayed as Aphrodite. Through syncretism, however, they were often equated with Osiris and Isis and considered to be actual incarnations of the divinities. The coexistence of Greek and Egyptian culture is evident in the portraits of the deified Ptolemies. Depending on which elements of the population were more likely to view the representation, kings and queens might be depicted in purely Egyptian style, in purely Greek style, or in some combination of the two.

Figure 12.5. This gold octodrachm showing Ptolemy II and Arsinoe II was minted by Ptolemy III (246–221 BC).

Figure 12.6. Limestone statue of Arsinoe II. A hieroglyphic inscription on the back pillar of Arsinoe's portrait indicated that the figure was dedicated not long after her death and deification in 270. Her corn curls were painted black, and the face and parts of the body were originally gilded. The full, curved lips, highly-arched brows, and large, wide-open eyes are depicted in the Egyptian style, but the queen carries a double cornucopia, an attribute of Greek goddesses referring to their powers of fertility.

The apparent rationality of Hellenistic state organization greatly impressed late nineteenth- and early twentieth-century historians, leading them to view the Hellenistic kingdoms as essentially Greek institutions with few ties to their Persian and Egyptian predecessors. Closer scrutiny of Egyptian and Cuneiform texts and the Greek sources, however, has revealed greater continuity with Egyptian and ancient Near Eastern political traditions in the administration of the Macedonian kingdoms than earlier historians had realized. These regions maintained many of their traditional administrative structures, together with many of their key institutions. The administrative organization of Ptolemaic Egypt and Seleucid Asia, for example, remained divided into traditional subdivisions, such as nomes and satrapies, just as they had been under the Macedonians' Persian predecessors. Not surprisingly, the Greek terminology of many of our sources often proves upon analysis to be a facade, hiding traditional institutions and practices.

In Hellenistic Egypt and Asia, the temples still played major roles in the social and economic lives of their peoples. In Egypt, the priests used the names of the Greek gods, equated the months of the Macedonian and Egyptian calendars, and translated the royal titulary into Greek in order to give a Hellenic cast to the millennia-old traditions of Egyptian religion and kingship. This continuity with the past is not surprising, since, like Alexander, the Ptolemies and Seleucids were simultaneously both Macedonian kings and pharaohs and kings of Babylon, whose responsibilities included support of traditional institutions.

In addition to continuities between the Egyptian and Near Eastern past and the organization of the later Hellenistic kingdoms, scholars have also observed "irrationalities" and inefficiencies in their everyday operations. Ptolemaic Egypt and Seleucid Asia were personal autocracies. Official documents describe their governments as consisting of the "king, his friends" (the king's personal entourage), "and the army." The only effective limit on the kings' exercise of their power was fear of losing the support of their armies and generals, who alone had the power to unseat a king if provoked too far. Government officials were political appointees with often multiple and sometimes even overlapping responsibilities, who fulfilled whatever position the king posted them to irrespective of their previous service.

Instead of the smoothly functioning bureaucratic machines envisioned by their late nineteenth- and early twentieth-century predecessors, therefore, the sources reveal that the Hellenistic governments were inefficient and often arbitrary instruments, primarily designed to extract the maximum revenue from their rulers' subjects. Documents such as Ptolemy II's (282–246 BC) recently discovered order for a complete economic survey of Egypt, and his letter forbidding lawyers from assisting individuals in disputes concerning taxes, bear witness not to rational central planning but to the Hellenistic kings' insatiable need for money to support their ambitious foreign policies and domestic projects. Similarly, the numerous royal orders forbidding government officials from exploiting the king's subjects for personal gain, and the frequent recourse to blanket amnesties for unfulfilled obligations owed the government and for charges of wrongdoing by government officials, attest to the inherent inefficiency and corruption of these systems in actual practice.

HELLENISTIC SOCIETY

While the emergence of new Macedonian monarchies in the early third century BC posed a significant threat to the independence of the cities of Aegean Greece, they also created unprecedented opportunities for individual Greeks from those same cities. Whatever Alexander's plans for the governance of his empire may have been, his successors clearly judged that he had made a serious mistake in appointing Iranians to important posts. In staffing the upper levels of their governments, therefore, they relied on Greek immigrants instead.

New Opportunities in a Colonial World

The resulting opportunities were greatest for the male members of the Greek elite, who quickly formed a powerful class of expatriate civilian and military officials. Inscriptions and papyri amply document the wealth and influence of members of this new governing class—men such as Apollonius, the chief financial officer of Ptolemy II, and Zenon, the Carian immigrant who managed his estate. Less glamorous, but equally real and far more numerous, were the opportunities created by the kings' incessant need for Greeks to serve in their armies and to fill the multitude of minor, but potentially lucrative, administrative jobs required to govern their kingdoms. For ambitious men of this sort, the court poet Theocritus spoke the literal truth when he described Egypt as a land of opportunity for immigrants and characterized Ptolemy II as a "good paymaster."

Document 12.2 Letter of King Ptolemy II to Apollonius concerning the revenues of Egypt (259 BC)

King Ptolemy to Apollonius, greeting. Since some of the advocates listed below are intervening in fiscal cases to the detriment of the revenues, issue instructions that those advocates shall pay to the crown twice the additional tenth and that they shall no longer be allowed to serve as advocates in any matter. And if any of those who have harmed the revenues be discovered to have served as advocate in some matter, have him sent to us under guard and have his property assigned to the crown.

The Amherst Papyri *(eds. B. P. Grenfell and A. S. Hunt, Vol. 2, London, 1901, Nr. 33) translated by Stanley M. Burstein,* The Hellenistic Age from the Battle of Ipsos to the Death of Kleopatra VII. *Cambridge: Cambridge University Press, 1985, pp. 121–122.*

Opportunities were not limited, however, to men; they expanded also for women, although not to the same extent. As in the case of men, they were greatest for women of wealth. Queens like Arsinoe II and Cleopatra VII of Egypt stand out in the ancient sources, but some Greek cities allowed women to hold minor public offices in return for their willingness to use their wealth for civic purposes. Education, which became common for upper-class women in the Hellenistic period, also created the possibility of careers for individual women, such as the Cynic philosopher Hipparchia and the professional musician Polygnota of Thebes, whose career is documented in a series of inscriptions from Delphi. More women, however, probably benefited from the modest but significant changes in their rights that occurred in the colonial society of the Macedonian kingdoms, where marriage contracts and other legal documents preserved on papyrus reveal women capable of conducting their own business and seeking legal redress for their husbands' misconduct. Not surprisingly, the explosion of new opportunities made the Hellenistic period one of the great creative ages of Greek civilization.

ALEXANDRIA AND HELLENISTIC CULTURE

Alexandria was the most famous and enduring of Alexander's foundations, and the site of his tomb. Responsibility for embellishing the city, however, lay with the first three Ptolemies, who transformed it into the foremost city of the Hellenistic world. A liberal immigration policy created a multiethnic population including Macedonians, Greeks, Egyptians, and a vibrant Jewish community occupying one-fifth of the city's area. Perhaps the clearest symbol of the dynamism and originality of early Hellenistic Alexandria was its signature monument, the Pharos. Built by the architect Sostratus of Cnidus for Ptolemy II, the Pharos was the first skyscraper, a 400-foot-high polygonal tower topped by a statue of Zeus Soter ("Savior") whose beacon fire, reflected far out to sea by giant mirrors, guided ships to Alexandria. The Pharos was considered one of the Seven Wonders of the Ancient World. It is no accident that three of the seven creations that wound up on this list dated from the Hellenistic period, for this was a time when rulers were particularly eager to advertise their cities' wealth and prestige; the

Figure 12.7. Tetradrachm of the Roman Emperor Commodus (180–192 AD) struck at Alexandria showing ship(s?) passing the Pharos.

other two were the Colossus of Rhodes and the temple of Artemis at Ephesus. In scale and style these were all appropriate monuments to an age of competition and larger-than-life historical figures.

🮑🮑🮑🮑🮑🮑🮑🮑🮑🮑🮑🮑🮑🮑🮑🮑🮑🮑🮑🮑🮑🮑🮑🮑🮑🮑🮑🮑🮑🮑🮑🮑

Document 12.3 Marriage Contract of Heracleides and Demetria

(311 BC) The improved legal position of married women in the Hellenistic period is clear in this marriage contract from Egypt. The diverse origin of Greek immigrants to Egypt is evident in the variety of ethnics among the witnesses to Heracleides' and Demetria's marriage contract.

Seventh year of the reign of Alexander, the son of Alexander, fourteenth year of the satrapy of Ptolemy, month of Dius. Marriage contract of Heracleides and Demetria. Heracleides, a free born man, takes as his lawful wife Demetria, a free born woman from Cos, from her father Leptines, from Cos, and from her mother Philotis. Demetria will bring with her clothing and ornaments worth 1,000 drachmas. Heracleides will furnish to Demetria everything that is appropriate for a freewoman. We shall live together in whatever place seems best in the common opinion of Leptines and Heracleides.

If Demetria shall be detected devising something evil for the purpose of humiliating her husband Heracleides, she shall be deprived of everything she brought to the marriage. Heracleides shall declare whatever charge he may make against Demetria before three men whom both approve. Heracleides may not introduce another woman into their home to insult Demetria, nor have children from another woman, nor devise any evil toward Demetria for any reason. If Heracleides shall be detected doing any of these things and Demetria declares this before three men whom both approve, Heracleides shall return to Demetria the dowry of 1,000 drachmas which she brought, and he shall pay to her in addition 1,000 silver Alexandrian drachmas. Demetria, and those with Demetria, shall be able to exact payment, just as though there were a legal judgment from Heracleides himself, and from all of Heracleides' property on both land and sea.

This contract shall be wholly valid in every way wherever Heracleides produces it against Demetria, or Demetria and those with Demetria produce it against Heracleides, in order to exact payment. Heracleides and Demetria each have the right to preserve their contracts and to produce the contracts against each other. Witnesses: Cleon of Gela, Anticrates of Temnos, Lysis of Temnos, Dionysius of Temnos, Aristomachus of Cyrene, Aristodicus of Cos.

Elephantine Papyri (ed. O. Rubensohn, Berlin, 1907, Nr. 1, lines 1–18).

🮑🮑🮑🮑🮑🮑🮑🮑🮑🮑🮑🮑🮑🮑🮑🮑🮑🮑🮑🮑🮑🮑🮑🮑🮑🮑🮑🮑🮑🮑🮑🮑

The Ptolemies also strove to make Alexandria the cultural center of the Greek world. Like Alexander, whose entourage had included artists and intellectuals such as Aristotle's nephew, Callisthenes, his court historian, Ptolemy I and his immediate successors encouraged prominent Greek scholars and scientists to come to Egypt. With the enormous wealth of Egypt at their disposal, the Ptolemies could afford to subsidize intellectuals, encouraging artistic and scientific work by establishing cultural institutions of a new type.

Their principal cultural foundation was the research center known as the "Museum" because of its dedication to the nine Muses, the patron goddesses of the arts. There distinguished scholars, supported by government stipends, could pursue their studies in congenial surroundings including dormitories, dining facilities, and pleasant gardens. To assist the Museum's scholars, Ptolemy I established (with the aid of Demetrius of Phalerum) a library intended to contain copies of every book written in Greek. The library's collection is said to have ultimately reached 700,000 papyrus rolls.

The Ptolemies' passion for expanding the royal library's collections was legendary. The Greek translation of the Jewish Bible, the *Septuagint*, was supposedly produced on order of Ptolemy II, and the official Athenian copy of the works of the three canonical tragedians was allegedly stolen by Ptolemy III. Even the books of visitors to Egypt were scrutinized and seized—the owner received a cheap copy—if they were not in the library. However its books were acquired, the library offered unprecedented resources for scholarly research in every field of intellectual endeavor (although an envious rival might sneer at the successful occupants of Ptolemy's "bird coop" with some justification, since subsidized intellectuals were expected to earn their keep). Doctors and writers receiving government stipends served as physicians and tutors to members of the royal family, and celebrated its achievements. The scholar and poet Callimachus created a monumental catalogue in 120 books of the library that laid the foundation for the history of Greek literature. In his poem *The Lock of Berenice* Callimachus also celebrated the transformation into a comet of a lock of hair dedicated by Berenice II in 246 BC to commemorate the beginning of the Third Syrian War. In a similar vein, Theocritus' seventeenth *Idyll* extravagantly praised the first decade of Ptolemy II's reign.

New Directions in Literature

The work of Alexandrian intellectuals was not limited, however, to satisfying the whims of their royal patrons. Alexandrian writers made important innovations in Greek literature. In his *Idylls*, brief dialogues or monologues set in an idealized countryside, Theocritus introduced the pastoral mode into western literature. Callimachus inaugurated the tradition of "learned" poetry in works such as his *Hymns* and *Aetia*, in which he retold in elegant verse obscure myths and the origins of strange customs and festivals collected from all over the Greek world. Callimachus' younger contemporary and rival Apollonius of Rhodes reinvigorated the old epic genre with his acute psychological portraits of Jason and Medea in his vivid retelling of the story of Jason and the Argonauts, the *Argonautica*. Another contemporary of Callimachus, Euhemerus, an ambassador of Cassander to Ptolemy I, put forward a radical and important theory about the origins of mythology: he invented the utopian travel romance in order to propound in his *Sacred Tale* the notion that the gods were great rulers worshiped after their deaths for their gifts to humanity.

The Visual Arts

The visual arts reflect the combination of old and new that is a distinctive feature of the Hellenistic age. In the Classical period artists had devoted themselves to the perfection of a limited number of artistic genres or types. For example, the epitome of fifth-century sculpture was the idealized figure of an unemotional youthful nude male. This type of figure continued to be sculpted as a heroic representation of Hellenistic kings. Though Hellenistic art evolved from Classical, it is characterized by variety and experimentation. Sculptors perfected an idealized figure of the youthful female nude and also produced realistic renderings of a cross section of the population of the cosmopolis displaying a variety of human emotions. Sculptures, both large and small, are additional testimony to the new focus on the individual as special and unique, rather than as an equal member of a democratic polis.

The production of small terracotta figures began in the fourth century and continued to flourish in the Hellenistic period. These figurines were made in molds in multiple copies, and were relatively inexpensive. Like the people they represented, they were widespread in the Greek world. The figurines are our best evidence for the visual arts as a reflection of reality. As we have mentioned previously in our discussion of Menander's plays, art could be considered a mirror of life. The figurines portray people of all ages, every social status, and a range of ethnicities, including chubby children; stooped, stout, and wrinkled elderly people; elegant and graceful society women; and members of the lower classes. Small bronze sculptures, though more expensive, also depict a broad variety of people.

The development of portraiture on coins and in sculpture was fostered by interest in the individual and in the personality: such things were particularly important for people whose lives were subject to the whims of monarchs. As the portrayals of Alexander and his successors in this chapter and Chapter 11 indicate, a portrait was not only an attempt to portray the actual features of the subject, but also an attempt to influence the viewer's perception of the character. Coins may be small, but because they are numerous and circulate widely they are very influential. In larger works as well, art not only reflects the world but attempts to shape it. The Ptolemies, for example, were adept at the use of visual imagery as propaganda to gain support for their reign. Like Alexander, who encouraged belief in his own divinity and was worshiped as a god after his death, the Hellenistic rulers manipulated religion in their own interests. The monarchs' definition of themselves as divine was not mere immodesty; it also served to legitimize their use of absolute power. Members of the ruling dynasties were commonly portrayed on coins and in sculpture with the attributes and epithets of

a   b   c

Figure 12.8. Miniature Hellenistic sculptures. **a.** Terracotta figurine of old nurse and child. Late fourth century BC. **b.** Terracotta figurine of school girl reading a papyrus roll. **c.** Bronze statuette of black youth in craftsman's garb. Third to second century BC.

gods and heroes. The value of sculpture as a political tool is obvious in the image of Alexander in the company of Egyptian divinities (Chapter 11, Figure 11.5) and in the sculpture of Arsinoe II (this chapter, Figure 12.6) that portrays the queen as an Egyptian goddess. Even an illiterate viewer would immediately understand the message: Alexander and his successors are not mere mortals but incarnations of divinities. Furthermore, they are rightful heirs to the throne of the pharaohs as well as monarchs who rule over the Greek world.

Larger-than-life monarchs strutted proudly on the huge stage of Egypt and the eastern Mediterranean. Many of the monuments they commissioned are now fragmentary or have completely disappeared, but like the Pharos they are known through images on coins, copies made by the Romans, and verbal descriptions. They convey a vivid impression of the wealth and power of the monarchs and proud cities who constructed them. Artists were available to travel when such patrons beckoned. Bravura characterizes many major Hellenistic sculptures like one of the best-known, the Victory (Nikē) of Samothrace. This huge work was dedicated by the people of Rhodes to commemorate their victories over Antiochus III of Syria (222–187 BC). It was erected at Samothrace, an international religious center where it would be seen by travelers. Victory alights on the prow of a ship. Her wet and windblown dress reveals the contours of her body, while the cloth flaring out behind the goddess symbolizes the agitation, restlessness, and continuous change characteristic not only of the art but also of life in the Hellenistic period. Her raised wings also suggest that her presence is not necessarily permanent, but linked to the donor's fortune. Like the goddess Tyche (Fortune), Victory can be fickle.

The visual arts also reveal nostalgia for the past, which must have seemed a safer, more secure time. Portraits of philosophers, poets, and other historical figures decorated public areas and private enclosed spaces such as libraries (cf. Demosthenes, Chapter 10, Figure 10.4). Some authors and other intellectuals were worshipped as divine. They had become as immortal as their words and thoughts. For example, portrait busts of Homer (about whose appearance nothing was known), were common, no doubt because the *Iliad* was the mostly widely read book in the Greek world, and was used as a text in primary school. Nevertheless, despite the reverence for the past, the evidence of the visual arts leaves no doubt that the world had changed drastically since the days of Achilles and the bards who first recited his exploits in regular lines of verse.

Scholarship and Science

The greatest achievements of Hellenistic intellectuals, however, were in the areas of literary scholarship and applied science, where their works remained unmatched during the rest of antiquity. Callimachus, together with other scholars such as the philologists Zenodotus and Aristarchus, founded the critical study of Greek language and literature, and prepared standard texts of Homer and the other poets that are the ancestors of those we still use. The mathematician and geographer Eratosthenes established the principles of scientific cartography, and produced a strikingly accurate estimate of the circumference of the earth on the basis of evidence collected by Hellenistic explorers. The physicist Ctesibius pioneered the study of ballistics and the use of compressed air as a source of power, while other scientists experimented with the use of steam to operate simple machines. More mundanely, an unknown Ptolemaic technician invented the *saqqiyah*, an animal-powered water wheel that is still used today in Egypt and the Sudan.

The doctors Herophilus and Erasistratus made fundamental discoveries concerning the anatomy and functions of the human nervous, optical, reproductive, and digestive systems by dissecting corpses, and even vivisecting criminals whom the government provided for the advancement of science. The Hippocratic Oath, which in many parts of the western world physicians take upon graduation from medical school, dates to the Hellenistic period. In the oath the physicians promise to respect the physicians who taught them and to hand on their knowledge only to their teachers' sons and paying apprentices. They swear to abstain from using their craft to harm or wrong any person and to refrain from

Figure 12.9. Victory (Nikē) of Samothrace. The massive statue known as the Winged Victory dates from around 200 BC and is one of the best-known works of art in the Louvre Museum in Paris.

Figure 12.10. This sculpted relief of the Apotheosis of Homer by Archelaus of Priene, found in Bovillae, Italy, dates from around 221–205 BC. The deified poet, seated at the lower left holding a scroll and scepter, is crowned by the Muse of epic poetry. The other figures include Zeus and Mnemosyne (Memory) and their daughters, the Muses. The sculpture was probably made for a poet who was victorious in a competition at Alexandria.

practicing abortion and euthanasia and from divulging what patients tell them in confidence. Since there was no licensing of physicians in antiquity and many conflicting medical doctrines and views of the physician's ethical role, the oath was by no means universally adhered to by Greek physicians, as is obvious from other medical texts that do discuss abortion, and from the use of vivisection.

The importance of royal patronage in Ptolemaic cultural activity did, however, have a drawback. Areas that did not receive royal largess tended to stagnate.

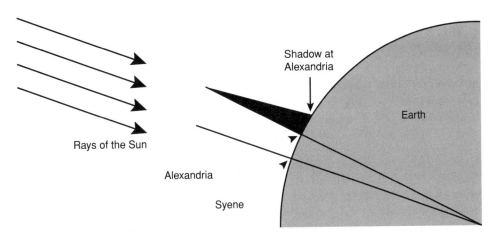

Figure 12.11. Eratosthenes' Calculation of the Circumference of the Earth. Eratosthenes measured at Alexandria the shadow cast by a pointer on the interior of a hemispherical bowl at noon on the day of the summer solstice when the sun was directly overhead at Aswan. By applying two simple geometrical theorems—the angles of similar triangles are equal and equal angles sweep out equal arcs—he concluded that the 5000 stade distance between Alexandria and Aswan represented 1/50 of a sphere with a circumference of approximately 250,000 stades. Despite minor errors of fact that Eratosthenes could not know, his procedure was methodologically correct and resulted in a measurement of the circumference of the earth that was either almost exactly correct or, at the most, 20 percent too large, depending on whether Eratosthenes' stade should be counted as equal to 10 to the mile or 8 1/3 to the mile. *(Diagram of Eratosthenes' procedure for calculating the circumference of the earth.)*

Thus, apart from the works of the mathematician Euclid, whose *Elements* is still used to introduce students to geometry, the Alexandrian contribution to the theoretical sciences and philosophy, which were of limited interest to the Ptolemies, was undistinguished in quality and limited in quantity.

SOCIAL RELATIONS IN THE HELLENISTIC WORLD

The importance of their cultural achievements tends to obscure the fact that Greeks were a minority in the Hellenistic world everywhere outside the Aegean. This was true even in cities like Alexandria and Antioch, which were themselves only islands of Greek domination and culture in a predominantly non-Greek world. Not surprisingly, therefore, the relationship between immigrant Greeks and the native populations is one of the central issues of Hellenistic historiography. Those Hellenistic historians who wrote early in the twentieth century were heartened by the results of the encounter between Greeks and non-Greeks in the Hellenistic period. They viewed the Hellenistic cities as "melting pots" in which Greek and non-Greek cultures and peoples blended into a new cosmopolitan civilization. A much harsher interpretation of Hellenistic social relations has become popular recently, reminiscent of Isocrates' dream of a conquered Asia in which natives worked just as hard to support the new Greek colonists and their Macedonian masters as they had for their Persian overlords. Supporters of this new interpretation view the Macedonian kingdoms as segregated societies in which social status and privilege were primarily determined by ethnicity. Needless to say, in this interpretation the ethnicities that counted were Macedonian and Greek.

A considerable degree of social and cultural segregation was inherent in the demography of the Hellenistic kingdoms. As Greek settlement was predominantly urban, the countryside inevitably was largely cut off from Greek influence. Studies of Egyptian villages have revealed an almost total absence of either Greek residents or Greek influence on daily life.

Ethnic separation was not limited, however, to the countryside. Non-Greeks were denied citizenship and lived in separate residential quarters in the cities of the Hellenistic East. In Egypt distinct legal systems were even maintained for Greeks, Egyptians, and Jews. Ethnic prejudices and tensions are also well documented in the sources. Theocritus characterizes petty street crime as "an Egyptian game," and an agricultural worker complains that his supervisors hold him

---

Figure 12.12. The Rosetta Stone. 27 March 196 B.C. Fragment of a black granite stele found at the Rosetta mouth of the Nile containing a trilingual decree (Greek, Hieroglyphic [Middle Egyptian], and Demotic [vernacular late Egyptian]) passed by a synod of the priests of Egypt commemorating the coronation of Ptolemy V (204–180 BC) as king of Egypt: In the reign of the young god who received the kingship from his father, Lord of crowns, great of fame, who established Egypt, and is reverent toward the gods, victorious over his enemies; who improved the life of men, lord of the thirty-year cycle just as Hephaistus the Great, and king just as Helios; great king of the upper and lower lands, son of the gods Philopatores, whom Hephaistus approved, to whom Helios gave victory, living image of Zeus; son of Helios, Ptolemy, living forever, beloved of Ptah. When he [sc. Ptolemy V] arrived at Lycopolis in the Bousirite nome, which had been seized and had been readied for a siege with an abundant store of weapons and all other provisions since the conspiracy had been prepared over a long period of time by impious men who had gathered together in it and who had committed many evil acts against the temples and the inhabitants of Egypt, he encamped opposite it and surrounded the city with mounds and ditches and wondrous walls. As the Nile flood in the eighth year was great and normally covered the plains, he restrained it by blocking in many places the mouths of the canals. Having spent not a little money on these things and, having stationed cavalry and infantry to guard them, in a short time he took the city by force and destroyed all the impious men in it, just as Hermes and Horus, the son of Isis and Osiris, dealt with the rebels in these same places formerly. Those who had led the rebels in the time of his own father [sc. Ptolemy IV] and caused disorder in the land and desecrated the temples, when he arrived at Memphis to avenge his father and his realm, he punished all of them fittingly at the time he arrived to perform the rites connected with his coronation.

Orientis Graeci Inscriptiones Selectae (ed. W. Dittenberger, 2 vols., Leipzig: S. Hirzel, 1903–1905, Nr. 90); *translated by Stanley M. Burstein,* The Hellenistic Age from the Battle of Ipsos to the Death of Kleopatra VII. *Cambridge, Cambridge University Press, 1985, pp. 131–132 (excerpted).*

in contempt and refuse to pay him "because I am a barbarian" (cf. Figure 12.2), while the personal papers of a Greek recluse at Memphis are filled with references to incidents of personal harassment by his Egyptian neighbors. Finally, longing for the end of Macedonian rule is a common theme in both Hellenistic Egyptian and Jewish literature, and the history of Ptolemaic Egypt and Seleucid Asia is replete with examples of rebellions intended to achieve that goal. The

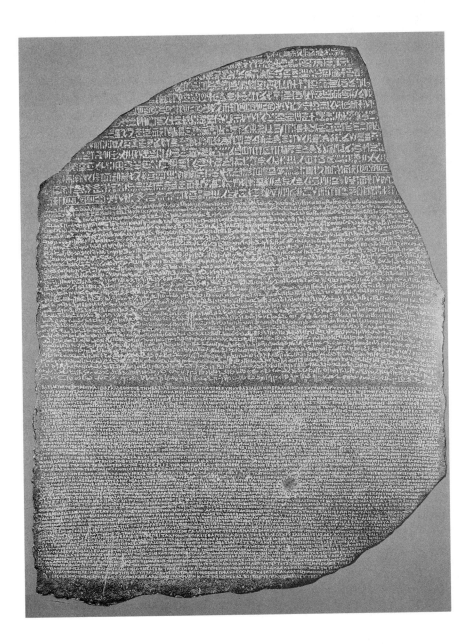

Rosetta Stone alludes to such a rebellion in the first years of the reign of Ptolemy V. Some Egyptians even dreamed of the miraculous return of Nectanebo II, the last pharaoh of a free Egypt who had fled to Nubia when the Persians reconquered Egypt in the 340s BC.

The Place of Non-Greeks

Nevertheless, the picture of the Hellenistic kingdoms as divided into two almost totally isolated societies—one Greek and the other non-Greek—distorts ancient social reality almost as much as the earlier ideal of a harmoniously mixed Hellenistic civilization. The existence of Greek versions of the Nectanebo story, such as "The Dream of Nectanebos," proves that at least some Greeks were interested in contemporary Egyptian culture. More important, serious social divisions and conflicts within the native populations of the Hellenistic kingdoms themselves precluded any unified native resistance to Macedonian rule.

In the theocratic monarchies of Egypt and the ancient Near East, the security of the state relied on the support of the gods and their priesthoods, and that remained true during the Hellenistic period. The Ptolemies subjected the temples of Egypt to greater supervision than their pharaonic predecessors, but they also maintained and even expanded the scale of state subsidy of religion, as can be seen from the vast extent of temple building that occurred during the Hellenistic period. Study of the extensive Egyptian evidence for Hellenistic Egypt is only in its infancy. But already it has revealed that under the Ptolemaic regime the priestly families prospered, accumulating large estates and actively engaging in business transactions of all kinds, while expending large sums on the traditional Egyptian indicators of personal success: dedications to the gods and lavish tomb furnishings. Their prosperity also provided the basis for a vigorous revival of Egyptian culture, resulting in a variety of new and interesting literary and artistic works that are only now being studied and appreciated. It is not surprising, therefore, that in the Rosetta Stone Ptolemy V is congratulated for his brutal suppression of a native rebellion at Lycopolis in Lower Egypt that threatened the welfare of the Egyptian priesthood just as much as it did their Macedonian overlord.

Opportunity was not limited to the religious elite. Analysis of the personal archives of village officials—individuals dismissed by early Hellenistic historians as lowly and insignificant figures—has shown that such people could grow rich by exploiting their role as essential intermediaries between the Greek-speaking central government and its Egyptian subjects. Not surprisingly, priests and local officials were loyal supporters of the Ptolemaic regime, and both were singled out for reprisal during native uprisings in the late third and second centuries BC. Similar patterns of royal patronage for the temples and priestly prosperity characterize Seleucid Asia, where the Seleucid monarchs generously supported both Babylonian temples and the temple of Yahweh at Jerusalem, receiving in return the loyal support of their respective priesthoods.

There were, moreover, social and cultural factors that tended to moderate the strong impulse toward social segregation in Ptolemaic Egypt and elsewhere in the Hellenistic world. The most important of these factors was demography. At the beginning of the Hellenistic period intermarriage between Greeks and non-Greeks may have been relatively common, since the majority of Greek immigrants were soldiers and therefore predominantly male. Moreover, although the Ptolemies and their rivals actively encouraged Greek immigration with generous rewards, the actual number of immigrants was relatively small, and the majority of those came in the early years of Macedonian rule. The number of ethnic Greeks in Ptolemaic Egypt and elsewhere in the Hellenistic East was, therefore, probably small. Furthermore, those Greeks who lived in the countryside, where the tendency toward intermarriage was greatest, assimilated somewhat to the social and cultural mores of their non-Greek neighbors. This was particularly true in the area of religion, since Greeks, like other polytheists, were already predisposed to honor the gods of countries in which they lived.

Hellenistic Religion

Throughout the Hellenistic world, Greek religion underwent a profound change, as some of the old polis gods came to appear anachronistic or irrelevant to the multiethnic populations of Egypt and Asia. Paganism and polytheism were flexible, nondogmatic religious systems, amenable to the introduction of new divinities and to the reshaping of old ones. In many instances, the powers of the old Olympian gods were redefined, for plainly their mission could no longer be conceived as defending Greek interests against those of non-Greeks.

In Egypt, for example, a Hellenized form of Egyptian religion developed. The most striking product of this Hellenization of Egyptian religion was to be found in Alexandria, where Ptolemy I called on the Egyptian priest Manetho and the Athenian ritual expert Timotheus to create a new god to serve as the city's new patron deity. The new god, Sarapis, was a synthesis of Egyptian and Greek elements, combining aspects of Hades, Osiris, Dionysus, and Zeus. Outside Alexandria, Greeks worshiped traditional Egyptian gods such as Isis and Osiris. Acceptance of these strange deities was aided by the centuries-old Greek practice of identifying their own gods with those of other peoples (syncretism), but the process of identification itself entailed losses as well as gains.

Native Egyptian practices that too obviously conflicted with Greek religious traditions, such as animal worship or mummification, were purged from the new Hellenized cults, while the Egyptian gods took on the identities of the Greek gods with whom they were identified. The result is evident in the case of Isis. Originally the devoted wife of Osiris and mother of Horus in the charter myth of the Egyptian monarchy, Isis, through her identification with Greek goddesses like Aphrodite, Demeter, and Athena, assumed a character that was unprecedented in Egyptian tradition: queen of the universe, benefactress of all people, and creator of civilization. When accommodation between Greek and non-Greek culture occurred, therefore, it occurred in such a way that the result did not challenge the dominance of Greek culture and values.

⟦decorative border⟧

Document 12.4 The Praises of Isis (first century BC or first century AD)
The Hellenization of Egyptian religion is evident in this inscription from the city of Cyme in northwest Anatolia with its universalization of Isis' power and identifications of Greek and Egyptian gods (Hephaestus=Ptah, the creator god of Memphis; Hermes=Thoth, god of wisdom and inventor of writing; and Cronus=Geb, god of the earth and father of the royal gods of Egypt).

Demetrius, the son of Artemidorus, who is also called Thraseas, a Magnesian from Magnesia on the Maeander, an offering in fulfillment of a vow to Isis. He transcribed the following from the stele in Memphis which stands by the temple of Hephaestus.

I am Isis, the tyrant of every land; and I was educated by Hermes, and together with Hermes I invented letters, both the hieroglyphic and the demotic, in order that the same script should not be used to write everything. I imposed laws on people, and the laws which I laid down no one may change.

I am the eldest daughter of Cronus. I am the wife and sister of King Osiris. I am she who discovered the cultivation of grain for people. I am she who is called goddess by women. By me the city of Bubastis was built. I separated earth from sky. I designated the paths of the stars. The sun and the moon's course I laid out. I invented navigation.

I caused the just to be strong. Woman and man I brought together. For woman I determined that in the tenth month she shall deliver a baby into the light. I ordained that parents be cherished by their children. For parents who are cruelly treated I imposed retribution. Together with my brother Osiris I stopped cannibalism.

I revealed initiations to people. I taught people to honor the images of the gods. I established precincts for the gods. The governments of tyrants I suppressed. I stopped murders. I compelled women to be loved by men. I caused the just to be stronger than gold and silver. I ordained that the true be considered beautiful. I invented marriage contracts. Languages I assigned to Greeks and barbarians. I caused the honorable and the shameful to be distinguished by Nature. I caused nothing to be more fearful than an oath. Anyone who unjustly plotted against others I gave into the hands of his victim. On those who commit unjust acts I imposed retribution. I ordained that suppliants be pitied. I honor those who justly defend themselves. With me the just prevails.

I am mistress of rivers and winds and the sea. No one becomes famous without my knowledge. I am the mistress of war. I am the mistress of the thunderbolt. I calm and stir up the sea. I am in the rays of the sun. I sit beside the course of the sun. Whatever I decide, this also is accomplished. For me everything is right. I free those who are in bonds. I am the mistress of sailing. The navigable I make unnavigable whenever I choose. I established the boundaries of cities.

I am she who is called Thesmophoros. The island from the depths I brought up into the light. I conquer Fate. Fate heeds me. Hail Egypt who reared me.

Inscriptiones Graecae 12.14; translated by Stanley M. Burstein, The Hellenistic Age from the Battle of Ipsos to the Death of Kleopatra VII. *Cambridge: Cambridge University Press, 1985, p. 147.*

These considerations have important implications for understanding the course of relations between Greeks and non-Greeks throughout the Hellenistic world. Since apartheid was never characteristic of Greek society, the combination of a relatively small number of ethnic Greeks and the Hellenistic kings' constant need for a Greek elite to provide a reliable base of support for their rule could have only one result. As time passed, many individuals referred to as "Greeks" in Hellenistic sources were not so much persons of Greek birth as of Greek culture: people, that is, who had received a Greek education, adopted a Greek lifestyle (and frequently a Greek name), and worshiped their old gods under Greek names.

Likewise, many "Greek cities" in the Near East were more and more often simply renamed local settlements whose citizen-bodies were composed largely of such acculturated non-Greeks. Some Jews sought to transform Jerusalem into a Greek polis in the early second century BC, but other Jews, under the leadership of the family of the Maccabees, opposed these efforts to Hellenize the community. The conflict escalated when Antiochus IV was drawn into it, forbade the Jews to carry on their traditional religious practices, and in 167 BC rededicated the temple of Yahweh at Jerusalem to Olympian Zeus. When Jews celebrate the festival of Chanukah today, they commemorate their triumph over Antiochus and his supporters. The history of this conflict is recorded in *Maccabees* I and II, two books of the *Apocrypha* that provide a unique picture of the Hellenistic world from the viewpoint of a subject people. They also clearly reveal the chief limitation of the process of Hellenization: its inability to affect significantly the lives of the mass of the population of the Hellenistic kingdoms.

*   *   *

Although Macedonian rule in Egypt and western Asia lasted for almost three centuries, assessments of the significance of this period of foreign rule vary widely. Some scholars emphasize the positive effects of the spread of Greek culture in the region, while others view it as a transitory period of colonial rule in which Greek culture was little more than a veneer, beneath which traditional social and cultural traditions survived and even flourished. Not surprisingly, the truth is more complex than is supposed by the supporters of either extreme. Hellenization did occur, but its effects were little felt outside the major urban centers of the region. Likewise, native traditions did survive and were even, as has been noted earlier in this chapter, patronized by the Ptolemies and Seleucids. Still, their vigor was short-lived, having largely spent itself by the late first century BC. Education, culture, and elite status had always been closely connected in the region. Persian rule had not threatened that connection, because the Persians themselves recognized the primacy of Mesopotamian culture in their empire. The privileged position enjoyed by Greek culture, however, severed the link between culture and status, thus providing a strong incentive for ambitious members of the local elites gradually to abandon their traditional cultures and Hellenize. Without anyone intending it, therefore, the establishment of the Macedonian kingdoms marked the beginning of the end of the ancient civilizations of Egypt and the ancient Near East.

SUGGESTED READING

Green, Peter. 1990. *Alexander to Actium: The Historical Evolution of the Hellenistic Age*. Berkeley and Los Angeles: University of California Press. Brilliantly written comprehensive history of the Hellenistic period.

Green, Peter, ed. 1993. *Hellenistic History and Culture*. Berkeley and Los Angeles: University of California Press. Wide-ranging collection of essays on various aspects of Hellenistic culture.

Lewis, Naphtali. 1986. *Greeks in Ptolemaic Egypt*. Oxford: Clarendon Press. Lucid account of life in Ptolemaic Egypt as reflected in the careers of eight Greeks and Egyptians.

Momigliano, Arnaldo. 1975. *Alien Wisdom: The Limits of Hellenization*. Cambridge, Eng.: Cambridge University Press. Pioneering study of the nature of cultural interaction in the Hellenistic period.

Onians, John. 1979. *Art and Thought in the Hellenistic Age: The Greek World View 350-50 BC*. London: Thames & Hudson. Provocative study of the relationship between art and thought in the Hellenistic Age.

Pollitt, J. J. 1986. *Art in the Hellenistic Age*. Cambridg, Eng.: Cambridge University Press. Standard treatment of Hellenistic Art.

Pomeroy, Sarah B. 1984, 1989. *Women in Hellenistic Egypt: From Alexander to Cleopatra*. New York: Schocken Books (1984); with a new foreword and addenda, Detroit: Wayne State University Press (1989). Wide-ranging survey of the social, economic, and legal status of women in Ptolemaic Egypt.

EPILOGUE

In many ways the early third century BC was the climax of ancient Greek history. For a brief period Macedonian power and Greek culture reigned supreme in the Near and Middle East. New Greek cities were founded at strategic points throughout this enormous region. A person could travel from Egypt to the borders of India speaking only Greek. The heyday of the Hellenistic kingdoms, however, was brief. Internal and external threats called their survival itself into question within a generation of their foundation.

The Seleucids' kingdom proved the most vulnerable. From their capital at Antioch the Seleucids struggled with limited success to maintain control of the Asian territories of Alexander's empire. Already before the end of the fourth century BC Seleucus I (311–281) had ceded his dynasty's claims to Alexander's conquests in India to Chandra Gupta (ca. 324–300), who had conquered northern India and founded the Maurya dynasty. Further territorial losses followed in the third century BC. While Seleucus' successors fought bitterly among themselves over the succession to the throne, enemies attacked their western and eastern frontiers. In the west, the Attalids of Pergamum seized control of much of Anatolia; in the east, the Parthians (Iranian-speaking nomads) and rebellious Greek settlers carved out kingdoms for themselves in eastern Iran and Bactria.

The Ptolemies were more secure in their Egyptian fortress than their Seleucid rivals. For over a century and a half no enemy succeeded in breaching Egypt's defenses. Nevertheless, Ptolemaic authority in Egypt also weakened significantly in the third century BC. Native rule was reestablished in southern Egypt in the last decades of the century, while succession crises sapped the dynasty's strength. By 200 BC, the Ptolemies ruled only Lower and Middle Egypt. With total collapse of the Hellenistic state system virtually in sight, Antiochus III (223–187 BC) and Ptolemy V (204–180 BC) launched vigorous counteroffensives that seemingly restored their dynasties' authority over most of their former territory. Before the Seleucids and Ptolemies could fully consolidate their hold on their kingdoms, however, disaster struck in the form of the Romans. Roman expansion into the eastern Mediterranean was so dramatic and unexpected that the historian Polybius could justifiably begin his great history with the deceptively simple ques-

471

tion: How could anyone not be interested in knowing how the Romans overthrew the world created by Alexander in less than half a century?

Although Roman relations with the Hellenistic kingdoms dated to the 270s BC, Rome first intervened decisively in the political life of the eastern Mediterranean in the first decade of the second century BC, inflicting severe defeats on Philip V of Macedon and Antiochus III. The Romans did not annex any territory after decisively defeating the two kings, preferring instead to pose as the defender of Greek freedom. The Roman Senate's refusal to brook potential rivals to Roman preeminence in the region, however, effectively undermined all the major Hellenistic kingdoms. By the mid-second century, the kingdom of Macedon had disappeared, transformed into a Roman province. Meanwhile, the Seleucids, weakened by dynastic rivalry and internal subversion often abetted by Rome, were locked in a losing struggle with the Parthians. This struggle gradually reduced the once mighty Seleucid kingdom to a few cities in Syria that Rome finally occupied in 63 BC. The Ptolemies survived their Seleucid rivals by a generation, but only because the Roman Senate could not agree on which senator would take credit for the annexation of Egypt. That debate ended in 31 BC, when Octavian defeated Antony and Cleopatra VII at Actium in northwest Greece. With their suicides in 30 BC the long succession of Alexander's successors finally ended.

In the end, Rome and Parthia turned out to be the ultimate heirs of Alexander's legacy, having extinguished the kingdoms of his successors. The demise of the Hellenistic state system did not mark the end of Greek civilization in the lands conquered by Alexander, but it did change its character and role. In the eastern portions of Alexander's empire, Greek civilization gradually disappeared as a coherent force. Macedonian and Greek rulers were responsible for the flowering of Greek culture in the Hellenistic East, and their patronage ended with the disappearance of their kingdoms in the late second and first centuries BC. Deprived of political support, Greek culture withered as the new Parthian rulers of the Mid-

Figure Epilogue 1. Coin portrait of Cleopatra VII, who ruled Egypt from 51 to 30 BC.

dle East sought to rally support for their regime from the non-Greek elites of their territory by favoring local traditions. In the western part of the Hellenistic world, Greek culture did not merely survive. It flourished thanks to Roman support.

That Rome was the savior of Greek culture in the Near East is one of the paradoxes of history. A brutality that belied the promise of "freedom" the Romans had made to the Greeks in 196 BC after the defeat of Philip V marked the Roman conquest of the eastern Mediterranean. Incidents such as the enslavement of 150,000 people from Epirus by Aemilius Paulus in 168 BC, the destruction of Corinth in 146 BC, and Sulla's devastation of Attica in 86 BC made clear to the Greeks that the Romans had come to the East as masters, not liberators. Nevertheless, while the disruption of Greek life during the almost two centuries during which Rome consolidated its rule over the eastern Mediterranean was enormous, it was not the whole story.

Like their Macedonian predecessors, the Romans were no strangers to Greek culture. Greek influence on Rome dated from the beginning of the city's history and had become an integral part of Roman culture by the time Rome intervened in the affairs of the Hellenistic East. That influence continued long after Greece had ceased to be a political and military power and had become a minor province of the Roman empire. Not surprisingly, Greek literature and art were familiar to many upper-class Romans. Some senators, like Fabius Pictor (c. 220 BC), the father of Roman history, were sufficiently fluent in Greek to write books in the language. By the first century BC Roman aristocrats routinely acquired a Greek education. Roman culture was suffused with Greek influence. Rome's gods and myths had been recast in terms of Greek mythology. Latin writers constantly echoed their Greek predecessors, so that a work like Virgil's *Aeneid*, Rome's national epic, has to be read against the background of the *Iliad* and *Odyssey* for its artistry to be fully appreciated. The first-century-BC Roman poet Horace was only recognizing reality when he wrote that "Greece, though a captive, captured her fierce conqueror, and brought the arts to rustic Latium" (*Epistles* 2.1).

One important result of the Hellenization of the Roman upper class was the Senate's adoption of the concept of Greek freedom as the framework for the exercise of Roman supremacy in the eastern Mediterranean. In spite of the suffering they inflicted on the cities and kingdoms of the Greek East, therefore, the Romans made the support of Greeks and Greek culture the linchpin of their rule of the region. Greeks enjoyed privileged status, and Greek cities provided the framework for Roman provincial administration. The result was a remarkable renaissance in the cultural life of the Greek cities of old Greece and the Near East during the first two centuries of the Christian era. Evidence of this renaissance is visible in the ruins of the splendid public buildings that everywhere in the eastern Mediterranean dominate the remains of Greek cities and in the innumerable honorary statues that crowd our museums.

Greek writers, such as the historian Appian and the orator Aelius Aristides, had good reason to celebrate the benefits of the *Pax Romana* ("Roman Peace"), although conscientious Roman governors like Pliny the Younger complained about the costs of the ambitious building projects undertaken by the Greek cities in their efforts to outdo each other in public splendor and distinction. The renaissance was not limited to architecture and the visual arts. The second and third centuries AD also saw a remarkable upsurge of Greek literary activity that historians of Greek literature call the Second Sophistic. The Second Sophistic is named after the great public orators such as Aelius Aristides who dominated the public culture of the period, but new works appeared in almost every genre of Greek literature. Many of these works such as the biographies and essays of the biographer and moralist Plutarch and the histories of Arrian were of considerable distinction and exercised significant influence on the development of later western thought.

Science and philosophy also flourished. Galen and Ptolemy compiled syntheses of Greek medicine, astronomy, and geography that remained authoritative for more than a millennium. Indeed, medical students still studied the works of Galen in the early nineteenth century AD. The Egyptian-born Neo-Platonist Plotinus created the last great philosophical system of antiquity, a philosophical mysticism based loosely on the works of Plato that was Christianity's most formidable intellectual rival. Only in one area of Greek life was there no renaissance: the civic and political culture of the Greek cities themselves. Instead, during these same two centuries, the last vestiges of the polis tradition of self-government disappeared.

Officially, the Romans treated the Greek cities of the eastern Mediterranean as self-governing entities. Epigraphical records of their government's activities are numerous, but the spirit was gone. City assemblies no longer met, and city councils were controlled by narrow aristocratic oligarchies. Even the freedom of action of these oligarchic regimes was increasingly limited by the Roman government's practice of employing officials such as Pliny the Younger to monitor their conduct of affairs. Plutarch candidly assessed the situation in an essay written in response to a young friend's request for advice about a possible political career. "Nowadays," he wrote, "when the affairs of the cities no longer include leadership in wars, nor the overthrowing of tyrannies, nor acts of alliances, what opening for a conspicuous and brilliant public career could a young man find?" Plutarch answered his own question by pointing out that "there remain the public lawsuits, and embassies to the Emperor" (*Precepts of Statecraft* 805a–b; Fowler). Greek patriots such as Plutarch, who considered holding the traditional magistracies in his home city of Chaeronea a sacred obligation, found the contrast with the freedom of fifth- and fourth-century BC Greece painful. Other Greeks were more pragmatic. Men such as Arrian, who was governor of Cappadocia under the emperor Hadrian (117–138 AD) and historian of Alexander, and Dio Cassius, a historian of Rome who held the offices of consul and praetorian prefect during the early third century AD, abandoned their poleis, and found rewarding careers in the service of Rome.

While Greeks and Greek culture prospered under Roman rule, the same was not true of the non-Greek cultures of Egypt and the Near East. The Roman emperors' patronage of the Greek cities of the eastern Mediterranean heightened the value of Greek culture and Roman citizenship. The former was the key to social and cultural prestige and the latter to a political career and its rewards. Non-Greek cultural traditions and institutions were not repressed, but they were devalued. In the second century AD the Syrian writer Lucian expressed the cultural priorities of the new regime in his autobiographical essay *The Dream,* stating that without a Greek education a man could only be an "artisan and commoner, always envying the prominent and fawning on the man who was able to speak," while the educated man was "honored and praised, in good repute among the best people, well regarded by those who are preeminent in wealth and breeding . . . and considered worthy of public office and precedence" (*The Dream* 9–11). Lucian's calculation was correct. His Greek education and literary skill brought him fame and a lucrative post on the staff of the Prefect of Egypt.

Some peoples, such as the Jews, resisted the assimilatory pressures of Roman imperial society, sometimes violently. Others found in the new Christian church opportunities for the satisfaction of the ambitions of their elites. Not surprisingly, however, over time increasing numbers of non-Greeks followed Lucian's example and sought to acquire the advantages of Greek status, especially after 212 AD when the emperor Caracalla erased the legal barriers between Greeks and non-Greeks by conferring Roman citizenship on virtually all inhabitants of the empire.

The process of assimilation was not always free of friction. Complaints of Greek prejudice and cultural chauvinism are frequent in the writings of Hellenized non-Greeks such as, for example, the Hellenized Syrian rhetorician Tatian, who urged Greeks not to despise non-Greeks and their ideas since most Greek practices "took their origin from barbarian ways" (*Address to the Greeks* 1.1). Nevertheless, by late antiquity a significant portion of the social and intellectual elite of the eastern provinces of the Roman empire consisted of Hellenized non-Greeks. The local languages of the region did not disappear. They survived in the vernacular speech of the urban lower classes and the countryside and even found new written expression in the literatures of Syriac and Coptic Christianity. But the traditional cultures of Egypt and the Near East died, as the native elites that had patronized them for millennia gradually deserted them. Harassed by the government of the Christian Roman emperors, they survived only in the esoteric knowledge of the priests of a few remote and impoverished temples before finally disappearing completely in late antiquity. Meanwhile, the dominant strand in the intellectual life of the eastern Mediterranean basin became what scholars call Hellenism, essentially a cosmopolitan form of Greek culture loosely based on the canon of Classical Greek literature. This literature formed the basis of both pagan and Christian education and thought, although the civic culture of the Greek city-states that had given birth to it almost a millennium earlier had disappeared. In this form Greek culture continued to flourish in the lands conquered by Alexander the Great and influenced the medieval civilizations of Byzantium and Islam and through them the culture of western Europe and the Americas.

TRANSLATIONS

Fowler, Harold N. 1936. *Plutarch's Moralia.* Vol. X. Loeb Classical Library. Cambridge, Mass. and London: Harvard University Press.

GLOSSARY

Academy—The school founded by Plato at Athens during the 380s BC in the groves sacred to the hero Academus. Its most famous pupil was Aristotle. The Academy continued to function until the Christian emperor Justinian ordered it closed, along with other pagan schools, in 529 AD.

acropolis—Literally, the "upper city," the citadel of a city or town. Many citadel hills had been the sites of Mycenaean palaces and remained as special places in *polis* life. The most famous is the Acropolis of Athens, the religious center of the city, which was magnificently adorned with temples in the fifth century.

agora—In Homer, the term for the "place of gathering," the assembly of the people. In the city-state period it denoted the public space of a city or town, being both the marketplace and civic center. Lingering in the agora was the best way to inform oneself about public affairs, make business contacts, and collect gossip.

Amphictyonic Council—The governing body of an ancient league of Delphi's neighbors, the Delphic Amphictyony, that administered the oracle. The Amphictyony also conducted the Pythian games and dealt with transgressions against the oracle and its territory. The members were *ethnē*, of which the most important were the Thessalians, Phocians, Boeotians, Dorians, and Ionians. Votes were unequally divided among the members, so that Philip II's acquisition of the twelve Thessalian and two Phocian votes gave him a majority of the council's twenty-two votes and control of the Amphictyony.

archon—A common title (meaning "leader") for the highest ranking magistrate in the early city-states. During the Classical period, even when the *stratēgoi* had become the most important officials in Athens, nine archons continued to be chosen (by lot) to serve judicial and administrative functions. The archontate was used in larger contexts as well; for example, as the title of the civil and military head of the Thessalian League. This archon was elected by the League assembly and served for life.

aristocracy—The term *aristokratia* ("power in the hands of the best men") was coined, probably in the fifth century, as the word the elite used to describe their hold on power, in preference to the less noble-sounding *oligarchia*. (Plato defines aristocracy as the good form of oligarchy.) Aristocratic power and exclusiveness were strongest in the early Archaic period and gradually weakened as strong democratic sentiments emerged in the city-states.

assembly—Along with the "council" (*boulē*, *gerousia*), one of the two primary elements of Greek governance. From the Dark Age on it was made up of the adult males of the community. In the Dark Age, the assembly (called *agora* in Homer) had limited power vis-à-vis the chiefs, although its concurrence was crucial. Despite attempts by the oligarchical rulers of the Archaic period to curtail further the authority of the assembly, it eventually became the deciding body of state policy. In Athens, the assembly or *ekklēsia* met in the open air on the hill called the Pnyx about forty times a year.

barbaros—The term used by the ancient Greeks for all people who were not Greek in language and culture. The contrast did not necessarily imply uncivilized crudity and savagery (the highly civilized and generally admired Egyptians and Persians were *barbaroi* to the Greeks), although increasingly from the fifth century on *barbaroi* came to be stigmatized as the inferior "others," lacking the mental and moral capabilities that belonged naturally to Hellenes.

basileus—The term for the legitimate single ruler, the "king." In Mycenaean society, the title *pasireu* denoted an official who had charge of a village or district; with the breakup of the Mycenaean kingdoms it became (in the form *basileus*) the title of the warrior-chiefs who ruled the villages and districts in the Dark Age. The hierarchy of *basileis* was replaced in the Archaic Age by landed aristocrats who ruled as an oligarchy.

boule—The commonest term for the "council," which, along with the assembly, was one of the two primary governing institutions of the Greeks. Composed of the chiefs and other influential men in the Dark Age, it became the major organ of aristocratic power in the Archaic Age. In the democratizing city-states, the council became increasingly an organ of popular will. In Classical Athens, the *boulē* consisted of five hundred men chosen by lot; it prepared business for the assembly. It could also try certain court cases.

Cadmea—The acropolis of Thebes. Its seizure by Sparta in 382 BC provoked a major diplomatic crisis in Greece.

cella—The inner shrine of a temple. The gold and ivory statue of Athena, over 40 feet high and now lost, stood in the cella of the Parthenon.

city-state—See polis.

Common Peace—The term used to describe a number of fourth-century-BC treaties beginning with the King's Peace in 387 and ending with that sponsored by Philip II after the Battle of Chaeronea in 338. The characteristic feature of these treaties was that they guaranteed the autonomy of all subscribing states.

Corinthian League—The term used by modern scholars to designate the alliance organized to implement the Common Peace established by Philip II in 338 BC. The League included the principal cities and *ethnē* of Greece except Sparta and guaranteed its members: freedom, autonomy, collective action against states who broke the peace, and protection against proposals to cancel debts and liberate slaves. The Corinthian League provided the framework for Macedonian domination of Greece until it was dissolved by Antipater in 322 BC.

currency, Athenian—Units of Athenian currency included the obol, the drachma, the mina, and the talent. Six obols made a drachma; one hundred drachmas made a mina; and sixty minas (i.e., 6000 drachmas) added up to a talent. A man who had a talent was rich. In fifth-century Athens, a silver drachma coin was considered good pay for a day's labor by an unskilled worker and probably represented a living wage for a small family. A drachma was the standard pay for a rower in the fleet. Maintaining a trireme cost a talent a month.

Delian League—The modern name for the confederacy organized under Athenian leadership after the end of the Persian wars. Founded in 477 BC, the League was slowly converted into an Athenian empire as Athens began forcing unwilling states to remain in the organization, or to join it if they were not already members.

demagogos—Literally, a "leader of the people." This was the term some Athenians used to categorize the politicians who arose in Athens after Pericles' death. Usually it had negative connotations and suggested that such a man was interested only in his own well-being, unlike a true statesman, who cared for the welfare of the state. Unlike the word "demagogue" today, however, it was occasionally used in a neutral way.

democracy—A form of government in Classical Greece that permitted all free men some degree of participation in politics, regardless of wealth or family background. Ideologies of equality were preached, though economic inequalities prevailed and generally brought political inequalities with them. Athens encouraged democratic governments in its allies. Like other forms of Greek government, democracies denied voting rights to women and assumed the appropriateness of slavery.

demos—A territory and the people who live in it; thus, "the land" and "the people." It occurs in the Linear B tablets in the form *damo*, meaning, apparently, a village community and its free inhabitants. Originally a neutral term, it came to be used by aristocrats (probably in the seventh century) as an exclusive term for the "commoners," or the "masses," although technically (as in legal inscriptions) it retained its inclusive meaning as "the (whole) people."

Demotic—The "popular" script, an extremely simplified cursive form of the hieroglyphic script used in the Hellenistic period to write Egyptian. Demotic was the principal Egyptian script in Ptolemaic Egypt and was used for writing both literary and nonliterary texts.

dicasteries (dikastēria)—The people's courts at Athens. As Athens was notoriously litigious, these courts tried an enormous number of cases. A dicasterion was composed of hundreds of adult male citizens who were chosen by lottery at the last minute from those who had presented themselves for membership in the pool of jurors known as the heliaia (q.v.) Both the last-minute element of the choice and the large size of the juries discouraged bribery, especially since Athenian court cases had to be decided in a single day. Since the large jury was considered to be acting in the stead of the people, there could by definition be no appeal from its decisions. Beginning around the middle of the fifth century, jurors received a small amount of pay for their services.

dokimasia—The scrutiny Athenian citizens had to undergo before assuming a position in the government. Political enemies often used this procedure as a means of keeping a man out of public office.

drachma—See currency, Athenian.

ekklesia—See assembly. The Athenian assembly (*ekklēsia*) met about thirty to forty times a year on the hill known as the Pnyx. In its meetings it voted on business prepared by the *boulē*.

ephor (*ephoros*)—"Overseer," an office found in Sparta and in other Dorian states. In Sparta a board of five ephors was elected annually by the assembly; the senior ephor gave his name to the year. The ephors had great power in the Spartan state, including general control over the kings' conduct.

epikleros—A brotherless Athenian girl who was compelled to marry her nearest male relative able to procreate so that her son, who was slated to inherit her father's property, would be descended from his grandfather through the male line. The word is often translated "heiress," but in fact the epikleros could herself inherit nothing, which was the whole point of her forced marriage.

ethnos—The term used to describe a large group of people who shared a common identity and territory, but were not politically united, preferring local self-government. The story of the Greek *ethnē* is their growing ability from the sixth century BC on to act as unified states by forming federations of local and regional segments of the *ethnos*. By the fourth century, ethnic confederacies and leagues were playing a prominent, and even a dominant, role in the geopolitics of Greece.

Freedom of the Greeks—Propaganda slogan used by various Hellenistic kings and the Romans to attract the support of Greek cities. Although proclamations of "freedom" included guarantees that cities would be free, autonomous, and un-garrisoned, in practice kings did not hesitate to interfere in city affairs to achieve their goals.

genos—"Clan." A social group composed of families who claimed descent from a single male ancestor. A *genos* was led by its most prominent family and played a prominent part as a political group in the Archaic Age. The power and influence of the aristocratic *genē* (plural) waned in the Classical period, but continued to confer social prestige on the member families.

gerousia—The "council of elders" (from *gerōn* = "old man"). This was the term used at Sparta and in other *poleis* for the aristocratic council. The Spartan *gerousia* consisted of the two kings plus twenty-eight men over age 60 who served for life.

graphe paranomon—The procedure the Athenians began to use in the late fifth century BC to indict a man for making an illegal proposal in the assembly. Since the Athenians had no real constitution, it was very difficult to tell what laws might be illegal, and the procedure was usually used as a form of political attack. Those convicted were generally fined; three convictions barred a citizen from making further proposals.

guest-friendship (*xenia*)—A form of ritual friendship, whereby a "stranger" (*xenos*) entered into a relationship of mutual friendship with a man from another *dēmos*, each obliged to offer hospitality and aid when they visited each other's community. The bond was perpetuated down through generations of the two families. A prominent feature of Homeric society, *xenia* continued throughout antiquity, evolving in the city-states into the more formal diplomatic relationship of proxeny (q.v.).

hegemon—A state or individual who headed an organization of states. Athens, for example, was the hegemon of the Delian League, Sparta of the Peloponnesian League. A hegemon was said to exercise hegemony, hence the period of Theban ascendancy in the 360s BC is known as the Theban hegemony. Hegemon was also the title of the leader of the Corinthian League. This hegemon was officially elected by the League council and was its chief executive and commander-in-chief of the League's military forces with full authority to conduct its military and diplomatic activities.

hektemoroi—A term used in Solonian Athens meaning "sixth-parters," referring, presumably, to poor farmers who had fallen into debt to wealthy landowners and had to hand over to them a sixth of their produce under penalty of enslavement for their debt.

heliaia—The body of prospective jurors from which dikasteria (q.v.) were selected. Any adult male citizen might present himself for participation.

Hellenes—The name the Greeks called themselves (and still do). They had a myth of an eponymous ancestor, Hellen, who was the son of Deucalion, the Greek Noah, and the father of the eponymous ancestors of the Dorians, Ionians, and Aeolians. There is some reason to believe that the common name (and the supporting myth) arose relatively late, perhaps in the eighth century BC.

helots—The term used to describe groups of conquered people in Greece who were forced by their conquerors to work as serfs on their former lands. The word is most commonly associated with Sparta, where helots probably outnumbered citizens by a ratio of seven to one. The Spartan way of life both depended on and was formed by the state's ownership of the labor of thousands of helots in Laconia and Messenia. Fear of helot uprisings often discouraged the Spartans from becoming engaged in campaigns far from home.

hetaira—Meaning literally "female companion," this was the term normally used for courtesans in Classical Athens. *Hetairai* usually came from the metic class. They were generally more cultivated than citizen women; they were trained (usually by older hetairai) to be entertaining and interesting rather than to be thrifty managers of households. Since Pericles' citizenship laws of 451–450 made it impossible for a man to marry a metic woman and still have his children enjoy citizenship rights, many Athenian men chose to have long-term associations with hetairai simultaneously with their legal marriages to Athenian women. Some hetairai functioned as entrenched mistresses or even common-law wives, but others less fortunate were essentially prostitutes.

hetaireiai—The military systems of some cities such as those in Crete grouped men in *hetaireiai* or "bands of companions," but the word is most commonly associated with Athens. There young men of the upper class frequently belonged to hetaireiai or social clubs with political overtones, often of an antidemocratic nature. The mutilation of the herms in 415 was rumored to be the work of such a hetaireia, and the subversive activity of hetaireiai probably played a part in the oligarchic revolutions of 411 and 404.

hetairos—"Companion" or "comrade." In the Dark Age, follower-bands of *hetairoi* formed the military and political support of the chiefs who recruited and rewarded them. Associations of hetairoi for political purposes continued to function in the city-states (see *hetaireiai*). In Macedonia, the hetairoi were an elite band of warriors and advisors who formed the retinue and personal bodyguard of the kings.

hippeis—See Solonic system.

hoplite—*Hoplitēs*. The heavily armored infantryman, named from his distinctive shield (*hoplon*). Hoplites were the dominant military arm from the seventh century on, gradually undergoing changes in weaponry and tactics. Because Greek governments did not issue arms to their soldiers, hoplites tended to come from the middle class, men able to afford armor and swords, unlike the rowers in the fleets, who were likely to be *thētes* (see thes).

King's Peace—The agreement that ended the Corinthian War in 387 BC. A key role was played by Artaxerxes II of Persia, and Greeks were chagrined by the wording of the peace, which began, "I, King Artaxerxes, regard the following arrangements as just. . . ."

kleros—An allotment of farmland sufficient to support a citizen-family; it was passed on in perpetuity in the male line. In oligarchic states, full citizenship was frequently tied to the possession of a certain amount of land.

kore—"Maiden." A term used to describe the life-size or larger marble Archaic statues of clothed females, made as cult offerings or grave markers. The term *kouros* ("youth") is used of the corresponding nude male statues.

liturgies—An indirect system of taxation whereby the rich were required to spend their own money in the service of the state. Liturgies included financing the training of a chorus for dramatic performances or financing a delegation to a religious festival in another state. The most expensive liturgy was the trierarchy, which required a man to maintain a trireme for a year and to pay for the training of its crew.

Lyceum—The school founded by Aristotle in Athens in 335 BC. It became a major center for scientific study, and Aristotle's pupils also collected the constitutions of 158 states.

megaron—A large rectangular building that served as the focal point of Mycenaean palaces. Its function as the "great hall" of the ruler continued in the reign of the Dark Age chiefs. In the city-states the ancient *megaron* achieved immortality as the basic plan of the Greek temple.

metics—Resident aliens in a Greek state. There were probably metics throughout Greece, but we know only about metics in Athens. Although they lacked citizenship, metics mingled comfortably in Athenian society and were often called on for help in wartime. The women known as *hetairai* were generally metics, though most metic women were probably housewives.

metropolis—"Mother-city," describing a *polis* that sent out a colony under its aegis. The relationship between the mother-city and the new *polis* was normally very close, combining economic, political, and spiritual ties.

mina—See currency, Athenian.

mothax (pl. mothakes)—The *mothakes* were a new class that arose in Sparta during the Peloponnesian War. Some were the offspring of Spartan fathers and helot mothers, others the sons of impoverished Spartans who were no longer able to maintain their status in the corps of "equals" by contributing to the common meals.

myth—All cultures possess myths, traditional tales that treat aspects of life that are important to the collective group (e.g., marriage, initiation, food, cultural institutions, human-divine relations, etc.). The Greeks had an immensely rich storehouse of such orally transmitted stories going back to the second millennium BC and continually infused by additions from the mythologies of the Near East. The Greek historians depended on ancient myths to reconstruct the preliterate past. Modern researchers attempt to glean from them historical or psychological realities.

nomos—Custom or law. Sometimes it corresponds to the English word "mores," connoting a way of doing things that is deeply embedded in a value system. It can also be used, however, in a legal context; thus for example the rules laid down by Solon were called his *nomoi*.

nomothetai—Athenian officials set up after the restoration of the democracy in 403 BC. The *nomothetai* reviewed and ratified the laws of Athens.

obol—See currency, Athenian.

oikist—The *oikistēs* (note the root of *oikos*) was the "founder" and the leader of a colony sent out by a mother-city (*mētropolis*). As the founder, he had great authority in the new settlement, and was usually highly honored after his death.

oikos—"Household." The fundamental social and economic unit in Greek society, comprehending the family group, its house, land, animals, and property, including slaves.

oligarchy—*Oligarchia* ("rule by a few men") was the standard form of government in the early city-states, having replaced the system of ranked chieftains. Opposition from below the narrow ruling circle caused most oligarchies to broaden inclusion in state affairs, while other states adopted democratic governments. Democratic *poleis* were subject to oligarchic revolutions, as in Athens in 411 and again in 404 BC. Throughout the fifth and fourth centuries, tension between oligarchs and democrats—which often added up to tension between rich and poor, especially in the difficult economic times of the decades after the Peloponnesian War—was a constant factor in Greek political life and sometimes erupted in bloodshed.

paramount—An anthropological term referring to the highest ranking leader of a community or group. The major warrior-heroes of the Homeric epics, who rule over other leaders as a "first among equals," represent the paramount chiefs who ruled during the tenth to eighth century BC.

pediment—The elongated triangular spaces that sat on top of the columns on the front and back of Greek temples. They were frequently adorned with elaborate relief sculpture.

Peloponnesian League—The modern name for an organization led by Sparta and dated to some time in the sixth century BC. Scholars have joked that it was neither Peloponnesian nor a league. It consisted of Sparta and less powerful allied states who swore to have the same friends and enemies as the Spartans. Thus they were tied to Sparta but not really to each other, and some important members of the League, such as Thebes, were outside the Peloponnesus. The most important member after Sparta was Corinth, which provided naval power. After its victory over Athens in the Peloponnesian War (431–404 BC), Sparta increasingly interfered in domestic affairs in allied states, causing substantial friction. The League finally dissolved in the 360s.

peltasts—Lightly armed Greek soldiers who carried light throwing spears and small, round shields. They functioned as skirmishers and could be deployed either alone or in concert with hoplites. Although they were utilized during the Peloponnesian War, they increased dramatically in importance in the fourth century. The Athenian commander Iphicrates owed his successes to his well-trained peltasts.

pentakosiomedimnoi—See Solonic system.

perioikoi—"Those who dwell about," the term used to describe neighboring peoples who were in a subordinate relationship to a dominating *polis*. The most prominent example is Sparta, which treated the people of the perioecic communities of Laconia and Messenia as half-citizens, granting them local autonomy but obligating them to military service and allowing them no say in the conduct of policy.

phalanx—The tactical formation of a hoplite army, consisting in the Archaic and Classical periods of ranks of heavy infantry, usually eight deep. The phalanx underwent change and experiment in the fifth and fourth centuries. The highly successful form of phalanx introduced by Philip II of Macedon consisted of six brigades of fifteen hundred men each, recruited on a regional basis. Macedonian "phalangites" were armed with a short sword, a small round shield, and a long pike (*sarissa*) up to 18 feet long, and they fought in rectangular formations sixteen men deep.

phratry—A subdivision of the tribe (*phylē*) and, at least theoretically, a kin grouping. In Classical times phratries were well-defined social groups concerned with defining descent and therefore citizenship. Every citizen family in Athens belonged to a phratry.

phylai—The term for the large, ancient descent groups into which a *dēmos* was divided. Ionian communities had four such "tribes," as moderns call them, Dorian communities three. The tribes functioned as organizational units in the city-states. In his reform of the Athenian government, Cleisthenes bypassed the four traditional tribes and divided Attica politically and militarily into ten new *phylai*.

polemarch—The office of *polemarchos* ("war leader") was common to many early city-states. As army commander for a specified term, usually a year, and subject to the policy of the aristocratic council, the polemarch was limited in his power. In 500 BC at Athens the polemarch was eclipsed by the board of ten *stratēgoi*, military commanders elected from the ten new *phylai*. After 487 BC, when the polemarch became appointed by lot, his functions became mainly legal and ceremonial.

polis—"City," "town." Beginning in the eighth century, *polis* came to designate a political community, composed of a principal city or town and its surrounding countryside, which together formed a self-governing entity, the "city-state." The small polis was the principal form of Greek community throughout antiquity, numbering in the high hundreds by the fifth century BC. With the exception of Sparta, *poleis* were generally governed by some sort of republican government, whether oligarchic or democratic. Since the polis system implied some degree of political self-awareness, it was an open question whether a city ruled by a tyrant could be a polis.

probouleutic—The term for the council's (*boulē's*) function of preparing state business for consideration in the assembly.

probouloi—In Athens, a committee of ten older men that was set up to direct the government in 413 BC. The establishment of the *probouloi* resulted from the shock engendered by the disaster in Sicily.

proskynesis—Greek name for the Persian ritual greeting that social inferiors offered to their superiors and all Persians offered to the Persian king. In its simplest form, *proskynēsis* involved merely blowing a kiss. Proskynesis to the Persian king, however, required full prostration before the ruler. Although Persians did not believe that their king was divine, Greeks and Macedonians considered the performance of proskynesis to be appropriate only to deities and resented attempts to make them perform it.

proxeny—The term used for a diplomatic arrangement whereby citizens in one state, called *proxenoi*, looked after the interests of other states in their communities. The *proxenos* was highly honored by the foreign state he represented. The system of proxeny (*proxenia*) developed from an earlier system of *xenia* or private "guest-friendship" (q.v.).

prytanis—One of the titles for the presiding magistrate (or a college of magistrates) in a city-state. In the reorganization of the Athenian *boulē* (508 BC), ten boards of fifty *prytaneis* each, chosen by lot from the ten new "tribes" (*phylai*), took turns as the officials in charge of the daily business of the *boulē* and *ekklēsia* for a tenth of the year. Each group of fifty men comprised a prytany.

redistributive system—The term for the kind of economic and political arrangements found in the Bronze Age kingdoms of the Near East and Greece, where most of the agricultural and manufactured production of a region was controlled from the center (the king and his palace), which redistributed the resources as it saw fit. In the Greek city-states, by contrast, the government exercised only limited control over production and distribution. See liturgies.

rhetores—The men who chose to involve themselves intensively in Athenian politics during the fourth century, proposing decrees and making speeches in the assembly. It is often translated "politicians."

Royal Pages—The Royal Pages were a body of young men recruited, probably while still in their teens, from the Macedonian aristocracy. The pages lived at the royal court and were the king's personal attendants, guarding him while he slept, accompanying him on hunting expeditions, and performing whatever other tasks he might require of them. The institution was established by Philip II and served as the first step in the career of Macedonian aristocrats.

Sacred Band—Elite Theban infantry formed about 378 BC. The Sacred Band consisted of 150 pairs of lovers. It played a major role in the Spartan defeat at Leuctra in 371 and later Theban military campaigns until it was totally destroyed at the Battle of Chaeronea in 338 BC.

Satrap—Title of the governors of the principal territorial subdivisions of the Persian empire, then of Alexander III's empire, and later of the Seleucid kingdom. During the Peloponnesian War, the coastal satraps Tissaphernes and Pharnabazus enjoyed considerable independence from the king and entered freely into negotiations with the warring states.

satrapy—Originally a province of the Persian empire. Alexander III retained the satrapal system of the Persian empire as the administrative framework of his empire. After the division of Antigonus the One-Eyed's empire in 301 BC, the term was used to designate the largest territorial subdivisions of the Seleucid kingdom.

Second Athenian Confederacy—A voluntary organization led by Athens which many Greek states joined, some at the inception in 377 and others later. Though member states sent delegates to a common deliberative body known as the *synedrion* and hence had far greater say in policy decisions than the helpless allies of the Delian League, disaffection nonetheless developed and the alliance began to disintegrate in the late 370s. It suffered substantial defections in the 350s and was finally dissolved when the Corinthian League was established in 338 BC.

Solonic system—According to the reforms made early in the sixth century BC by Solon, Athenian citizens were allotted political power in accord with the amount their land produced (a figure that correlated roughly with the amount of land they owned). Making use of property classes that had existed for some time, Solon divided citizens into four groups. To qualify for membership in the highest class, the *pentakosiomedimnoi* or "500-measure men," a man needed an estate that produced at least 500 *medimnoi* (bushels) of produce in any combination of oil, wine, or grain. Below these were the *hippeis* ("horsemen," since they were the men who could afford to keep a horse for the cavalry), whose income was more than 299 *medimnoi* but less than 500. After them came the *zeugitai*, men who could afford to own a team of oxen, with 200 to 299 measures. The lowest class (above the slaves) consisted of the *thētes*, poor people whose land produced fewer than 200 measures; some had no land at all and so produced no measures.

sophists—The itinerant intellectuals who taught and gave speeches during the latter part of the fifth century BC. Some were primarily teachers of oratory, while others engaged in thoughtful speculation about society that challenged entrenched conventions. Sophists were drawn to the climate of Athens, where response to them was mixed. Plato made the discrediting of the sophists an important part of his dialogues, accusing them of substituting showy rhetorical displays for real wisdom such as Socrates possessed.

stasis—The term first for a group of men who take the same "stand" in a political dispute—a faction—and then by extension the act itself of taking sides. In the city-states *stasis* (civil strife) occurred between oligarchical factions and between the rich and the poor. At its worst stasis entailed bloodshed; thus containing it within nonviolent bounds was a principal objective of the city-states.

stele—A stone slab inscribed with a text, a decoration, or both. Stelae could be used to indicate graves, military victories, or property boundaries. Important texts such as legal decrees and treaties might also be inscribed on them.

strategos—The common term for a "military leader." In the city-states, this office was usually political as well as military. In Athens, after 487, the ten *stratēgoi* were the only elected high officials (the others being selected by lot); thus most of the powerful politicians of the fifth century were strategoi. In the Hellenistic era, during the reigns of Alexander III, Philip III, and Alexander IV, *stratēgos* (general) was the title of the highest ranking Macedonian military commander in Europe and Asia. The four attested strategoi of this period were Antipater, Polyperchon, and Cassander in Europe and Antigonus the One-Eyed in Asia.

symposion—In Archaic and later periods the after-dinner "drinking party," made up of a small number (between fourteen to thirty) of men, was a frequent event in adult male social life, primarily among the elite. The *symposion* was an important bonding ritual among young aristocrats and (like the *hetaireiai*, q.v.) was often the occasion of factional plotting. Meaning "drinking together," it is the origin of the English word symposium.

synedrion—A representative council such as that of the Second Athenian Confederacy (q.v.) or the Corinthian League (q.v.). The *synedrion* of the Second Athenian Confederacy was composed of a single representative from each member state and ruled the confederacy jointly with the Athenian assembly; policy decisions had to be ratified by both bodies. The synedrion of the Corinthian League consisted of representatives of the member cities and *ethnē* of the league. The latter synedrion was responsible for upholding the Common Peace (q.v.) that established the Corinthian League and was empowered to arbitrate disputes among its members and to try individuals accused of betraying its goals.

synoecism (*synoikismos*)—The term used for the process whereby several separate communities were formed into a single political union. Synoecism also referred to the actual movement of people from several communities into a brand new composite settlement.

talent—See currency, Athenian.

temenos—In Mycenaean times and in the Dark Age, a *temenos* was a parcel of choice land given as a due to the preeminent families. *Temenos* was also the term for a sacred precinct of land given to a god or hero, containing an altar, and often other buildings, for cult and ritual. This became the prevalent meaning in the Archaic and later periods, as the custom of giving land to the leaders waned (though it did not completely vanish) with the shortage of good land.

Theoric Fund—A special fund established at Athens probably in the 350s BC by Eubulus. In peacetime it received the fiscal surplus remaining after all annual expenditures mandated by law had been made. The purpose of the fund was to enable poor Athenians to attend public festivals, but it was also used for various other purposes including work on the dockyards and the public arsenal. In wartime use of the surplus for military purposes was possible by vote of the Athenian assembly, but such use was unpopular.

thes—The term for a free man who was forced by his poverty to hire out as a laborer for wages. In Athens, according to the economic divisions attributed to Solon (c. 600 BC), the *thētes* (plural) formed the lowest class of citizens.

Thirty Tyrants—The pro-Spartan puppet government installed in Athens by Lysander in 404. After murdering over a thousand citizens, as well as metics whose property they coveted, the Thirty were overthrown the following year.

tholos (plural tholoi)—A type of monumental above-ground stone tomb (shaped like a beehive) favored by the elites of the Late Bronze Age. In the Classical period, circular structures, also called *tholoi*, served as temples and public buildings.

trireme—The modern term for the standard form of Greek warship (*triērēs*) in the Classical period. Propelled by three banks of oars, and attaining speeds of nine knots, the trireme used its bronze ram to disable enemy ships. Athenian oarsmen were the best at this maneuver, and Athenian fleets dominated naval warfare during the fifth century.

tyranny (*tyrannis*)—The illegal seizure and control of governmental power in a *polis* by a single strong man, the "tyrant" (*tyrannos*). Tyranny occurred as a phase in many city-states during the seventh and sixth centuries, and is often seen as an intermediate stage between narrow oligarchy and more democratic forms of polity. In the late fifth and the fourth century, a new kind of tyrant, the military dictator, arose, especially in Sicily.

wanax—"Lord," "master." The title of the monarchical ruler of a Mycenaean kingdom. In the form *anax* it appears as the title of gods and high-ranking chiefs in Homer.

xenia—See guest-friendship.

zeugitai—See Solonic system.

ART AND ILLUSTRATION CREDITS

1.1a Plan of the Minoan palace at Knossos. From Raimond Higgins, *The Archaeology of Minoan Crete* (London: The Bodley Head, 1973), p. 41.

1.1b View of the ruins of the Minoan palace at Phaistos. Photo: The J. Allan Cash Photo Library, London.

1.2 Fresco of a fisherman from Thera. Athens, National Archaeological Museum. Photo: Bildarchiv Preussischer Kulturbesitz, Berlin.

1.3a Inlaid dagger. Athens, National Archaeological Museum. Photo: Hirmer Fotoarchiv, Munich.

1.3b Plan and cross section of the Kato Phournos *tholos* tomb, Mycenae. Photo: British School, Athens.

1.3c Interior vault of a *tholos* tomb, Mycenae. Photo: Hirmer Fotoarchiv, Munich.

1.3d Gold mask from shaft graves, Mycenae. Athens, National Archaeological Museum. Photo: Foto Marburg/Art Resource, New York.

1.4b The *megaron* hall at Pylos. Photo: Alison Franz.

1.4c "The Lion Gate." Photo: Bildarchiv Preussischer Kulturbesitz, Berlin.

1.5a Linear B tablet from Mycenaean Knossos. From J. Chadwick, *The Mycenaean World* (Cambridge: Cambridge University Press, 1976), p. 16. Reprinted by permission of publisher.

1.5b A chariot tablet from Mycenaean Knossos. After J. Chadwick, *The Decipherment of Linear B,* 2nd ed. (Cambridge: Cambridge University Press, 1976), p. 108.

1.6a Statue of goddess figure from Knossos. Herakleion, Crete, Archaeological Museum. Photo: Foto Marburg/Art Resource, New York.

1.6b Gold ring from Knossos. Herakleion, Crete, Archaeological Museum. Photo: Hirmer Fotoarchiv, Munich.

1.7 Bronze plate armor and boar's tusk helmet. Nauplion Museum. Photo: German Archaeological Institute, Athens.

2.1a Submycenaean vase. Athens, Kerameikos Museum K2616. Photo: German Archaeological Institute, Athens.

2.1b Late Protogeometric vase. Athens, Kerameikos Museum K576. Photo: German Archaeological Institute, Athens.

2.2a "Village chieftain's house" at Nichoria. From William A. McDonald et al., *Excavations at Nichoria in Southwest Greece: Vol. III, Dark Age and Byzantine Occupation* (Minneapolis: University of Minnesota Press, 1983), pp. 36–37, Figs. 2-22 and 2-23. Reprinted by permission of publisher.

2.2b "Ordinary" Dark Age house. From William A. McDonald, *Progress into the Past: The Rediscovery of Mycenaean Civilization,* rev. ed. (Bloomington: Indiana University Press, 1990), p. 368, fig. 103. Reprinted by permission of publisher.

2.3 Gold jewelry from the tomb of a rich Athenian Woman. Athens, Agora Museum. Photo: American School of Classical Studies at Athens.

490

2.4a Graffiti on eighth-century vases. Transcriptions: L. H. Jeffery, LSAG in J. N. Coldstream, *Geometric Greece* (Huntingdon, England: A&C Black Publishers Ltd., 1977), p. 298. Reprinted by permission of publisher.

2.4b Late Geometric vase from the Dipylon cemetery. Athens, National Archaeological Museum NM192. Photo: German Archaeological Institute, Athens.

2.5a Large Late Geometric grave amphora from the Dipylon cemetery. Athens, National Archaeological Museum 804. Photo: German Archaeological Institute, Athens.

2.5b A detail of Figure 2.5a. Athens, National Museum. Photo: German Archaeological Institute, Athens.

2.6 Bronze statuette of man and centaur. New York, The Metropolitan Museum of Art 17.190.2072. Gift of J. Pierpont Morgan, 1917. Photo: Museum.

3.2 Corinthian vase with depiction of a hoplite battle. Rome, National Museum of the Villa Giulia. Photo: Hirmer Fotoarchiv, Munich.

3.3a Athenian amphora. Boston, The Museum of Fine Arts 01.8037. Henry Lillie Pierce Fund. Photo: Museum.

3.3b A *symposion* scene on an Athenian red-figure calyx krater. Munich, Staatliche Antikensammlungen und Glyptothek. Photo: Museum.

3.4 Statue of an Egyptian nobleman. Boston, The Museum of Fine Arts 07.494. James Fund Purchase and Contribution, August 8, 1907. Photo: Museum.

3.5 Marble *kouros*. New York, The Metropolitan Museum of Art 32.11.1. Fletcher Fund, 1932. Photo: Museum.

3.6 Marble *kouros*. Athens, National Archaeological Museum NM3938. Photo: Museum.

3.7 Late Archaic *korē* from the Acropolis. Athens, Acropolis Museum. Photo: German Archaeological Institute, Athens.

3.8 Relief sculpture depicting the battle of the Gods and the Giants. Delphi, Archeological Museum. Photo: Nimatallah/Art Resource, New York.

3.9 The *agora* in the Archaic period, c. 500 BC. After J. Travlos 1974. Used with permission of the American School of Classical Studies at Athens, Agora Excavations.

4.2 Laconian cup depicting rider on horseback. London, The British Museum. Photo: Museum, courtesy of trustees.

4.3 Bronze statuette of a running girl. London, The British Museum. Photo: Museum, courtesy of trustees.

4.4 Hilaire Germain Edgar Degas' "Young Spartans." London, The National Gallery. Photo: Museum, courtesy of trustees.

5.1 *Tetradrachm*, Athens. New York, American Numismatic Society 1957.172.1033. Photo: Society.

5.2 Detail of Attic red-figure *psykter*. New York, The Metropolitan Museum of Art 1989.281.69. Gift of Norbert Schimmel Trust, 1989. Photo: Museum.

5.3 Statues of the tyrannicides Harmodius and Aristogiton. Naples, National Museum. Photo: Hirmer Fotoarchiv, Munich.

5.5 Delegations bringing tribute to Persepolis. Photo: Barbara Grunewald © Bildarchiv Preussischer Kulturbesitz, Berlin.

5.7 Herm of Themistocles. Ostia, Archaeological Museum. Photo: Antike Porträts © Bildarchiv Preussischer Kulturbesitz, Berlin.

5.8 *Ostraka* discovered in the Athenian agora. Agora Excavations. Photo: American School of Classical Studies at Athens.

5.9 Reconstruction of the Athenian trireme of the Classical period. Photo: Paul Lipke/Trireme Trust, Montague, Mass.

6.2 Section of Athenian Tribute List incription. Athens, Epigraphic Museum. Photo: Museum.

6.3 Aerial view of Piraeus. From Raymond Schoder, *Wings over Hellas: Ancient Greece from the Air* (New York: Oxford University Press, 1974), p. 175. Copyright © 1989 Loyola University of Chicago. Reprinted by permission of Loyola University of Chicago.

6.4 Bronze charioteer. Delphi Museum. Photo: Foto Marburg/Art Resource, New York.

6.5 Roman copy of *diskobolos*. Rome, National Museum. Photo: Hirmer Fotoarchiv, Munich.

6.6a Reconstructions of the east pediment of the temple of Zeus at Olympia. From Bernard Ashmole, *Architect and Sculptor in Classical Greece* (London: Phaidon Press, 1972), p. 25.

6.6b Seer from east pediment. Olympia Museum. Photo: Museum.

6.7 Marble relief depicting girl with doves. New York, The Metropolitan Museum of Art 27.45. Fletcher Fund, 1927. Photo: Museum.

6.8 Attic vase c. 470 BC. Boston, The Museum of Fine Arts 63.1246 Ca. 470. William Francis Warden Fund. Photo: Museum.

6.9   Attic black-figure vase depicting crafts people at work. Boston, The Museum of Fine Arts, 01.8035. Henry Lillie Pierce Fund. Photo: Museum.

6.10   The family of Megacles. After J.K. Davies, *Athenian Propertied Families 600–300 B.C.* (Oxford: Oxford University Press, 1971), Table I.

6.11   Detail of Attic red-figure wedding bowl by the Washing Painter. Munich, Staatliche Antikensammlungen und Glyptothek. Photo: Museum.

6.12   Black-figure vase, attributed to the Amasis Painter. New York, The Metropolitan Museum of Art 31.11.10. Fletcher Fund, 1931. Photo: Museum.

7.3   Model of Periclean Acropolis. Toronto, The Royal Ontario Museum 956.118. Photo: Museum.

7.4   The Doric and Ionic orders. From John Boardman, ed., *The Oxford History of Classical Art* (New York: Oxford University Press, 1997). Reprinted by permission of publisher.

7.5   Ground plan of the Parthenon. From John Boardman, ed., *The Oxford History of Classical Art* (New York: Oxford University Press, 1997). Reprinted by permission of publisher.

7.6   The Parthenon today. Photo: Werner Forman Archive/Art Resource, New York.

7.7   Parthenon east frieze, slab V. London, British Museum. Photo: Foto Marburg/Art Resource, New York.

7.8   Statue of Athena. Nashville, Tenn., Parthenon Museum. Photo: Gary Layda © Metropolitan Government of Nashville/Davison County. Sculptor: Alan LeQuire.

7.9   Ground plan of Erechtheion. From J. Travlos, *Pictorial Dictionary of Ancient Athens* (New York: Praeger Publishers), 1971, pp. 216–217. Reprinted by permission of Greenwood Publishing Group, Inc.

7.10   Erechtheion, Athens Acropolis. Photo: The J. Allen Cash Photo Library, London.

8.2   Herm of Pericles by Cresilas. Photo: © Bildarchiv Preussischer Kulturbesitz, Berlin.

8.3   Aerial view of the Pylos and Sphacteria. From Raymond Schoder, *Wings over Hellas: Ancient Greece from the Air* (New York: Oxford University Press, 1974), p. 177. Copyright © 1989 Loyola University of Chicago. Reprinted by permission of Loyola University of Chicago.

8.4   Bronze shield with graffiti. Agora Excavations. Photo: American School of Classical Studies at Athens.

8.5   Diagram of Syracuse and Epipolae. Reprinted from Donald Kagan, *The Peace of Nicias and the Sicilian Expedition.* Copyright © 1981 by Cornell University Press. Used by permission of publisher.

8.6   Coin struck by Tissapherenes. New York, American Numismatic Society 1967.152.462. Photo: Society.

9.1   Decree of Aristoteles. Athens, Epigraphic Museum. Photo: Museum.

9.2a   Fragment of the kleroterion. Athens, Agora Museum. Photo: American School of Classical Studies of Athens.

9.2b   *Klepsydra* ("water clock"). Athens, Agora Museum. Photo: American School of Classical Studies at Athens.

10.2   Miniature ivory head of Philip II. Thessaloniki, Archaeological Museum. Photo: Museum.

10.3   The Macedonian Phalanx. From Arther Ferrill, *The Origins of War: From the Stone Age to Alexander the Great* (New York: Thames and Hudson, 1985), p. 177. Reprinted by permission of publisher.

10.4   Portrait of Demosthenes. Naples, National Museum 6018. Photo: Museum.

10.5   Burial monument at Chaeronea. Photo: SEF/Art Resource, New York.

11.2   Portrait of Alexander as hero-king. Paris, Louvre Museum. Photo: Giraudon/Art Resource, New York.

11.3   Plan of the Battle of Issus. From Arther Ferrill, *The Origins of War: From the Stone Age to Alexander the Great* (New York: Thames and Hudson, 1985), p. 201. Reprinted by permission of publisher.

11.4   Mosaic from Pompeii. Naples, National Museum 10020. Photo: Alfredo D'Agli Orti, 1990 © Bildarchiv Preussischer Kulturbesitz, Berlin.

11.5   Alexander as Pharaoh. Chicago, The Oriental Institute of the University of Chicago P.38387/N.43812/CHFN 9246. Photo: Museum.

11.6   Plan of the Battle of Gaugamela. From Arther Ferrill, *The Origins of War: From the Stone Age to Alexander the Great* (New York: Thames and Hudson, 1985), p. 209. Reprinted by permission of publisher.

11.7   The Greek view of the inhabited world. From N. G. L. Hammond, *A History of Greece to 322 BC.* 3rd ed. (Oxford: Oxford University Press, 1986). p. 622. Reprinted by permission of publisher.

11.8   Islamic manuscript depicting Alexander in Indian costume. New York, The Pierpont Morgan Library f.330. Photo: The Pierpont Morgan Library/Art Resource, New York.

11.9   Silver five-shekel coin from Babylonia. London, The British Museum. Photo: Museum, courtesy of trustees.

12.1   Statue of old market woman. New York, The Metropolitan Museum of Art 09.39. Rogers Fund, 1909. Photo: Museum.

12.2   Letter to Zenon. New York, Columbia University Rare Books and Manuscript Library. Papyrus P. Col. Zen. 2 66 (P Col. Inv. 274). Photo: Library.

12.4 Roman bronze statuette copy of the Tyche of Antioch by Eutychides. New York, The Metropolitan Museum of Art 13.227.8. Rogers Fund, 1913. Photo: Museum.

12.5 Gold octodrachm showing Ptolemy II and Arsinoe II. New York, American Numismatic Society 1977.158.112. Photo: Society.

12.6 Limestone statue of Arsinoe. New York, The Metropolitan Museum of Art 20.2.21. Rogers Fund, 1920. Photo: Museum.

12.7 Tetradrachm of Commodus. London, The British Museum. Photo: Museum, courtesy of trustees.

12.8a Miniature sculpture of old nurse with child. New York, The Metropolitan Museum of Art 10.210.38. Rogers Fund, 1910. Photo: Museum.

12.8b Miniature sculpture of school girl reading a papyrus roll. Hamburg, Museum für Kunst und Gewerbe. Photo: Museum.

12.8c Bronze statuette of black youth. New York, The Metropolitan Museum of Art 18.145.10. Rogers Fund, 1918. Photo: Museum.

12.9 The "Winged Victory." Paris, Louvre Museum 2369. Photo: Alinari/Art Resource, New York.

12.10 Sculpted relief of the Apotheosis of Homer. London, The British Museum. Photo: Werner Forman Archives/Art Resource, New York.

12.12 The Rosetta Stone. London, The British Museum. Photo: © Bildarchiv Preussischer Kulturbesitz, Berlin.

Epi. 1 Coin portrait of Cleopatra VII. London, The British Museum. Photo: Museum, courtesy of trustees.

INDEX